# Group Decision Making

This is a volume in
EUROPEAN MONOGRAPHS IN SOCIAL PSYCHOLOGY

Series Editor: Henri Tajfel

EUROPEAN MONOGRAPHS IN SOCIAL PSYCHOLOGY 25
Series Editor: HENRI TAJFEL

# Group Decision Making

Edited by

**HERMANN BRANDSTÄTTER**
*University of Linz, Austria*

**JAMES H. DAVIS**
*University of Illinois at Urbana-Champaign, USA*

**GISELA STOCKER-KREICHGAUER**
*University of Augsburg, West Germany*

1982

*Published in cooperation with*
EUROPEAN ASSOCIATION OF EXPERIMENTAL
SOCIAL PSYCHOLOGY
*by*
ACADEMIC PRESS
*A Subsidiary of Harcourt Brace Jovanovich, Publishers*
*London    New York*
*Paris    San Diego    San Francisco    São Paulo*
*Sydney    Tokyo    Toronto*

ACADEMIC PRESS INC. (LONDON) LTD.
24/28 Oval Road
London NW1

*United States Edition published by*
ACADEMIC PRESS INC.
111 Fifth Avenue
New York, New York 10003

**British Library Cataloguing in Publication Data**

Group decision making.
  1. Decision-making, Group
  I. Brandstätter, H.    II. Davis, J.H.
  III. Stocker-Kreichgauer, G.
  302.3      HM131

  ISBN   0-12-125820-3
  LCCN  81-66398

Printed in Great Britain at the Alden Press
Oxford London and Northampton

# European Monographs in Social Psychology

## *Series Editor:* HENRI TAJFEL

C.P. WILSON
Jokes, Form, Content, Use and Function, 1979

J.P. FORGAS
Social Episodes: The Study of Interaction Routines, 1979

R.A. HINDE
Towards Understanding Relationships, 1979

A-N. PERRET-CLERMONT
Social Interaction and Cognitive Development in Children, 1980

B.A. GEBER and S.P. NEWMAN
Soweto's Children: The Development of Attitudes, 1980

S.H. NG
The Social Psychology of Power, 1980

P. SCHÖNBACH, P. GOLLWITZER, G. STIEPEL and U. WAGNER
Education and Intergroup Attitudes, 1981

C. ANTAKI (ed)
The Psychology of Ordinary Explanations of Social Behaviour, 1981

W.P. ROBINSON (ed)
Communication in Development, 1981

J.P. FORGAS (ed)
Social Cognition: Perspectives in Everyday Understanding, 1981

H.T. HIMMELWEIT, P. HUMPHREYS, M. JAEGER and M. KATZ
How Voters Decide: A Longitudinal Study of Political Attitudes and Voting
extending ever Fifteen Years

*In Preparation*

P. STRINGER (ed)
Confronting Social Issues: Applications of Social Psychology, Vol. 1

# List of Contributors

JOHN ADAMOPOULOS: *Department of Psychology, University of Illinois, Champaign, IL 61820, USA.*

HERMANN BRANDSTÄTTER*: *Johannes Kepler Universität Linz, 4040 Linz-Auhof, Austria.*

EUGENE BURNSTEIN*: *Research Center for Group Dynamics, Institute for Social Research, University of Michigan, Ann Arbor, MI 48106, USA.*

W. CROTT*: *Psychologisches Institut der Universität Freiburg, Peterhof, D-7800 Freiburg i. Br., W. Germany.*

JAMES H. DAVIS*: *Department of Psychology, University of Illinois, Champaign, IL 61820, USA.*

JOE HATCHER*: *Universiteit te Leuven, Laboratrrium voor Experimentele Social Psychologie, Tiesestraat 102, B-3000 Leuven, Belgium.*

VERLIN B. HINSZ: *Department of Psychology, University of Illinois, Champaign, IL 61820, USA.*

AUSTIN C. HOGGATT: *School of Business Administration, University of California, Berkeley, CA 94720, USA.*

IRVING JANIS*: *Department of Psychology, Yale University, New Haven, CT 06520, USA.*

NORBERT KERR*: *Department of Psychology, Michigan State University, East Lansing, MI 48824, USA.*

ZOLTÁN KOVÁCS*: *Institute for Psychology at the Hungarian Academy of Sciences, Postafiók 398, H-1394 Budapest 62, Hungary.*

PATRICK LAUGHLIN*: *Department of Psychology, University of Illinois, Champaign, IL 61820, USA.*

DIETER H. LUTZ: *Psychologisches Institut der Universität Hamburg, von-Melle-Park 6, D-2000 Hamburg 13, W. Germany.*

BEATE MICHELS: *Psychologisches Institut der Universität Freiburg, Peterhof, D-7800 Freiburg i.Br., W. Germany.*

IAN MORLEY*: *Department of Psychology, University of Warwick, Coventry, CV4 7AL, England.*

*Participants of the Reisenburg Symposium on Group Decision Making

GABRIEL MUGNY*: *Faculté de psychologie et des sciences de l'éducation, Université de Genève, 3 Place de l'Université, CH-1211 Genève, Switzerland.*

DAVID G. MYERS*: *Department of Psychology, Hope College, Holland, MI 49423, USA.*

CHARLAN NEMETH*: *Department of Psychology, University of California, Berkeley, CA 94720, USA.*

J. VAN OOSTRUM: *Universiteit te Utrecht, Institute of Social Psychology, Jacobstraat 14, NL Utrecht, Netherlands.*

J. M. RABBIE*: *Universiteit te Utrecht, Institute of Social Psychology, Jacobstraat 14, NL Utrecht, Netherlands.*

LUTZ von ROSENSTIEL*: *Universität München, Abt. für Organisations- und Wirtschaftspsychologie, Widenmayerstrasse 46a D-8000 München 22, W. Germany.*

BRUNO RÜTTINGER*: *Institut für Psychologie der Universität Darmstadt, Hochschulstrasse 1, D-6100 Darmstadt, W. Germany.*

ROLAND W. SCHOLZ: *Psychologisches Institut der Universität Freiburg, Peterhof, D-7800 Freiburg i. Br., W. Germany.*

HEINZ SCHULER*: *Lehrstuhl für Psychologie der Universität Erlangen, Bismarckstrasse 1, D-8520 Erlangen, W. Germany.*

BLAIR H. SHEPPARD: *Department of Psychology, University of Illinois, Champaign, IL 61820, USA.*

IVAN D. STEINER*: *Department of Psychology, University of Massachusetts, Amherst, MA 01003, USA.*

GEOFFREY STEPHENSON*: *University of Kent at Canterbury, Social Psychology Research Unit, Beverley Farm, Kent CT2 7NS, England.*

GISELA STOCKER-KREICHGAUER*: *Lehrstuhl für Psychologie, Universität Augsburg, Memmingerstrasse 6-14, D-8900 Augsburg, W. Germany.*

L. VISSER: *Universiteit te Utrecht, Institute of Social Psychology, Jacobstraat 14, NL Utrecht, Netherlands.*

DAVID A. VOLLRATH: *Department of Psychology, University of Illinois, Champaign, IL 61820, USA.*

JANETTE WEBB: *University of Kent at Canterbury, Social Psychology Research Unit, Beverly Farm, Kent CT2 7NS, England.*

ERICH WITTE*: *Psychologisches Institut der Universität Hamburg, von-Melle-Park 6, D-2000 Hamburg 13, W. Germany.*

MARYLA ZALESKA*: *Laboratoire de psychologie sociale, Université Paris VII, 18 rue de la Sorbonne, F-75005, Paris, France.*

# Preface

It has been a pleasure to edit a book in which contributors have generally given a fairly comprehensive account of some important aspect of group decision making, rather than merely interpreting results from a study or two. Thus we believe this volume provides an up-to-date survey of theoretical notions as well as empirical findings concerning important issues in group decision and related social processes which are currently salient both in Europe and North America. Various conceptual approaches and research strategies are illustrated, although the laboratory experiment continues as the dominant general mechanism for data-gathering. While most researchers would surely agree that the problem dictates the method, the last decade has seen repeated calls for field investigations. Whatever the research location preferred on logical grounds, there are often troublesome issues of ethics, legality, practicality, and simple availability which cannot be easily brushed aside; however attractive naturally occurring groups may be in the abstract, a realistic appraisal suggests that, in practice, experimental studies are likely to remain the chief research tool for some time to come—as the work discussed in this volume illustrates.

Group decision includes a large number of phenomena, and the boundaries of the category are somewhat fuzzy. None the less, the prototypic decision making group is a set of task-oriented individuals who interact and reach consensus on one or another alternative defined by the task, although quite disparate preferences and interpersonal disagreement may arise along the way. Various tasks and various aspects of the attendant social processes have been emphasized by the authors of the different chapters. We have grouped these topics into six parts on the basis of apparent similarities, but we readily confess that other categorizations might work as well.

Part 1 (Social Decision Schemes) contains chapters in which the primary concern is with the molar characterization of how interaction combines member preferences to produce the solution, decision, or whatever, and how the successful model for accomplishing this may depend on the task itself. Part 2 (Choice Shifts) is a collection of papers which focus on the comparison of individuals and groups, or of individuals before and after discussion. Part 3 (Social Emotions in Group Decisions) is composed of papers which focus on perceptions, attitudes and feelings of interaction participants rather than on predominantly intellective behaviour as in the first two sections. Part 4 (Bargaining) deals with situations in which at least part of the task is the reconciliation of divergent interests or preferences among the group members themselves—a situation which often arises in even the most apparently cooperative circumstances. The contributions to Part 5 (Social Influences on Individual Judgement), although quite different in other respects, have in common that they focus on enduring or transitory effects of social situations on individual processes, i.e. on individual cognitive development, and on conforming behaviour as a means of maintaining the optimal level of arousal. Part 6 (Groupthink) is the last section and contains papers which elaborate on explanations of why some naturally occurring groups have produced some markedly unwise decisions in critical situations, whereas other groups seem to have behaved prudently despite considerable pressure. How the areas of research, samples of which are represented in this volume, are related to each other, and what else has happened recently in the field of group decision making is reviewed in an introductory and also in a final chapter.

The Symposium was co-sponsored by the European Association of Experimental Social Psychology and its American counterpart, the Society of Experimental Social Psychologists. Financial support came from the Deutsche Forschungsgemeinschaft, enabling participants to spend a very stimulating, productive and pleasant week at the Castle Reisenburg in Bavaria. More importantly, we have seen the emergence of a number of cooperative research endeavours among participants and among several of their departments and institutes. We owe thanks to Åse Lie for her kind and efficient secretarial assistance, and we are grateful to our colleagues for their ready response to our editorial requests.

HERMANN BRÄNDSTATTER
JAMES H. DAVIS
GISELA STOCKER-KREICHGAUER                    September 1981

# Contents

# II
# Choice Shifts

## III
## Social-Emotional Aspects of Group Decision Making

IV
Bargaining

# 1
# Current Research Problems in Group Performance and Group Dynamics

James H. Davis and Verlin B. Hinsz

In a recent summary, Nagao *et al.* (1978) traced the historical development of several small group research problems and forecast a renewed interest in such questions. Their discussion was organized around three research areas: (a) Cooperative interaction: cognitive aspects; (b) Cooperative interaction: social—emotional aspects; and (c) Mixed-motive interaction. McGrath (1978) has also written an historical account of small group research, and Davis (in press) has reviewed from an historical perspective seminal theories offered during the last several decades to account for small group behavior. All of these accounts have concluded that the study of small groups has been in eclipse for at least the past decade and a half, but predict a renewal of research vigor in the years ahead. Whether such a resurgence is a recognition of needs dictated by current social "engineering" questions (as implied by Davis, 1980), a recognition of social trends in society at large (as implied by McGrath, 1978), or some recognition of the basic importance of the topic in general, current research on small groups appears to be very diverse in substance and geographically diffuse (as implied by the varied character of contributions to the book by Brandstätter *et al.* 1978, and the contents of this book).

The major aim of the present chapter, however, is less to identify the historical roots of prevailing research trends than to summarize briefly the status of current research themes, many of which are evident in the contributions to this volume. In the sections to follow

Preparation of this chapter was supported by NSF Grant BNS-77-15216.

we attempt a brief summary of only a few research themes, many of which are closely related to each other but have been separated here for ease of discussion.

## Group problem solving

Almost any area of research having to do with the collective performance of a set of persons working at a task was at one time called "group problem solving." According to at least one system of group task classification (Davis, 1969, a), problem solving tasks emphasize the processing of information in order to formulate an answer, and may be contrasted with decision-making tasks which emphasize less a construction of some response than a specification of one alternative out of several defined by the task. Such a system, of course, is largely a matter of convenience and cannot easily be maintained in strict logical form. The important point is that, while virtually all group performance in the past was called group problem solving, a number of useful distinctions are now normally made. For example, consider a town council where the selection of a policy which obliges some larger constituency is perhaps less a matter of processing information and seeking a "correct" solution than adjudicating among the various "political forces," proposals, and points of view conveyed by the community representatives.

Group problem solving is well illustrated in the classic study by Marjorie Shaw (1932) in which small *ad hoc* groups were asked to discuss and solve word puzzles collectively, and more recently by the work of Laughlin (see Chapter 4 in this volume), and others (e.g., Davis, 1964, 1969, b). Perhaps the most active period of group problem solving research ranged from the mid-1930s until the late 1950s. Like so many other trends in psychological research, the activity of this period was in part traceable to the demands or needs of society at large.

For example, it might be argued with some merit that a large portion of the efforts in the late 1930s and early 1940s was stimulated by the desire to demonstrate that "democracy is good at solving problems". Lewin and his associates (e.g., Lewin *et al.*, 1939) were anxious to show that a democratic approach to group work indeed produced solutions as good or nearly as good as those produced in a more autocratic group atmosphere. At the time, the world political order was very much in turmoil, with democracy largely retreating before political systems emphasizing authoritarianism. Somewhat later and, in part, contemporaneous with this movement, a considerable effort was being devoted to industrial applications of psychology. "Troubleshooting" was a frequent assignment of small groups in industrial settings and not very surprisingly psychologists began research on how to go about such problem solving efficiently.

By the early 1950s a substantial body of group problem solving research in the United States had arisen in response to military applications ranging from air crews to human relations problems associated with training recruits drawn from a heterogeneous society. A somewhat different area of group problem solving arose from a concern with fostering creativity in industry: "brain-storming" (Osborn, 1953; Lamm and Trommsdorff, 1973). The purpose of brain-storming was the creation of a group atmosphere especially conducive to creative problem solving on the part of the participants. Originating in the advertising industry, the method proved popular in various commercial enterprises, surviving in one form or another to the present time. Numerous anecdotal reports suggest that brain-storming is usually perceived as a stimulating exercise by many of the participants who also judged it to be valuable. On the other hand, we know of no systematic studies of the technique which have demonstrated its value in fostering group performance. Carefully controlled studies by Taylor *et al.* (1958) and Dunnette *et al.* (1963) are in substantial agreement that the production of ideas, the creation of new ideas, etc., when working on highly abstract problems do not demonstrably benefit by the "free wheeling atmosphere" and the rules for creative interaction laid down by brainstorming proponents.

The idea of inefficiency in group relative to individual problem solving in brainstorming situations presupposes some *a priori* theoretical expectations about the way member contributions are optimally elicited, combined, or integrated during discussion. Steiner (1972) has presented a very general model which conceptualizes "actual group productivity" as "potential productivity" minus "losses due to faulty process". The form of suitable "potential productivity" models poses an interesting conceptual problem, and Chapter 2 by Davis in this volume suggests various ways this problem may be attacked. The "faulty process" characterization of social interaction as a key theoretical problem need not and has not been limited to brainstorming groups; the approach is useful for a very broad array of group problem solving tasks and social contexts (cf. Davis, 1969, a; in press).

Attention has frequently been devoted to engineering group interaction discussion with the aim of overcoming the "faulty process" noted by Steiner. Indeed, brainstorming was an attempt to achieve just such an improvement in performance, albeit a largely unsuccessful attempt. (See Lamm and Trommsdorff, 1973, for a summary of results from brainstorming studies.) However, other techniques and other problem-group formats have been the subject of efforts to engineer better group problem solving (Hackman and Morris, 1975), though perhaps less dramatic in style.

One line of research which currently holds some promise is the "Delphi Method." Like brainstorming, the Delphi Method arose outside of psychology. The technique is an attempt to recognize and combat the social sources of inefficiency in group problem solving — Steiner's process losses. The idea is to separate persons and bring them together again in an orderly fashion, to secure the advantages long recognized for isolation in the solution of difficult abstract problems (e.g., Davis and Restle, 1963), but at the same time to use discussion for catching errors and exercising solution criteria which may not be evident to individuals alone. In other words, "correctness" may not always be self-evident, and requires some component of consensus to be established, or at least publicized.

Laughlin (Chapter 4) has studied group problem solving at least partially as a function of member abilities. Creating groups with different levels of member abilities, Laughlin has touched upon one of the generally ignored problems in group performance — individual differences. In this volume Laughlin, working close to the distinction we have drawn between group decision making and group problem solving, distinguishes between tasks which engage existing axiomatic systems and those which depend upon consensual validation for the establishment of collective criteria for response.

In summary, while the investigation of problem solving is the precursor of most group performance research, it is today not the most active area of work. Task-oriented groups in society at large are, of course, charged with a number of important jobs, and problems to be solved constitute only a single category. As the papers in this volume demonstrate, there is at present a remarkably diverse array of group tasks that have been brought under study by researchers.

## Choice shifts

The substantial literature on choice shift phenomena (once called risky shift) has been so thoroughly and so often summarized (e.g., Clark, 1971; Dion et al., 1970; Vinokur, 1971) that little remains to be said. A large research effort followed the initial findings by Stoner (1961) and Wallach et al., (1962) that the average group was more inclined than its average individual member (prior to discussion) to recommend an apparently risky course of action for a central character faced with a dilemma. Such a difference between individuals and groups, while often observed before and variously interpreted (see Davis, in press; Chapter 2 in this volume), was contrary to prevailing conventional wisdom that group decisions were generally moderate relative to individual inclinations (Cartwright, 1973). It thus appeared that groups might even harbor an inherent bias toward adventurous strategies or attractive but improbable goals, rather than a system of interpersonal constraints generally supposed to foster prudence. If so, powerful decision-making bodies such as town councils, legislative committees, advisory groups, cabinets, and the like, might pose something of a hazard for their constituents and others dependent on their actions.

More than a decade and a half of research on choice dilemma items, and related decision tasks, has shown that a number of originally attractive hypotheses can be ruled out as *necessary* explanations (e.g. risky alternatives are especially attractive, individual responsibility is diffused by group decision, discussion encourages revision in the direction of the norm engaged by the "dilemma," etc.). But, the so-called individual-group shift need not be interpreted in terms of risk at all. (Even the concept of risk is poorly defined in the literature of psychology.) Not only were items later written which generally produced a "cautious shift" (e.g., Stoner, 1968), but risk-neutral items and risk-irrelevant decision tasks often displayed similar individual-group decision shifts (e.g., Davis et al., 1974; Kerr et al., 1975). The importance of the particular task in interpreting the significance of social decisions was again evident. More importantly, once group decision research was "freed" of its preoccupation with risk as the dominant ingredient in the process, investigators were able to broaden the range of group tasks to be studied, and theoretical explanations to be considered. (See Myers and Lamm, 1976, for a discussion of the role of risk in "misdirecting" explanations of choice shifts.)

Research effort on choice shifts has been waning in recent years. But, closely related phenomena such as "group polarization" (Moscovici and Zavalloni, 1969, and Myers, Chapter 6 in this volume) and "groupthink" (Janis, 1972, and Chapter 20) have enjoyed increased attention. Although we have labeled one section of this volume "Choice Shifts" in the interest of generality, it is notable that the chapters therein are considerably more heterogeneous in content than such a title might suggest.

Choice shift research may seem in retrospect to have been generally beset with difficulties in experimental design (e.g., procedural problems particularly pertinent to "within subjects" designs), conceptual ambiguities in the very definition of risk, a multitude of difficult-to-refute informal theories, and so on (see Davis et al., 1974, and Zajonc et al., 1968, for a more thorough discussion of these issues). However, hindsight is always clear, and it is important to acknowledge the role of the choice shift research tradition in focusing attention on the possibility of increased *extremity* in group, relative to individual, response (see Zaleska, Chapter 7, for an insightful discussion of response extremity from a somewhat different point of view).

## AGGREGATION PROCESSES IN CHOICE SHIFTS AND OTHER GROUP DECISIONS

Most of the usual choice shift explanations assume that individual group members are induced by one means or another to change their personal choices among response alternatives. The major theoretical focus has generally been on how such change was worked. (The response is usually a selection of a category from among an ordered set, such as the n-point rating scale of minimum acceptable odds in the case of choice dilemma items.) The group choice is in turn determined by the group members who have discussed the item and reached consensus; on the average, the group response is then observed to be different (more cautious or risky) from the mean prediscussion, personal choices of its members. A different kind of explanation which is often at least sufficient to predict the choice shift (as well as many other individual-group differences) has been proposed by Zajonc (e.g., Zajonc, 1966; Zajonc et al., 1968) and Davis (e.g., 1973, 1980; Davis et al., 1974). In many situations, individual members need not change their position up to the point of reaching consensus (by formal vote or publicizing their position informally during discussion). This point of view assumes that the social interaction process effectively aggregates member responses (whatever their origin) to establish the group decision, i.e. selection of a response category.

The intricacies of social influence, mutual accommodation etc., are most complex, and have occupied the attention of social psychologists for many years. However, summary principles (group decision rules, social decision schemes, etc.) have proved useful to describe the process efficiently at the group level. Many group decision rules are familiar: majority rules, plurality decides, equal factions compromise, and so on. Other decision rules, however, may be unfamiliar and quite complex — the product of particular group tasks and social contexts.

Table 1 gives an *example* of how a group shift (i.e., an average individual—group difference) might occur, without individual members *necessarily* changing their personal preferences, whether or not they do so later. (The values reported in Table 1 were composed for this example.) It is sufficient that the unconvinced members acquiesce in the choice established by the process we sometimes summarize in a social decision rule. The example uses ten response categories, in which the larger scale value might indicate, say, increased risk preferences.

The ten groups of four members in our example have acted strictly on a plurality principle. That is, each group in the "sample" has chosen the most popular position among its members. Note that the distribution of opinion within groups is generally toward the upper end of the scale at the outset, implying that the members have been drawn from a population skewed in that direction. (Population distribution shapes are themselves important topics for investigation, suggesting as they may something about influential cultural values and norms.) Observe, too, that as a consequence of such initial skew and the plurality rule, the distribution of group decisions, $Pl(X)$, is generally *more extreme* than that of individual members, $X$. For a particular group, the resulting difference, $\bar{X} - Pl(X)$, between the average of individual pregroup preferences, $\bar{X}$, and their group decision, $Pl(X)$, generally shows a shift, and the overall (sample) mean difference, $-0.975$, is significantly different from zero, $t(9) = 5.54, P < 0.001$.

Of course, this is only an example, but it demonstrates that the effects of such aggregation principles can be very strong. A social

TABLE 1

*An example of how a sample of four-person groups, acting on a plurality principle, could produce a "shift" (upward) along a ten-category scale*

| Group no. | Prediscussion preference | $X$, Response category value | $X$, Members' prediscussion average | $Pl(X)$ Plurality rule choice | $[X_I-Pl(X)]$ Ind.-Gp. difference |
|---|---|---|---|---|---|
|   | 1 | 9 |      |   |       |
| 1 | 2 | 8 | 7.50 | 8 | −0.50 |
|   | 1 | 5 |      |   |       |
|   | 1 | 8 |      |   |       |
| 2 | 2 | 7 | 6.25 | 7 | −0.75 |
|   | 1 | 3 |      |   |       |
|   | 3 | 6 |      |   |       |
| 3 | 1 | 5 | 5.75 | 6 | −0.25 |
|   | 2 | 8 |      |   |       |
| 4 | 1 | 6 | 6.50 | 8 | −1.50 |
|   | 1 | 4 |      |   |       |
|   | 1 | 9 |      |   |       |
| 5 | 2 | 7 | 6.50 | 7 | −0.50 |
|   | 1 | 3 |      |   |       |
|   | 3 | 7 |      |   |       |
| 6 | 1 | 4 | 6.25 | 7 | −0.75 |
|   | 2 | 9 |      |   |       |
| 7 | 1 | 7 | 7.00 | 9 | −2.00 |
|   | 1 | 3 |      |   |       |
|   | 2 | 6 |      |   |       |
| 8 | 1 | 4 | 4.75 | 6 | −1.25 |
|   | 1 | 3 |      |   |       |
|   | 2 | 7 |      |   |       |
| 9 | 1 | 6 | 6.25 | 7 | −0.75 |
|   | 1 | 5 |      |   |       |
| 10 | 3 | 8 | 6.50 | 8 | −1.50 |
|   | 1 | 2 |      |   |       |
| Total/ Average | 40 |  | 6.325 | 7.30 | −0.975 |

decision scheme can be a very useful picture of complex group decision processes and as such can summarize conveniently very complex social phenomena. Such a view does not imply that choice shifts, or any other individual—group difference, must necessarily be an artifact. Indeed a group—individual difference (whether representing risky or cautious shifts, or something else), along with the summary social decision scheme (majority, plurality, weighted averaging, and so on) for that task and social context, may serve to direct efficiently the subsequent study of the underlying social and individual processes. In other words, a social decision scheme may not only serve as a statistical consequence of summary of interpersonal process, but "exist" as one picture of a social norm — itself a summary abstraction, albeit verbal in character.

## Group polarization

Whether members change before or after a group decision, or as a result of discussion alone, the possibility of increased extremity in individual opinions excited considerable attention during the past decade. Called, perhaps inconveniently, *group polarization,* such an effect of group discussion ran counter to conventional wisdom, which as we note above, implied that group decisions or positions should be moderate relative to the initial distribution of individual preferences. The group polarization effect was identified by Moscovici and Zavalloni (1969) who observed that French university students sometimes displayed more extreme attitudes following free discussion than they had prior to the interaction. Originally associated with attitudes, the polarization effect has more recently been observed to apply to a wide range of judgement and decision tasks.

The original Moscovici and Zavalloni report fitted easily into the political climate of the times in which student unrest was widespread and intense. Such results seemed to confirm the puzzling observations many had made informally — namely that students sometimes were even more extreme in their opinions *after* what should have been moderating discussion (see also Moscovici, 1976). Traditionally, "polarization" has been a label applied to increased movement toward opposite poles, that is increased bi-modality in a preference distribution, as a result of some social event or force. The current use of polarization is as a label for members' post-discussion mean responses when this value is more extreme than, and "in the *same* direction," as the prediscussion mean (see Myers, Chapter 8.)

Prior to Myers and Lamm (1976), the *"location"* of the polarization effect was not always clear. That is to say, it was not always clear whether polarization was to be regarded as a group-level phenomenon, as group performance outcomes such as choice shift tended to be, or a phenomenon at the individual level. The problem is that in group research the distinction between these two is often unclear. Myers and Lamm appear to imply that the group polarization phenomenon is at the individual level. In other words, we might take this to mean that individual group members change their position as a function of the discussion, mutual accommodation, and so on, which can be described as extremization (a change in either "direction") or polarization (a change in the same "direction"), and this in turn produces changes in response (e.g. shifts) at the group level.

Thus, a change in the group position or decision may be the consequence of a change in position of at least some subset of members or the way in which the opinions are aggregated to reach consensus, or both. More generally, it seems intuitively probable that group performance outcomes are a function of individual opinions, preferences or responses and the social interaction which combines them to produce the group result. Social decision scheme theory yields an overall description of this input—output relation, and social polarization can describe individual-level consequences in before—after designs. However useful these notions may be, a deeper consideration of the interpersonal dynamics remains to be achieved if a closer conceptual connection is to be achieved between individual cognitive behavior and group responses. In other words, why and when do polarizations occur? Why does a social decision scheme arise in one social context or task, and a different summary is required to describe group performance in another? It would seem that answers might appropriately be sought at the interpersonal level.

## Groupthink

Several research themes of recent years can be identified as relevant to the questions posed above. One particular line of work, "groupthink" (Janis, 1972) traces decision fiascos (extreme or bizarre choices) to the collective push for consensus and other antecedent conditions, which sometimes mark actual discussion groups pressing to reach decision (see Chapter 20.) Janis provides a valuable conceptual link between the level of group action and the individual level of opinion and motivation by emphasizing the role of various social-contextual variables (see Fig. 1, Chapter 20). At the same time, he constructs a rich picture of social dynamics using *both* popular accounts (Janis, 1972) of past and present groups making policy decisions, and empirical data (Janis and Mann, 1977; and Chapter 20) — an all too rare synthesis.

Though widely cited and discussed the groupthink phenomenon has been somewhat slow in receiving the attention of empirical researchers. Such a lag may have developed because the attention of investigators has been so closely tuned to (social) cognitive processes at the individual level during the latter half of the seventies. In any event, it is likely that we shall see increased research effort directed at the collection of issues associated with groupthink. For example, Steiner (Chapter 21) has made important heuristic connections with several earlier lines of research (viz., group problem solving, choice shifts, and lynching mobs), thus providing a further foundation within familiar problem areas.

## Interpersonal processes

The dominant concern of research on task-oriented groups has, of course, been with the output *per se* (solution, decision, judgement, etc.). More recently, such an interest has been balanced by a concomitant interest in the social processes responsible — a trend noted by Nagao *et al.* (1978). We might supplement their prediction of increased future research in this direction by observing that various levels of interpersonal dynamics may be identified. Just as the emphasis upon group performance (output) is one of degree, so is the turn to the group's internal workings a relative matter.

### SUBGROUPS AND FACTIONS

Task-oriented groups are often observed to form distinct subgroups. Various factions, coalitions, cliques, and the like, may be identified, depending upon the variable used in differentiating them. The potential number of different structures or interpersonal systems can thus be very large even within the same group. Different sets of subgroups would result as one chooses to classify on age, religion, sex, socioeconomic status, and so on. However, in task-oriented groups, subsets of members likely to be of interest are those which are distinguishable by virtue of their differences concerning what they prefer the group decision, solution, etc., to be. These distinguishable distributions of opinion can create the basis of sometimes intense inter-subgroup interaction (e.g. in juries, city zoning councils, government study commissions, and many other groups likely to debate divisive issues).

For many years, the study of task-defined subgroups focused upon the sometimes awesome power of the majority to influence deviants to conform to the prevailing opinion (Asch, 1956; see Allen, 1965, 1975). Such an emphasis is perhaps not surprising in cultures making a virtue of formal majority rule in political and policy matters. However, with the adoption of a research paradigm (Asch, 1956; Crutchfield, 1955) that minimized free-flowing interaction, the bidirectional nature of influence during discussion preceding a decision or solution was overlooked. Thus, it fell to the "minority influence" research effort (Moscovici, 1976; Nemeth, 1974) to restore some balance to the investigation of majority and minority subgroups each of which is attempting to prevail (see Nemeth, Chapter 8.)

Actually, many tasks permit or even encourage a great many more subgroups than the majority—minority dichotomy. Consider tasks which allow more than two response options. In general, if the group size is $r$ and $n$ is the number of response alternatives, $\binom{n+r-1}{r}$ is the number of distinguishable distributions possible, given that alternatives but not persons are distinguishable (see Davis, 1973; Chapter 2; and Stasser *et al.*, 1980.) Clearly there may be many subgroups, factions, pluralities, minorities, or the like, depending upon conditions. Future research on inter-subgroup influence processes will presumably address not only the multiple subgroup problem, but the basis of persuasion, coercion, and the like, which are at work.

One approach which has addressed the content of interaction is the notion of persuasive arguments as suggested by Vinokur and Burnstein (1974). Persuasive arguments theory is similar in certain respects to informational social influence as a conformity explanation (Deutsch and Gerard, 1955), early information exchange explanations of choice shifts (e.g., Bateson, 1966), and to recent proposals by Bishop and Myers (1974) and Anderson and Graesser (1976) for explaining interaction effects on certain group tasks. Persuasive arguments theory holds that some positions or response alternatives on an issue or point of contention permit or foster argument generation to a greater extent than other positions (see Burnstein, Chapter 5, for a more comprehensive discussion). Culturally shared experiences, given a particular decision task, explain why majorities in at least some groups (and perhaps why resolute minorities in some situations) are so effective in guiding the decision for all.

Despite some contrary trends (e.g. Nisbett and Wilson, 1977), current ideas of (social) information processing seem to reflect a fairly "rational" view of human social judgement (e.g. Fishbein and Ajzen's (in press) account of the citizen voter's reasons for the choices made). The work on persuasive arguments appears to fall within the same general approach which places little emphasis upon the role of motivation, emotion and other such psychological factors which are often poorly represented in conscious experience.

## BARGAINING

Just as distinguishable subgroups holding different positions, preferences, or opinions might emerge during the course of discussion about the group decision, so can a more formal deliberation format recognize the disparate, and sometimes conflicting, aims which characterize different sets of members. Rarely regarded as a subarea of group dynamics or group performance, bargaining and negotiation situations are also aimed at achieving consensus, albeit in a task often characterizable as a zero-sum game (note that the Davis *et al.* (1976) literature review was one of the few such summaries dealing with group dynamics and performance to include bargaining topics). In other words, the typical freely-interacting decision group whose members are not initially unanimous in their opinions may form factions, coalitions, and so on during the struggle for consensus. Sometimes a minor exercise in dispute resolution, other tasks and social contexts may result in considerable conflict, requiring protracted negotiation if the group is to remain intact and achieve consensus. Social contexts which formally recognize the conflicting aims of the subgroups, especially those in which one player's gain is at the expense of another, tend to be regarded as bargaining situations. A useful distinction, it is perhaps also valuable to recognize a continuum of situations, at least in principle; subgroups may emerge during interaction, or they may be officially recognized at the beginning of debate (see Chapter 15 by Rabbie *et al.*).

Bargaining and negotiation have long been active research themes in social psychology, but constitute a relatively small portion of the total effort compared to the attention accorded in the administrative sciences and economics. However, the emphasis upon normative models and prescriptive theories which is routine in the latter have few counterparts in psychology which is much more inclined to study empirically bargaining and negotiation *behavior*.

It is perhaps premature to conclude that a new surge in bargaining research is imminent, but activity in the area is currently at a high level. McGrath (1978) in his brief history of small group research implies that social research questions reflect the surrounding society, its current needs and problems — an observation echoed by Nagao *et al.* (1978). Researchers are, of course, members of their society, and moreover, research on current social problems is likely to enjoy better support than other types of investigation, and relevant scholars are likely to be enlisted in various programs of targeted inquiry. Just as McGrath pointed to the existing level of international conflict as a stimulus for parallel social research in the late 1950s and early 1960s, so might we suggest that negotiation and bargaining research will respond to ecological social limitations and widespread economic problems apparently in store for the 1980s. Empirical inquiries into the effects of third parties in negotiation is one consensus-seeking format very likely to receive special attention (see Stephenson and Webb, Chapter 17), along with a number of related problems (see Morley, Chapter 18, and Crott *et al.,* Chapter 16).

Research on social disagreement seems likely to be a lively topic of research in the immediate future, as in the immediate past, whether the work focuses upon conflict among individuals, subgroups, or groups; motives or cognitions (opinions, preferences, etc.); or emerging factions, coalitions, or formally designated bargaining units. If, indeed, future societal conditions foster increased attention to disagreements, conflicts, etc., as we are implying, it seems likely that a number of other concerns will also become more salient. As a general organizing principle in this regard, we might conclude along with McGrath (1978) that the focal problem at the end of the seventies might be posed: ". . . how can individuals effectively relate to one another amidst the complex physical and social forces of this highly technical and interdependent world?" (p. 655).

SOCIAL EMOTIONS IN GROUP DECISION MAKING

It has been precisely the personal (emotional) reaction to the task and other members which has routinely been missing from theoretical accounts of group performance. Thus, of all the contemporary research topics considered here, the study of personal emotional reactions during and/or associated with interaction is the least common. Research at the level of interpersonal exchanges has generally been sporadic, since the classic work of Bales and his associates (e.g. 1950). However, as Nagao *et al.* (1978) suggested near the close of their summary of research trends, several efforts appear to be emerging which hold considerable promise for the direct study of interaction (e.g. Bakeman and Dabbs, 1976; Gottman and Bakeman, 1979). This research generally stresses the assessment of group members' interactions (see Duncan and Fiske, 1977; Lamb *et al.*, 1979).

A somewhat different approach, but one which also emphasizes the person-to-person level of interaction, is illustrated by Brandstätter (Chapter 13), Rüttinger (Chapter 14), Schuler (Chapter 12), and Stocker-Kreichgauer and von Rosenstiel (Chapter 11). The common theme in this work is the concern with the perceptions of participants and the emotional reactions to the interaction. Much of the work on social cognition and emotion during the past two decades employed research settings which remove the individual from the group. It has frequently been difficult to recognize conceptually that the feature distinguishing the special character of *social* cognition is indeed the dynamic exchanges between and among persons.

Thus, if the increased attention to the study of small groups develops as forecast by McGrath (1978) and Nagao *et al.* (1978), it seems probable that considerably more effort than in the past will be devoted not only to the assessment of interpersonal acts, but to the examination of perceptions, emotions, and motives of those involved. A major problem is, of course, to develop further the theoretical connections between the individual level of response and the aggregate level of action.

## Concluding remarks

The purpose of this chapter was to identify current research problems in small group performance, relate those themes to past and present research efforts, and key these developments to some of the topics covered by the various chapters of this book. However, the coverage of this volume is not exhaustive, and several areas have not been addressed — especially those for which there is no "critical mass" of research reports yet in the literature. For example, there is considerable interest in an area of group decision making called "social choice." Primarily developed within economics and to some extent political science, the field has largely been devoted to normative models and the derivation of consequences (sometimes unexpected) of formal group decision plans. More specifically, social choice theorists have sought to study how a set of individual preferences are mapped into a group choice by means of some social choice function (see especially Black, 1958; Fishburn, 1973; Murakami, 1968). Unlike their counterparts in social psychology, social choice theorists have been concerned more with the selection of whole preference orders (of response alternatives) rather than a most-preferred alternative; committees, votes and elections rather than informal discussion groups interacting freely to consensus; and the construction of theoretical models in which the issue is efficiency, consistency, etc., of axioms rather than empirical estimates of social behavior. However, change appears imminent. For example, empirical verification of social choice propositions seems to be increasingly attractive to social choice theorists (in particular, see Plott, 1977; Plott and Smith, 1976).

Other examples would include the continuing problems created by the lack of a viable task taxonomy for use with performing groups. Long recognized as a serious impediment to small group research (see, for example, Roby and Lanzetta, 1958; Steiner, 1972; Shaw, 1976), group engineering for efficiency through task redesign also requires a better understanding of task-social process dependencies (e.g., Hackman and Morris, 1975, also Davis, Chapter 2). Yet another example might be the effects of interaction which linger in individuals after the group's work is finished. Lewin's (1958) work on group-based attitude change was a prototype of such a focus, but has been largely superceded as a popular paradigm by the "Yale approach" (Fishbein and Ajzen, 1975) which stresses persuasive messages and single individuals, and permits tidier experimental control. Current perspectives which emphasize interaction effects on post-group individuals range from research on jurors (e.g., Davis et al., 1977) to information integration (e.g. Anderson and

Graesser, 1976), and suggest future development may include an important emphasis upon group discussion.

## Summary

We have attempted to relate here the several areas of research represented in this volume to group performance research topics at large. It is clear that work is spread widely not only over geographical areas, but over topic areas as well. However, systematic research has developed along several themes as the sections of this book attest. It is perhaps notable that these themes are focused upon particular problems rather than research "traditions" or philosophical approaches to the study of group behavior we believe to have often been characteristic of much earlier work.

We hope this volume supports an answer of sorts to Steiner's (1974) famous question, "Whatever happened to the group in social psychology?"; the group is well, if not wholly robust, but it is to be found under study in many different places, with many different research techniques, and in response to questions posed at several different levels of social organization. No school of thought appears to be dominant, and this is probably a good development.

## References

Allen, V. L. Situational factors in conformity. In L. Berkowitz (Ed.), *Advances in Experimental Social Psychology*. New York and London: Academic, 1965.

Allen, V. L. Social support for nonconformity. In L. Berkowitz (Ed.), *Advances in Experimental Social Psychology*. New York and London: Academic, 1975.

Anderson, N. H. and Graesser, C. C. An information integration analysis of attitude change in group discussion. *Journal of Personality and Social Psychology*, 1976, 34, 210–222.

Asch, S. E. Studies of independence and submission to group pressure: I. On minority of one against a unanimous majority. *Psychological Monographs*, 1956, 70, (9, Whole No. 417).

Bakeman, R. and Dabbs, J. M. Social interaction observed: Some approaches to the analysis of behavior streams. *Personality and Social Psychology Bulletin*, 1976, 2, 335–345.

Bales, R. F. *Interaction Process Analysis*. Cambridge, Ma: Addison-Wesley, 1950.

Bateson, N. Familiarization, group discussion, and risk taking. *Journal of Experimental Social Psychology*, 1966, 2, 119–129.

Bishop, G. D. and Myers, D. G. Information influence in group discussion. *Organizational Behavior and Human Performance*, 1974, 12, 92–104.

Black, D. *The Theory of Committees and Elections*. Cambridge: Cambridge University Press, 1958.

Brandstätter, H., Davis, J. H. and Schuler, H. C. (Eds) *Dynamics of Group Decisions*. Beverly Hills, Ca: Sage, 1978.

Cartwright, D. Determinants of scientific progress: The case of the risky shift. *American Psychologist*, 1973, 28, 222–231.

Clark, R. D. III Group-induced shift toward risk: A critical appraisal. *Psychological Bulletin*, 1971, 76, 251–270.

Crutchfield, R. S. Conformity and character. *American Psychologist*, 1955, 10, 191–198.

Davis, J. H. The solution of simple and compound word problems. *Behavioral Science*, 1964, 9, 359–370.

Davis, J. H. *Group Performance*. Reading, Ma: Addison-Wesley, 1969a.

Davis, J. H. Individual-group problem solving, subject preferences, and problem type. *Journal of Personality and Social Psychology*, 1969b, 13, 362–374.

Davis, J. H. Group decision and social interaction: A theory of social decision schemes. *Psychological Review*, 1973, 80, 97–125.

Davis, J. H. Group decision and procedural justice. In M. Fishbein (Ed.), *Progress in Social Psychology*. Hillsdale, NJ: Erlbaum, 1980.

Davis, J. H. Group performance: Theories and concepts. In C. G. McClintock and J. Maki (Eds), *Social Psychological Theory*. New York: Holt, in press.

Davis, J. H. and Restle, F. The analysis of problems and prediction of group problem solving. *Journal of Abnormal and Social Psychology*, 1963, 66, 103–116.

Davis, J. H., Kerr, N. L., Sussman, M. and Rissman, A. K. Social decision schemes under risk. *Journal of Personality and Social Psychology*, 1974, 30, 248–271.

Davis, J. H., Laughlin, P. R. and Komorita, S. S. The social psychology of small groups: Cooperative and mixed-motive interaction. *Annual Review of Psychology*, 1976, 27, 501–541.

Davis, J. H., Bray, R. M. and Holt, R. W. The empirical study of decision processes in juries: A critical review. In J. L. Tapp and F. J. Levine (Eds), *Law, Justice and the Individual in Society: Psychological and Legal Issues*. New York: Holt, 1977.

Deutsch, M. and Gerard, H. A study of normative and informational social influence on individual judgment. *Journal of Abnormal Social Psychology*, 1955, 51, 629–636.

Dion, D. L., Baron, R. S. and Miller, N. Why do groups make riskier decisions than individuals? In L. Berkowitz (Ed.), *Advances in Experimental Social Psychology*. New York and London: Academic Press, 1970.

Duncan, S. and Fiske, D. W. *Face-to-face Interaction: Research, Methods, and Theory*. New York: Halsted Press, 1977.

Dunnette, M. C., Campbell, J. and Jaastad, K. The effect of group participation on brainstorming effectiveness for two industrial samples. *Journal of Applied Psychology*, 1963, 47, 30–37.

Fishbein, M. and Ajzen, I. *Belief, Attitude, Intention and Behavior: An Introduction to Theory and Research*. Reading, Ma: Addison-Wesley, 1975.

Fishbein, M. and Ajzen, I. Attitudes and voting behavior: An application of the theory of reasoned action. In G. Stephenson and J. H. Davis (Eds), *Progress in Applied Social Psychology*. London: Wiley, in press.

Fishburn, P. C. *The Theory of Social Choice.* Princeton, NJ: Princeton University Press, 1973.

Gottman, J. M. and Bakeman, R. The sequential analysis of observational data. In M. E. Lamb, S. J. Suomi and G. R. Stephenson (Eds), *Social Interaction Analysis: Methodological Issues.* Madison, WI: University of Wisconsin Press, 1979.

Hackman, J. R. and Morris, C. G. Group tasks, group interaction process, and group performance effectiveness: A review and proposed integration. In L. Berkowitz (Ed.), *Advances in Experimental Social Psychology.* New York and London: Academic, 1975.

Janis, I. L. *Victims of Groupthink.* Boston: Houghton Mifflin, 1972.

Janis, I. L. and Mann, L. *Decision Making: A Psychological Analysis of Conflict, Choice, and Commitment.* New York: Free Press, 1977.

Kerr, N. L., Davis, J. H., Meek, D. and Rissman, A. K. Group position as a function of member attitudes from the perspective of social decision scheme theory. *Journal of Personality and Social Psychology,* 1975, 31, 574–593.

Lamb, M. E., Suomi, S. J. and Stephenson, G. R. (Eds) *Social Interaction Analysis: Methodological Issues.* Madison, Wi: University of Wisconsin Press, 1979.

Lamm, H. and Trommsdorff, G. Group versus individual performance on tasks requiring ideational proficiency (brainstorming): A review. *European Journal of Social Psychology,* 1973, 3, 361–388.

Lewin, K. Group decision and social change. In E. E. Maccoby, T. M. Newcomb and E. L. Hartley (Eds), *Readings in Social Psychology.* New York: Holt, 1958.

Lewin, K., Lippitt, R. and White, R. K. Patterns of aggressive behavior in experimentally created "social climates." *Journal of Social Psychology,* 1939, 10, 271–299.

McGrath, J. E. Small group research. *American Behavioral Scientist,* 1978, 21, 651–674.

Moscovici, S. *Social Influence and Social Change.* New York and London: Academic Press, 1976.

Moscovici, S. and Zavalloni, M. The group as a polarizer of attitudes. *Journal of Personality and Social Psychology,* 1969, 12, 125–135.

Murakami, Y. *Logic and Social Choice.* New York: Dover, 1968.

Myers, D. G. and Lamm, H. The group polarization phenomenon. *Psychological Bulletin,* 1976, 83, 602–627.

Nagao, D. H., Vollrath, D. A. and Davis, J. H. Group decision making: Origins and current status. In H. Brandstätter, J. H. Davis and H. C. Schuler (Eds), *Dynamics of Group Decisions.* Beverly Hills, Ca: Sage, 1978.

Nemeth, C. (Ed.) *Social Psychology: Classic and Contemporary Integrations.* Chicago: Rand McNally, 1974.

Nisbett, R. E. and Wilson, T. D. Telling more than we can know: Verbal reports on mental processes. *Psychological Review,* 1977, 84, 231–259.

Osborn, A. F. *Applied Imagination.* New York: Scribner, 1953.

Plott, C. R. Externalities and corrective policies in experimental markets. Social Science Working Paper, 180. Pasadena, Ca: California Institute of Technology, 1977.

Plott, C. R. and Smith, V. L. An experimental examination of two exchange institutions. Social Science Working Paper, 83. Pasadena, Ca: California Institute of Technology, Revised 1976.

Roby, T. B. and Lanzetta, J. T. Considerations in the analysis of group tasks. *Psychological Bulletin*, 1958, 55, 88–101.

Shaw, M. E. A comparison of individuals and small groups in the rational solution of complex problems. *American Journal of Psychology*, 1932, 44, 491–504.

Shaw, M. E. *Group Dynamics: The Psychology of Small Group Behavior.* New York: McGraw-Hill, 1976.

Stasser, G., Kerr, N. L. and Davis, J. H. Influence processes in decision making: A modeling approach. In P. Paulus (Ed.), *Psychology of Group Influence.* Hillsdale, NJ: Erlbaum, 1980.

Steiner, I. D. *Group Process and Productivity.* New York and London: Academic Press, 1972.

Steiner, I. D. Whatever happened to the group in social psychology? *Journal of Experimental Social Psychology*, 1974, 10, 94–108.

Stoner, J. A. F. A comparison of individual and group decisions involving risk. Unpublished Master's thesis, Massachusetts Institute of Technology, 1961.

Stoner, J. A. F. Risky and cautious shifts in group decisions: The influence of widely held values. *Journal of Experimental Social Psychology*, 1968, 4, 442–459.

Taylor, D. W., Berry, P. C. and Block, C. H. Does group participation when using brainstorming facilitate or inhibit creative thinking? *Administrative Science Quarterly*, 1958, 3, 23–47.

Vinokur, A. A review and theoretical analysis of the effects of group processes upon individual and group decisions involving risk. *Psychological Bulletin*, 1971, 76, 231–250.

Vinokur, A. and Burnstein, E. The effects of partially shared persuasive arguments on group induced shifts: A group problem solving approach. *Journal of Personality and Social Psychology*, 1974, 29, 305–315.

Wallach, M. A., Kogan, N. and Bem, D. J. Group influence on individual risk taking. *Journal of Abnormal and Social Psychology*, 1962, 65, 75–86.

Zajonc, R. B. *Social Psychology: An Experimental Approach.* Belmont, CA: Brooks/Cole, 1966.

Zajonc, R. B., Wolosin, R. J., Wolosin, M. A. and Sherman, S. J. Individual and group risk-taking in a two-choice situation. *Journal of Experimental Social Psychology*, 1968, 4, 89–106.

# I
# Social Decision Schemes

# Introduction

David A. Vollrath and James H. Davis

The development of theories and formal models of small group behavior has historically lagged behind corresponding efforts at collecting data about groups. Steiner (1972) has suggested that the extent to which empirical research outstripped theory contributed to the decline of interest in small groups following their popularity as an object of study in the 1950s. Another contribution to this decline, which highlighted the limited theoretical approaches in group psychology, was a wave of provocative and stimulating theories of individual social psychology, chief among which was cognitive dissonance (e.g. Festinger, 1957).

Today, however, one finds more vigor in theorizing about small group phenomena — evident, for example, in the recent work by Myers and Lamm (1976) and Shiflett (1979). The papers which appear in this section of the book are related by their use of a rather general theoretical approach, the social decision scheme model (Davis, 1973). The basic description of the social decision scheme approach is presented in each of the following chapters, and will not require a general description here.

The historical roots of individual-into-group pooling models, of which social decision scheme theory is a general case, are evident in the work of Taylor (1954), Marquardt (1955), and Lorge and Solomon (1955). Such formulations were stimulated in large measure by the earlier, individual v. group comparisons (e.g., Marjorie Shaw, 1932), and in turn prompted a "second generation" of models which resulted in the general cases of social decision scheme theory and the account of group process and productivity proposed by Steiner (1972). A more detailed treatment of these historical developments is available elsewhere (Davis, in press). Suffice it to say that group versus individual comparison continues to occupy the attention of researchers to this day and to stimulate research, e.g. concerning choice shifts.

The chapter by Davis in this section of the book represents a somewhat more narrow historical review, focusing on the development of the social decision scheme approach and related theory, as well as supporting research. The results of a variety of experiments show how the apparent social process by which a group performs varies with the nature of the task. Tasks high in uncertainty, often encountered in problem solving, encourage groups to perform as if the allocation of work time is egalitarian with respect to competence. Group decision tasks, however, seem to be more variable with regard to member uncertainty about relevant task features. High uncertainty in tasks seems to be associated with an equiprobability social decision process, while moderate and low task uncertainty fosters plurality and majority processes, respectively. If such a generalization relating group process to task features proves reliable, Davis suggests, it should be valuable both in limiting the number of plausible decision schemes in a given situation and in simulating group performance where it cannot be directly observed. Other factors of social context, individual differences and the like may prove to be of overriding importance in any particular application.

In the second chapter, Laughlin and Adamopoulos also address differences in group process as a function of the experimental task. They propose a dimension of consensus which distinguishes intellective from judgmental tasks. The former are evaluated demonstrably within an agreed-upon set of axioms; the latter are decided by social consensus. Moreover, the authors argue that social consensus ultimately operates to establish the axiomatic system by which demonstrability proceeds. The results of several investigations are summarized to suggest that in group intellective performance the social decision process may be described as "truth wins" or "truth-supported wins," depending upon the demonstrability of proposed answers. By contrast, group judgments are often described by a majority process. (It is possible that Davis's task uncertainty, like demonstrability for intellective tasks, may serve to indicate more specifically whether majority, plurality, or equiprobability processes are expected for a certain judgmental task.)

In the final chapter, Kerr introduces social transition schemes, an extension of social decision scheme theory to a more dynamic form. Here the focus is on changes in the distribution of member preferences during the discussion, rather than on the final group product. Kerr reports a study designed to assess the potential re-activity of periodic polling procedures, which are necessary for testing such dynamic models. These procedures may reduce the time required to reach group consensus, but in the cases studied there is no evidence that the position agreed upon is significantly affected. The author then discusses two existing examples of the transition scheme approach and at the same time distinguishes be-tween model-fitting and model-testing methodologies. Kerr also makes a distinction between *shift* and *rate* models of social process, which corresponds closely to the *event* and *timed-event* types of sequential data considered by Gottman and Bakeman (1978) and their associates who have been studying interpersonal processes directly.

These chapters have presented the development of social decision scheme theory from its historical antecedents through some of its present applications in a wide variety of group decision making and problem solving tasks. Of course, many possible topics remain unexplored. The future is likely to see further theoretical develop-ments concerning the social processes responsible for group per-formance, greater attention to sampling multiple populations of individuals, increased reliance on the simulation of proposed changes to groups and their parent institutions prior to undertaking the actual social engineering, and more frequent use of tasks requiring a social consensus rather than the discovery of a correct answer.

## References

Davis, J. H. Group decision and social interaction: A theory of social decision schemes. *Psychological Review*, 1973, 80, 97–125.

Davis, J. H. Group performance: Theories and concepts. In C. G. McClintock and J. Maki (Eds), *Social Psychological Theory*. New York: Holt, in press.

Festinger, L. *A Theory of Cognitive Dissonance.* Evanston, Ill.: Row, Peterson, 1957.

Gottman, J. and Bakeman, R. The sequential analysis of observational data. In M. Lamb, S. Suomi and G. Stephenson (Eds), *Methodological Problems in the Study of Social Interaction*. Madison, Wisc., University of Wisconsin Press, 1978.

Lorge, I. and Solomon, H. Two models of group behavior in the solution of Eureka-type problems. *Psychometrika*, 1955, 20, 139–148.

Marquardt, D. I. Group problem solving. *Journal of Social Psychology*, 1955, 41, 103–113.

Myers, D. G. and Lamm, H. The group polarization phenomenon. *Psychological Bulletin*, 1976, 83, 602—627.

Shaw, M. E. Comparison of individuals and small groups in the rational solution of complex problems. *American Journal of Psychology*, 1932, 44, 491—504.

Shiflett, S. Toward a general model of small group productivity. *Psychological Bulletin*, 1979, 86, 67—79.

Steiner, I. D. *Group Process and Productivity*. New York and London: Academic Press, 1972.

Taylor, D. W. Problem solving by groups. In Proceedings XIV, International Congress of Psychology, 1954. Amsterdam: North Holland Publishing, 1954.

# 2
# Social Interaction as a Combinatorial Process in Group Decision

James H. Davis

The aim of this chapter is to trace the history and origin of what one might call an individual-into-group approach (Davis, 1969a) to the study of group performance. First, we shall consider the comparison of individuals and groups, one of the oldest "problems" in social psychology, and then describe how this comparison leads rather naturally to the representation of task-oriented social processes as combinatorial processes. Finally, we shall discuss the use of this idea in a research program primarily, though not exclusively, concerned with group performance.

## Individuals versus groups

Over the years the simple notion of comparing the performance of a set of individuals with that of a sample of groups has been repeatedly discovered and rediscovered. The motivation for the comparison can sometimes be traced to highly practical aims. For example, the question of efficiency and cost per man-hour has long been an issue in industrial work groups of all kinds. Organizational efficiency of course does not entirely depend upon small group performance, but is often closely related. A second kind of motivation may derive from the realization that the individual-group comparison is at the point of demarcation between individual psychology and social psychology.

The nature of the task has always been crucial in determining the importance of the individual-group comparison. The idea of a group

Preparation of this chapter was supported by NSF Grant BNS 77-15216.

task should be expanded for our purposes to mean a *task-role system*: task and subtask performance roles as well as response alternatives and requisite cognitive activity are defined by the task demands in some sense. Moreover, we will confine our attention to essentially intellective tasks, perhaps the most frequent object of study in any event. However, the early studies by Triplett (1898) compared how rapidly individuals in isolation could wind a fishing reel, with the performance of those persons doing the same task in each other's company.

A number of such "coaction" or "audience" studies during the ensuing two or three decades reported highly inconsistent results in that sometimes social facilitation and sometimes inhibition was reported. It was not until Zajonc (1965) that a theoretical analysis of the research (using tasks which ranged from the reel-winding task of Triplett to the more intellective tasks of Dashiell, 1930) brought some order to the findings. The nature of the task was critical; learning (or processing information) versus performance of well-practised responses fostered inhibition or facilitation according to task demand.

Although the work of Triplett, among others just described, focused on individual rather than group level action, other research focused on the comparison of group level action with that of individuals. Perhaps the classic study in the latter category was the investigation of group problem solving by Marjorie Shaw (1932) — long regarded as the basic empirical support for group superiority in view of her finding that a higher proportion of groups than individuals solved some common problems. Her general explanation and that of many who followed her was that group interaction stimulated intellective activity, permitted the mutual catching of errors, and allowed partial ideas to be integrated by social interaction. The activity known as "group brainstorming" (Osborn, 1957) was an outgrowth of such thinking and attempted to apply interpretations of why groups were superior to individuals. Until the middle to late 1950s social psychologists appeared to regard groups in one place engaged in one kind of task very much like those in another place engaged in a different kind of task. In other words, there was little critical attention devoted specifically to the importance of either the task or the associated role-contextual demands.

However, by the mid-1950s there was considerable concern over such issues. First Taylor (1954), then Marquardt (1955), and most incisively Lorge and Solomon (1955) showed in a rather simple form that Shaw's interpretation of the apparent group performance superiority could be seriously challenged. These workers introduced a model of the problem solving process that permitted an evaluation of Shaw's results in terms of efficiency. It is now well known that the "superiority" of group problem solving cannot in general be maintained, and for many (though not all) intellective tasks could be seriously questioned. We shall return later to this fundamental change in interpretation of results from group-individual perform-ance comparisons, and the change in theoretical approach which was responsible.

*Individual versus groups: conceptual issues*
Of course, the important theoretical issue is not just the finding that group performance is or is not different in one way or another from that of individuals. The important question is why and how might this come about. It is this theoretical question which is the primary concern of this paper.

We will generally be concerned with *ad hoc,* freely interacting, task-oriented groups of perhaps as many as a dozen people, but usually less than half that many. Such groups have been widely studied in social psychology, partly for their convenience, but also because they resemble in certain respects a great many groups in contemporary society. A surprising variety of important groups do not have a long history of mutual association; juries, study com-missions, organization evaluation teams etc., are all examples of short-lived, *ad hoc* groups that perform important tasks. Moreover, we shall focus on group level action: the aggregation of individual task proposals or the process whereby initially independent and perhaps disparate individuals coordinate their activities to establish a consensus for a group response.

## Interaction as the pooling of resources

Perhaps the most important "metatheory" or conceptual tradition in the study of small groups was the group dynamics of Kurt Lewin (e.g., 1947). Lewin apparently saw the group as the site of social forces in dynamic interaction. These ideas sustained not only Lewin's own active empirical research efforts, but stimulated a long list of well known theorists and researchers. However, by the early sixties, group research had begun to languish. Steiner (1972) mentions in the preface to his book on group process and productivity that empirical research on groups simply outran the available theory. Certainly prior to the middle 1960s attention had shifted to "individual" social cognition, although methodological refinement and experimental control may have been as important as newly available theory focusing on individuals rather than groups (e.g. cognitive dissonance).

### Individual-into group as "pooling" of resources

Whatever the reason for the decline of group dynamics as the dominant conceptual force in small group research, one might take the position that a somewhat separate tradition was developing during the late 1950s. This second approach was more concerned with the group product or intellective aspects of the goal to be achieved than it was with social interaction *per se*. Whereas the Lewinian tradition emphasized interpersonal relations or structural properties of the group, the new approach emphasized the task-relevant resources of the members and the way in which these were aggregated, concatenated, or the like in order to perform the task. The difference in the two traditions is one of relative emphasis.

The basic idea was that members of a small group contribute or pool their resources (variously defined) to solve a problem or reach a decision. The pooling notion seems to have started in several places at about the same time, and was inherent in several early efforts (cf. Davis, 1969a). Taylor (1954) was perhaps the first to propose resource pooling in a clear way, but the most succinct is the formal statement ("Model A") by Lorge and Solomon (1955):

$$P = 1 - (1 - p)^r. \tag{1}$$

This simple pooling notion was based upon the hypothesis that the probability, $p$, of a correct solution by an individual was constant for all persons being studied, and that individuals in group problem solving situations acted rather much as they did when alone. They further assumed that social interaction is neither deleterious nor facilitating to such efforts, members behave independently, and a solution was adopted if it arose in discussion. In other words, the probability, $P$, of a group solving a problem was simply the probability that the group of size $r$ contained at least one individual solver.

The notion that people would interact without affecting each other's tendency to solve a problem is surely false in general. The point is the model provided a conceptually useful standard against which the familiar individual--group comparison could be judged (see Steiner and Rajaratnam, 1961, for a modification of the Lorge—Solomon model in order to provide a more nearly descriptive model). To be sure, the Lorge—Solomon, and Taylor model was cast in the language of problem solving, and thus the idea of correct and incorrect solutions. However, its usefulness is not limited to problem solving situations (i.e. to tasks requiring the social processing of information). Decision making situations, where the primary requirement is to select one response out of several defined by the task, may be equally relevant, and "correctness" or "optimality" may not be involved.

In summary, the pooling of abilities or aggregating of resources may seem a relatively passive notion in comparison to the dynamics that characterized the Lewinian approach. However, we may extend the notion beyond the mere "pooling" of ideas to the active combination of task responses or resources. In other words, we can regard the social interaction that achieves a solution, or establishes a consensus on the group decision, as an active combinatorial process.

## Social combination processes

Social interaction as a combinatorial process implies that elements (whether they be ideas, partial task responses, or position preferences on a social issue) must be aggregated. Arithmetic averages of individual members' positions or task responses is a very common, though often ill-advised, aggregation principle. Also, some elements may predominate or receive special weight during discussion. An hypothesis of social averaging may not always be incorrect, but a great many group tasks define response alternatives that do not form an ordered set much less represent points along a continuum.

In the following sections a sequence of empirical studies is described in just such combinatorial terms. The basic goal which lies behind this effort is to treat the emerging social process as largely a function of the task to be performed. We propose to review a number of studies conducted over several years which, although not identical as to subject population and conditions of research, are nonetheless quite similar in both respects. The subjects were typically university undergraduates and the groups were *ad hoc* aggregations of randomly assembled subjects given no special instructions (except as noted) as to how they should interact or organize their social effort.

## Problem solving: the combination-of-contributions model

Restle and Davis (1962), taking a "combinatorial" approach, constructed a formal model which dealt with both the individual solving of word puzzles (the task in question) and group problem solving. These problems were of a sort commonly used in group problem solving in that they possessed a single correct solution, and often a correct answer was self-evident. The classic water jar problem of Luchins (1942) was an example of such puzzles, although the research literature contains a great many other examples as well. From earlier research which need not concern us here, Restle and Davis concluded that for subjects working as individuals, the time, $t$, to a solution should be gamma-distributed, and thus,

$$g(t; \lambda, k) = \frac{\lambda}{\Gamma(k)} e^{-\lambda t} (\lambda t)^{k-1}. \tag{2}$$

Here, $\lambda$ and $k$ are respectively the rate parameter and the number of "stages" in the problem. (A stage in this sense is a separate idea which must be conjoined to the next, and the solver is finished when the various subproblems or ideas have all been correctly achieved.) An additional assumption of this model for individual problem solving is that the times to solve each of the $k$ stages are independently and identically distributed (exponential) random variables.

What concerns us here is that Restle and Davis next took up the question of how group members might pool or combine their contributions when each of them had been drawn from a population of problem solvers described by Equation 2. Imagine we have a group of $r$ persons facing a problem that must be solved in $k$ equally difficult stages. Imagine first of all that none of the subjects arrives at a wrong solution. All subjects are solvers, and thus the group solves at the increased rate of $r\lambda$, where $\lambda$ is of course the rate at which an individual solves the problem. In other words, the solution rate has been increased by a factor of $r$, leading to the expression,

$$g(t; r\lambda, k) = \frac{r\lambda}{(k-1)!} e^{-r\lambda t} (r\lambda t)^{k-1}. \tag{3}$$

Restle and Davis next undertook the construction of two extreme forms of this general combination of contributions model, since the ideal that all group members can solve the problem is not plausible in general.

In one special case, called the hierarchical model, they assumed that some subjects will "go off the track," in the sense that a group is likely to contain at least some members who do not or cannot solve the problem. In this sense non-solvers would be non-functional or, in the most extreme case, have no effect upon the group process at all. In other words, the group social process is hierarchically arranged such that only those able to solve the problem consume any of the group's working time. This means the "best" people (the solvers) are working on the problem, while the "incompetent" (the non-solvers) are somehow suppressed. Such a view constitutes a plausible "upper boundary" for problem solving groups, and may be shown to be analogous to the Lorge and Solomon Model A (cf. Restle and Davis, 1962). If there are $A$ solvers in a group and $B = r - A$ non-solvers, the distribution of solution times should be a gamma distribution, $g(t; A\lambda, k)$. Now, if $a$ is the probability of an individual worker ultimately solving the problem, then the probability that a group of size $r$ has precisely $A$ members who will solve the problem is

$$P(A) = \binom{r}{A} a^A (1 - a)^{r-A},  \tag{4}$$

the familiar binomial distribution. Taking Equations 3 and 4 together we have the distribution of group solution times to be

$$f_H(t) = \sum_{A=0}^{r} P(A)g(t; A\lambda, k),  \tag{5}$$

if the hierarchical model is correct. In other words, from the perspective of this "upper boundary," groups solve according to the social process that allows those people on the "right track" to consume time, but not those who are on the "wrong track."

At the other extreme, Restle and Davis constructed an egalitarian model, which they viewed as another special case of the combination of contributions model, but one establishing a kind of "lower boundary" for group problem solving of the sort in question. This model assumes, in contradistinction to the hierarchically organized group, that persons not contributing to solution continue to consume their proportionate share of the group's working time, and the rate is reduced from $\lambda$ to $(A/r)\lambda$. However, only A solvers are at work on a problem in any event, and thus we have

$$g(t; A(A/r)\lambda, k) = g(t; (A^2/r)\lambda, k). \tag{6}$$

Thus, since once more we must weight this expression by the probability of A solvers in the group, we have for the egalitarian model the density function,

$$f_E(t) = \sum_{A=0}^{r} [P(A)g(t, (A^2/r)\lambda, k)], \tag{7}$$

if the egalitarian model is correct.

Although Restle and Davis proposed a number of other theoretical ideas for different situations, we shall be concerned with the empirical test of only these two. Davis and Restle (1963) compared predictions of each model in turn with the response times of *ad hoc* groups of four working on each of three separate problems in succession. (One problem was a word puzzle concerning the escape of a prisoner from a castle; the second problem was a typical "tongue twister" requiring cancellation of several mutually contradictory phrases; and the third was a standard Luchins water jar problem modified for use in these circumstances.) These results are given in Fig. 1.

As confirmed both statistically and by inspection, the hierarchical model is seriously in error, and does not afford an adequate description of the results. To our surprise, the egalitarian model provided a close fit, and could not be confidently rejected. In other words, whereas we had initially anticipated group performance to fall between these two extremes (which we have regarded as "boundaries" of a sort), it appears that the distribution of solution times was very well described by what we have considered to be a lower boundary (see Larntz and Regal, 1978, for a general, technical discussion of estimation and a reanalysis of these data using a different approach).

The result was somewhat counterintuitive, but we subsequently obtained sociometric data which closely supported the equalitarian hypothesis.[1] One summary of what we have observed might be that

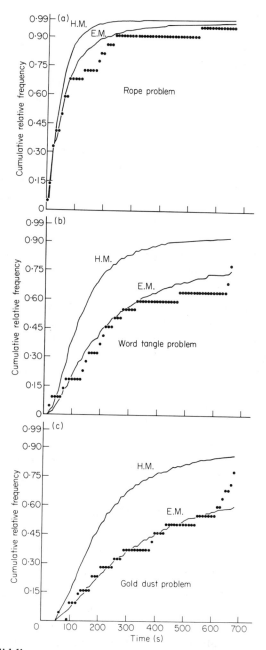

Fig. 1. The solid lines represent cumulative relative frequency predicted by the hierarchical and egalitarian models for groups of size 4. (Observed group performance is given by solid points.) (From Restle and Davis, 1962. Copyright American Psychological Association. Reproduced with permission.)

one group member's proposed solution is as acceptable as another in such a context. (It is worth noting at this point that the equalitarian social hypothesis is not simply another name for random guessing on the part of the subjects; such models are easily rejected.) These results were subsequently replicated (Davis, 1969b) with smaller groups ($r = 3$) and longer allowable working times.[2] It would appear then that at least some kinds of group problem solving are well described by an egalitarian assumption about the social process.

One likely influence on the way in which members socially combine task contributions is their familiarity with each other, especially in regard to past task performance of a similar nature. In a study by Davis et al. (1971), a number of groups whose members had substantial experience with working together at a succession of intellective tasks which were part of a prolonged business game in an administrative science curriculum were assigned one of the problems (the modified water jar problem called the "gold dust" problem) used earlier by Davis (1969b) and Davis and Restle (1963). Somewhat surprisingly the same egalitarian form of the combination of contributions model closely predicted the solution time distribution of the experienced groups. These results are given in Fig. 2. Whereas the equalitarian model could not be rejected, the hierarchical model could once more be rejected confidently, confirming the relative goodness-of-fit evident by inspection.

In summary, problem solving groups, under several different conditions, appear to be well described by a social decision process that assumes an equalitarian input or contribution. At this point, we elected to move from the study of group problem solving to group decision making — a task classification of some convenience.

### Social decision schemes and group decision making

Many decision tasks, unlike most problem solving tasks, have a fairly well circumscribed set of response alternatives which are mutually exclusive and exhaustive. For example, there may be two or three courses of action, whether or not one or more of the response alternatives can be interpreted as correct, optimal, or in some other fashion. Moreover, depending upon the task, these may or may not be ordered alternatives or reflect an underlying continuum. The initial problem was to adapt the general combination of contributions idea to the discrete case where response alternatives not time was at issue.

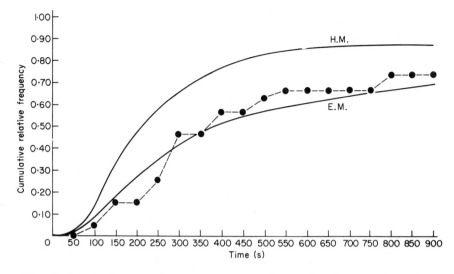

Fig. 2. The higher smooth curve represents the predicted cumulative relative frequency of group solutions under the hierarchical model, and the lower curve the same for the equalitarian model. The data obtained from three-person groups (broken curve) was acceptably described only by the equalitarian model. (From Davis *et al.*, 1971. Copyright Academic Press. Reproduced with permission.)

Imagine that a decision maker must select one of $n$ mutually exclusive and exhaustive response alternatives, $A_j, j = 1, 2, \ldots, n$. We assume that individual decisions are characterized by a discrete probability distribution, $p = (p_1, p_2, \ldots, p_n)$, over these alternatives, and that groups are described by a probability distribution, $P = (P_1, P_2, \ldots, P_n)$, over the same response alternatives. (The number of response alternatives available for groups may be different from the number defined for individuals, but we shall not consider that possibility here.) The theoretical problem is one of mapping the individual distribution onto or into the group distribution. One way of summarizing the social process responsible for such mapping uses the idea of a social decision scheme.[3] Basically, a social decision scheme may reflect a social (task) norm, or it may be an emergent phenomenon that is simply a consequence of individuals from some particular population and setting working together. The point is that group discussion begins with any one of a large number of possible arrays of member opinion and ends with a group decision. We assume the discussion which establishes the consensus on one or another response alternative is representable as a social decision scheme. "Majority rules" is an example of a well known social decision scheme, although it is not well defined in the sense we shall discuss below.

*Social decision scheme theory*
It is convenient at this point to describe a very general combinatorial model for translating the social decision scheme approach into an explicit account of group decision making. (Prior to the derivation of the general model (Davis, 1973), many of the theoretical notions to be described made use of special case models involving rather tedious algebra.) As before, imagine that a decision task defines a set of mutually exclusive and exhaustive response alternatives, $A_1, A_2, \ldots, A_n$. The probability of any alternative being chosen is given by the probability distribution, $p = (p_1, p_2, \ldots, p_n)$ for individuals, and similarly for $r$-person groups, $P = (P_1, P_2, \ldots, P_n)$.

Next, we recognize that at the beginning of discussion individual members may disagree on the response alternative for the group. Consequently, individuals may array themselves over the $n$ response alternatives in $m = \binom{n + r - 1}{r}$ different ways. An array is sometimes referred to as a distinguishable distribution since alternatives are distinguishable but not individuals. The probability of the $i$-th distribution occurring, $\pi_i$, may in some research applications be estimated directly by counting the relative frequency, $\hat{\pi}_i$, of the $i$-th array. But, in other instances, $\pi_i$ must be estimated indirectly by substituting the estimates $(\hat{p}_1, \hat{p}_2, \ldots, \hat{p}_n)$ from a sample of individuals in the expression

$$\pi_i = \binom{r}{r_1, r_2, \ldots, r_n} p_1^{r_1} p_2^{r_2} \cdots p_n^{r_n}, \tag{8}$$

the well known multinomial distribution which defines the probability of the $i$-th distinguishable distribution occurring.

Given a particular distribution or array of opinions in a group, what is the probability that a group will choose a particular alternative? This process is obviously a function of the social interaction that establishes the consensus and to which we have earlier given the name social decision scheme. To provide the social decision scheme with more explicit form, we define the conditional probability, $d_{ij}$, which is the probability of the group choosing the

$j$-th response alternative given the $i$-th distinguishable distribution. The general statement of theoretical relations between initial distribution and final outcome may be cast in a $m \times n$ social decision scheme matrix, $D$. Examples of social decision scheme matrices for $15 \times 3$ matrices are given in Table 1.

TABLE 1

*Examples of various 15 × 3 social decision scheme matrices for groups of size r = 4 and n = 3 response alternatives*

| Disting. Distrib. | Equiprobability | | | Proportionality | | | Plurality—Equiprobability | | |
|---|---|---|---|---|---|---|---|---|---|
| | $A_1$ | $A_2$ | $A_3$ | $A_1$ | $A_2$ | $A_3$ | $A_1$ | $A_2$ | $A_3$ |
| (4, 0, 0) | 1.00 | 0.00 | 0.00 | 1.00 | 0.00 | 0.00 | 1.00 | 0.00 | 0.00 |
| (0, 4, 0) | 0.00 | 1.00 | 0.00 | 0.00 | 1.00 | 0.00 | 0.00 | 1.00 | 0.00 |
| (0, 0, 4) | 0.00 | 0.00 | 1.00 | 0.00 | 0.00 | 1.00 | 0.00 | 0.00 | 1.00 |
| (3, 1, 0) | 0.50 | 0.50 | 0.00 | 0.75 | 0.25 | 0.00 | 1.00 | 0.00 | 0.00 |
| (3, 0, 1) | 0.50 | 0.00 | 0.50 | 0.75 | 0.00 | 0.25 | 1.00 | 0.00 | 0.00 |
| (1, 3, 0) | 0.50 | 0.50 | 0.00 | 0.25 | 0.75 | 0.00 | 0.00 | 1.00 | 0.00 |
| (1, 0, 3) | 0.50 | 0.00 | 0.50 | 0.25 | 0.00 | 0.75 | 0.00 | 0.00 | 1.00 |
| (0, 3, 1) | 0.00 | 0.50 | 0.50 | 0.00 | 0.75 | 0.25 | 0.00 | 1.00 | 0.00 |
| (0, 1, 3) | 0.00 | 0.50 | 0.50 | 0.00 | 0.25 | 0.75 | 0.00 | 0.00 | 1.00 |
| (2, 2, 0) | 0.50 | 0.50 | 0.00 | 0.50 | 0.50 | 0.00 | 0.50 | 0.50 | 0.00 |
| (2, 0, 2) | 0.50 | 0.00 | 0.50 | 0.50 | 0.00 | 0.50 | 0.50 | 0.00 | 0.50 |
| (2, 1, 1) | 0.33 | 0.33 | 0.33 | 0.50 | 0.25 | 0.25 | 1.00 | 0.00 | 0.00 |
| (1, 2, 1) | 0.33 | 0.33 | 0.33 | 0.25 | 0.50 | 0.25 | 0.00 | 1.00 | 0.00 |
| (1, 1, 2) | 0.33 | 0.33 | 0.33 | 0.25 | 0.25 | 0.50 | 0.00 | 0.00 | 1.00 |
| (0, 2, 2) | 0.00 | 0.50 | 0.50 | 0.00 | 0.50 | 0.50 | 0.00 | 0.50 | 0.50 |
| | Majority—Proportionality | | | Averaging | | | Majority—Averaging | | |
| | $A_1$ | $A_2$ | $A_3$ | $A_1$ | $A_2$ | $A_3$ | $A_1$ | $A_2$ | $A_3$ |
| (4, 0, 0) | 1.00 | 0.00 | 0.00 | 1.00 | 0.00 | 0.00 | 1.00 | 0.00 | 0.00 |
| (0, 4, 0) | 0.00 | 1.00 | 0.00 | 0.00 | 1.00 | 0.00 | 0.00 | 1.00 | 0.00 |
| (0, 0, 4) | 0.00 | 0.00 | 1.00 | 0.00 | 0.00 | 1.00 | 0.00 | 0.00 | 1.00 |
| (3, 1, 0) | 1.00 | 0.00 | 0.00 | 1.00 | 0.00 | 0.00 | 1.00 | 0.00 | 0.00 |
| (3, 0, 1) | 1.00 | 0.00 | 0.00 | 0.50 | 0.50 | 0.00 | 1.00 | 0.00 | 0.00 |
| (1, 3, 0) | 0.00 | 1.00 | 0.00 | 0.00 | 1.00 | 0.00 | 0.00 | 1.00 | 0.00 |
| (1, 0, 3) | 0.00 | 0.00 | 1.00 | 0.00 | 0.50 | 0.50 | 0.00 | 0.00 | 1.00 |
| (0, 3, 1) | 0.00 | 1.00 | 0.00 | 0.00 | 1.00 | 0.00 | 0.00 | 1.00 | 0.00 |
| (0, 1, 3) | 0.00 | 0.00 | 1.00 | 0.00 | 0.00 | 1.00 | 0.00 | 0.00 | 1.00 |
| (2, 2, 0) | 0.50 | 0.50 | 0.00 | 0.50 | 0.50 | 0.00 | 0.50 | 0.50 | 0.00 |
| (2, 0, 2) | 0.50 | 0.00 | 0.50 | 0.00 | 1.00 | 0.00 | 0.00 | 1.00 | 0.00 |
| (2, 1, 1) | 0.50 | 0.25 | 0.25 | 0.00 | 1.00 | 0.00 | 0.00 | 1.00 | 0.00 |
| (1, 2, 1) | 0.25 | 0.50 | 0.25 | 0.00 | 1.00 | 0.00 | 0.00 | 1.00 | 0.00 |
| (1, 2, 2) | 0.25 | 0.25 | 0.50 | 0.00 | 1.00 | 0.00 | 0.00 | 1.00 | 0.00 |
| (0, 2, 2) | 0.00 | 0.50 | 0.50 | 0.00 | 0.50 | 0.50 | 0.00 | 0.50 | 0.50 |

As a final step, we may relate the individual probability distribution, $p$, with the group probability distribution, $P$, by the expression

$$\pi D = (\pi_1, \pi_2, \ldots, \pi_m) \begin{bmatrix} d_{11} & d_{12} & \cdots & d_{1n} \\ d_{21} & d_{22} & \cdots & d_{2n} \\ \cdot & & & \cdot \\ \cdot & & \cdots & \cdot \\ \cdot & & & \cdot \\ d_{m1} & d_{m2} & \cdots & d_{mn} \end{bmatrix} = (P_1, P_2, \ldots, P_n)$$

(9)

One advantage of the social decision scheme approach is evident from Table 1. All possible ways, distinguishable distributions, that four individuals may array themselves over three alternatives is shown by these matrices. The first matrix, labeled equiprobability, is one that is conceptually comparable to the equalitarian model of the problem solving research discussed earlier. Observe that each alternative advocated by one or more members is as likely to be the decision as any other alternative advocated by one or more members. Observe that this is not like a "random" coin tossing exercise, in that no alternative without an advocate can be chosen. In contrast, observe the proportionality social decision scheme matrix in which the probability of a response alternative being chosen is the proportion of persons advocating that alternative. Next, is the plurality, equiprobability otherwise model. That social decision scheme makes explicit an assumption about a social process in which the group chooses with probability near 1.00 that alternative which possesses a plurality of members; but, if no alternative possesses a plurality, then equiprobability prevails as a subscheme. A majority, proportionality otherwise, social decision scheme matrix has a similar interpretation. In that case, the majority defines the alternative with probability near 1.00, but if no majority exists the probability of an alternative being chosen requires a subscheme which, as illustrated there, is the proportionality principle. The averaging model assumes that the group chooses an alternative with probability near 1.00 which is nearest the arithmetic average of the alternatives advocated. Of course, such a subscheme assumes that the alternatives are ordered, whereas the preceding social decision schemes can operate on a nominal scale. The final matrix illustrates a majority, otherwise averaging social decision scheme.

It is perhaps obvious that the general social decision scheme model reflects an approach to the study of group performance which easily admits of special case models of the sort we have mentioned above. These special case models carry the substantive theory which makes explicit, by means of the social decision scheme matrix, those notions only implied by such phrases as "majority action." The entries of $D$ thus provide a precise rendition as to the order of majority (simple, 5/6, 3/4, 2/3, or the like), the form of the sub-scheme acting when no majority exists, the force of the majority (the probability of a majority prevailing) as well as the minority, and many other factors usually left unstated by the deceptively simple label, "majority effect." Of course, the social decision scheme is a macro-level summary of social process, for all of its explicit-ness, and the investigator's interest may ultimately be on the de-tailed interpersonal events responsible for the group's action or differences in individual motivation, cognition, and so on, respon-sible in turn.

The research described in the following sections emphasizes the role of the task confronting the group in influencing the particular social process responsible for collective performance. In other words, we varied the task to observe how the social decision scheme changed accordingly, while holding (relatively) constant some variables (e.g., social context), and "randomizing out" others (e.g., individual differences).

## Decisions under high task uncertainty

A number of group decision studies have used tasks devoid of social content in order to minimize normative and other influences on the decision making process. For example, Zajonc et al. (1968) required subjects to make a choice as to which of two lights would appear on each of several trials. Zajonc et al. were interested in studying choice shifts when no obvious social content was present in the task to engage social norms etc., as a number of choice—shift theories required (see Dion et al., 1970, or Vinokur, 1971, for reviews of the choice shift literature). The major point for our purposes is that the subject, individual or group, was quite uncertain about task features or parameters.

In fact, when the subject is unaware of the probability associated with an outcome the custom is to speak of decisions under uncertainty. However, if the subject is aware of the probabilities, then such choices are called decisions under risk. Thus, making decisions about a fair die are decisions under risk because the probability of a side is known in the sense that it is deducible from plausible assumptions. The two-choice situation used by Zajonc *et al.* required decisions under uncertainty, because the subject was unaware of such essential task parameters except as he or she developed an impression by the end of the experiment.

Johnson and Davis (1972) made use of a similar two-choice task, paying subjects a small amount for a correct choice. Defining risky choices as the decision to adopt the less frequent but potentially higher payoff light, the risky choices of three-person groups may be plotted as in Fig. 3.

We have hypothesized, as a result of the problem solving research described earlier, that an equalitarian social process is likely to arise under conditions of substantial task uncertainty. Consequently, the most plausible social decision scheme is the one defined by the equiprobability matrix in Table 1. (Note that the values for $n$ and $r$ will differ study to study, and thus from those given in Table 1.) Calculations were carried through under that model, and the cumulative risks predicted for group decisions are also given in Fig. 3. As evident by inspection, there is a rather close fit between model predictions and data.[4]

Davis *et al.* (1970) carried out a similar sequential decision task, requiring individual subjects and groups to make decisions under

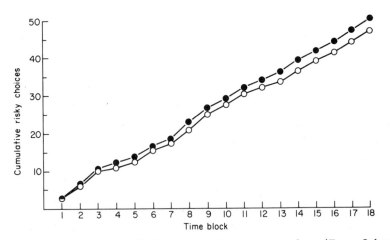

Fig. 3. Equiprobability predictions in relation to group data. (From Johnso and Davis, 1972. Copyright Academic Press. Reproduced with permission.)

substantial task uncertainty. In this Davis *et al.* study subjects chose which one of four lights would appear on a trial. Four-person groups discussed and individuals pondered strategy between each block of trials. Moreover, subjects, whether individuals or groups, were encouraged to think of the task as a problem to be solved in that optimal responding could be achieved, although correct choices on all trials were not a realistic possibility. The results were consistent with the Johnson–Davis findings. By the third block of trials, several models such as plurality, majority, etc., could be rejected, and an equiprobability model was the only statistically acceptable account of the group response distribution.

In summary, it would appear from several points of view that substantial task uncertainty, whether a problem to be solved or a sequential decision making task, forces an egalitarian/equiprobability social process. Although not mentioned previously, groups in all studies were closely observed by experimenters, and interpersonal relations assessed sociometrically. In every case, sociometric questionnaire responses and informal observations converged to support the notion of an egalitarian social process. Thus, several lines of evidence seem to suggest that an egalitarian social process attends group decision making under the task uncertainty conditions we have described.

## Decisions under moderate task uncertainty

In the absence of a good task typology, or even a clear theory of tasks in individual or group decision making, it is difficult to manipulate task uncertainty with precision. Therefore, it is necessary to rely on intuition and rather gross changes in task structure. In one such variation, Davis *et al.* (1968) modified a task used earlier by Myers and Sadler (1960). A slide appeared before a subject on each of several trials, and indicated whether he or she had won or lost a unit, as signaled by $(-1)$ or $(+1)$. The subject could elect to "stay" with this known outcome or to take a risk of sorts by choosing an "unknown" event — a slide which appeared shortly after the known event. The unknown event was one where the subject could win up to 11 units or lose up to 11 units, indicated by a $+11, +10, \ldots, -10, -11$. Like the known event $(-1, +1)$, the values of the unknown event appeared equally often. Again, neither individuals nor groups were instructed as to the exact nature of the best strategy, but were encouraged to seek one which would permit them to maximize the number of their wins over trials.

The result from this study most important for our purposes was that a plurality social decision scheme provided an acceptable account of group decisions. The analysis of individual and group choices employed a rather complicated set of hypothetical strategies to which individuals and/or groups might ascribe, and this makes summarizing the data graphically somewhat difficult. However, suffice it to say that group risk-taking decisions were well described (on both those trials where subjects lost a unit and those where they had gained a unit) by a plurality social decision scheme (see Table 1 for an example).

In summary, it is tempting to suggest that departure from a strict egalitarianism is fostered by a task where there is somewhat more definite grounds about which to disagree and deliberate. A task with more distinct features may offer grounds for forming disagreeing subgroups, and hence create a need for a decision rule of some "decisiveness" (e.g., plurality, majority, etc.) based on relative numbers of adherents.

### Decisions under low task uncertainty

In the final variation, we undertook to create a substantial decrease in task uncertainty by not only choosing a task where the parameters governing outcomes were quite obvious but by training subjects in the meaning of "probability of winning," amount of money liable to be lost, etc. For this task, Davis et al. (1974) adopted the duplex bet (e.g. Slovic and Lichtenstein, 1968). Duplex bets possess a number of desirable properties for the study of decision making under risk. We will not have space to discuss these here, but, as shown in Fig. 4, a subject sees two "pies" divided to illustrate the probability of winning (left-hand) or losing (right-hand), as well as the amount which can be won or lost. The separation of winning or losing events in this way is not familiar to most subjects, and thorough training was undertaken to insure a high level of understanding.

Both individuals and four-person groups were asked to rate the attractiveness of each of the 16 bets along a ten-point scale. Later a pair of bets would be selected at random, and the higher rating would determine which bet they would play (i.e., wager some of the small stake (wage) they had been paid). In other words, the initial decision figured heavily in the total amount of money one would acquire in the future.

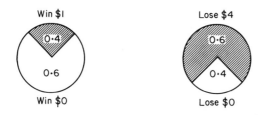

Fig. 4. The two discs represent a single duplex gamble. (The left-hand disc represents the amount that can be won, and the probability of winning that amount, as well as the probability of winning nothing. Similarly, the right-hand disc indicates the amount that can be lost, and the probabilities of losing that amount, or losing nothing.) (From Davis *et al.*, 1974. Copyright American Psychological Association. Reproduced with permission.)

We have not the space here to discuss the several results of what was a relatively large study. However, we might point out that individual decisions were closely correlated with the bets' expected values (which ranged from −3.00 to +3.00). Such scales are bounded, like any rating scales, and we found that the individual decision distributions were negatively skewed for bets with high positive expected values, while bets with low, negative expected values were positively skewed. Bets with expected values near zero produced decision distributions that were rather symmetrically distributed with mean near the mid-point of the rating scale. These distributional properties are important, since the social decision scheme model depends upon the individual distribution.

In the Davis *et al.* (1974) study, predictions from six models, judged applicable at the outset on intuitive grounds, were contrasted with the data. These were equiprobability; proportionality; majority, otherwise equiprobability; majority, otherwise proportionality; plurality, otherwise equiprobability; and plurality, otherwise proportionality. Some of the social decision schemes for these matrices were given earlier for the 15 × 3 case in Table 1, and the others are deducible from the labels given above. The only statistically acceptable fit was provided by the majority, otherwise proportionality model; data and predictions from this model are given in Fig. 5. As is evident by inspection, this form of the majority model provided a very close account of the group decision distribution both for bets with positive expected values as shown in Fig. 5a, and for bets with negative expected values as shown in Fig. 5b.

Again, not only did the majority model provide a close account

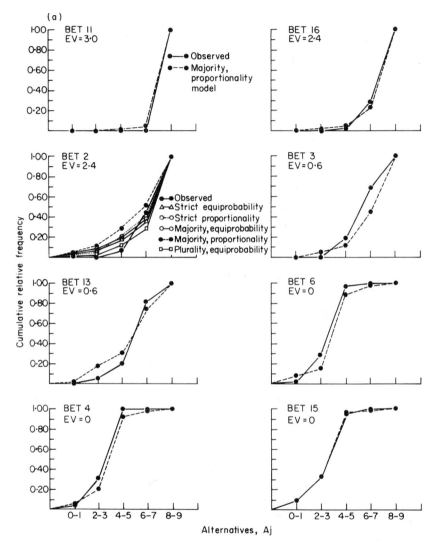

Fig. 5(a). Cumulative relative frequency observed at Period 2 for male group preferences (solid curve) for the alternatives, $A_j$, on each bet and predictions (broken curve) under the majority-proportionality model. (Predictions under several other social decision scheme models are illustrated for Bet 2.) (From Davis *et al.*, 1974. Copyright Americal Psychological Association. Reproduced with permission.)

of the data, but post-group questionnaire responses showed a majority to be the most frequent nomination to describe the consensus process. The majority scheme was more popular yet as the ideal social decision process for such tasks.

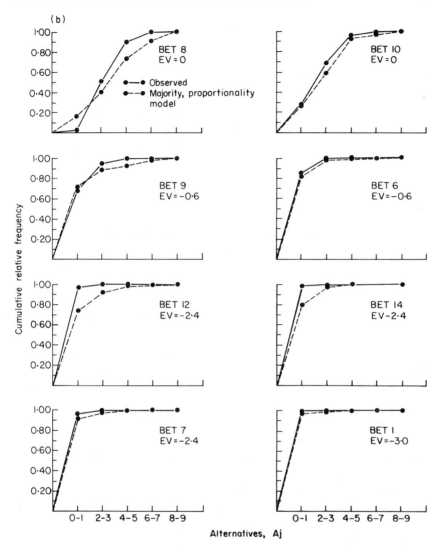

Fig. 5(b). Cumulative relative frequency observed at Period 2 for male preferences (solid curve) for the alternatives, $A_j$, on each bet and predictions (broken curve) under the majority-proportionality model. (Predictions under several other social decision scheme models are illustrated for Bet 2 in Fig. 5a.) (From Davis *et al.*, 1974. Copyright American Psychological Association. Reproduced with permission.)

These and other analyses strongly support the notion of a majority process arising in groups confronted with duplex bets. Our interpretation is that in such cases the task role system requires a more decisive or explicit social decision scheme than has been observed on the previous decision and problem solving experiments. Such a change in social decision scheme may come about because the opportunity for disagreement was heightened when clear positions could be established concerning rather definite features of the task. It is also possible the particular task-role system engaged a prevalent social norm imported into the situation; this seems less likely since little extra-group social content was attached to the gambling decisions of duplex bets — indeed one of the major reasons they were chosen for study.

### Decision making in mock juries

We next turn to decision tasks, which are not bereft of social content in the sense that the decision has larger implications or engages extra-group issues to some extent. The uncertainty associated with task features is necessarily low.

Studies with which we will be concerned below required mock juries to reach a decision concerning the guilt of a defendant who had been accused of rape. The subjects, after viewing a (closed circuit) television presentation of a mock trial, were asked to give their personal opinion about the guilt of the defendant. Some of these individuals were later assigned the role of juror, and they deliberated as a jury to reach a verdict of guilty or not guilty. Some juries failed to reach a verdict after a considerable length of time, and were thus declared hung. The first study (Davis et al., 1975) was undertaken in part to ascertain the effect on the jury verdict distribution of two variables: (a) size (six or 12 persons), and (b) assigned decision rule (instructions to reach a 2/3 majority or a unanimous decision). (Observe that the number of decision outcomes is $n = 2$ for individuals, guilty and not guilty, but $n = 3$ for juries since they can be hung.)

As is evident from Table 2 there was no significant effect upon the relative frequency of guilty, not guilty, or hung verdicts due to jury size or assigned decision rule. The next step was to seek an account of jury decisions given the individual guilt-preference distribution, $\hat{p}_G = 0.22$ and $\hat{p}_{NG} = 0.78$, observed in the independent samples of individuals and among pre-deliberation jurors, and assuming in turn a number of social decision scheme models which seemed intuitively plausible for six- and 12-person juries (examples of social decision scheme matrices appropriate to juries are given in Table 3).

TABLE 2

*Distribution of guilty, not guilty, and hung juries of 12 and six members assigned unanimous and two-thirds majority decision rules, and predictions under the one most accurate model of the 13 studied*

| | Six-person | | | Jury size 12-person | | | Total | | |
|---|---|---|---|---|---|---|---|---|---|
| Experimental condition | G | NG | H | G | NG | H | G | NG | H |
| Individuals | | | | | | | $0.22^a$ | 0.78 | |
| Assigned social decision scheme | | | | | | | | | |
| Unanimity | 0.00 | 0.89 | 0.11 | 0.00 | 0.72 | 0.28 | 0.00 | 0.81 | 0.19 |
| 2/3 Majority | 0.00 | 0.89 | 0.11 | 0.00 | 0.94 | 0.06 | 0.00 | 0.92 | 0.08 |
| Total | 0.00 | 0.89 | 0.11 | 0.00 | 0.83 | 0.17 | 0.00 | 0.86 | 0.14 |
| Predictions (2/3 Majority; proportionality)$^b$ | 0.02 | 0.88 | 0.10 | 0.00 | 0.90 | 0.10 | 0.01 | 0.89 | 0.10 |

Note: There were 18 juries assigned to each cell and 73 individuals. Abbreviations are as follows: $G$ = guilty, $NG$ = not guilty, $H$ = hung. Adapted with permission from Davis *et al.* (1975), copyright with American Psychological Association.
[a]Predeliberation individual jurors and second-tested (post-reflection responses) individuals who were never in juries gave identical guilty/not guilty response distributions, namely, 0.22, 0.78.
[b]See $D_4$ and $D_8$ in Table 3.

From amongst the predictions generated by various social decision scheme models suitable to juries (15 more or less plausible schemes were entertained) only one (2/3 majority, otherwise hung) closely predicted the outcome distributions of both six- and 12-person juries. These predictions are given at the bottom of Table 2. The social decision scheme matrices in question are listed in Table 3 as $D_4$ and $D_8$ for six- and 12-person juries respectively. Again, ancillary data offered additional support for a majority social decision scheme.[5]

Individual jurors developed opinions about the defendant's guilt, and were asked to record their personal verdict preference. Jury deliberation, often quite intense, involved developing support for either a guilty or not guilty verdict. It is our interpretation at this point that the jury decision task more closely resembles the duplex bet situation than the uncertain tasks studied earlier. Task features are well drawn (according to which people can take definite positions) and involve evidence, testimony, and the like, as well as the verdict.

In support of the basic majority nature of the social decision process, we turn next to a study by Davis *et al.* (1977a) which also investigated two independent variables — the effect of victim suffering

TABLE 3

*Selected examples of social decision scheme matrices for 12- and six-person juries, showing the probability, $d_{ij}$, of the j-th verdict given the i-th distribution of member preferences*

| Distribution of jurors | | Verdict distribution | | | | | | | | | | |
|---|---|---|---|---|---|---|---|---|---|---|---|---|
| | | G | NG | H | G | NG | H | G | NG | H | G | NG | H |
| G | NG | | $D_1$ | | | $D_2$ | | | $D_3$ | | | $D_4$ | |
| 12 | 0 | 1.00 | 0.00 | 0.00 | 1.00 | 0.00 | 0.00 | 1.00 | 0.00 | 0.00 | 1.00 | 0.00 | 0.00 |
| 11 | 1 | 1.00 | 0.00 | 0.00 | 1.00 | 0.00 | 0.00 | 1.00 | 0.00 | 0.00 | 1.00 | 0.00 | 0.00 |
| 10 | 2 | 1.00 | 0.00 | 0.00 | 1.00 | 0.00 | 0.00 | 1.00 | 0.00 | 0.00 | 1.00 | 0.00 | 0.00 |
| 9 | 3 | 0.00 | 0.00 | 1.00 | 0.75 | 0.13 | 0.13 | 0.00 | 1.00 | 0.00 | 1.00 | 0.00 | 0.00 |
| 8 | 4 | 0.00 | 0.00 | 1.00 | 0.67 | 0.17 | 0.17 | 0.00 | 1.00 | 0.00 | 1.00 | 0.00 | 0.00 |
| 7 | 5 | 0.00 | 0.00 | 1.00 | 0.58 | 0.21 | 0.21 | 0.00 | 1.00 | 0.00 | 0.00 | 0.00 | 1.00 |
| 6 | 6 | 0.00 | 0.00 | 1.00 | 0.50 | 0.25 | 0.25 | 0.00 | 1.00 | 0.00 | 0.00 | 0.00 | 1.00 |
| 5 | 7 | 0.00 | 0.00 | 1.00 | 0.21 | 0.58 | 0.21 | 0.00 | 1.00 | 0.00 | 0.00 | 0.00 | 1.00 |
| 4 | 8 | 0.00 | 0.00 | 1.00 | 0.17 | 0.67 | 0.17 | 0.00 | 1.00 | 0.00 | 0.00 | 1.00 | 0.00 |
| 3 | 9 | 0.00 | 0.00 | 1.00 | 0.13 | 0.75 | 0.13 | 0.00 | 1.00 | 0.00 | 0.00 | 1.00 | 0.00 |
| 2 | 10 | 0.00 | 1.00 | 0.00 | 0.00 | 1.00 | 0.00 | 0.00 | 1.00 | 0.00 | 0.00 | 1.00 | 0.00 |
| 1 | 11 | 0.00 | 1.00 | 0.00 | 0.00 | 1.00 | 0.00 | 0.00 | 1.00 | 0.00 | 0.00 | 1.00 | 0.00 |
| 0 | 12 | 0.00 | 1.00 | 0.00 | 0.00 | 1.00 | 0.00 | 0.00 | 1.00 | 0.00 | 0.00 | 1.00 | 0.00 |

| | | G | NG | H | G | NG | H | G | NG | H | G | NG | H |
|---|---|---|---|---|---|---|---|---|---|---|---|---|---|
| | | | $D_5$ | | | $D_6$ | | | $D_7$ | | | $D_8$ | |
| 6 | 0 | 1.00 | 0.00 | 0.00 | 1.00 | 0.00 | 0.00 | 1.00 | 0.00 | 0.00 | 1.00 | 0.00 | 0.00 |
| 5 | 1 | 1.00 | 0.00 | 0.00 | 0.83 | 0.00 | 0.17 | 1.00 | 0.00 | 0.00 | 1.00 | 0.00 | 0.00 |
| 4 | 2 | 0.00 | 0.00 | 1.00 | 0.67 | 0.00 | 0.33 | 1.00 | 0.00 | 0.00 | 1.00 | 0.00 | 0.00 |
| 3 | 3 | 0.00 | 0.00 | 1.00 | 0.33 | 0.33 | 0.33 | 0.00 | 0.75 | 0.25 | 0.00 | 0.00 | 1.00 |
| 2 | 4 | 0.00 | 0.00 | 1.00 | 0.00 | 0.67 | 0.33 | 0.00 | 1.00 | 0.00 | 0.00 | 1.00 | 0.00 |
| 1 | 5 | 0.00 | 1.00 | 0.00 | 0.00 | 0.83 | 0.17 | 0.00 | 1.00 | 0.00 | 0.00 | 1.00 | 0.00 |
| 0 | 6 | 0.00 | 1.00 | 0.00 | 0.00 | 1.00 | 0.00 | 0.00 | 1.00 | 0.00 | 0.00 | 1.00 | 0.00 |

Note: Some entries ($d_{ij}$) are given as 0.00 or 1.00 for convenience; the true corresponding parameter values should be regarded as very near but not equal to 0.00 or 1.00.
$D_1$ and $D_5$: 5/6 majority, hung otherwise. $D_2$: 5/6 majority, otherwise proportionality and equiprobability mixture. $D_3$: A not-guilty advocate supported "wins." $D_4$ and $D_8$: 2/3 majority, otherwise proportionality. $D_6$: Proportionality-hung mixture, equiprobability otherwise. $D_7$: 2/3 (simple) majority, defendant protection-hung otherwise mixture.

(two levels) in the same but slightly modified mock trial,[6] and the severity of the potential penalty (two levels) in the event of a guilty verdict. Neither variable exerted significant effects, and the data from all (six-person) juries were combined to increase the power for testing social decision scheme models.

Predictions from various social decision scheme models were tested against the verdict distributions of juries as before. Again, a 2/3 majority model provided the most accurate account of the data, and was in keeping with other self-report and observational results.

However, a different subscheme was required in the second study —
perhaps an important though subtle difference (see matrix $D_7$ in
Table 3).

We will not further discuss jury decisions. Comprehensive summaries of the mock jury studies described above, as well as discussions of several other similar investigations not mentioned here,
may be found in Davis (in press). However, it seems at this juncture
that the shift from egalitarian/equiprobability social processes,
which we believe to be associated with highly uncertain decision
tasks, to the majority principle, which may be related to the less
uncertain (duplex bets), has continued. That is, we see in the case
of jury verdicts an even more "decisive" social decision scheme or
stronger (higher order) majority norm emerging — that is, a 2/3
rather than a simple majority.

## Social decisions: opinions and social issues

We observed earlier that group performance research has been
handicapped by the absence of a satisfactory task typology. Consequently, our observations that tasks have varied with regard to
explicit task parameters or prominent structural features have
rested largely on intuitive grounds. At the same time we must recognize that there has been an increasing level of "personal involvement" in the decisions required of groups. For example, even casual
observation suggests there is considerably less involvement in achieving an optimal strategy in the distribution of one's choices among
four lights over a series of trials[7] than at the other extreme where
one plays the role of a juror.

The question of personal involvement suggests an important
type of group decision rarely studied until recently: taking a position
on a social issue. If the issues are carefully chosen, substantial personal involvement of members already exists prior to group discussion. While "taking a position" may not be very well defined
after the fashion of, say, duplex bet ratings, the social object may
be familiar and one's feelings about a social issue may indeed be very
explicit. Clearly, such opinion decisions do not possess an intuitively
compelling location on the task uncertainty "dimension" we have
been considering heretofore.

From this point of view a study by Kerr *et al.* (1975) is especially
pertinent. We will discuss only a portion of the study in which
subjects (both individuals and four-person groups) were asked to

take a position on each of four social issues or social objects. The position was an alternative along a seven-category scale ranging from "bad" to "good." Discussion to establish consensus preceded the group endorsement of a position on each issue. Individuals similarly expressed again their preference after reflection.

Unfortunately, the social decision scheme matrices that would translate various plausible conjectures about the consensus-establishing process are very large, 210 by 7. However, as in the applications we have discussed up to this point, the entries of the matrices are not parameters to be estimated, but are parameters fixed by assumption once the overall social decision scheme has been defined.[8] A large number of intuitively relevant social decision schemes were considered prior to this research on opinion decisions. The closest approximation to the data was given by the majority, otherwise averaging, social decision scheme, although a median model was also fairly accurate. The distribution of group decisions for each opinion is given in Fig. 6 along with predictions assuming a majority-averaging model.

It is evident by inspection that the majority, otherwise averaging model provides a fairly close description of the data. The opinion task for which decisions were required in this study is interesting on several grounds. We observed earlier that tasks such as "position-taking" on social issues would seem to engage majority norms (in this case, simple majority) in a rather natural way. However, a scale, as opposed to nominal categories, allows (perhaps even encourages) compromises — compromises which may be described by averaging, weighted averaging, taking the median, or perhaps constructing some other similar function of member positions. Such a task is quite different from choosing among lights, developing strategy over several trials, or reaching a guilty/not guilty verdict — all sets of response alternatives which do not easily admit of compromise in the usual sense of choosing an alternative located somewhere between positions of contending members.[9]

## Discussion

We have viewed a series of studies beginning in the early 1960s and continuing to the present rather like a grand experimental manipulation — which implies some degree of planning. While there has been

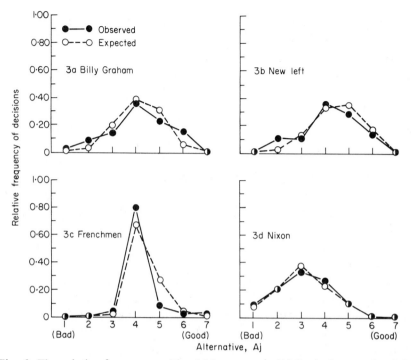

Fig. 6. The relative frequency with which groups (solid line) chose each of the response alternatives on the semantic differential items. (Predictions assuming a majority-averaging model are given by the broken line.) (From Kerr *et al.*, 1975. Copyright American Psychological Association. Reproduced with permission.)

considerable planning over this 15-year period, it has not been nearly as orderly as such *post hoc* summaries as this may make it seem. Moreover, other research using populations differing considerably in socioeconomic character, cultural background, or in other ways, might arrive at quite different conclusions. Obviously empirical research needs to check out these possibilities as well as other task variations. Our research has, as we mentioned at the outset, been carried out under relatively uniform conditions with relatively homogeneous subject populations. While the typical undergraduate population is not uniform, the interpersonal variation is not nearly as great as we typically find in the social world at large.

Overall, it is difficult to escape the impression that social decision schemes do depend to a considerable extent upon the task confronting the group. To what extent a social decision scheme is a picture of a social norm that is engaged by the task and context and to what extent the social decision scheme is an emergent conse-quence of other conditions in the group situation is not yet clear. However, it seems plausible that both increasing social involvement and increasing conflict, as a consequence of members being able to take explicit positions with regard to task/structural features, re-quire a more decisive or explicit social decision scheme in order to achieve consensus. If this interpretation of the research record is correct, we then have a guide for deciding, *a priori,* which categories of social decision scheme models (and there are many *a priori* can-didates) might be applicable in particular situations. This reduction of the large number of viable possibilities is important, partly be-cause of economy in conducting social research, but also partly because we need to select some workable number of relevant social decision models for purposes of simulating group decision effects under conditions difficult or impossible to research directly. One thinks here of such applications as jury deliberations or sensitive meetings of government decision-making bodies which are not open to direct empirical study, but for which important social engineering changes (e.g. size, procedure, etc.) cannot be delayed because of political or ethical pressures to alter the system.

No social decision scheme model, however accurate or intuitively pleasing its predictions, can be proved unique. On the contrary, for any set of data there may exist another social decision scheme matrix that will equally well predict the data. This can be seen mathemati-cally by noting that if one writes out Equation 9 as a system of simultaneous linear equations it possesses no unique solution in general. Obviously, there are always competing explanations for any theoretical interpretation. Subsequent tests of earlier inferences continue the familiar chain. The difficulty in social research is that, given the ill-defined character of the phenomena we study and the imperfect state of psychological measurement, we must be par-ticularly careful about attributing much permanence to conceptual explanations, whether translated by social decision schemes or something else.[10] It is less that social knowledge "perishes" than that social researchers and consumers alike sometimes fail to ap-preciate its dynamic character. Temporal and cultural inconstancies are very much a fact of social life.

Finally, we might notice that we have ignored two extremely important characteristics of small group performance. The first of these is that we have treated all individuals as being well characterized by a single probability distribution with regard to the decision task. Fortunately, we have recently been able to derive social decision scheme models which provide for individual differences by allowing the subject population to be partitioned into subpopulations, each characterized by its own probability distribution (see Davis *et al.*, 1978, and Davis, in press.) A second problem concerns the static nature of the social decision scheme models as we have discussed them. Recall that we generally begin with the initial array of member task preferences, and by various social assumptions predict the final outcome. Obviously, this approach underemphasizes the dynamic quality of social interaction which intervenes between the two events. Recently, however, social decision scheme models have been developed which directly accommodate social dynamics (Davis *et al.*, 1976, Stasser and Davis, 1977, and Stasser *et al.*, in press). We anticipate that these two developments should prove useful in the future for both empirical research and theoretical simulations oriented toward application.

## Notes

1. Group performance is the phenomenon, variously measured, in all of the studies to be reported. However, other data concerned with various facets of group activity and interaction were routinely collected in each case, and their internal consistency examined. Goodness-of-fit between theoretical prediction and the observed value of the performance variable in question is of course the main interest and necessary conceptual achievement. But, the value of this or any other theoretical notion does not rest on a single data set, or even single kind of data; a major appeal of programmatic research is the availability of a cumulative record for evaluating conceptual notions.

2. Bray *et al.* (1978) have recently reported an extensive investigation of group performance in which they varied both problem difficulty and group size, and explored the usefulness of the combination of contributions model under a variety of conditions.

3. This terminology directly reflects the continuity between the work reported here and that of Smoke and Zajonc (1962) in which the term "decision scheme" also occurs.

4. The Johnson and Davis study was carried out before social decision theory was efficiently formalized (Davis, 1973), and hence made use of somewhat more laborious calculations to achieve the same result. Finally, more than one theoretical construction can sometimes yield statistically acceptable predictions for a particular data set. In the case at hand, the Zajonc *et al.* two-stage model (1968) could not be rejected, but in an absolute sense was not quite as accurate an account as the Johnson—Davis equiprobability model. In the general case, the matrix $D$ is not unique. That is to say, more than one $D$ will solve the expression $\pi D = P$. See Kerr *et al.* (in press) for a comprehensive discussion of this issue.

5. It is perhaps worth noting that in general a conclusion that group size is inefficacious in juries operating on a majority social decision scheme, as in this study, constitutes a contradiction. As mentioned in Davis *et al.* (1975), if the majority, otherwise hung social decision scheme is true, then there must be a difference in the verdict distribution of six- and 12-person juries. Davis *et al.* discussed this conceptual issue at length and it is again discussed in Davis (in press). The problem is that the true difference is necessarily small; samples typically used in empirical research, including the present study with 720 subjects, are simply too small to detect such small theoretical differences (see also Davis *et al.*, 1977b).

6. To our surprise we were able to increase the guilty preferences of individuals from $\hat{p}_G = 0.22$ in the first study to $\hat{p}_G = 0.53$ in the second investigation by relatively subtle alterations in the script. A case less "slanted" to one or the other verdicts offers a better opportunity for various treatments to manifest themselves.

7. In the various studies described herein, subjects were sometimes volunteers, sometimes able to win small amounts of money, sometimes paid modestly, and sometimes worked only for "points." We have never observed systematic differences due to financial status of subjects; the amounts of money involved were apparently too small. In general, subjects appeared to be well motivated by the prospect of accumulating points and a sense of achievement as by financial renumeration at the modest level we could afford.

8. Research (Laughlin *et al.*, 1975) emphasizing parameter estimation rather than theory testing has also been carried out when the lack of plausible theory or even appealing "folklore" dictated such an approach. Also, see Kerr *et al.* (in press) for a discussion of model-testing and model-fitting research strategies.

9. During *post hoc* analyses, the authors constructed a rather complicated model that employed normative beliefs of subjects as well as personal preferences and the subsequent predictions were also close to the group decision distributions. This *post hoc* model is not considered here partly because there are no other data supporting such a notion, and partly because subsequent, though informal, studies have cast doubt on its generality.

10. At this writing, preliminary analyses (Davis *et al.*, unpublished data; Nagao and Davis, unpublished data) of the sequence of mock jury studies (Davis *et al.*, 1975, 1976, 1977, 1978; Kerr *et al.*, 1976) suggest that some subject parameters have changed over the course of a relatively short period of time. See Davis *et al.* (1978), Davis *et al.* (unpublished data) and Nagao and Davis (unpublished data) for a more comprehensive discussion.

# References

Bray, R. M., Kerr, N. L. and Atkin, R. S. Effects of group size, problem difficulty, and sex on group performance and member reactions. *Journal of Personality and Social Psychology*, 1978, 36, 1224–1240.

Dashiell, J. F. An experimental analysis of some group effects. *Journal of Abnormal and Social Psychology*, 1930, 25, 190–199.

Davis, J. H. *Group Performance*. Reading, Mass.: Addison-Wesley, 1969a.

Davis, J. H. Individual-group problem solving, subject performances, and problem type. *Journal of Personality and Social Psychology*, 1969b, 13, 362–374.

Davis, J. H. Group decision and social interaction: A theory of social decision schemes. *Psychological Review*, 1973, 80, 97—125.

Davis, J. H. Group decision and procedural justice. In M. Fishbein (Ed.), *Progress in Social Psychology*. Hillsdale, N. J.: Erlbaum, in press.

Davis, J. H. and Restle, F. The analysis of problems and a prediction of group problem solving. *Journal of Abnormal and Social Psychology*, 1963, 66, 103—116.

Davis, J. H., Hoppe, R. A. and Hornseth, J. P. Risk-taking: Task, response pattern, and grouping. *Organizational Behavior and Human Performance*, 1968, 3, 124—142.

Davis, J. H., Hornik, J. A. and Hornseth, J. P. Group decision schemes and strategy preferences in a sequential response task. *Journal of Personality and Social Psychology*, 1970, 15, 397—408.

Davis, J. H., Bates, P. A. and Nealey, S. M. Long-term groups and complex problem solving. *Organizational Behavior and Human Performance*, 1971, 6, 28—35.

Davis, J. H., Kerr, N. L., Atkin, R. S., Holt, R. and Meek, D. The decision processes of 6- and 12-person juries assigned unanimous and 2/3 majority rules. *Journal of Personality and Social Psychology*, 1975, 32, 1—14.

Davis, J. H., Stasser, G., Spitzer, C. E. and Holt, R. W. Changes in group members' decision preferences during discussion: An illustration with mock juries. *Journal of Personality and Social Psychology*, 1976, 34, 1177—1187.

Davis, J. H., Kerr, N. L., Sussmann, M. and Rissman, A. K. Social decision schemes under risk. *Journal of Personality and Social Psychology*, 1974, 30, 248—271.

Davis, J. H., Kerr, N. L., Stasser, G., Meek, D. and Holt, R. Victim consequences, sentence severity, and decision processes in mock juries. *Organizational Behavior and Human Performance*, 1977a, 18, 346—365.

Davis, J. H., Bray, R. M. and Holt, R. W. The empirical study of decision processes in juries: A critical review. In J. Tapp and F. Levine (Eds), *Law, Justice and the Individual in Society: Psychological and Legal Issues*. New York: Holt, Rinehart & Winston, 1977b.

Davis, J. H., Spitzer, C. E., Nagao, D. and Stasser, G. The nature of bias in social decisions by individuals and groups — an example from mock juries. In H. Brandstätter, J. H. Davis and H. Schuler, *Dynamics of Group Decisions*. Beverly Hills, Ca.: Sage, 1978.

Dion, K. L., Baron, R. S. and Miller, N. Why do groups make riskier decisions than individuals? *Advances in Experimental Social Psychology*, 1970, 5, 306—372.

Johnson, C. E. and Davis, J. H. An equiprobability model of risk taking. *Organizational Behavior and Human Performance*, 1972, 8, 159—175.

Kerr, N. L., Davis, J. H., Meek, D. and Rissman, A. K. Group position as a function of member attitudes: Choice shift effects from the perspective of social decision scheme theory. *Journal of Personality and Social Psychology*, 1975, 31, 574—593.

Kerr, N. L., Atkin, R. S., Stasser, G., Meek, D., Holt, R. W. and Davis, J. H. Guilt beyond a reasonable doubt: Effects of concept definition and assigned decision rule on the judgments of mock jurors. *Journal of Personality and Social Psychology*, 1976, 34, 282—294.

Kerr, N. L., Stasser, G. and Davis, J. H. Model testing, model fitting and social decision schemes. *Organizational Behavior and Human Performance*, in press.

Larntz, K. and Regal, R. R. Likelihood methods for testing group problem solving data. *Psychometrika*, 1978, 43, 353—366.

Laughlin, P. R., Kerr, N. L., Davis, J. H., Halff, H. M. and Marciniak, K. A. Group size, member ability, and social decision schemes on an intellective task. *Journal of Personality and Social Psychology*, 1975, 31, 522—535.

Lewin, K. Frontiers in group dynamics (1947). In D. Cartwright (Ed.), *Field Theory in Social Science*. New York: Harper, 1951.

Lorge, I. and Solomon, H. Two models of group behavior in the solution of Eureka-type problems. *Psychometrika*, 1955, 20, 139—148.

Luchins, A. S. Mechanization in problem solving : The effect of Einstellung. *Psychological Monographs*, 1942, 54, No. 6 (Whole No. 248).

Marquardt, D. I. Group problem solving. *Journal of Social Psychology*, 1955, 41, 103—113.

Myers, J. L. and Sadler, E. Effects of range of pay-offs as variable in risk-taking. *Journal of Experimental Psychology*, 1960, 60, 306—309.

Osborn, A. F. *Applied Imagination*. New York: Scribners, 1957.

Restle, F. and Davis, J. H. Success and speed of problem solving by individuals and groups. *Psychological Review*, 1962, 69, 520—536.

Shaw, M. E. Comparison of individuals and small groups in the rational solution of complex problems. *American Journal of Psychology*, 1932, 44, 491—504.

Slovic, P. and Lichtenstein, S. Relative importance of probabilities and pay-offs in risk taking. *Journal of Experimental Psychology Monograph*, 1968, 78, No. 3, Part 2.

Smoke, W. H. and Zajonc, R. B. On the reliability of group judgments and decisions. In J. H. Criswell, H. Solomon & P. Suppes (Eds), *Mathematical Methods in Small Group Processes*. Stanford, Ca.: Stanford University Press, 1962.

Stasser, G. and Davis, J. H. Opinion change during group discussion. *Personality and Social Psychology Bulletin*, 1977, 3, 252—256.

Stasser, G., Kerr, N. L. and Davis, J. H. Social influence and group decision making. In P. Paulus (Ed.), *Psychology of Group Influence*. Hillsdale, N.J.: Erlbaum, in press.

Steiner, I. D. *Group Process and Productivity*. New York and London: Academic Press, 1972.

Steiner, I. D. and Rajaratnam, N. A model for the comparison of individual and group performance scores. *Behavioral Science*, 1961, 6, 142—147.

Taylor, D. W. Problem solving by groups. In *Proceedings XIV, International Congress of Psychology, 1954*. Amsterdam: North Holland Publishing, 1954.

Triplett, N. The dynamogenic factors in pacemaking competition. *American Journal of Psychology*, 1898, 9, 507—533.

Vinokur, A. Review and theoretical analysis of the effects of group processes upon individual and group decisions involving risk. *Psychological Bulletin*, 1971, 76, 231—250.

Zajonc, R. B. Social facilitation. *Science*, 1965, 149, 269—274.

Zajonc, R. B., Wolosin, R. J., Wolosin, M. A. and Sherman, S. J. Individual and group risk taking in a two-choice situation. *Journal of Experimental Social Psychology*, 1968, 4, 89—106.

# 3
# Social Transition Schemes: Model, Method, and Applications

Norbert L. Kerr

Although an enormous amount of research has been carried out on what may be called the social psychology of small groups, distressingly little is understood about the process of group decision-making. Most prior research, including our own, has employed product theories or models. By using this designation I do not mean that this work has not spoken to the processes whereby a group product is forged; rather, I mean that most traditional small-group research has validated its theoretical notions by examining the effects of sundry variables on some product of group interaction, such as the group's decision, proposed solution, and the like. Such a strategy can speak to process issues but does so indirectly, i.e. successful prediction of the group product provides support for the theory's process assumptions. However, the process itself has been directly observed and analyzed infrequently.

The primary purpose of this chapter is to present a stochastic model of the group decision-making process, termed the social transition scheme (STS) model. I will argue that this model provides a useful framework within which to carry out systematic research on the group decision-making process (called the GDM process in this chapter). The paper will consist of three parts. The first will outline the origins and logic of the STS model. The second part reports a methodological experiment designed to see whether collecting the data required for a STS analysis disrupts or alters the GDM process. The paper will conclude with a brief summary of existing applications of the STS model and a description of some of the theoretical problems which the model is particularly well suited to answer in future research.

## The social transition scheme model

ORIGINS: THE SOCIAL DECISION SCHEME (SDS) MODEL

The STS process model has grown out of Davis' (1973) social decision scheme (SDS) product model which Davis outlines in his chapter in this volume. To briefly recapitulate, the SDS model is a stochastic model of group decision-making with which one may predict the distribution of group decisions. In the simplest version of the model two parameters are fixed: (a) the group size = $r$, and (b) the number of response alternatives = $n$. To make its predictions, the model then requires only two additional pieces of information: (a) the overall distribution of individual preferences, and (b) a social decision scheme. The latter is a rule which specifies $d_{ij}$ = the probability that the group will adopt the $j$'th decision alternative when it begins discussion with the $i$'th possible internal distribution of opinion (there are $m = \dbinom{n + r - 1}{r}$ such "distinguishable distributions"). Such a rule must be exhaustive in the sense that every distinguishable distribution of member opinion is accounted for. Thus, the familiar "simple majority" decision rule would not in general constitute a decision scheme because it does not make a prediction in cases of non-majority. However, by adding a secondary rule or "subscheme" to handle such troublesome cases, one can construct a social decision scheme (e.g. majority-averaging). The logic of the SDS model is quite straightforward. Given the distribution of individual opinion, and the assumption of random composition of groups (which is usually procedurally guaranteed), one can use the multinomial expansion to compute the probability of each distinguishable distribution occurring, $\pi_j$, $j = 1, 2, \ldots, m$. Then, for any decision scheme of interest, one may generate a predicted probability distribution of group decisions by partitioning the $\pi_j$ among the response alternatives in accordance with the decision scheme and accumulating across the distinguishable distributions (see Davis, 1973, for a more detailed explanation of the model). Formally, this is accomplished by post-multiplying the row vector $\pi$ by the decision-scheme matrix $D$ (i.e., $\hat{P} = \pi \cdot D$). The application of the SDS model may take one of two forms: a model-fitting or a model-testing approach. Under the model-fitting strategy, one attempts to estimate the best-fitting social decision scheme from one set of data and either cross-validate on another sample or examine the plausibility of one's estimate vis-a-vis other evidence (e.g., Kerr *et al.*, 1976; Kerr *et al.*, 1979; Laughlin *et al.*, 1975). The more popular technique to date has been the model-testing approach within which one compares the adequacy of fit for several social decision schemes which are plausible, *a priori*, or span the range of reasonable alternatives. The latter procedure has been automated for several decision schemes (Kerr and Davis, 1976).

The social decision scheme model has been able to make reasonably accurate predictions in a variety of decision-making tasks. Most of the studies applying the model have suggested that some type of majority primary decision scheme provides the best fit to the group data; this has been shown for attitudinal items (Kerr *et al.*, 1975), duplex bets (Davis *et al.*, 1974) and, more recently, verdicts by mock juries (Bray, 1974; Davis, 1973; Davis *et al.*, 1975, 1977; Davis and Kerr *et al.*, 1976; Kerr *et al.*, 1979). Collectively, these experiments document the utility of the SDS model for predicting the product of the group decision-making process. They also allow us to make tentative, general inferences about the process itself, e.g. in the mock jury setting, jurors rarely successfully oppose a large majority, and having minimal support (e.g. one ally) at the onset of group deliberation seems to be of little value, etc. Furthermore, a social decision scheme which predicts the group product accurately provides a baseline against which to judge the plausibility of particular process models; that is, a process model whose implications for the group product are consistent with the accurate decision scheme's is more plausible than a model whose implications are contrary to those of a well-fitting decision scheme. However, in applying the SDS model one need not explicitly make any assumptions about the process whereby the group hammers out a mutually acceptable decision. Rather, the model suggests that a knowledge of the initial distribution of opinion along with a particular decision scheme is often sufficient to account for the results of that process. The SDS model says nothing directly about the dynamics of the process after the initial expression of opinion, save that the outcome of that process will be alternative i with probability $d_{ij}$, although as noted previously, the $d_{ij}$ may be indirectly informative.

It is very encouraging that one can often account for the group product so well using such a simple model. It is also clearly desirable to develop a better understanding of the process itself. Such an understanding is not only of fundamental theoretical interest but could also serve as a basis for even more accurate product models. But the SDS model is not only a potential beneficiary of a powerful model of the GDM process, it may also serve as a basis for such theory by providing a useful unit of analysis.

Developing useful process models seems at some point to require the direct observation and analysis of group interaction. The reluctance of most researchers to do this is appreciable by anyone who has attempted it. Social interaction in decision-making groups is characterized by such variety, complexity, and apparent disorder that it seems to defy neat analysis. The key difficulty seems to be choosing an appropriate aspect of the group's behavior for observation, i.e. deciding upon a useful unit of analysis. Nearly all prior analyses of group processes have focused upon verbal communication in the group: its content, temporal flow, patterning, etc. (e.g., Bales, 1950; Fisher, 1970; Leavitt, 1951; Schachter, 1951; Stephan and Mishler, 1952; Vinokur and Burnstein, 1974). The basic unit of analysis of the SDS model is the distribution of group member preferences. Since this unit has repeatedly been shown to be highly predictive of the group's product, it holds great promise as a unit for the analysis of the group decision-making process.

AN OUTLINE OF THE SOCIAL TRANSITION SCHEME (STS) MODEL

The social transition scheme (STS) model is an extension of the SDS approach. A simple example will illustrate the nature of this extension. Suppose a twelve-person jury must choose between two decision alternatives, guilty and not guilty. Furthermore, suppose that the initial distinguishable distribution of the group is (8 $G$, 4 $NG$). The standard SDS logic would specify a decision scheme which would predict the likelihood of the group choosing each alternative; for example, if a majority primary scheme were hypothesized, the SDS model would predict that the group would ultimately convict. The D matrix summarizes the likelihood of such initial-split to final-decision transitions.

By contrast, the STS model does not focus upon the group's final decision, but rather upon the successive changes in group members' positions during group decision-making. In other words, the STS model either estimates or predicts (depending upon one's research strategy) the likelihood of transitions from one distinguishable distribution of group members' opinion to another. In our hypothetical example, an application of the model would result in an estimation or prediction of the likelihood of shifting from the group "state" (8 $G$, 4 $NG$) to (9 $G$, 3 $NG$), (7 $G$, 5 $NG$), etc. Under a set of simplifying assumptions discussed more fully below, the STS representation of the process can be summarized by a single $m \times m$ transition matrix, $T$, the $i$'th row of which specifies the probabilities of transition from the $i$'th distinguishable distribution to each of the $m$ distinguishable distributions (see Table 4 for an illustration of an estimated $T$).

Any discussion of process implies changes in behavior across time. Therefore, it is important to specify how the passage of time will be incorporated into any process model. There are at least two potentially useful ways to break up group behavior across time for the STS model, defining two classes of STS models. One class of models, the STS shift models, takes each transition from one state to another as a moment in time at which the sequential process is observed. For a shift model, a group has either satisfied a decision criterion (e.g. unanimity) or will shift with certainty; no allowance is made for indefinite stalemate. Formally, the shift models assume that the entries in the T matrix,

$t_{ij}$ = probability that a group shifts from state $i$ to state $j$,

$$= \begin{cases} 1.0, \text{ if } i = j \text{ and state } i \text{ satisfies the decision criterion or} \\ \quad \text{rule (e.g. unanimity),} \\ 0, \text{ if } i = j \text{ and state } i \text{ does not satisfy the decision} \\ \quad \text{criterion, and} \\ \text{some probability determined by the particular process} \\ \quad \text{model's assumptions, if } i \neq j. \end{cases}$$

The rate model is the other type of STS model. Here, the end of some fixed interval defines the moment at which the group state is determined. We shall refer to this interval as the "trial interval." Rate models allow groups to remain within non-absorbing states from trial to trial. Every diagonal entry of the T matrix, $t_{ii}$, may take on some non-zero value for a rate model. Thus, it is possible to predict both the group process data (vis. the transition data) and the group product data using sufficiently elaborate STS rate models, including cases of no decision (e.g. hung juries).

Although they are related, the shift and rate models give somewhat different representations of the group decision-making process. Shift models are concerned only with the path that process takes, while rate models are concerned with both where the group is headed and how quickly it is moving. A single theoretical question can raise somewhat different issues when framed in one or the other class of models.

## The social transition scheme methodology

Before describing some of the completed and potential applications of the STS model, the model's methodological requirements warrant discussion. To estimate T or validate a predicted T, the positions of each group member must be monitored more or less continuously throughout the entire course of group deliberation. Two techniques have been used to accomplish this. The first technique involves polling the entire group at regular intervals (see Davis et al., 1976, for an illustration). The primary advantage of this technique is that it is fairly simple to use, requiring no expensive monitoring equipment. One apparent disadvantage is that several shifts may occur during a trial interval if one chooses an interval that is too long; a less detailed description of the GDM process may result. Another potential disadvantage is that such periodic polling may disrupt or alter the process under study. In the other technique, a group member makes a response only when a change in opinion has occurred (see Godwin and Restle, 1974, for an illustration). This technique seems less likely to disrupt the process and also permits a detailed account of the locus and timing of all shifts in opinion in the group. Its primary drawback seems to be that elaborate monitoring equipment may be required if one wants to obtain subjects' opinion changes privately and unobtrusively. Furthermore, while this technique seems, on the face of it, less reactive than the first technique, it could also disrupt the group decision-making process in some significant way.

Since the generality of any analysis using the STS model is dependent upon the assumption of non-reactivity (or perhaps minimal reactivity) of the observational techniques, it seemed advisable that this assumption be checked empirically. As noted above, the technique employed in the earlier work of Davis et al. (1976) (viz. polling the entire group at fixed intervals) seemed potentially more disruptive than the technique used by Godwin and Restle (1974) (viz. having subjects respond only when a change of opinion occurred). We chose to consider the "worst case" first, i.e. it was decided to carry out a study to examine the Davis procedure. If there were little actual disruption of the process with this technique, then it seems unlikely that there would be a problem with less obstrusive measurement techniques.

The plan of the study was to contrast an experimental group of mock juries which was polled once every minute with a control group of mock juries which was never polled during group deliberation. Of primary concern was the extent to which the two conditions differed in their group decisions (i.e. verdicts), the time required for deliberation, and members' perceptions of the decision-making process.

METHOD

*Subjects*

The subjects were students drawn from introductory psychology classes at the University of California, San Diego. Eleven experimental and eleven control groups were scheduled; decision data for two experimental groups were lost due to equipment failure. The decision data reported here are based on 120 subjects (61 males, 59 females). Most of the groups were six-person groups; three groups (one five-person experimental group, two four-person control groups) were smaller due to "no-shows". Most groups had nearly equal numbers of males and females.[1]

*Materials and equipment*

The group decision task was to arrive at a unanimous verdict for each of six one-page summaries of armed robbery cases. The cases had been developed through pilot work to produce roughly equal numbers of convictions and acquittals by individual pilot subjects. Subjects indicated their predeliberation verdicts, and in the experimental condition their current verdicts throughout deliberation, by pressing one of two buttons (for Guilty and Not Guilty) on a response panel. Each subject had his/her own panel and low partitions prevented any subject from seeing the response of any other subject. In addition, the arbitrarily designated foreman had a response station through which he/she recorded the group verdicts.

When a subject made a response, the response and the time on a system clock were automatically encoded and temporarily stored in a microprocessor memory. The data were later stored permanently on magnetic tape from which they could be retrieved, decoded, and analyzed.

*Procedure*

Subjects were greeted and told that the study was concerned with how jurors arrive at a verdict. They were told that they would consider summaries of six actual cases of armed robbery tried in the local courts within the last two years, and that they were to attempt to reach a unanimous group verdict on each case. The operation of the response stations was then explained. After reading over the one-page case summary, each subject was to privately consider the evidence and individually record his/her personal verdict at his/her response station. Groups were given a maximum of seven minutes to reach a unanimous verdict. After deliberation began a tone was sounded every minute. The control groups were told that the tones were to help them keep track of the passage of deliberation time. The members of the experimental groups were told to indicate "the verdict you support at the moment" on their response stations every time the tone sounded. They were to resume their deliberations after making this response. Groups were instructed to work through the cases in the order they were provided. Each pair of experimental and mock juries received an independently randomized ordering of cases. When a group had finished all six cases, or when the available time had elapsed, all group members individually completed a questionnaire which probed their perceptions of the group's deliberations.

RESULTS

*Predeliberation individual verdicts*

The predeliberation, individual verdicts and the group verdicts are presented in Table 1 for each of the six cases separately. The distributions of individual verdicts for experimental and control subjects were reasonably similar; statistical tests revealed no significant differences between the two groups for any case (although there was a clear trend on Case $C$, $\chi_1^2 = 3.31$, $P < 0.07$), nor did the overall distributions, summed across cases, differ significantly, $\chi_1^2 = 1.64$. Apparently periodic polling did not tend to make subjects more or less prone to convict or acquit at the onset of group deliberation.

*Group verdicts and deliberation times*

The distributions of experimental and control groups' verdicts are

TABLE 1

*Individual and group verdicts*

| Individual verdicts | | | | Cases | | | |
|---|---|---|---|---|---|---|---|
| Experimental subjects | A | B | C | D | E | F | Total |
| G | 32 | 14 | 28 | 13 | 11 | 18 | 116 |
| NG | 15 | 33 | 19 | 28 | 36 | 29 | 160 |
| % G | 68.1 | 29.8 | 59.6 | 31.7 | 23.4 | 38.3 | 42.0 |
| Control subjects | | | | | | | |
| G | 39 | 27 | 43 | 15 | 17 | 21 | 162 |
| NG | 11 | 35 | 12 | 35 | 45 | 41 | 179 |
| % G | 78.0 | 43.5 | 78.2 | 30.0 | 27.4 | 33.0 | 47.5 |
| Group verdicts | | | | | | | |
| Experimental groups | | | | | | | |
| G | 6 | 0 | 6 | 1 | 0 | 2 | 15 |
| NG | 2 | 6 | 1 | 7 | 6 | 5 | 27 |
| H | 1 | 2 | 1 | 0 | 3 | 2 | 9 |
| Control groups | | | | | | | |
| G | 6 | 2 | 8 | 0 | 0 | 1 | 17 |
| NG | 2 | 2 | 0 | 7 | 7 | 6 | 24 |
| H | 1 | 7 | 2 | 2 | 4 | 3 | 19 |

also reported in Table 1. For the group verdicts there seemed to be a tendency for the control groups to hang more often, which was most evident for Case B. However, there were no significant associations between the variables experimental-control and verdict (guilty and not guilty)-no verdict (hung), either across all cases or for any of the cases separately (tested by Fisher's exact test), although the small number of verdicts limits the power of these tests. When one excluded hung juries and compared the distribution of verdicts of the experimental and control groups, again there were no significant differences for any particular case, nor did the distributions of verdicts across all cases differ significantly.

The SDS literature indicates that the likelihood of obtaining a hung jury is strongly related to the initial distribution of individual opinion in the group (cf. Kerr *et al.,* 1976). Therefore, a revealing way of probing for experimental-control group differences was to examine the relative frequency of initial-split to final-verdict transitions; in effect, one compares estimates of the social decision schemes operative in the experimental and control conditions. These data are presented in Table 2. Again, the tendency for control groups to hang more often than the experimental groups was evident (see

TABLE 2

*Initial split to final decision transition frequencies and deliberation times*

| Initial distribution | Experimental Groups | | | | Control Groups | | | | Test on time | |
|---|---|---|---|---|---|---|---|---|---|---|
| | Verdicts | | | Deliberation time mean | Verdicts | | | Deliberation time mean | t | d.f. |
| | G | NG | H | | G | NG | H | | | |
| 6:0 | 2 | 0 | 0 | 10.0 | 6 | 0 | 0 | 7.0 | 1.03 | 6 |
| 5:1 | 5 | 0 | 0 | 238.2 | 9 | 0 | 1 | 225.4 | 0.15 | 13 |
| 4:2 | 4 | 1 | 1 | 250.2 | 1 | 1 | 2 | 413.5 | 2.65[a] | 8 |
| 3:3 | 1 | 6 | 5 | 321.8 | 1 | 2 | 7 | 379.0 | 1.49 | 20 |
| 2:4 | 0 | 4 | 3 | 313.9 | 0 | 8 | 4 | 362.3 | 0.77 | 18 |
| 1:5 | 0 | 6 | 0 | 166.8 | 0 | 9 | 5 | 255.3 | 1.26 | 18 |
| 0:6 | 0 | 9 | 0 | 75.6 | 0 | 4 | 0 | 12.0 | 1.30 | 11 |
| Overall: | 12 | 26 | 9 | 222.4 | 17 | 24 | 19 | 263.5 | 1.29 | 106 |

[a] $p < 0.05$

*Notes:* (1) These data are summed across all cases and groups for which initial distribution was available.

(2) For the 4- and 5-person groups, initial splits were classified according to the number in the minority for inclusion in the above table. Thus, for example, 4:1 was treated as 5:1; 3:2 was treated as 4:2; 3:1 was treated as 5:1; etc.

(3) Groups which were hung were given the maximum of 420-second deliberation time, unless, as occasionally happened, the group reported a deadlock before the time lapsed.

especially groups which began with a 3:3 or 1:5 split), although again the relationship was not significant for any of the initial splits. The mean time required to reach consensus is also presented in Table 2. When there was no initial unanimity, the control groups tended to deliberate somewhat longer, which is consistent with the trend for more hung juries in the control groups. This difference was statistically significant only for the 4:2 split, $t(8) = 2.65, P < 0.05$.

*Group members' perceptions of deliberation*
All subjects also responded to the following questions on appropriately anchored seven-point bipolar scales: (a) How satisifed were you with your group deliberations? (b) Generally, how hard was it for your group to reach unanimous verdicts? (c) How much did your foreman dominate your deliberations? (d) How hurried were your deliberations? (e) How committed did you feel to your initial verdict? (f) To what degree were your deliberations dominated by a few jurors v. having everyone contribute equally? Comparisons of the experimental and control groups resulted in a significant difference for item (b) only; the control groups reported that it was harder to reach a unanimous verdict, $t(18) = 2.24, P < 0.05$. This result was consistent with the trend for more hung juries in the control group. The experimental groups also responded to two additional items: (g) To what extent did being polled regularly on your Juror Box interfere with your deliberations? ("not at all" to "very much"). (h) Do you think that being polled regularly on your Juror Box affected the final verdicts you reached? ("yes" or "no"); if yes, how? The mean response to question (g) was 2.43, which was significantly $(P < 0.01)$ closer to the "not at all" than the "very much" anchor. The majority of subjects (67%) responded "no" to the final question. Among those who said "yes" several reasons were given. The modal response was that polling forced careful reconsideration of one's opinion, which could produce either change or even stronger commitment. A few subjects felt that polling made group pressure more salient. In a similar vein, some said the polling helped to identify deviates. Finally, a few felt hurried by the polling.

*Independence of initial verdicts*
Although it did not bear directly upon the methodological issues addressed by this study, another pattern which emerged from these data was of interest. In experimental groups, there was a clear

tendency for subjects who were in the minority for one case to choose the opposite verdict on the very next case; for example, a subject who was the only one advocating conviction on the first case would be relatively more likely to favor acquittal on the next case than the members of the majority faction. Table 3 presents the relevant data. Based on the predeliberation votes, the members of a group were identified as either in the majority or minority faction for each case separately. Occasionally this classification could not be made, e.g. when the group was already unanimous prior to deliberation. Also equivocal were cases in which there was initially an even split. No majority/minority classification was made if such a group failed to reach a verdict for that case; however, when one side did eventually prevail, its members were identified as belonging to the majority faction. We then tallied the number of times members of each faction on the $i$'th case began deliberation on the $i + 1$'th case with the same verdict or the opposite verdict. The data in Table 3 represent the totals across $i = 1, 2, \ldots, 8$. The relationship suggested by the tabled data is a significant one in the experimental (i.e. polled) condition, $\chi_1^2 = 7.79, P < 0.01$; the control (i.e. non-polled) subjects did not exhibit this relationship, $\chi_1^2 = 0.03$. It is as if the experimental subjects tended to avoid a position which had recently placed them in the role of a deviant.[2]

TABLE 3

*Frequencies of switches of predeliberation verdicts for minority and majority jurors*

| Polled groups | Produced same individual verdict for Case $i + 1$ | Produced different individual verdict for Case $i + 1$ |
|---|---|---|
| In the majority faction on Case $i$ | 58 | 58 |
| In the minority faction on Case $i$ | 14 | 40 |
| No-polled groups | | |
| In the majority faction on Case $i$ | 65 | 78 |
| In the minority faction on Case $i$ | 26 | 28 |

DISCUSSION

The results of this study seem to justify the following conclusions: (a) the periodic polling of deliberating juries did not systematically affect individual predeliberation verdicts. (b) There was some indication that such polling might increase the likelihood of achieving unanimity and, hence, decrease the time required for deliberations and the perceived difficulty of reaching a unanimous verdict. (c) although polling may have had some weak effect on the likelihood of reaching a verdict, there was no indication that it affected the verdict for those who did achieve unanimity. (d) With the exception of perceived difficulty, polled groups had perceptions of their deliberations which were very similar to those who were not polled. The overall pattern of these data suggest that periodic polling did not materially disrupt the group decision-making process. Informal observation of these groups reinforced this conclusion; the polling usually took only a few seconds and discussion seemed to continue without interruption (often in mid-sentence). These results increase our confidence that the periodic-polling technique represents a viable, non-reactive method for the analysis of the group decision-making process. It seems probable that the other measurement technique in use (viz. subject responds only when shifting positions) will be even less reactive.

The only (non-significant) effect of periodic polling seemed to be one of accelerating the movement towards consensus. The rather low power of some of the tests, particularly those with groups as replicates, as well as the consistency of group product (i.e. verdict), process (e.g. deliberation time), and self-perception data suggest that this effect may be a genuine one, worthy of further research attention. Besides its relevance to STS methodology, validation of this effect may also be of some practical value, i.e. periodic polling may help prevent a stalemate or deadlock in the decision-making group.

## Applications of the social transition scheme model

Having described the origin, logic, and methodology of the STS model, this chapter will conclude with a description of some of the ways in which the STS model has been and might be applied.

Like the SDS model, the STS model may employ either a model-fitting or a model-testing strategy. In the former case, the objectives of the model are primarily descriptive; a descriptive summary of the GDM process can be produced within the framework of the STS model. The relative frequencies of observed transitions, an estimated $T$ matrix, is the model's formal representation of the process. The pattern of the entries in such $\hat{T}$ matrices under various conditions can be examined to answer questions about the decision-making process of interest. The emphasis of the model is primarily predictive when the model-testing strategy is employed. The investigator constructs a T matrix whose entries are constrained by theoretical assumptions about the nature of the group decision-making process. To the extent that the model can accurately predict the observed transition (and hence, final product) data, those theoretical assumptions receive support. Although the STS model's logic has been applied only a very few times, both research strategies are well illustrated in the literature.[3]

STS MODEL-FITTING

The Davis *et al.* (1976) study of mock juries may be classified as a model-fitting application of an STS rate model. Davis *et al.* were interested in the effects on the GDM process of the accountability of groups for their decisions. Half of their groups were told that video recordings of their deliberations would be reviewed by a panel of psychologists and legal experts who were investigating the accuracy of such juries, and were also told that they might later be invited to discuss their participation in deliberation (public-accountable condition); the rest of the juries were instructed that their deliberations would be private (private condition). Using a trial interval of one minute, jurors were periodically polled by the experimenter during a deliberation period with a 30-minute time limit. The transition data, summarized in estimated $\hat{T}$ matrices, were classified according to the accountability manipulation and trial block (the 30-minute session was divided into five blocks of six minutes each). $\hat{T}$ for public-accountable juries, Block 1, is presented in Table 4 to illustrate such a $\hat{T}$.

Just as a Bales's (1950) IPA profile summarized certain features of a group's verbal interaction, the $\hat{T}$s provide a summary of what Godwin and Restle (1974) have termed "the road to agreement." By comparing certain features of the $\hat{T}$, one may better understand whether public-accountable groups travel down the same road as the non-accountable, private groups. For example, using an index which summarized the magnitude of off-diagonal entries of $\hat{T}$, the timing of group member movement was shown to differ for accountability conditions; the public-accountable juries tended to increase their rate of shifting across blocks but the private jury members tended to shift positions more rapidly during the early stages of deliberation. Both

TABLE 4

*Davis et al. (1976): $\hat{T}$ for private juries, Block 1*

| Distinguishable distribution on trial i | Distinguishable distribution on trial i + 1 | | | | | | |
|---|---|---|---|---|---|---|---|
| | 6:0 | 5:1 | 4:2 | 3:3 | 2:4 | 1:5 | 0:6 |
| 6:0 | 0.93 | 0.07 | | | | | |
| 5:1 | 0.03 | 0.95 | 0.02 | | | | |
| 4:2 | | 0.01 | 0.95 | 0.03 | 0.01 | | |
| 3:3 | | | | 0.85 | 0.13 | 0.02 | |
| 2:4 | | | | 0.05 | 0.90 | 0.05 | |
| 1:5 | | | | | 0.03 | 0.97 | |
| 0:6 | | | | | | | 1.0 |

*Note*: 6:0 means 6 votes for conviction, 0 notes for acquittal. $t_{ij}$ are the averages of the relative frequencies with which mock juries moved from distinguishable distribution i on trial k to distinguishable distribution j on trial k + 1. Zero entries have been left blank.

types of juries also seemed to demonstrate an asymmetry in their shifts, viz. movement was generally more rapid toward acquittal than toward conviction (hints of this can be seen in the $\hat{T}$ presented in Table 4; in particular, see the fourth row of the matrix); the accountability conditions were fairly similar in this regard except for the fourth block, during which this bias was dramatically stronger for the public-accountability juries. Most interestingly, the observed distributions of verdicts did not differ between accountability conditions. Thus, even though the analyses demonstrated marked and reliable differences in the decision-making process, they were not reflected in product differences. This result illustrates the notion that the identity of group product does not ensure the identity of group process and underscores the importance of a process-oriented analysis.

STS MODEL-TESTING

In this chapter's terminology, Godwin and Restle's (1974) study represents a model-testing application of several STS shift models. Groups of 3–6 persons attempted to reach consensus on which of four multidimensional stimulus arrays another (bogus) group had chosen as "most outstanding." Each member's current opinion was continuously monitored from the outset of group discussion. Godwin and Restle proposed a series of theoretical models which might explain the groups' choices at the forks in the road to agreement. For example, a random model which predicted that

group members randomly changed their opinions until group consensus was reached could be confidently rejected. They also tested
a dyadic model which assumed that each member at a different
position than one's own exerts the same degree of attraction as every
other such member. The dyadic model was also refuted by their data:
for example, they found that the likelihood of transition from
(3, 1, 0, 0) to a (2, 2, 0, 0) split occurred much less frequently
than would be predicted by the dyadic model. Two "subgroup"
models were also examined. The first assumed that each subgroup
(i.e. faction) of a fixed size had a unique "attractiveness" which
determined the probability of another member joining that position.[4]
This model was found to be significantly less accurate than a more
complicated one in which the attractiveness of a faction depended
not only upon the size of the faction, but also upon the overall size
of the group. The estimated parameters for this fourth model
suggested the factions including all but one group member were
extremely attractive, and all factions with at least a majority were
also very much more attractive than submajority factions.

An analysis like Godwin and Restle's is useful in several ways. It
narrows the range of plausible models of the group decision-making
process, e.g. it suggests that the relative size of a faction is more
informative about its attractiveness than its absolute size and that
the majority/non-majority distinction is central to defining the
attractiveness of a faction. Such information can also speak to
broader theoretical issues. For example, there is currently a lively
controversy surrounding the importance of informational v. normative processes for choice shift phenomena. The extremely sharp
drop in faction attractiveness observed by Godwin and Restle as
one moves from majorities to minorities to minorities of one is
inconsistent with any persuasive-argument (i.e. informational)
model which assumes even a rough correspondence between the size
of a faction and the number of persuasive arguments they generate.[5]

FURTHER APPLICATIONS OF THE STS MODEL

As the preceding (nearly-comprehensive) review of extant STS
applications shows, the STS model provides a general descriptive
framework within which one can examine the effects on the GDM
process of any individual, task, or group characteristic of interest,
and provides a predictive framework within which the implications
of many theoretical notions may be worked out, made explicit,

embodied in a model which makes point predictions, and tested. Our own in-progress and planned research tends to emphasize the former, model-fitting (i.e. descriptive) strategy. This reflects our judgement that although we know a good deal about the effects of group discussion on individual and group products (cf. Myers, 1973), and a reasonable amount about the dynamics of such discussion (cf. Fisher, 1970), we know relatively little about how groups move along the road to agreement. Thus, our current work is devoted to expanding the data base in this area.

However, our objectives are not solely descriptive; we also seek answers to key theoretical questions which must be addressed before simple and powerful models of the GDM process can be constructed. Two such key questions are: (a) Is the group decision-making process stationary? (b) Is the process path independent? Stationarity means that the process doesn't change over time; that is, the likelihood of a particular transition is the same at every point in group discussion.[6] Path independence means that the likelihood of shifting in to a particular "state" (i.e. distinguishable distribution) is independent of all previous states of the group except the one it is now in; in other words, where our group is going depends only upon where it is right now, but not upon how we got here.[7]

These are key questions for several reasons. Clearly, STS models which need not be concerned with the passage of "time" nor any history of the group other than its current configuration will be considerably more parsimonious than models which must somehow incorporate these factors. In particular, if these conditions are met, the STS model becomes a Markov chain, a familiar and extensively studied class of models. Furthermore, when these assumptions are met, the SDS product model and the STS process model may be explicitly and simply related.[8] But the investigation of these issues represents more than preliminary steps to the construction of parsimonious predictive models; the issues of stationarity and path independence represent fundamental psychological questions about the nature of small group interaction; viz. how does it vary over time and how does the history of the group alter its future course? Although there is suggestive theory and research bearing on these questions (e.g., Bales and Strodtbeck, 1951, Fisher, 1970; Komorita and Brenner, 1968), they remain open questions. They are also questions which arise naturally from the structure of the STS model and which must be answered before we can determine whether and when simple and elegant or more complex STS models will be required. Research is now underway to explore these key questions.

## Conclusions

The social transition scheme model provides a novel and potentially useful framework for analyzing the group decision-making process. It employs a unit of analysis (the distribution of member preferences) which is simply and nonreactively measured and known (through SDS research) to be reliably predictive of the group product. The small set of existing applications have demonstrated the descriptive and explanatory utility of an STS analysis and represent a promising beginning to the search for accurate models of the group decision-making process. Much more work still remains to be done before we can judge whether the STS model can provide us with a legible map of the group's road to agreement.

## Notes

1. An equal number of males and females were scheduled at each session. Due to no-shows and late arrivals, not every group had exactly three males and three females. However, 18 of the 20 juries departed from an equal sex split by only one person; one experimental group had a 5:1 male-to-female ratio and one control group had a 6:0 ratio.

2. Further research should explore the generality of this effect (e.g., must members be polled to produce it?) as well as its explanation (e.g., is it the result of normative pressures ("I'll switch my verdict to avoid the distasteful role of deviate again"), or perhaps an attributional process ("Maybe I'm in the minority because my personal criterion for conviction is too high or low")?).

3. It should be noted that none of the previous applications employ the STS model notation used here; however, the logic and methods are those of the STS model.

4. This probability was computed in much the same manner as in the dyadic model except that rather than assuming the attractiveness of a position was equal to a sum of equal, individual attractiveness valences, Godwin and Restle took these to be free parameters. That is:

$$P_{ij} = \text{the predicted probability that a member moves from position } i \text{ to position } j$$

$$= \beta_{n_j} / \sum_{k \neq i} \beta_{n_k}$$

where $n_j$ = number of persons at position $j$ and $\beta_n$ is the attractiveness of a faction of size $n$. For the dyadic model, $\beta_n = n\alpha$ where $\alpha$ = a constant.

5. Note that this argument assumes that the positions group members support during deliberation accurately reflect members' personal opinions. Godwin and Restle's findings need not contradict a persuasive-argument explanation of choice shift in individual decisions if this assumption is invalid.

6. Formally, if

$t_{ijk}$ = probability of moving from state i to state j on trial k, then stationarity requires that

$t_{ijk}$ = $t_{ijm}$ for all i, j, k, and m.

Because the meaning of a trial differs for shift and rate models, the stationarity assumption has a somewhat different interpretation as well. Stationarity for a shift model means that the likelihood of a given shift is independent of the number of shifts which have already taken place. Stationarity for a rate model means that the likelihood of a given shift is independent of the amount of time that has elapsed during group discussion.

7. Formally, if

$S_1$ = an arbitrary sequence of group states, and

$t_{ijk}/S_1$ = the probability of a group shifting into state i from state j on trial k, where $S_1$ preceded the $k$'th trial,

then path independence requires that

$t_{ijk}/S_1$ = $t_{ijk}/S_m$ for all i, j, k, l, and m.

8. Recall that the SDS theory predictions were generated by the formula,

$\hat{P}_{1 \times n'}$ = predicted distribution of group decisions across the $n'$ alternatives

= $\pi_{1 \times m} D_{m \times n'}$.

(The subscripts represent the order of the matrices.) If one can assume that the STS (shift or rate) transition matrix, **T**, satisfies the assumptions of a Markov-chain model transition matrix (i.e. path independence and stationarity), one could rewrite this formula as follows:

$$\hat{P}_{1 \times n'} = \pi_{1 \times m} (T_{m \times m})^{l} R_{m \times n'}.$$

The matrix **R** summarizes the decision rule under which the group operates. This decision rule is the consensus criterion for group decision. Decision rules may be explicit and formal (e.g. the voting rules specified in an organization's bylaws) or implicit and informal (e.g. a husband and wife's rule for settling disputed decisions). For the present purposes, the decision rule must be explicit and sufficiently detailed to handle every possible internal distribution of opinion; a good example is the unanimity rule. Decision rules should not be confused with decision schemes. The latter specify the likelihood of reaching certain decisions based on the initial distribution of opinion; the former specify the consensus necessary at the conclusion of discussion for group decision. The value of $l$ in the above equation will depend upon whether the STS **T** matrix summarizes a shift or rate model. If **T** represents a rate model, $l$ is just the maximum number of trial intervals which are allowed for group discussion.

If **T** represents a shift model, if all groups reach a decision, and if the **T** matrix is a Markov chain which will achieve a steady state (Coombs *et al.*, 1970, p.254), then $l$ represents some extremely large number. Strictly speaking, for STS shift models, the above equation should be rewritten:

$$\hat{P}_{1 \times n'} = \pi_{1 \times m} \left( \lim_{l \to \infty} T_{m \times m}^{l} \right) R_{m \times n'}.$$

## References

Bales, R. F. *Interaction process analysis.* Reading, MA: Addison-Wesley, 1950.

Bales, R. F., and Strodtbeck, F. L. Phases in group problem solving. *Journal of Abnormal and Social Psychology*, 1951, **46**, 485–495.

Bray, R. M. *Decision rules, attitude similarity, and jury decision making.* Unpublished doctoral dissertation, University of Illinois, 1974.

Coombs, C. H., Dawes, R. M., and Tversky, A. *Mathematical psychology: An elementary introduction.* Englewood Cliffs, NJ: Prentice-Hall, 1970.

Davis, J. H. Group decision and social interaction: A theory of social decision schemes. *Psychological Review*, 1973, **80**, 97–125.

Davis, J. H., Kerr, N. L., Sussman, M., and Rissman, A. K. Social decision schemes under risk. *Journal of Personality and Social Psychology*, 1974, **30**, 248–271.

Davis, J. H., Kerr, N. L., Atkin, R. S., Holt, R., and Meek, D. The decision processes of 6- 12-person mock juries assigned unanimous and 2/3 majority decision rules. *Journal of Personality and Social Psychology*, 1975, **32**, 1–14.

Davis, J. H. Stasser, G., Spitzer, C. E., and Holt, R. W. Changes in group members' decision preferences during discussion: An illustration with mock juries. *Journal of Personality and Social Psychology*, 1976, **34**, 1177–1187.

Davis, J. H., Kerr, N. L. Stasser, G., Meek, D., and Holt, R. Victim consequences, sentence severity, and decision processes in mock juries. *Organizational Behavior and Human Performance*, 1977, **18**, 346–365.

Fisher, B. A. *Small group decision making: Communication and the group process.* New York: McGraw-Hill, 1974.

Godwin, W., and Restle, F. The road to agreement: Subgroup pressures in small group consensus processes. *Journal of Personality and Social Psychology*, 1974, **30**, 500–509.

Kerr, N. L., Atkin, R., Stasser, G., Meek, D., Holt, R., and Davis, J. H. Guilt beyond a reasonable doubt: Effects of concept definition and assigned decision rule on the judgements of mock jurors. *Journal of Personality and Social Psychology*, 1976, **34**, 282–294.

Kerr, N. L., and Davis, J. H. VOTE: A computer program to analyze group decision data under Social Decision Scheme theory. *Behaviour Research Methods and Instrumentation*, January 1976.

Kerr, N. L., Davis, J. H., Meek, D., and Rissman, A. K. Group position as a function of member attitudes: Choice shift effects from the perspective of social decision scheme theory. *Journal of Personality and Social Psychology*, 1975, 35, 574–593.

Kerr, N. L., Harmon, D. L., Graves, J. K., and Sawyers, G. W. Independence of multiple verdicts by jurors and juries. *Journal of Applied Social Psychology*, (in press.)

Kerr, N. L., Nerenz, D., and Herrick, D. Role playing and the study of jury behavior. *Sociological Methods and Research*, 1979, 7, 337–355.

Komorita, S., and Brenner, A. R. Bargaining and concession making under bilateral monopoly. *Journal of Personality and Social Psychology*, 1968, 9, 15–20.

Laughlin, P. R., Kerr, N. L., Davis, J. H., Halff, H. M., and Marciniak, K. A. Group size, member ability, and social decision schemes on an intellectual task. *Journal of Personality and Social Psychology*, 1975, 31, 522–535.

Leavitt, H. J. Some effects of certain communication patterns on group performances. *Journal of Abnormal and Social Psychology*, 1951, 46, 38–50.

Myers, D. G. Summary and bibliography of experiments on group-induced response shift. JSAS *Catalog of Selected Documents in Psychology*, 1973, 3, 123. (MS #478)

Schachter, S. Deviation, rejection, and communication. *Journal of Abnormal and Social Psychology*, 1951, 46, 190–207.

Stephan, F. F., and Mishler, E. G. The distribution of participation in small groups: An exponential approximation. *American Sociological Review*, 1952, 17, 598–608.

Vinokur, A., and Burnstein, E. Effects of partially shared persuasive arguments on group-induced shifts: A problem solving approach. *Journal of Personality and Social Psychology*, 1974, 29, 305–315.

# 4
# Social Decision Schemes on Intellective Tasks

Patrick R. Laughlin and John Adamopoulos

One theoretical approach to small group performance conceptualizes the social combination processes of cooperative problem-solving and decision-making groups as a social decision scheme (e.g. Davis, 1973; Lorge and Solomon, 1955; Smoke and Zajonc, 1962; Thomas and Fink, 1961). Given a set of mutually exclusive and exhaustive response alternatives, the individual group members may initially prefer different alternatives, and the group task is essentially to map this distribution of individual preferences to a collective group decision. A social decision scheme is a model of the underlying group process, formal or informal, explicit or implicit, which guides this mapping. The most comprehensive statement of this approach is presented by Davis (1973). After a summary of the general social decision scheme model this paper discusses intellective and judgemental group tasks, and then presents the results of competitive tests of ten formal theories of the social combination process of cooperative groups on four classes of verbal intellective tasks.

## The general social decision scheme model

Davis (1973) assumes a set of $n$ mutually exclusive and exhaustive response alternatives, $A_1, A_2, \ldots, A_n$. A given population of individuals defines a probability distribution, $(p_1, p_2, \ldots, p_n)$, of individual preferences for the $n$ alternatives. If a group of $r$ individuals is assembled at random from this population, the distribution of group member preferences for the $n$ alternatives will be $r_1, r_2, \ldots r_n$ in each group, with $r_j$ the number of group members from zero to group size $r$ who favor the $j$th alternative. Considering response alternatives (but not people) as distinguishable, the number, $m$, of distinguishable distributions of member preferences for the $n$ alternatives (type of groups) in a group of $r$ members is given by Equation 1:

$$m = \binom{n + r - 1}{r}. \tag{1}$$

For example, there are five possible distinguishable distributions for a four-person group $(r = 4)$ with the two response alternatives $(n = 2)$, $A_C$ = correct and $A_I$ = incorrect: four members correct and none incorrect $(4-0)$, three members correct and one incorrect $(3-1)$, two members correct and two incorrect $(2-2)$, one member correct and three incorrect $(1-3)$, no members correct and four incorrect $(0-4)$.

Given the probability distribution of individual preferences for the $n$ response alternatives, the probability of occurrence, $\pi_i$, of each of these $m$ distinguishable distributions is given by Equation (2):

$$\pi_i = \binom{r}{r_1, r_2, \ldots, r_n} p_1^{r_1} p_2^{r_2} \ldots p_n^{r_n}. \tag{2}$$

Equation 2 is the general term of the multinomial expansion of $(p_1 + p_2 + \ldots + p_n)^r$, and reduces to the general term of the binomial expansion of $(p_1 + p_2)^r$ for the special case of two alternatives, such as correct and incorrect.

Davis (1973) next introduces the concept of a social decision scheme, which corresponds to the group decision scheme of Smoke and Zajonc (1962). From a theoretical perspective a social decision scheme is a method of formalizing any set of assumptions about the social combination process, thus enabling quantitative predictions of the actual distribution of group responses over a sufficiently large number of groups. Formally, a social decision scheme is an $m \times n$ matrix, $D$, with entries $[d_{ij}]$, in which each element is the probability that the group will select the $j$th response alternative given the $i$th distribution of member preferences. The predicted probability distribution of group responses, $(P_1, P_2, \ldots, P_n)$ is obtained by postmultiplying the known vector, $(\pi_1, \pi_2, \ldots, \pi_m)$ by the assumed $m \times n$ social decision scheme matrix, $D$, as in Equation 3:

$$(P_1, P_2, \ldots, P_n) = (\pi_1, \pi_2, \ldots, \pi_m) \begin{bmatrix} d_{11} & d_{12} & \cdots & d_{1n} \\ d_{21} & d_{22} & \cdots & d_{2n} \\ \cdot & \cdot & & \cdot \\ \cdot & \cdot & & \cdot \\ \cdot & \cdot & & \cdot \\ d_{m1} & d_{m2} & \cdots & d_{mn} \end{bmatrix}$$

$$(3)$$

The predicted probability distribution of group responses from each social decision scheme may be compared with the actual distribution of group responses as a test of the particular theories of the social combination process of interest. If the predicted and obtained distributions do not differ significantly by standard goodness-of-fit statistics, the assumptions formalized by the particular social decision scheme matrix may be considered a sufficient and plausible theory of the group process. Conversely, a significant difference indicates that the particular theory of the social combination process is not plausible for the conditions of the experiment. Further details on the general social decision scheme approach are given in Davis (1973).

## Intellective and judgemental group tasks

We may distinguish two fundamental types of tasks in cooperative group problem solving and decision making, intellective and judgemental tasks. Many group tasks involve a definite objective criterion of success within the axioms, definitions, rules, operations, theorems, and relationships of a particular conceptual system. Such group tasks emphasize the solution of a problem or formulation of a decision within some set of constraints, proceeding by a demonstrable series of permissable operations to a solution or decision which may be evaluated within the conceptual system. The criterion of success on such problems or decisions is defined by the relationships of the conceptual system. We may call such group tasks intellective tasks. The classic example is the three problems involving transfer of objects under constraints of Marjorie Shaw (1932), the Tartaglia (husbands and wives), Alcuin (cannibals and missionaries), and Tower of Hanoi (disk transfer). Other examples include anagrams (e.g. Faust, 1959), modified water-jar problems (e.g. Davis and

Restle, 1963), concept-attainment problems (e.g., Laughlin and Sweeney, 1977), and most of the tasks in the earlier group problem-solving literature (see Kelley and Thibaut, 1969, for a review).

In contrast, many other group tasks involve political, ethical, aesthetic, or behavioral judgments for which there is no demonstrably correct solution within a conceptual system. On such tasks the criterion of success is subjective group consensus, either the consensus of the interacting group members themselves or the consensus of an external group of judges, raters, or observers. Success or failure is not defined by demonstrable operations within a conceptual system, but by judgemental consensus. We may call such group tasks judgemental tasks. Most current work in group processes involves judgemental rather than intellective tasks, primarily in the two areas of jury decision making (e.g. Davis *et al.*, 1977a; Davis *et al.*, 1975; Davis *et al.*, 1977b; Davis *et al.*, 1976; Gelfand and Solomon, 1973, 1974, 1975; Kerr *et al.*, 1976), and evaluative attitudinal judgements (e.g. Cvetkovitch and Baumgardner, 1973; Kerr *et al.*, 1975; Moscovici and Zavalloni, 1969). The large amount of research on the "risky shift," and the more fundamental question of the group "choice shift," is based almost entirely on judgemental tasks (see Davis *et al.*, 1976; Lamm and Myers, 1978; and Myers and Lamm, 1976, for recent reviews.).

Similarily, the majority of research applying the social decision scheme approach has used judgemental tasks. However, two recent studies have compared ten social decision schemes as competitive theories of the social combination process on verbal intellective tasks. Laughlin *et al.* (1975) used a difficult English vocabulary test, Part I of the Terman (1956) Concept Mastery Test, Synonyms and Antonyms. This test consists of 115 pairs of English synonyms or antonyms, such as "squeamish" and "qualmish," or "disingenuous" and "artless." Since accepted English usage, as formalized in standard dictionaries, defines a correct answer, the identification of the pairs as synonyms or antonyms is an intellective group task with two responses, correct and incorrect. A large sample (510) of college students first took the test as individuals, and were then assigned to groups of sizes of two to five (34 groups at each size) or control individual conditions for a second administration of the same test. The 510 first-test responses defined the probability distribution $(p_c, p_I)$ of correct and incorrect individual responses on each item, and these 115 distributions were used in Equation 2. The groups were instructed to discuss each item and reach a collective decision, but no social decision scheme or social combination process was prescribed by the instructions.

Nine *a priori* social decision schemes were tested as theories of the group process: (a) strict equiprobability; (b) strict proportionality; (c) truth wins; (d) truth-supported wins; (e) majority, equiprobability otherwise (adding an equiprobability subscheme when no majority existed); (f) majority if correct, equiprobability otherwise; (g) majority if incorrect, equiprobability otherwise; (h) error wins; and, (i) error-supported wins. These nine *a priori* social decision scheme matrices are given in Table 1 for four-person groups. Further details on these nine social decision schemes, which formalize a wide range of current theory (e.g. truth wins), recent research (e.g. strict majority), plausible intuition (e.g. truth-supported wins), and implausible baselines (e.g. error wins), are given in Laughlin *et al.* (1975). The best-fitting *a priori* social decision scheme suggested a basic truth-supported wins process.

In addition to these competitive tests of nine *a priori* social decision schemes, the best-fitting *a posteriori* decision scheme was estimated from another large sample of 240 four-person groups on the same task administered to a comparable college population under the same instructions (Laughlin and Branch, 1972). This was done by rewriting Equation 3 as a system of linear equations, adding an item index for the 115 items, and solving the resulting set of 230 simultaneous equations by numerical methods (for details see Laughlin *et al.*, 1975). This best-fitting *a posteriori* scheme is labeled DEST in Table 1, and represented a combination of a truth-supported wins process when three or four members knew the correct answer and a slight decrement from the truth-supported wins process when two were correct and two incorrect. These 2–2 groups had a probability of 0.78 of giving the correct answer, approximately midway between the truth-supported wins and equiprobability predictions. This DEST scheme was then tested as a tenth *a priori* scheme on the data of Laughlin *et al.* (1975), and fit somewhat better than the other nine.

A second study (Laughlin *et al.*, 1976) tested the ten social decision schemes of Table 1 on 106 four-person groups with two different intellective tasks. The first task was the Otis Quick-Scoring Mental Ability Test (Gamma Test, Form Fm; Otis, 1954), which includes 80 general verbal achievement items such as vocabulary,

## TABLE 1

Matrices, $D_h$, corresponding to social decision schemes for two decision alternatives (correct, incorrect) for four-person groups, where entries are probabilities of a given preference distribution yielding a correct or incorrect response

| Member Preference Distribution | | Social Decision Scheme | | | | | | | | | | | | | | | | | | | |
|---|---|---|---|---|---|---|---|---|---|---|---|---|---|---|---|---|---|---|---|---|---|
| | | STEQ | | STPR | | TWIN | | TSWIN | | MAEQ | | MCEQ | | MIEQ | | EWIN | | ESWIN | | DEST | |
| Cor. | Inc. | Cor. | Inc. | Cor. | Inc. | Cor. | Inc. | Cor. | Inc. | Cor. | Inc. | Cor. | Inc. | Cor. | Inc. | Cor. | Inc. | Cor. | Inc. | Cor. | Inc. |
| 4 | 0 | 1.00 | 0.00 | 1.00 | 0.00 | 1.00 | 0.00 | 1.00 | 0.00 | 1.00 | 0.00 | 1.00 | 0.00 | 1.00 | 0.00 | 1.00 | 0.00 | 1.00 | 0.00 | 1.00 | 0.00 |
| 3 | 1 | 0.50 | 0.50 | 0.75 | 0.25 | 1.00 | 0.00 | 1.00 | 0.00 | 1.00 | 0.00 | 1.00 | 0.00 | 0.50 | 0.50 | 0.0 | 1.00 | 1.00 | 0.00 | 1.00 | 0.00 |
| 2 | 2 | 0.50 | 0.50 | 0.50 | 0.50 | 1.00 | 0.00 | 1.00 | 0.00 | 0.50 | 0.50 | 0.50 | 0.50 | 0.50 | 0.50 | 0.0 | 1.00 | 0.0 | 1.00 | 0.78 | 0.22 |
| 1 | 3 | 0.50 | 0.50 | 0.25 | 0.75 | 1.00 | 0.00 | 0.0 | 1.00 | 0.0 | 1.00 | 0.50 | 0.50 | 0.00 | 1.00 | 0.0 | 1.00 | 0.0 | 1.00 | 0.18 | 0.82 |
| 0 | 4 | 0.0 | 1.00 | 0.0 | 1.00 | 0.0 | 1.00 | 0.0 | 1.00 | 0.0 | 1.00 | 0.0 | 1.00 | 0.00 | 1.00 | 0.0 | 1.00 | 0.0 | 1.00 | 1.00 | 0.82 |

*Note:* Abbreviations of social decision schemes: STEQ: strict equiprobability; STPR: strict proportionality; TWIN: truth wins; TSWIN: truth-supported wins; MAEQ: majority, equiprobability otherwise; MCEQ: majority if correct, equiprobability otherwise; MIEQ: majority if incorrect, equiprobability otherwise; EWIN: error wins; ESWIN: error-supported wins; DEST: estimated *a posteriori* as best-fitting scheme in Laughlin and Branch (1972). Entries for which $d_{ij} = 1.00$, 0.00, should be regarded as values very close to 1.00 and 0.00, respectively, i.e. 0.999 . . . , and 0.0 . . . 01, representing a liberty taken for convenience of exposition.

information, antonyms, etc., and probably samples a wider domain of intellective verbal tasks than the Terman. The best-fitting *a priori* social decision scheme was again truth-supported wins, with DEST again providing a somewhat better fit and indicating an attenuation from the truth-supported wins process in the 2–2 groups. The second intellective task was the Mednick and Mednick (1967) Remote Associates Test, which consists of 30 sets of three words that can be related by a common associate. For example, an item from the instructions presents the three words "cookies," "sixteen," and "heart," indicating that they can be related by the common associate "sweet." The 30 items were selected so that the correct answer would be immediately obvious once proposed. Thus a truth-wins (Lorge and Solomon, 1955, Model A; Smoke and Zajonc, 1962, minimal quorum group decision scheme; Steiner, 1966, 1972, disjunctive task) social combination process should accurately predict group performance: if any group member proposes the correct answer it should be recognized and adopted as the group response. This prediction was supported, as the truth-wins social decision scheme fit better than any of the other nine. Thus, different social decision schemes fit the social combination processes of the same groups on two different intellective tasks.

The present study tested the same ten social combination processes for four-person groups on a fourth class of intellective tasks, four-term verbal analogies of the form $A : B :: C : D$. Each group took two different analogies tests. The first was the Terman Concept Mastery Test, Part II, Analogies (Terman, 1956), consisting of 75 items with three possible answers. The second was the Visualizing Relations (W. P. Laughlin, 1964), consisting of 30 items with five possible answers. Both tests sample a wide domain of quite sophisticated analogies, and require fairly extensive verbal knowledge and comprehension of relationships. Verbal analogies should be intermediate on a continuum of demonstrability between the highly demonstrable items of the Remote Associates Test and the relatively less demonstrable vocabulary and verbal achievement items of Part I of the Terman and the Otis. Verbal analogies involve demonstrable relationships on parallel conceptual dimensions, but not the strong immediately obvious demonstrability which guided item selection on the Remote Associates Test. However, the relationships on conceptual dimensions of verbal analogies should be more demonstrable than the essentially arbitrary correspondences which associate meaning and symbols in individual vocabulary words. Thus, the best-fitting social decision scheme on both verbal analogy tests was hypothesized to be truth-supported wins, corresponding to a social combination process where two or more correct members of a four-person group are necessary and sufficient for a correct group response.

## Method

The subjects were 260 college students (130 male and 130 female) who were fulfilling required experimental participation in introductory psychology courses at the University of Illinois. Each person took both Part II, Analogies, of the Terman Concept Mastery Test (Terman, 1956), and the Visualizing Relations analogies (W. P. Laughlin, 1964) in a counterbalanced order, either alone (26 males, 26 females) or in a four-person same-sex group (26 male, 26 female). The groups were instructed to take each test as a cooperative group, discussing each item and reaching a collective decision, but no social decision scheme was prescribed or implied by instructions. Over the 52 individuals there was a correlation of 0.57 between the two analogies tests.

## Results

The predicted proportions of correct group responses for the ten social decision schemes are given in Table 2, together with the obtained proportion of 0.71 correct responses on the Terman and 0.76 on the W. P. Laughlin analogies.

TABLE 2

*Predicted and obtained proportions of correct group responses for ten social decision schemes for Terman and W. P. Laughlin analogies*

| | | | | | Social decision scheme predictions | | | | | |
|------|------|------|-------|------|------|------|------|-------|------|----------|
| STEQ | STPR | TWIN | TSWIN | MAEQ | MCEQ | MIEQ | EWIN | ESWIN | DEST | Obtained |
| | | | | | | Terman | | | | |
| 0.59 | 0.58 | 0.87 | 0.68 | 0.59 | 0.67 | 0.48 | 0.30 | 0.48 | 0.65 | 0.71 |
| | | | | | | W. P. Laughlin | | | | |
| 0.61 | 0.58 | 0.89 | 0.71 | 0.60 | 0.69 | 0.47 | 0.22 | 0.48 | 0.68 | 0.76 |

Inspection of Table 2 indicates that the most accurate prediction was, as hypothesized, from the truth-supported wins social decision scheme, which predicted 0.68 against the obtained 0.71 proportion of correct answers on the Terman, and 0.71 against the obtained 0.76 on the W. P. Laughlin analogies.

Using the ten social decision scheme matrices from Table 1, the probability of a correct response on each item from the control individual distributions, and Equation 3, the distribution of correct-incorrect group responses was predicted for each of the ten models for each item on each analogies task. Goodness-of-model-fit for each of the ten decision schemes was then tested by forming a likelihood ratio, $LR$, over the set of 75 Terman items or 30 W. P. Laughlin items as a whole.

Assume that for the $i$th item $n_{Ii}$ out of $N_{Ii}$ individuals were correct and $n_{Gi}$ out of $N_{Gi}$ groups were correct. Assuming a general binomial model for both individual and group problem solving, if $p_{Ii}$ is the probability that an individual will solve the $i$th item, and $p_{Gi}$ is the probability that a group will solve the $i$th item, the likelihood of the observed frequencies of individual and group correct responses is:

$$L_i = \binom{N_{Ii}}{n_{Ii}} p_{Ii}^{n_{Ii}} (1 - p_{Ii})^{N_{Ii} - n_{Ii}} \binom{N_{Gi}}{n_{Gi}} p_{Gi}^{n_{Gi}} (1 - p_{Gi})^{N_{Gi} - n_{Gi}}.$$

(4)

In the general case we assume no necessary relation between individual and group performance. Hence, the maximum likelihood estimators of $p_{Ii}$ and $p_{Gi}$ are the observed proportions of correct individual and group responses, that is, $\hat{p}_{Ii} = n_{Ii}/N_{Ii}$, and $\hat{p}_{Gi} = n_{Gi}/N_{Gi}$. Substituting these values into Equation 4 yields the maximum likelihood of the $i$th item data under the general model. The maximum likelihood of the entire data set over the 75 items of the Terman, and over the 30 items of the W. P. Laughlin analogies, would be given by the product of the itemwise maximum likelihoods:

$$L = \prod_{i=1}^{75} L_i.$$

(5)

(The $\Pi$ product in Equation 5 is from 1 to 30 on the W. P. Laughlin analogies.) Equation 5 represents the numerator of the $LR$.

Under a particular social decision scheme $p_{Ii}$ and $p_{Gi}$ are functionally related. For example, the truth-wins social decision scheme (TWIN) posits the simple function:

$$p_{Gi} = 1 - (1 - p_{Ii})^r . \tag{6}$$

Thus, under the truth-wins social decision scheme, Equation 4 has only one unknown parameter. The maximum likelihood estimator of this parameter, $p_{Ii}^*$, under the truth-wins (TWIN) social decision scheme was found using the STEPIT iterative search program of Chandler (1969). The corresponding maximum likelihood $L_i^*$ comprises a component of the maximum likelihood of the entire data set under a truth-wins model:

$$L^* = \prod_{i=1}^{75} L_i^* . \tag{7}$$

Thus, the $LR$ under the truth-wins model is:

$$LR = L/L^* . \tag{8}$$

$-2 \log_e LR$ is distributed approximately as $X_{75}^2$ when the truth-wins model holds. Although the functional relationship between $p_{Ii}$ and $p_{Gi}$ is more complex for other social decision schemes, the same procedures were followed to compute an $LR$ similar to Equation 8 for each of the nine other social decision scheme models.

Results of these $LR$ tests for each of the ten social decision scheme models for each of the two analogies tests are given in Table 3. The smaller the value of $X^2$, the better the fit of the model. As indicated in Table 3, the best-fitting social decision scheme on both analogies tests was, as hypothesized, truth-supported wins (TSWIN).

## Discussion

The best-fitting theory of the social combination process on two different verbal analogies tests (which correlated 0.57 with each other for individuals) was truth-supported wins: two or more correct members of a four-person group were necessary and sufficient for a correct group response. This basic truth-supported wins social

TABLE 3

*Likelihood-ratio tests showing relative goodness-of-fit of each model across all 75 Terman analogies items, and across all 30 W. P. Laughlin analogies items.*

| Social decision scheme | Terman | W. P. Laughlin |
|---|---|---|
| STEQ | 514.60 | 418.34 |
| STPR | 372.14 | 307.64 |
| TWIN | 503.47 | 221.06 |
| TSWIN | 115.17 | 105.62 |
| MAEQ | 273.33 | 214.19 |
| MCEQ | 145.19 | 143.81 |
| MIEQ | 759.47 | 536.20 |
| EWIN | 2378.11 | 1275.31 |
| ESWIN | 633.42 | 388.71 |
| DEST | 150.21 | 138.36 |

*Note*: Tabled values are $-2 \log_e LR$, which is distributed approximately as $X^2$ with 75 d.f. for the Terman items and 30 d.f. for the W. P. Laughlin items. The smaller the value of $X^2$, the better the relative fit of the model. Thus, best-fitting model is truth-supported wins (TSWIN) on both analogies tasks.

combination process provided a better fit than a wide range of other plausible theories, including the classic truth-wins assumption, which overpredicted performance, and majority, proportionality, and equiprobability assumptions, which underpredicted performance. Moreover, the truth-supported wins process was not attenuated in the 2—2 groups, as indicated by the poorer fit of the DEST model.

The three studies in this series (including the present experiment; Laughlin *et al.,* 1975, 1976) indicate that there is a continuum of demonstrability on verbal intellective tasks. The fundamental social combination process for four-person groups is truth-supported wins, as exemplified most strongly on verbal analogies. The dimensions of analogies are apparently demonstrable by a single correct person only if supported by a second correct person. In contrast, a single correct person is able to demonstrate a correct answer on the class of strong verbal associations represented by the Remote Associates Test, while there is a slight attenuation from the basic truth-supported wins process on English vocabulary and general verbal achievement items (represented by Part I of the Terman and by the Otis), as indicated by the better fit of the DEST scheme. On this class of intellective tasks the 2—2 group has a probability of about 0.78 of giving the correct response, intermediate between the probability of 1.00 for a truth-supported wins social combination process and the probability of 0.50 for the majority, equiprobability (or proportionality) otherwise process.

In contrast, the best-fitting social decision scheme on judgemental tasks is a majority social combination process. A two-thirds majority social decision scheme has provided the best fit for both six-person and twelve-person mock juries in three extensive studies (Davis *et al.*, 1975, 1977b; Kerr *et al.*, 1976). There is also evidence that majority is the fundamental social combination process on evaluative attitudinal judgements, especially when the majority is in the direction of prevailing group norms (Cvetkovitch and Baumgardner, 1973; Davis *et al.*, 1974; Kerr *et al.*, 1975). In contrast to intellective tasks, the criterion of successful group performance on judgemental tasks is necessarily group consensus, and the majority social combination process seems to be necessary and sufficient to achieve such group consensus in the absence of demonstrably correct solutions.

Intellective and judgemental tasks may be considered regions on a dimension of consensus. In an intellective task the consensus is a given, and in a judgemental task the consensus is an objective. Intellective tasks are embedded in conceptual systems representing the consensus of previous groups on the meaning of words, the relevant dimensions of analogies, the axioms of a mathematical system, or, perhaps most importantly, on the epistemological criteria of relevant questions, evidence, and proof. Given the conceptual system, a problem may be posed within the system, and the proposed solution evaluated within the demonstrable relationships of the system. In a judgemental task the conceptual system in which the task is embedded has not been developed, particularily to the level of axiomatization, sufficiently to enable demonstrable solutions within the system. On a judgemental task the fundamental group problem is to achieve consensus, rather than to operate within the previously given consensus.[1]

All social knowledge, and hence social discourse and intellectual communication, is predicated upon social consensus on the axioms of a given conceptual system, whether the formal axiomatization of many mathematical and some philosophical systems, the less formal axiomatization of language and legal systems, or the still less formal axiomatization of the systems of social norms and relationships which guide interpersonal behavior. The achievement of group consensus on the axioms is a judgemental task guided by a majority process. Given this basic achievement, the further achievement of problem solutions within the conceptual system is an intellective task guided by a truth-supported wins process, where "truth" is defined by the previous social judgemental consensus on the axioms.

## Note

1. It is perhaps worth distinguishing between procedural and outcome consensus. Procedural consensus involves group agreement on the manner or modus operandi of the group process, such as the formal procedures of Robert's Rules of Order or other manuals of prescribed operating rules. Outcome consensus involves group agreement on the value of the group decision on some negative to positive continuum such as bad to good, inappropriate to appropriate, or other evaluative dimension. Outcome consensus presupposes procedural consensus or agreement on the "rules of the game." Such procedural consensus represents the achievement of previous groups on the modus operandi of the group process. Indeed, we may propose that political systems are fundamentally solutions to the group task of achieving procedural consensus.

## References

Chandler, J. P. STEPIT: Finds local minima of a smooth function of several parameters. *Behavioral Science*, 1969, 14, 81–82.

Cvetkovitch, G., and Baumgardner, S. R. Attitude polarization: The relative influence of discussion group structure and reference group norms. *Journal of Personality and Social Psychology*, 1973, 26, 159–165.

Davis, J. H. Group decision and social interaction: A theory of social decision schemes. *Psychological Review*, 1973, 80, 97–125.

Davis, J. H. and Restle, F. The analysis of problems and prediction of group problem solving. *Journal of Abnormal and Social Psychology*, 1963, 66, 103–116.

Davis, J. H., Kerr, N. L., Atkin, R. S., Holt, R. and Meek, D. The decision processes of 6- and 12-person mock juries assigned unanimous and two-thirds majority rules. *Journal of Personality and Social Psychology*, 1975, 32, 1–14.

Davis, J. H., Laughlin, P. R. and Komorita, S. S. The social psychology of small groups: Cooperative and mixed-motive interaction. *Annual Review of Psychology*, 1976, 27, 501–541.

Davis, J. H., Stasser, G., Spitzer, C. E. and Holt, R. Changes in group members' decision preferences during discussion: An illustration with mock juries. *Journal of Personality and Social Psychology*, 1976, 34, 1177–1187.

Davis, J. H., Bray, R. M. and Holt, R. W. The empirical study of decision processes in juries: A critical review. In J. Tapp & F. Levine (Eds), *Law, justice, and the individual in society: Psychological and legal issues*. New York: Holt, Rinehart, & Winston, 1977a.

Davis, J. H., Kerr, N. L., Stasser, G., Meek, D. and Holt, R. Victim consequences, sentence severity, and decision processes in mock juries. *Organizational Behavior and Human Performance*, 1977b, 18, 346–365.

Faust, W. L. Group versus individual problem-solving. *Journal of Abnormal and Social Psychology*, 1959, 59, 68–72.

Gelfand, A. E. and Solomon, H. A study of Poisson's models for jury verdicts in criminal and civil trials. *Journal of the American Statistical Association*, 1973, 68, 271–278.

Gelfand, A. E. and Solomon, H. Analyzing the decision-making process of the American jury. *Journal of the American Statistical Association*, 1974, 69, 32–37.

Gelfand, A. E. and Solomon, H. Modeling jury verdicts in the American legal system. *Journal of the American Statistical Association*, 1975, **69**, 32–37.

Kelley, H. H. and Thibaut, J. W. Group problem solving. In G. Lindzey and E. Aronson (Eds), *The handbook of social psychology*. Vol. 4. Reading, Mass.: Addison-Wesley, 1969, pp. 1–101.

Kerr, N. L., Davis, J. H., Meek, D. and Rissman, A. K. Group position as a function of member attitudes: Choice shift effects from the perspective of social decision scheme theory. *Journal of Personality and Social Psychology*, 1975, **31**, 574–593.

Kerr, N. L., Atkin, R. S., Stasser, G., Meek, D., Holt, R. W. and Davis, J. H. Guilt beyond a reasonable doubt: Effects of concept identification and assigned decision rule on the judgements of mock jurors. *Journal of Personality and Social Psychology*, 1976, **34**, 282–294.

Lamm, H. and Myers, D. G. Group-induced polarization of attitudes and behavior. In L. Berkowitz (Ed.), *Advances in experimental social psychology*. New York and London: Academic Press, 1978. Vol. 11, pp. 145–195.

Laughlin, P. R. and Branch, L. G. Individual versus tetradic performance on a complementary task as a function of initial ability level. *Organizational Behavior and Human Performance*, 1972, **8**, 201–216.

Laughlin, P. R. and Sweeney, J. D. Individual-to-group and group-to-individual transfer in problem solving. *Journal of Experimental Psychology: Human Learning and Memory*, 1977, **3**, 246–254.

Laughlin, P. R., Kerr, N. L., Davis, J. H., Halff, H. M. and Marciniak, K. A. Group size, member ability, and social decision schemes on an intellective task. *Journal of Personality and Social Psychology*, 1975, **31**, 522–535.

Laughlin, P. R., Kerr, N. L., Munch, M. M. and Haggarty, C. A. Social decision schemes of the same four-person groups on two different intellective tasks. *Journal of Personality and Social Psychology*, 1976, **33**, 80–88.

Laughlin, W. P. *Visualizing relations*. Elmhurst, Illinois: Author, 1964.

Lorge, I. and Solomon, H. Two models of group behavior in the solution of Eureka-type problems. *Psychometrika*, 1955, **20**, 139–148.

Mednick, S. A. and Mednick, M. T. *Examiner's manual: Remote Associates Test*.

Moscovici, S. and Zavalloni, M. The group as a polarizer of attitudes. *Journal of Personality and Social Psychology*, 1969, **12**, 125–135.

Myers, D. G. and Lamm, H. The group polarization phenomenon. *Psychological Bulletin*, 1976, **83**, 602–627.

Otis, A. S. *Manual of directions for Gamma Test*. New York: Harcourt, Brace, & World, 1954.

Shaw, M. E. A comparison of individuals and small groups in the rational solution of complex problems. *American Journal of Psychology*, 1932, **44**, 491–504.

Smoke, W. H. and Zajonc, R. B. On the reliability of group judgements and decisions. In J. H. Criswell, H. Solomon, and P. Suppes (Eds), *Mathematical methods in small group process*. Stanford: Stanford University Press, 1962.

Steiner, I. D. Models for inferring relationships between group size and potential group productivity. *Behavioral Science*, 1966, **11**, 273–283.

Steiner, I. D. *Group process and productivity*. New York and London: Academic Press, 1972.

Terman, L. M. *Manual for Concept Mastery Test*. New York: Psychological Corporation, 1956.

Thomas, E. J. and Fink, C. F. Models of group problem solving. *Journal of Abnormal and Social Psychology*, 1961, **68**, 55–63.

# II
# Choice Shifts

# Introduction

Blair H. Sheppard and James H. Davis

As Davis (in press) suggests, inspection of the literature on small group behavior reveals that many phenomena naturally arising in groups and originally studied in that setting are now primarily the property of "individual social" psychology. This drift from the group to the individual as the level of analysis has, in many cases, followed a particular pattern. First, an unexpected finding is generated regarding group performance, particularly as contrasted to individual performance (for example, Shaw, 1932) or expectations regarding the combination of individual endeavors (e.g., Lorge and Solomon, 1955). Effort is next focused on determining the validity and ability to be generalized of the finding using different stimuli, research settings, etc. Finally, interest in repeated demonstrations of the unexpected phenomenon itself wanes and is replaced with attempts to identify the process(es) through which the phenomenon arises. At this point manipulations related to specific hypotheses (intended to simulate some aspect of group interaction) are performed, often upon isolated individuals, to determine the validity of a particular explanation. In this way, one might argue that the study of group cohesiveness became the study of interpersonal attraction (e.g. see Byrne, 1971); interpersonal influence processes among a group of interacting people were redefined as the social conformity of one individual to a majority (e.g. see Allen, 1965); and intra-group conflict and cooperation were transformed to the study of cooperation and competition in a minimal social setting (e.g. see Deutsch, 1949).

Much of the movement to the individual as the level of analysis results from great savings in time, money and subjects, increased experimental control, improved measurement and simplification of the problem under study. It is also, however, the quite natural result of a healthy interest in the cognitive dynamics underlying the phenomena originally detected in a group setting, which in many instances would be simply impossible to study further in a collection of people. One unfortunate consequence, however, is that the group often seems to be forgotten and the steps back to the original question are usually not retraced conceptually or empirically. Without confirmation of results in a group setting we remain uncertain that the explanations from individuals have sufficiently cogent applicability to social interaction.

Choice shift research has followed a very similar pattern, but without losing contact with the group according to the familiar pattern. (Myers, Chapter 6, traces the history of choice shift research.) The original finding, that groups can be more risky than individuals, has been translated (cf. Doise, 1969; Moscovici and Zavalloni, 1969; Myers and Lamm, 1976) to an investigation of a wide range of potential mechanisms through which individual post-discussion attitudes may have been polarized. The set of papers in this section presents a sample of the current range of explanations (limitations) of group-induced opinion polarization. As a result of the diversity of positions on polarization this series of papers implies a highly heterogeneous literature. All, however, concentrate upon the influence of actual group discussion on opinions. Through their common concern for the consequences of entering discussion, the authors in this section have all maintained a direct concern with the level of interpersonal interaction. Thus, it appears that, in the case of choice shift research, the retracing of steps to recover the group nature of the phenomenon is unnecessary; the group setting was never abandoned.

A further commonality amongst the chapters in this section is that each, either directly or indirectly, addresses the two general classes of explanation for polarization offered as most viable by Myers and Lamm (1976), specifically persuasive arguments theory and social comparison theory. Persuasive arguments theory suggests that post-discussion opinion change is the result of hearing new belief statements during discussion, while social comparison theory suggests change results from comparing one's position to that of others in the group or that position valued by the group. The first three chapters are directly concerned with these two ideas.

Myers' first chapter presents a history of his own work and the general literature on choice shifts and polarization in which he describes in some detail a progression from the demonstration of an interesting phenomenon to the study of underlying processes. At the same time, he indicates the potential implications of the choice shift phenomenon for many non-laboratory settings, including the potentially debilitating effects of placing like-minded persons in prison, as well as the positive role of interaction in Alcoholics Anonymous and religious fellowships. The last section of the paper discusses the presently available theoretical explanations of group-induced attitude polarization. In this section, Myers reviews two series of studies in which he and his colleagues purportedly demonstrate that argumentation and social comparison processes are both sufficient to induce polarization. He concludes, however, that the two are inextricably bound, since it is inconceivable that social comparison-induced opinion change does not result in, at least, some cognitive reorganization by the individual.

In the second chapter, Burnstein also adopts Myers' position that social comparison results in some self-generated cognitive (belief) change, but in contrast to Myers suggests that argument, either by self or others, is both a necessary and sufficient cause of attitude polarization. To support this view Burnstein discusses the results of several studies on depolarization in which attitudes of individuals in two extreme groups become less extreme after discussion. Burnstein argues that Festinger's social comparison theory (1954) would predict increased identification with like-minded others and thus increased polarization of the two opposing groups. Persuasive arguments theory, on the other hand, suggests that, since individuals at each of the opposing poles are probably hearing more novel arguments supporting the opposing position, the two groups should, as the results show, become less extreme. Also, Burnstein shows how reinterpreting results of the Asch (1956) conformity paradigm in terms of persuasive arguments provides a reasonable explanation for the sharp reduction in conformity with increases in group size beyond three or four — a problem which has eluded explanation by social conformity theorists. The author concludes that the utility of a persuasive arguments approach in explaining results from the bastion of social comparison research (Asch paradigm) is compelling support for his position.

In the third chapter, Witte and Lutz attempt to directly assess the underlying cognitive factors (cognitive structure) influencing choice behavior in risky situations. They reasoned that, if group discussion does induce new cognitions which in turn results in polarization, then post-discussion attitude change should be accompanied by predictable changes in risk-related cognitive structure. In the first portion of the study Witte and Lutz successfully reproduce, on a very different subject population, four factors developed in an earlier study by Witte and Arez (1974). Further, a multiple regression using these factors effectively predicted individual risk behavior. Thus, Witte and Lutz argued that they had identified those aspects of cognition important to risk preference. However, while individual risk preferences changed after discussion there was no accompanying predictable change in the regression weights for the equation predicting risk preference. Clearly, a firm statement of the implications of this research will require verification of the findings with other analytical techniques, since it is possible that the authors did not assess the relevant cognitions. However, it is a tantalizing possibility that attitude change is not a result of, or even accompanied by, changes in related cognitions (see the Burnstein and Myers chapters for a discussion of the arguments supporting the need for related cognitive change).

The remaining three chapters in this section are rather different from the first three. Kovács argues that the degree of discussion-induced attitude polarization is related to the level of uncertainty arising from two sources: (a) the inherent complexity of the issue, and (b) the discrepancy between the certainty with which group members hold their respective positions on the issue (structural uncertainty). Using the familiar information measure, $H = -\Sigma_i p_i \times \log_2 p_i$ where $p_i$ is the probability of the $i$-th category, as a measure of uncertainty, Kovács determines that uncertainty is inherent when the task and structural uncertainty interact to increase or limit polarization. The author concludes that the effects are mediated by differential tendencies to process available information which results from the two types of uncertainty.

Chapter 7 by Zaleska considers attitude polarization in the light of social judgement theory, a viewpoint developed by Sherif (1965) from the study of individual attitude change. One derivation of Sherif's theory is that persons holding extreme attitude positions should be less likely to change their opinion after discussion than persons holding moderate positions. In a review of 26 studies, Zaleska indicates that this prediction only holds when persons identify themselves with an extreme group. She provides an interesting anecdotal example of a devout Catholic who supported the state-proposed abortion laws in order not to be identified with a group of leftist students who felt that the proposed law was not liberal enough. She concludes that past research on individual attitude change may have confused extremity of attitude for identification with an extreme group. Thus, social judgement theory may have a basis in social identification or comparison processes. It is of note that Zaleska's paper provides a striking example of the potential insights to be gained by taking questions traditionally studied at the individual level into the group level.

In Chapter 8, Nemeth presents another approach to polarization research. Her strategy uses polarization as an experimental device for studying another related phenomenon, minority—majority processes in conformity. Nemeth's position regarding conformity research is that the stability of the position held by each faction will determine the degree to which that side will (a) induce change by the other faction, and (b) itself remain resolute. Nemeth relied on polarization as a means of inducing greater stability in minority and majority positions. In some conditions, members of a jury holding the same position (either minority or majority) in a personal injury case met with each other before jury deliberation. Members of these like-minded groups were expected to polarize, thus inducing more stable minority—majority positions relative to juries whose factions did not meet before deliberation. This use of polarization as an experimental manipulation was generally successful. Nemeth's discussion of the implications of the results for minority—majority influence are particularly interesting in light of Burnstein's treatment of group size effects in Chapter 5.

In summary, the present chapters all use actual group interaction to investigate the potential mechanisms underlying polarization. As in most psychological research the articles appear to have generated as many questions as they have answered. One firm conclusion which can be drawn from the chapters as a whole is simply that answers to group-related questions can usefully be sought using actual groups. The richness of results coming from this set of studies augurs well the future usefulness of increased group research where subjects interact freely. In fact, Zaleska's novel chapter suggests it may be time to turn the tables and take much of what had traditionally been studied as individual social psychology into the group.

# References

Allen, V. L. Situational factors in conformity. In L. Berkowitz (Ed.), *Advances in Experimental Social Psychology*. New York and London: Academic Press, 1965.

Asch, S. E. Studies of independence and submission to group pressure: I. On minority of one against a unanimous majority. *Psychological Monographs*, 1956, 70, (9, Whole No. 417).

Byrne, D. *The Attraction Paradigm*. New York and London: Academic Press, 1971.

Davis, J. H. Group performance: Theories and concepts. In C. G. McClintock and J. Maki (Eds), *Social Psychological Theory*. New York: Holt, in press.

Deutsch, M. A theory of cooperation and competition. *Human Relations*, 1949, 2, 199–231.

Doise, W. Intergroup relations and polarization of individual and collective judgments. *Journal of Personality and Social Psychology*, 1971, 1, 511–518.

Festinger, L. A theory of social comparison processes. *Human Relations*, 1954, 7, 117–140.

Lorge, I. and Solomon, H. Two models of group behavior in the solution of Eureka-type problems. *Psychometrika*, 1955, 20, 139–148.

Moscovici, S. and Zavalloni, M. The group as a polarizer of attitudes. *Journal of Personality and Social Psychology*, 1969, 12, 125–135.

Myers, D. G. and Lamm, H. The group polarization phenomenon. *Psychological Bulletin*, 1976, 83, 602–627.

Shaw, M. E. A comparison of individuals and small groups in the rational solution of complex problems. *American Journal of Psychology*, 1932, 44, 491–504.

Sherif, C. W., Sherif, M. and Nebergall, R. E. *Attitude and Attitude Change: The Social Judgment-Involvement Approach*. Philadelphia: W. B. Saunders, 1965.

Witte, E. H. and Arez, A. The cognitive structure of choice dilemma decisions. *European Journal of Social Psychology*, 1974, 4, 313–328.

# 5
# Persuasion as Argument Processing

Eugene Burnstein

Our interest in the informational basis of social influence was piqued several years ago as a result of trying to understand group polarization or what, during this period, was called the "risky shift." At that time virtually every explanation for this phenomenon said it was due to normative influence. Although other explanations have been proposed since then, many of these also insist on the primacy of the latter process. According to this view individual choice and, consequently, group decision making are controlled by hedonic factors.

For instance, when a person values his membership in a group and finds his position on an important issue differs from that of other members, he anticipates that they will disapprove of him, which is distressing; to reduce this distress the person ostensibly abandons his position and shifts toward the consensus. As this example might suggest, normative influence models require that the individual knows the attitude of others and compares the latter to his own. Let us therefore call them comparison theories.

From the very beginning we found little or no evidence that polarization depended in the slightest on the normative influence mediated by a comparison mechanism (see the review in Burnstein and Vinokur, 1977). As a result we began to think of a different kind of explanation for group polarization, one based on informational influence. In general, such an explanation assumes that the impact of an argument depends on the information it contains and on the manner in which the person processes this information. Our particular formulation was called persuasive-arguments theory (Vinokur and Burnstein, 1974). Other versions of informational

The research reported in this paper was supported by grants from the National Institute of Mental Health.

influence have been proposed by Bishop and Myers (1974) and by Anderson and Graesser (1976). The basic idea of persuasive-arguments theory is that when the person evaluates (or re-evaluates) alternative positions, points of view, courses of action, etc., say, *J* versus *K*, he generates or constructs arguments, namely, ideas, images, or thoughts describing the attributes of *J* and *K*. This is based on the assumption that there exists in memory a culturally given pool of arguments speaking to each alternative. On some occasions these arguments are accessible, on others, they are not. In order to judge the relative merits of these alternatives the person samples (retrieves arguments) from this pool. Up to now we have focused on the following pro- perties of such arguments: their availability or accessibility (the probability of coming to mind), direction (pro-*J* and pro-*K*), and persuasiveness. When the preponderance of arguments in the pool favors a particular alternative, the average prior attitude reflects the direction and magnitude of this preponderance. Further thought or discussion leads to polarization toward the alternative that initially elicits more and/or better arguments. The extent of polarization will depend on whether the initial argument samples overlap or exhaust the larger pool. This implies that polarization will increase under conditions in which the person's initial position is based on a less than complete processing of the information available in the argument pool. The latter can be due to real ignorance (e.g. some people may never have encountered a particular idea even though the idea is known to many of their peers) or to a frailty of thought (e.g. some people may momentarily forget an idea or find there is insufficient time to recall it). Whatever the reason, under these conditions when the person begins to rethink the issue, there still remain many arguments which have not yet come to mind, or when several individuals discuss the issue with each other, the arguments which have come to mind are only partially shared.

A persuasive-arguments analysis of discussion effects may be illustrated with a simple example. Consider a choice in which the culturally given pool contains six pro-*J* arguments, *a, b, c, d, e,* and *f,* and three pro-*K* arguments, *l, m,* and *n*. One of several distinct outcomes would be expected, depending on the distribution of arguments among members. Suppose all three of our discussants had thought of the same arguments. In this case their prior attitude toward *J* would be identical and discussion would produce no change. On the other hand, if *a, b,* and *m* had come to mind in one discussant, $c$, $d$, and $m$ in the second, and $e$, $f$, and $m$ in the third (i.e. if each has different pro-$J$ arguments, but the same pro-$K$ arguments) then, although they again hold identical prior attitudes, the discussion would produce marked polarization toward $J$. Finally polarization toward $K$ would be predicted if one member had generated $a$, $b$, and $l$, another $a$, $b$, and $m$, and the third $a$, $b$, and $n$ (i.e. if each had initially thought of the same pro-$J$ but different pro-$K$ arguments). Normally individual argument samples are representative of the larger pool (Vinokur and Burnstein, 1974). Therefore, average prediscussion preferences can be estimated from the balance of pro-$J$ and pro-$K$ arguments in the pool. Post-discussion preferences can be predicted just as readily if in addition we know the degree of partial sharing, that is, the extent of overlap among individual argument samples.

During the past several years we have tried to isolate the conditions under which persuasive-arguments theory and comparison theory make conflicting predictions and then to pit these predictions against each other in experiments. I do not think it an unfair summary of this work to say we have demonstrated that (a) if an individual could argue but not compare, polarization still occurred (Burnstein and Vinokur, 1973); (b) if he could compare but not openly argue, polarization vanished (Burnstein and Vinokur, 1973, 1975) or was greatly attentuated (Burnstein et al., 1973); but (c) even in attentuated form, polarization seemed to depend directly on tacit argumentation (Burnstein and Vinokur, 1975). In short, persuasive-arguments theory (or probably any theory based on informational influence) seems to provide a more adequate explanation of group polarization than theories based on normative influence, particularly those that assume comparison processes are important.

For the remainder of this paper I want to discuss our most recent research on informational influence. Three issues will be examined. First, and most closely related to our past work comparing informational and normative influence theories, I will present some findings on group depolarization, contrasting what might be anticipated in respect to such effects from the point of view of persuasive-arguments and from that of comparison theories. This will be followed by a brief analysis of our conception of informational influence as argument processing. And finally, I would like to describe an experiment in which this analysis is applied in an Asch-like conformity situation.

### Depolarization

It is well known that in the typical polarization situation, attitudes also depolarize (converge) and become less extreme. To take one example, Ferguson and Vidmar (1971) demonstrated that group members with relatively extreme prior attituded either change very little as a result of discussion or shift to a more moderate position. (Moderate members, of course, shift to a more extreme position, and often this shift is of sufficient magnitude to produce polarization for the group as a whole, so that the average post-discussion attitude is more extreme than the average pre-discussion attitude.) Also it is worth noting that about a quarter of choice-dilemmas are neutral in respect to polarization, that is, discussion leads initially riskier group members to become more cuatious to the same extent that it leads the initially more cautious group members to become riskier — thus, depolarization alone is observed. Although this pervasive effect, by its neglect, seems to be considered theoretically unimportant, we think it can be demonstrated that in certain circumstances the two types of theories in question, comparison and persuasive-arguments, make grossly different predictions regarding the relative magnitude of polarization and depolarization. Let me now describe these circumstances.

In an analysis of neutral choice dilemmas (Vinokur and Burnstein, 1974) it was demonstrated that these items depolarize (and do not polarize) because their argument pools contain a similar number of partially shared persuasive arguments in favor of the certain and uncertain courses of action (also see Vinokur *et al.*, 1975). The identical state of affairs may on occasion also occur with items that are known to polarize. Consider an item that typically shifts toward $K$. According to persuasive-arguments theory, the average individual will have access to more pro-$K$ than pro-$J$ arguments, and owing to this, his prior attitude will be pro-$K$. Suppose, however, there is an unusual group in which half of the members are pro-$J$ (and, thus, for the moment, have more pro-$J$ than pro-$K$ arguments), and half are pro-$K$ (and, thus, for the moment, have more pro-$K$ than pro-$J$ arguments). Even though discussion typically leads to polarization toward $K$, persuasive-arguments theory must predict that depolarization will occur in this group — the pro-$J$ subgroup will become more pro-$K$, the pro-$K$ subgroup more pro-$J$, and there will be relatively little polarization. Furthermore, if the proportions of pro-*J* and pro-*K* arguments in the larger pool are known, even roughly, then an estimate can be made of which subgroup will depolarize the most. For example, on dilemmas that usually polarize toward risk, the number of pro-risk arguments in the pool is larger than the number of pro-caution arguments. It follows that in discussion, pro-risk members are likely to have available and, thus, to present a greater number of additional arguments supporting their position (and to have more impact on pro-caution members) than the reverse. As a result, pro-caution individuals should shift (toward risk) more than pro-risk individuals (toward caution). A similar line of reasoning would predict that pro-risk members will exhibit a greater shift (toward caution) than pro-caution members (toward risk) on dilemmas which typically polarize in a cautious direction. Finally, recall that on neutral dilemmas, the proportion of pro-risk and pro-caution arguments in the larger pool are similar. According to persuasive-arguments, therefore, pro-risk and pro-caution subgroups should depolarize to the same extent.

Unfortunately, in the above circumstances (i.e. when the group contains equally large subgroups with diametrically opposite points of view) comparison theories are somewhat vague as to how members decide which position is more socially desirable and, thus, who they will choose to compare themselves with. Nevertheless, reasonable inferences are possible on the basis of Festinger's classical formulation (1954) which serves as the common framework for all later versions of comparison theory (cf. Sanders and Baron, 1977).

From the point of view of comparison theories, as they are used in the analysis of polarization, the fact that, prior to discussion, attitudes are generally pro-*K* and that, following discussion, they polarize further toward *K* signifies that this alternative is more socially desirable than *J*. Given our hypothetical half pro-*J* and half pro-*K* group, these theories suggest two possible outcomes, both of which differ from that proposed by persuasive-arguments theory. First, upon observing that others prefer *K*, the pro-*J* subgroup may realize its *faux pas* and change in the socially desirable direction (toward *K*) while the pro-*K* subgroup should at least maintain its initial position or, what is more likely, become increasingly pro-*K*. In short, the group as a whole will polarize toward *K* and the effect should be robust. A second possibility is that pro-*J* members will find pro-*K* members too dissimilar for purposes of comparison, and vice versa. By categorizing the opposing subgroups as non-comparable, pro-$J$ members in effect define $J$ (not $K$) as the socially desirable alternative while pro-$K$ members define $K$ (not $J$) as the socially desirable alternative. Comparisons then would be made within, not between, the two attitude subgroups. As a result, pro-$J$ members will become increasingly pro-$J$ and pro-$K$ members increasingly pro-$K$. Thus, the first derivation from comparison theories suggests that polarization will be unidirectional and the second, that polarization will be bidirectional. The latter, however, seems much more likely than the former when each subgroup clearly favors opposte sides of the issue and the difference between them is sizable.

Two experiments were recently performed to test these ideas. In the first experiment groups of six individuals discussed the standard choice-dilemma items. Each group was composed of two attitudinally homogenous subgroups, with the position taken by members of one subgroup being markedly different (and opposite) from that taken by members of the other. This state of affairs either was not mentioned at all or was explained in detail prior to discussion and kept salient throughout by an appropriate seating arrangement and the assignment of highly visible labels. The second experiment also involved group discussion. However, the items, compared to those used in the first experiment, are highly variegated. They were selected so as to allow us to demonstrate not only that depolarization of attitudes is a very general phenomenon but also that the magnitude of this effect varies in a manner predicted by persuasive-arguments theory.

The results of the first experiment were unambiguous. Neither the mean amount of polarization (shift) nor the mean amount of depolarization on any single item, or on all items pooled, significantly differed as a function of subgroup salience. Therefore, the data from the two experimental conditions were combined and are summarized in Table 1. As can readily be seen, the creation of distinct subgroups with divergent points of view did not affect the shifts typically found with such items. That is to say, there was a significant shift toward risk on risky items, a significant shift toward caution on the cautious items, and no reliable shift whatsoever on the neutral items. It is quite important to keep in mind, however, that polarization in this as well as in the second experiment is comparable to that observed in past studies only at the gross level of group averages. The pattern of changes that underlies the gross effect is rather different. In past research polarization reflected

TABLE 1

*Mean choice and mean gap before (I) and after (II) group discussion, mean shift and mean depolarization for choice dilemma items*

| Item type | N | Mean choice | | Mean shift[c] | Mean gap[d] | | Mean depolarization[e] |
|---|---|---|---|---|---|---|---|
| **Risky items** | | | | | | | |
| A | 14 | I.[a] | 4.71 | $-1.21^\dagger$ | I. | 5.09 | $3.09^\dagger$ |
| | | II.[b] | 3.50 | | II. | 2.00 | |
| B | 16 | I. | 5.03 | $-0.58^*$ | I. | 4.31 | $1.95^\dagger$ |
| | | II. | 4.44 | | II. | 2.35 | |
| C | 19 | I. | 4.58 | $-0.70^*$ | I. | 4.79 | $2.59^\dagger$ |
| | | II. | 3.88 | | II. | 2.19 | |
| K | 19 | I. | 5.25 | $-0.78^*$ | I. | 4.47 | $2.08^\dagger$ |
| | | II. | 4.47 | | II. | 2.38 | |
| **Neutral items** | | | | | | | |
| D | 14 | I. | 6.59 | 0.18 | I. | 4.90 | $1.92^\dagger$ |
| | | II. | 6.77 | | II. | 2.97 | |
| H | 18 | I. | 6.45 | $-0.10$ | I. | 4.79 | $2.01^\dagger$ |
| | | II. | 6.35 | | II. | 2.77 | |
| **Cautious items** | | | | | | | |
| E | 19 | I. | 6.22 | $0.98^\dagger$ | I. | 5.96 | $3.36^\dagger$ |
| | | II. | 7.21 | | II. | 2.59 | |

[a] I = Mean choice before discussion (initial choices).
[b] II = Mean choice made after group discussion in private.
[c] Negative values indicate shifts toward risk. Positive values indicate shifts toward caution.
[d] This mean indicates the absolute difference between the two subgroups (i.e. the gap) before (I), and after (II) group discussion.
[e] Mean depolarization indicates changes in the mean gap between the two subgroups following group discussion. Positive value indicates decrease in the gap, i.e. depolarization. Negative value indicates an increase in the gap, i.e., polarization.
$^*P < 0.01.$
$^\dagger P < 0.001.$

a pattern of changes whereby the more moderate members become more extreme. In our experiment, the two subgroups contain members who are equally extreme to begin with and in every case following discussion they converge, i.e. become less extreme. On converging, however, one subgroup depolarizes more than the other (e.g. on items known to shift in a cautious direction, the subgroup that initially is extremely cautious will move in a risky direction and the subgroup that is initially extremely risky will move in a cautious direction, but the latter subgroup will move more than the former). Thus, while both subgroups always depolarize and never polarize, the average position of group members will appear more extreme.

Which is a lengthy way of saying that because of the differential rate of depolarization, the average post-discussion preference will be more cautious on cautious-shifting items and more risky on risky-shifting items than the average prediscussion preference.

The depolarization effect itself is sweeping. The initial mean gap between subgroups which amounted to 4.90 scale points (on a ten point scale), decreased by half, to a mean of 2.46 scale points. Hence, a short discussion of six minutes halved the large difference between two subgroups whose members were clearly aware of their being in opposition. Furthermore, on each item the magnitude of depolarization on the part of one subgroup relative to that of the other subgroup was just what would be anticipated on the basis of persuasive arguments theory.

Persuasive-arguments theory implies that if each individual weighs all the relevant information before choosing (i.e. if the argument sample he or she generates exhausts the larger pool), the impact of discussion will be nil. Nothing anyone may say can change that person's mind because he has already taken everything into account. In other words, discussion will produce a shift in attitude to the extent that the relevant information is only partially (rather than completely) shared (Kaplan, 1977; Kaplan and Miller, 1977; Vinokur and Burnstein, 1974; Vinokur et al., 1975). In our second experiment, a reasonable guess was made as to how information is shared in respect to different kinds of issues. If the guess is correct, then we have distinguished those issues in which discussion will have a pronounced effect on attitudes from those in which it will not. Later we shall present some evidence, gathered as an afterthought, in support of this guess. Now let us simply describe the reasoning behind it: it is not far-fetched to assume that the commerce individuals have with an issue (the extent to which they read, think about, and discuss the matter) is a rough index of information and interest. If individuals often read, think about, and discuss a topic, they will know much of what there is to know about it. Hence, their knowledge is likely to overlap considerably. Moreover, since they are interested in the issue, under appropriate conditions they will be motivated to retrieve and encode this knowledge. A well-known example of the latter process is the tendency to construct counter-arguments in a response to persuasion (Brock, 1967; Greenwald, 1968; 1969; 1970; McGuire, 1964; Miller and Baron, 1973). On the other hand, if individuals rarely read, think about, and discuss a topic, they will know only a small part of what is to be known. Hence, their knowledge is likely to overlap very little. Since their interest is meager, they also will have little incentive to retrieve and encode this limited knowledge. Thus, the more popular the topic, the more widely shared the arguments, and the more widely shared the argument, the weaker the impact of group discussion.

Given this line of reasoning, we then conjectured that, in our population, individuals were likely to have most commerce with certain matters of social value (e.g. "Is capital punishment justified?"), a moderate amount with certain matters of personal taste (e.g. "Is attending a classical music concert more interesting than visiting an art museum?"), and least commerce with obscure matters of fact (e.g. "How far below sea level is the town of Sodom?"). According to persuasive-arguments theory, then, if attitudinally divergent subgroups discuss these topics, depolarization will be greatest for matters of fact, moderate for matters of taste, and least for matters of social value.

Except for the items, our second experiment was identical to the previous one. Again the results indicate that the manipulation of subgroup salience had no significant effects on polarization or depolarization. The data from the two experimental conditions were therefore combined and are shown in Table 2.

As can readily be seen, one value item and two factual items exhibited statistically significant polarization; the two taste items gave no shifts. Consistent with persuasive-arguments theory, the strongest depolarization was exhibited by the factual items, a moderate amount by the taste items, and the least depolarization by the value items. Depolarization on the choice-dilemma items fell between the factual and the taste items (thus, the dilemmas do not behave as if they engage social values, although comparison theories assume this to be the case). The proportional reduction in the initial (pre-discussion) gap was 0.81 for the factual items, 0.49 for the dilemma items, 0.35 for the taste items, and 0.18 for the value items.

Finally, remember that our predictions regarding differences in depolarization over items assumed corresponding differences in knowledge and interest in the issues. We made a modest attempt to assess the validity of this assumption by asking another group of individuals to perform four rank orderings of the seven items that were used in the second experiment. The rankings were made

TABLE 2

*Mean choice and mean gap before (I) and after (II) group discussion, mean shift and mean depolarization for factual, taste, and value items*

| Item type | N | Mean choice | | Mean shift[c] | Mean shift[d] | | Mean depolarization[e] |
|---|---|---|---|---|---|---|---|
| Value items | | | | | | | |
| A | 29 | I.[a] | −0.06 | 0.12 | I. | 5.53 | 1.66[†] |
| | | II.[b] | 0.05 | | II. | 3.86 | |
| B | 20 | I. | −0.28 | −0.41* | I. | 7.23 | 0.50 |
| | | II. | −0.70 | | II. | 6.73 | |
| Taste items | | | | | | | |
| C | 22 | I. | 0.18 | 0.01 | I. | 6.22 | 1.95[†] |
| | | II. | 0.19 | | II. | 4.27 | |
| D | 15 | I. | 0.23 | 0.15 | I. | 5.84 | 2.28[†] |
| | | II. | 0.38 | | II. | 3.55 | |
| Factual items | | | | | | | |
| F | 23 | I. | 7.25 | 0.62 | I. | 7.89 | 6.76[†] |
| | | II. | 7.87 | | II. | 1.13 | |
| F | 18 | I. | 9.18 | −1.02* | I. | 6.88 | 5.68[†] |
| | | II. | 8.16 | | II. | 1.20 | |
| G | 23 | I. | 8.89 | 2.58[†] | I. | 7.72 | 5.76[†] |
| | | II. | 11.47 | | II. | 1.95 | |

[a]I = Mean choice before discussion (initial choices).

[b]II = Ɔean choice made after group discussion in private.

[c]Negative values indicate shifts toward risk. Positive values indicate shifts toward caution.

[d]This mean indicates the absolute difference between the two subgroups (i.e. the gap) before (I), and after (II) group discussion.

[e]Mean depolarization indicates changes in the mean gap between the two subgroups following group discussion. Positive value indicates decrease in the gap, i.e. depolarization. Negative value indicates an increase in the gap, i.e., polarization.

*$P < 0.01$.

†$P < 0.001$.

in respect to (a) "How many ideas do you have about the issues? When you try to make up your mind about these issues, can you think of many ideas or only a few ideas?" (b) "How often have you read about these issues?" (c) "How often do you discuss these issues?", and (d) "How interesting are these issues?" The rankings on all four dimensions were perfectly correlated, with strong inter-judge agreement, demonstrating that our subjects had most commerce with and interest in, matters of social value, a moderate amount, regarding matters of personal taste, and least regarding matters of fact.

Let me now summarize what can be concluded on the basis of these two recent experiments. That the "risky shift" is simply a special case of group polarization was initially suggested by Moscovici and Zavalloni (1969). Since then, numerous studies have demonstrated that group discussion will lead to polarization on a variety of issues, most having nothing to do with risk (see Myers and Lamm, 1976). At the same time, two kinds of theories were developed to explain this phenomenon. One says that polarization is the result of normative influences (e.g. a desire for approval from others) operating through the mechanism of interpersonal comparison (Sanders and Baron, 1977). The second kind of theory attributes the effect to informational influences based on the processing and dissemination of partially shared persuasive arguments (Burnstein and Vinokur, 1977). Nearly all of the past research on polarization involved groups in which a large majority of the members, or even the entire membership, initially favored one side of the issue. Under these conditions, both comparison theory and persuasive-arguments theory predict that polarization will follow group discussion. If, however, the members are split so that one half of them takes a point of view highly discrepant from that of the other half, then the two theories make rather different predictions. A comparison theory, analysis implies that following discussion, the gap between these subgroups should increase a persuasive-arguments analysis, on the other hand, leads one to expect a decrease in this gap. When such subgroups were in fact created, massive depolarization effects were observed. Furthermore, consistent with persuasive arguments theory, the magnitude of depolarization was inversely related to commerce with the issue, that is, matters of social value (rated as most popular and most interesting) depolarized the least, matters of personal taste (rated as moderately popular and moderately interesting) depolarized a moderate amount, and obscure matters of fact (rated as least popular and least interesting) depolarized the most. Our reasoning here was that the more someone has discussed, read, and thought about an issue, the more relevant arguments he or she will possess and the more motivated he or she will be to retrieve and encode these arguments (e.g. to counter-argue) in a discussion. Both these factors together presumably lead to a state of affairs prior to the discussion, say, of a popular topic, whereby the information about to be communicated is already widely shared among participants. As a result, the arguments raised by those on one side will have little impact because they have been taken into account by those on the other side.

## The informational basis of persuasion

For the most part we have called an argument persuasive simply on operational grounds, i.e. on the basis of judges' ratings. Our theoretical description of persuasiveness, however, is quite undeveloped. Nevertheless, we have ventured that this property of an argument depends on its validity and its originality (Burnstein and Vinokur, 1977). I would now like to provide some framework for explicating these terms.

People will be influenced by an argument if, among other things, they are able to grasp its meaning. In other words, interpretation is a necessary condition for persuasion. The fullness of the interpretation, the amount of information squeezed from an argument, depends on the depth and breadth of prior knowledge, plus the time and incentive to access this knowledge. The deeper the existing knowledge, the more levels of meaning can be found in the argument; the broader the knowledge at a given level, the more differentiated the meaning at that level.

Many of you will recognize these general ideas as stemming from a model of a semantic memory proposed by Craik and Lockhart (1972; also see Craik and Tulving, 1975). From this perspective memory is simply "an automatic by-product" of cognitive analysis, or, in particular, of elaborative coding. Hence, the duration of the memory for a statement is a function of the depth and spread of processing. If one takes some small liberties with Craik and Lockhart, then their work suggests much about the impact of an argument. Let us examine the issue of retention, that is, the question "How long does an argument endure in memory?" Considering the problem in gross, depth of processing implies that coding an argument in terms of its visual or phonetic features (e.g. according to the color of the ink it is printed in or according to some rhyming rule) is a much less effective mnemonic device than semantic coding (e.g. fitting the argument into a contextual paragraph or story). However, in most circumstances all arguments are processes at the semantic level. Differences in retention, therefore, would depend on how elaborate or widespread the processing an argument received at this level. Spread of processing refers to the integration of information contained in the argument with information already existing in the person, to the establishment of implicative links or paths between the argument and prior knowledge. Conceptually, it may be useful to think of relevant prior knowledge as a schema (Bartlett, 1932; Markus, 1977); it is also often considered as context, and since such contextual information pertains to the same issue as the argument, it constitutes at least in part the argument pool. In general, however, spread of processing merely suggests an interdependence between (new) communicated and (old) stored arguments, whereby access to the latter depends on it being implied by (congruent with) the former.

Research on spread of processing (e.g. Craik and Tulving, 1975) indicates retention of an argument is enhanced if it is congruent with the network of knowledge already existing in the person. For our purposes the relation "congruent with" describes the line of reasoning a person is likely to follow, that is, it denotes an implicative link or path existing between two sets of ideas, here in particular, between the ideas contained in the argument and those in prior knowledge. Once the two sets are integrated, gaining access to an element (idea, opinion, etc.) in one provides a path to an element in the other. Indeed, if called upon to express an opinion after receiving a relevant argument, the person may be unable to discriminate the information contained in the latter from prior knowledge (see Bartlett, 1932; Bransford and Frank, 1973; Brockway et al., 1974; Cofer, 1973; Johnson et al., 1973).[1]

Let me now try to indicate what processing of arguments says about social influence. Our conjecture is that the impact of an argument will depend on (a) the size of the information network with which it makes contact, (b) on the relative number of paths in this network congruent with the position advocated in the argument, and (c) the extent to which the knowledge retrieved thereby — as a result of the argument activating these paths — would not have been accessible to the person otherwise. Hence, validity and originality, the two properties of an argument that we proposed earlier as determining persuasiveness, take on special meaning. Validity in this context refers to the soundness of an argument. It is congruent with the line of reasoning that leads to or follows from it? Does the argument fit into the network of knowledge associated with it? Originality has to do with the richness of this network. An original argument has many ramifications *and* the latter contain information that ordinarily is rather inaccessible. An original argument, therefore, is one that lends itself to elaborate processing; as a consequence it is rich in meaning. And as a final conjecture, an argument may be given equally elaborate processing by the sender or the receiver. As a result, when one either generates or comprehends a valid argument, the greater its originality, the more new ideas are brought to mind.

So far it has been possible to demonstrate crudely that if an argument is valid, its perceived as well as its actual persuasiveness increases with its originality (Vinokur and Burnstein, in press). In this study arguments were rated by judges for their validity, defined as ". . . the extent to which the argument is true and accepted as such by most people" and originality, defined as ". . . the extent to which the argument relies on information that is already contained in the description of the choice dilemmas situation or is new and novel." The former rating was made on a scale ranging from "Definitely untrue, completely invalid and implausible, nearly everyone would reject it as untrue," to "Definitely true, completely valid and plausible, nearly everyone would accept it as true." The latter rating involved a scale ranging from "Complete reiteration of elements or relationships between elements which are contained and spelled out in the item" to "Introduction of new elements and/or new relationships (between new or old elements)." In our first experiment these same arguments were presented to a large number of people who judged their persuasiveness. In a second experiment people expressed their attitude after receiving either (a) several valid and original pro-risk arguments and an equal number of valid but unoriginal pro-caution arguments, or (b) several valid but unoriginal pro-risk arguments and an equal number of valid and original pro-caution arguments. The results were straightforward. First, valid and original arguments were perceived as more persuasive than either valid and unoriginal arguments or invalid and original arguments. Second, after reading the samples of arguments, the subject's attitude polarized toward the position advocated by the original arguments rather than toward advocated by the unoriginal arguments. The latter effect may be especially interesting to those who have worked with the choice dilemmas, that is, on items which typically shift toward risk, when the more original arguments supported the cautious course, a small shift toward caution was observed instead; similarly, on items which typically shift toward caution, when the more original arguments favored the risky course, a small shift toward risk was observed.[2]

In summary, at the heart of our analysis is the idea that an argument is persuasive because it stimulates people to think further, to see implications, to pursue a line of reasoning. This means that an argument is persuasive to the extent that it is linked to (implies) elements of a larger network of congruent knowledge and, thereby, brings to mind information not otherwise available. In providing access to new ideas an argument persuades us to change our mind.

## Informational influence and conformity

Argument processing sometimes may seem irrelevant in the light of common sense. After all, there are experimental situations in which shifts in attitude occur when there seems to be virtually no information available with which to think about (or discuss) one's attitude (e.g. Sherif's autokinetic paradigm), or when the available knowledge appears to argue for an attitude quite different from the one actually observed (e.g. Asch's line judgement paradigm). Of course, informational influence cannot be dismissed just because introspection says that informational events are feeble. Such introspections, however, touch on an interesting problem and I would like to speculate about this problem in the context of the Asch conformity situation (Asch, 1951, 1956). Whether or not Asch's line judgement task is in fact "unthinkable" (and "undiscussable"), we will assume for the moment that argument processing does occur but is difficult to tap directly. Let us now show that this assumption has testable implications.

A number of situational factors guide (bias) the person in processing arguments. For instance, knowing that a disagreement with the majority will be made public may change the pool of relevant arguments and lead the individual to consider implications that would never have entered his mind were the disagreement to remain private. Indeed in terms of a persuasive-arguments analysis, some widely used experimental procedures for changing attitudes may actually do so because they introduce new information which inadvertantly redefines the universe of relevant arguments for the subject. As a consequence implications that were inaccessible or had no bearing on the issue, become accessible or pertinent. Redefining the pool, in the sense of enlarging it, may be critical for polarization when there would be few arguments available otherwise (e.g.

when the person is uninformed about the issue). Suppose an individual is asked to state his opinion about something with which he is quite unfamiliar, say, kumquats. Then before discussing his opinion with others, he learns that this fruit has been condemned by a highly credible source, say, a group of gourmet oncologists. Although the person's familiarity with the kumquat itself has not increased, in all likelihood this additional information would greatly enlarge the universe of kumquat-relevant implications so that the number and kind of arguments contained in subsequent samples (e.g. those expressed in discussion) will be mardedly different from those contained in the initial sample.

The biases that concern us here stem from the fact that individuals know the attitude of their peers. Let us briefly consider the effects of such knowledge in relation to some well known results from Asch (1951, 1956) having to do with the size of a majority (for an analysis of other results from Asch, see Burnstein and Vinokur, 1977). A still puzzling finding is that agreement with a unanimous majority increased with the size of the majority but only up to the size of three (Asch, 1956). Hence, a unanimous majority need not be large to exert all of its potential influence. Keep in mind, however, that in this famous experimental paradigm individual attitudes are revealed in series. Since the critical subject is always next to last, he receives more information about the preferences of others and has a greater amount of time to generate arguments as majority size increases. The knowledge that another prefers, say, alternative $J$ rather than $K$, focuses the person's attention on the former. The larger the majority, the more this alternative will monopolize his attention and lead him to generate a disproportionately large number of arguments explaining why $J$ might be preferred. Therefore, the tendency to agree with a majority would continue to increase over a large range of sizes. Asch, as we know, did not obtain such an effect. Persuasive-arguments suggest why: while others reveal their preferences for $J$, the person, at some point in this string of revelations, will have exhausted the pool of pro-$J$ arguments. From that instant, knowing that still another member favors $J$ can have no impact because the person simply will be unable to think of additional reasons for being pro-$J$. Whether this point occurs early or late in the series obviously depends on the number of pro-$J$ arguments in the pool. In Asch the alternative preferred by the majority is unlikely to elicit many favorable arguments. Hence, according to persuasive-arguments theory, under these conditions the tendency to conform will not increase with the majority size beyond some relatively small value.

Keith Sentis and myself are testing this analysis and I would like to tell briefly something of this work in progress. We have assumed that if (a) there is an appreciable number of arguments for $J$ as well as $K$ in the pool, (b) the majority preference, $J$, biases a person's line of reasoning so that a relatively large number of pro-$J$ arguments come to mind, and (c) the biasing effect increases with the size of the majority, then the more time the person has to think about the majority preference and the larger the majority, the more likely it is that he will conform and prefer $J$. In the experiment six person groups were confronted with 24 issues, twelve choice dilemma items and twelve items involving obscure facts similar to those described earlier in the study of depolarization. The groups were told that they were participating in a study of the technical feasibility of television voting. Members would sit in separate cubicles containing a video monitor and a six-button response panel and respond in series, so as to simulate a voting queue. Thus an issue would appear on the minitor followed some time later by a signal to vote, the interval presumably depending on the member's position in the queue. A member was led to believe that on some items he would be the first to respond, on others, the fourth to respond, and on still others, the sixth to respond. Of course, the response of others whose turn in the voting queue came prior to that of the member would appear on the latter's video monitor. Hence, before indicating their position on an issue, members learned the position either of no other members (on a third of the items when they were first in the queue), of three others (on a third of the items when they were fourth in the queue), or of five others (on a third of the items when they were sixth in the queue). The pattern of others' responses displayed was contrived so as to be either highly typical or highly atypical for the item in question. The important variable was the length of time given to an individual for considering the position of the majority. On half the items a short (ten second) interval was given and on the other half a long (forty second) interval. The results, collapsed across the two types of items, are presented in Fig. 1. These curves describe how much the average individual preference under a three or five person majority (i.e. when the member was fourth or sixth, respectively, in the voting queue)

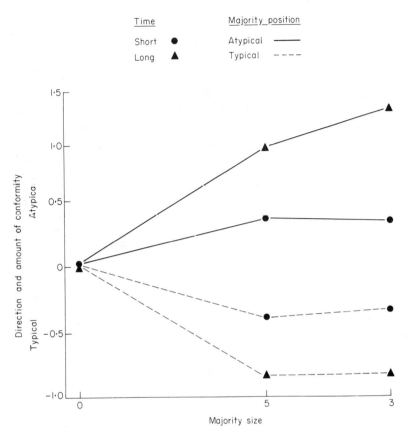

Fig. 1. Conformity as a function of time to consider the majority position when the majority varies in size and its position is typical or atypical. Conformity is measured in terms of deviations from the position held in the absence of knowledge about the attitude of others (zero majority size). The values on the vertical axis refer to units on a six point attitude scale.)

deviated from that under no majority (i.e. when the member was first in the voting queue). Keep in mind that when the majority position is typical for the item in question there is by definition little difference between the latter and the position taken by the average member in the absence of a majority. Thus, the opportunity for the majority to exert influence is extremely limited. In fact, instances in which typical distributions are presented correspond to those trials in Asch in which the confederates made the correct choice.

The data indicate, as you would expect, that in the face of an atypical majority, members reliably shift in an atypical direction and in the face of a typical majority, in a typical direction, even though in the latter case the distance available for a shift to occur is meager. More interesting is the finding that the longer a member has to consider the majority position, the more he conforms. This holds regardless of majority size. In addition, a large majority has no more impact than a small majority, only if the member has little time to think about the majority position. When there is much time to do so, however, conformity increases regularly with majority size, which is what an argument processing approach would suggest.

## Conclusions

These latest findings, as well as the others I discussed earlier, are difficult to explain in terms of normative influence. It would seem, therefore, that the hypothesis that such changes in opinion serve a hedonic function, is, to say the least, inadequate. On the other hand, the data make good sense from the point of view of informational influence and argument processing. Indeed, it was one such formulation, persuasive-arguments theory, that led us to anticipate these very results. Finally, the findings attest to a need for changing our conception of persuasion, especially in group research where normative and informational processes are still seen as equally important bases for social influences. According to our analysis this distinction is a phenotypic one. It may remain convenient for practical purposes, but there are increasing signs that social influence can be explained in information processing terms alone.

In any case, at least in the area of group polarization I feel confident in saying that the problem of social influence is reasonably well understood: it is essentially informational. I believe that this is no longer an issue and that nothing further is to be gained by invoking hedonic mechanisms. Of course, settled problems are not interesting. But I do not expect that work on this point is about to peter out. Not only do we know very little about the nature of argument processing, but also, I am confident that many of my colleagues are sure this analysis is dead wrong, and, as scientists, will act accordingly.

## Notes

1. Research on semantic memory, of course, is not directly concerned with social influence. Nevertheless, current work on social influence especially in the

area of attitude change, often asks just those questions that would follow from a level of processing approach. For instance, when people code a persuasive argument do they elaborate on the ideas contained therein and, thus, generate new ideas, ones not immediately given in the argument? Are the new ideas congruent with or incongruent with those in the argument (Brock, 1967; Burnstein and Vinokur, 1977; Kaplan and Miller, 1977; McGuire, 1964; Petty and Cacioppo, 1977)? It should be no surprise then that the hypothetical cognitive events used by these researchers to describe attitude change seem quite compatible with those used to describe the dynamics of semantic memory. Indeed, the current explanation of why the memory for an argument is relatively independent of its impact makes attitude change sound much like a spread of processing phenomenon, without even using the phrase (e.g. Greenwald, 1968).

2. I might also mention some new research along these lines that is being carried out by Yakov Schul. In this work we inform respondents that another person has a certain trait. Theoretically this information is an argument in the sense that we have been using the term. When equally positive or equally negative traits are used, the respondent, in forming an opinion of the person, gives more weight to the trait that implies many rather than few other characteristics. In brief, the persuasiveness of a trait seems to depend on its originality. At the same time a persuasive trait, presumably because it implies much and, thus, lends itself to further processing, ought to require more processing time. In respect to this point we find that the time needed by resoondents to identify and determine the meaning of a trait seems to increase with its originality (or persuasiveness), although I want to be cautious on this point because we have not yet completed this part of the research. On the other hand, because it provides access to more information, an original trait should allow the respondent to form an opinion about the person so characterized more readily than a trait low in originality. In this case there's less need for caution. The opinion forming time clearly and reliably decreased as the originality of the trait increased.

# References

Anderson, N. H. and Graesser, C. C. An information integration analysis of attitude change in group discussion. *Journal of Personality and Social Psychology,* 1976, 34, 210—222.

Asch, S. E. Effects of group pressure on the modification and distortion of judgements. In H. Geutzkow (Ed.), *Groups, Leadership, and Men.* Pittsburgh: Carnegie, 1951.

Asch, S. E. Studies of independence and submission to group pressure: I. On minority of one against a unanimous majority. *Psychological Monographs,* 1956, 70 (9, Whole No. 417).

Bartlett, F. C. *Remembering.* Cambridge: Cambridge University Press, 1932.

Bransford, J. D. and Franks, J. J. The abstraction of linguistic ideas. *Cognitive Psychology,* 1971, 2, 331—350.

Bishop, G. D. and Myers, D. G. Information influence in group discussion. *Organizational Behavior and Human Performance,* 1974, 12, 92—104.

Brock, T. C. Communication discrepancy and intent to persuade as determinants of counterargument production. *Journal of Experimental Social Psychology,* 1967, 3, 296—309.

Brockway, J., Chmielewski, D. and Cofer, C. N. Remembering prose: Productivity and accuracy constraints in recognition memory. *Journal of Verbal Learning and Verbal Behavior,* 1974, 13, 194–208.

Burnstein, E. and Vinokur, A. Testing two classes of theories about group-induced shifts in individual choice. *Journal of Experimental Social Psychology,* 1973, 9, 123–137.

Burnstein, E. and Vinokur, A. What a person thinks upon learning he has chosen differently from others: Nice evidence for the persuasive-arguments explanation of choice shifts. *Journal of Experimental Social Psychology,* 1975, 11, 412–426.

Burnstein, E. and Vinokur, A. Persuasive arguments and social comparison as determinants of attitude polarization. *Journal of Experimental Social Psychology,* 1977, 13, 315–332.

Burnstein, E., Vinokur, A. and Trope, Y. Interpersonal comparison versus persuasive argumentation: A more direct test of alternative explanations for group induced shifts in individual choice. *Journal of Experimental Social Psychology,* 1973, 9, 236–245.

Cofer, C. N. Constructive processes in memory. *American Scientist,* 1973, 61, 537–543.

Craik, F. I. and Lockhart, R. S. Levels of processing: a framework for memory research. *Journal of Verbal Learning and Verbal Behaviour,* 1972, 11, 671–684.

Craik, F. I. and Tulving, E. Depth of processing and the retention of words in episodic memory. *Journal of Experimental Psychology,* 1975, 104, 268–294.

Festinger, L. A theory of social comparison processes. *Human Relations,* 1954, 7, 117–140.

Festinger, L. A theory of social comparison processes. *Human Relations,* 1954, 7, 117–140.

Ferguson, D. A. and Vidmar, N. Effects of group discussion on estimates of culturally appropriate risk levels. *Journal of Personality and Social Psychology.* 1971, 20, 436–445.

Greenwald, A. G. Cognitive learning, cognitive response to persuasion, and attitude change. In A. G. Greenwald, T. C. Brock and T. M. Ostrom (Eds), *Psychological Foundations of Attitudes.* New York and London: Academic Press, 1968.

Greenwald, A. G. The open-mindedness of the counterattitudinal role player. *Journal of Experimental Social Psychology,* 1969, 5, 375–388.

Greenwald, A. G. When does role playing produce attitude change? Toward an answer. *Journal of Personality and Social Psychology,* 1970, 16, 214–219.

Johnson, M. K., Bransford, J. D. and Solomon, S. Memory for tacit implications of sentences. *Journal of Experimental Psychology,* 1973, 98, 203–205.

Kaplan, M. F. Discussion polarization effects in a modified jury decision paradigm: Informational influences. *Sociometry,* 1977, 40, 262–271.

Kaplan, M. F. and Miller, C. E. Judgements and group discussion: Effect of presentation and memory factors on polarization. *Sociometry,* 1977, 40, 337–343.

Markus, H. J. R. Self-schemata and processing information about the self. *Journal of Personality and Social Psychology,* 1977, 35, 63–78.

McGuire, W. J. Inducing resistence to persuasion: Some contemporary approaches. In L. Berkowitz (Ed.) *Advances in Experimental Social Psychology,* Vol. 1. New York and London: Academic Press, 1964.

Miller, N. and Baron, R. S. On measuring counterarguing. *Journal for the Theory of Social Behavior*, 1973, 3, 101–118.

Moscovici, S. and Zavalloni, M. The group as a polarizer of attitudes. *Journal of Personality and Social Psychology*, 1969, 12, 125–135.

Myers, D. G. and Lamm, H. The group polarization phenomenon. *Psychological Bulletin*, 1976, 83, 602–627.

Petty, R. E. and Cacioppo, J. T. Forewarning cognitive responding and resistance to persuasion. *Journal of Personality and Social Psychology*, 1977, 35, 645–655.

Sanders, G. and Baron, R. S. Is social comparison irrelevant for producing choice shifts? *Journal of Experimental Social Psychology*, 1977, 13, 303–314.

Vinokur, A. and Burnstein, E. The effects of partially shared persuasive arguments on group induced shifts: A group problem solving approach. *Journal of Personality and Social Psychology*, 1974, 29, 305–315.

Vinokur, A. and Burnstein, E. Novel argumentation and attitude change: The case of polarization following group discussion. *European Journal of Social Psychology*, in press.

Vinokur, A., Trope, Y. and Burnstein, E. A decision-making analysis of persuasive argumentation and the choice-shift effect. *Journal of Experimental Social Psychology*, 1975, 11, 127–148.

# 6
# Polarizing Effects of Social Interaction

David G. Myers

Research on the effects of social interaction in small groups, a central concern of social psychology in Kurt Lewin's day, has been relegated to the background for much of the past 20 years while social psychologists concentrated on the intrapersonal dynamics of attitude change and other aspects of social cognition. Recently there has been renewed interest in the interplay between psychological and social processes, particularly in the small group and its effects on attitudes, decisions, and behaviors.

The most striking example is the many recent studies of group-induced shifts in attitudes and behavior. Scholarship is a community enterprise and it is difficult to disentangle my insights from those achieved, sometimes simultaneously, by investigators elsewhere. Since our research program on group-polarization is now coming to an end, this symposium does, nevertheless, seem like an appropriate occasion to summarize it. I shall, therefore, describe the development of our research with occasional reference to the larger body of scholarship into which it fits.

This research was stimulated by a surprising effect of group discussion uncovered by James Stoner in 1961. For his master's thesis in industrial management at the Massachusetts Institute of Technology, Stoner decided to compare risk-taking by individuals and groups. He wanted to test the old adage that groups are more cautious and less creatively daring than individuals. His procedure is worth describing because it has been followed in dozens of later experiments.

A small number of participants — usually about five — are scheduled for a given session. First they individually respond to a series of story problems, here called dilemma situations. Each problem describes a decision faced by a fictional character. The participant's task is to advise the protagonist how much risk he should take. The following sample problem illustrates the task.

> Henry is a writer who is said to have considerable creative talent but who so far has been earning a comfortable living by writing cheap Westerns. Recently he has come up with an idea for a potentially significant novel. If it could be written and accepted it might have considerable literary impact and be a big boost to his career. On the other hand, if he was not able to work out his idea or if the novel was a flop he would have expended considerable time and energy without remuneration.
>
> Imagine that you are advising Henry. Please check the *lowest* probability that you would consider acceptable for Henry to attempt to write the novel.
>
> Henry should attempt to write the novel if the chances are at least:
>
> 1 in 10 that the novel will be a success.
> 2 in 10 that the novel will be a success.
> 3 in 10 that the novel will be a success.
> 4 in 10 that the novel will be a success.
> 5 in 10 that the novel will be a success.
> 6 in 10 that the novel will be a success.
> 7 in 10 that the novel will be a success.
> 8 in 10 that the novel will be a success.
> 9 in 10 that the novel will be a success.
> Place a check here if you think Henry should attempt the novel only if it is certain (i.e. 10 in 10) that the novel will be a success.

After individually marking their advice on all the items, the participants then assemble as a group and discuss each item until they agree. The discovery that groups are on the whole more risk-prone than the average individual member was immediately dubbed the "risky shift" phenomenon, and it was followed by a wave of investigations of group risk taking. These subsequent studies have taken place in a dozen different nations, indicating that Stoner's results are not peculiar to MIT graduate students. They also reveal that group decision-making is not an essential component of the procedure; a brief period of discussion followed by individual decision-making will also produce a shift in the group average.

This interest in the risky shift was stimulated not by any great magnitude of the group change — the average shift was only about one scale unit or less — but rather because the reliable effect was unexpected and its cause was not obvious. As one might expect, group members tended to converge after conversation, but the point towards which they converged was usually a lower number than their initial averages. A lively controversy developed over what was producing the shift. Here was a new puzzle for social psychologists. As always, it was hoped that the solution might yield some important new understandings about human behavior in social situations. Does discussion in juries, in business committees, and in military decision groups generally increase risk-taking?

After about five years of research and speculation on the great proneness to risk of human groups, it became evident that the risky shift was not as general as first thought. For example, some dilemmas did not yield a reliable risky shift, and some items were found to yield reliable shifts to greater caution after discussion. One such dilemma concerned "Roger," a young married man with two school-age children and a secure but low-paying job. Roger can afford life's necessities, but few of its luxuries. He hears that the stock of a relatively unknown company may soon triple in value if its new product is favourably received or decline if it does not sell. Roger has no savings, but he is considering investing his life insurance money in the company.

Is there a general principle that will allow us to predict why most people give riskier advice after discussing Henry's situation and more cautious advice after debating Roger's? Fortunately, an excellent predictor exists. These cases differ not only in whether they elicit group shift toward the risky or cautious ends of the scale, but also in the average of the initial prediscussion responses. Chances are that the reader would advise greater risk to Henry than to Roger, even without any discussion with others. As Fig. 1 illustrates, there turns out to be a strong relationship between the average initial response on an item and the average shift elicited by that item. In general, items which usually elicit risky shift will have an initial response average about 5 in 10 or less (as with Henry), and items which elicit a shift toward caution will have an initial response average around 7 in 10 or higher (as with Roger). We therefore see that what the research with dilemmas indicates is not a consistent risky shift tendency, as was originally assumed, but rather a tendency for group discussion to enhance the initially dominant point of view. This was our first insight, in 1966, and it suggested that the group-change effect discovered on dilemmas might better be conceptualized as a group-polarization phenomenon: the average post-discussion response will tend to be more extreme in the same direction as the average of the pregroup responses (the term "group polarization"

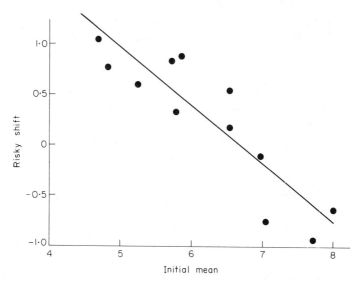

Fig. 1. The mean risky shift on a dilemma item is a linear function of the mean of the initial degree of risk-taking selected on a scale of 1 (high risk) to 10 (low risk). Items which elicit high-risk initial tendencies generally elicit shift toward the high-risk extreme after discussion. Items which elicit caution are more likely to elicit shift toward the cautious extreme. (Correlation = 0.89 across 12 items, Myers and Arenson, 1972.)

originated later in the pioneering work of Moscovici and Zavalloni (1969) and Doise (1969).)

With this group polarization hypothesis now in mind our research program developed in two directions. First, we explored the generality of the phenomenon by laboratory and field experimentation and, more recently, by searching the literature for examples of naturally occurring group polarization in real life situations. Second, we sought to help develop a satisfactory theoretical explanation of the phenomenon. We hoped that understanding the dynamics of group polarization might enrich our understanding of the nature of social influence.

## Generality of group polarization

### EXPERIMENTS ON GROUP POLARIZATION

Viewing the risky shift phenomenon as a general tendency for group discussion to amplify the prevailing pregroup inclination stimulated us to see whether polarization could, in fact, be demonstrated on other, non-risk, dimensions. If it could this would not only confirm the validity of the concept but also disconfirm those explanations of risky shift which were risk specific and those which attributed the shift effect to peculiarities in the instructions or the metric of the dilemma items.

Two research strategies have been used in these studies. In the first procedure, people discuss topics on which they are generally predisposed to feel pro or con. Then it is determined whether talking in groups tends to enhance this dominant leaning, as happens with the choice dilemma items. The general prediction for these experiments is intensification of the initial average.

Our first study (Myers and Bishop, 1971) engaged students in discussion of imaginary decision situations, in each of which a protagonist faced two alternative courses of action. The dominant prediscussion preference was noticeably in the pro or con direction on the Likert scale attached to each item and, sure enough, discussion tended to accentuate these tendencies, but other control treatments did not.

We also experimented with group-induced change in a simulated jury setting (Myers and Kaplan, 1976). As Kalven and Ziesel (1966) concluded, "The jury deliberation process. . . is an interesting combination of rational persuasion, sheer social pressure, and the psychological mechanism by which individual perceptions undergo change when exposed to group discussion" (p. 489). Do decisions following jury deliberation differ in any predictable way from the average of the predeliberation opinions of individual jury members? Participants discussed traffic cases which elicited a dominant predisposition of either guilty or not guilty. Figure 2 indicates that when the defendants were made to appear low in guilt, the jurors, after discussion, were even more definite in their judgements of innocence and more lenient in their recommended punishments. After discussing high-guilt cases, the participants polarized toward harsher judgements of guilt and punishment. Likewise, Hans and Doob (1976) engaged a heterogeneous sample of adult Canadians in individual or group judgement of a burglary case in which the jurors were informed or not informed of the defendant's prior conviction record. Group discussion magnified the effect of this independent variable. As Hans and Doob put it, "What is most striking about the overall pattern of results obtained is that what is apparently a weak manipulation (one prior conviction) in the individual verdict

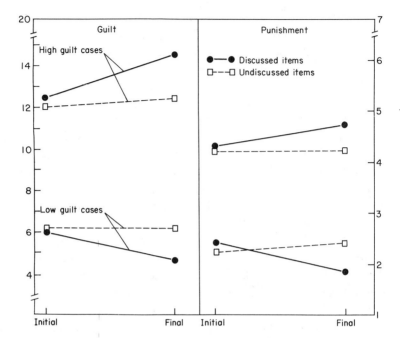

Fig. 2. Discussion in simulated juries magnified initial judgement tendencies on the cases discussed. For each case, subjects rated the degree of guilt from definitely not guilty (0) to definitely guilty (20). Then, assuming the person was found guilty, they recommended punishment from the minimum provided by law (1) to the maximum (7).

condition proves to be a strong manipulation in the group verdict conviction."

Group discussion also helps shape our perceptions of other people — take gossip, for example. To see if conversation could polarize the opinions of people who share a mutual feeling, we asked students to respond to 200-word descriptions of hypothetical faculty members made to appear relatively good or bad (Myers, 1975). A "good" faculty member might be described as an effective teacher, though not an outstanding researcher, while the great researcher with little time for students tended to be rated as bad. As predicted by the group-polarization hypothesis, "good" faculty were rated and paid even more favorably after the group discussion, and the contrary was true for the "bad" faculty.

Finally, we have also taken a second look at some previous studies of group risk-taking which used risk tasks other than dilemmas (Lamm et al., 1976). It turns out that the group-polarization hypothesis fits quite well here, too. If a betting situation is constructed that initially induces individuals to take large gambles (e.g. when there is little at stake), then groups generally take even larger gambles. But if the initial tendency is to bet cautiously, this usually becomes strengthened by the group. For example, McCauley and his associates (1973) observed at a Philadelphia race track that individuals generally preferred the horses with good odds (the favourites) and avoided betting the long shots. He then formed small groups of these Saturday-afternoon betters and offered them money to bet as a group. In groups they bet even more cautiously than they did as individuals.

Collectively, the results of experiments in our laboratory and elsewhere indicate that the group-polarization hypothesis does have external validity on measures other than those used to derive the hypothesis in the first place. Response tendencies generally favored by the subject population tend to be strengthened by group interaction.

A second set of experiments has explored group polarization using a different strategy. Instead of introducing items that elicit a dominant initial tendency toward one pole or the other, this strategy picks issues where opinion is mixed and isolates people who share common attitudes. Their average shift may then be compared with that of other groups of people who share the opposite tendency. The group-polarization hypothesis predicts that discussion with similarly minded other people will increase the attitude gap between the two groups.

For example, we composed groups of relatively high-, medium-, or low-prejudice high school seniors using a measure of racial attitudes (Myers and Bishop, 1970). Group members then responded to new racial attitude items (e.g. concerning federal v. local control of desegregation) before and after discussion. The discussion with others having similar racial attitudes significantly increased the gap between the high- and low-prejudice groups.

There is ample evidence that people tend to associate mostly with others who have similar attitudes and values. Most of us need only to look at our friends to demonstrate this point. Does separation on the basis of shared values generally produce increased polarization between groups? This is an important question.

Other experiments using this homogeneous grouping procedure have yielded only mixed support for the group-polarization

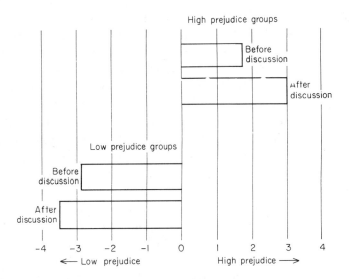

Fig. 3. Discussion increased polarization between homogeneous groups of high-
and low-prejudice high school students.

hypothesis. We separated relatively pacifistic and relatively militaristic students into two groups — doves and hawks (Myers and
Bach, 1974). Although we predicted that discussion of relevant
materials within the two homogeneous "communities" would
increase the polarization between them, both the hawks and doves
increased in pacifism after discussion.

   Other evidence is more supportive. In another experiment we used
a measure of sex-role attitudes to separate subjects into conservative
(chauvinist) and liberal (feminist) populations (Myers, 1975). As
predicted, discussing statements about the role of women, e.g.
"women with children should not work outside the home if they
don't have to financially", increased the attitude gap between the
two groups. This outcome resulted from an increased liberalism in
the already liberal feminist population — a demonstration of
"consciousness-raising" through discussion among the like-minded.

   The social psychological research on group polarization has
stimulated a number of attempts to explore the phenomenon in
business and political arenas. One fascinating experiment (reported
separately by Minix, 1976, and Semmel, 1976) engaged groups of
Army officers, ROTC cadets, or university students in discussion of
hypothetical but credible international military crises, each of which
involved some threat to the United States. Instead of the usual

10-point numerical scale, the respondents chose one of ten response options, ranging from bilateral negotiations to use of nuclear force. On each of the six cases the student groups were more inclined to recommend diplomatic alternatives than were the Army officers and in each case these student v. officer differences were further polarized by deliberation within their own groups. Regardless of whether the discussion proceeded to consensus or to a majority vote, the officers groups generally came to recommend even more forceful responses. The ROTC cadets were intermediate in both initial and shift scores. These new results closely parallel our observations of increased intergroup polarization following discussion within groups of like-minded. They also underscore Sidney Verba's contention that face-to-face groups "are important transmission points in political communications, and they exercise a major influence on the political beliefs and attitudes of their members" (1961, p. 2).

Our reviews of other experimental research on the generality of group-induced polarization further confirms the reality of the phenomenon (Myers, 1973; Myers and Lamm, 1975, 1976; Lamm and Myers, 1978). With the reliability of this phenomenon established, we were prompted to wonder whether natural occurrences of the phenomenon could also be detected. Is the phenomenon something more than a hothouse laboratory effect?

NATURALISTIC OBSERVATIONS OF GROUP POLARIZATION

If group polarization is something more than a laboratory creation of social psychologists then we may expect that instances of it will already have been observed and noted by social scientists who are unfamiliar with the experimental literature. Before offering some examples a word of caution is in order. While these observations carry the force of naturally occurring reality it is difficult to disentangle causes, correlates, and effects. The most that can be said is that these interesting observations are consistent with the experimental literature.

*Student change during college*
Investigations of student change during college have revealed an "accentuation phenomenon." As Feldman and Newcomb (1969) describe it, "initial differences among students in different colleges and in different curricula are accentuated or amplified as students

progress through college. Instances of this same phenomenon also occur with respect to initial differences among students entering different types of residences" (p. 209). For example, attitude differences between American fraternity members and independents are modest at the freshman level — for example, fraternity members are slightly more politically conservative — and accentuated by the senior level.

Chickering and McCormick (1973) concluded from their decade of research on student development at various colleges that if the students who enroll at a particular college have a predominantly practical-vocational outlook they will emerge even more that way. Colleges which attract more intellectually oriented or non-conformist students will further strengthen these tendencies in their students. Another more recent study provides the same conclusion: "In short, the qualities students bring to college generally tend to persist and become accentuated as a result of their college education" (Wilson et al., 1975, p. 123). Other data gathered by Astin and Panos (1969) and Clark et al. (1972) confirm the same point.

It is, to be sure, not entirely clear what produces this accentuation phenomenon. Students are not only attracted to and interacting with similar others, they are also taking classes and concentrating their attention on activities which are compatible with their inclinations. It seems, none the less, reasonable to expect that, as Feldman and Newcomb (1969) surmise, the accentuation phenomenon occurs partly because "the reciprocal influences of members of one another reinforce and strengthen extant orientations" (p. 223).

*Social conflict*

The possibility that intra-group discussion might enhance inter-group polarization was suggested by our experiments noted earlier. Some field observations are consistent with these laboratory findings. Coleman (1957) concluded from his analyses of opinion polarization during community conflict that "group discussion. . . is such an important phenomenon in the community controversies that in the case studies examined most descriptions of behavior during the intense part of the controversy were descriptions of discussion and of attempts to persuade or reinforce opinion" (p. 18). Homogeneous grouping was an apparent source of community polarization and the occurrence of social conflict further heightened "the proliferation of associations among those who feel one way, and the attenuation of association between those who feel differently. One's statements meet more and more with a positive response; one is more and more free to express the full intensity of his feeling" (p. 14). We have seen this happen in our own local community. Proposals for establishment of a halfway house or a correctional institution have typically elicited private apprehensions which, after discussion, become polarized into overt paranoia and hostility.

This dynamic can be seen at work in the well-known Robbers Cave experiment (Sherif, 1966) in which the competition and intra-group dynamics moved the rival groups to extreme antagonism and perceptions of one another; in the Stanford Prison Experiment (Zimbardo, 1975) in which the aggressive reactions of guards appeared to feed on one another in spiraling escalation; and in the emergence of the radical student movement of the late 1960s. Evidence indicates that conservative and radical students existed in two separate social worlds and that interpersonal influence was a substantial contributor to leftist tendencies within the radical sub-culture (Gold et al., 1976).

Group interaction may magnify conflict partly because, as we have observed in the laboratory, the tendency of individuals to justify their own behavior when in conflict is intensified by discussion with one's group — people are even more inclined toward self-justification when in groups than when alone (Myers and Bach, 1976). This phenomenon of group-enhanced self-justification is part of the "groupthink" process which Janis (1972) has proposed to help explain political decision fiascoes, such as the escalation of the Vietnam War.

Gang delinquency provides yet another example. Enduring gangs reportedly differ sharply from one another but develop homogeneous within-group attitudes. Cartwright (1975) concludes that this occurs as a result of group processes such as "interstimulation" among gang members and "a process of summation, or progressive urging on of members from one deed to another" (p. 7). We observed an analogous tendency in an experiment involving young male felons residing at a correctional institution (Myers et al., 1974). Given some simple ethical-legal dilemmas (e.g. a scenario in which a mature-minded but underage teenager is deciding whether to order a drink), the inmates initially tended to favor the illegal behavior and they favored it even more following discussion among themselves. Prisons are just one example of closed environments which seem to produce debilitating effects by grouping people with shared deviant traits.

Riley and Pettigrew (1976) have observed that dramatic events can polarize attitudes. Surveys of white Texans — before and after the desegregation of the Little Rock, Arkansas schools in 1957, and the assassination of Martin Luther King and subsequent civil disorders in 1968 — revealed that the initial opinion tendencies of various demographic groups tended to polarize following the dramatic events, a phenomenon Riley and Pettigrew labelled the "counterceiling effect." Moreover, within each demographic group, attitudes toward formal inter-racial contacts were initially most positive and were also the most likely to become even more positive, and vice versa for intimate racial contacts. These two findings parallel the two types of laboratory evidence for group polarization — from studies indicating that positive items elicit positive shift and vice versa.

It seems likely that dramatic events stimulate discussion. When the event is subject to multiple interpretations, intra-group discussion may intensify the dominant local viewpoint. In the absence of dramatic events and their accompanying intra-group discussion, social influences that are common to all groups (e.g. the national media) may reduce attitude polarization.

Urban crowding sometimes seems to exaccerbate individual reactions. Freedman (1975) has researched this effect of social density. Crowding, he suggests

> *serves to intensify the individual's typical reactions to the situation.* If he ordinarily would find the circumstances pleasant, would enjoy having people around him, would think of the other people as friends, would in a word have a positive reaction to the other people, he will have a more positive reaction under conditions of high density. On the other hand, if ordinarily he would dislike the other people, find it unpleasant having them around, feel aggressive toward them, and in general have a negative reaction to the presence of the other people, he will have a more negative reaction under conditions of high density. And if for some reason he would ordinarily be indifferent to the presence of other people, increasing the density will have little effect one way or the other (p. 91).

Although this sounds like a social facilitation effect, Freedman concludes — as have most theorists regarding group polarization — that the density-intensity effect is not an arousal phenomenon. Freedman believes it rather occurs because "high density makes other people a more important stimulus and thereby intensifies the typical reaction to them" (p. 105). This fits in with Moscovici and Lecuyer's (1972) finding that less group polarization occurred when people sat in a straight line with reduced face-to-face contact than when they talked face-to-face — which surely made the other people more salient stimuli.

*Group counseling*

If the group polarization principle helps explain some seemingly negative effects of group interaction, then it may also help us understand beneficial group effects. Malamuth (1975) had groups discuss what advice they would give to real human beings whom they met and who were believed to be facing life dilemmas similar to some of those in the dilemmas questionnaire. Malamuth's peer counseling experiment, which was an analog to actual peer counseling programs, indicated that "such group counseling experiences result in a more extreme advice than that given by individuals" (p. 53).

Toch (1965) describes additional examples of the power of mutual assistance in small self-help groups. Social interaction in Alcoholics Anonymous groups strengthens the members' commitment to shared goals. Members of TOPS (Take Off Pounds Sensibly) sing their weekly pledge:

The more we get together
Together, together —
The more we get together,
The slimmer we'll be.
For your loss is my loss;
And my loss is your loss,
The more we get together
The slimmer we'll be.

*Religious fellowship*

Another apparent example of group polarization in natural settings is provided by various religious social support systems. Heightened religious identity is usually achieved by a substantial amount of interaction among members of the religious body and a certain amount of insulation from the surrounding society. As Thomas à Kempis advised, "a devout communing on spiritual things sometimes greatly helps the health of the soul, especially when men of one mind and spirit in God meet and speak and commune together."

Emile Durkheim theorized that "dynamic density" (the extent of intra-group communication) determines the intensity of religious commitment. Some sociologists of religion (e.g. Hoge, 1974) suggest that this may be one reason why the increasing individualism and social mobility of the modern age is associated with decreased religious commitment.

Perhaps American culture's most striking example of intense religious identity emerging from separation with similar others is provided by the Amish, who live, go to school, work, and worship only among themselves. In earlier eras small interacting groups contributed significantly to the dynamic of the early Christian church and, during the 18th century, to John Wesley's Methodist movement. According to a Wesley biographer, the mutual edification and commitment which occurred in these "classes" and "bands," as they were called, was the chief feature of the movement's structure (Schmidt, 1972). Close scrutiny of religious social support systems in *When Prophecy Fails* confirms the power of the small group to amplify the religious impulse (Festinger *et al.,* 1956, see also related observations by Hardyck and Braken, 1962, and Batson, 1975).

In summary, it seems that the group polarization phenomenon uncovered in laboratory experiments is, indeed, manifest in important real-life situations as well.

## Theoretical explanation

Having established the reality and generality of group polarization our next task was to understand what is causing the phenomenon. Might group polarization research stimulate new insight into human social influence? An adequate theoretical explanation of group polarization will serve the functions of any good theory in the social sciences: it will account for the known conditions under which group polarization occurs, and it will also predict the effects of other conditions not yet studied and suggest when group polarization is not to be expected. This predictive function allows us to test the truth of the theory, and it may suggest some useful applications.

By now the reader may have conjectured his or her own explanations of group polarization. One idea often suggested involves leadership. Someone probably emerges as the most forceful group member and may sway the others. Although this was one of the first explanations seriously advanced by social psychologists who studied the phenomenon, it will not explain the results. For example, while it is indeed true that some members of the group are more verbally aggressive than others, an additional assumption is required to explain group polarization — namely, that those who emerge as leaders are also more extreme in the dominant direction than their fellow group members. Yet we have found that there is no relationship between the extremity of persons and the extent to which they dominate the discussion (Myers and Murdoch, 1972). It is, however, still possible that relatively extreme positions will tend to be more persuasive than neutral positions.

Research in our laboratory and elsewhere has also discounted some other plausible ideas. For example, polarization is not simply the result of becoming more familiar with the materials: private study of the items does not yield the same effect as discussion.

More attention has been devoted to group decision rule explanations which predict shift by using statistical schemes for combining individual preference distributions into an expected group product. Perhaps, for example, a "majority-rule" decision process could predict the polarization effect without postulating any real attitude change. If the deviant minority in the tail of a skewed distribution is being pressured into conformity with the dominant opinion, an artifactual polarization of the mean response would result. Skewness does, in fact, often exist when the initial average response departs from neutrality and polarization obtains, so majority-rule is an especially plausible decision scheme.

It is something of a surprise, then, that decision schemes which depend on skewness have generally not been supported by our findings (some of which have also been observed in other laboratories). Specifically, we have observed that:

(1) Group polarization occurs even when there is no opportunity for combining pretest decisions (e.g. when there has been no pretest and no awareness of the response scale while discussing. This involves a between-groups design in which post-discussion responses are compared with a no-discussion control group, c.f. Myers *et al.*, 1974).

(2) There generally occurs not only a polarization of the group's mean score but also of its median (middle) score (e.g. Myers and Aronson, 1972). The middle member is, of course, a member of the majority.

(3) Some group shift occurs in dyads, where obviously there can be no skewness in the initial responses (see Myers and Lamm, 1976).

(4) Group shift can occur without group convergence, that is, without the emergence of any implicit group product (Myers *et al.*, 1974; Myers, 1977b).

While these data raise questions about the majority-rule scheme as a complete explanation of group polarization, they do not bear upon the general usefulness of decision models. Not only are decision schemes compatible with other explanations which follow, they may sometimes operationalize purported social psychological processes (as noted by James Davis, Norbert Kerr, and Patrick Laughlin in their excellent contributions to this symposium).

With several other plausible explanations of group polarization also set aside, our sleuth continued as we turned our attention to two other theories which we hoped might solve the mystery and expand our understanding of group influence. The informational influence explanation stresses our rational capacities — persuasive discussion arguments are presumed to predominantly favor the initially preferred alternative, thereby enhancing it. Social comparison explanations stress social motivation — people presumably want to perceive and present themselves favorably, so exposure to others' positions may stimulate them to adjust their responses in order to maintain a desirable image.

INFORMATIONAL INFLUENCE

The informational influence explanation postulates that during discussion each subject is processing and weighing information by a process akin to Anderson's (1971) information integration scheme. The average initial response to an item presumably reflects the prevailing direction in the pool of relevant arguments. As arguments are drawn from this pool during discussion they may reinforce the average initial opinion, especially since it is unlikely that any given person will have already considered all these arguments or found them all salient. In discussing Henry, for example, someone may point out that Henry has little to lose since if his novel flops, as he can always go back to writing cheap Westerns. This thought may be compelling to other group members who have not entertained it before.

We examined this theory with two types of investigations: experimental manipulations of the availability of arguments, and content analyses of arguments generated by individuals and groups. The first group of experiments attempted to disentangle the argument-exchange component of group discussion from exposure to others' positions to see if one of these components — exposure to others' arguments or to their positions — is necessary and sufficient for changed responses. These experiments clearly indicated that when, by various methods, subjects are exposed to relevant arguments but gain no information about others' positions, they none the less evidence the expected shift. For example, in one experiment, the typical polarization effect was obtained even when the subjects were prohibited from mentioning their initial choices (and the effectiveness of this treatment was empirically confirmed, Myers *et al.*, 1971). In another experiment subjects shared arguments relevant to the substance of the items without awareness of the response scale on which they were eventually to indicate their individual choices, and polarization was still obtained (Myers *et al.*, 1974). Burnstein and Vinokur (e.g. 1973) have obtained similar results when using other clever manipulations to keep subjects from learning the actual opinions of the other group members. It thus seems clear that arguments have a persuasive impact above and beyond any impression they convey about the positions of the persons who spoke them.

The second type of investigation looks inside the "black box" of discussion to examine the arguments which are actually expressed. First we ascertained that the initial average response to an item does indeed reflect the trend of privately considered prediscussion arguments. The initial average also predicts the trend of the arguments expressed during discussion, which in turn predicts the average group shift (Myers and Bishop, 1971). Thus we concluded that the predictive power of the average initial response is captured by the content of the subsequent discussion, suggesting that it is the nature of the expressed arguments which mediates the relationship between initial mean and mean shift.

We next proposed a mathematical model of information influence which assumed that the amount of group shift is determined by three factors: the direction of each argument (which side it favors), its cogency, and its novelty (the degree to which the argument is not already known to group members before discussion). The potency of an argument is presumed low if, being trivial or irrelevant, it lacks cogency or if all group members have considered the argument before discussion. By detailed analysis of the discussion content we were able to demonstrate support for the model (Bishop and Myers,

1974). Our research also confirmed that if, in a given discussion, the spoken arguments depart from the initial responses, it will be the arguments and not the initial response mean which will predict the direction of group shift (Myers and Bach, 1974). Simultaneously, Vinokur and Burnstein (1974; in press) derived a similar model and independently confirmed that the discussion content — its direction, cogency, and novelty — is a causal determinant of group polarization.

This explains why, on a given item, a group that is already quite extreme before discussion will often not show as much polarization as a less extreme group. The initially polarized group already shares the most persuasive arguments, whereas the less polarized group has more to learn from exchanging the available arguments. The theory also clearly implies the conditions under which group polarization is to be expected: when discussion generates potent information predominantly in one direction. Although the average initial tendency gives an index to the direction of available arguments and thus generally predicts shift, the initial tendency is not a direct cause of the shift. It is possible to imagine situations in which a known alternative A is initially favored over unknown B, but shift would be expected toward B because the impact of new information in support of B would be greater than the impact of old arguments for A.

Subsequent research has applied the sophistication of information integration theory to informational influence in group discussion (e.g. Anderson and Graesser, 1976; Kaplan and Schersching, in press). These new experiments further confirm the causal role of cognitive learning in producing group polarization.

But it seems that cognitive learning is not a complete explanation by itself. We and others have observed that passive exposure to arguments outside an interactive discussion content generally produces less shift than actual participation in discussion. Actual discussion stimulates more change than passively reading or listening to the same arguments. This finding is reminiscent of early work by Kurt Lewin (1947) on the superiority of group discussion to lecture in producing behavior change; of more recent educational research indicating that participative discussion has a greater effect than mere information presentation (McKeachie, 1968); of experiments demonstrating the impact of active role-playing as contrasted with passive exposure (see Jones and Gerard, 1967); and of Thomas Crawford's report (1974) of the minimal impact of passively received sermons on racial tolerance.

The work of attitude researchers is germane here, for it appears that passive comprehension of arguments is not a sufficient condition for internalization of attitude change. As Greenwald (1968) has demonstrated, passive learning about the target of an attitude is not sufficient to change the attitude; the subject must actively reformulate, or rehearse, the information in order for an internalization of attitude change to result. (This observation parallels the thinking of theorists like Jerome Bruner and Jean Piaget, who have concluded that children's intellectual development takes place more by self-generated activities, such as active play, than by being passive while taught.) It seems quite reasonable to presume that the social confrontation inherent in debate and discussion motivates covert as well as overt rehearsal, as when people quietly think about their next contribution. Eugene Burnstein's contribution to this symposium speculates creatively concerning the cognitive processes engaged by discussion.

Arguments that are openly expressed may be additionally important as a public verbal commitment toward whatever alternative is defended. We have found that spoken arguments tend to favor the socially preferred choice more predominantly that do privately processed arguments. Responding to other people in conversation elicits a more one-sided line of thought than does private contemplation of an issue. The self-attribution and dissonance reduction dynamics that accompany such overt expression likely contribute to attitude intensification. Although these and other possible mechanisms of group influence have not yet been fully explored it nonetheless seems reasonable to presume that informational influence in group discussion involves group dynamics as well as a pooling of individually processed information. These group dynamics might be incorporated within the information integration perspective by studying how they affect such factors as the distribution and weighting of pieces of information.

SOCIAL COMPARISON

There is little doubt that the substantive information which is communicated and rehearsed in group discussion in an important source of group polarization. But in addition to this information processing, are there also social-emotional processes at work? Might interpersonal comparisons, motivated by a concern for perceiving and presenting oneself favorably, contribute to the amplification of responses? Several variations on social comparison theory suggest that mere exposure to others' preferences should be a sufficient condition for polarization. In general, this group of theories (see Pruitt, 1971a, b; Baron *et al.,* 1975; Jellison and Arkin, 1977) proposes that people modify their responses when they discover that others share their inclinations more than they would have supposed. This prompts change either because the group norm is discovered to be more in the preferred direction than previously imagined (and people act to keep themselves a step ahead of the average) or because people are released to more strongly act out their secret preference after observing someone who embodies their ideal more strongly than they do.

This latter idea, called "release theory," is consistent with conformity studies which indicate that the example of only one person freely deviating from an imposed norm can liberate other individuals to act out their own impulses. If there is any commonality in the sources of polarization in small laboratory groups and in large crowds and mobs, it probably lies in the contribution of social-emotional forces to both. For example, release theory is compatible with observations of the contagion effects of actions by "trigger persons" in crowds of people who share a common impulse.

Although the available research does not so unambiguously confirm social comparison processes theory as it does informational influence processes, the sometimes mysterious and counter-intuitive results of research on social comparison have provided us with a challenging intellectual puzzle.

### Differences between self, presumed other, and ideal

The foundational assumption of social comparison theories is that people are motivated to see and to present themselves as better embodiments of socially desired abilities, traits, and attitudes than are most other members of their groups and that they therefore enter the discussion misperceiving the likely positions of their fellow group members. There are many studies, performed in our own laboratory and elsewhere, which have asked participants, after they have responded to questionnaire items, to go back over the items and guess how their average peer would respond and then to go back over the items a third time and indicate what response they would actually admire the most. People typically estimate that the group norm is more neutral than their own initial responses and indicate their ideal as even more extreme.

This is an interesting phenomenon which, like some of our other laboratory results, seems also to operate in the real world. For example, most business people perceive themselves to be more ethical than the average business person (Baumhart, 1968, Brenner and Molander, 1977). Most people perceive their own views as less racially prejudiced than the norm of their community or of their friends and neighbors (Fields and Schuman, 1976; Lenihan, 1965; O'Gorman and Garry, 1976). An exhaustive series of investigations with adolescent and adult French people confirms the same strong and consistent tendency: people tend to perceive themselves as superior to the average member of their groups (Codol, 1976).

These perceptions are, of course, distorted; the average person is not better than the average person. This self-flattery is probably also a source of much human discontent. When an employer awards merit rises and half of the employees receive less than the median increase, perceptions of injustice are likely to be widespread since few will perceive themselves as less competent than their average peer.

We have observed a puzzling order effect, however (Myers, 1974). The tendency to perceive others as "behind" oneself on the dilemma items exists only when the self response is made prior to estimating the group norm. Evidently it is after people have acted or decided that there is then a tendency to consider their own action as relatively admirable.

One version of social comparison theory suggests that in the group context people typically discover that the group norm is more supportive of their positions than they had supposed (they are therefore outshining the other group members less than they had presumed). Consistent with this line of thinking, we have found that subjects do, indeed, realistically revise their estimates of the group norm after discussion. This even happens if arguments are exchanged but explicit mention of scale responses is prohibited (e.g. Myers et al., 1971, 1974), indicating that under normal circumstances arguments may serve to implicitly convey information about others' positions in addition to their direct persuasive impact.

While these findings are all well established, their theoretical significance is still somewhat ambiguous. Just as social comparison theorists have argued that spoken arguments convey implicit cues about others' positions and may only serve to rationalize shifts once people are socially motivated to change, so also have informational theorists argued that there are plausible informal influence explanations of these self v. presumed other differences. Burnstein *et al.* (1974), for example, show that people who adopt extreme choices are presumed to possess cogent arguments and are, perhaps, therefore admired for their ability. Furthermore, the fact that subjects are much less confident about their estimates of others' choices than about the correctness of their own choices suggests that the tendency to perceive others as more neutral than oneself may simply reflect ignorance about others' choices. If you really do not know how other people feel, is it not reasonable to check a response near the middle of the scale?

In sum, the group polarization literature provides well-documented confirmation of hypotheses derived from the assumption that people are motivated to see and present themselves in a favorable light, relative to others. But the results are somewhat ambiguous because it is possible to construct a scenario which explains these findings without reference to normative social pressures or desire to engage in rank-order evaluation.

It is therefore fortunate that support for the social comparison assumption has recently emerged from some independent lines of research. Schlenker (1975) has shown that people present themselves with a positive bias, unless public exposure is forthcoming that would debunk a positive self-presentation. Fromkin (1970, 1972) provides evidence that people want to perceive themselves as somewhat different from others. Although a considerable body of research on conformity and reactions to being markedly deviant indicates that people are discomfited by being substantially different from others, it now appears that people also find it unpleasant to sense that they are undistinctive. Fromkin demonstrates that people feel better when they understand themselves to be unique and they will act in ways which will create a sense of individuality.

These conclusions are reinforced by Lemaine's (1974) analysis of the contribution to one's identity of differentiating oneself from others. McGuire and Padawer-Singer's (1976) observation that self concept is defined by differences from comparison others further strengthens the point. When simply asked to describe themselves, sixth grade children were most likely to mention spontaneously their distinctive attributes. Foreign-born children were the most likely to mention their birthplace, redheads their hair color, and so forth. These contemporary research findings will come as no surprise to personality theorists. As Fromkin notes, Fromm (1941), Horney (1937), and Maslow (1962) long ago proposed that people have a "need for separate identity" or "need for uniqueness." Situations which diminish one's sense of individuality purportedly revive the threat of "ego diffusion" (Erikson, 1959), an uncomfortable state of confused self concept. These assorted observations lend strength to social comparison theory's assumption that people are motivated to see themselves as basically similar to others, yet different — in the right direction and to the right extent.

*Perceived differences and shift*
Given this diverse support for the foundational assumption of social comparison theory, the next question is whether this social motivation does, in fact, contribute to the observed effects of group discussion. We pursued this question in two ways. The first was to inquire whether the perceived difference between oneself and others correlates with an individual's shift score on a specific item. The expectation here is that people who most perceive themselves as outshining their peers will suffer most disconfirmation of their perceived relative position and so should be most stimulated to shift when informed of the actual group norm. But to the contrary, there is no such correlation between perceived deviation from the norm and subsequent shift, even when one's own initial choices are held statistically constant (Myers *et al.,* 1971). This is a troubling finding for social comparison theory, although Baron *et al.* (1975) suggest that this low correlation may occur because even those who do not actually feel different beforehand may wish to present themselves as strong embodiments of the ideal once they get in the group context. They suggested, as we have, that the extent to which people feel that their present positions underplay their ideals may be a more crucial element of social comparison dynamics. This conclusion is supported by Lamm's findings that groups composed of individuals with high self-ideal discrepancy on issues discussed, evidenced more shift than did groups with low self-ideal discrepancy (Lamm *et al.,* 1971), but that there was no difference in shift between groups of subjects who strongly underestimated peer positions and those who did not underestimate peer positions (Lamm *et al.,* 1972).

*Polarizing effects of attitude comparison*

Because the social comparison explanations assume that the exchange of arguments in discussion is unnecessary, one way to test them is to examine their prediction that mere exposure to others' responses is sufficient to produce the effect. Our last series of experiments does just this. In contrast to numerous social psychological experiments which provide subjects with contrived misinformation about others' responses, these investigations provide accurate feedback concerning others' attitudes, just as happens in many social situations and when opinion polls are published or election returns are broadcast.

Several early studies using this procedure, including one of our own, found minimal polarization from pretest to post-test after mere exposure to others' choices. We later realized that the pre-exposure commitment was probably a sure recipe for inhibiting response change, or so some of the classic conformity studies seemed to suggest (e.g. Asch, 1956).

Our next experiment therefore removed the pretest commitment by having people respond to three risk-eliciting dilemma items after being informed of the distribution of responses by 40 other people in a control condition (Myers *et al.,* 1974). As predicted, their responses were more polarized than the average of the control responses they were shown — the opposite of conformity! The participants were fairly accurate in their guess of the average observed response, and yet this knowledge stimulated a deviation (polarization) from the observed norm.

Our subsequent experiments have explored further the attitudinal effects of mere exposure to others' attitude responses. Their purpose was, first, to ascertain whether the phenomenon would generalize across a variety of methods and materials and, second, to explore some psychological dynamics which might mediate the phenomenon.

Since, comparing our first two experiments, it seemed that binding oneself to a pre-exposure choice might, indeed, have been inhibiting response change, a follow-up study (unpublished data) put this conclusion to experimental test. Half of those who observed others' choices did so after first making a pretest commitment and half did so without pretest. Attitude materials requested subjects to evaluate hypothetical positively or negatively described college professors. Although the social comparison effect was small, only those who had not made a pretest commitment evidenced significantly more polarized responses than the control distribution which had been observed.

Our next experiment (Myers, 1978) compared two versions of social comparison theory. One version (e.g. Brown, 1974) presumes that exposure to the group norm, or average, is sufficient to stimulate a more polarized response, because people want to keep a step ahead of the average. Release theory (Pruitt, 1971a, b) postulates that the key is not discovery of the peer group average, but rather observation of a group member who models the person's ideal in a relatively extreme form.

These two explanations of attitude polarization were experimentally contrasted by showing some people a complete percentage distribution of others' opinions (therefore incorporating the necessary exposure to some extreme models), while others learned only of the group average (norm). Two types of stimulus materials were drawn from previous research — jury problems and dilemma items. The experimental groups were exposed, in balanced fashion, to the pretest responses on some items but not on others, making each subject his or her own control. With both item sets we observed (see Tables 1 and 2) that responses were significantly more polarized ($P < 0.01$) on items where subjects had observed others' responses than on items where they had not. Contrary to release theory, exposure merely to the average other response was sufficient to polarize responses. Those exposed to the full distribution of others' choice were not significantly more polarized than those who merely witnessed the group norm.

A follow-up experiment (Myers, 1978) used a between-groups comparison to examine the exposure effect (instead of the more sensitive within-subjects design) and it asked an additional question of empirical interest: what if we took the relatively polarized responses of those who had observed others' choices and exposed a third group to these? Would additional polarization occur with a second iteration of the exposure treatment?

The dependent variable in this experiment was, again, a polarization score, defined as the mean gap between responses to four cautious and four risky dilemma items. In the first stage of the experiment 30 pretest subjects completed each item individually. In a second stage 30 more subjects were shown the exact distribution of responses by the 30 subjects preceding them in the pretest condition while thirty control subjects answered without feedback,

TABLE 1

*Mean choice dilemma response, by condition*

|  |  | No exposure | | | Exposure | | |
| --- | --- | --- | --- | --- | --- | --- | --- |
| Condition | N | Risky items | Cautious items | Polari- zation | Risky items | Cautious items | Polari- zation |
| Pretest | 67 | 4.34 | 7.62 | 3.28 | | | |
| Average exposure | 52 | 4.45 | 7.80 | 3.35 | 4.04 | 7.92 | 3.88 |
| Percent exposure | 52 | 4.27 | 7.55 | 3.28 | 3.79 | 7.98 | 4.19 |

TABLE 2

*Mean jury item response, by condition*

|  |  | No exposure | | | Exposure | | |
| --- | --- | --- | --- | --- | --- | --- | --- |
| Condition | N | Low guilt | High guilt | Polari- zation | Low guilt | High guilt | Polari- zation |
| Pretest | 67 | 35.43 | 70.75 | 35.32 | | | |
| Average exposure | 52 | 36.54 | 71.83 | 35.29 | 27.12 | 72.79 | 45.67 |
| Percent exposure | 52 | 40.19 | 74.71 | 34.52 | 31.15 | 78.37 | 47.21 |

TABLE 3

*Computer experiment mean choice dilemma polarization scores*

| Stage One | Stage Two | Stage Three |
| --- | --- | --- |
| Pretest — 3.55 | $Exposure_1$ = 4.45 | $Exposure_2$ = 4.75 |
|  | Control = 2.87 | Control = 3.73 |

*Note*: $N = 30$ for each cell

just as did the pretest subjects. In the third stage of the experiment, two more groups were given the same treatments, except that those in the exposure condition were shown the responses of the preceding thirty people in their own condition.

The entire experiment was run by a computer as the subject sat at a high speed terminal. This not only eliminated any possibility of experimenter effects but, more importantly, enabled the instant tabulation of responses and their instant presentation to subsequent subjects with precisely controlled format. As can be seen in Table 3, responses in the two exposure conditions were significantly more polarized than in the control conditions ($P < 0.001$). The second iteration of feedback did not, however, significantly exaggerate the polarization effect.

Our two most recent experiments explored some additional empirical questions (Myers *et al.,* 1980). In the first experiment we observed that even a small number of others' responses (rather than a large distribution, as in previous experiments) will still produce the effect and we found again that making a public pretest commitment attenuates the polarization effect. Inspired by recent demonstrations of the impotence of abstract, "base rate" information (e.g. Borgida and Nisbett, 1978), we also wondered whether face-to-face exposure to others' choices would produce a greater polarization than when that same information was presented as dry statistics. It did, but not to a statistically significant extent.

What do these comparison effects actually represent? Does learning others' opinions really change one's opinion, or have we simply elicited a change in scale marking behavior? Perhaps subjects' perceptions of the response scale has been altered by exposure to more extreme raters, but their judgements of the issue at hand have been unaffected. In our second experiment of this pair, we observed that the polarizing effect of observing others' judgements generalized to a separate, but related judgement scale. This suggests that the phenomenon represents a genuine attitude change, not just a response effect that is specific to the scale on which others' responses have been observed. This result is compatible with Burnstein and Vinokur's (1977) contention that exposure to others' choices biases subjects' processing of information regarding the item, thus producing genuine attitude change.

Can this reliable comparison effect in laboratory studies also be observed in a field setting? Another experiment asked whether exposure to others' attitudes in a real world setting could polarize initial attitude tendencies (Myers *et al.,* 1977). Evidence from previous studies indicates there is no powerful bandwagon effect resulting from the publication of election polls (Klapper, 1964), but these studies generally present poll results from the general public, rather than from a significant social reference group. We expected that a small bandwagon effect might be obtained if exposure to the opinions of significant others informed people that their preferences were shared more strongly than they were aware. Our second purpose was, much as in one of the preceding experiments, to contrast release theory with the assumption that correctly perceiving the group norm (average) is sufficient to produce shift.

As Fig. 4 suggests and as statistical analyses confirmed, those exposed merely to the average pretest opinion were intermediate between the control and percentage exposure conditions. In this experiment it appeared that exposure to the group norm and to extreme models had small additive effects.

An additional finding evaluated the presumption that if attitude comparison is strengthening the initially dominant point of view, then items for which there is clearly a socially preferred tendency should elicit greater polarization than items initially near the neutral point. This supposition was confirmed by correlational analysis.

Each of the comparison effects reported to this point might

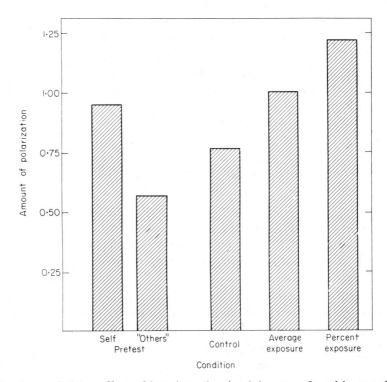

Fig. 4. A polarizing effect of learning others' opinions was found in an opinion survey of 269 members of a local church who were randomly divided into four groups. *Pretest* condition participants indicated their opinions on issues. (As the figure indicates, they guessed their average fellow member would respond less strongly in the preferred direction on these issues.) After these pretest responses were tabulated, *control* participants completed the same items without information about others' opinions, while other participants were shown either the *average* or complete *percentage* distribution of the personal opinions of people in the pretest condition.

plausibly be interpreted (as by Burnstein and Vinokur, 1975) as resulting from stimulation to think up arguments which others might have had to justify their choices. Thus what appears at first glance to be a social comparison effect might in reality be an information processing effect.

Our last experiment (unpublished data) attempted to examine this by using a simple judgement task which we presumed could not engage rationally considered arguments. Under such conditions an informational influence explanation would predict little comparison effect. Two people at a time judged the attractiveness of attractive and unattractive faces pictured on slides. The second respondent always viewed and rated the slide after hearing the first response. As Table 4 indicates, the second respondent seldom duplicated the first judgement and was almost twice as likely to deviate in the dominant direction — to go the first person one better — as to deviate in the contrary direction.

This is a relatively pure demonstration of comparison-induced polarization of judgements and it also again suggests that a large distribution of judgements is not a necessary requirement for polarization. It is conceivable, however, that even in this argument-poor situation, hearing another's judgement may have stimulated the listener to think up arguments which the other person might have had to justify that judgement (although the two seconds or so in between responses hardly allowed for much of this). The possibility of this type of cognitive mediation of the social comparison effect is difficult to rule out and, indeed, may support any motivation to outshine others.

What have these experiments established? First, they indicate that comparison-induced polarization occurs using a variety of methodologies and stimuli. The phenomenon appears to be reliable and generalizable, although subtle. Second, some theoretical explanations

TABLE 4

*Frequency of second judgements exceeding, matching, or moderating first judgements*

| Stimuli | Second judgement compared to first | | |
| | More positive | Same | More negative |
| --- | --- | --- | --- |
| Attractive | 99 | 26 | 75 |
| Unattractive | 52 | 29 | 119 |

for the phenomenon appear incapable of handling the results. It is difficult to conceive how all the findings could be fully explained by implicit group decision mechanisms (as when only two persons were present) or by the releasing effects of observing extreme models. The experiments do not, however, clearly indicate whether observing others' responses liberates people to express their secret inclinations (Levinger and Schneider, 1969) or motivates them to "one up" the self-presentations of other people as a self-enhancement strategy (Brown, 1974; Jellison and Arkin, 1976; Sanders and Baron, 1977), nor do the experiments rule out a mediational role of self-generated persuasive arguments.

The likelihood of self-enhancement dynamics is apparent from some independent lines of research noted earlier (e.g. Fromkin, 1970, 1972). These add credence to the presumption that there is a human concern for perceiving and presenting oneself favorably which may contribute to the amplification of socially desirable response tendencies. The present research is congenial to the presumption of this personality research and theory — that people want to differentiate themselves from others, to a small extent and in the right direction. By "one-upping" the self-presentations of others, people can see and present themselves as basically similar, yet desirably distinctive. This suggestion complements social psychology's historic emphasis on conformity and the avoidance of deviance.

A UNIFYING CONCEPTUAL SUMMARY

We have seen that argument exchange and rehearsal — with or without social comparison — has significant attitudinal effects. Informational influence is clearly occurring. Comparing positions without argument exchange also has a reliable effect, but this might be due to cognitive processing stimulated by exposure to others' choices. A fundamental issue thus remains: does social comparison directly prompt changed responses, or is its effect entirely mediated by the biased information processing which it induces? Eugene Burnstein's provocative chapter in this volume concludes by posing the issue in even more general terms: is there any social influence that is not mediated by information processing?

In reality, information processing and social comparison are interwoven. Arguments imply one's position and are constrained by one's perception of others' positions. Sometimes people secretly want to act on an impulse, but are inhibited from fully doing so by their perception of an external social norm. When several such people find themselves in a group, they soon verbalize their inclinations and discover that others are emitting similar opinions. Since arguments consistent with their shared inclinations are likely to be expressed, received, and rehearsed with greatest enthusiasm, the discussion arguments are more one-sided than are arguments privately processed by each individual (see Myers and Lamm, 1976). The net result is that when people feel a conflict between what they ought to do (an external norm) and what they want to do (an internal preference), discussion with similar others generally induces information processing in support of the internal preference.

This formulation integrates social-motivational concerns (as suggested by Levinger and Schneider, 1969) with the information processing mechanisms which have demonstrable importance. It explains the many experiments in which the initial statistical tendency of a subject population has been magnified by group discussion and it has the virtue of also incorporating other effects of discussion which do not exemplify polarization of the initial average.

Let us briefly consider some of these exceptions to group polarization and see how they, too, are explained. Ivan Steiner's chapter in this volume offers two instances in which this process seems to have occurred. In Lewin's (1947) visceral meat studies the women subjects apparently were well aware of government pleas to buy the sweetbread meats and willing to do so, but, until the group interaction, were apprehensive about appearing lower class. The lynching situations likewise embodied a conflict between external social constraints and private inclinations. Both situations liberated and amplified what people secretly wanted to do — in the one case with pro-social consequences and in the other case with anti-social results. As Professor Steiner notes, the groupthink situations summarized by Irving Janis seem to exhibit this same pattern.

A number of similar findings have been reported in the more recent experimental literature. Walker and Main (1973) observed that civil liberties decisions made by individual federal district court judges were predominantly conservative, apparently reflecting their awareness of public sentiment. By contrast, civil liberties decisions made by three-judge panels composed from the same pool of judges were far more libertarian. Walker and Main surmise that the group context enhanced the expression of the judge's private sympathies for constitutional rights.

Several experiments have faced subjects with a conflict between self-sacrificial altruism and self-serving selfishness. Aggression which benefits oneself is exhibited more strongly by groups than by individuals (Mathew and Kahn, 1975; Wolosin et al., 1975; Yinon et al., 1975). Here again, the secret urges of individuals were accentuated by group interaction, regardless of whether this tendency was reflected in their individual pregroup decisions.

J. M. Rabbie's fourth experiment, reported in this volume, offers fresh new documentation of group-enhanced selfishness. Rabbie's earlier finding (Rabbie and Visser, 1972) that the demands of simulated labor groups polarized following discussion probably reflects a similar process. Lutz von Rosenstiel (pers. comm.) reports that when German university students were asked whether television should be primarily informative or entertaining, they individually advised the former. After group discussion they shifted to an expressed preference for entertainment, which probably better reflected their secret preference.

While these results conflict with the group polarization phenomenon (defined as accentuation of the initial average response), they are entirely consistent with the explanation of that phenomenon. This conclusion should not be surprising. The statistical average cannot cause group polarization; it is only an indicator of some underlying social process which generally occurs when groups discuss issues where they share an acknowledged initial leaning. When social inhibitions cause the initial private leaning to remain unacknowledged prior to group interaction, the same accentuation of private inclinations may nevertheless occur.

It appears, then, that a fundamental social process, including both social motivation and information processing, can explain group polarization and its variants. To repeat the synopsis stated earlier, group interaction will affect responses when people secretly want to act in a given way, but are restrained from fully doing so by their perception of an external social norm. When several such people find themselves in a group, they soon verbalize their inclinations and discover that others are emitting similar arguments and opinions. Since information consistent with their shared inclinations is expressed and received most warmly, the discussion arguments become polarized. The net result is that when people feel a conflict between what they ought to do and what they want to do, discussion with similar others generally induces information processing in support of their internal preference and this tendency is therefore magnified.

## Note

1. This paper summarizes research previously reported in a number of separate papers. The support of a National Institute of Mental Health small starter grant (MH 15999) and of subsequent grants from the National Science Foundation (GS 2891, GS 2891A#1, BNS-7420465) is gratefully acknowledged. (A previous draft of this paper received the 1977 Gordon Allport Intergroup Relations Prize of the Society for the Psychological Study of Social Issues.)

## References

Anderson, N. H. Integration theory and attitude change. *Psychological Review*, 1971, 78, 171—206.

Anderson, N. H. and Graesser, C. C. An information integration analysis of attitude change in group discussion. *Journal of Personality and Social Psychology*, 1976, 34, 210—222.

Asch, S. E. Studies of independence and conformity: A minority of one against a unanimous majority. *Psychological Monographs*, 1956, 7, (9, Whole No. 416).

Astin, A. W. and Panos, R. J. *The educational and vocational development of college students*. Washington, D.C.: American Council on Education, 1969.

Baron, R. S., Sanders, G. S. and Baron, P. H. Social comparison reconceptualized: Implications for choice shifts, averaging effects, and social facilitation. Unpublished manuscript, University of Iowa, 1975.

Batson, C. D. Rational processing or rationalization? The effect of disconfirming information on a stated religious belief. *Journal of Personality and Social Psychology*, 1975, 32, 176—184.

Baumhart, R. *An honest profit*. New York: Holt, Rinehart & Winston, 1968.

Bishop, G. D. and Myers, D. G. Informational influence in group discussion. *Organizational Behavior and Human Performance*, 1974, 12, 92—104.

Borgida, E. and Nisbett, R. E. The differential impact of abstract vs. concrete information on decisions. *Journal of Applied Social Psychology*, 1977, 7, 258—271.

Brenner, S. N. and Molander, E. A. Is the ethics of business changing? *Harvard Business Review*, 1977, January-February, 57—71.

Brown, R. Further Comment on the risky shift. *American Psychologist*, 1974, 29, 468—470.

Burnstein, E. and Vinokur, A. Testing two classes of theories about group-induced shifts in individual choice. *Journal of Experimental Social Psychology*, 1973, 9, 123—137.

Burnstein, E. and Vinokur, A. What a person thinks upon learning he has chosen differently from others: Nice evidence for the persuasive-arguments explanation of choice shifts. *Journal of Experimental Social Psychology*, 1975, 11, 412—426.

Burnstein, E. and Vinokur, A. Persuasive arguments and social comparison as
   determinants of attitude polarization. *Journal of Experimental Social
   Psychology*, 1977, 13, 315–332.
Cartwright, D. S. The nature of gangs. In D. S. Cartwright, B. Tomson and H.
   Schwartz (Eds), *Gang Delinquency*. Monterey, Calif.: Brooks/Cole, 1975,
   pp. 1–22.
Chickering, A. W. and McCormick, J. Personality development and the college
   experience. *Research in Higher Education*, 1, 1973, 62–64.
Clark, B. R., Heist, P., McConnell, T. R., Trow, M. A. and Yonge, G. *Students
   and colleges: Interaction and change*. Berkeley: Center for Research and
   Development in Higher Education, University of California, 1972.
Codol, J. P. On the so-called 'superior conformity of the self' behavior: Twenty
   experimental investigations. *European Journal of Social Psychology*,
   1976, 5, 457–501.
Coleman, J. S. *Community conflict*. New York: Free Press, 1957.
Crawford, T. J. Sermons on racial tolerance and the parish neighborhood con-
   text. *Journal of Applied Social Psychology*, 1974, 4, 1–23.
Doise, W. Intergroup relations and polarization of individual and collective
   judgements. *Journal of Personality and Social Psychology*, 1969, 12,
   136–143.
Erikson, E. H. Identity and the life cycle. *Psychological Issues*, 1959, 1, 1–171.
Feldman, K. A. and Newcomb, T. M. *The Impact of College on Students*. San
   Francisco: Jossey-Bass, 1969.
Festinger, L., Riecken, H. W. and Schachter, S. *When Prophecy Fails*. Minnea-
   polis: University of Minnesota Press, 1956.
Fields, J. M. and Schuman, H. Public beliefs about the beliefs of the public.
   *Public Opinion Quarterly*, 1976, 40, 427–448.
Freedman, J. L. *Crowding and Behavior*. New York: Viking Press, 1975.
Fromkin, H. L. Effects of experimentally aroused feelings of undistinctiveness
   upon valuation of scarce and novel experiences. *Journal of Personality
   and Social Psychology*, 1970, 16, 521–529.
Fromkin, H. L. Feelings of interpersonal undistinctiveness: An unpleasant af-
   fective state. *Journal of Experimental Research in Personality*, 1972,
   6, 178–185.
Fromm, E. *Escape from Freedom*. New York: Farrah and Rinehart, 1941.
Gold, A. R., Christie, R. and Friedman, L. N. *Fists and Flowers: a social psy-
   chological interpretation of student dissent*. New York and London:
   Academic Press, 1976.
Greenwald, A. G. Cognitive learning, cognitive response to persuasion, and
   attitude change. In A. G. Greenwald, T. C. Brock and T. M. Ostrom
   (Eds), *Psychological Foundations of Attitudes*. New York and London:
   Academic Press, 1968.
Hans, V. P. and Doob, A. N. S.12 of the Canada Evidence Act and the delibe-
   rations of simulated juries. *Criminal Law Quarterly*, 1976, 18, 235–253.
Hardyck, N. A. and Braden, M. Prophecy fails again: A report of a failure to
   replicate. *Journal of Abnormal and Social Psychology*, 1962, 65, 136–
   141.
Hoge, D. R. *Commitment on Campus: changes in religion and values over five
   decades*. Philadelphia: Westminster Press, 1974.
Horney, K. *The Neurotic Personality of our Time*. New York: Norton, 1937.
Janis, I. L. *Victims of Groupthink*. Boston: Houghton Mifflin, 1972.

Jones, E. E. and Gerard, H. B. *Foundations of Social Psychology*. New York: Wiley, 1967.

Kalven, H. G. Jr. and Zeisel, H. *The American Jury*. Boston: Little, Brown, 1966.

Kaplan, M. F. and Schersching, C. Juror deliberation: An information integration analysis. In B. D. Sales (ed.), *Perspectives in Law and Psychology, The jury, judicial, and trial process: Vol. II.* Plenum Press, in press.

Kelman, H. C. Attitudes are alive and well and gainfully employed in the sphere of action. *American Psychologist*, 1974, 29, 310–324.

Klapper, J. T. *Bandwagon: A review of the literature*. Office of Social Research, Columbia Broadcasting System, 1964.

Lamm, H. and Myers, D. G. Group-induced polarization of attitudes and behavior. Pp. 145–195 in L. Berkowitz (ed.), *Advances in Experimental Social Psychology*, Vol. 11, New York and London: Academic Press, 1978.

Lamm, H., Schaude, E. and Trommsdorff, G. Risky shift as a function of group members' value of risk and need for approval. *Journal of Personality and Social Psychology*, 1971, 20, 430–435.

Lamm, H., Trommsdorff, G. and Rost-Schaude, E. Self-image, perception of peers' risk acceptance and risky shift. *European Journal of Social Psychology*, 1972, 2, 255–272.

Lamm, H., Myers, D. G. and Ochsmann, R. On predicting group-induced shift toward risk or caution: A second look at some experiments. *Psychologische Beitrage*, 1976, 18, 288–296.

Lemaine, G. Social differentiation and social originality. *European Journal of Social Psychology*, 1974, 4, 17–52.

Lenihan, K. J. Perceived climates as a barrier to housing desegregation. Unpublished manuscript, Bureau of Applied Social Research, Columbia University, 1965.

Levinger, G. and Schneider, D. J. Test of the "risk is a value" hypothesis. *Journal of Personality and Social Psychology*, 1969, 11, 165–169.

Lewin, K. Group decision and social change. In T. M. Newcomb and E. L. Hartley (Eds), *Readings in Social Psychology*. New York: Holt, 1947.

Malamuth, N. M. A systematic analysis of the relationship between group shifts and characteristics of the choice dilemmas questionnaire. Unpublished doctoral dissertation, UCLA, 1975.

Maslow, A. H. *Toward a Psychology of Being*. New York: Van Nostrand, 1962.

McCauley, C., Stitt, C. L., Woods, K. and Lipton, D. Group shift to caution at the race track. *Journal of Experimental Social Psychology*, 1973, 9, 80–86.

McGuire, W. J. and Padawer-Singer, A. Trait salience in the spontaneous self-concept. *Journal of Personality and Social Psychology*, 1976, 33, 743–754.

McKeachie, W. J. Psychology at age 75: The psychology teacher comes into his own. *American Psychologist*, 1968, 23, 551–557.

Minix, D. A. The role of the small group in foreign policy decision making: A potential pathology in crisis decisions? Paper presented to the Southern Political Science Association, 1976.

Jellison, J. M. and Arkin, R. M. Social comparison of abilities: A self-presentational approach to decision making in groups. In J. M. Suls and R. L. Miller (Eds), *Social Comparison Processes*, Halsted Press, 1977, pp. 235–257.

Moscovici, S. and Lecuyer, R. Studies in group decision I: Social space, patterns of communication and group consensus. *European Journal of Social Psychology*, 1972, 2, 221—244.

Moscovici, S. and Zavalloni, M. The group as a polarizer of attitudes. *Journal of Personality and Social Psychology*, 1969, 12, 125—135.

Myers, D. G. Summary and bibliography of experiments on group-induced response shift. *JSAS Catalog of Selected Documents in Psychology*, 1973, 3, 123.

Myers, D. G. Interpersonal comparison processes in choice dilemma responding. *Journal of Psychology*, 1974, 86, 287—292.

Myers, D. G. Discussion-induced attitude polarization. *Human Relations*, 1975, 28, 699—714.

Myers, D. G. The polarizing effects of social comparison. *Journal of Experimental Social Psychology*, 1978, 14, 554—563.

Myers, D. G. and Arenson, S. J. Enhancement of dominant risk tendencies in group discussion. *Psychological Reports*, 1972, 30, 615—623.

Myers, D. G. and Bach, P. J. Discussion effects on militarism-pacifism: A test of the group polarization hypothesis. *Journal of Personality and Social Psychology*, 1974, 30, 741—747.

Myers, D. G. and Bach, P. J. Group discussion effects on conflict behavior and self-justification. *Psychological Reports*, 1976, 38, 135—140.

Myers, D. G. and Bishop, G. D. Discussion effects on racial attitudes. *Science*, 1970, 169, 778—779.

Myers, D. G. and Bishop, G. D. The enhancement of dominant attitudes in group discussion. *Journal of Personality and Social Psychology*, 1971, 20, 386—391.

Myers, D. G. and Kaplan, M. F. Group-induced polarization in simulated juries. *Personality and Social Psychology Bulletin*, 1976, 2, 63—66.

Myers, D. G. and Lamm, H. The polarizing effect of group discussion. *American Scientist*, 1975, 63, 297—303.

Myers, D. G. and Lamm, H. The group polarization phenomenon. *Psychological Bulletin*, 1976, 83, 602—627.

Myers, D. G. and Murdoch, P. Is risky shift due to disproportionate influence by extreme group members? *British Journal of Social and Clinical Psychology*, 1972, 11, 109—114.

Myers, D. G., Wong, D. W. and Murdoch, P. Discussion arguments, information about others' responses, and risky shift. *Psychonomic Science*, 1971, 24, 81—83.

Myers, D. G., Bach, P. J. and Schreiber, B. F. Normative and informational effects of group interaction. *Sociometry*, 1974, 37, 275—286.

Myers, D. G., Schreiber, B. J. and Viel, D. J. Effects of discussion on opinions concerning illegal behavior. *Journal of Social Psychology*, 1974, 92, 77—84.

Myers, D. G., Wojcicki, S. B. and Aardema, B. S. Attitude comparison: Is there ever a bandwagon effect? *Journal of Applied Social Psychology*, 1977, 7, 341—347.

Myers, D. G., Bruggink, J. B., Kersting, R. C. and Schlosser, B. Does learning others' opinions change one's opinions? *Personality and Social Psychology Bulletin*, 1980, 6, 253—260.

Mynatt, C. and Sherman, S. J. Responsibility attribution in groups and individuals: A direct test of the diffusion of responsibility hypothesis. *Journal of Personality and Social Psychology*, 1975, 32, 1111—1118.

O'Gorman, H. J. and Garry, S. L. Pluralistic ignorance — A replication and extension. *Public Opinion Quarterly*, 1976, 40, 449–458.

Pruitt, D. G. Choice shifts in group discussion: An introductory review. *Journal of Personality and Social Psychology*, 1971a, 20, 339–360.

Pruitt, D. G. Conclusions: Toward an understanding of choice shifts in group discussion. *Journal of Personality and Social Psychology*, 1971b, 20, 495–510.

Rabbie, J. M. and Visser, L. Bargaining strength and group polarization in inter-group polarization. *European Journal of Social Psychology*, 1972, 2, 401–416.

Riley, R. T. and Pettigrew, T. F. Dramatic events and attitude change. *Journal of Personality and Social Psychology*, 1976, 34, 1004–1015.

Schlenker, B. R. Self-presentation: Managing the impression of consistency when reality interferes with self-enhancement. *Journal of Personality and Social Psychology*, 1975, 32, 1030–1037.

Schmidt, M. *John Wesley: A theological autobiography*, Vol. II (translated by Normal P. Goldhawk), Abingdon, 1972.

Semmel, A. K. Group dynamics and the foreign policy process: The choice-shift phenomenon. Paper presented to the Southern Political Science Association, 1976.

Sherif, M. *In Common Predicament: social psychology of inter-group conflict and cooperation.* Boston: Houghton Mifflin, 1966.

Toch, R. *The Social Psychology of Social Movements.* Indianapolis: Bobbs-Merrill, 1965.

Vinokur, A. and Burnstein, E. The effects of partially shared persuasive arguments in group-induced shifts: A group problem solving approach. *Journal of Personality and Social Psychology*, 1974, 29, 305–315.

Vinokur, A. and Burnstein, E. Novel argumentation and attitude change: The case of polarization following discussion. *European Journal of Social Psychology*, 1978, 8, 335–348.

Walker, T. G. and Main, E. C. Choice-shifts in political decision making: Federal judges and civil liberties cases. *Journal of Applied Social Psychology*, 1973, 2, 39–48.

Wilson, R. C., Gabb, J. G., Dienst, E. R., Wood, L. and Bavry, J. L. *College Professors and their Impact on Students.* New York: John Wiley, 1975.

Wolosin, R. J., Sherman, S. J. and Mynatt, C. R. When self-interest and altruism conflict. *Journal of Personality and Social Psychology*, 1975, 32, 752–760.

Yinon, Y., Jaffe, Y. and Feshbach, S. Risky aggression in individuals and groups. *Journal of Personality and Social Psychology*, 1975, 31, 808–815.

Zimbardo, P. G. Transforming experimental research into advocacy for social change. In M. Deutsch and H. A. Hornstein (Eds), *Applying Social Psychology: implications for research, practice, and training.* Hillsdale, N.J.: Erlbaum, 1975.

# 7
# The Stability of Extreme and Moderate Responses in Different Situations

Maryla Zaleska

In the extensive literature on the choice shift phenomenon, recently reviewed by Myers and Lamm (1976), little, if any, reference is made to the results of years of previous research on the effects of persuasive communication on attitude change. On first glance, this research, which focuses mostly on the characteristics of the source, the message and the receiver (cf. McGuire, 1969), does not appear to be directly related to the study of group decision processes. However, since persuasive argument is considered by some authors to be the only determinant of opinion change (Burnstein and Vinokur, 1977), or, at least, as a major factor facilitating change (Sanders and Baron, 1977; Tesser and Leone, 1977), it may be interesting to examine the extent to which findings concerning the effects of persuasive arguments emitted by an outside source can be generalized to the group setting. Of particular interest in this respect is the research on the relations between extremism, position stability and involvement, stimulated by the publication of social judgement theory by Sherif and Hovland (1961).

According to the theory proposed by these authors, an individual's own stand on an issue serves as a strong reference point for judging attitude statements or persuasive communications. Around this position, there is a range of similarity, called "latitude of acceptance," such that an opinion of an outside source falling within this range is perceived as lying very close to one's own position. Beyond the lattitude of acceptance is a range of positions to which an individual is indifferent (region of non-commitment). Any position beyond an individual's zone of indifference is seen as highly dissimilar from the person's own position and thus within their latitude of rejection. The central assumption of the theory is that the effects of a persuasive message depend upon the manner in which it is categorized by the individual. If it falls within his latitude of acceptance, the individual's opinion is likely to change toward that of the outside source, and, if it falls within his latitude of rejection, the individual's opinion would either be reinforced, or change away from that of the source.

A major proposition of social judgement theory, particularly in its later formulation (Sherif *et al.*, 1965), is that an individual's susceptibility to attitude change decreases with increased ego-involvement in his or her own stand. It is assumed that for an individual highly involved in an issue, his or her position serves as a very strong anchor, resulting in a broad latitude of rejection and a narrow latitude of non-commitment.

Another assumption of the theory is that extremity of initial attitude position is associated with high involvement (although, in principle, the involvement effects do not depend on endorsement of an extreme position). Since there is a high probability that the individual extreme in his position will also be highly involved with that position, persons holding extreme positions should be more resistant to persuasion than those adopting a moderate stand.

The predictions of social judgement theory concerning the relations between extremity of position, stability and involvement are in agreement with intuitive beliefs and expectations. Not surprisingly, the stability of extreme as compared to moderate positions has been confirmed not only by the numerous studies performed or quoted by Sherif and his co-authors, but also by the results or more recent experiments designed to study the effects of persuasive communication (Allen, 1970; Halverson and Pallack, 1978). The latter results are, however, less clear-cut than the former.

Thorough discussion of social judgement theory and of the research designed to test the implications of this theory are beyond the scope of this paper. However, since involvement and extremism are central to this paper, a few comments are necessary on their definition.

In order to demonstrate the effects of involvement, Sherif and Hovland chose as subjects natural groups who were deeply committed to a strong stand on an issue and compared them to less committed subjects. Thus, involvement was initially defined in terms of group membership. As pointed out by Kiesler *et al.* (1969), the question then would be whether the main variable is public commitment, strong affect, or a deep conviction.

In the later presentation of his theory, Sherif (Sherif *et al.*, 1965) suggests that involved individuals are those identified by a narrow latitude of non-commitment and a broad latitude of rejection which, though characteristic of extreme subjects, may also be found with those in the middle-of-the-road. However, in many studies position extremity and involvement are confounded. For example, Allen (1970) and Halverson and Pallak (1978) apparently assume that extreme subjects are also highly involved in the issue.

This assumption is questionable in view of the variety of possible definitions of position extremity. Positions referred to as extreme in the experimental literature are most often end-positions on Likert-type scale, but if Thurstone-type scales are used they may correspond to the most extreme of a series of statements. It may be argued that an individual expressing total approval of a moderate statement on a scale ranging from $+3$ (absolutely pro) to $-3$ (absolutely con) is not extreme in the same sense as a person who selects a very extreme statement as best representing his own opinion. While Sherif and his co-authors used the latter method of assessing extremism, Halverson and Pallak's subjects indicated their positions on a Likert-type scale.

## Social judgement theory and group discussion: study description

Whatever the method of measuring involvement and position extremity, all experiments designed to test the differential resistance to persuasion of extreme and moderate individuals have exposed subjects to a written or tape-recorded message from an outside source. To my knowledge, no specific predictions have been derived from the social judgement theory concerning the relative stability of extreme and moderate responses in the group setting. The question raised here is whether the extreme, as compared to the moderate, positions would also be less likely to change when exposed to persuasive arguments from other group members.

The applicability of social judgement theory to group discussions was investigated using data collected in the course of several group discussion experiments (Zaleska, 1972, 1974, 1976).[1] These studies were carried out on eight different population samples, composed of university students in psychology and in other disciplines, from Paris and from Rennes, as well as juvenile delinquents and adolescent boys attending a technical school. The subjects gave their answers on probability and on Likert-type attitude scales in a variety of situations: hypothetical risk-taking dilemmas, betting for money, deciding on alternative conditions of a high-prize game contest, and expressing attitudes or opinions on various issues. In each case, initial and final private responses of subjects were compared and the average percent change for individuals holding either extreme or moderate positions was computed for each population.

Figure 1 shows the mean post-discussion change (percentages) as a function of three dichotomous variables describing individuals' prediscussion position. The first is extremity v. moderation, the second is whether the response is located on the dominant v. the non-dominant pole of the scale, and the third whether the position is held by a majority or minority of individuals.

Positions defined here as extreme are those situated at both scale ends; they were either labelled "absolutely pro" and "absolutely con" (+3 and −3 on Likert-type attitude scales), or they corresponded to the 1/10 and 10/10 chances of success on probability scales. The term "moderate" refers here to all other positions with the exception of the neutral point.

There are extreme and moderate positions on both the dominant and the non-dominant poles of the scale. The dominant pole is defined as that attracting the greater proportion of subjects' initial choices, while the non-dominant pole is the opposite one, i.e. atracting less than half of the initial choices in the whole population. With very few exceptions, the subjects' responses were not distributed symmetrically: the proportion of those situated on the dominant pole varied, however, from 51% to 96%.

As to the third variable, i.e. majority v. minority position, it should be stressed that it does not correspond to the majority or minority within each group but to the position on each pole favoured by the highest proportion of subjects in the whole population. In other words, the majority position corresponds to the modal position (on each end of the scale) of the initial distribution of all individual choices and the minority position to all other points on that end of the scale.

RESULTS

If extreme positions are associated with higher involvement, persons holding them should be more resistant to persuasive arguments from moderate group members than individuals holding moderate positions would resist attempts at persuasion by extreme group members. This difference should be particularly accentuated on the non-dominant pole, since individuals holding extreme positions on that pole of the scale would be exposed mostly to arguments in favour of the opposite stand, thus falling within their latitude of rejection. For example, if the attitude of most subjects is "pro" on a given problem, private post-discussion attitude of individuals who initially were "absolutely con" should change less often than the opinion of those who were more moderately con. According to social judgement theory, it may be expected that in this case extreme positions should be reinforced rather than modified.

Figure 1 shows the mean percentage of individual post-discussion change (ordinate) as a function of position extremity v. moderation (represented by two points on the $x$ axis). The points having different subscripts are significantly different (two-tailed $t$ test, $P < 0.05$).

Examination of Fig. 1 shows that the difference between the percent change of extreme, as compared to moderate positions, is significant only for responses situated on the dominant pole of the

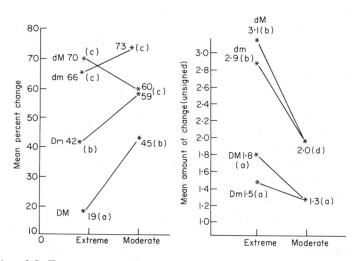

Figs. 1 and 2. Two measures of post-discussion attitude change averaged across eight experiments as a function of the extremity, dominance and popularity of initial attitude position. Note: (a) Points bearing different subscripts are significantly different ($P < 0.05$ or better) and (b) D = dominant pole; d = non-dominant pole; M = modal (majority) positions on the corresponding pole; m = other (minority) positions on the same pole.

scale, i.e. the pole attracting most of the initial choices in the population. On the opposite pole, extreme and moderate positions are about equally unstable.

A more detailed analysis of the data suggests that the difference between the overall stability of extreme and moderate positions on the dominant pole is due to a ceiling effect. Extreme responses have only the possibility of becoming more moderate, while moderate positions may also polarize, i.e. become more extreme. A comparison of the relevant data, presented in Tables 1 and 2, shows that on the dominant pole, the average proportion of change for the extreme positions (29%) is slightly higher than the average proportion of moderate positions which become more moderate (20%), while the percentage of moderate position polarization is 35%. On the opposite pole, however, the moderate positions seldom polarize (9%) and move predominantly in one direction, toward the middle of the scale and the dominant pole (59%). Consequently, their average stability is not significantly different from that of extreme responses moving in the same direction (70%).

Further inspection of Fig. 1 reveals that the stability of responses is mainly determined by their position on the dominant or on the non-dominant pole. It should also be noted that on the dominant pole, and only on that pole of the scale, both the extreme and the moderate positions are significantly more stable when they are initially adopted by a majority than by a minority of subjects in the population.

These results suggest a relation between the initial frequency of a position and its stability. In fact, significant correlations between these two variables are found for all positions (0.57), as well as for extreme (0.58) and for moderate positions (0.60) separately. Thus, the larger the proportion of individuals initially adopting a given position, the greater the proportion of responses which remain unchanged following discussion.

Another question of interest is that of direction of change. As would be expected, a high negative correlation is found between the initial proportion of extreme choices in the population and the proportion of those becoming more moderate (−0.66). Moreover, the degree of post-discussion extremism is related to its initial frequency. Specifically, the percentage of initial extreme positions in the population is significantly correlated (0.78) with the percentage of moderate choices which become extreme following

TABLE 1

*Mean percent of individuals changing their initial position for 20 studies*

| | Dominant pole Extreme positions | Dominant pole Moderate positions | Non-dominant pole Extreme positions | Non-dominant pole Moderate positions | Total Dominant pole | Total Non-dominant pole |
|---|---|---|---|---|---|---|
| I. Group experiments (N = 8) (7 and 6 point scales) | 29% (a) | 55% (b) | 70% (c) | 68% (c) | 39% (a) | 61% (b) |
| II. Augsburg experiments (N = 11) | | | | | | |
| A. Observation experiments (N = 6; 21 point scales) | 35% (a) | 75% (b) | 29% (a) | 83% (b) | 61% (a) | 74% (b) |
| B. Interaction experiments (N = 5; 11 point scales) | — | 58% (a) | — | 65% (a) | | |
| C. Observation experiments (7 point transformed scales) | 19% (a) | 62% (b) | 29% (c) | 72% (b) | 40% (a) | 55% (b) |
| III. Individual study at Rennes (7 point scales) | (24%) | (61%) | (33%) | (65%) | (46%) | (61%) |

*Note*: 1. Extreme positions here are these situated at both scale ends, and moderate positions all others with the exception of the neutral point on the attitude scales. 2. Figures in the same row bearing different subscripts are significantly different ($P < 0.05$).

TABLE 2

*Direction of change of initial moderate responses for 19 studies*

| | Dominant pole | | | Non-dominant pole | | |
|---|---|---|---|---|---|---|
| | % Polarization | % change in opposite direction | % total change | % polarization | % change in opposite direction | % total change |
| I. Group experiments | 35% a | 20% a | (55%) a | 9% a | 59% a | (68%) ab |
| II. Augsburg experiments | | | | | | |
| A. Observation experiments (21 point scales) | 41% a | 34% bc | (75%) b | 36% b | 47% ab | (83%) a |
| B. Interaction experiments (11 point scales) | 13% b | 45% c | (58%) a | 14% a | 51% ab | (65%) bc |
| C. Observation experiments (7 point transformed scales) | 38% a | 24% ab | (62%) a | 35% b | 37% bc | (72%) ab |

*Note:* 1. Polarization is the movement toward more extreme positions on the same pole. 2. Means in the same column not sharing the same subscript are significantly different ($P < 0.05$, by two tailed $t$ test).

discussion, and also with the difference between the percent change in both directions (0.79). For the population samples participating in the experiments reported here, the breaking point is 40%. When the initial proportion of extreme responses is above this figure, the percentage of moderate positions becoming extreme is higher than that of extreme positions becoming moderate, while the reverse is true when this proportion is below 40%. The correlation of 0.79 indicates that the higher the proportion of extreme positions in the population, the greater the extremization effect of discussion on the final private responses of individuals.

Finally, we investigated the amount of change. Presumably, this amount should be greater for individuals holding extreme positions, when they change, since they have the possibility of moving a greater distance on the scale than moderate ones. However, the prediction based on social judgement theory would be the opposite. The more involved extremists should change to a lesser extent than uninvolved moderates. Inspection of Fig. 2 shows that the latter prediction is not borne out and that the extreme positions change more than the moderate responses. However, the difference is significant only on the non-dominant pole ($P < 0.001$, two-tailed $t$ test). On this pole, the average amount of change is three scale points for extreme positions, and two scale points for moderate ones; the corresponding figures on the dominant pole being 1.6 and 1.3.

Thus, initial disagreement with a dominant tendency results not only in a greater proportion of change following discussion, but also to a significantly greater amount of change. This difference is not surprising. As pointed out elsewhere (Zaleska, 1972, 1978), the responses which are most frequently chosen by a population of individuals are more likely to gain wider acceptance following discussion than responses which are relatively infrequent.

First of all, the differences in the initial choice frequencies suggest that one position may, in fact, be stronger. Thus, individuals defending the dominant tendency tend to be more confident in their position and in the arguments supporting it. Moreover, they have majority support in most groups. Because of its numerical superiority, a majority is liable to produce more arguments than a minority and may even prevent the minority from expressing itself at all. Finally, the greater the number of individuals defending the same tendency, the greater the probability that one of them at least will find a novel and persuasive argument. A majority has thus generally more chance of convincing the group than a minority, unless it is scarcely convinced itself.

However, in contrast to the results reported by Sherif and his co-authors, extreme responses are not resistant to persuasive arguments from individuals advocating the opposite stand, since, as shown in Fig. 1, on the non-dominant pole extreme responses are not more stable than moderate ones. In fact, for positions on the non-dominant end of the scale the mean percentage of extreme positions moving in the direction of the dominant tendency is 70%, while only 59% of the moderate individuals moved in the dominant direction (see Tables 1 and 2).

These figures are very different from those found, for example, in the well-known prohibition study (Hovland *et al.*, 1957), in which the highest percentage of change in the direction advocated is for moderate subjects (28.3%), while those adopting extreme stands changed only about 4%. Since the crucial factor in social judgement theory is involvement, rather than extremism as such, could it be that the two are not related?

## Does extremism necessarily mean involvement?

The relations between extremity of position, its stability, involvement and information were examined in another study. About a hundred students from the same class at the University of Rennes were requested to express their attitudes and opinions on 14 problems. They were first asked to give, as usual, their own position, and then to indicate on another seven-point scale all the positions that appeared to them as acceptable as the initially given position. Finally, they were requested to indicate how involved and how well informed they considered themselves to be on each problem.

As predicted, high and significant correlations were found between average extremism, the number of positions considered as acceptable, involvement and information. The more extreme subjects' mean attitude score, the lower the number of positions they find acceptable, the greater the degree of self-attributed involvement, and the higher the amount of information subjects feel they know about the topic.

However, the correlations across problems are much lower than those across subjects. The relatively low, non-significant correlation between mean extremity and involvement scores for the 14 problems suggests the existence of a sort of "conventional" extreme response. Thus, for example, all students were very strongly in favour of the lowering of the retirement age but their rated involvement in the issue was relatively low.

It is interesting to note that in the experiment by Allen (1970), university students who were extremely opposed to "prosecution of students by both city and university officials," and extremely in favour of "lowering the voting age," did not exhibit change on the former issue, but, contrary to expectations, changed in the direction of decreased favourability on the latter, due to persuasive communication. Commenting on these contradictory findings, Allen remarks that students were actively protesting "prosecution by both city and university officials," while nothing approaching a high level of support for "lowering of the voting age" was apparent.

It would appear then that extremism defined by total approval of a statement is not necessarily associated with high involvement. The examples given above suggest that an extremely favourable attitude may denote only an unqualified approval of a general principle and may be relatively easy to modify. The high correlations between average extremism, involvement and amount of information across subjects found in the Rennes study are probably due mostly to the tendency of some individuals to adopt a response set. Both the extreme response set and the neutral response set have been analysed and discussed by various authors (e.g. Innes, 1977).

## Social judgement theory and group discussion: summary and discussion

The change of response observed in the group discussion experiments does not necessarily indicate a genuine change of attitude or opinion, but may only be a modification of their expression. The results reported here show that, following group discussion, this modification (or genuine change) is less likely to occur if a given response represents a dominant tendency in the population since the stability of a position is strongly correlated with its initial frequency. As for the extreme positions, not only their stability, but also their attraction power within groups depend to a large extent on their initial proportion in the population. It should also be noted that if this proportion of extreme initial positions is relatively high and, instead of being concentrated at one pole of the scale, is divided between the two opposite poles an accentuated bi-polarization of responses is observed in the population (in some cases). Thus, when a population is randomly divided into small discussion groups, not only convergence but also divergence of attitudes or opinions may be accentuated depending on their initial distribution in the population.

However, the results of a recent experiment with Serge Moscovici suggest that the relative stability of extreme and moderate responses may also be determined by the climate of interpersonal relations within the group. According to the hypothesis proposed by Moscovici, most individuals would not adopt publicly an extreme stand and would show moderation rather than extremism, if they feared rejection by the group. When interpersonal relations are positive, group members feel secure to express and defend extreme attitudes and opinions; extreme positions also are more easily accepted in a friendly climate. Hence, the extremization effect should be more frequent in groups of friends, and compromise situations in groups of strangers.

In order to test this hypothesis, in the experimental condition randomly assembled groups of students were led to believe that they had been formed on the basis of observed similarities of personality traits among their members. An opinion questionnaire, previously submitted to all subjects, was alleged to be an adequate instrument for detecting these similarities. Eight experimental and eight control groups of four members each discussed their attitudes on a series of problems and gave their responses on seven-point attitude scales.

As predicted, group decisions in the control condition were consistently less extreme than initial choices and the average group decision for all the seven problems was significantly more moderate than in the experimental condition. These results give support to the hypothesis proposed by Moscovici.

The results of the comparison between the initial and final private responses of subjects in both conditions are presented in Fig. 3. The percentage of responses remaining stable after discussion is shown on the $y$ axis, while the absolute values of the attitude scores are shown on the $x$ axis.

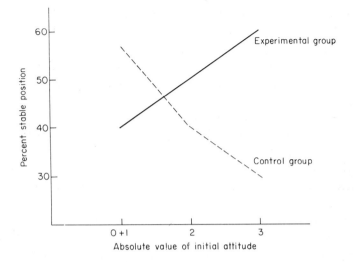

Fig. 3. Position stability in experimental and control groups as a function of extremity of initial positions.

Inspection of Fig. 3 clearly shows that the stability of responses increases with the extremity of opinion in the experimental condition, while it decreases in the control condition.

## Social judgement theory and attitude change following observation: study description

The relations between extremism and position stability were further investigated by examining some of the data obtained by the Augsburg University Research Group in the course of 11 experiments.[2] The essential differences between the Augsburg studies and those reported earlier are a lack of group discussion and controlled argumentation. That is, in the Augsburg studies individuals either observed a discussion or interacted with only one other person and the quality and number of arguments for either side were determined by the experimenter.

In six of these experiments the subjects were observing a discussion between two or three persons on the TV or on the radio. In each case, an equal number of pro and con arguments was produced by the discussants, while the third person, when present, adopted a neutral position. The problems discussed were whether members of radical parties should be employed in the German Civil

Service and whether the severity of punishment for drug possession should be increased. Subjects indicated their attitude on 21-point scales ranging from 100% pro to 100% con. The subjects were students from various university departments and Augsburg citizens. Except for one experiment with 42 subjects, the number of subjects was over 100 in each study. These experiments were designed to study the effect of approving or disapproving behaviour of an audience, of discussion style and of personality characteristics of the discussants on attitude change.

In five other experiments the subjects participated in a discussion and expressed their attitudes on 11-point scales. In three of the experiments subjects were made to choose among prearranged arguments, which they were led to believe they presented/received to/from another subject by means of a computer. The problem to be discussed by sending the selected arguments was whether to hire a job applicant whose record threw some doubt about his abilities. The same problem was given to the subjects in a fourth experiment in which they interacted with a fictitious partner by exchanging written arguments prepared by the experimenter. In the fifth experiment, in which the question debated was whether to plead guilty before a disciplinary court in a case involving a teacher and a pupil, the naive subject was discussing with an experimenter's confederate. The independent variables studied was friendly or unfriendly behaviour of the partner, his liking of the subject, his perceived similarity to the subject, his competence and expectation or no expectation of future interaction. The number of subjects participating in these experiments varied between 69 and 143; subjects were mostly students from various university departments.

## Social judgement theory and observation: results

As may be seen from Table 1, the average proportion of attitude change tends to be lower on the dominant than on the non-dominant pole ($P < 0.05$, two-tailed $t$ test), but the difference is slight as compared to that in the group experiments. In the six observation studies, extreme positions (100% pro and 100% con) are significantly more stable than all other positions on the same pole, dominant and non-dominant. The corresponding comparison could not be made for the interaction experiments, because hardly any subjects adopted an extreme attitude when discussing the problem of hiring a hypothetical job applicant, and there were no individuals holding extreme positions on the question of whether to plead guilty before the court.

In order to make the data more comparable to those observed in the group experiments, the 21-point scales used in the six observation experiments were transformed into seven-point scales by pooling together the immediately adjacent positions three-by-three. As would be expected, position stability is thus increased (see Table 1, II C). The overall results do not appear, however, very different. On each pole, the extreme responses are more stable than moderate ones, and those situated on the dominant pole change less often than those situated on the opposite pole. The comparison of the proportions of change calculated with the transformed seven-point scales to the corresponding proportions in the eight group experiments shows that the only striking difference is that between the percentage of change of extreme responses situated on the non-dominant pole.

Inspection of Table 2 reveals another difference between the group experiments and the Augsburg observation experiments. In this table, the total proportion of change of moderate positions is divided into those moving toward more extreme positions on the same pole, and those moving in the opposite direction. The displacement toward the end of the scale of positions situated on the same pole may be called polarization or extremization. As may be seen, the lowest figure in Table 2 is that representing the polarization of responses on the non-dominant pole in the group experiments (9%). This figure would be even lower if the results corresponding to bimodal distributions were not taken into account, because in this case a bipolarization of responses is generally observed. When these distributions are excluded from the data, the average proportion of responses becoming more extreme on the non-dominant pole following group discussion falls to 3%, with their range being from 0% to 6%. In three of the five Augsburg interaction experiments, the proportion of polarization is of comparable magnitude (between 4% and 6%) on the non-dominant pole, but the mean proportion is around 13%.

As to the amount of change, if the 21-point scales are reduced to seven-point scales, all figures in the Augsburg observation experiments are of similar magnitude, and vary between a minimum of

1.42 and a maximum of 1.83 scale points. As expected, the displacements of the extreme positions are slightly greater than those of the moderate responses, but the difference is not significant. It may also be noted that the average amount of change is the same on both poles, and that it is of very similar magnitude to that observed on the dominant pole in the group experiments. The average displacement of extreme responses on the non-dominant pole is however about twice as great in the group experiments (see Fig. 2).

To summarize these results, it appears that, after having watched and/or listened to a discussion between persons defending two opposite points of view, individuals tend to less often modify their initial opinion when it is situated on the dominant than on the non-dominant pole. Thus, students who are against excluding members or radical parties from Civil Service are more firm in their attitude than the students who are pro exclusion. On the contrary, Augsburg citizens, sampled at random from the telephone directory, tend to be more stable in their opinion when they are in favour of exclusion. In both cases, the majority opinion seems to correspond to a slightly greater stability of attitude. The finding that the percentage of stable opinions and the proportion of polarization on both poles are comparable to those observed in the group for responses situated on the dominant pole suggests that individuals exposed to conflicting arguments are more sensitive to those supporting their own point of view than to those opposing it, particularly if their opinion corresponds to the dominant opinion in the population. Finally, it appears that in this type of situation, the proportion of movement toward the middle of the scale and toward the opposite pole is about the same for extreme and for moderate positions.

In the interaction experiments, subjects were participating in a discussion, but they had only one opponent, and in some cases also a neutral partner. Because they had no supporting partner, their situation was to some extent similar to that of subjects defending a non-dominant position in the group experiments; the latter, however, had generally more than one opponent, the groups being composed of four or five members. In the interacting pairs, as shown in Table 2, moderate subjects holding the dominant position tend to show more polarization and less change in the direction advocated by the opponent than group members defending the non-dominant positions, but the observed differences are not significant.

It is interesting to report that in the Augsburg experiments very few subjects changed the polarity of their attitude. Whether they were observing a discussion, or participating in it, on average only 4% of all individuals holding initially the dominant positions, and 9% of those holding the non-dominant positions, declared themselves "pro" at the end of the experiment when they were "con" at the beginning, or vice versa. In contrast, while 5% (on the average) of all group members defending the dominant opinion modified it following discussion by moving to the opposite pole of the scale, the corresponding percentage for group members defending the non-dominant positions was 48%. This last value is significantly different from all the others ($P < 0.01$, by two-tailed $t$ test).

## Integration of discussion and observation studies

At first sight, it would seem that the results reported here could be explained by persuasive arguments theory. Since in the Augsburg observation experiments, the proportion of pro and con arguments exchanged during discussion is carefully balanced, the theory would predict that, whatever the initial opinion of subjects observing these discussions, the proportion of change should be approximately the same. In contrast, the theory would also predict that the proportion, direction and amount of change, of subjects participating in the group discussions would depend on their initial opinion, because group members defending the dominant positions would be exposed mostly to supportive arguments, while those defending the non-dominant positions would be generally exposed to the arguments of an opposing majority.

An explanation in terms of the persuasive arguments theory as formulated by Burnstein and Vinokur (1977), however, is not fully satisfactory. Though the importance of argument as one of the major determinants of response change is unquestionable, the process of yielding and of resisting to influence attempts does not depend only on purely cognitive factors.

First of all, it is contended here that the quantity, the quality and the novelty of arguments are not the only factors determining response modification; repetition of the same argument or the approval of it by several persons can have a significantly greater persuasive impact than the same argument once stated by a single person. In the Augsburg observation experiments, the approval of a speaker's argumentation by an audience does have a significant effect on opinion change (Brandstätter, 1978).

Also, as repeatedly shown by Eiser (Eiser, 1975; Eiser and Mower White, 1974, 1975), evaluatively biased language has a significant effect on attitude change. Attaching positive or negative labels to concepts, persons and groups is one of the most widely used means of persuasion. In the betting experiments reported here, calling a cautious group member "stingy" or "boring," accusing him of having the mentality of an "old miser" and the like, constituted the bulk of arguments produced by the proponents of risky bets. Any explanation of choice shifts or of group induced opinion change in terms of persuasive argumentation is incomplete if the effect of positive and negative linguistic labels is not taken into account.

Furthermore, as shown by Moscovici and Faucheux (1972) and confirmed by other authors, change may also be induced by consistent repetition of the same response by a minority. Since Burnstein and Vinokur (1977) extend their persuasive arguments theory to the conformity experiments in which consistency over persons is generally considered as the determinant of yielding to a unanimous majority, they may apply the same reasoning to consistency over time, i.e. to the systematic repetition of the same response by a minority. It is, however, difficult to prove that the reasons for giving an erroneous response, presented by the subjects after having participated in a conformity experiment, and quoted by Burnstein and Vinokur (1977), are the actual determinants of yielding. It seems more likely that they are justifications aimed at restoring the damaged self-image of subjects who repeated the obviously erroneous response of the unanimous majority. In other words, the arguments given by a person to justify a particular behaviour are not necessarily the actual cause of that behaviour.

Finally, other results of the Augsburg experiments also suggest that persuasive arguments are not the only factor influencing attitude change. For example, in one of the observation experiments, the person arguing in favour of increasing the amount of information on the TV at the expense of entertainment induced about the same amount of change when using "good" arguments (18%) and "poor" arguments (20%), the quality of arguments being defined by the experimenter. However, the frequency of response modification in the direction advocated was significantly lower when unfriendly

(12%) rather than friendly or neutral (32%) behaviour was adopted by that person ($P < 0.05$, $\chi^2$, 1 d.f.). Also, in the Augsburg inter- action experiments it appeared that the subjects were more in- fluenced by a friendly than by an unfriendly partner, by the liked partner than by a neutral one, and by a similar partner than by a different one, though the arguments presented by each were strictly identical (Brandstätter, 1978).

These results show that the same argument may be accepted or refused depending on various affective factors, such as friendly or unfriendly relations with the person presenting the arguments. In my opinion, therefore, one of the most powerful determinants of yielding or resisting influence attempts is the identification with groups and persons.

## Extremism as identification with an extreme group

Before concluding, let me report a case which will illustrate my point. In one of the group experiments, subjects were requested to discuss their opinion about the recent law legalizing abortion in France. In our sample of students, almost all considered that this law was not radical enough and most of them, for that reason, expressed a more or less strong "con" attitude. In one group, a member discovered during discussion that, while he was also against the law, it was because, as a Catholic, he was strongly opposed to any legalization of abortion. On finding that his apparent agreement with the group was in fact a deep disagreement, he adopted a position in favour of the law in order to differentiate himself from the group. He apparently preferred not to be seen as a member of the group of leftist students at the cost of declaring himself in favour of the law, against which his own reference group, the Catholics, have actively fought. This case of paradoxical change, motivated by a high involvement in a position, illustrates the importance of the relation between central values, group membership, and reactions to influence attempts.

A strong identification with and commitment to groups advo- cating certain values and opinions would prevent acceptance of other values and opinions. Thus, the very low proportion of change of extreme subjects toward the direction advocated in the already quoted prohibition study by Hovland *et al.* (1957) may be attributed to their commitment to groups strongly favouring prohibition. It should be recalled that the subjects participating in this study were sought from Women Christian Temperance Union groups, the Salvation Army, and strictly denominational colleges to represent the "dry" side. The similar results obtained in a field study of political attitudes prior to the 1960 presidential election could be explained by commitment to political parties. In this study, the percentage of change among those taking a moderate position was about twice as frequent as the percentage of change among those with extreme stands (Sherif *et al.* 1965).

It should be stressed that, while in their studies, Sherif and his co-authors generally compared members of extreme groups or highly committed individuals to unselected subjects, all individuals participating in the group experiments reported here were unselected subjects sought from relatively homogeneous populations of peers. Most probably, the results would have been very different, and more similar to those of Sherif, if extremism had been defined by membership in extreme groups, rather than by extremity of position on attitude or on risk scales.

If group identification and commitment are of primary importance, it is not surprising that extreme individuals generally resist attempts at persuasion from an outside source when they are committed to opinions and values of their reference group, while they most often modify their initial position when it appears to be different from that of their peer group. Attitude and opinions, beliefs and preferences of any individual do not exist in a "social vacuum" but are tied to reference groups and engaged with value systems of these groups. They are part of the social identity of the individual in which his self-identity is deeply rooted.

In conclusion, it is suggested here that position stability depends not only on the value of arguments presented during discussion but also on the degree of involvement with the issue as compared to the involvement with the group supporting the issue; on the importance of holding a particular stand, as compared to that of perceiving oneself, and being perceived as a member of a given group. By moving their initial opinion toward that expressed during discussion by the group, or away from it, individuals probably indicate not only to what extent they are convinced by the argumentation developed during the interaction with other group members, but also to what extent they identify themselves, and wish to be identified, with that group.

As shown in the remarkable work by Nuttin (1975), response modification on an attitude scale may be maintained by the subjects for a long time following the experimental manipulation without corresponding to a genuine change of attitude or opinion. Though Nuttin studied a very different experimental situation, the same may be true of response modification induced by discussion in *ad hoc* groups. However, repeated interaction within the same, or similar groups, may progressively induce genuine change particularly if membership in these groups is sought for.

A final word of caution is necessary: the conclusions proposed here are only tentative hypotheses which have to be tested by developing research on opinion change in relation to identification and differentiation processes in groups.

## Notes

1. Not all these experiments are published as yet.
2. The experimental data were communicated by courtesy of Professor Hermann Brandstätter to whom I wish to express my gratitude. Full description of the method and results can be found in the doctoral dissertations by Rüttinger, Augsburg, 1974 and by Stocker-Kreichgauer, Augsburg, 1976, and in the papers by Peltzer, Rosenstiel, Rüttinger, Schuler and Stocker-Kreichgauer, to whom I extend my thanks. The papers are published in *Problem und Entscheidung*, 1972, 8; 1974, 12; 1975, 14; 1976, 18.

## References

Allen, B. P. Demonstrations in attitude change and persuasive communication. *Psychological Reports*, 1970, 27, 703–706.

Brandstätter, H. Social emotions in discussion groups, In: Brandstätter, H., Davis, J. H., Schuler, H. (Eds). *Dynamics of Group Decisions*, 1978, Beverly Hills, Sage, pp. 93–111.

Burnstein, E. and Vinokur, A. Persuasive argumentation and social comparison as determinants of attitude polarization. *Journal of Experimental Social Psychology*, 1977, 13, 315–332.

Eiser, J. R. Attitudes and the use of evaluative language: a two-way process. *Journal for the Theory of Social Behavior*, 1975, 5, 235–248.

Eiser, J. R. and Mower White, C. J. The persuasiveness of labels: attitude change produced through definition of the attitude continuum. *European Journal of Social Psychology*, 1974, 4, 89–92.

Eiser, J. R. and Mower White, C. J. Categorization and congruity in attitudinal judgement. *Journal of Personality and Social Psychology*, 1975, 31, 769–775.

Halverson, R. R. and Pallak, M. S. Commitment, ego-involvement and resistance to attack, *Journal of Experimental Social Psychology*, 1978, 14, 1–12.

Hovland, C. I., Harvey, O. J. and Sherif, M. Assimilation and contrast effects in reactions to communication and attitude change, *Journal of Abnormal and Social Psychology*, 1957, 55, 244–52.

Innes, J. M. Extremity and "don't know" sets in questionnaire response. *British Journal of Social and Clinical Psychology*, 1977, 16, 9–12.

Kiesler, C. A., Collins, B. E. and Miller, N. Social Judgement Theory, *In: Attitude Change. A Critical Analysis of Theoretical Approaches*, 1969, New York, John Wiley, pp. 238–301.

McGuire, W. J. The nature of attitude and attitude change. In: Lindzey, G., Aronson, E. (Eds). *The Handbook of Social Psychology* (2nd ed.), Vol. 3, The individual in a social context. 1969, Reading Mass.: Addison-Wesley, pp. 136–314.

Moscovici, S. and Faucheux, C. Social influence, conformity bias, and the study of active minorities. *In:* Berkowitz, L. (Ed.). *Advances in Experimental Social Psychology*, Vol. 6, 1972, New York and London, Academic Press, pp. 149–202.

Myers, D. G. and Lamm, H. The group polarization phenomenon. *Psychological Bulletin*, 1976, 83, 602–627.

Nuttin, J. M. Jr. *The Illusion of Attitude Change: Towards a Response Contagion Theory of Persuasion*, 1975, London and New York, Academic Press and Leuven University Press.

Sanders, G. S. and Baron, R. S. Is social comparison irrelevant for producing choice shifts? *Journal of Experimental Social Psychology*, 1977, 13, 303–314.

Sherif, M. and Hovland, C. I. *Social judgement: assimilation and contrast effects in communication and attitude change*. 1961, New Haven, Conn.: Yale University Press.

Sherif, C. W., Sherif, M. and Nebergall, R. E. *Attitude and attitude change; the social judgement-involvement approach*. 1965, Philadelphia, Pa.: W. B. Saunders Company.

Tesser, A. and Leone, C. Cognitive schemas and thought as determinants of attitude change. *Journal of Experimental Social Psychology*, 1977, 13, 340–356.

Zaleska, M. Comparaison des décisions individuelles et collectives dans des situations de choix avec risque. 1972. (Unpublished doctoral dissertation.)

Zaleska, M. The effects of discussion on group and individual choices among bets. *European Journal of Social Psychology*, 1974, 4, 229–250.

Zaleska, M. Majority influence on group choices among bets. *Journal of Personality and Social Psychology*, 1976, 33, 8–17.

Zaleska, M. Individual and group choices among solutions of a problem when solution verifiability is moderate or low. *European Journal of Social Psychology*, 1978, 8, 37–53.

# 8
# Stability of Faction Position and Influence

Charlan Nemeth

In Festinger's classic paper arguing that there are pressures to uniformity in groups, it became apparent that people assume that truth lies in consensus and that disagreement is an unpleasant state that sets in motion pressures for agreement. Since the 1950s and Asch's classic work, a good deal of work has been directed toward one way in which such consensus can be achieved, i.e. the conformity process. In that situation, the deviant or minority changes their position in the direction of the position of the majority, thus evidencing a process of social control.

In the decades of studies that followed, considerable evidence was amassed which demonstrated repeatedly that discomfort was engendered by disagreement and that people "strained toward uniformity". Deutsch and Gerard (1955), for example, illustrated these elements in their distinction between normative and informational influence. Normative influence, according to Deutsch and Gerard, is "an influence to conform with the positive expectations of another". In other words, some subjects may have conformed because of anticipations of rewards and avoidance of punishment from the other members for such behavior. Informational influence, on the other hand, is defined as "an influence to accept information obtained from another as evidence about reality".

The fact of discomfort in disagreement is evidenced by reports of Asch's subjects that they did not want to "stick out like a sore thumb" and our own work, (Nemeth, 1976; Wachtler and Nemeth, 1978), in which minorities who face a majority in disagreement with them report considerable stress. The assumption that truth lies in consensus is an underlying premise of informational influence. When there is no physical way of determining the truth or falsity of a position, people rely on others to determine the correctness of their perceptions or opinions. Thus, some of Asch's subjects reported concern over their own opinions and judgements because others disagreed; "they can't all be wrong and I'm right". This questioning of one's judgements was presumably due to the belief that truth lies in agreement; when there is disagreement, there are pressures for consensus in order to validate one's opinions.

During the present decade, considerable interest has focused on another way in which consensus can be achieved, i.e. minority influence. Here, the process is one in which the majority changes its position in the direction of that espoused by the minority. Again, we find evidence for the discomfort engendered by disagreement and the strains for uniformity. Only now, the process by which this is achieved and the particular form that characterizes the discomfort and "strains" are different. In fact, it is by promoting the discomfort engendered by disagreement and relying on the attendant strains toward uniformity and consensus that the minority appears to effect the acceptance of its position. In many of the studies (Moscovici *et al.*, 1969; Nemeth *et al.*, 1974; Nemeth and Wachtler, 1974), it is precisely maintenance of the minority position that is necessary for minority influence; it is the maintenance of the disagreement, of the viability of the alternative position, that creates the necessary discomfort and the necessary strains toward consensus on the part of the majority that serves to make the minority position influential.

In previous papers, we have addressed some of the major differences between the processes of conformity and minority influence (Nemeth, 1976, 1978; Wachtler and Nemeth, 1978). One difference is that conformity is often evidenced on the first trial or in the first few moments of a discussion. In contrast, minority influence takes more time to be evidenced; it is rarely seen in early trials or in early minutes of a discussion. Secondly, the opposition in conformity situations, i.e. the majority, is better liked than the opposition in minority influence. The deviant, the persistent minority, is rarely liked; they are in fact highly disliked. Thirdly, the conformity process appears to involve more stress on the part of the naive subjects (i.e. the minority), than does the minority influence process (i.e. where the naive subjects are a majority). Such high levels of stress in the conformity process appears to cause the naive subjects to focus on who is correct, themselves or the disagreeing majority.

In contrast, the minority influence process appears to be characterized by sufficient conflict to "reassess" the position but does not cause the members of the majority to reduce the world of alternatives to two, i.e. themselves and the minority. Rather, there is evidence (Nemeth and Wachtler, 1981) that maintenance of position by the minority causes the majority to find new alternatives, ones not suggested by the minority nor previously considered by the majority. As such, there appears to be a creative contribution of conflict engendered by the maintenance of a minority position.

In this paper, we will concentrate instead on the similarities between the conformity and minority influence phenomena and, indeed, among, influence processes in general. In particular, we will argue that much of the literature on each process indicates that it is the stability of the "anchor" or position that is proposed by the majority v. the minority that will dictate whether the process is one of conformity v. minority influence v. compromise. Finally, we will outline a study just completed which strengthens the stability of the "anchor", by means of another social psychological phenomenon, i.e. the polarization process. Depending on which faction is strengthened by this process, we predict different outcomes of the majority/minority interaction.

First, let us consider the existing literature regarding stability as a factor in influence. The conformity studies have, by and large, concentrated on stability between persons, i.e. inter-individual consistency. The majority starts out with numbers on its side and the extent of their unanimity appears to dictate the extent of their influence. Most of the available literature (Asch, 1956; Rosenberg, 1961; Goldberg, 1954), indicates that conformity may increase as the number in the majority increases from 1 to 2 to 3 but, thereafter, increases in size appear to make little difference. Thus, size appears not to be a determining factor of the power of conformity. Unanimity, on the other hand, appears to be highly important.

In Asch's early studies (1955), the power of the majority was found to be broken by the presence of a dissenter in addition to the naive subject. In one variation, this supporter was another naive subject; in a second variation, a confederate who was instructed to give correct answers throughout the trials was the supporter. In both these conditions, the amount of conformity manifested by the naive subject was reduced to one fourth. However, other conditions pointed to the fact that it was not social support *per se* which reduced the impact of the majority but, rather, the fact that the majority position was broken, i.e. there was a break in unanimity. In one condition, this break was created by a confederate who gave incorrect answers, but in-between the naive subject and the incorrect majority; in another condition, this confederate gave even more incorrect answers than the majority. Both conditions led to decreased conformity; in fact, the extreme dissenter led to even greater reduction in conformity, the errors dropping to only 9%. Asch concluded that "dissent *per se* increased independence and moderated the errors that occurred, and that the direction of dissent exerted consistent effects" (p. 34).

We are assuming that the stability of the position proposed by the majority is lessened when there is a break in the judgements offered by others. In contrast to a unanimous majority, the presence of another individual who disagrees with the majority, whether or not he/she agrees with oneself, serves to lessen the likelihood that a stable consensus will revolve around the majority position. Thus, subjects may be more likely to maintain their own opinion.

Even greater evidence for such a contention comes from other conditions manipulated by Asch. The desertion of a social supporter appears to heighten the likelihood of conformity. In one experiment, Asch had a confederate support the subject's correct position for six trials; on the seventh trial, this supporter joined the majority. Conformity abruptly increased after the six trials, reaching a level close to the condition where the individual was faced with a unanimous majority throughout the trials.

Indeed, we suspect that the fact of desertion may have been additionally useful to the majority since it may have added credence to the majority position. Asch was surprised that the six trials of social support did not "strengthen the individuals' independence" (p. 34). It appears that it did when one considers the fact that when the social supporter simply left the room (rather than deserting the subject) "the partner's effect outlasted his presence" (p. 34). Thus, it may well be that desertion was even more potent for conformity than a pre-existing unanimous majority since one had to overcome the conformity of one's own judgement achieved during the period of support. We would hypothesize that desertion adds credence to the majority position and, in addition, reflects adversely on the minority position. Further, it makes even clearer that a consensus revolving around the majority position is likely to be stable.

In minority influence, the emphasis has been not so much on inter-individual consistency but rather intra-individual consistency. Available data show that minority influence is rarely evident on early trials or early moments in a discussion; in fact, the deviant or minority is usually the subject of derision, particularly in these early moments. Asch (1952) reports laughter when an individual made incorrect judgements in disagreement with a group of 16 naive subjects. Schacter (1951) reports that most communication is directed toward the deviant in an attempt to change his/her mind; when unsuccessful, the majority responds by rejecting the person sociometrically. In one of our own studies (Nemeth and Wachtler, 1974), naive subjects laughed at and ridiculed a confederate who maintained a position of low compensation in a personal injury case. One naive subject threatened him with physical harm in order to illustrate the "pain and suffering" involved in the case.

Not only is the minority not initially effective nor compelling but it is precisely its behavior over time, the orchestration and patterning of its verbal and nonverbal cues in the presentation of its position, that appears to render it effective. The most important aspect of this patterning and representation of position appears to be consistency, the maintenance of position over time.

It is this intra-individual consistency, the stability of the position being promoted that is necessary, though not always sufficient, for minority influence. Moscovici et al. (1969), demonstrated that a minority of two who repeatedly stated that they saw "green" to blue slides were followed 8.42% of the time. A minority of two who said "green" on 2/3 of the slides and "blue" on 1/3 of the slides was ineffective, i.e. the naive subjects judged the stimuli as "blue". Subsequent studies (e.g. Nemeth et al., 1974), demonstrated that repetition per se was not a prerequisite for minority influence but that the perception that the minority had a position in which it was fully convinced was such a prerequisite. In their study, responses of "blue-green" on half the trials and "green" on half the trials led to a significant amount of minority influence when the responses were patterned with a property of the stimulus. When unpatterned, i.e. random, the perception was one of inconsistency and no influence was exerted. In fact, the "correlated" conditions were as effective as a repetitive "blue-green" response and significantly more effective than a repetitive "green" response. The important part of the minority's behavioral style appeared to lie in the perception that they had a consistent position, one that was stable and one in which they were convinced. Such perceptions can be fostered by more subtle behavior than repetition. Again, however, it appears that a process where the consensus revolves around the minority position requires that the minority position be stable, i.e. consistent, over time.

Other evidence is consistent with such a formulation. If one analyzes the process of minority influence over time, it becomes clear that the "break" in the majority is an aid to the position promoted by the minority. We suggest that this creates the perception that concensus revolving around the minority position is likely to be more stable than that revolving around the majority position. Repeatedly, our data show a "group effect". The naive subjects constituting the majority are more like each other than they are like members of another majority. In addition, we find a "first half/last half" main effect for influence data. Descriptively, the process appears to be one of derision of the minority during early trials; if the minority maintains its position, a member of the majority may then show doubt or, more importantly, change his position in the direction of the minority; when this happens, the process appears to "snowball", i.e. other members of the majority start to change their position in the direction of the initial minority.

Thus, we suggest that each faction needs to, firstly, consistently maintain its position over time and, secondly, maintain the agreement of its members. At one level, this requires resistance to the others' influence attempts. At another level, it requires the active promotion of one's position.

The preceding point finds support in a study we conducted using natural majorities and minorities (Nemeth, 1977). In that study, we pretested individuals on a criminal case involving a charge of first degree murder and from those individuals who indicated a clear opinion of "guilty" or "not guilty", we invited participation such that the first ballot would split 4:2. In half of the groups, the minority believed "not guilty"; in the other half of the groups, the minority believed "guilty".

This study was conducted with reference to a recent US Supreme Court decision regarding the allowance of non-unanimity for jury verdicts. Very briefly, both Oregon and Louisiana allow for non-unanimous verdicts and two suits were brought against these states by individuals convicted by less than unanimous verdicts. The legal basis was the alleged violation of the defendants' constitutional rights under the Fourteenth Amendment of the US Constitution. "Due process" and "equal protection under the law" were the key concepts invoked.

In ruling on this issue, the Supreme Court split 5:4. Five Justices ruled that allowance of non-unanimity did not violate the constitutional rights of a defendant whereas four Justices dissented from this decision. However, since the Supreme Court is ruled by majority decision, the five Justices prevailed. The difference in opinion on this case involved theories of social influence, of interactions between majorities and minorities in a decision making situation. These theories and our data relevant to this decision can be found in Nemeth (1977) and Nemeth et al. (1976).

Very briefly, all the Justices were concerned that there be full and just consideration of all viewpoints, majority and minority opinions. The Court opinion (five Justices) was that the majority would not impose its will on a minority whose votes it did not need for a verdict as long as the minority had reasoned arguments in support of its position. The four dissenting Justices feared such imposition of will, arguing that safeguards were necessary. Further, they concerned themselves with whether or not the deliberation would be as robust if unanimity were not required.

Our study of this issue involved the variation of majority v. unanimity instructions and created groups that had four majority and two minority opinions present. In addition, we conducted a study utilizing a set of simulated trials in an actual courtroom with a judge presiding, witnesses appearing, etc. These involved both civil and criminal cases and the 12 person "jury" was randomly split into two groups of six, one deliberating to unanimity, the other being required to reach at least a majority vote.

While the specific legal issues and the issue revolving around the majority/unanimity requirement are less pertinent here, the influence processes evolving between majority and minority are pertinent. Lest the work on minority influence create the perception that minorities are as effective as majorities, we should be reminded that most decisions go in the direction of the initial majority. Kalven and Zeisel's (1966) classic work comparing judge and jury decisions pointed out that over 90% of the final jury verdicts are in the direction of the position held by a majority of jurors on the first ballot. Our own study showed very similar results. In the courtroom simulations, every group, whether majority or unanimity instructed, whether deliberating a criminal or civil case, came to a verdict in the direction of the position held by a majority of the jurors at first ballot.

The only place where minority influence was evidenced was in the experimental setting, particularly when the minority took the position of "not guilty" on the case involving first degree murder. That experiment involved 37 groups deliberating the same case and, as can be seen from Table 1, the minority occasionally prevailed when they argued "not guilty".

TABLE 1

|  | Minority "win" | Majority "win" | Hung |
|---|---|---|---|
| Minority "not guilty" Majority "guilty" | 7 | 7 | 5 |
| Minority "guilty" Majority "not guilty" | 1 | 16 | 1 |

From Nemeth (1977).

Even though it is only when the majority held the position of "guilty" and the minority held the position of "not guilty" that we can compare a "majority win" v. a "minority win" in this study, some of the data are suggestive. Each of the deliberation tapes was coded in terms of who talked, to whom it was addressed and the nature of the comment as determined by Bales categories.

By reanalyzing these data in terms of what categories were initiated by majority v. minority members in groups where the minority prevailed v. where the majority prevailed, the direction of the means indicates that the "winning faction" made more comments in the categories of friendliness (1), dramatization (2), agreement (3), giving suggestions (4), giving opinions (5), giving information (6), and disagreement (10). The "winning faction" gave fewer comments in the categories of asking for opinions (8), showing tension release (11), and interruptions or showing unfriendliness (12). While these means are not significantly different from one another, partly because of a small sample size and high variability, the systematic patterns are suggestive that the winning faction is one that exhibits a relatively larger number of comments in the fairly active and forceful categories and fewer comments that are ingratiating. In keeping with this pattern, there is a fairly clear tendency for the losing faction to receive more opinions and information.

As could be predicted from the pattern illustrated above it was also the case that the winning faction uttered more comments in general than the losing faction. Consistent with this finding is one piece of data which we found particularly revealing since it argues that not just "talk' *per se* but active argument in defense of a given position is a predictor of influence.

In the above referenced jury study, we used a procedure derivative of Hoffmann and Maier (1964), known as "valence" in which we coded every comment in terms of whether it was pro-prosecution or pro-defence. When we cumulated the comments for "guilty" and "not guilty" respectively, regardless of who uttered the comments, we found that *when the difference between such sums exceeded 7, all but one of the 37 groups' verdicts could be predicted.* Thus, predictions of outcome were made on the basis of number of comments uttered in the promotion of a particular position, not on the number of people making such comments. This meant that the minority needed to utter twice as many comments each in order to "stay even". The active promotion of a position by the minority where their total number of comments equalled or exceeded those of the majority was related to the eventual success of the minority position.

With the data repeatedly indicating the importance of maintenance of position as well as active argumentation in support of one's position, be that of the majority or the minority, the question then arises as to how such passive resistance and active persuasion can be achieved. Most of the studies have used confederates in order to assess behavioral styles and the importance of unanimity. Our recent studies corroborate such conclusions even when the majorities or minorities are "natural" factions, i.e. all are naive subjects who have different positions.

Most factions do not, however, operate in a vacuum. Many have opportunities for discussion among themselves, and some recent evidence on the polarization phenomenon suggests an interesting way of achieving greater confidence by one or the other faction as well as, we hypothesize, creating a greater psychological sense of belonging to a "group". It amounts to simply giving a faction the opportunity for discussion with each other.

One of the more interesting and replicable phenomenon that has been researched by social psychologists recently is this polarization process. While, originally, attention was addressed to the "risky shift" and the search was to understand greater risk taking, it soon became clear that the risky shift was an example of a more general process, i.e. polarization. As a recent comprehensive review (Myers and Lamm, 1976) suggests, the findings have been quite consistent for issues as diverse as jury decision, ethical decisions, judgements, person perception, negotiations and risk taking. The phenomenon is that "the postgroup response will tend to be more extreme in the same direction as the average of the pregroup responses" (Myers and Lamm, 1967, p. 603). One of the reasons given for such a polarization phenomenon is that discussion with like-minded others increases certainty; another reason is that subjects may moderate their initial viewpoints in anticipation of opposing viewpoints from others (Walker and Main, 1973); still another reason is that "the reciprocal influences of members on one another reinforce and strengthen extant orientations" (Feldman and Newcomb, 1969, p. 223).

It should be pointed out, however, that not all studies conducted show the polarization phenomenon. Some studies show nonsignificant changes in the expected direction. Others show changes in an opposite direction to that predicted. For example, Myers and Bach (1974) show separated pacifistic and militaristic subjects became more pacifistic after discussion with like-minded individuals. Yet, the overwhelming evidence is consistent with the polarization hypothesis even across many different kinds of judgement situations.

Utilizing this phenomenon, we hypothesize that if prior discussion by a given faction, be that a majority or minority opinion, leads to polarization and increased confidence of opinion, such prior discussion should cause both maintenance of position and increased activity in the promotion of such a position when the two factions are brought together for a decision. In addition, we hypothesize that such prior discussion increases the psychological sense of belonging to a faction, a sub-group. As such, individuals may be even more reluctant to change in their own opinion since they may perceive such a change as leaving a group, perhaps even leaving a "cause". Though for a different reason, such views should increase the unanimity and maintenance of position and ultimately, we would hypothesize, influence.

If the above process ensues as a result of prior discussion, it should be manifested in the ultimate decision reached. Thus, if the minority is given an opportunity for prior discussion while the majority does not have this opportunity, the minority should resist conformity and argue its own position with more confidence. Thus, we would predict that the resulting decision should be more in the direction of the minority. Similarly, where the majority has prior discussion and the minority does not, the decision should be more in the direction of the majority. If both are given an opportunity for prior discussion or if neither are given such an opportunity, the verdict (decision) should be in-between. However, we would also predict some differences between the "both" and "neither" conditions.

Though both involve equality of the factions, at least where prior discussion is concerned, we would expect the "neither" condition to reach a decision more easily than the "both" condition. With greater committment created by prior discussion may come an unwillingness to compromise or change. Thus, we would predict that when neither are given the prior discussion opportunity, there will be a greater number of decisions reached; the "both" condition should "hang" more often. However, we would not predict any differences in the decision reached, if they reached a decision, between the "both" and "neither" conditions.

During this past year, we conducted exactly the study proposed above. While we had hoped to report the full results of this study for this conference, the data collection was only recently completed and only preliminary data analyses were available at the time of this writing. Let us first consider the procedures utilized for this study.

The procedure involved the pretesting of approximately 1200 undergraduates at the University of California, Berkeley on a series of four personal injury cases. Taking the case which gave the best bimodal split, we asked persons who indicated an opinion of either $100,000 or $200,000 to volunteer for an experiment on jury decision making. In fact, the largest number of subjects gave $200,000 as their position; the second mode of $100,000 involved half as many subjects. Participants were scheduled such that four persons would take the position of $200,000 and two persons would take the position of $100,000. By this method, we were able to

construct 40 groups of six persons each. Ten were run in each of
four conditions described below.

Upon meeting in a common room, the four representing the
$200,000 position were taken to one room and the two representing
the $100,000 position were taken to another room. None knew the
positions of the other subjects at this point. Depending on the
condition, the factions were either instructed to discuss the case,
exploring their views, for 15 minutes or they were asked to simply
wait for around 15 minutes while the experiment was being set up.
The latter were asked not to discuss anything with one another. In
one condition (minority only), the minority discussed the case and
the majority waited; in a second (majority only), the majority
discussed the case and the minority waited; in a third (both), both
discussed the case; and in a fourth condition (neither), neither were
allowed discussion. At the end of this waiting/discussion period,
subjects completed a very short questionnaire basically asking for
their private judgement and confidence ratings.

All subjects were then placed in a third room and asked to
deliberate the case as a jury. They were instructed to deliberate for
a maximum of 35 minutes and to reach a unanimous verdict of
compensation in the personal injury case. These discussions were
videotaped. Upon reaching a verdict (or 35 minutes discussion),
subjects were then asked to complete a rather lengthy questionnaire
on perceptions of the process and impressions of each individual.
What follows is only a preliminary analysis of the data since the data
was coded only a week prior to this writing.

Originally, we had expected that "prior discussion" would cause
the minority to take a position of $100,000 or less and the majority
to take a position of $200,000 or more and for the factions to feel
increased confidence in their position. As Table 2 points out, it
appears that prior discussion did not make the factions more
extreme in their judgement. All subjects appear to have increased
the amount of compensation they thought to be proper from that
reported on the pretest. However, prior discussion does seem to
affect the degree of confidence that each faction has in its own
position. As Table 3 points out, the minority faction that was
allowed prior discussion (the "minority only" and the "both"
conditions), appears to be more confident than a minority faction
not allowed discussion (the "majority only" and the "neither"
conditions). Similarly, the majority faction allowed discussion

TABLE 2

*Private position after prior discussion*

|                   | Minority only | Majority only | Both    | Neither | $\bar{X}$ |
|-------------------|---------------|---------------|---------|---------|-----------|
| Minority subjects | 114 150       | 115 000       | 116 800 | 118 400 | 116 088   |
| Majority subjects | 213 475       | 224 250       | 216 775 | 184 650 | 212 288   |

TABLE 3

*Confidence[a] of private position after prior discussion*

|                   | Minority only | Majority only | Both | Neither | $\bar{X}$ |
|-------------------|---------------|---------------|------|---------|-----------|
| Minority subjects | 2.2           | 3.3           | 2.2  | 2.7     | 2.6       |
| Majority subjects | 1.8           | 1.2           | 1.7  | 2.3     | 1.8       |

[a]Confidence is rated on a seven-point scale with 1 being "very confident" and 7 being "very unconfident".

(the "majority only" and "both" conditions), appears more confident than the majority faction not allowed discussion (the "minority only" and "neither" conditions).

With regard to the final verdict, our hypothesis that the "both" and "neither" conditions would differ as to the number of decisions reached appears to have been borne out. As noted in Table 4, the "both" condition leads to the most "hung" juries. It is closely followed by the "minority only" condition. On the other hand, most decisions are made when the majority had prior discussion but the minority did not. As will be noted from Table 3, this is also the condition where the majority appears most confident and the minority least confident, possibly the reason why verdicts were reached, usually in the direction of the majority.

The amount of compensation agreed upon by those groups which

TABLE 4

*Number of verdicts reached*

|                                                | Minority only | Majority only | Both    | Neither |
|------------------------------------------------|---------------|---------------|---------|---------|
| Verdicts                                       | 4             | 8             | 3       | 6       |
| Hung                                           | 6             | 2             | 7       | 4       |
| Compensation by groups which did reach agreement | 187 000       | 184 375       | 200 000 | 187 333 |

did reach consensus is less straightforward. As can be observed in Table 4, the amount of compensation does not appear to differ greatly as a result of discussion opportunities. However, it would be premature to speculate on these findings since they are based on very specific groups and await a finer analysis of questionnaire data as well as the coding of interactions between majority and minority members.

In this study, we are asking for a high degree of regularity in the influence processes and the hypotheses require a tracking that is contingent on previous dependent variables. We assumed polarization of opinion in terms of amount of compensation considered appropriate as a function of discussion opportunities. The data, however, indicate an increase in "compensation judgement" for both majority and minority individuals. This may be due to the fact that there is a value on higher compensation for victims of personal injury and the ethical considerations may have come into play during discussion. We also predicted greater confidence in whatever position was taken as a result of discussion opportunities. This appears to be borne out by the data. The factions allowed prior discussion appear to be more confident of their judgements.

The important link in this process, however, is that such increased confidence should manifest itself in behavioral styles that create the perceptions of consistency and confidence. It should also manifest itself in resistance to the persuasion tactics of the other faction. These will have to be tested by an analysis of the interaction patterns on our videotapes. It is the styles of interaction that should provide an understanding of why a decision is reached or not and the direction of the decision when agreement is reached.

While our hypotheses are relatively straightforward, it is undoubtedly clear to those working with natural majorities and minorities in interaction that the processes are very complex. Even if our premises concerning the importance of resistance and active argument are correct, and even if our premises concerning the efficacy of prior discussion for the manipulation of confidence are correct, it still may be that increased confidence does not always manifest itself in appropriate behavioral styles. It is the tracking of this process that is our greatest challenge.

As a starting point, I believe that the principles of stability are an appropriate way to view the influence patterns of majorities and minorities. In so doing, however, we have concentrated on the similarities in the processes of conformity and minority influence, of compromise and polarization. Yet, faction size or, more appropriately, the notion of being in a majority v. a minority does have consequences as we ourselves have pointed out. Our data may well remind us that the processes are different for our two factions and that the decision making process is, once again, more complex, than our theories.

## References

Asch, S. E. *Social Psychology*. Englewood Cliffs, N. J.: Prentice-Hall, 1952.

Asch, S. E. Opinions and social pressure. *Scientific American*, 1955, 193, 31–35.

Asch, S. E. Studies of independence and conformity: A minority of one against a unanimous majority. *Psychological Monographs*, 1956, 7, (9, Whole No. 416).

Deutsch, M. and Gerard, H. B. A study of normative and informational social influences upon individual judgement. *Journal of Abnormal and Social Psychology*, 1955, 51, 629–636.

Feldman, K. A. and Newcomb, T. *The impact of college on students*. San Francisco: Jossey-Bass, 1969.

Goldberg, S. C. Three situational determinants of conformity to social norms. *Journal of Abnormal and Social Psychology*, 1954, 49, 325–329.

Hoffman, R. and Naier, Norman, R. F. Valence in the adoption of solutions by problem-solving groups: Concept, method and results. *Journal of Abnormal and Social Psychology*, 1964, 69, 264–271.

Kalven, Harry Jr. and Zeisel, Hans. *The American Jury*. Boston: Little, Brown & Co., 1966.

Moscovici, S., Lage, E. and Naffrechoux, M. Influence on a consistent minority on the responses of a majority in a color perception task. *Sociometry*, 1969, 32, 365–380.

Myers, D. G. and Lamm, H. The group polarization phenomenon. *Psychological Bulletin*, 1976, 83, 602–627.

Nemeth, C. A comparison between conformity and minority influence. Paper presented to International Congress on Psychology, Paris, France, July 1976.

Nemeth, C. Interactions between jurors as a function of majority v. unanimity decision rules. *Journal of Applied Social Psychology*, 1977, 7, 38–56.

Nemeth, C. The role of an active minority in inter-group conflict. In W. G. Austin and S. Worchel (Eds) *The Psychology of Intergroup Relations*. Belmong, Cal.: Brooks-Cole Publishing Co., 1978, in press.

Nemeth, C. and Wachtler, J. Creating the perceptions of consistency and confidence: A necessary condition for minority influence. *Sociometry*, 1974, 37, 529–540.

Nemeth, C. and Wachtler, J. Creative problem solving as a function of majority vs minority influence. Submitted to *Journal of Personality and Social Psychology*, 1981.

Nemeth, C., Swedlund, M. and Kanki, B. Patterning of the minority's responses and their influence on the majority. *European Journal of Social Psychology*, 1974, 4, 53–64.

Nemeth, C., Endicott, J. and Wachtler, J. From the '50s to the '70s: Women in jury deliberations. *Sociometry*, 1976, 39, 293—304.

Rosenberg, L. A. Group size, prior experience and conformity. *Journal of Abnormal and Social Psychology*, 1961, 63, 436—437.

Schacter, S. Deviation, rejection and communication. *Journal of Abnormal and Social Psychology*, 1951, 46, 190—207.

Walker, T. G. and Main, E. C. Choice-shifts in political decision making: Federal judges and civil liberties cases. *Journal of Applied Social Psychology*, 1973, 2, 39—48.

# 9
# Group Decision under Uncertainty: Group Structure and the Shift Phenomenon

Zoltán Kovács

In past years, several experiments have been directed toward particular aspects of human information processing and the characteristic methods used to eliminate uncertainty. According to Hogarth (1974), the basic characteristics of human information processing are the following: (1) human perception of information is not comprehensive but selective; (2) simplifying cognitive mechanisms (heuristic methods) are frequently used; (3) man is not able to integrate great quantities of information and he is therefore forced to process information sequentially.

Recently, research has focused on the discovery and examination of those simplifying cognitive mechanisms which are the typical methods used to eliminate uncertainty. According to Tversky and Kahnemann (1973), the characteristics of probabilistic judgements can be derived from three heuristic methods appearing regularly in the process of making judgements: "representativeness," "availability," and "anchoring and adjustment." Cohen et al. (1969) have demonstrated experimentally that when subjects had to choose from among segments of a field of equal (objective) probabilities they tried to structure the fields by considering some parts more probable than others. On the basis of several experiments, Engländer (1976) concluded that subjects ascribe a deterministic role to certain structural characteristics. Their probability assessments were significantly influenced by the spatial and temporal traits of the field of events, which are in a normative sense irrelevant.

These conclusions are very convincing in view of the empirical data, but are subject to the condition that the subject will make a decision or is forced to make one. These experiments do not allow choices which are frequent in everyday life, such as avoiding a decision or avoiding individual decision. Very often one has to decide in a group situation under great uncertainty; in these cases, even when the decision is individual, the influence of the group cannot be excluded. A social environment is thought to eliminate uncertainty, and there are certain groups which are created for just this reason (juries, committees, and so on). The implicit or explicit aim is to increase reliability by eliminating uncertainty. Can groups comply with this requirement? Though for decades group performance has been a popular research area, neither experimental social psychology nor decision-theory research can give a definite answer to this question. The main reason for this may well be the fact that the approach of most workers in this field is normative: the main aim is to evaluate group products, to determine the additivity combinatorial rules of individual responses, and so on. Research in this field is thoroughly discussed by Davis (1969) and Seaver (1976).

Group performance can be examined from another perspective as well. The main aim of this approach is not to evaluate but to discover the special traits and characteristic features of group performance. Among the research results of the past 10–15 years, findings concerning the "risky-shift" phenomenon fall into line with this approach. As is already well-known, characteristic differences are shown in individual and group answers given to the so-called "Choice Dilemmas Questionnaire". (1) When subjects are asked to decide first which of two alternatives to choose individually, then within a group, and finally individually again, the average of the second individual decisions shows a greater inclination toward risk than the average of the preliminary individual decisions. (2) In most cases, group decision results in a riskier alternative being chosen than the average of preliminary decisions by members of the group. This phenomenon has been demonstrated in various situations, and the literature has already been discussed in detail (Cartwright, 1971; Dion *et al.,* 1970; Vinokur, 1971; Moscovici and Lecuyer, 1972; Myers and Lamm, 1976). The results of many experimental studies suggest that it would be better to speak in general of the "shift-phenomenon" because, beside risky shifts, so-called cautious shifts can be detected in certain test items. Both Moscovici and Myers and Lamm attempt to emphasize the occurrence of shifts in different situations by speaking of group polarization. Despite the widespread research effort in connection with this phenomenon the underlying principles which would explain and describe the ubiquitousness and development of the shift mechanism is yet to be discovered.

Two hypotheses repeatedly occur in the shift literature. The first considers the shift as a social motivation induced by interpersonal comparison (this may be called an hypothesis of the source effect). According to the second hypothesis, the cause of a shift is the special way a group handles information; the shift is explained as a cognitive learning process (and this may be called an hypothesis of the message effect). Some researchers (Davis, 1973; Zajonc *et al.*, 1972) try to predict the shift-phenomenon by certain social decision schemes (mainly the majority-rule), particularly when the greater part of pregroup preferences converge to one point (this may be called an hypothesis of the effect of the process).

Myers and Lamm (1976) examined the validity of these three hypotheses in a review of the literature. Summarizing arguments for and against the different theoretical positions, they developed an explanatory model in which a shift is the result of the interaction of the factors described by the above three hypotheses. From these hypotheses the existence of the shift can be predicted and we can identify some factors influencing the degree of the shift.

The experiments of Myers and Aronson (1972) using the "Choice-dilemma Questionnaire" show that there is a close connection between the risk-level of pregroup response and the degree of the shift. Items which elicit high-risk initial tendencies generally produce shifts toward the high-risk extreme after discussion. Consequently, a high degree of certainty (as defined by population consensus) induces a further increase of certainty.

The degree of shift is also influenced by group composition. Vidmar (1972) compared the decisions of highly dogmatic groups with those by groups with members low in dogmatism. According to his findings, the former groups arrived at decisions which were more extreme and severe than those of the latter groups, even though prior decisions of dogmatic and less dogmatic individuals did not differ significantly.

Laughlin and Izzett (1973) found shifts in groups of people having similar attitudes, but not in the case of people having different attitudes. These data relate to the connection between group-homogeneity and the shift. Rarely are groups in everyday life as thoroughly homogeneous as in an experimental situation. Naturally-occurring groups are mostly heterogeneous: the pregroup preferences of their members held with different degrees of certainty.

An important question is whether the degree of within group heterogenity influences the degree of shift. Can a similar degree of shift be expected in groups where the uncertainty-level of pregroup responses differs slightly as those in which certainty differs a great deal? An example of such groups might be those in which, say, half of the members are extremely uncertain while the other half are extremely certain.

To answer this question, it is necessary to create an experimental situation in which both the decision uncertainty of group members and the division of uncertainty among the group members are variable. This is possible by considering the supply of information available to each group member.

In a given group consisting of $n$ members, the information necessary for performing some task must be introduced as many times as there are members of the group. In this case, every person will receive all necessary information; thus, there are theoretically no persons who are uncertain. Consequently, if the necessary information is introduced less than $n$ times, there would be persons lacking either all or a part of the information that is needed for performing the task. In such cases, the existing information could be distributed among the group members in many ways; thus different patterns of uncertainty among group members may exist at the outset.

Within the same group, some members may have all the information while others have no information at all, but it is also possible that all members receive the same or varying amounts of the necessary information. In such cases the group-output is hypothesized to be influenced by two factors simultaneously: (1) the decision-uncertainty of group members (uncertainty in approaching the task); (2) the pattern of information-distribution within the group, defining the uncertainty of the group as a whole (therefore, called structural uncertainty).

## Experiment

### STIMULI

We elaborated two experimental problems:

(1) *Murder task.* The subjects received a short record of evidence on a fictitious murder: a woman engineer who headed a Mongolian

TABLE 1

*The relationship between criteria and suspects in the "murder task"*

| Suspects | Criteria | | | | | | | |
|---|---|---|---|---|---|---|---|---|
| | 1 | 2 | 3 | 4 | 5 | 6 | 7 | 8 |
| $A_1$ | + | − | + | + | + | + | − | + |
| $A_2$ | + | + | + | + | + | − | − | − |
| $A_3$ | + | + | − | − | − | + | + | − |

TABLE 2

*The relationship between criteria and islands for the "treasure hunt task"*

| Island | Criteria | | | | |
|---|---|---|---|---|---|
| | 1 | 2 | 3 | 4 | 5 |
| $A_1$ | + | + | − | + | + |
| $A_2$ | + | + | + | − | − |
| $A_3$ | + | + | + | − | − |

delegation to Hungary was found dead in her hotel room. She was probably murdered. From the record it can be inferred that the detectives have eight criteria by which to decide who the murderer is. They suspect three persons: $A_1$, $A_2$, and $A_3$; six, five and four criteria fit the respective suspects.

Results of the investigations are available; they contain some facts which explicitly meet the criteria for the suspect in question and some which do not. The material also contains data irrelevant to the investigation (age, marital status, character, poise, and so on). The task is to estimate the probability of $A_1$, $A_2$ and $A_3$ being the murderer, assuming that one and only one of the three was the person who committed the murder.

(2) *Treasure hunt task.* The subjects received a fictitious map of an island. The map is alleged to be several hundred years old. It is known that in the 17th century a boat full of treasure sank near the island, but part of the ship's cargo was saved and hidden in a cave. The difficulty in finding this treasure is that the name of the island does not appear on the map. In the course of previous searches, the number of possible islands was reduced to three. Certain data available on these islands makes it possible to guess the identity of the island shown on the map. According to the data, four characteristics of the first island ($A_1$), three of the second ($A_2$), and two of the

third $(A_3)$ match the five characteristics that can be obtained from the map. The task is to estimate with what probability the treasure would be found on the different islands.

PROCEDURE

Subjects solved the problems in groups of four. First, they received the story of the murder or the map. When they understood the task, the evidence on the three suspects or the information about the three islands was played to each subject separately from a tape-recorder through earphones (they were allowed to take notes).

There were two different recordings for each task. In one case, noise was added to the recording where information necessary for the solution was presented (denoted as $B$). In the other case, noise was also added as in the first recording but not where relevant data were presented (marked $T$). Members of the experimental groups of four received one or the other recording according to the scheme shown in Table 3. Of the many possible combinations for groups of four, we chose four for each experiment.

The subjects were asked first to make an individual estimate of the probability based on the written and tape-recorded text (they were allowed to use their notes), and then to make a unanimous group decision after discussion. Finally, after the group decision everyone was again individually asked to give his opinion of the probabilities. The time for discussion was not limited, and the whole discussion was recorded by hidden video cameras.

Sixty engineers (aged 28–35) were involved in the experiment. At the time of the experiment, they were in their first year of the three-year-long postgraduate correspondence course of the Technical

TABLE 3

*The scheme according to which members of the experimental groups received one or the other recording*

| Scheme | | | Probabilities | | Entropy |
|---|---|---|---|---|---|
| $A_1$ | $A_2$ | $A_3$ | $p_B$ | $p_T$ | $H$ |
| $B$ | $B$ | $B$ | 1.000 | 0.000 | 0 |
| $B$ | $B$ | $T$ | 0.667 | 0.333 | 0.918 |
| $T$ | $B$ | $B$ | 0.333 | 0.667 | 0.918 |
| $B$ | $T$ | $T$ | 0.333 | 0.667 | 0.918 |
| $T$ | $B$ | $T$ | 0.333 | 0.667 | 0.918 |
| $T$ | $T$ | $B$ | 0.333 | 0.667 | 0.918 |
| $T$ | $T$ | $T$ | 1.000 | 0.000 | 0 |

TABLE 4

*Experimental plan by group type and member for each task*

| Task | Member | I | | | II | | | III | | | IV | | |
|---|---|---|---|---|---|---|---|---|---|---|---|---|---|
| | | $A_1$ | $A_2$ | $A_3$ | $A_1$ | $A_2$ | $A_3$ | $A_1$ | $A_2$ | $A_3$ | $A_1$ | $A_2$ | $A_3$ |
| First | $x_1$ | B | T | T | B | B | B | B | T | T | T | T | T |
| task | $x_2$ | T | B | B | B | T | T | T | T | T | B | B | B |
| (murder) | $x_3$ | B | T | T | T | B | T | B | B | B | T | T | T |
| | $x_4$ | T | B | B | T | T | B | T | B | B | B | B | B |
| Second | $x_1$ | T | T | B | B | B | B | T | T | B | T | T | T |
| task | $x_2$ | B | B | T | T | T | B | T | T | T | B | B | B |
| (treasure | $x_3$ | T | T | B | T | B | T | B | B | B | T | T | T |
| hunt) | $x_4$ | B | B | T | B | T | T | B | B | T | B | B | B |

University in Budapest. Every subject took part in the solution of both problems (the order was not fixed) in such a way that in the second task the information-conveying scheme, the type of the group, and the members in the group were all different. Thus, we managed to form a group type in both experiments other than those in Table 4 (control group), the members of which received information in the scheme *TTT*. Thus, we obtained six experimental groups of each type in both tasks, i.e. 60 experimental groups in all. However, when analysing the results we took into consideration only the data of five groups of each type (50 groups) because the others could not be evaluated in every respect due mostly to the bad quality of the video-recording.

*Principal experimental measures*
In both tasks, the goal of the subjects and the groups was to evaluate the probabilities of given alternatives. The only objective basis for doing so was the number of criteria fitting each alternative. Let $i$ be the index of the alternatives in the experiment, $i = 1, 2, \ldots, n$, and $j$ be the index of the criterion in relation to the alternatives, $j = 1, 2, \ldots, m$ (accordingly, each alternative can be identified).
    Let

$$X_{i,j} = \begin{cases} 0, & \text{if the } j\text{-th criterion does not fit the } i\text{-th alternative,} \\ 1, & \text{when it does.} \end{cases}$$

If there is more than one alternative corresponding to a given criterion, $j$, then we say that theoretically the alternatives will be chosen with equal probabilities. That is,

$$P_{ij} = \begin{cases} 0, & \text{if } X_{i,j} = 0 \\ 1/\sum_{i=1}^{n} X_{i,j} & \text{if } X_{i,j} = 1. \end{cases}$$

The probability of the $i$-th alternative is given by

$$P(A_i) = \frac{\sum_{j=1}^{m} P_{ij}}{m}. \tag{1}$$

In this way the objective distribution of probabilities can be specified for both problems and the respective entropies can be calculated by the well-known formula:

$$H(X_r) = -\sum_{j} P(A_i) \log_2 P(A_i), \tag{2}$$

where $P(A_i)$ is the value of the $P_i$-th probability of the discrete distribution $A_i$ and where $X_r$ represents individual $r$ for one of the tasks. This is, of course, a theoretical value and there is no reason to suppose that pregroup, post-group or group responses will have this value as well. This need not be assumed even if every experimental group was purposely formed to allow two subjects each hear the $T$ and the $B$ recordings of each alternatives (see Table 4). In this way every group was equally informed.

According to the hypothesis of risky shift, one supposes that there will be a difference between the average entropy of pregroup responses and that of group responses, and also between the average entropy of pregroup responses and that of post-group responses.

Joint entropy of pregroup responses and that of post-group responses is calculated by the following equation:

$$H_k(X_1, X_2, X_3, X_4) = \sum_{r=1}^{4} H(X_r), \tag{3}$$

where $H_k$ is the joint entropy for group $k$. However, the aim of this experiment was to investigate whether the structural uncertainty of groups has any influence on the shift phenomenon. Therefore, it was necessary to determine the exact structural uncertainty of each group type. This was done, by Equation 3, on the basis of the entropies of Table 3, taking into account the combinations in Table 4. The values of structural uncertainty calculated for each group type are contained in Table 5.

TABLE 5

*Values of structural uncertainty for each group type*

| Group type | Structural uncertainty | |
|:---:|:---:|:---:|
| | Murder | Treasure hunt |
| I | 3.673 | 3.673 |
| II | 2.755 | 2.755 |
| III | 1.873 | 1.837 |
| IV | 0.000 | 0.000 |
| Control group | 0.000 | 0.000 |

TABLE 6

*Average pregroup, group, and post-group respones and percent differences for each group type on each task*

| Group type | Structural uncertainty | Pre-group | Group | Post-group | Average entropy Pregroup group difference in percent | Pregroup post-group difference in percent |
|:---|:---:|:---:|:---:|:---:|:---:|:---:|
| Murder | | | | | | |
| I | 3.67 | 4.16 | 4.61 | 4.49 | −10.8 | −7.9 |
| II | 2.75 | 3.84 | 4.10 | 3.82 | − 6.7 | +0.5 |
| III | 1.83 | 3.27 | 3.36 | 2.51 | − 2.7 | +23.2 |
| IV | 0.00 | 5.10 | 4.30 | 4.22 | +15.6 | +17.2 |
| Control groups | 0.00 | 3.98 | 2.62 | 2.94 | +34.1 | +26.1 |
| Treasure hunt | | | | | | |
| I | 3.67 | 4.20 | 3.97 | 3.59 | + 5.4 | +14.5 |
| II | 2.75 | 4.43 | 3.68 | 3.62 | +16.9 | +18.2 |
| III | 1.83 | 4.45 | 3.06 | 3.08 | +31.2 | +30.7 |
| IV | 0.00 | 3.99 | 1.95 | 1.46 | +51.1 | +63.4 |
| Control groups | 0.00 | 2.47 | 1.99 | 1.40 | +19.4 | +43.3 |

## Results and discussion

The average pregroup, post-group and group responses are shown in Table 6 according to structural uncertainty, along with the percentage differences of group responses and post-group responses from the average pregroup estimations.

## THE SHIFT-PHENOMENON

Within our data, the shift phenomenon can be detected both in the average group responses and in the average post-group individual responses. In most cases the shift phenomenon is reflected by a shift towards greater certainty (+), i.e. the entropy of the group responses as well as that of the post-group responses decreases. However, in the first task there is a negative shift in group-types I, II, and III where the structural uncertainty is greater, i.e. the average uncertainty of group responses is greater than that of pregroup responses. The average entropy of post-group individual responses of group-type I shows the same tendency. With regard to structural uncertainty, however, these cases are not basically different nor incompatible with the others. If all the above data are examined as a function of structural uncertainty similar trends can be found in both situations: as structural uncertainty decreases there is a gradual shift towards greater certainty of decision.

The question of this tendency manifesting itself in one situation as a diminishing increase of uncertainty and in the other case as a gradual increase of certainty requires, of course, some further explication. As the two problems were specifically created to differ on one important factor (i.e. entropy), it may be supposed that the divergence of the direction of shift in the two problems is caused by this factor. To explicate this point we should first estimate the theoretical probabilities for each alternative in task one. Calculated by Equation 1, they are: $P_1 = 0.49$, $P_2 = 0.29$, $P_3 = 0.22$. The

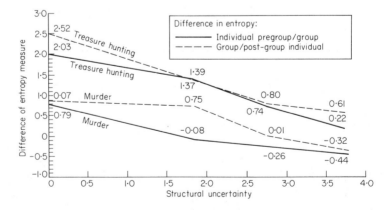

Fig. 1. Difference in entropy as a function of structural uncertainty.

entropy of the above calculated by Equation 2 is: $H = 1.5028$. The same values for the second task are: $P_1 = 0.57, P_2 = 0.27, P_3 = 0.16$ and $H = 1.3953$. Thus, subjects were facing greater entropy in the first task than in the second one. It appears, therefore, that the greater the uncertainty inherent in the task the less the resultant shift.

On the basis of the above, the following hypothesis can be formulated. The efficiency in eliminating uncertainty of the different groups is influenced by at least two factors: the uncertainty of decision within the task and the structural uncertainty caused by the distribution of uncertainty among the members of the group. From the experimental data it can be deduced that the above two factors — though probably not clearly separated in the psychological experience of the individual — influence separately the tendencies eliminating uncertainty. Increased structural uncertainty appears to hinder the activation of the simplifying cognitive mechanisms which accompany such decisions: it compels the group to make an effort in collecting and evaluating information. Increased information processing by the group results, in this experiment, in decreased shift (note that there is a limited pool of information available). Decreased structural uncertainty, on the other hand, gives the illusion of certainty of the answer and thus reinforces trends toward the strongest position, i.e. increased shift.

This supposition is supported by some further experimental data. The duration of discussions in both problem-situations gradually diminished as structural uncertainty decreased. This can be regarded both as one of the indicators of the uncertainty of decision of the group members and as the sign of a decrease in effort. Table 8 shows how many times on the average groups of different structural uncertainty repeated the criteria necessary to form a judgement. As can be seen, the number of repetitions decreases with structural uncertainty. These data relate to those on duration but the distribution in percentages of the criteria for each alternative itself indicates that our hypothesis is correct. As structural certainty increases, the experimental groups tend to repeat more often arguments for the most probable alternative (marked $A_1$); as shown by the earlier data, this causes an increase in the value of the estimated probabilities and a decrease in the entropy value of the probability distribution.

Regarding decision uncertainty, it is less clear why the results

occur; it can only now be concluded that increased decision uncertainty appears to induce decreased shift.

## Summary

The analysis of our experimental data lead to the formulation of the
hypothesis that structural uncertainty of groups influences the

TABLE 7

*Duration of discussion and structural uncertainty by group types for each task*

| Task | Group type | Structural uncertainty | Duration in minutes |
|------|-----------|------------------------|---------------------|
| Murder | I | 3.67 | 16.3 |
| | II | 2.75 | 14.6 |
| | III | 1.83 | 12 12.2 |
| | IV | 0.00 | 10.2 |
| | Control groups | 0.00 | 9.7 |
| Treasure hunt | I | 3.67 | 15.2 |
| | II | 2.75 | 12.9 |
| | III | 1.83 | 8.3 |
| | IV | 0.00 | 10.5 |
| | Control groups | 0.00 | 13.2 |

TABLE 8

*Average frequency with which groups of various types on each task repeat the
criteria necessary to form a judgement*

| Task | Group type | Structural uncertainty | Criteria repetition, sum | Distribution of criteria repeated in percent | | |
|------|-----------|------------------------|--------------------------|--------------------------------------------|--|--|
| | | | | $A_1$ | $A_2$ | $A$ |
| Murder | I | 3.67 | 30 | 36 | 30 | 3 |
| | II | 2.75 | 25 | 34 | 30 | 3 |
| | III | 1.83 | 22 | 40 | 33 | 2 |
| | IV | 0.00 | 19 | 45 | 27 | 2 |
| | Control groups | 0.00 | 16 | 56 | 26 | 1 |
| Treasure hunt | I | 3.67 | 25 | 41 | 24 | 3 |
| | II | 2.75 | 25 | 45 | 37 | 1 |
| | III | 1.83 | 20 | 45 | 25 | 3 |
| | IV | 0.00 | 19 | 58 | 20 | 2 |
| | Control groups | 0.00 | 19 | 64 | 20 | 1 |

effectiveness with which groups can reduce decision uncertainty. Great structural uncertainty hinders the activation of tendencies to diminish decision uncertainty (including repetition of arguments supporting one point of view and short decision time) so that in such experimental situations a relatively smaller shift can probably be expected. Trends to reduce uncertainty are gradually reinforced as structural uncertainty decreases and this results in an increasing shift in group responses.

## References

Cartwright, D. Risk taking by individuals and groups: An assessment of research employing choice dilemmas. *Journal of Personality and Social Psychology*, 1971, 20, 361–378.

Cohen, J., Boyle, L. E. and Chesnick, E. I. Patterns of preference in locating targets. *Occupational Psychology*, 1969, 43, 129–144.

Davis, J. H. *Group Performance*. Reading, Ma: Addison-Wesley, 1969.

Davis, J. H. Group decision and social interaction: A theory of social decision schemes. *Psychological Review*, 1973, 80, 97–125.

Dion, K. L., Miller, N. and Magnan, M. A. Cohesiveness and social responsibility as determinants of group risk taking. Proceedings of the 78th Annual Convention of the American Psychological Association, 1970, 5, 335–336.

Engländer, T. *Valószinuségi konfigurációk szerepe a dontéselókészitésben* (Kandidátusi értekezés). Unpublished manuscript, 1976.

Hogarth, R. M. *Cognitive processes and the assessment of subjective probability distributions.* Unpublished manuscript, 1974.

Laughlin, E. R. and Izzett, R. R. *Juror-defendant attitude similarity and choice shift in the jury trial.* Paper presented at the meeting of the Midwestern Psychological Association, May 1973.

Moscovici, S. and Lecuyer, R. *Studies on, polarization of, judgements: III.* Majorities, minorities and social judgements. *European Journal of Social Psychology*, 1972, 2, 221–244.

Myers, D. G. and Aronson, S. J. Enhancement of dominant risk tendencies in group discussion. *Psychological Reports*, 1972, 30, 615–623.

Myers, D. G. and Lamm, H. The group polarization phenomenon. *Psychological Bulletin*, 1976, 83, 602–627.

Seaver, D. A. *Assessment of group preferences and group uncertainty for decision making.* University of Southern California Research Report, 1976.

Tversky, A. and Kahneman, D. *Judgement under uncertainty: Heuristics and biases.* Fourth Research Conference on Subjective Probability, Utility and Decision Making. Rome, 1973.

Vidmar, N. *Group-induced shifts in simulated jury decisions.* Paper presented at the meeting of the Midwestern Psychological Association, May 1972.

Vinokur, A. A review and theoretical analysis of the effects of group processes upon individual and group decisions involving risk. *Psychological Bulletin*, 1971, 76, 231–250.

Zajonc, R. B., Wolosin, R. J. and Wolosin, M. A. Group risk taking under various
    group decision schemes. *Journal of Experimental Social Psychology*, 1972,
    8, 16–30.

# 10
# Choice-shift as Cognitive Change?

Erich H. Witte and Dieter H. Lutz

Research on the polarizing effect of group discussion has stimulated many new insights into the nature of group influence. However, we have ignored some of the main difficulties associated with the use of the choice dilemma research paradigm. First, many researchers have analysed the mean shift summed over choice dilemma items, even though the correlations between choice dilemma items are near zero (Slovic, 1962, 1964, 1972; Witte, 1971a). Second, many researchers postulate that a social value or the like, which is hypothesized to govern the discussion, directly or indirectly causes the shift effect.

Although research on this basic assumption is somewhat technical, it is generally concluded that people want to be more risky or more cautious than the majority. But what is the underlying reason why one choice dilemma produces a risky and another a cautious shift? The answer to that requires a content analysis of the items to discover discriminating cues. That implies we must know more about the cognitive structure of these choice dilemmas. Only then can we confirm the next basic assumption — that the discussion induced changes in subjects' perception of the choice dilemma items results in changes in their risk levels.

It may be the case, however, that change is only occurring in the interpretation of the risk levels. The existence of "Walter Mitty" effects (Higbee, 1971; Jellison and Riskind, 1970; McCauley *et al.*, 1971; Pruitt, 1969) should alert us to the possibility that the choice shift may also consist only of a change in the risk levels, without any cognitive reorientation with respect to the choice dilemmas. The "Walter Mitty" effect illustrates the relatively loose connection that exists between a given risk level and its interpretation.

It seems possible, therefore, that group discussion may serve to strengthen the view of the choice dilemma situation but change the view of the risk level. Perhaps confidence in the "correct" view increases (and is followed by a polarizing effect) because increasing knowledge leads to a greater polarization of opinion (Gamson and Modigliani, 1966). All of these and other problems will remain unsolved unless we try to identify the cognitive structure of choice dilemma items.

In one attempt to find out why subjects chose a specific risk level, Witte and Arez (1974) constructed a questionnaire consisting of 30 statements concerning various aspects of the content of choice dilemmas and administered it to 61 field officers. A factor analysis of the 30 statements over the ten choice dilemmas yielded a structure of four cognitive elements. By using these four factors as predictors in a regression analysis, a large part of the variance in individual risk level in each choice dilemma could be accounted for. The regression analysis was conducted with normal product-moment-correlations as well as scalar-products with both analyses yielding similar results. However, it seemed preferable to use scalar-products because one could then use the information about the means. The four cognitive elements were interpreted as (1) decision-making strategy, (2) responsibility for others, (3) reputation, (4) socially valued riskiness.

The best supported theoretical explanation of the choice shift phenomenon seems to be the social argumentation hypothesis, a combination of the social value and informational exchange hypotheses (Witte, 1979). The most commonly accepted interpretation of this explanation is based on the assumption that discussion, biased in the socially desired direction, results in a cognitive re-orientation on the part of the subject with regard to the choice dilemma items. It is this reorientation which then produces a shift in the risk levels. With this interpretation in mind we planned our study to address the following questions: (1) Would the cognitive structure Witte and Arez (1974) found be replicated with another reference group? (2) Is it possible to predict risk levels from the cognitive structure? (3) Is a choice shift followed by cognitive change? (4) How will independent ratings of the riskiness of arguments proposed during discussion compare with the average risk level?

Hence, the following study had two tasks — to validate the results of Witte and Arez (1974) concerning cognitive structure and to extend the research concerning discussion-induced change in the cognitive structure.

## Method

### SUBJECTS

The subjects were 75 male students from a technical school with an average age of 21.5 years. For our purposes we wanted the sample to be homogeneous with regard to (1) sex, because male and female subjects have different social values; (2) age, because the perception of the choice dilemma items varies with age, and (3) education. By fulfilling those requirements we obtained a homogeneous reference group different from that used by Witte and Arez (1974).

### CHOICE DILEMMA ITEMS AND QUESTIONNAIRE STATEMENTS

The six choice dilemma situations used were originally constructed by Witte (1971b, 1979) and constitute a subsample of the ten situations employed by Witte and Arez (1974). A short description of the content of the items follows. The number of each item corresponds to the notation in Witte (1971a, b).

(12) Mr A. B. is a managing director and has to meet an important business connection at the airport. Since he is very late he has to decide whether to drive through a crossing at high speed or to let the business connection wait.

(13) Mr A. M. is a politician and an expert in economics. In a newspaper interview he has to decide whether to give his own opinion, which is different from that of his party (meaning he will have some troubles), or to represent the official opinion of his party (which will help him with his career).

(17) Mr A. Q. is an underground engineer who has received an offer to change to a newly founded firm where his earnings will depend upon the profits of the firm. He has to decide whether to change jobs or not.

(19) Mr A. S. has a spinal wound. He must decide whether to remain bedridden his whole life or to undergo a dangerous surgical operation.

(26) Mr A. Z. is unmarried and has a scar over his left eye. This scar disfigures his whole face. He has to decide whether or not to try a surgical operation, which may lead to blindness in the left eye.

(40) Mr B. N. is an electrical engineer. He has an opportunity to

earn more money in a new job further away from home. However, it entails staying away from his family for several days every week. His wife has spoken about divorce. Now he has to decide whether to take this job or not.

Next we used a revised questionnaire of 40 items, 21 of which were taken from Witte and Arez (1974), with the other 19 especially constructed for this study. Examples of the 40 items include:

(1) Here, it is possible to fall back farther than the point one has previously achieved.

(16) I try to estimate how my actions impress other people.

(23) I have learned to master that kind of danger.

(25) My behaviour will afford me new intellectual stimulation.

(27) I can't influence the conditions for success alone.

Each statement was judged as to its importance for the risk level decision required for each decision situation. (See Appendix for a description of the 40 items.) The rating scale ranged from 0 (no importance for the choice of the risk level) to 6 (very high importance), perhaps called "*attribution* of social reasons".

TEST PROCEDURE

In the first part of the study each subject read six randomly ordered choice dilemmas, and then chose a risk level for each item. Next, subjects responded to one of six different orders of the 40 item questionnaire. One week later eight groups of five pupils and two groups of four were formed; four of the six choice dilemma situations were discussed (no. 13, 19, 26 and 40). (The reason for using four rather than six was due to time limitations.) All discussions were recorded on tape. Following the group discussions individuals completed the 40-item questionnaire a second time with the instructions that they should indicate how important each of the statements were for the group decision. A control group of 17 subjects was treated identically except for the group discussion.

## Results

Q-FACTOR ANALYSIS OF THE SUBJECTS

The first thing we wanted to know was the extent to which subjects viewed the choice dilemma situations as similar with respect to the questionnaire statements. Since we had no specific hypothesis about the similarity function which might exist between the subjects, we employed the common linear model. For that reason we correlated the subjects' risk choices over the vector of the choice dilemmas × the statements (6 × 40 = 240 importance ratings). The first principal component extracted 25% of the total variance. This is in the normal range and means an average loading of 0.50 on the first factor. There is place enough for a more idiographic viewpoint, but otherwise we can consider our sample as a more or less homogeneous reference group. Of course, if we were interested in more methodological questions we could not be satisfied with such a result. However, reference group theory is not our research intention.

## TWO-MODE FACTOR ANALYSIS OF THE STATEMENTS

Our next question focused on the nature of the factor structure that might exist over subjects (initial responses) and situations (75 × 6 = 450) for the 40 statements and whether it would be possible to predict the individual risk levels from them. Our expectations were that a structure similar to that found by Witte and Arez (1974) would also be found here.

A two-mode factor analysis was conducted and with four factors 43% of the total variance was extracted. The varimax rotated matrix was then compared with the solution of Witte and Arez (1974). The factor congruency coefficients were: $c_{11} = 0.84$; $c_{22} = 0.98$; $c_{33} = 0.95$; $c_{44} = 0.93$. The reduced similarity of the first factor is a function of the smaller loadings. If we compare the factors over loadings $\geq 0.40$, we arrive at a congruency coefficient of $c_{11} = 0.97$. Statements with loadings $\geq 0.40$ on one factor only and no other loading $\geq 0.40$ were:

Factor I: 1, 10, 14, 19, 30, 31, 34, 36, 39.
Factor II: 18, 21, 28, 32, 40.
Factor III: 2, 4, 7, 8, 9, 11, 13, 16, 20, 22, 26, 29, 33, 35.
Factor IV: 5, 12, 15, 23, 24, 25, 38.
Residual statements: 3, 6, 17, 27, 37.

(For a description of the 40 items see the Appendix).

The loading matrix is presented in Table 1. An interpretation of the factors might be:

Factor I: Decision-making strategy.
Factor II: Responsibility for others.
Factor III: Reputation.
Factor IV: Socially valued riskiness.

Note that these factors correspond exactly to those found by

TABLE 1

Varimax rotated factor loading matrix of the 40 statements concerning the choice dilemma situations

| Item/Factor | 1 | 2 | 3 | 4 |
|---|---|---|---|---|
| 1 | −0.4369 | −0.0543 | −0.1994 | 0.1966 |
| 2 | −0.1463 | 0.1125 | −0.6306 | 0.1952 |
| 3 | −0.1632 | 0.0155 | −0.0856 | 0.2912 |
| 4 | −0.2185 | −0.1889 | −0.5869 | 0.1403 |
| 5 | −0.1745 | −0.0442 | −0.3002 | 0.4770 |
| 6 | −0.2808 | −0.1071 | −0.2386 | 0.2408 |
| 7 | 0.0337 | 0.2893 | −0.5821 | −0.0213 |
| 8 | −0.1450 | 0.3334 | −0.6271 | 0.0175 |
| 9 | 0.0300 | 0.3495 | −0.5770 | 0.0218 |
| 10 | −0.4468 | 0.0600 | −0.2358 | −0.3061 |
| 11 | −0.3678 | 0.1221 | −0.6397 | 0.1054 |
| 12 | −0.1438 | −0.1202 | −0.1765 | 0.5480 |
| 13 | 0.1635 | −0.0423 | −0.5527 | 0.3082 |
| 14 | −0.4176 | 0.0847 | −0.1849 | 0.0679 |
| 15 | −0.0646 | −0.1196 | −0.2111 | 0.6818 |
| 16 | −0.0695 | 0.1769 | −0.5847 | 0.2293 |
| 17 | −0.0559 | 0.1243 | −0.4188 | 0.6343 |
| 18 | 0.0044 | 0.6327 | −0.3990 | −0.1341 |
| 19 | −0.4518 | 0.1103 | −0.2038 | 0.1430 |
| 20 | −0.2410 | −0.2894 | −0.4333 | 0.3639 |
| 21 | −0.3699 | 0.5922 | −0.0493 | −0.0329 |
| 22 | −0.2497 | 0.1165 | −0.5903 | 0.2972 |
| 23 | −0.1511 | −0.0502 | −0.3858 | 0.4730 |
| 24 | −0.1288 | 0.0740 | −0.0787 | 0.4857 |
| 25 | −0.1083 | 0.0721 | −0.3223 | 0.6754 |
| 26 | −0.2688 | 0.0820 | −0.6741 | 0.0681 |
| 27 | −0.3474 | 0.0228 | 0.0028 | 0.3913 |
| 28 | −0.0078 | 0.5598 | −0.2124 | 0.2464 |
| 29 | −0.2316 | 0.0947 | −0.6226 | 0.0633 |
| 30 | −0.5001 | 0.1135 | 0.1288 | 0.3200 |
| 31 | −0.6133 | 0.0057 | −0.1773 | 0.2189 |
| 32 | 0.1465 | 0.7156 | −0.2053 | −0.0480 |
| 33 | −0.2527 | 0.3282 | −0.5339 | 0.1071 |
| 34 | −0.5585 | −0.1169 | −0.3432 | 0.3118 |
| 35 | −0.3462 | −0.0753 | −0.4653 | 0.0593 |
| 36 | −0.5414 | 0.1257 | −0.1100 | 0.1842 |
| 37 | −0.4340 | 0.1408 | −0.5805 | 0.0555 |
| 38 | −0.2826 | 0.1019 | −0.0148 | 0.5681 |
| 39 | −0.5748 | 0.0540 | −0.0694 | 0.3304 |
| 40 | −0.2236 | 0.6638 | 0.0265 | −0.0247 |

Witte and Arez (1974). However, the question as to whether we can account for a large part of the variance in individual risk levels with these four factors still remains.

PREDICTION OF THE INDIVIDUAL RISK LEVELS

It is now our intention to show that the variance of the individual risk levels can be adequately explained by the cognitive elements (i.e., the four factors). We decided to use a linear model to generate the risk level predictions for several reasons: (1) it facilitates the development of a complex information processing model similar to that of Anderson's (1971) integration theory; (2) linear models have been previously found to provide a theoretical explanation of very different small group phenomena (Witte, 1979); (3) the continued use of such models more easily permits theoretical integration with previous research.

Since we had no specific hypotheses about the combination rule, we chose to optimize our prediction of the risk levels by use of multiple regression analysis. The four cognitive elements were employed as predictors by summing, for each factor, the rating scale values for statements with loadings $\geq 0.40$ on that factor. We then considered whether or not to eliminate the information of the means by use of a normal multiple regression based on product-moment correlations. Witte and Arez (1974) utilized a regression analysis based on the normed scalar products and found such information useful. However, other difficulties may then arise. The normed scalar product, however, can hardly reach a value of $r_{ns} = 0.00$ due to the limited range the discrepancy between predictor and criterion could take. That is, the scalar product itself can only reach a value of zero when all the predictors are zero valued. This result is an overestimation of the similarity between individual risk levels and the linear combination of the predictors. For that reason we constructed a reference figure supposing the following:

|  | Predictor | Criterion |
|---|---|---|
| 19 subjects react | 6 | 10 |
| 19 subjects react | 6 | 1 |
| 19 subjects react | 0 | 10 |
| 19 subjects react | 0 | 1 |

These data give (for $N = 76$ subjects) a product-moment correlation of $r = 0.00$. The normed scalar product is then $r_{ns} = 0.55$. A significant difference at the 0.01 level for d.f. $= 73$ then requires a value of $r_{ns} = 0.785$ or greater. A better coefficient for interpretational purposes, however, is the percentage of variance accounted for, that is, $\eta_{ns}^2$.

As indicated in Table 2, the multiple correlation $(R_{ns})$ for all six of the choice dilemma situations was satisfactory (although the $R_{ns}$ for item 19 just barely attainéd the 0.01 significance level). The signs of the beta weights for the fourth predictor were all negative, indicating a weight for greater riskiness. The relevance of the second factor (Reputation) increased over that observed by Witte and Avez. This may, in part, reflect the difference in average age between our student subjects (21.5) as compared to the field officer subjects (32) of Witte and Arez. The rank order of the four beta weights over the six identical situations in both studies is equivalent with the exception of one exchange from place three to two and vice versa.

In summary, these results essentially replicate those of Witte and Arez (1974) with another sample possessing different reference group characteristics with respect to the perception of the choice dilemma situations. We shall next consider the question of cognitive change in combination with risk level changes.

CHOICE SHIFTS AND COGNITIVE CHANGE

Since research concerning cognitive structures is just beginning and because of our small sample of choice dilemma situations, we chose

TABLE 2

*Beta weights and multiple correlations $(R_{ns})$ from the regression analyses of risk levels with the four cognitive elements as predictors*

| Choice-dilemma situation | Predictors | | | | $R_{ns}$ | $R_{ns}^2$ |
|---|---|---|---|---|---|---|
| | $P_1$ | $P_2$ | $P_3$ | $P_4$ | | |
| 12 | 0.357 | 0.804 | 0.169 | −0.393 | 0.955 | 0.912 |
| 13 | 1.585 | 0.256 | −0.398 | −0.592 | 0.904 | 0.816 |
| 17 | 1.063 | 0.211 | 0.126 | −0.490 | 0.931 | 0.867 |
| 19 | 0.795 | 0.389 | −0.197 | −0.197 | 0.787 | 0.620 |
| 26 | 1.252 | 0.282 | −0.512 | −0.144 | 0.896 | 0.803 |
| 40 | 0.339 | 0.697 | 0.115 | −0.180 | 0.967 | 0.935 |
| All situations together | 0.959 | 0.442 | 0.128 | −0.652 | 0.905 | 0.816 |

*Note.* $N = 75$. Regressions are based on the normed scalar products.

to focus only on those groups which evidenced a change in risk level which was predictable from the mean of the first individual reactions. That is, choice dilemma situations with means greater than 6.1 are usually expected to shift in the cautious direction and the others in the risky direction, ignoring those items that do not show any mean shift (Witte, 1979). As shown in Table 3, there were large significant changes in the risk levels of the "selected" experimental group, no significant differences between experimental and control groups ($E_1$ versus $C_1$) at the first treatment but large differences at the second treatment ($E_2$ versus $C_2$). Under these extreme shift conditions we expected cognitive change to have occurred in the experimental group.

However, we have yet to define what we mean by "cognitive change". We will look at three operationalizations: as changes in the (1) mean of each cognitive element, (2) multiple scalar product, or (3) beta weights.

A simple hypothesis with respect to mean differences in the cognitive elements is as follows: if a cautious shift occurred the importance-rating for cognitive elements (predictors) with a positive sign in the regression analysis should increase from the first testing to the second, whereas those with a negative sign should decrease, while the reverse should be true if a risky shift occurred. With four cognitive elements and four choice dilemma situations there are 16 possible predictions about the sign of the mean importance shift. In total, there were nine incorrect and seven correct predictions, which was not significantly different from the null hypothesis of an equal distribution of incorrect and correct predictions (by the binomial test).

TABLE 3

*Mean risk levels of the selected experimental group and controls at test periods one ($E_1$, $C_1$) and two ($E_2$, $C_2$) for four choice-dilemma situations*

| Experimental condition | Dilemma situations | | | |
| | 13 | 19 | 26 | 40 |
|---|---|---|---|---|
| $E_1$ | 5.00* | 2.97* | 5.63* | 8.78* |
| $E_2$ | 3.43* | 1.65* | 2.44* | 9.66* |
| $C_1$ | 5.35 | 3.47 | 5.29 | 8.71 |
| $C_2$ | 4.53 | 3.76 | 6.29 | 7.82 |

*Note.* The sample sizes for the experimental group for each of the choice dilemmas (13, 19, 26, 40) were 34, 33, 23, 27, respectively. For the control group $N = 17$ for each item. Entries in a column marked with * differ at the $P < 0.01$ level (one tailed $t$ test).

However, the beta weights involved in the preceding analysis were derived from the full sample of 75 subjects. These may or may not be appropriate for the restricted sample (i.e. those showing choice shifts). Hence, the multiple regression analyses were recomputed for the restricted sample. The new beta weights appear in Table 4. A comparison of these weights with those derived from the total sample revealed three sign changes. A reanalysis of the importance ratings with respect to the predictions generated by the new beta weights now revealed eight correct and eight incorrect predictions.

Apparently, discussion does not result in a systematic change in the mean importance ratings of the four cognitive elements. One interesting aspect of the mean ratings considered over all situations (see Table 5) is the high importance apparently attached to predictor $P_3$ (Reputation). Obviously the subjects were other directed.

The second operationalization of cognitive change concerns the multiple scalar product. We hypothesized that it should be possible to predict the individual risk levels better after a socially valued discussion, because discussion may serve to resolve the individual differences in the cognitive systems. This should result in individual risk levels (post-discussion) which are more in accordance with the

TABLE 4

*Beta weights and multiple correlations $(R_{ns})$ from the regression analyses of risk levels with the four cognitive elements as predictors for the selected sample at test periods one $(E_1)$ and two $(E_2)$*

|  | Choice-dilemma situation | $P_1$ | $P_2$ | $P_2$ | $P_4$ | $R_{ns}$ | $R_{ns}^2$ |
|---|---|---|---|---|---|---|---|
| | 13 | 0.248 | 1.300 | −0.048 | −0.652 | 0.941 | 0.886 |
| | 19 | 0.584 | 1.175 | −0.341 | −0.662 | 0.778 | 0.606 |
| $E_1$ | 26 | 0.038 | 1.344 | 0.363 | −0.886 | 0.893 | 0.797 |
| | 40 | 0.094 | −.653 | 1.060 | 0.509 | 0.988 | 0.975 |
| | All situations together | 0.253 | 0.921 | 0.494 | −0.805 | 0.902 | 0.813 |
| | 13 | 0.156 | 0.748 | 0.126 | −0.609 | 0.953 | 0.907 |
| | 19 | −0.087 | 0.298 | 0.186 | 0.503 | 0.892 | 0.796 |
| $E_2$ | 26 | 0.190 | 0.951 | 0.092 | 0.432 | 0.807 | 0.651 |
| | 40 | −0.042 | 0.169 | 0.789 | 0.077 | 0.982 | 0.965 |
| | All situations together | 0.588 | 0.684 | 0.493 | −0.975 | 0.873 | 0.762 |

*Note.* $N = 34, 33, 23,$ and $37$ for choice dilemmas 13, 19, 26, and 40, respectively. Regressions are based on the normed scalar products.

TABLE 5

*Mean importance-ratings of the four cognitive elements for the selected experimental group at test periods one $(E_1)$ and two $(E_2)$*

| | Choice-dilemma situation | Cognitive element | | | |
|---|---|---|---|---|---|
| | | $P_1$ | $P_2$ | $P_3$ | $P_4$ |
| | 13 | 4.02 | 3.58 | 4.28 | 3.92 |
| | 19 | 2.93 | 3.21 | 4.92 | 3.84 |
| $E_1$ | 26 | 2.65 | 3.43 | 4.63 | 3.06 |
| | 40 | 3.54 | 3.77 | 5.54 | 2.93 |
| | All situations together | 3.29 | 3.50 | 4.84 | 3.44 |
| | 13 | 3.77 | 3.65 | 3.69 | 3.77 |
| | 19 | 3.46 | 3.52 | 5.55 | 3.92 |
| $E_2$ | 26 | 2.83 | 3.64 | 3.26 | 3.61 |
| | 40 | 4.06 | 3.57 | 5.63 | 2.54 |
| | All situations together | 3.56 | 3.60 | 4.53 | 3.46 |

*Note.* $N = 34, 33, 23$ and 37 for choice dilemmas 13, 19, 26 and 40, respectively. The average importance rating of a given cognitive element was computed by taking the average of the importance ratings of the content statements loading on that element (factor). The range of value the importance rating may take is $0 =$ no importance for the choice of the risk level to $6 =$ very high importance.

common view than those before discussion. This prediction was disconfirmed. As is evident in Table 4 the percentage of variance accounted for by the four predictors considered over all situations was reduced after discussion from 81% to 76%. Inspection of each situation shows an increase for two and a decrease for two.

The third operationalization of cognitive change concerned changes in the beta weights. We hypothesized that discussion should serve to increase the highest beta weight, but not any of the others. The rationale underlying this hypothesis is that a socially biased discussion may effectively serve to reduce the complexity of the interpretation of a situation. That is, a one-sided discussion may result in a one-sided cognitive reorientation which then produces a choice shift. Thus, those subjects evidencing a choice shift should exhibit cognitive change in the now more salient direction.

In each of the four situations, however, the beta weights with the largest absolute value were reduced. In addition, inspection of Table 4 indicates that there was no apparent systematic variation in the beta weights, in fact, they remained relatively stable. Of course, beta weights are not very reliable measures but they are, perhaps, a first approximation to addressing the problem fo cognitive change in a repeated sampling situation.

All in all, we did not find evidence of systematic cognitive change occurring as a result of discussion, even though our analyses were restricted to only those subjects who showed choice shifts. The remaining problems and a possible interpretation of this result are discussed later.

## ANALYSIS OF THE GROUP DISCUSSION

The tape recordings of the group discussions were transcribed and then coded by three raters who were instructed to rate the amount of riskiness each argument conveyed by indicating the choice of risk level they thought would follow from that argument (because of technical problems two discussions were not recorded. Hence, there were ten ratings each for dilemma situations No. 13 and 26 but only nine each for items No. 19 and 40).

We shall define the risk value of the discussion as the mean of the arguments in the group averaged over the three raters and the argumentation value of the whole choice dilemma situation as the mean risk value over all groups.

The correlation between the raters was always greater than 0.90 and the slope of the regression line between any two raters for each respective choice dilemma situation is near 1.00. From these figures it follows that a combination of the raters should increase the reliability. The mean ratings for a choice dilemma considered over all groups and raters (i.e. argumentation values) were: $A_{13} = 5.6$; $A_{19} = 4.0; A_{26} = 5.8; A_{40} = 7.3$.

We can compare the mean argumentation values with the mean individual initial risk level of the whole sample $(M_1)$ and the mean pre- and postdiscussion risk levels of the experimental group $(m_1$ and $m_2$, respectively). These means are presented in Table 6. Note that the rank order of the mean argumentation values and the mean risk levels remains stable. The absolute mean differences between the argumentation values and the risk levels summed over choice dilemma situations were: $D_{A-M_1} = 0.74$; $D_{A-m_1} = 0.85$; $D_{A-m_2} = 1.42$.

The mean ratings of the arguments are in all cases less extreme than the mean risk levels. The fact that the prediscussion $(m_1)$ risk level decreases from 5.75 to 4.79 after discussion $(m_2)$ seems to support Witte's (1979) contention that the neutral point on the risk

TABLE 6

*Mean risk levels for the total sample* $(M_1)$ *and the selected experimental group* $(m_1$ *and* $m_2)$

| Sample | Choice-dilemma situation | | | |
|---|---|---|---|---|
| | 13 | 19 | 26 | 40 |
| Total $(M_1)$ | 4.86 | 3.34 | 5.57 | 8.63 |
| Experimental $(m_1)$ | 4.77 | 3.00 | 5.75 | 8.83 |
| Experimental $(m_2)$ | 3.91 | 2.62 | 4.79 | 9.02 |

*Note.* $N = 75$ for $M_1$, $N = 34$, 33, 23 and 37 for choice dilemmas 13, 19, 26 and 40, respectively, for both $m_1$ (prediscussion choice) and $m_2$ (post-discussion choice).

scale is not 5.0 but 6.1. Note further that the shift in the mean risk levels from pre- to post-discussion ratings results in a greater discrepancy between the mean argumentation value and mean risk levels. One conclusion we might draw from this result is that the riskiness or cautiousness of the arguments itself can hardly be the reason for the choice shift. This does not, however, contradict the finding that the percentage of risky and cautious arguments in the group discussion and the resulting shift are usually correlated (Myers and Bishop, 1970; Silverthorne, 1971). A relationship has been found between the mean prediscussion risk level and mean argumentation value. Given the high correlation usually found between the initial mean and the magnitude of the shift on a given choice dilemma item, both results are equivalent. However, it appears that the content of the arguments concerning the risk-dimension could not have directly caused the shift primarily because of the fact that the argumentation values were less extreme than both the pre- and post-discussion risk levels.

## Discussion

The results concerning the stability of the cognitive structure and its determination of the individual risk levels are encouraging. Further research should consider other reference groups, such as females and elderly people. The next step should, ideally, involve the classification of choice dilemma situations according to their content on the four cognitive aspects. Knowledge of an adequate combination rule for any given reference group, given the content classification, should allow the prediction of the direction and magnitude of the choice shift following group discussion. Such knowledge might then be profitably used to counteract the socially biased nature of the discussion thereby facilitating a more rational group decision. In addition to the possible application possibilities, a deeper understanding of the perception of choice dilemma-like situations can aid in the formulation of more adequate theories of group process.

We would also suggest that research on cognitive structure change be intensified, even though there was no clear evidence that any systematic cognitive reorientation occurred when it was expected to (i.e. for those subjects exhibiting a clear choice shift). However, operationalizing cognitive change as a change in the beta weights may not have been the best solution because of their instability. If we had found a combination rule with less technical weights it may have been possible to have provided a more adequate demonstration. We must recall, however, that the analysis of the arguments raised during discussion also seems to indicate that systematic cognitive reorientation did not occur; that is, the mean ratings of the arguments were less extreme than the mean risk levels.

The preceding seems to indicate that the arguments raised during discussion were not attempts directly to persuade others to be more risky or cautious. In fact, the average discussion appears to involve the exchange of socially valued, but not too extreme, arguments. Given such interaction, the subjects may, in fact, be reinforced for their views by the other group members and their (similar) arguments. As a consequence they may not feel the need to change their perception of the choice dilemma situations.

A comparable result was also found by Vinokur and Burnstein (1974) who tested a model which assumed that information must be partially shared among the group members if a shift is to occur. Such a model would also have to assume some degree of cognitive change (due to the fact that at least some of the subjects would learn new information as a function of participating in group discussions). However, this complicated model was not found to be any more convincing than a simpler one, as Vinokur and Burnstein (1974) have indicated. For that reason the analogy to a group problem solving model is not as direct as assumed.

In normal cases discussions of social problems without a clear solution are usually socially biased and result, through a social support process, in greater member confidence in the obtained group product, but without cognitive change. However, problems with objective solutions that are known only by few group members might be followed by real cognitive change.

Given the above, is it possible to explain the choice shift without postulating the occurrence of cognitive change? Is the whole choice shift phenomenon something like a Walter Mitty effect? Indeed, it could be argued that the choice shift is nothing more than a risk level change under a constant orientation of what to do. Just as subjects might change the meaning of a risk level under constant riskiness they may similarly be able to change risk levels under constant meaning. What we then have is a reverse Walter Mitty effect.

As is evident from the preceding the connection between risk level and its interpretation is not very close. We do not hold such an explanation, however; we prefer another. As Stroebe and Fraser (1971) have shown, the well-known relationship between confidence and extremity is also valid for choice dilemma situations. If we accept this relationship as a law, then increases in confidence should, on average, result in increases in extremity.

Thus, argumentation during discussion may serve no other purpose but to provide group members with mutual reinforcement (i.e. social support) that their initial view was the correct one, thereby increasing their confidence in the "right" perception. This, in turn, may free subjects to choose a more extreme risk level depending upon the social value. This can also be construed as diffusion of responsibility, but in a broader sense, with subjects diffusing responsibility on to the entire reference group. Given that, then shifts in the socially valued direction could also be viewed as an increase in conformity.

Unfortunately, most of our everyday problems contain at least some social aspects to them. Groups thinking they have found creative solutions may, in fact, only be reproducing the commonly shared opinion, but with an accompanying feeling of increased confidence in the solution. These remarks, however, should be taken only as speculative generalizations, the validity of which will await further empirical test.

Is there any empirical support for the existence of a cognitive reorientation process within the choice dilemma paradigm? There is some evidence that seems to indicate that change in a non-socially valued direction can be induced by the controlled selection of arguments given to a sample (Witte, 1971b) or by controlled group discussion with the help of confederates (Baron et al., 1971). Under such conditions it should also be possible to detect cognitive change, if the instrument (questionnaire) and the methods (mean differences, regression analyses) are valid. More of this kind of experimentation is necessary in the future if we are to arrive at a more subtle understanding of the risky shift phenomenon and its theoretical integration.


## Conclusions


Of course, research oriented towards detecting whether choice shifts do or do not occur is not very interesting and one may question the utility of such research. However, because of its complexity and connections with other areas of research it maintains a paradigmatic, heuristic character capable of stimulating research into other small group phenomena. Furthermore, a better understanding of the influence processes in group discussions could help to avoid simple conformity behaviour, thus encouraging a more applied aspect.

In our opinion, one promising research avenue is the analysis in depth of reasons why subjects, on average, choose a more extreme cautious or risky level. We have provided, through the present study, what we hope is an illustrative example of such an approach.

We have demonstrated that the structure of the four cognitive elements is reasonable and that the prediction of the individual risk levels from them is good enough to speak about their possible determination by the cognitive elements. In addition, the present study replicates quite well the results obtained by Witte and Arez (1974) but with a different reference group (Witte and Arez, 1974). We were unable, however, to find any evidence of systematic cognitive change in a sample of subjects who exhibited large choice shifts following group discussion. This is in agreement with both the results obtained by Vinokur and Burnstein (1974) in their test of their hypothesis of partially shared information and the content analysis of the arguments (where the average riskiness of the arguments raised during group discussion was found to be less extreme than the mean individual risk levels). Our conclusion is that the choice shift depends upon the higher confidence in the initial view, a social argumentation and support hypothesis.

# References

Anderson, N. H. Integration theory and attitude change. *Psychological Review*, 1971, 78, 171—206.

Baron, R. S., Dion, K. L., Baron, P. H. and Miller, N. Group consensus and cultural values as determinants of risk taking. *Journal of Personality and Social Psychology*, 1971, 20, 446—455.

Gamson, W. A. and Modigliani, A. Knowledge and foreign policy: Some models for consideration. *Public Opinion Quarterly*, 1966, 30, 187—199.

Higbee, K. L. Expression of "Walter-Mitty-ness" in actual behavior. *Journal of Personality and Social Psychology*, 1971, 20, 416—422.

Jellison, J. M. and Riskind, J. A social comparison of abilities interpretation of risk-taking behavior. *Journal of Personality and Social Psychology*, 1970, 15, 375—390.

McCauley, C., Teger, A. I. and Kogan, N. Effect of the pretest in the risky shift paradigm. *Journal of Personality and Social Psychology*, 1971, 20, 379—381.

Myers, D. G. and Bishop, G. D. Discussion effects on racial attitudes. *Science*, 1970, 169, 778—789.

Pruitt, D. G. The "Walter Mitty" effect in individual and group risk-taking. *Proceedings of the 77th Annual Convention of the American Psychological Association*, 1969, 4, 425—426.

Silverthorne, C. P. Information input and the group shift phenomenon in risk taking. *Journal of Personality and Social Psychology*, 1971, 20, 456—461.

Slovic, P. Convergent validation of risk-taking measures. *Journal of Abnormal and Social Psychology*, 1962, 65, 68—71.

Slovic, P. Assessment of risk-taking behavior. *Psychological Bulletin*, 1964, 61, 220—233.

Slovic, P. Information processing, situation specificity, and the generality of risk-taking behavior. *Journal of Personality and Social Psychology*, 1972, 22, 128—134.

Stroebe, W. and Fraser, C. The relationship between riskiness and confidence in choice dilemma decisions. *European Journal of Social Psychology*, 1971, 1, 519—526.

Vinokur, A. and Burnstein, E. The effects of partially shared persuasive arguments on group induced shifts: A group problem-solving approach. *Journal of Personality and Social Psychology*, 1974, 29, 305—315.

Witte, E. H. Das 'risky-shift'-Phänomen: Eine kritische Untersuchung der Dimensionalitat von hypothetischen Entscheidungssituationen. *Psychologie und Praxis*, 1971a, 15, 22—25.

Witte, E. H. Das 'risky-shift'-Phänomen: Eine kritische Untersuchung der bestehenden Hypothesen. *Psychologie und Praxis*, 1971b, 15, 104—117.

Witte, E. H. *Das Verhalten in Gruppensituationen. Ein theoretisches Konzept.* Göttingen: Hogrefe Verlag, 1979.

Witte, E. H. and Arez, A. The cognitive structure of choice dilemma decisions. *European Journal of Social Psychology*, 1974, 4, 313—328.

## Appendix: Statements of the questionnaire

1. Especially here it is possible to fall back farther than the point one has previously achieved.
2. Other people should know that they can rely on me.
3. This situation is of great importance to me.
4. It is of importance that my behaviour meets with approval.
5. Here I want to have great influence on the world.
6. Here I take into consideration that I as a man behave in another way than women in general.
7. I do not like to exploit other people.
8. I do not like to behave in such a way that I disappoint the expectations of other people.
9. Sometimes one has to give up his own advantage for the advantage of other people.
10. I do not want to regret my decision afterwards.
11. Sometimes I am forced to conform to the expectations and hopes of other people, because they have a specific image of my personality.
12. I think that my self-confidence is influenced.
13. My behaviour should be worthy of imitation.
14. Here I am not sure whether my behaviour will make me happier if everything worked well.
15. Only if I risk something can I win.
16. I try to estimate how my actions impress other people.
17. Here especially I have the possibility of intellectually analysing the situation.
18. I must seriously consider whether my behaviour hurts other people.
19. Here I am not sure whether my behaviour will make me happier if everything worked well. (A double-item for reliability estimation.)
20. Here the general impression I leave on other people is important for me.
21. The position of friends is influencing my behaviour here.
22. Here I try to justify my behaviour.
23. I have learned to master that kind of danger.
24. I know for sure that I have to expect trouble.
25. My behaviour will afford me new intellectual stimulation.

26. I consider carefully how my behaviour would be judged by other people.
27. I cannot influence the conditions for success alone.
28. I have to think about the advantage not only for me but also for other people.
29. The opinion of other people about my behaviour is especially important in this situation.
30. I bear in mind my age.
31. My professional position is very important for me.
32. I must consider that my decision can influence the life of other people deeply.
33. I also conform to the expectation of other people.
34. My social position is important for me.
35. Other people's opinion about me do not leave me untroubled.
36. I am not sure because I cannot influence all factors of the situation.
37. Sometimes I have to take in mind the expectations of other people.
38. I want to keep my life as variable as possible.
39. Here I consider my income.
40. I also have to think of my family.

*Note.* This study was conducted in German and the statements given above are fairly literal English translations.

# III
# Social-Emotional Aspects of Group Decision Making

# Introduction

Hermann Brandstätter

In explaining the choice shifts following a group discussion two concepts seem to be stressed most: information integration and social comparison. The reasoning is well documented by Burnstein as well as by Myers (both in this volume). Burnstein relates choice shift mainly, if not exclusively, to the number and quality of arguments that support one or the other alternatives.

Myers takes both the processing of arguments as well as comparing one's own position with the other's position into account. This distinction can be traced back to the concepts of informational and normative influence (Deutsch and Gerard, 1955). Brandstätter (1978) proposed a further differentiation within the concept of normative influence: perceiving the other's stand on the issue, and perceiving the other's demand for compliance. Whether, and to what degree, the influence processes in groups are informational or normative is often difficult to tell. Usually both components are involved, and disentangling them calls for rather sophisticated experimental devices. There is, however, quite a simple way left to study the normative influence without interfering with the informational influence, that is by holding constant the arguments, and varying the social-emotional aspects of interaction. Positive or negative emotional responses to a discussion partner may be called forth by perceived similarity/dissimilarity, by learning that one is liked/disliked by him, or by his friendly/hostile interaction style. To focus the attention of a person on the social-emotional cues of interaction means to make salient the normative influence.

The chapters in this section all share this perspective, which has been developed cooperatively during the time when the five authors were working together at the University of Augsburg on a research project concerning group decision making sponsored by the Deutsche

Forschungsgemeinschaft. Meanwhile each of them has moved to a different University, and this chapter is a memorial to the pleasant and stimulating years spent together at Augsburg.

Two of the chapters presented in this section attempt a theoretical integration of a number of experiments. Stocker-Kreichgauer and von Rosenstiel analyse various aspects of normative influence on observers of controversial discussions. Applause v. disapproval of an audience or consent v. dissent of a moderator increase the influence which the applauded or consented speaker has on the observers. If the arguments of a speaker are responded to by his opponent with friendly or unfriendly remarks, the speaker who is treated in a friendly manner by his opponent (who nevertheless stays firm in his opposition) gains more influence on the observers. These results can be explained by concepts of vicarious social reinforcement (operant conditioning) as well as by concepts of attribution theory.

Schuler reviews four experiments dealing with normative influence in the interaction setting. The social-emotional responses to the opponent in the discussion were elicited in different ways. Whether a person is informed before the discussion starts that the other likes him, or that he adheres to similar values, or whether he receives verbal or non-verbal signals of friendliness from his opponent during the discussion, he responds more favourably to the other as well as to the other's arguments than the person who thinks the other dislikes him, has different values, or is treated in an unfriendly way by the opponent. In his theoretical integration of the experimental results Schuler combines concepts of classical conditioning of emotions with concepts of cognitive interpretation of the situation and voluntary goal directed behaviour.

Rüttinger as well as Brandstätter and Hoggatt report on single experiments, each designed in order to test whether liking does promote yielding to the partners' expectations in a distributional conflict, as well as in discussions of less well structured judgemental and evaluative conflicts. Because both experiments have been designed to test the generalizability of hypotheses originally related to the social-emotional influence in discussion groups, these reports are subsumed under the heading of this section rather than under Section IV.

Rüttinger used a matrix with a structure similar to a PDG, and varied the advantage to be expected from a competitive choice. His assumption that liking would increase the frequency of cooperative choices only if the advantage expected from competition was low, was weakly supported by the data.

Following Pruitt and Kimmel (1977, p. 381) one may surmise that liking could have strengthened the expectation of cooperation from the other at a later stage when the players, after having experienced the unsatisfactory results of mutual non-cooperation, developed the goal of mutual cooperation. Since Rüttinger's experiment provided only two games leaving the subjects unsure at each stage whether another one would follow, there was no time and no incentive to develop the goal of mutual cooperation.

Brandstätter and Hoggatt learned from their bargaining experiment that the effect of liking on yielding to the partner's demand is not as simple as they had thought. Bargaining among players who liked each other compared to those who did not like each other did not result in a higher frequency of agreement. But liking made a difference in the number of steps needed to reach agreement or to end in conflict. When the situation was difficult, i.e. when one or both players had high costs, liking players reached agreement in fewer steps and ended up in conflict after a greater number of steps than disliking players. If players in the liking condition do not reach agreement at an early stage, disappointed expectations are supposed to increase the resistance to the other's demands thus delaying, but not actually preventing a breakdown of the negotiations.

One important aspect seems to be common to the discussion experiments reported by Schuler and the experimental games reported by Rüttinger and by Brandstätter and Hoggatt: the subjects perceive the others demand or expectations for yielding to his position, and tend to meet the expectation of a liked opponent more readily than that of a disliked one. If the other fails to reciprocate the cooperation there is disappointment which leads to increasing resistance.

## References

Brandstätter H. Social emotions in discussion groups. In: Brandstätter, H., Davis, J. H. and Schuler, H., *Dynamics of Group Decisions*. Beverly Hills: Sage 1978.

Deutsch, M. and Gerard, H. B. A study of normative and informational social influence upon individual judgement. *Journal of Abnormal and Social Psychology* 1955, 51, 629–636.

Pruitt, D. G. and Kimmel, M. J. Twenty years of experimental gaming. Critique, synthesis and suggestions for the future. *Annual Review of Psychology* 1977, 28, 363–392.

# 11
# Attitude Change as a Function of the Observation of Vicarious Reinforcement and Friendliness/Hostility in a Debate

Gisela Stocker-Kreichgauer and Lutz von Rosenstiel

Today, people often find themselves in situations where they are able to observe or listen to controversial discussions without actually participating in the debate. Observers of such discussions are generally able to express agreement or disagreement to the arguments of the speakers. However, such reactions are not possible when the discussion is media-transmitted (e.g. through television, radio, or newspapers). Thus, the media-user can only observe the described reactions of the audience present at the debate.

In three separate experiments we studied how media-transmitted *applause or disapproval by an audience* (von Rosenstiel and Rüttinger, 1976; von Rosenstiel and Stocker-Kreichgauer, 1975, 1978) or by a *mediator* (Stocker-Kreichgauer, 1976) affected the attitudes of observers. In all three studies it could be shown that observers' attitudes were influenced more by speakers receiving applause than by those who elicited either no reaction or disapproval. In fact, when the audience disapproved of the speaker, observers were actually found to shift away from the speaker's position (von Rosenstiel and Stocker-Kreichgauer, 1975, 1978). We proposed that the concept of vicarious social reinforcement could be used to explain these changes in observers' attitudes.

In many media-transmitted discussions there may not be an audience's evaluative reaction to observe simply because no audience was present. However, usually one can observe the *friendliness or hostility* the speakers show to one another. Schuler and Peltzer (1978), in a study of the effect of *non-verbal* friendliness and hostility in direct interaction, found that a friendly speaker proved to be more influential than an unfriendly one, both with respect to his discussion partner as well as an observer of the discussion. Stocker-Kreichgauer and von Rosenstiel (1976) investigated how the *verbal* friendliness and hostility of two discussants affected observer attitudes. They expected that direct interaction with the friendly speaker would be more effective in changing observers' attitudes than the unfriendly one. This hypothesis, based on the theory of classical conditioning of emotions by friendliness or unfriendliness (Brandstätter, 1976; Bandura, 1969; Staats, 1968), was not confirmed.

While reviewing our previous experiments concerning the influence of an audience's applause or disapproval and the speakers' friendliness or hostility on the attitudes of observers, we became increasingly unhappy with out attempt to explain the attitude change effects by means of different theoretical frameworks. In this paper we will explore some of the implications of these different frameworks in an attempt to discover which of these may provide the best account for the different effects we have observed. To do this we will need to examine the data of the different experiments once more, but in a unifying way.

## Theoretical frameworks

The frameworks we shall examine are: (1) vicarious social reinforcement based on operant or instrumental conditioning; (2) vicarious social reinforcement based on classical conditioning, and (3) attribution theory. From each of the preceding, hypotheses about the effects of an applauding/disapproving audience or a friendly/hostile speaker on the attitudes of observers can be derived.

### VICARIOUS SOCIAL REINFORCEMENT BASED ON OPERANT OR INSTRUMENTAL CONDITIONING, LEARNING BY AWARENESS OF CONTINGENCIES

One can assume that a speaker is positively reinforced when he is applauded immediately after presenting his argument. Furthermore, to the extent that he identifies with the applauded speaker, an observer will be vicariously reinforced by the applause (Kelman, 1967). An awareness of the contingency between the argument (or more specifically the position expressed by this argument) and the applause should shift the observer in the direction of the applauded speaker. In the case of audience disapproval, the observer should move away from the position of the punished speaker. As Staats *et al.* (1973) have pointed out, stimuli-eliciting positive emotions within a person reinforces his immediately preceding behaviour and induces him to display impulsive appetence behaviour to that stimulus (see Brandstätter, 1976); contingently given stimuli which are negatively evaluated, however, induces impulsive avoidance behaviour and reduces the frequency of the immediately preceding behaviour.

In our experiments the vicarious social reward or punishment was given only in response to some of the arguments transmitted (partial reinforcement). One could assume that the attitude change was confined only to the reinforced arguments. However, it may be the case that the observer generalizes that reinforcement to the attitudes expressed by the other, non-reinforced arguments. If so, then these non-reinforced arguments may also influence an observer's attitude. This was the explanation that von Rosenstiel and Rüttinger (1976) proposed to account for their finding that changes in observers' attitudes did not specifically refer to the positively reinforced arguments, but to all arguments of the applauded speaker.

In our friendliness/hostility experiments, the speakers made friendly/unfriendly remarks after their partner's argument and immediately afterwards expressed their own controversial attitude. From the perspective of vicarious social reinforcement, based on an instrumental conditioning framework, we assume that these remarks also act as social rewards or punishments for the respective partner and vicariously for observers. It should be pointed out that in our experimental design an interval of about four seconds occurred between the argument of one speaker and the subsequent friendly or hostile remark of the other. Within that interval subjects were required to mark their current preference on an attitude scale. In addition, it should also be noted that the friendliness of a given speaker was defined relative to the remarks of his partner; i.e. neutral remarks were interpreted as "friendly" when the speaker's partner used hostile remarks, and as "hostile" when his partner used friendly remarks. Unfriendly remarks were interpreted as vicarious punishment.

Given the preceding we can derive the following hypotheses. (1) The speaker rewarded by applause will influence, in a direction congruent with the speaker's position, the attitudes of observers to a greater extent than the punished speaker (we do not differentiate here between "experienced" and "reported" attitude change). (2) The speaker treated in a friendly manner will influence the attitudes of observers to a greater extent than the speaker treated in an unfriendly manner.

## VICARIOUS SOCIAL REINFORCEMENT BASED ON CLASSICAL CONDITIONING

The applause/disapproval experiments can be viewed from a classical conditioning perspective, if we assume that an argument combined with applause is, in general, a positively evaluated reaction (see Landy, 1972); while arguments combined with audience disapproval tend to elicit negative emotional reactions. To take such a perspective, however, we do need to make some additional assumptions. Classical conditioning works most effectively when the unconditioned stimulus is given simultaneously with the response and immediately after the neutral stimulus. In our experiment, however, it was given immediately after the argument was finished. We assume that the recognition of the argument induced "post-mental excitations" in the observer and that the latter were still going on when the applause was recognized.

As to the friendliness/hostility experiments, we assume that friendliness produces positive emotional responses (see Byrne and Clore, 1970) in the observer. These emotions may then be related to the speaker himself (e.g. in the form of sympathy, Byrne and Griffith, 1973) or to his arguments or to the attitude expressed by the arguments. The observer should shift towards the positively evaluated speaker and his arguments (see Staats, 1968). Conversely, the unfriendly speaker should produce negative evaluative responses in the observers. These implicit evaluative responses can be attached both to the perception of the person and of his arguments.

From the preceding perspective we can derive the following hypotheses: (1) The speaker rewarded by the audience's applause will influence observers' attitudes in the direction of the speaker's position more than the punished speaker will. (2) The friendly speaker will have more influence than the unfriendly speaker.

## ATTRIBUTION THEORY

Here, the approach taken involves a much stronger cognitive component. In particular, the applause condition (a positive social consequence) is thought to be very differently interpreted by the observer. We assume, in accordance with the relevant norms of our culture, that observers interpret applause as a sign of social success and attribute it to the competence or persuasive power of the arguments of the applauded speaker or to the speaker himself. As a result, his arguments may be attended to, and accepted, by the observer to a greater degree than those of his non-applauded and/or sometimes disapproved opponent (see Landy, 1972; Baron, 1970) (of course, the observer's evaluation of the applauding audience is also an important factor; one which we have addressed elsewhere, von Rosentiel and Stocker-Kreichgauer, 1978.)

Given the preceding, we would expect the apparently more competent, and socially influential, speaker to produce more attitude change in the direction of his arguments than an opponent who received no reactions from the audience. Conversely, the speaker who gets disapproving reactions from the audience should be seen as being less competent and less socially influential, and therefore should be less successful in changing the observers' attitudes in his direction.

In the friendliness/hostility experiments, the friendly remarks may be attributed to very different personality characteristics and intentions of the friendly speaker. One cannot, however, isolate the perception of friendliness from the situation in which it occurs because the context is important for its interpretation. In our experiment the display of friendliness is shown within the context of a discussion meeting. Different observers, of course, may have different ideas about the purposes of such discussion meetings. For example, some may think that they serve to exchange information or beliefs (stand and information), while others may believe that their aim is to influence the beliefs of the others in a specific way (demand; e.g. of unanimity). Still others may interpret the discussion meeting as a competitive situation in which one will emerge the victor (social power).

Each of the preceding cognitive conceptualizations of discussion meetings will influence the perception of friendliness in a specific way. In the information exchange conceptualization, friendliness could be viewed as indicating both a positive social attitude as well as acceptance of the other speaker. In the demand conceptualization, friendliness might be attributed to a desire to influence the other speaker in a somehow unfair way, perhaps in the conviction that one's own position is weak and that attempts to persuade the other must be supported by positive social-emotional means. In the competitive conceptualization of discussion meetings, friendliness might be taken to indicate an actual weakness of the friendly speaker compared to the unfriendly one; the attribution here being that the latter seems so sure about his victory that he can even afford to speak to the other in a hostile way. Unfriendliness in this latter case may be attributed to social power in the sense of withholding rewards. Along these lines, Heider (1958) has pointed out that there is no doubt that power, as an abstract variable, is evaluated positively and weakness negatively. Heider suggests that this may be due to the fact that power, in a subjective utility model, implicates the ability to cause events which are useful to $p$ or his follower, and to avoid situations which could be harmful to $p$. Furthermore, powerful people are not likely to hurt those who join them (see Argyle, 1969).

In our experiments, friendliness and hostility are expressed toward an opponent who does not share the position of the friendly/hostile speaker, Considering the antagonism of the positions, it is possible that an observer may actually perceive unfriendliness as being more appropriate in that situation than friendliness. Indeed, in another slightly modified version of the friendliness/hostility experiments (as yet unpublished), we found that observers watching a dyadic discussion of controversial issues did, in fact, negatively interpret the friendliness of the speaker.

The experiments we have discussed did not include questions about the perceived friendliness/hostility of the speakers. Therefore, we make no assumptions about that particular topic. Given the preceding discussion, however, we can derive the following hypotheses. (1) The applauded speaker will produce more consistent attitude change than the disapproved speaker. (2) The unfriendly speaker will produce more consistent attitude change than the friendly one.

Note that the hypotheses derived from the first and third theoretical frameworks correspond to each other. Confirming, or disconfirming, evidence for these hypotheses requires experimental designs which allow us to differentiate between the concept of vicarious social reinforcement and the observational learning or modelling based on attribution processes concerning social power and success.

## Experimental designs

The experiments we shall reanalyse are described in detail by von Rosenstiel and Rüttinger (1976), von Rosenstiel and Stocker-Krieichgauer (1975), Stocker-Kreichgauer (1976) and Stocker-Kreichgauer and von Rosenstiel (1976). In the first experiment the effects of applause by an audience on attitude change was studied by having the audience either applaud or express disapproval immediately after a given speaker presented his argument. In the second experiment three levels of audience reaction (applause, no reaction, and disapproval) to the two speakers which were communicated across three types of media (television, radio, and paper) were studied. The third experiment used consent and rejection by a moderator as the experimental variable. Each of the preceding three studies focus on the influence of applause or disapproval on observer attitudes. Their experimental designs are further illustrated in Table 1.

TABLE 1

*Experimental conditions involving applause/disapproval in a discussion situation with two speakers*

| | | | Audience reactions to | | Medium | | |
| | | | 1st speaker | 2nd speaker | TV | radio | paper |
|---|---|---|---|---|---|---|---|
| (a) | von Rosenstiel and Rüttinger (1976) | Control group | No reaction / | No reaction | x | | |
| | | Experimental group | Applause / | No reaction | x | | |
| (b) | von Rosenstiel and Stocker-Kreichgauer (1975) | Control group | No reaction / | No reaction | x | x | x |
| | | Experimental groups[a] | Applause / | Disapproval | x | x | x |
| | | | Applause / | No reaction | x | x | x |
| | | | No reaction / | Disapproval | x | x | x |
| | | | Disapproval / | No reaction | x | x | x |
| | | | No reaction / | Applause | x | x | x |
| | | | Disapproval / | Applause | x | x | x |
| (c) | Stocker-Kreichgauer (1976) | Control group | No reaction[b] / | No reaction | x | | |
| | | Experimental groups | Consent / | No reaction | x | | |
| | | | Consent / | Rejection | x | | |

[a]Only the experimental groups have been reanalysed.
[b]In this experiment a moderator, rather than an audience, provided the reactions to each of the speakers.

TABLE 2

*Experimental conditions concerning friendliness/hostility in discussion meetings with two speakers presenting their arguments in a friendly/neutral/hostile way*

|  |  | Presentation style | | Medium | | |
|  |  | 1st speaker | 2nd speaker | TV | radio | paper |
| --- | --- | --- | --- | --- | --- | --- |
| Stocker- | Control | Neutral / | Neutral | x | x | x |
| Kreichgauer and | groups | Friendly / | Friendly | x | x | x |
| von Rosenstiel | | Hostile / | Hostile | x | x | x |
| (1976) | Experi- | Friendly / | Hostile | x | x | x |
| | mentalq | Friendly / | Neutral | x | x | x |
| | groups[a] | | | | | |
| | | Neutral / | Hostile | x | x | x |
| | | Hostile / | Neutral | x | x | x |
| | | Neutral / | Friendly | x | x | x |
| | | Hostile / | Friendly | x | x | x |

[a] Only the experimental groups have been reanalysed.

The remaining experiment focused on the influence of the friendliness or hostility of the speaker's presentation style on the attitudes of observers of the debate. Stocker-Kreichgauer and von Rosenstiel (1976) employed a design somewhat similar to that used by von Rosenstiel and Stocker-Kreichgauer (1975). However, in contrast to the latter study the former one included three, rather than one, control groups (Table 2).

In the von Rosenstiel and Rüttinger (1976), von Rosenstiel and Stocker-Kreichgauer (1975) and Stocker-Kreichgauer and von Rosenstiel (1976) experiments the topic of discussion was the "Radikalenerlass der Ministerpräsidenten" (members of radical political parties should/should not be refused public employment). In the Stocker-Kreichgauer (1976) experiment two speakers were introduced by a moderator and then proceeded to discuss, for and against respectively, a personnel problem.

The subjects in the von Rosenstiel and Rüttinger (1976) and Stocker-Kreichgauer (1976) studies were students from the University of Augsburg. In two of the other studies the subjects were citizens from Augsburg chosen at random from the Augsburg phone directory. All subjects were male.

## A reanalysis and new evaluation of the experiments

For the purposes of this paper we are not interested in the continuous process of attitude change or in the observer's reactions to specific arguments (e.g. reinforced and not reinforced arguments), but in the "lasting influence" of the experimental manipulations. We shall define the latter as the difference between the attitude position at the beginning and at the end of the discussion (post-discussion position minus prediscussion position). Because of the problems related to such difference measures (Cronbach and Furby, 1970; Albers *et al.*, 1975), and to neutralize individual differences in using the preference scale, we disregarded the magnitude of the preference change and noted only the direction of the attitude change for each subject. Here, like in the other experiments, we did not distinguish between those observers who held the same position as the speaker from those who did not.

## Results

The results of the preceding reanalysis of the applause/disapproval experiments are summarized in Table 3. This pattern of results supports the hypothesis that applause increases the influence of a speaker in changing the attitudes of observers while disapproval reduces it.

The results of the reanalysis of the friendliness/hostility experiment are shown in Table 4. If one chooses the hypothesis derived from the first or third theoretical framework, then the observed shifts are in the predicted direction, although not significant. The assumption derived from the theory of classical conditioning (framework two) that the friendliness of a speaker influences observers' attitudes in the direction he advocates must be rejected.

## Discussion

The effects we have described cannot be explained by differences in argument quality because there were symmetric reinforcement and friendliness conditions. A theoretical integration of the experimental results would seem to need only two of the three frameworks we examined, i.e. the learning by vicarious social reinforcement based on instrumental conditioning (awareness of contingencies) and modelling based on the attribution of competence, social power, and success. The theory of classical conditioning, in its original

TABLE 3

*Number of persons yielding to speaker (M) (pro) or speaker (B) (con) in the applause/disapproval experiments*

|  |  | Yielding to | |  |
|---|---|---|---|---|
|  |  | Speaker M | Speaker B |  |
| Audience | B | 21 | 37 | $\chi^2 = 7.86$ |
| supports | M | 26 | 14 | $P < 0.01$ |

Von Rosenstiel and Rüttinger (1976) and von Rosenstiel and Stocker-Kreichgauer (1975) combined.

|  | Yielding to | |  |
|---|---|---|---|
|  | Speaker M | Speaker B |  |
| Neutral | 21 | 12 | $\chi^2 = 5.41$ |
| Moderator |  |  |  |
| favours B | 33 | 50 | $P < 0.05$ |

Stocker-Kreichgauer (1976).

TABLE 4

*Number of persons yielding to speaker M (pro) or speaker B (con) in the friendliness/hostility experiment. (Stocker-Kreichgauer and von Rosenstiel, 1976.)*

|  |  | Yielding to | |  |
|---|---|---|---|---|
|  |  | Speaker M | Speaker B |  |
| Less friendly | M | 24 | 15 | $\chi^2 = 3.35$ |
| speaker | B | 21 | 29 | $P < 0.10$ |

form, is based on the principle of repeated contiguity of two external stimuli, a neutral (later conditioned) and an unconditioned one, with the optimal interval between the two stimuli being, roughly speaking, a split second. In the case of our applause/disapproval experiments the audience's (or moderator's) reactions were presented immediately after the speaker's argument; hence, the connection between the two stimuli is theoretically clear. In our friendliness/unfriendliness experiments, however, a minor interval occurred between the two stimuli, i.e. between the appearance of the speaker and his voice (neutral stimuli) and his verbal friendliness/unfriendliness (quasi-unconditioned stimuli). As discussed earlier, the friendliness/unfriendliness of the speaker would give the speaker himself a positive/negative value.

There is another possibility regarding the connection of stimuli (Brandstätter, 1976, 1979) which abandons the more behaviouristic view of orthodox classical conditioning in favour of a more cognitive point of view: the observer still has in mind the predecessor's argument when the next speaker gives his friendly/unfriendly statement and attaches, corresponding to the intention of the friendly/unfriendly speaker, his evaluation of the emotional response to the predecessor, or his argument, instead of the author of the emotional response. Brandstätter points out that every learning process has at least two different components: a problem-solving component (cognitive side of the learning process) and a classical conditioning component (emotional side of the learning process). In the former, the learner learns contingencies between reactions and consequences (see the first theoretical framework) while in the latter the learner learns an emotional connection between reaction and consequences (see the revised second theoretical framework).

The former distinction between instrumental and classical conditioning is here given up in favour of a more integrated point of view with the focus on the learning individual and his cognitive and emotional responses. The predictions of this revised view of classical conditioning would be the same as those made on the basis of the first and third theoretical frameworks.

The finding that a speaker who receives applause increases his influence with respect to observers' attitudes is not surprising and has been found in other studies (see Landy, 1972). However, the trend we observed that suggested that a friendly speaker was less influential in changing the attitudes of observers than a hostile speaker was somewhat unexpected (although in Stocker-Kreichgauer and von Rosenstiel, 1976, the same effect was significant). This result stands in contrast to our original hypothesis (Stocker-Kreichgauer and von Rosenstiel, 1976) and in part to the results of Schuler and Peltzer (1978) who found positive effects of friendliness on attitude change in a direct interaction situation. This surprising result concerning observed friendliness must be considered in the light of the many studies of direct interaction and modeling which report an influence-enhancing effect of sympathy (see Schuler, 1975; Stocker-Kreichgauer, 1976).

The differential effects of observed and directly experienced friendliness in discussion meetings seems to be well known to judicial experts. According to H.A. Hartmann (pers. comm.), the judicial expert behaves differently when speaking directly to the judge than when he addresses the expert of the other party in front of the judge.

He shows friendliness and politeness when he addresses the judge (whom he wants to influence in his direction), but behaves in a hostile and aggressive way when he speaks to the expert of the opponent in front of the judge (whom he wants to impress by that hostility). When he is alone with the expert of his opponent and wants to persuade him, however, he again chooses a friendly style of interaction.

How can we explain these differences in the effects of friendliness? Possibly by the theory of social exchange (Homans, 1958; Thibaut and Kelley, 1959, Adams, 1965; Bierhoff, 1974; Kelley and Thibaut, 1978). In the direct interaction situation the friendly speaker may view his friendliness as a "present" which he hopes to be answered by a "return present" by his partner (perhaps in the form of changes in attitude or beliefs in his direction). He cannot count upon unfriendliness having these positive effects. With respect to norms existing in our society, it is possible that the partner treated in a friendly way feels that friendliness cannot be taken for granted but requires a "return present" from his side (demand characteristics). The social exchange not only takes place with social-emotional goods, but also on the cognitive side. For example, if friendliness will have persuasive effects on the opponent in direct interaction, the opponent, in general, may evaluate the maintenance of a positive emotional interaction (the "rewards" he expects) higher than the consistency of his own cognitions about the issue and may change his attitude to correspond to that of his friendly partner (provided that his prediscussion position was not taken by chance but deliberately).

The observer of a media-transmitted discussion presumably does not interpret his relations to the speakers within a social exchange concept. He probably does not view the observed friendliness as a gift to himself but instead, as described earlier, as being indicative of a lack of power and competence. Additionally, he can see that the speaker in question is friendly though his opponent does not give up his position (awareness of contingencies).

We do have some doubts about the generalizability of our results concerning the relative success of the hostile speaker since all of our discussion topics had a hostile or punitive component. However, the attitude expressed towards that punitive topic did not seem to be correlated to personality traits. (The correlation between the initial position and personality traits as measured by the FPI, Fahrenberg and Selg, 1971, was not significant.)

As we have already mentioned, the results of our evaluation of the five experiments are compatible with the predictions of two of the theoretical frameworks: the learning of vicarious social reinforcement based on instrumental conditioning (awareness of contingencies) and modelling based on the attribution of social power and success. Within our data we have found no information to decide for one framework against the other. In fact, it may even be the case that the processes underlying the two frameworks are both operative in the learning process.

Further information about which framework best describes the processes going on within the subjects during observation and continuous attitude scaling requires an experiment testing the two. Perhaps one possibility could be the following. Before the media-transmitted discussion begins, subjects could be informed that one speaker is especially competent, successful or powerful. This should give him acceptance as a powerful model within a framework of social discussion norms which must be specified further. In the experiment, however, only the other speaker should be contingently reinforced. Furthermore, the reinforcements should be such that they could not be interpreted as reinforcements for competence or success or social power, e.g. "sunshine" after his argument; otherwise he would be seen as a competent model himself.

With regard to the generalizability of our results, we hasten to note that in different cultures and social classes there may exist quite different norms concerning how one should react in situations involving persuasion. Our findings were with members of the German middle class who were probably aware of the fact that the result of the discussion of the specific topics would have no real life consequences to them. Other cultures, social classes, topics, and degrees of ego involvement could possibly yield quite different results.

## References

Adams J. S. Inequity in social exchange. In Berkowitz, L. (ed.), *Advances in Experimental Social Psychology*, vol. 2, New York and London: Academic Press, 1965, 267–299.

Albers, G., Brandstätter, H. and Peltzer, U. Zum Problem der Messung von Einstellungsänderungen durch Meßwiederholung. *Problem und Entscheidung*, 1975, 14, 9–16.

Argyle, M. *Soziale Interaktion* (engl. Social interaction, London: Methuen, 1969) Köln: Kiepenheuer, 1972.

Bandura, A. *Principles of Behaviour Modification*. London: Holt, Rinehart and Winston, 1969.

Baron, R. A. Attraction toward the model and model's competence as determinants of adult aggressive behaviour. *Journal of Personality and Social Psychology*, 1970, 14, 345–351.

Bierhoff, H. W. Attraktion, hilfreiches Verhalten, verbale Konditionierung und Kooperation: eine Integration durch die Austauschtheorie. *Zeitschrift für Sozialpsychologie*, 1974, 84–107.

Brandstätter, H. Soziale Verstärkung in Diskussionsgruppen. In Brandstätter, H. and Schuler, H. (eds.) *Entscheidungsprozesse in Gruppen*, Bern: Huber, 1976, 65–82.

Byrne, D. and Clore, G. L. A reinforcement model of evaluative responses. *Journal of Personality*, 1970, 1, 103–128.

Byrne, D. and Griffith, W. Interpersonal attraction. *Annual Review of Psychology*, 1973, 24, 317–336.

Cronbach, L. J. and Furby, L. How we should measure "change" or should we? *Psychological Bulletin*, 1970, 74, 68–80.

Fahrenberg, J. and Selg, H. *Das Freiburger Persönlichkeitsinventar. FPI.* Göttingen: Hogrefe, 1970.

Heider, F. *The Psychology of International Relations*. New York: Wiley, 1958.

Homans, G.C. Social behavior as exchange. *American Journal of Sociology*, 1958, 63, 597–606.

Kelley, H. H. and Thibaut, J. W. *Interpersonal Relations: A theory of Interdependence*. New York: Wiley, 1978.

Kelman, H.C. Compliance, identification, and internalization: Three processes of attitude change. In Fishbein, M. (ed.) *Readings in Attitude Theory and Measurement*. New York: Wiley, 1967, 469–476.

Landy, D. The effects of an overhead audience's reaction and attractiveness of opinion change. *Journal of Experimental Social Psychology*, 1972, 8, 176–288.

Rosenstiel, L, von and Rüttinger, B. Die Wirkung von Applaus für Beiträge in Fernsehdiskussionen auf die Einstellungsänderung der Diskussionsbeobachter. In Brandstätter, H. and Schuler, H. (eds.) *Entscheidungsprozesse in Gruppen*. Bern: Huber, 1976, 83–104.

Rosenstiel, L, von and Stocker-Kreichgauer, G. Vicarious social reinforcement. In Brandstätter, H., Davis, J. H. and Schuler, H. (eds.) Dynamics of Group Decisions. Beverly Hills: Sage, 1978, 133–148.

Rosenstiel, L. von and Stocker-Kreichgauer, G. Der Einfluß stellvertretender sozialer Verstärkung auf den Entscheidungsverlauf der Beobachter von Gruppendiskussionen. *Problem und Entscheidung*, 1975, 14, 17–77.

Schuler, H. *Sympathie und Einfluß in Entscheidungsgruppen*. Bern: Huber, 1975.

Schuler, H. and Peltzer, U. Friendly versus unfriendly nonverbal behaviour: The effects in partner's decision-making perferences. In Brandstätter, H., Davis, J. H. and Schuler, H. (eds.) *Dynamics of Group Decisions*. Beverly Hills: Sage, 1978, 113–132.

Staats, A. W. *Learning, Language, and Cognition*. London: Holt, 1968.

Staats, A. W., Gross, M. C. Guay, P. F., and Carlson, C. C. Personality and social systems and attitude-reinforcer-discriminative theory: interest (attitude) formation, function, and measurement. *Journal of Personality and Social Psychology*, 1973, 26, 251–261.

Stocker-Kreichgauer, G. *Stellvertretende Verstärkung und Einfluß in Entscheidungsgruppen.* Augsburg, Diss., 1976.

Stocker-Kreichgauer, G. and von Rosenstiel, L. Der Einfluß der Sprecherfreundlichkeit auf den Entscheidungsverlauf der Beobachter von Gruppendiskussionen. *Problem und Entscheidung,* 1976, **18,** 23–78.

Thibaut, J. W. and Kelley, H. H. *The Social Psychology of Groups.* New York: Wiley, 1959.

# 12
# Liking and Influence in Group Decision Making: a Test in Four Different Experimental Settings

Heinz Schuler

Anyone who has ever taken part in group decision making has suspected that more than the "rational" parts of arguments are of importance for the decision. One additional influence is the liking-relations between the interacting persons. Besides the agreement or disagreement concerning the facts of the case, decisions also depend on social-emotional relations (i.e. whether another participant is conceptualized as a partner or as an opponent). Positive feelings should enhance attention towards a speaker, facilitate attributions of credibility, and thus reduce mechanisms of perceptual and attitudinal defence.

This intuitive notion is supported by a large number of social psychological and learning theories. Virtually all of the consistency theories (Abelson *et al.*, 1968) would predict yielding as one of the mechanisms for the reduction of cognitive inconsistency, which is produced by the perception of a positive liking-relation on one side, and a large attitudinal discrepancy on the other. In terms of concepts from exchange theory, such as justice (Homans, 1961), equity (Adams, 1965) and interpersonal relations (Kelley and Thibaut, 1978), yielding would be expected with higher probability when it can serve as a response to a liked participant's argumentation. Like-wise, several other psychological theories would support the notion of a liking—yielding relationship (cf. Schuler, 1975). Although the predictions derived from these concepts lack precision and dif-ferential validity, there is literally no viable theory predicting the contrary.

Part of a larger research project on "social emotions in discussion groups" (Brandstätter, 1978), our experimental approach to testing the liking-influence relationship in interaction was not originally founded on any special or explicitly formulated theory. Rather, the theoretical approach was developed parallel to experimental advancement. In short, the present state of our theoretical assumptions (following Brandstätter, 1976, 1978) can be stated as follows: (1) there is a close connection between emotions and motives; (2) a person reacts emotionally (positively or negatively) to situations facilitating or hindering need satisfaction; therefore, the type and intensity of motivational states determine the type and intensity of the emotions which are elicited by the given situation; (3) following classical conditioning concepts, emotions which were originally only evoked by motivationally relevant situational characteristics can become conditioned also to irrelevant elements of the situation (or to their cognitive representations); and (4) consideration of possible consequences, or alternative lines of action, can transform drive-controlled behaviour (impulsive action) into will-controlled behaviour (problem solving).

To predict a person's responses to his partner's behaviour on the basis of this theory of social emotions, the following need to be known or inferred: (1) whether this behaviour evokes positive or negative feelings; (2) to which characteristics of the situation these feelings are particularly conditioned; and (3) how the person interprets the situation. For example, another participant's positively evaluated remark ("I have always admired your thoughtful behaviour, but in this case you should agree with me") should lead to a more positive evaluation of the other person and of the other's attitude than before, but only if one does not have to worry that the other's remark is only a rhetorical phrase intended to induce flattery. Further determinants of the outcome are the needs of the interacting persons (persons with a high need for social approval will tend to interpret remarks as more laudatory than others do and will react more positively), and characteristics of the situation, including the partner's personality (his status, e.g. from which is inferred his necessity to flatter).

It is difficult to control all relevant parameters in a single experimental test of this theory. Therefore, it is important for construct validity and empirical generalizability to create a number of experimental settings which are as different as possible, but still comparable, in order to test the critical elements in each of them. From the convergence of these parameters, confirming evidence for the theory should be gained, and its "hard core" (Lakatos, 1970) should be submitted to increasingly strict tests relative to the less essential parts.

Explicit tests of this theory are still lacking. As mentioned above, it was developed over a number of years to reach its present form; this development was influenced less by the results of experiments than reasoning about the phenomenon in question.

The following four experiments explored the liking–influence relationship. Some share an experimental design which was used in several slightly different experiments, and, as far as appropriate, some of these additional results will be mentioned. It will be apparent that experimental complexity changed during the course of the research process. While the first experiment was very complex (involving an almost "natural" interaction of a three-person group), the second and third designs were characterized by vigorously enhanced control. By the last setting we had profited from our experience, and had gained enough confidence to work with a rather high level of experimental complexity once again.

The central independent variable consisted of the establishment of a liking-relation between the subjects. This was accomplished in different forms. In the first and second experiments subjects were informed that one of the other participants liked them very much. Our expectation was that this would create sympathy in kind; this was confirmed. The slight variation was that in the first experiment the manipulated liking-relation information concerned already well-acquainted respondents, which complicated the relationship some-what. In the later designs subjects were pre-experimentally (and sometimes even during the experimental discussion) unknown to each other. In the third design, liking was manipulated by attitudinal similarity information; additionally, verbal friendliness during presentation of the arguments was varied. In the fourth experiment confederates were trained to behave with a friendly or unfriendly non-verbal stance towards their partners.

In all these designs the social-emotional dimension was varied. The rather wide variation of the central independent variable should help to "encircle" the construct and to ensure some generalizability. For the sake of this second aim the following peripheral character-istics were also varied: group size (because of research economy only two- and three-person groups); discussion topics (in all cases we tried

TABLE 1

*Four types of experimental settings to test the liking-influence relationship in group decision making.*

| Type | Complexity | Group size | Medium of Interaction | Independent variables Controlled | Independent variables Manipulated | Dependent variables | Results |
|---|---|---|---|---|---|---|---|
| I | Very high: real interaction; self-produced arguments of different quality; no time limit | 3 | Free verbal interaction | Starting position in view of the discussion topic; enduring attraction among acquainted partners | Information of being liked by one of the partners | Changes in decision making preferences | Interaction of liking and positional distance |
| II | Low: fictitious interaction; choice of given arguments; time limited | 3 | Quasi-interaction written | Starting position (= extremity); sequence of argumentation; mutual impression rating | Information of being liked by one of the partners | Sum of changes in decision making preferences; changes in course of discussion; partner impression rating | Liking, extremity and first position enhanced influence liking-effect diminished during discussion |
| III | Low: fictitious interaction; choice of given arguments and remarks; time limited | 2 | Discussion via computer-terminals; partner simulated by dialogue program | FPI (personality inventory); values; starting position (extremity) | Similarity; verbal friendliness/unfriendliness status; expectation to see partner again | Sum of changes in decision making preferences; changes in course of discussion; partner impression rating; use of remarks; wish for contact | Similarity enhanced influence; friendliness induced friendliness (and some yielding) status and expectation of minor effect |
| IV | High: real interaction with confederate; self-produced arguments; no apparent time-limit | 2 | For subjects free verbal interaction; instructed confederate | Starting position (extremity); mutual impression rating | Non-verbal friendliness | Sum of changes in decision making preferences; changes in course of discussion; partner evaluation and discussion behaviour | Non-verbal friendliness effected partner's evaluation enhanced influence (even 8 weeks later); positive evaluation diminished by time; negative evaluation deteriorated |

to find topics of interest to the subjects); form of interaction (real, written, or via computer terminal); presence v. absence of an observer; all subjects naive v. confederate interaction; visible v. invisible scaling of preferences. Constant in all these variations was the scale of the decision preferences. This was an 11-point quasi-ratio scale where respondents stated their opinions before discussion and then either after each argument (own or other) or after every minute. Discussion usually lasted for 20–30 minutes. Subjects were asked to weigh the arguments favouring one side against the arguments supporting the other side of the case. The sum of weights was kept constant at 100. (See Table 1 and Fig. 1.)

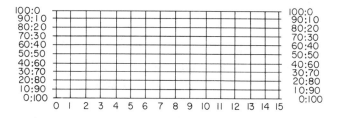

Fig. 1. Quasi-ratio scale used in the reported experiments. The length of the scale varied up to 30 scaling points.

This scale enabled us to compare start-end differences and also to analyse sequences and the development of influence processes. Different tests were conducted to clarify the characteristics of the scale and the scaling process. This allowed us to ascertain that the process of preference scaling itself did not bias the scores and that the principles of cardinal scaling can be assumed for this quasi-ratio scale (Stehle, 1977).

Different methods of data analysis were used: analysis of variance, trend analysis, regression analysis, start-end difference scores, and some attempts to adopt probabilistic sequence models like Markov chains (Peltzer, 1979). As far as necessary for the interpretation of the data, the methods used will be mentioned.

In the first of the four reported experiments (presented in more detail by Brandstätter et al., 1971) we started our empirical work with almost unreduced interactional complexity.

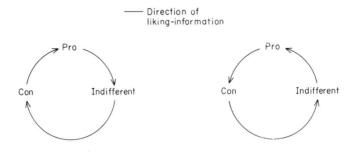

Fig. 2. Alternative directions of liking-information in reference to prediscussional preferences of triad-members in experiment I.

## Experiment I

METHOD

Thirty male and female students participated in this experiment. They were assigned to ten groups of three persons. Within each of the sex-homogeneous triads the subjects were pre-experimentally known to each other.

In the prediscussion phase the respondents individually stated their preferences regarding a set of relevant decisional propositions, most of which concerned university politics or didactics (e.g. "voting in plenary discussions should be performed anonymously in the future"). For the group discussions items were chosen which allowed composition of three-person groups in which one supported the proposition, one rejected it, and the third one was indifferent.

After a discussion on "probation" the participants of each group rated one another on a semantic differential containing an affective factor. This rating served as preparation for the liking manipulation, as well as to control the factual attraction between the discussants. Subsequently, every person was informed that one of his partners had rated him as "very likable." To avoid confounding liking and decisional preference, information was directed alternatively as is shown in Fig. 2. Thereafter, every triad discussed their topic for about half an hour. To maintain about the same degree of participation for each group member, every person was given the same number of "tokens"; one argument or statement had to be supplied for each token received. Following each contribution, the participants marked their preferences on the quasi-ratio scale. Finally, the

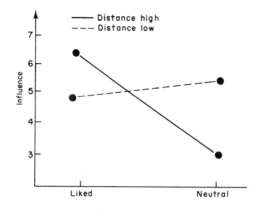

Fig. 3. Interaction between liking and positional distance on interpersonal influence. (Data from Brandstätter et al., 1971.)

respondents were asked about their hypotheses concerning the experiment and the credibility of the liking-manipulation.

RESULTS

Although there was a difference in influence between the liked and the neutral partner in the direction of our hypothesis, it did not reach statistical significance. However, there was a significant interaction in that liking did have an influence-heightening effect, but only when the distance of preferences between speaker and listener was high; it had no effect when the positional distance was low.

The interaction between distance and liking in Experiment I seems to be interpretable in terms of Sherif and Hovland's assimilation-contrast theory (1961); the low distance partner's arguments are "assimilated," i.e. their distance is underestimated, so they deliver no incentive for a remarkable change of preferences whatever the liking-relations. On the other hand, the high distance partner's arguments for a neutral or disliked participant lie in a region Sherif and Hovland called the "latitude of rejection" and are expected to evoke no impulse for yielding or even a "boomerang effect." In this condition, a liked partner's distant position could not be rejected as much, and thus would induce greater acceptance and more yielding.

Brandstätter et al. (1971) preferred a balance theory interpretation of the data. They felt that in the high distance condition, but not in the low distance condition, there is an imbalance between liking-relations and object-relations (Heider, 1958), and this leads to yielding as one possible strategy to balancing the situation.

The specificity of the liking-induction as shown in Fig. 3 causes us to ask if there may not be an alternative methodological interpretation. If the manipulation of liking worked — and we know from post-discussion ratings that it did — and a subject approached the participant who supposedly liked him very much, he must find it odd that this one of all people turned away and sought contact with the third person. This third person, on the other hand, while ignored by our subject, approached him.

Thus, we created a situation which, while being quite interesting concerning the special group dynamics, could have had some conflicting appeal for the subjects and rather unintended characteristics. There is no direct evidence, but it may have been this problem that suppressed the main effect of the liking-manipulation. In fact, the liking-distance-interaction was never again observed in the later experiments.

Other problems which hindered interpretation were the pre-experimental acquaintance of the participants which could have interacted with the liking-information, the differing lengths and qualities of the arguments used in discussion, and other aspects of what we called here the "experimental complexity." These impose difficulties in interpretating the results unambiguously.

Our reaction to this first experiment was a drastic improvement of experimental control in the second experiment, while the central variable, the liking manipulation, was in principle held constant.


## Experiment II

METHOD

In this experiment different groups of persons were hired as subjects. Of the 137 male respondents, 43 were middle managers of a large bank, 35 were economics students, 42 were participants in management training coming from different firms, and 17 were student officers of a military academy.

The subjects decided on a personnel decision case. In the pre-discussion phase they were informed about the details (i.e. a job description and a rather detailed description of an applicant). Afterwards they stated individually their preference to hire or to reject the applicant, received a list of arguments favouring their own position, and had to choose five they considered best for the discussion.

The respondents were told that they would lead a discussion with two others of the 15–20 people present in the room who were all acquainted with each other, but that they would not be identified personally. First, they rated five group members of their own choice on a likable/not likable semantic differential item. After the fictitious analysis of the scores, each subject was told that one of his future discussion partners (marked as A, B, or C) had rated him as "especially likable" and that the other one did not give any evaluation of him. Again, it was assumed that expression of liking would evoke a positive attitude towards that person. Subsequently, each subject was represented by a set of 15 arguments in a standardized sequence, every five of them arguing for a pro, con or an indifferent position (i.e. not to decide now, but first to collect additional information). One of the three positions was represented by the very arguments he had chosen before, the other two by the arguments stemming from his fictitious partners, called A, B, or C (actually, the discussion sets were prearranged for the parts of the two discussion partners). After reading each argument, the respondents had to state their decision preferences on the same quasi-ratio scale used in Experiment I.

After the discussion the respondents performed some additional scaling (e.g. evaluation of discussion partners) and were interviewed and thoroughly debriefed.

RESULTS

The number of subjects was large enough for sample-splitting; thus, the hypotheses could be tested with two sets of data.

There were significant main-effects for the three independent variables liking (induced by the liking-manipulation), extremity, and sequence of argumentation (both induced by design). Liked participants had more influence than neutral ones, arguments favouring extreme positions induced more yielding than those representing a position of indifference, and arguments directly following the subjects' own statements were more influential than those coming in the second position.

In terms of explained variance, extremity had the greatest effects, sequence of argumentation was second, and liking third. It seems worth noting that these three variables were additive for both sets of data. A liked participant arguing extremely pro or con and being first with his statement was most influential; a disliked discussant arguing

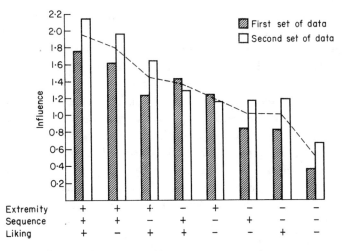

| Extremity | + | + | + | − | + | − | − | − |
| Sequence | + | + | − | + | − | + | − | − |
| Liking | + | − | + | + | − | − | + | − |

Fig. 4. Mean influence for eight different conditions. (From Schuler, 1975, p. 134.)

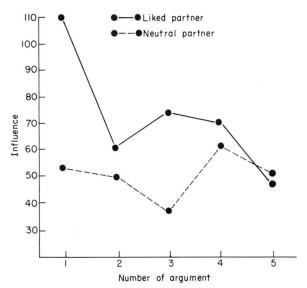

Fig. 5. Sums of influence for liked and neutral discussion partners for arguments 1–5 in the course of the discussions. (Data from Schuler, 1975.)

for deletion of the decision in the second place of the sequence was least influential (see Fig. 4).

A trend analysis for the arguments of the liked and neutral discussants showed a diminution of influence of the liked partners during the discussion (from their first to their fifth argument, with an intermediate low level at the second). The neutral discussants' arguments by and large kept their level of influence throughout the discussion and, thus, at the fifth argument both ended with an equal amount of influence (see Fig. 5).

This second experiment, primarily designed as an improvement of the first one, showed a rather clear-cut influence of the liking variable. However, this effect is not as large as the other two variables, extremity and sequence of argumentation. The diminution of the liking effect during the course of the discussion showed up in similar form in the following experiments.

In Experiment III we took advantage of a computer with a dialogue program to simulate the discussion partner. One aspect of complexity, group size, was reduced from three to two. The decisional case and the selection of preformulated arguments was held constant as in Experiment II. Attraction was manipulated via attitudinal similarity supplied by a variation in the friendliness of remarks added to the arguments.

## Experiment III

METHOD

Experiment III took place in a highly artificial setting. Eighty-four Augsburg University students participated in groups of 12 to 20 in a room equipped with 20 computer terminals. Subjects were made to believe that there were connections between these terminals and that they would interact in dyads with one human partner. In fact, there was no connection, and they interacted with a dialogue program (named LIDIA).

After playing some computer games to train the subjects in handling the terminals, the subjects were given the same personnel problem used in Experiment II and were similarly instructed. As was the case there, they first stated their prediscussion preference to employ the applicant or not. As a preparation of the liking-manipulation, they were asked to answer some questions concerning "general attitudes and beliefs" (ten items of an Allport-Vernon-type, or F scale-type, respectively). They were then shown the bogus answers of their partner. These answers were either very similar to their own (i.e. with only one difference) or very dissimilar (nine differences out of ten). They then rated their partner on seven semantic differential items.

During the computerized discussion each contribution consisted of an argument and an introduction phrase. Subjects were given lists of arguments that corresponded to their initial decisions and with lists of phrases, friendly, neutral, and unfriendly in character. From those lists, they had to choose one phrase and one argument for each of their contributions (e.g. "I respect your view of this matter, but . . ." v. "I strongly oppose this position, because . . ."). Both were marked with a number which was to be typewritten in order to be displayed on their own monitor and seemingly to be communicated to the other discussant.

The fictitious partner (i.e. the dialogue program) represented the adverse position of the subject's arguments. For one half of the subjects friendly phrases were used, for the other half unfriendly ones. Subject and partner followed each other in giving their contribution. The dialogue program was developed to a state of credibility such that it was taken for a human partner by all of the subjects. For example, twice in every discussion the respondents saw a message on their monitor informing them that they would have to wait for a further moment because either their partner had not yet decided which argument to use or he had made a mistake in typewriting.

Subjects and their "partners" argued alternatively by communicating five contributions each. After every argument subjects stated their preferences on a version of the quasi-ratio scale especially adapted to the computer terminal. After discussion had ended, respondents stated their final position, again gave a rating of their partner, and were asked about their interpretation of the experiment.

RESULTS

The intended liking-manipulation via information about attitudinal similarity was successful. Ratings showed that similar partners were rated as being more likable than dissimilar discussants (2.05 v. 4.25 on a six-point scale).

Both independent variables, similarity and friendliness, had an effect on yielding. However, an analysis of linear trends was insignificant for the time x similarity and the time x friendliness interaction, as well as the main effect of time, although all of them were in the hypothesized directions. Figure 6 demonstrates that both curves have similar shapes for both variables. An analysis of variance for the

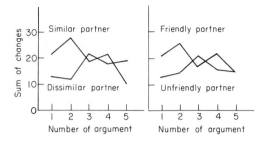

Fig. 6. Sums of changes of preferences on partner's arguments. Left: similar v. dissimilar partners. Right: friendly v. unfriendly partners. (From Peltzer and Schuler, 1976, p. 111.)

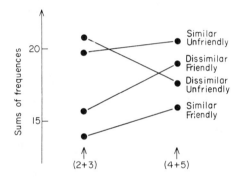

Fig. 7. Sums of frequencies of use of unfriendly discussion remarks dependent on partner's similarity and friendliness for second and third v. fourth and fifth argument. (From Peltzer and Schuler, 1976, p. 112.)

combined values of the first and second v. third, fourth, and fifth arguments (roughly first v. second half of the discussion) was statistically significant for similarity and marginally significant for friendliness.

The use of unfriendly remarks by the respondents was also defined as a second dependent variable. The analysis of variance was significant for friendliness. Friendly arguing partners led to the use of less unfriendly remarks compared to unfriendly partners. No analogous effect was demonstrated for similarity.

The combined sums of second and third v. fourth and fifth argument show an interesting, although not completely consistent pattern (the first argument could not be included as half of the subjects started themselves, while in the other half partners started the discussion) (see Fig. 7).

As Byrne (1969) and others had shown with high reliability, information about attitudinal similarity was suitable to evoke positive feelings towards the partner. Similarity was shown to have more effect on yielding, while verbal friendliness seemed to be more important for eliciting the same style of argumentation with the discussion partner. In this respect, a former study in this series (Schuler, 1974) had shown an interesting interaction between extroversion and style. While introverts responded rather independent from their partners' remarks, extroverts showed more conciliation to unfriendly discussants than to friendly ones. However, this result has failed in attempted replications.

The chronological sequence of similarity/dissimilarity and friendliness/unfriendliness could be viewed in terms of gain-loss (Aronson and Linder, 1965). As can be seen in Fig. 7, similar and friendly participants elicited the fewest but an increasing number of unfriendly remarks. Similar but unfriendly partners provoked the most unfriendly style and also a diminishing number of unfriendly remarks in response to a dissimilar and unfriendly participant is in full concordance with gain-loss. Only one of the four conditions does not fit expectations; this is the increase in unfriendly phrases for dissimilar but friendly partners, who should theoretically gain most in positive evaluation.

An influence heightening effect of similarity-induced liking was found in a further experiment of this type (Schuler and Peltzer, 1975), combined there with two other variables, status and expectation of future interaction.

The fourth experiment in this series profited from our experience with the earlier experimental settings. What had shown to be too complex to be manageable at the start of our project, seemed to be feasible at this later date. For discussion in a real interaction setting, this time we trained confederates, and controlled the time and quality of argumentation. In this fourth experiment the liking variable was introduced in the form of non-verbally expressed friendliness.


## Experiment IV

METHOD

Sixty-nine male students participated either as participants in dyads or as observers of these dyads. This time the form of communication was face-to-face interaction. The respondents had to imagine they were members of a disciplinary court making a decision on a case where a teacher was accused of an indecent assault on a pupil. To avoid the social-desirability components of a decision in *dubio pro reo*, the accusing girl, who was of full age, was said to be in danger of being condemned for having committed perjury. In this way, a decision had to be made between a negative consequence for the teacher or a negative consequence for the pupil. The case was pre-tested until a balance was obtained regarding the alternatives.

The central independent variable, expression of positive emotions, took the form of non-verbal friendliness or unfriendliness of one of the discussion partners. Four students were trained (with the help of an acting school) to express unambiguously non-verbal friendliness (frequent eye contact, friendly countenance, e.g. smiling if suitable, bodily orientation towards the partner, and emotionally warm voice) and non-verbal unfriendliness (avoidance of eye contact, neutral or hostile countenance, bodily orientation away from partner, and indifferent or aggressive voice). In addition, each of the confederates learned to argue for as well as against the facts of the case.

A second independent variable was the presence or absence during the discussion of an "observer" — a third student who watched and listened to the participants and performed the same ratings and decisions but stayed in a passive role. The observer was introduced to assess the importance of an observer for the discussion and to compare the responses of active and passive participants.

At the beginning of each experimental session the subjects had the opportunity to become briefly acquainted with each other. The con-federates behaved neutrally during this period, since they did not know which role they would have to play afterwards. The case was presented to the subjects in written form. After an individual decision the subjects were assigned to the experimental conditions. Prior to discussion the members of each group rated each other on a nine-item semantic differential.

The discussion took place in the form of alternative argumentation. The subjects were asked to try to come to a joint decision. Every minute the participants as well as the observer had to state their decision preferences on the quasi-ratio scale. After 22 minutes the discussion was ended by the experimenter. Then the discussion participants rated each other once more on the semantic differential items used before the discussion. Following the discussion, the

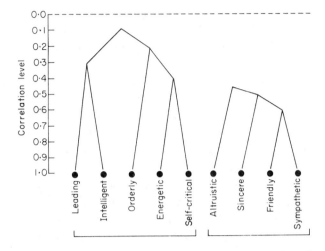

Fig. 8. Hierarchical clustering of the partner rating by means of a semantic differential. (From Schuler and Peltzer, 1978, p. 120.)

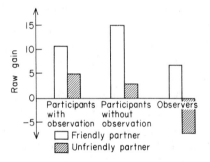

Fig. 9. Effects of friendly and unfriendly behaviour on participants' and observers' preferences. (From Schuler and Peltzer, 1978, p. 123.)

respondents were interviewed individually in order to get information about the individual course of the decision, and to reconcile possible strain caused by the partner's unfriendly behaviour.

RESULTS

The inter-correlation matrix of the nine semantic differential items of all 69 subjects was submitted to an hierarchical cluster analysis. Two rating factors were clearly discriminated: one factor of social-emotional evaluation and one factor of dominance or potency. The

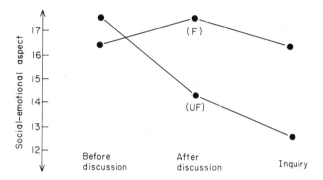

Fig. 10. Changes of partner ratings (liking factor) for friendly (F) and unfriendly (UF) participants at three points in time. (From Schuler and Peltzer, 1978, p. 127.)

two factor scores were not significantly correlated ($r = 0.157$) and so offered no evidence against an hypothesis of independence (see Fig. 8).

Non-verbal, but friendly, participants influenced their partners' decision preferences more than unfriendly acting persons (see Fig. 9). The presence of observers had no influence on the participants' behaviours or preferences. Observers reacted similarly to discussants, but somewhat more critically; i.e. they withdrew from the unfriendly debater's point of view, while the active participants in this condition only showed a lesser degree of yielding. These effects were diminished somewhat when measured with a post-experimental questionnaire eight weeks later, but still reached a statistically significant level.

The analysis of variance for the partner rating (social-emotional aspect) at three points of time (before discussion, immediately after discussion, and eight weeks later) showed effects of time and the time × friendliness interaction to be significant (see Fig. 10). The main effect of friendliness scarcely missed the 0.05 level of significance, which may be explained by a slight initial difference in favour of the later unfriendly debaters. While the friendly partners' gain in liking during the discussion was almost diminished after eight weeks, the evaluation of unfriendly discussion partners deteriorated even further.

The success in distinguishing the two factors of behaviour (or behaviour rating), liking and dominance (see Fig. 8), supports Argyle's assumption (1969) of two orthogonal factors of non-verbal behaviour.

There was no indication of a third activity factor as postulated by Mehrabian (1972).

Especially remarkable in the data from Experiment IV is the change in partner rating from the first to the second post-discussion inquiry. Contrary to the impression of the friendly acting person, the rating of the unfriendly partner became even worse during the following period. This could be explained by the partner's failing to correspond to social norms of politeness and kindness. Presumably there is a difference in information processing between the encoding and retrieval of observations of positively and negatively evaluated behaviour when one is the adressee.

As to the effect of behavioural style, this kind of emotionally positive behaviour enhanced the influence on the partner's decisional preference. In a second experiment of the same type, but with confederates acting verbally instead of non-verbally friendly or aggressive, the same effect was demonstrated to an even greater extent (Klein-Moddenborg and Brandstätter, 1978). Friendly behavioural style enhanced the influence on the partner's preference scaling, unfriendly style reduced it, and behavioural style had more impact on discussion partners than on observers.

## Summary

To sum up the reported results, a liked participant had higher influence on his partner's decisional preferences than a neutral or disliked one. This effect was rather small in magnitude, but quite reliable. Stable interactions with other variables were not observed.

Comparing the four types of experiments, the way in which liking was induced, or, formulated in behavioural terms, in what special way social reinforcement was expressed seemed to be relatively unimportant. Although phenomenally quite different, the diverse types of social reinforcement had about the same effect. The information that one is liked by another person, the high attitudinal similarity, the perception of arguments with conciliant, friendly remarks, and the view of one's discussion partner as behaving in a non-verbally warm and friendly way — all these different expressions of the liking construct evoked positive evaluation in reverse and some willingness to correct one's decisional preference in direction of the partner's arguments.

Thus, it does not seem to be a question of a specific behavioural dimension or even of special elements of behaviour, but of the characteristic common to all of this information — that they are interpreted by the addressee as expressions of benevolence, as positive evaluation and as such evoke positive emotions. In terms of Brandstätter's theory of social emotions (Brandstätter, 1976, 1978), these emotions are conditioned to the position represented in the other participant's arguments and, by making it more favourable, elicit a process of reformulation of one's own preferences and position.

As was outlined earlier, the following three parameters are conceptualized as the most important for a discussant's reaction to his or her partner's discussion style: (a) whether this behaviour evokes positive or negative feelings, (b) to which situational characteristics these feelings are conditioned, and (c) how the participant interprets the situation. Concerning the first parameter, we can state that each one of our different experimental operationalizations seemed to have had this effect. We tried to control the second parameter, the interpretation of the situation, by means of experimental design and setting. Beyond that, however, there is a residual variance dependent on individual differences in interpreting the situation. For more precise predictions of participants' reactions, this should be a source of additional capacity for explanation. A special theoretical problem is posed by the conditioning of feelings. It should make a lot of difference whether positive feelings are conditioned to the attitudinal position of another person, or to their own arguments spoken just before the partner reacted in such a pleasant way. In the first case we should expect yielding, in the second one the contrary. Regarding our results, we can conclude that it was the other's position rather than the own arguments; but the low, although reliable, amount of influence could well mean that a potentially higher effect was suppressed in that subjects (with an unknown amount of variance between them) came not only to find their partner's arguments attractive, but also were reinforced in their own position to a certain extent.

In this connection, Experiment III, where two different kinds of reinforcements (similarity and verbal friendliness) were varied, seems to be of special importance. Similarity had a higher influential effect than friendliness, while verbal statements of a friendly or unfriendly kind were more important in eliciting the same style of argumentation. This could be interpreted as an indication that all of our different types of reinforcements did have the effect of evoking positive or negative feelings, but had differing effect as well, i.e. the elements of the situation they were conditioned to.

Since the experiments conducted so far were not explicitly designed as tests of the "theory of social emotions," we can only answer these questions speculatively. In some cases, thorough post-experimental interviews provided interesting interpretive hints, but we still lack formal algorithms to combine these with the other results. Empirical answers of more stringency could be expected from experiments aimed directly at these explanatory details (by strictly separating and controlling the different reinforcing processes). However, as in our Experiment III, special difficulties will be posed by interactional effects.

To date, we must be content with describing the more global effects of liking or of liking-inducing properties of a person on his partner's preferences in decision making groups: it seems to work.

## References

Abelson, R. P., Aronson, E., MacGuire, W. J., Newcomb, T. N., Rosenberg, M. J. and Tannenbaum, P. (Eds) *Theories of Cognitive Consistency: a Sourcebook.* Chicago: Rand McNally, 1968.

Adams, J. S. Inequity in social exchange. In L. Berkowitz (Ed.) *Advances in Experimental Social Psychology,* vol. 2, New York and London: Academic Press, 1965, 267–299.

Argyle, M. *Social Interaction.* London: Tavistock, 1969.

Aronson, E. and Linder, D. Gain and loss of esteem as determinants of interpersonal attractiveness. *Journal of Experimental Social Psychology,* 1965, 1, 156–171.

Brandstätter, H. Soziale Verstärkung in Diskussionsgruppen. In H. Brandstätter and H. Schuler (Eds) *Entscheidungsprozesse in Gruppen.* Bern: Huber, 1976, 65–82.

Brandstätter, H. Social emotions in discussion groups. In H. Brandstätter, J. H. Davis and H. Schuler (Eds) *Dynamics of Group Decisions.* Beverly Hills: Sage, 1978, 93–111.

Brandstätter, H., Molt, W., von Rosenstiel, L., Rüttinger, B., Schuler, H. and Stocker-Kreichgauer, G. Der Einfluß in Entscheidungsgruppen als Funktion der Sympathie und des Unterschieds in den Handlungspräferenzen. *Problem und Entscheidung,* 1971, 6, 2–71.

Byrne, D. Attitudes and attraction. In L. Berkowitz (Ed.) *Advances in Experimental Social Psychology,* vol. 4, New York and London: Academic Press, 1969, 35–89.

Heider, F. *The Psychology of Interpersonal Relations.* New York: John Wiley, 1958.

Homans, G. C. *Social Behavior: its Elementary Forms.* New York: Harcourt Brace Jovanovich, 1961.

Kelley, H. H. and Thibaut, J. W. *Interpersonal Relations: a Theory of Interdependence.* New York: John Wiley, 1978.

Klein-Moddenborg, V. and Brandstätter, H. Kurz- und langfristige Wirkungen verbaler Aggression auf Beobachter und Teilnehmer von Gruppendiskussionen. *Problem und Entscheidung,* 1978, 22, 79—108.

Lakatos, I. Falsification and the methodology of scientific research programmes. In I. Lakatos and A. Musgrave (Eds) *Criticism and the Growth of Knowledge.* Cambridge: Cambridge University Press, 1970, 91—195.

Mehrabian, A. *Nonverbal Communication.* New York: Aldine-Atherton, 1972.

Peltzer, U. Interaktion und Entscheidung in Gruppen. Doctoral Dissertation, University of Augsburg, Augsburg: Maro, 1979.

Peltzer, U. and Schuler, H. Personwahrnehmung, Diskussionsverhalten und Präferenzänderung in Dyaden (LIDIA II). In H. Brandstätter and H. Schuler (Eds) *Entscheidungsprozesse in Gruppen.* Bern: Huber, 1976, 105—117.

Schuler, H. Soziale Verstärkung und Diskussionsverhalten bei simulierter Interaktion (LIDIA I). *Problem und Entscheidung,* 1974, 12, 26—37.

Schuler, H. *Sympathie und Einfluß in Entscheidungsgruppen.* Bern: Huber, 1975.

Schuler, H. and Peltzer, U. Ähnlichkeit, Kompetenz und die Erwartung künftiger Interaktion als Determinanten von Diskussionsverhalten und Partnerbeurteilung (LIDIA III). *Problem und Entscheidung,* 1975, 14, 78—107.

Schuler, H. and Peltzer, U. Friendly versus unfriendly nonverbal behavior: The effects on partner's decision-making preferences. In H. Brandstätter, J. H. Davis and H. Schuler (Eds) *Dynamics of Group Decisions.* Beverly Hills: Sage, 1978, 113—132.

Sherif, M. and Hovland, C. *Social Judgement.* New Haven: Yale University Press, 1961.

Stehle, W. Skalierung von Entscheidungspräferenzen. Ein experimenteller Skalenvergleich. Unpublished masters thesis. University of Augsburg, 1977.

# 13
# The Influence of Social Emotions on Bargaining Outcomes in a Bilateral Monopoly Game

Hermann Brandstätter and Austin C. Hoggatt

This study deals with the question of whether in a bargaining situation yielding to the opponent's demand is affected by emotional relations in a way similar to attitude change in a group discussion on matters of facts or values. The social emotional conditions of attitude change in discussion groups have been studied for some years at our Institute (cf. Brandstätter, 1978, for references). In general, perceived similarity of the partner as well as his verbal or non-verbal friendliness fosters agreement, particularly during the early stages of discussion.

Emotional responses to the discussion partner can modify attitude change by affecting the perception of the other's stand on the issue, the other's demand for conforming to his stand, and the other's arguments supporting his/her stand. Social comparison according to Festinger (1954) has its focus on the perception of the other's stand. Much of the research on conformity deals with perception of the other's implicit or explicit demand (cf. Hollander, 1976). The third means of influence, exchanging information on the issue, is analysed mainly with models of information integration (Anderson, 1971; Anderson and Graesser, 1976). Burnstein *et al.* (1973) as well as Ebbesen and Bowers (1974) may be mentioned here as well.

So far in explaining the function of social emotions on the influence process we have not been able to separate the three means of influence. However, we may speculate that it is mainly the perception of the other's demand that is dependent on social emotions. More experiments focusing on separating the three means of influence will be necessary in order to test this hypothesis. A step in this direction was taken by Mills and Aronson (1965) who showed that a physically attractive female speaker was more persuasive than an unattractive one only if she openly stated her desire to influence the listeners, i.e. if she announced her demand of the listeners to conform with her view.

Exchanging arguments in order to reach agreement upon a matter of fact or value is similar in one respect to exchanging offers in order to reach a compromise in sharing a scarce commodity: both imply the partner's demand for yielding. From our perspective, it is the expected reward or punishment that promotes yielding to the partner's demand, not the integration of new information about the issue, nor social comparison. Such reward or punishment may be expected from the other's behavior or from internalized social norms of equity or equality.

Rubin and Brown (1975) mention 17 bargaining studies focusing on perceived attractiveness or similarity of the other. However, we agree with Morley (1978) who does not subsume PD-games under "bargaining," since there is no sequence of concessions until agreement is reached. The experiments of Morgan and Sawyer (1967) and Benton (1971) are the only two out of the 17 studies mentioned by Rubin and Brown that deal with bargaining in the narrow sense. A recent study by Druckman and Bonoma (1976) has to be added here.

Morgan and Sawyer had dyads of fifth- and sixth-grade boys bargain for allocation of asymmetrically distributed rewards. They sat on opposite sides behind a "bargaining board" that was furnished with seven pockets on each side. The pockets contained on one side from zero up to six quarters, on the other side the pockets contained from zero to six nickels in a reversed order. The dyads could freely discuss their offers. If they agreed on a pair of directly opposite pockets, each got the contents of the pocket on his side; otherwise neither got anything. Side payments were not allowed. According to sociometric choices 14 pairs were composed of "friends" and the other 14 pairs were composed of "non-friends." Half of the pairs were informed of the partner's maximum and minimum expected outcome, the other half were not informed. Whereas non-friends generally settled for equal rewards (i.e., 25¢ and 25¢) in both information conditions, friends agreed on equitable rewards only if they were informed of the other's expectation; otherwise they agreed on equal rewards. Morgan and Sawyer thought that a subject who finds himself in the weaker position assumes that the other strives for an equitable solution. If the other is a friend, the person yields to the assumed expectancy of his partner; if he is not a friend, he insists upon the preferred equal distribution. Since boys of this age actually prefer equal solutions, even if they are in the stronger position, informing the pairs on the mutual expectancies would lead friends to agree on equal solutions. Without information on expectancies non-friends needed much more time to reach agreement than with information. For friends there was not such a difference. Friends seemed to enjoy the interaction and not to be in a hurry, whereas non-friends seemed to try to finish the interaction in a businesslike manner as soon as possible.

Benton (1971) was interested in reward allocation depending on merit and liking. Twenty-four dyads of boys and 24 dyads of girls, 9—12 years of age, were to bargain about which of four pairs of toys to choose for playing. The toys previously had been ranked individually by each child according to their attractiveness to the child. The first rank of one child was paired with the fourth rank of the other, the second rank was paired with the third, and so on: (1, 4), (2, 3), (3, 2), (4, 1). One third of the dyads of each sex were composed of friends, neutrals, and non-friends (according to socio-metric choices). At the beginning of the experimental session they had been informed that they were allowed to play with the toys only if at least one of them had been successful in a reading compre-hension test. One randomly selected child of each dyad had been made to appear successful in the test thus creating the possibility of choosing a pair of toys for both.

Prebargaining ratings of desirability of the various possible out-comes and actual outcomes of the bargaining were analyzed, as well as content of the discussions and the post-bargaining satisfaction ratings. In the prebargaining rating of the acceptability of the pairs of toys female friends preferred equality, whether successful in the verbal comprehension test or not; female non-friends who were successful in the test favored equity; those who were non-friends and unsuccessful favored equality. For boys there was no such a differential influence of friendship on prebargaining rating.

A difference between the prebargaining set of toys and the bargaining set may have been responsible for the fact that the impact of success (merit) and friendship on bargaining outcome was less clear. A sharp difference could be observed in the style of bargaining communication: female friends emitted a greater number of positive emotional responses than female non-friends. Such a difference could not be found for boys. The bargaining outcomes did not differ in a clear pattern. Since the prebargaining rating was based on five pairs of toys with ratings of 15, 24, 33, 42 and 51, whereas for the bargaining new pairs had been formed not containing the toys with the lowest rating, no equality solution existed. The results of the postbargaining satisfaction ratings were in agreement with the results of the prebargaining acceptability ratings.

Fifty-two eighth-grade boys from a junior high school participated in the experiment by Druckman and Bonoma (1976). In each session the two boys were to bargain for "imaginary grocery items" by exchanging written messages mediated by the experimenter. Both of them acted as buyers assuming the other would be the seller. At the beginning, each subject was given $1.25, and was informed that the other had paid between 50¢ and 60¢ for the items. The initial bargaining range was set equal for all subjects by requiring the subject to answer the first demand of the seller that was always $1.25 with an offer of 25¢. The subject's outcome was $1.25 minus the price he paid to the seller.

The opponent's perceived similarity was manipulated by the usual procedure. Half of the subjects bargained with an allegedly similar opponent, the other half with a dissimilar one. In one condition (increasing concession rate) the programmed seller started on Trial 3 with a concession that was one tenth of the last buyer's concession, and increased the concession rate by one tenth each time the subject made a concession, thus the concession rate moving upwards towards a maximum of 1.1 of the subject's previous concession. In the other condition (decreasing concession rate) the seller began with a concession rate of 1.1 and ended with a concession rate of 0.1.

Presumably the subjects were informed that there would be no award at all if they had not reached agreement by the 60th trial. At each step the subject was to record the seller's offer, his own offer, how far he would go at the moment, and what the other would offer next.

Although the authors analyzed their data and their experimental results in a rather confusing way, we may point to some of the effects of the opponent's similarity. The attraction to the similar other, at the beginning considerably higher than attraction to the dissimilar other, decreased as a result of the bargaining, whereas the initially low attraction to the dissimilar other increased somewhat.

Thirty-two percent (9 out of 28) of the subjects in the similar condition compared to 8% (2 out of 24) in the dissimilar condition were not able to reach agreement by the 60th trial, and therefore had to end the bargaining with no profit. This is explained by disappointed expectation: a buyer expects a similar seller to concede more and is ready to concede more himself; however, the buyer becomes increasingly disappointed if the seller does not meet his expectations and therefore becomes increasingly resistant himself.

Although the results of the three experiments are not completely consistent, some general conclusions may be drawn: (1) the perceived expectations of a liked other are more readily met than those of a disliked other; and (2) tough bargaining behavior of a liked other makes agreement more difficult than tough bargaining behavior of a disliked other.

Each of the three experiments implied bargaining with complete information on the other's payoff. The subjects were school children. Our experiment used a bargaining game with incomplete information, and the subjects were adults. Having only incomplete information on the other's payoff, a subject will guess it in order to understand and to predict the other's behavior. Such a design allows the experimenter to test one possible reaction to tough bargaining of a liked other: the other may be excused by perceiving him/her to be in a difficult payoff situation.

*Hypothesis 1: Liking promotes agreement by (a) diminishing the probability of deadlocks and (b) by leading the players closer to agreement in the case of deadlock.* If someone likes a bargaining partner, that person will accept the partner's demand more easily than when the partner is not liked, mainly for two reasons. (a) The person has been rewarded in the past by the partner; therefore, the person is ready to give the other some benefits in return. (b) The person perceives yielding as promising with respect to future returns from the other.

*Hypothesis 2: Liking promotes yielding to the partner's demand more if the stake is low than if it is high.* Being non-cooperative with a disliked other entails the risk of deadlock, losing any chance of gain. A person will allow feelings toward the opponent to interfere with bargaining only if there is little to lose by not being cooperative.

*Hypothesis 3: Liking promotes agreement more if the opponents are dependent on each other beyond the bargaining situation than if they are not.* Being non-cooperative with a disliked other may result in retaliation by the other at a later occasion. Therefore, a person will temper a bad mood if dependent on the other's benevolence in the future.

*Hypothesis 4: A liked opponent who is a tough bargainer is more often excused by being perceived in a difficult payoff situation than a disliked opponent.* If a liked other, who generally is expected to behave cooperatively, turns out to be a tough bargainer, the subject tries to regain cognitive consistency. One of the ways to achieve that is attributing the responsibility for the other's strange behavior to the situation.

## Method

### SUBJECTS

Thirty-two male adults, mostly businessmen, together with some university administrators, high school teachers, and university professors, were subjects. In each of the four experimental sessions eight subjects participated.

### BARGAINING GAME

We used the bargaining game with incomplete information (Hoggatt and Selten, 1978). The two players have to divide 20 money units between themselves if they reach agreement.

The subject only knows his own cost, which is told to him at the beginning of the game (high cost = 9 money units, low cost = 0 money units), he only knows that the other's cost is either low or high with a probability of $P = 0.50$. Both players decide on a demand independently from one another at each stage. As soon as both bargainers have made their demands they are reported to the players simultaneously. Each player guesses the cost of the other, and goes on to the next stage.

Agreement is reached if the sum of both demands is at most 20 money units. In this case the subject receives his last demand minus his cost. The amount by which the sum of demands falls short of 20 is split evenly.

Conflict occurs at any stage for which neither player makes a concession, i.e. both demands remain at the levels set in the previous stage. In case of conflict both players have a net payoff at zero. The original design of the game was modified in order to be able to test our hypotheses about liking and dependency.

## VARIATION OF LIKING

When the eight participants arrived at the laboratory they were seated around a table and asked to introduce themselves to the others by talking a little about their work and leisure activities. Each subject could be identified by a letter printed on a card and put before him on the table. Based on the first impression or prior acquaintance each subject marked on a scale ranging from 1 (very close) to 20 (very remote), with an indifference point between 10 and 11, how close he felt himself to each of the other participants. The liking rankings were typed on a computer terminal in order to find quickly a pairing of subjects that fit the experimental design as well as the real ordering of liking. We were concerned about avoiding any deception of the subjects. At the beginning of each game the subject was informed on whether he and his partner in the game liked each other or did not like each other, in order to learn "how liking based on first impression is affected by further interaction in a bargaining situation."

## DEPENDENCY

The participants of the second and the fourth group were informed that they could award the other player a bonus payment of 0, 1, or 2 money units (1 money unit = 10¢) at the end of each game. They were told that they would find out about the received bonus only after the end of all games.

## PERSON AND ROBOT GAMES

Based on the data of a previous experiment (Hoggatt and Selten, 1978) the laboratory computer was programmed to simulate a person's bargaining behavior (for more information on this program, see Hoggatt *et al.* 1978). The subjects were informed at the beginning of the experiment "that sometimes they will play one of the other persons and sometimes they will play a robot," without knowing whether the partner is a person or a robot. Each person played eight games. The games Number 1, 4, 5 and 8 were with the robot. Only the person games were analyzed for this report.

## FINAL RATING OF LIKING

After ending a game the subject marked on the 20-point scale how close he felt now to his partner in the game.

MEASURES OF INDIVIDUAL DIFFERENCES

Before entering the bargaining experiments the subjects took a test
on motivational orientation (cooperative, competitive, or individualistic) designed by Kuhlmann (cf. Kuhlmann and Marshello, 1975).
After finishing all of the eight games the subjects answered the
Machiavellism Scale (Christie and Geis, 1970). Since these measures
were not analyzed for the present report, we will not describe the
measures in detail.

THE INCOMPLETE BLOCK DESIGN

An incomplete block design with repeated measures was chosen in
order to balance the effects of major importance (Table 1). The
design was the same for low dependence (no bonus could be awarded
at the end of the game) and high dependence (bonuses could be
awarded). For the person games the eight players (A to H) were
paired as in Table 2.

TABLE 1

*Balanced incomplete block design*

| | | | | | | | |
|---|---|---|---|---|---|---|---|
| 11 2 4 | 22 1 1 | 32 2 2 | 41 1 3 | 51 1 2 | 62 2 3 | 72 1 4 | 81 2 1 |
| 11 2 1 | 22 1 4 | 32 2 3 | 41 1 2 | 51 1 3 | 62 2 2 | 72 1 1 | 81 2 4 |
| 11 1 3 | 22 2 2 | 32 1 1 | 41 2 4 | 51 2 1 | 62 1 4 | 72 2 3 | 81 1 2 |
| 11 1 2 | 22 2 3 | 32 1 4 | 41 2 1 | 51 2 4 | 62 1 1 | 72 2 2 | 81 1 3 |
| 11 1 4 | 22 2 1 | 32 1 2 | 41 2 3 | 51 2 2 | 62 1 3 | 72 2 4 | 81 1 1 |
| 11 1 1 | 22 2 4 | 32 1 3 | 41 2 2 | 51 2 3 | 62 1 2 | 72 2 1 | 81 1 4 |
| 11 2 3 | 22 1 2 | 32 2 1 | 41 1 4 | 51 1 1 | 62 2 4 | 72 1 3 | 81 2 2 |
| 11 2 2 | 22 1 3 | 32 2 4 | 41 1 1 | 51 1 4 | 62 2 1 | 72 1 2 | 81 2 3 |

*Note:* first digit: 1 to 8, sequence of games; second digit: 1 = robot; 2 = person; third digit:
1 = no liking; 2 = liking; fourth digit: cost state of the players (L = low cost; H = high cost).
1 = LL, 2 = LH, 3 = HL, 4 = HH.

TABLE 2

*Pairs of players in each of the four experimental sessions*

| Game number | | | |
|---|---|---|---|
| 2 | 3 | 6 | 7 |
|---|---|---|---|
| AB | AC | AC | AB |
| CD | BD | BD | CD |
| EF | EG | EG | EF |
| GH | FH | FH | GH |

*Note:* A to H identification of the players. Games 2 and 7 were played
by the same persons, and also games 3 and 6. The subjects were not
aware of the fact that they played the same partner in some games.

TABLE 3

*Relative frequency of conflict as dependent on cost and liking*

| Cost | Liking | n | P |
|------|--------|---|---|
| Low | Low | 8 | 0.00 |
| Low | High | 8 | 0.00 |
| Mixed | Low | 16 | 0.31 |
| Mixed | High | 16 | 0.38 |
| High | Low | 8 | 0.88 |
| High | High | 8 | 0.88 |

TABLE 4

*Sum of last demands as dependent on liking only for games that end in conflict*

| Liking | n | $\bar{x}$ | s |
|--------|---|-----------|---|
| High | 13 | 25.54 | 3.57 |
| Low | 12 | 29.42 | 4.94 |

TABLE 5

*Means and standard deviations of individual last demands as dependent on cost*

| Cost | Liking | n | $\bar{x}$ | s |
|------|--------|---|-----------|---|
| High | High | 32 | 11.78 | 2.11 |
| High | Low | 32 | 13.47 | 3.20 |
| Low | High | 32 | 9.94 | 3.22 |
| Low | Low | 32 | 10.03 | 3.03 |

## Results

As Table 3 shows there is no difference in frequency of conflict depending on liking. Therefore Hypothesis 1a has not been confirmed. Whereas liking does not influence the probability of conflict, it does influence the sum of last demands for those games that end in conflict (Table 4). Liking brings the players closer to agreement ($t = 2.26$ for 23 d.f., $P < 0.05$, two-sided). Therefore, Hypothesis 1b is confirmed.

In order to test Hypothesis 2 concerning interaction between liking and cost, we may focus on individual demands rather than on the sum of last demands. However, since individual demands of the two players are not independent from each other we cannot perform a significance test on these scores. Table 5 therefore displays means

TABLE 6

*Relative frequency of conflict as related to dependency and liking*

| Dependency | Liking | *n* | *P* |
|---|---|---|---|
| Low | Low | 16 | 0.38 |
| Low | High | 16 | 0.38 |
| High | Low | 16 | 0.38 |
| High | High | 16 | 0.44 |

TABLE 7

*Sum of last demands as related to dependency and liking for those games only that end in conflict*

| Dependency | Liking | *n* | $\bar{x}$ | *s* |
|---|---|---|---|---|
| Low | Low | 6 | 28.83 | 5.12 |
| Low | High | 6 | 26.17 | 2.86 |
| High | Low | 6 | 30.00 | 5.18 |
| High | High | 7 | 25.00 | 4.24 |

and standard deviations of the individual demands only. There is a tendency in the direction of Hypothesis 2, i.e. yielding to the liked partner's demand is observed mainly with players having high cost. For them little is at stake.

Hypothesis 3 (interaction of dependency and liking) is not confirmed, either by conflict probability (Table 6) or by sum of last demands for those games that end in conflict (Table 7). One may even notice a weak tendency in the opposite direction: liking seems to be a more potent factor if dependency is high.

Hypothesis 4 can be tested by counting the frequencies of overestimating and underestimating a partner's cost stage at the end of the game. The costs of a liked partner were overestimated in 16 out of 64 individual games (25%); the costs of a disliked partner were overestimated in 12 out of 64 individual games (19%). The difference is not significant. The proportion of underestimation is exactly the same for both groups (25%).

No hypothesis has been formulated in advance for the duration of the games as measured by the number of the last stage. Looking for further evidence of the specific relation between liking and yielding we thought that players in the liking condition should reach conflict later and agreement earlier than players in the disliking condition. Table 8 displays the means and standard deviations of the variable,

TABLE 8

*Duration of the game (number of stages) as dependent on liking for games that end in conflict*

| Liking | n | $\bar{x}$ | s |
|--------|-----|------|------|
| Low | 12 | 6.42 | 3.29 |
| High | 13 | 9.77 | 3.22 |

TABLE 9

*Duration of the game (number of stages) as dependent on liking and cost for games that ended in agreement*

| Cost | Liking | n | $\bar{x}$ | s |
|------|--------|-----|-------|------|
| Low | Low | 8 | 7.75 | 3.54 |
| Low | High | 8 | 9.00 | 2.45 |
| Mixed or high | Low | 12 | 10.17 | 2.52 |
| Mixed or high | High | 11 | 7.82 | 2.96 |

TABLE 10

*Analysis of variance of game duration as dependent on liking and cost for games that ended in agreement*

| Source of variance | SS | d.f. | MS | F |
|--------------------|--------|------|-------|------|
| Cost | 3.62 | 1 | 3.62 | |
| Liking | 2.85 | 1 | 2.85 | |
| Cost × liking | 30.56 | 1 | 30.56 | 3.72 $P < 0.10$ |
| Error | 287.21 | 35 | 8.21 | |

"duration of the game," as dependent on liking in the case of conflict. Since "duration" and "sum of last demand" are negatively correlated with $r = -0.61$ (liking) and $r = -0.68$ (disliking), this test is not independent from the test displayed in Table 4; $t = 2.57$ for 23 d.f. is significant, $P < 0.05$.

High cost games (conflict) and mixed cost games (conflict) did not differ in game duration as a function of liking. Therefore, they were combined in Table 8. There were no low cost games ending in conflict.

Agreement seems to have been reached earlier in the liking condition than in the disliking condition with mixed cost or high cost only (Table 9). Low cost games tended to take more steps if the

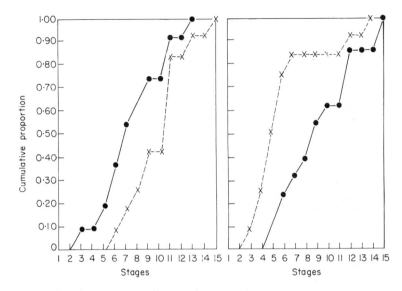

Fig. 1. Cumulative proportions of games with mixed costs and high costs having reached agreement at stage S (S = 1, 2, 3 ... 15).

Fig. 2. Cumulative proportions of games with mixed costs having ended in conflict at stage S (S = 1, 2, 3 ... 15). —— liking, – – – disliking.

players liked each other than if they did not like each other. However, the interaction (cost × liking) is not significant (Table 10).

Figures 1 and 2 display the cumulative proportions of mixed cost and high cost games that have reached agreement (conflict) at the various stages. In the liking condition 50% of the players had reached agreement already at Stage 7, whereas in the disliking condition the 50% score is not reached before Stage 10. The respective numbers for those games that end in conflict are Stages 9 and 5. Transforming the cumulative proportions of Figures 1 and 2 into logits $z$ ($z = \ln (p/1 - p)$) and determining the regression of $z$ on stage number (Linder and Berchtold, 1976) results in the values displayed in Table 11. There is a significant interaction of outcome × liking on the additive constants $a$.

Lastly, we may look at the final ratings of closeness to the partner (liking of the partner) as a function of subject's cost, partner's cost, dependency, and liking (Table 12). Only the main effect of partner's cost is significant ($F = 13.58, P < 0.001$).

TABLE 11

*Regression of logits z (z = ln (p/1 − p)) of the cumulative proportions of mixed cost and high cost games that have reached agreement or conflict at the various stages of the game*

| Outcome | Liking | a | b |
|---|---|---|---|
| Agreement | Low | −4.51 | 0.50 |
| Agreement | High | −3.88 | 0.53 |
| Conflict | Low | −2.21 | 0.40 |
| Conflict | High | −3.56 | 0.40 |

TABLE 12

*Means and standard deviations of final closeness rating as dependent on subject's cost (SUCO), partner's cost (PACO), and liking (LIK)*

| SUCO | PACO | LIK | n | $\bar{x}$ | s |
|---|---|---|---|---|---|
| Low | Low | Low | 16 | 7.94 | 4.23 |
| Low | Low | High | 16 | 7.69 | 4.73 |
| Low | High | Low | 16 | 11.57 | 6.17 |
| Low | High | High | 16 | 10.63 | 6.70 |
| High | Low | Low | 16 | 9.63 | 5.32 |
| High | Low | High | 16 | 8.57 | 5.39 |
| High | High | Low | 16 | 12.44 | 5.92 |
| High | High | High | 16 | 13.38 | 4.65 |

## Discussion

Liking does not significantly influence the probability of conflict (Table 3, Hypothesis 1a disconfirmed). However, among those games that end in conflict liking makes a difference in the sum of last demands: players who like each other come closer to agreement than players who do not like each other (Table 4). Related to this result is the fact that in the liking condition games end in conflict at a later stage than in the disliking condition (Hypothesis 1b confirmed).

One may wonder why liking players end as often in conflict as disliking players, although the former apparently strive harder for agreement. A plausible explanation would be to assume that the probability of yielding to the partner's demand is high at the beginning of the game in the liking condition but decreases in the course of the game because of disappointed expectation. If that is true, we would expect that liking players tend to reach agreement rather early or to end in conflict rather late. Particularly if the partner has high cost and therefore is a rather tough bargainer, a player may become increasingly irritated by the tenacity of his opponent. In the disliking condition the probability of yielding is supposed to be moderately low throughout the bargaining process.

In fact, the final rating of liking is almost independent from the liking condition. We know from many experiments that the kind of information on mutual liking we used in our experiment is efficient in eliciting liking. Therefore, the most probable explanation for the results of final liking ratings is that in the liking condition liking is reduced by bargaining, whereas in the disliking condition it is not. Druckman and Bonoma (1976) report similar results. The same happened consistently in all the Augsburg discussion experiments (Brandstätter, 1978), where the liked opponent insisted on his position throughout the discussion.

There is some additional evidence for the effect of disappointed expectancy: in six of 16 games (38%) involving mixed costs and liking, the low cost player surpassed the high cost player in his final demand. This never happened with disliking players. Low cost players who meet a liked partner with high costs may particularly be disappointed that the other does not meet their expectations, and therefore may increase their resistance.

The construction of a transition probability model is underway. It should represent the postulated differences in change of emotional states and its influence on the transition probabilies throughout the bargaining process.

As to Hypothesis 2 (joint influence of cost and liking on individual yielding), we also may point to the results of Table 5. There is some indication that liking does not lead to an early agreement if both players are low in cost. That liking, low-cost players need more time for reaching agreement than disliking, low-cost players is not easy to understand. It may be that they enjoy the interaction, and therefore are not in a hurry to end, like the pairs of friends in the experiment by Morgan and Sawyer (1967).

We are as yet not able to explain the failure of Hypothesis 3 (interaction dependency × liking, Tables 6 and 7). It may be that expecting a reward of 0, 1, or 2 money units from the opponent, i.e. 0, 10, or 20¢, is not at all experienced as being dependent on the other's benevolence.

The test of Hypothesis 4 (overestimation of the liked other's cost), the results of which were not significant, was based on the final guess of costs only. It may well be that the previous guesses reflect the differences in cost attribution as depending on liking more clearly. If the effect of liking variation is faded out during the bargaining process, then no big differences could be expected in the final attribution of costs. By analyzing the time series of guessing the other's costs the picture may become clearer.

Summarizing the results, we may state that in a bilateral monopoly game with incomplete information mutual liking of the players did not diminish the probability of conflict, but did delay the conflict. It can be assumed that in the liking condition the probability of yielding was rather high in the early stages of the game, allowing some of the players to reach agreement at an early stage. However, playing with a partner who had high cost and therefore yielded only little presumably resulted in disappointment and in decreased probability of yielding. This would lead to conflict at a later stage. If the players did not like each other, they did not expect that the other would be very cooperative. The probability of yielding is supposed to have been moderate throughout the game leading some to a rather late agreement and others to an early conflict.

## References

Anderson, N. H. Integration theory and attitude change. *Psychological Review*, 1971, 78, 171–206.

Anderson, N. H. and Graesser, C. C. An information integration analysis of attitude change in group discussion. *Journal of Personality and Social Psychology*, 1976, 34, 210–222.

Benton, A. A. Productivity, distributive justice, and bargaining among children. *Journal of Personality and Social Psychology*, 1971, 18, 68–78.

Brandstätter, H. *The Augsburg research project on social emotions in discussion groups.* In: Brandstätter, H., Davis, J. H., Schuler, H (Eds) Dynamics of Group Decision Making. Beverly Hills: Sage, 1978.

Burnstein, E., Vinokur, A. and Trope, Y. Interpersonal comparisons versus persuasive argumentation: a more direct test of alternative explanations for group induced shifts in individual choice. *Journal of Experimental Social Psychology*, 1973, 9, 236–245.

Christie, R. and Geis, F. L. (Eds) *Studies in Machiavellism.* New York and London: Academic Press, 1970.

Druckman, D. and Bonoma, T. V. Determinants of bargaining behavior in a bilateral monopoly situation II: opponent's concession rate and similarity. *Behavioral Science*, 1976, 21, 252–262.

Ebbesen, E. B. and Bowers, R. J. Proportion of risky to conservative arguments in a group discussion and choice shift. *Journal of Personality and Social Psychology*, 1974, 29, 316–327.

Festinger, L. A theory of social comparison processes. *Human Relations*, 1954, 7, 117–140.

Hoggatt, A. C., Brandstätter, H. and Blatman, P. *Robots as instrumental functions in the study of bargaining behaviour.* In: H. Sauermann (Ed.) Bargaining Behaviour. Tübingen: Mohr 1978, 179—210.

Hoggatt, A. C. and Selten, R. *Bargaining experiments with incomplete information.* In: H. Sauermann (Ed.) Bargaining Behaviour. Tübingen: Mohr 1978, 127—178.

Hollander, E. P. *Principles and Methods of Social Psychology,* 3rd ed. New York: Oxford University Press, 1976.

Kuhlman, D. M. and Marshello, A. F. J. Individual differences in game motivation as moderators of preprogrammed strategy effects in prisoner's dilemma. *Journal of Personality and Social Psychology,* 1975, 32, 922—931.

Linder and Berchtold, *Statistische Auswertung von Prozentzahlen,* Bern: Haupt, 1976.

Mills, J. and Aronson, E. Opinion as a function of the communicator's attractiveness and desire to influence. *Journal of Personality and Social Psychology,* 1965, 1, 173—177.

Morgan, W. R. and Sawyer, J. Bargaining, expectations, and the preference for equality over equity. *Journal of Personality and Social Psychology,* 1967, 6, 139—149.

Morley, I. E. *The character of experimental studies of bargaining and negotiation.* In: Brandstätter, H., Davis, J. H. and Schuler, H. (Eds) Dynamics of Group Decision Making. Beverly Hills: Sage 1978.

Rubin, J. Z. and Brown, B. R. *The Social Psychology of Bargaining and Negotiation.* New York and London: Academic Press, 1975.

# 14
# Partner Perception and Matrix Variation in a Mixed-motive Game

B. Rüttinger

The importance of different dimensions of partner perception for choices in mixed-motive games has been emphasized by several authors (cf. Deutsch, 1969; Krivohlavy, 1974; Nemeth, 1970; Rubin and Brown, 1975). However, empirical studies on that topic have not led to consistent results. Even in the studies in which the perceived friendliness or similarity of the co-player were manipulated, the results did not reveal consistent differences. Some studies (Baxter, 1970; Kaufman, 1967; McClintock and McNeal, 1967; Michelini, 1971; Swingle and Gillis, 1968; Tornatzky and Gleiwitz, 1968) suggest that perceived high friendliness or high similarity leads to greater cooperation than the perception of low friendliness or low similarity. Other studies, however, reported no consistent differences (Aranoff *et al.*, 1967, Bartos, 1967; Fisher and Smith, 1969; Marlowe *et al.*, 1966; Wrightsman *et al.*, 1969; Wyer, 1969).

For example, Oskamp and Perlman (1965, 1966) conducted three experiments which led to three different results. First, they studied, in a prisoner's dilemma game (PDG), the effect of friendship between the subjects, as indicated on a post-experimental questionnaire, on cooperation. No consistent relationship was found between cooperation and friendship.

In a later experiment they systematically varied the degree of friendship between the partners and studied its effect on cooperation in a PDG. A pre-experimental sociometric questionnaire was given to subjects to obtain their nomination of best friends, acquaintances, and disliked individuals. A fourth group of non-acquaintances was established by pairing subjects from different colleges. The subjects were assigned to one of the four conditions and paired with one of their sociometric nominees for that condition. The results of the experiment were significantly different for the two colleges studied. At one college there were significant differences between the four friendship groups and a strong positive relationship between degree of friendship and amount of cooperation. The subjects of the other college, on the other hand, exhibited almost the opposite relationship.

The latter results are surprising. When a player is led to believe that his partner is his friend, we would argue that this information is likely to induce cooperative behaviour, because to think of another as one's friend is to like and trust him, to expect him to behave cooperatively, and probably to behave cooperatively oneself. The ambiguous support received by this hypothesis led us to assume that the impact of perceived friendliness on game behaviour depends on other conditions.

One such condition seems to be the advantage one can gain from competitive behaviour (which can be calculated for a matrix game as we shall illustrate below). The greater this advantage is, the greater the profit which a player can expect to realize by competitive versus cooperative behaviour. The smaller this competitive advantage is, the less tempted a player is to show a behaviour which does not correspond to his attitude towards another player who was perceived to be friendly. On the other hand, the greater the competitive advantage is, the more likely it is that a player would be tempted to show a behaviour which did not correspond to his attitude towards a partner who he perceived to be likable. In other words, the larger the expected profit from competitive behaviour the more likely are friends and non-friends to be treated the same. The behaviour towards both is competitive, when the advantage is large.

Another possible reason for the discrepancy among published results may be the different approaches used to measure cooperation and competition. Some authors use a simple trial, others use an average score from many trials to define a person as behaving cooperatively or competitively.

Perceived similarity and friendliness can logically be assumed to affect the behaviour of a player in the first trial. The second trial is also affected by the results and consequences of the first trial. For example, desire to take revenge, or a wish to be fair to the underdog etc., may arise as a result of the unexpected response of the partner. These events can lead to substantial modification, even reversal of initial judgements of friendliness.

A large majority of the studies already referred to use the average score from 10, 30, or more trials to define a person's behaviour as cooperative or competitive. It seems therefore hardly surprising that in a large number of studies no effect of judged friendliness on game behaviour has been found.

The present study aims at an analysis of the dynamics of the process of choice behaviour and perceived friendliness; that is how a choice and the reactions to it may change the initially held opinion and vice versa. We have divided the process into three stages.

(1) The effect of perceived friendliness on the choice in the first trial.

(2) The effect of this choice on the subsequent rating of friendliness.

(3) The impact of judged friendliness from the first trial on the second trial.

We expect that competitive behaviour on the first trial will lead to a reduction in perceived friendliness of the partner. Besides friendliness two other variables included in this study are perceived dominance and conscientiousness.

To summarize our hypotheses, we expect:

(1) That initial perceived high friendliness leads to greater co-operation than perceived low friendliness, but that this tendency towards cooperation decreases with increasing advantages gained by competitive behaviour.

(2) That cooperative behaviour on the first trial increases the perceived friendliness while competitive behaviour reduces the perceived friendliness.

(3) That perceived high friendliness following the first trial causes more cooperation in the second trial than perceived low friendliness.

The basic question about the effect of perceived friendliness and competitive advantage on game behaviour is enlarged in two respects in this study. First, while the interrelation between partner perception and game behaviour is being investigated, the influence of game behaviour on partner perception will also be analysed. It is expected that a partner's competitive behaviour will diminish sympathy for him and that this will be all the more likely the smaller the competitive advantage is. In addition to investigating perceived friendliness, two other perceived characteristics of the partner, dominance and conscientiousness, were also included in the analysis.

Player 2

|  | $C_2$ | $D_2$ |
|---|---|---|
| $C_1$ | 1 , 1 [Re, Re] | 0, 10 [S, T] |
| $D_1$ | 10,0 [S , T] | 0,0 [P,P] |

Player I

Fig. 1. Basic form of the game matrix.

## Method

### SUBJECTS

The subjects were 88 male participants of advanced training courses from the medium-level management of economy and administration who knew one another for some time. Participation in the study was voluntary.

### MATERIALS

A 2 x 2 mixed-motive game was chosen as the decision task. The basic form of the matrix appears in Fig. 1. That matrix was presented in four variations by assigning the following values to the top cell $(C_1, C_2)$: (1, 1), (3, 3), (5, 5), (7, 7). Henceforth we shall use the $(C_1, C_2)$ entry to refer to each of the four matrices.

According to the terms of Rapoport and Chammah (1965) the values can be reported in the following order: $T > Re > (P = S)$. The matrices thus differ from the PDG matrix by the fact that $P$ is not greater than $S$. This form of game matrix was preferred to the PDG-matrix since it is easier to comprehend and, thus, reduces the likelihood of errors of understanding on the part of the subjects, who were inexperienced in psychological experiments. On the assumption of equal response frequencies in each cell, the average advantage of competition is defined as

$$\frac{T + P}{2} - \frac{Re + S}{2}$$

(Oskamp and Perlman, 1965). Thus, the competition advantage indices for the (1, 1), (3, 3), (5, 5) and (7, 7) matrices were 4.5, 3.5, 2.5, and 1.5, respectively.

PROCEDURE

Four experimental groups were established by randomly assigning pairs of subjects to the four different matrices. The first task the subjects did was to rate the other player on each of 11 semantic differential items. After completing the ratings the subjects played one of the four variations of the mixed-motive game. The game matrix and the instructions concerning it were both printed on a sheet of paper that was given to the subjects. Earnings in the form of chips (chewing-gums) valued at 20 Pfennigs a piece were given immediately after the trial. After the first trial the subjects again rated the other player on the 11 semantic differential items. This was followed by a second trial with the same matrix. The subjects were not informed regarding the number of trials.

## Results

### DETERMINATION OF THE PERCEIVED PERSONALITY CHARACTERISTICS OF THE PARTNER

The first set of semantic differential ratings were used for the determination of the original partner perception. In order to clarify what different dimensions were contained in the 11-item semantic differential questionnaire, the responses of all 88 subjects were submitted to a hierarchical cluster analysis as per Johnson (1967).

As shown in Fig. 2, three clusters can be discerned which are largely identical with Cohen's (1970) factors of dominance, likability, and conscientiousness. For further analysis the respective items were summed into three scores. The correlations of the three scores over all subjects were: $r_{dl} = -0.28; r_{dc} = 0.13; r_{lc} = 0.23$.

Thus, these clusters can be considered to be largely independent of one another. In the following the three scores will represent independent, perceived characteristics of the partner.

### THE EFFECT OF THE FIRST RATING ON THE FIRST CHOICE

As the results in Table 1 indicate, the choices depend very heavily on the form of the matrices. The proportion of C and D choices for

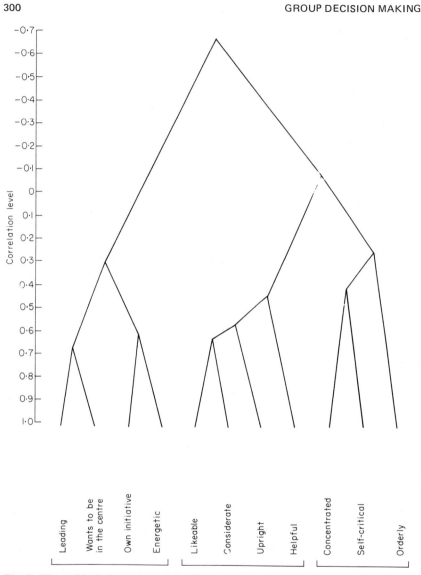

Fig. 2. Hierarchical clustering of the first set of semantic differential ratings.

the (1, 1), (3, 3) and (5, 5) matrices are approximately equivalent, whereas in the game involving the (7, 7) matrix 86% of the players chose a cooperative response. Apparently, the incentive to choose cooperative in the (7, 7) game matrix is so great that the matrix itself almost completely determines the choices. Therefore, the influence of the first ratings on the choices will be examined only with the (1, 1), (3, 3) and (5, 5) matrices.

TABLE 1

*Frequency of C and D choices*

| Matrix | (1, 1) | (3, 3) | (5, 5) | (7, 7) | Total |
|--------|--------|--------|--------|--------|-------|
| Choice |        |        |        |        |       |
| C      | 11     | 13     | 13     | 19     | 56    |
| D      | 9      | 9      | 11     | 3      | 32    |
| Total  | 20     | 22     | 24     | 22     | 88    |

TABLE 2

*Means and standard deviations of the perceived partner characteristics*

| Matrix | Dominance | | Likeability | | Conscientiousness | |
|--------|-----------|------|-------------|------|-------------------|------|
|        | Mean      | s.d. | Mean        | s.d. | Mean              | s.d. |
| (1, 1) | 16.95     | 3.58 | 20.30       | 3.84 | 13.40             | 3.76 |
| (3, 3) | 16.23     | 5.16 | 21.50       | 5.18 | 14.50             | 4.63 |
| (5, 5) | 17.83     | 6.06 | 20.29       | 5.17 | 13.46             | 3.89 |
| (7, 7) | 17.18     | 4.85 | 21.82       | 5.29 | 13.64             | 4.11 |

The means and standard deviations of the three scores for the four matrix conditions are shown in Table 2. Even though the differences are not significant, inspection reveals that the likability values, on the average, are the highest in the (7, 7) matrix condition. In part, this may have contributed to the fact that the C choices were so numerous in that condition.

In order to analyse the impact of the first rating on the choices, three discriminant analyses were performed. It was expected that cooperative players would have rated their partners higher on likability than would competitive players and that the discrimination between the two choice-groups would differ across the three levels of competition advantage. As Table 3 reveals, this prediction failed. The discriminant factor was not significant in any of the three matrix conditions. The perceived characteristics did not contribute to the discrimination of the two groups.

The same effect is also revealed by a rather rough classification of the values of likeability. That is, if we trichotomized individuals into high, moderate, and low likeability groups, we find that the proportion of C choices is roughly equivalent across the three matrix conditions. Table 4 shows the results of this classification.

THE IMPACT OF THE FIRST MOVE ON THE SECOND RATING

It might be expected that the initial rating causes variation in the second rating. Therefore, in order to assess the net impact of the

TABLE 3

*Discriminant analysis for the three matrix-conditions*

| Matrix | Eigenvalue | $V$ | d.f. $(V)$ |
|--------|-----------|-----|-----------|
| (1, 1) | 0.09 | 1.45 | 3 |
| (3, 3) | 0.16 | 2.75 | 3 |
| (5, 5) | 0.20 | 3.74 | 3 |

TABLE 4

*Relative frequencies of C choices for high, moderate and low likeability subjects*

| | | Likeability | |
|--------|------|----------|------|
| Matrix | High | Moderate | Low |
| (1, 1) | 4/20 | 2/20 | 5/20 |
| (3, 3) | 5/22 | 6/22 | 2/22 |
| (5, 5) | 4/24 | 6/24 | 3/24 |
| Total | 13/66 | 14/66 | 10/66 |

TABLE 5

*Means of the residual rating values*

| | | | | Other Player | | | | | |
|----------|---------|------|------|------|-------|------|------|-------|------|
| | | C | | | D | | | | |
| | $Do^a$ | Li | Co | Do | Li | Co | Do | Li | Co |
| Player C | −0.23 | 0.63 | 0.62 | 0.44 | −2.25 | 0.03 | 0.21 | −1.62 | 0.65 |
| Player D | −0.93 | 0.49 | −0.04 | 2.06 | −3.18 | 1.01 | 1.13 | −2.69 | 0.97 |
| | −1.16 | 1.12 | 0.58 | 2.50 | −5.43 | 1.04 | 1.34 | −4.31 | 1.62 |

[a]The abbreviations Do, Li and Co stand for Dominance, Likeability, and Conscientiousness, respectively.

choices on the second rating, the variance of the first rating was partialed out of the second rating. The means of the residual values are presented in Table 5. They reveal that a cooperative opponent gained on likeability but decreased in dominance, whereas a competitive opponent gained on dominance but decreased in likeability. There was also an interaction effect between the choices of the player and the choices of the other player: if the player chose D, the other player decreased more in likeability and gained more on dominance if he played D rather than C. However, if a player chose D and the other player played C, the latter decreased on conscientiousness. If the latter player played D instead, he gained on conscientiousness.

TABLE 6

*Results of multivariate analysis on residual rating values*

| Source | $\Lambda$ | d.f. (source) | $V$ | d.f. ($V$) |
|--------|-----------|---------------|-----|------------|
| Player | 0.98 | 1 | 1.68 | 3 |
| Other Player | 0.65 | 1 | 35.75[a] | 3 |
| Interaction | 0.89 | 1 | 9.67[a] | 3 |
| Error | | 84 | | |

[a] $P < 0.95$.

TABLE 7

*Number of C- and D-choices on second trial*

| Choice | | | Matrix | | |
|--------|-----|-----|-----|-----|-------|
| | 1/1 | 3/3 | 5/5 | 7/7 | Total |
| C | 7 | 14 | 14 | 19 | 56 |
| D | 13 | 8 | 10 | 3 | 32 |
| Total | 20 | 22 | 24 | 22 | 88 |

A multivariate analysis of the residual values indicated that the preceding effects were significant. The results of this analysis appear in Table 6.

THE IMPACT OF THE SECOND RATING ON THE SECOND MOVE

The number of C- and D-choices on the second move are presented in Table 7. The C- and D-proportion shows hardly any change when compared with the results obtained on the first move. Only in the 1/1-matrix is there an increase in the D-choices.

A total of 18 players changed their game behaviour: 10 from C to D and 8 from D to C. The amount of change is a function of the matrix involved (see Table 8): the lower the gain through competitive behaviour the less likely a change. This effect is statistically significant ($\chi^2 = 10.61$; d.f. 3; $P < 0.05$). The direction of change depends neither on the structure of the matrix nor on the behaviour of the co-player.

Three discriminant analyses were performed to analyse the influence of perceived personality characteristics on the second trial — the choices in the 7/7-matrix are again largely determined by the matrix itself. Here we expected that perceived likeability would primarily influence choices. We assumed that the cooperative player would rate the co-player higher on likeability than the competitive player.

The results show (see Table 9) that in the second trial, also, our

TABLE 8

*Number of persons changing and not changing in the 4 payoff
conditions*

| Matrix | Changers | Non-changers |
|--------|----------|--------------|
| 1/1 | 8 | 12 |
| 3/3 | 5 | 17 |
| 5/5 | 5 | 19 |
| 7/7 | 0 | 22 |
| Total | 18 | 70 |

TABLE 9

*Second discriminant analysis for three matrices*

| Matrix | Eigenvalue | $V$ | d.f. ($V$) | Sign. |
|--------|------------|-----|------------|-------|
| 1/1 | 0.76 | 4.46 | 3 | n.s. |
| 3/3 | 0.79 | 4.34 | 3 | n.s. |
| 5/5 | 0.91 | 1.98 | 3 | n.s. |

expectations were not fulfilled. Although the values are higher than
in the first trial, the discriminant factors do not differentiate in a
statistically significant manner between the two choice-groups.

## Discussion

The results confirm the influence of the competitive advantage on
choices.

On the one hand this influence is seen in the proportion of C- and
D-choices. The less one gains through competitive behaviour, the
more often one chooses C. This trend is more pronounced in the
second trial.

Between the matrices 5/5 and 7/7 we find a radical change. The
structure of the 7/7 matrix — the small advantage of competitive
behaviour — appears to determine the choices, whereas on the three
matrices which give a higher competitive advantage the C- and D-
choices are about equally distributed. This means that only after a
threshold value is reached are variables other than the matrix structure
seen to influence the choices.

On the other hand, the influence of the payoff-structure is seen in
the readiness to change strategy. The smaller the competitive

advantage, the greater the readiness to change one's choice on the second trial. This is understandable, because the advantage of either strategy is not so high, that the development of a pure strategy would be worthwhile.

The other variables which we studied in this context were perceived person characteristics. The hypothesis that these characteristics, mainly the perceived likeability, have a statistically significant effect on game behaviour was not confirmed.

On the other hand, the behaviour of the partner influences the social perception of the player and in the long run leads to increased congruence between perceived friendliness and choice behaviour.

It is surprising that the perceived likeability, an important dimension of social perception, does not have an immediate effect. However, our results do not support the conclusion made by Miller and Pyke (1973), who also failed to find a relationship between social perception and choices. According to these authors further investigations into the determinants of game behaviour should concentrate on the interactions of person and situation rather than on the interactions between the participants. Two points have to be considered in this context: first, the results show that only one kind of perceived friendliness or "likeability", the longer lasting sympathy, does not affect game behaviour in a definite way. This result corresponds to the findings of the Augsburg Research Group, where it was also found, that only manipulated sympathy (but not longer-lasting sympathy) affect the preferences of participants in group decisions (cf. Brandstätter et al., 1971; Schuler, 1975; Schuler and Peltzer, 1975). This may be primarily due to the fact that the longer-lasting sympathy is connected with other personality variables which, in part, have a contrary impact on choices. For instance, one person may find another one likeable because he is submissive whilst another finds a dominant partner more to his liking. The net impact of sympathy on game behaviour therefore seems to be controlled only by the manipulation of sympathy (e.g. by varying the similarity of preprogrammed choices).

Secondly, we should also take into account the motivational orientations of the subjects. It is well known that game behaviour is influenced by motivational orientations (McClintock, 1972; Rubin and Brown, 1975). Usually four such orientations are discussed; cooperative orientation (an effort to maximize joint profit), individualistic orientation (to gain as much as possible for oneself regardless of the interests of the partner), competitive orientation (to maximize relative gain) and defensive orientation (to minimize a maximum loss). Perceived friendliness probably has a different impact on these orientations. For example, a player with defensive orientation will trust a co-player, if he perceives him as friendly, and therefore chooses C, whereas he might choose D if he sees him as unfriendly and therefore distrusts him. On the other hand a person whose orientation is competitive or individualistic may perceive a friendly co-player as weak and thus provoke a D-choice. Finally a cooperatively oriented player will choose C regardless of the friendliness or unfriendliness of the other player. The interaction between motivational orientation and social perception means that a particular choice cannot be explained precisely as a function of perceived friendliness. For example, a D-choice can occur, depending on the motivational orientation, when the partner is perceived as friendly or unfriendly.

This hypothesis has received considerable support from some of the experiments that we have recently conducted in which motivational orientations were taken into account. Among others the results show:

(1) That cooperative-defensive players, who choose C, rate their co-players higher in friendliness than those, who choose D (5.02 v. 4.00 on a 6-point-scale).

(2) That persons with pure cooperative orientation choose C, even when the rated friendliness is in the medium range.

In later publications we shall present and discuss these data in greater detail.

## Summary

The effects of the perceived personality of the other player and of the possible competitive advantage on game behaviour and the effect of game behaviour on partner perception were examined in a $2 \times 2$ mixed-motive game with two trials. It was found that the possible competitive advantage influences the game behaviour in such a way that the number of D-choices decreases when this advantage is small. The readiness to change the choice on the second trial is increased when the possible competitive gain is small. The perceived personality characteristics, especially the perceived friendliness, do not directly affect the game behaviour, although on the second trial some evidence for such an influence was found. This latter result corresponds with the fact that game behaviour affects partner perception in such a way that the cooperative partner gains on perceived friendliness and loses on dominance, and the competitive partner loses on friendliness and gains on dominance.

# References

Aranoff, D., Burrill, D. A. Tedeschi, J. T. and Jones, B. *Techn. Report*, Dept. of Pyschology, University of Miami, Coral Gables, 1967.

Bartos, O. J. How predictable are negotiations? *Journal of Conflict Resolution*, 1967, 11, 481—496.

Baxter, G. W., Jr. The effects of information about other player and race of other player upon cooperation in a two-person game. *Dissertation Abstracts*, 1970, 30, 4544, 4545, A.

Brandstätter, H., Molt, W., von Rosenstiel, L., Rüttinger, B., Schuler, H. and Stocker-Kreichgauer, G. Der Einfluß in Entscheidungsgruppen als Funktion der Sympathie und des Unterschieds in den Handlungspräferenzen. *Problem und Entscheidung*, 1971, 6, 2—71.

Cohen, R. *Systematische Tendenzen bei Persönlichkeitsbeurteilungen*, Bern: Huber, 1969.

Deutsch, M. The effect of motivational orientation upon threat and suspicion. *Human Relations*, 1960, 13, 123—139.

Fisher, R. and Smith, W. P. Conflict of interest and attraction in the development of cooperation. *Psychonomic Science*, 1969, 14, 154—155.

Johnson, S. C. Hierarchical Clustering Schemes. *Psychometrika*, 1967, 32, 241—254.

Kaufmann, H. Similarity and cooperation received as determinants of cooperation rendered. *Psychonomic Science*, 1967, 9, 73—74.

Křivohlavý, J. *Zwischenmenschliche Konflikte und experimentelle Spiele*. Bern: Huber, 1974.

Marlowe, D., Gergen, K. J. and Doob, A. N. Opponent's personality, expectations of social interaction, and interpersonal bargaining. *Journal of Personality and Social Psychology*, 1966, 3, 206—213.

McClintock, Ch. G. Game behavior and social motivation in interpersonal settings. In Ch. G. McClintock (Ed.), *Experimental Social Psychology*. New York: Rinehart and Winston, 1972, 271—297.

McClintock, Ch. G. and McNeel, S. P. Prior dyadic experience and monetary reward as determinants of cooperative and competitive game behavior. *Journal of Personality and Social Psychology*, 1967, 5, 282—294.

Michelini, R. L. Effects of prior interaction, contact, strategy, and expectation of meeting on game behavior and sentiment. *Journal of Conflict Resolution*, 1971, 15, 97—103.

Miller, G. H. and Pyke, S. W. Sex, matrix variations, and perceived personality effects in mixed-motive games. *Journal of Conflict Resolution*, 1973, 17, 335—349.

Nemeth, C. Bargaining and reciprocity. *Psychological Bulletin*, 1970, 5, 297—308.

Oskamp, S. and Perlman, D. Factors affecting cooperation in a prisoner's dilemma game. *Journal of Conflict Resolution,* 1965, 9, 359—374.

Oskamp, S. and Perlman, D. Effects of friendship and disliking on cooperation in a mixed-motive game. *Journal of Conflict Resolution,* 1966, 10, 211—226.

Rapoport, A. and Chammah, M. A. *Prisoner's Dilemma. A study in Conflict and Cooperation.* Ann Arbor: The Univ. of Michigan Press, 1965.

Rubin, J. Z. and Brown, B. R. *The Social Psychology of Bargaining and Negotiation.* New York and London: Academic Press, 1975.

Schuler, H. Sympathie und Einfluß in Entscheidungsgruppen. Bern: Huber, 1975.

Schuler, H. and Peltzer, U. Ähnlichkeit, Kompetenz und die Erwartung künftiger Interaktion als Determinanten von Diskussionsverhalten und Partnerbeurteilung (LIDIA III). *Problem und Entscheidung,* 1975, 14, 78—107.

Swingle, P. G. and Gillis, J. S. Effects of the emotional relationship between protagonists in the prisoner's dilemma. *Journal of Personality and Social Psychology,* 1968, 8, 160—165.

Tornatzky, L. and Geiwitz, P. J. The effects of threat and attraction on interpersonal bargaining. *Psychonomic Science,* 1968, 13, 125—126.

Wyer, R. S. Prediction of behavior in two-person games. *Journal of Personality and Social Psychology,* 1969, 13, 222—238.

# IV
# Bargaining

# Introduction

Hermann Brandstätter

Looking back at "twenty years of experimental gaming" and its broader environment, Pruitt and Kimmel (1977) deplore that as yet little effort has been made to secure the external validity of experimental games. One of the remedies they suggest is to design experiments as more realistic simulations of natural settings and to combine "naturalistic observations" with laboratory research (p. 369–370). The contributions that make up this section are clearly concerned with the problem of the generalization of experimental results to natural settings. Morley looks at the preparatory phase of negotiation, a problem that has hitherto been neglected. By referring to reports on negotiations of great historical importance he gains a wider view over the complexity of the processes than the very specific and simple experimental games can give. Webb and Stephenson give an example of a bargaining experiment that seems to be quite successful in simulating important characteristics of labour-management negotiations. The experiment of Crott *et al.* aims at examining the effect of experience on bargaining behaviour, experience being a characteristic of bargainers in natural settings, which differentiates them from bargainers in most experimental settings. Rabbie *et al.* approach the problem by comparing inter-personal with inter-group behaviour in PD-games. Obviously most social conflicts of greater importance are resolved between groups rather than between individuals.

An important step towards a refinement of the theory of bargaining behaviour is to observe the process, and to consider how the bargainers interpret the situation, what goals they strive for, and what intentions they expect from their opponent. No doubt, each of the four contributions makes some progress in understanding the cognitive processes concurring with the overt bargaining behaviour.

Morley's paper on preparation for negotiation deals in the first instance with the circumstances found in natural settings. Negotiators, for instance, are representatives of groups, and share a common history of interaction, before they enter formal negotiations, and have to cope with complex difficulties. He presents historic examples, mainly from negotiations that preceded the Treaty of Versailles, in order to clarify the significance of these situational characteristics. In the second section there is a brief review of the experimental literature dealing with the preparation for negotiation.

Webb and Stephenson contribute to the understanding of the effect of mediation on process and outcome of bargaining, by studying how the mere presence of a third party introduced as an expert v. a naive observer, influences the bargaining behaviour of subjects playing the role of management or union representatives.

Crott et al. investigate how prior experience affects the exchange of information and bluffing in an asymmetrical bargaining situation. They based their hypotheses on concepts of equity and cognitive dissonance. The frequency of information exchange was about the same in all conditions, but bluffing as well as individualistic orientation increased with experience. The experienced player also gained a better outcome. Surprisingly the disadvantaged player, who was always inexperienced, frequently used overstatement bluffs. This may remind us of the rather bizarre ways in which a person can interpret and manipulate the situation in order to achieve his goal.

The overwhelming majority of experimental games have used an inter-personal rather than an inter-group conflict. Rabbie et al. discuss various theoretical assumptions that predict a difference between individuals and groups in an inter-party conflict and review the rather sparse empirical evidence. Since the motivation behind a choice in a PD-game remains unclear without any further information, Rabbie et al. measure the behaviour orientation (cooperative, individualistic, competitive, defensive) at different stages of the game by a questionnaire. The results of their experiments with a programmed opponent suggest that there are differences, but as yet clear cut generalizations are not possible. Whereas in PD-games dyads act more defensively than individuals or triads, in a task with less outcome interdependence the individualistic orientation is strongest with triads, and weakest with individuals. A theoretical integration of these and other results is not easily obtained. A closer look at the process of discussion by which groups come to their choices may give some useful hints. This is what the authors plan to do in future experiments.

## Reference

Pruitt, D. G. and Kimmel, M. J. Twenty years of experimental gaming; Critique, synthesis and suggestions for the future. *Annual Review of Psychology* 1977, 28, 363–392.

# 15

# Conflict Behaviour of Individuals, Dyads and Triads in Mixed-motive Games

J. M. Rabbie, L. Visser and J. van Oostrum

## Introduction

Conflict and strife between groups and nations are among the most pressing problems of our time. Against this background it is striking that most research on social conflict in experimental social psychology is based on mixed-motive games and other inter-personal bargaining tasks (Rubin and Brown, 1975). The dominant tradition to explain inter-group conflict in terms of intra-individual and inter-personal processes rather than studying inter-group relations at its own level has been severely criticized (Tajfel, 1972). Recently a heated discussion erupted among American and European social psychologists as to whether one approach to social conflict is more "fundamental" than another (Plon, 1974a, b; Deutsch, 1974; Nemeth, 1974). In our opinion one approach is not more "general" or "fundamental" than another; they complement each other (Doise, 1978). Moreover, such issues cannot be settled by debate, but should be made accessible to empirical research. For example, if it could be shown that groups would be less or more competitive than isolated individuals in experimental games, there would be some empirical grounds for believing that theories developed at the inter-personal level would be inadequate in explaining conflict behaviour between larger social systems. In any case such comparative research may help us to discover the crucial theoretical variables which may account for possible differences in conflict behaviour between individuals and groups.

There has been a long and venerable tradition to compare the

This research was supported by the Netherlands Organization for the Advancement of Pure Research (ZWO), Grant 57-7.

performance of individuals and groups. In fact this individual versus group-comparison is one of the oldest "problems" in experimental social psychology (Davis, 1978). In view of this work, it is striking how little systematic research has been conducted as to whether groups are less or more competitive than individuals (Brickman, 1974). Quasi-experimental studies by Sherif (1966) and Blake and Mouton (1961) indicate that highly cohesive groups may become very antagonistic toward outgroups. Janis (1972) in his analysis of "groupthink" at the highest levels of government comes to a very similar conclusion. In a single trial Prisoner's Dilemma Game (PDG) it was found that cooperatively inclined players placed in a group shifted more often toward competitive inter-group orientations than competitive players would shift toward inter-group cooperation (Pines, 1976). This study could imply that groups may induce a competitive rather than a cooperative orientation toward other groups. Apparently, under some circumstances, normative pressures may induce groups to become very competitive toward outgroups (Rabbie and de Brey, 1971; Janis, 1972). In view of the dominant inter-personal approach in the gaming literature it is not surprising that direct comparisons between individuals and groups are exceedingly rare. If we examine what little evidence there is, it appears that groups may be more or less competitive than individuals, depending upon the counter strategy of the other party they are faced with. Pylyshin et al. (1966) compared female dyads and individuals who played a 150 trial PD game against a programmed opponent who followed approximately a tit-for-tat strategy. They found that both individuals and pairs became more cooperative with trials, but that the rate of learning to play cooperatively was higher among dyads than among individuals, especially in the early stages of the game. Moreover dyads ". . . displayed less 'repentence' and less 'trust' than the individuals — i.e., were significantly more likely to continue non-cooperation once started" (p. 219).

Lindskold et al. (1969) compared in two experiments male triads in interaction with a single simulated opponent who followed a 50% non-contingent strategy in a 50 trial PD game. They found no differences in competitive behaviour between individuals and groups, but in one of the experiments triads appeared to be less "trustworthy", i.e. were less likely than individuals to make a cooperative choice after a joint cooperative outcome on the preceding trial. In a more recent article (Lindskold et al., 1977) two experiments were reported in which male and female subjects, either as individuals or preponderantly as triads, participated in a 50 trial PD game. In the first experiment, the subjects opposed a single life opponent, in the second they faced a simulated partner who followed mainly a 50% random (non-contingent) strategy. In both experiments groups were likely to be more competitive than individuals on the first five trials, but overall no differences between individuals and groups were obtained. When given the option, groups were likely, especially in the first experiment, to send more threatening, coercive messages to their opponents than individuals. In the second experiment, but not in the first, groups won more points than individuals. These experimental results suggest several hypotheses which do not exclude each other:

(1) *Groups may be more rational than individuals.* Wilson (1971) has pointed out that "against any non-contingent strategy, competition is optimal. It may be that groups differ from individuals the way males differ from females, namely, groups may be more competitive when competition is optimal and more cooperative when cooperation is optimal" (p. 186). This notion could imply that groups are more "rational" and better able to analyse the situation of this particular game and act accordingly (Barnlund, 1959). This point of view has been expressed by Pruitt and Kimmel (1977) in their recent review of experimental gaming in the last 20 years. In their view, experimental games such as the PDG confront people with "an unfamiliar strategic environment", in which they are trying to be as rational as possible in maximizing their own "individualistic" benefits. "The reward structure" in the PDG is such that each party is motivated not to cooperate and yet, paradoxically, both prefer cooperation to mutual non-cooperation. In other words, individual rationality leads to collective irrationality" (p. 372). Mutual cooperation is achieved when the interacting parties take a long range perspective of reaching the "goal of establishing and/or maintaining continued mutual cooperation". According to their "goal-expectation theory:" . . . three perceptions contribute to the development of this goal: (a) perceived dependence on the other, i.e. a recognition of the importance of the other's cooperation; (b) pessimism about the likelihood that the other can be exploited (i.e. that he will cooperate unilaterally for any period of time); and (c) insight into the necessity of cooperating with the other in order to achieve his cooperation. . .". The goal of achieving mutual cooperation ". . . must

be accompanied by an expectation that the other will cooperate either immediately or in response to the actor's cooperation" (Pruitt and Kimmel, 1977, p. 375). It should be noted that the "goal of mutual cooperation" is a strategic goal which serves as a means to realize the motivational goal of maximizing one's own benefit (McClintock, 1977, p. 53). When partners have reason to believe that they are able to maximize their own benefits by a competitive or non-cooperative response, they will compete rather than cooperate. According to Pruitt and Kimmel, when people have time to think, they will gain more insight in the reward structure of the game and will realize that it is more profitable to both parties to cooperate with each other than not to cooperate or defect. Thus, when people are forced to re-examine their experiences in the PDG, e.g. by filling out questionnaires about their behaviour (McClintock, 1972), by making provisional tries before making binding decisions (Pilisuk *et al.,* 1965) or engage in intra-team discussions about their strategic moves, they will become more cooperative than people who lack this insight. Therefore, groups will act more cooperatively than individuals provided the other group does the same. However, when the other does not reciprocate or even appears to have exploitative intentions groups will act more defensively or non-cooperatively than individuals.

(2) Another possible hypothesis might be that *groups may be more individualistic and "outcome oriented" than individuals.* Groups may want to maximize their own earnings regardless of their relationship with the other party. Relationship-oriented individuals or groups may compete or cooperate primarily because of the kind of relationship they want to establish with the other party. For the outcome oriented groups or individuals the opponent has merely an instrumental value. They will be responsive to the actions of the other party to the extent that it enables them to gain as much for themselves as possible (Rubin and Brown, 1975). Individuals might be more relationship oriented toward the other party than groups, since the minimal social situation of the PDG is highly ambiguous and confusing for the individual player (Nemeth, 1972). He is socially isolated and has no opportunity to compare his notions about the situation with those of others. Therefore he will become more socially dependent and responsive to the actions of the other party as compared with groups who will be more concerned with the internal affairs in the group. This might be one of the reasons why the individual shows a greater propensity of "trustworthy" behaviour

(Rapoport, 1964) than dyads (Pylyshin *et al.*, 1966) or triads (Lindskold *et al.*, 1969). Individuals also seem less likely than groups to run the risk of spoiling a good relationship by making coercive threats to the other party (Lindskold *et al.*, 1977).

(3) The results of the previous studies might also be interpreted as an instance of *group polarization* (Moscovici and Zavalloni, 1969; Rabbie and Visser, 1972). In an ambiguous situation like the PDG (Nemeth, 1972), people are motivated to arrive at a common norm on what the situation is about and on what is expected from them (Turner and Killian, 1972; Rabbie, 1978). Through a process of normative and informational comparisons during the group discussion (Festinger, 1954; Deutsch and Gerard, 1955; Myers and Lamm, 1976) groups may come to more extreme decisions than the average judgement of the individual members prior to the discussion. According to Moscovici and Zavalloni (1969) the group discussion creates a greater involvement and commitment to the issues being discussed. This commitment will move the individual further in the direction of his initial decision. Thus groups will polarize to that pole of the scale to which members are already attracted as individuals. This means that groups will strengthen those norms which prevail in the population from which they are recruited. It has been shown that these normative and "cognitive representations" of the task may have an important influence on how the game is played (Abric, 1970). Dependent on the kind of norms which prevail in the particular subculture the subjects belong to and the persuasiveness of the arguments which can be derived from these norms (Burnstein, 1978) groups may become more competitive or individualistic etc. than individuals. In their first study, Lindskold *et al.* (1969, p. 304) interpreted the greater "trustworthiness" of groups versus individuals as an instance of an "ethical shift to maximize gains". In the second study Lindskold *et al.* (1977) did not find any group polarization on behavioural measures, but some polarization on the post-experimental ratings of the opponent did occur. It should be noted however, that in both studies no pre- and post-discussion measures were obtained. Polarization or "choice shifts" were inferred on the basis of "between-subjects", rather than "within-subjects" comparisons.

In order to obtain more information about the tenability of these hypotheses, a series of experiments are reviewed which were originally conducted to explore the degree of inter-party differentiation of people who were engaged in inter-personal and inter-group conflict.

These studies were part of a research program designed to study the effects of inter-group competition and cooperation on intra- and inter-group relations (Rabbie, 1974, 1978, in press). Most of these experiments were more complex and involved more dependent variables. For the present purpose we will restrict our discussion to the differences in choice behaviour and motivational orientation between individuals and groups playing a Prisoner's Dilemma Game (PDG) or another mixed-motive game against a programmed or against a "natural" partner. A more comprehensive account of these studies will be reported elsewhere (Rabbie, 1979; Rabbie and Visser, 1975; van Oostrum, 1977; Visser, 1978; Rabbie, in press; Horwitz and Rabbie, in press).

## Experiment 1: comparison of individuals and dyads in a PDG

In a first experiment 34 individuals and 32 dyads were asked to play a five trial PDG. All subjects were male students at the University of Utrecht in their first year of study. They received six Dutch guilders or about $2.25 plus the money they could earn depending upon the actual outcome of the game. The payoff matrix of the game is displayed in Fig. 1. Although the subjects were made to believe that they placed against an actual partner, the choices of their opponents were preprogrammed. Irrespective of the subjects' strategy the opponent played the following pattern: C, D, D, C, C. It is well known that the motivational meaning of C or D choice in the PDG is somewhat ambiguous (McClintock, 1972). A C-choice might be seen as a *cooperative* move: as an effort to maximize joint profit, or might reflect an individualistic orientation: to gain as much for oneself, regardless of the interests of the other party. The D-choice is even more ambiguous: it can be made to maximize own gain (*individualistic* orientation), maximize relative gain (*competition*) or to minimize a maximum possible loss (*defensive* orientation).

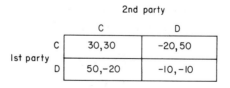

Fig. 1. Pay-off matrix of PDG (in Dutch cents).

In order to obtain information about the motivational meaning of the C and D choices on the part of our subjects, a motive question-naire was administered to them immediately after their first choice, but before they had received the choice of their opponent. This motive scale was administered again at the fifth and last trial of the game. In this 14-item questionnaire an attempt was made to assess the competitive, defensive, cooperative and individualistic orien-tations of the subjects. In the dyad condition all questionnaires were filled out after a discussion in the dyads. Their answers can be thus considered as group products. Obviously in the individual condition the questionnaire was filled out individually.

The subjects were told that we were interested in their reasons for their choice. Therefore, we asked the dyads permission to record their discussions on tape before they made their choice on each trial, while the individuals were urged to think "aloud" about their reasons for their choice which was also recorded on tape.


## Results

The subjects were classified as to whether they chose a C or D as their first choice. When this classification is included as a factor in the analysis of variance of the motive scores, it appeared that the C choice could be mainly considered as a cooperative move, while a first D choice reflected mainly a competitive-defensive orientation (Rabbie and Visser, 1975).

Overall dyads did not make more D-choices in this PDG than individuals, although they earned slightly more money than indi-viduals. The amount of money earned by individuals and dyads were respectively Dfl. 0.88 and Dfl. 0.98 ($P < 0.08$). However, the com-petitive behaviour of the opponent appeared to be an important variable. No significant differences were obtained between individuals and dyads on the first three trials. However, after having received two competitive and exploitive D-choices in a row after an initial C-choice, dyads tended to respond more with a D than individuals ($P < 0.04$). On the fifth and last trial dyads chose significantly more Ds than individuals ($P < 0.005$). Apparently, dyads become more defensive than individuals when the other party seems to use an exploitive, competitive strategy.

In this context, it is interesting to note that dyads seemed to be

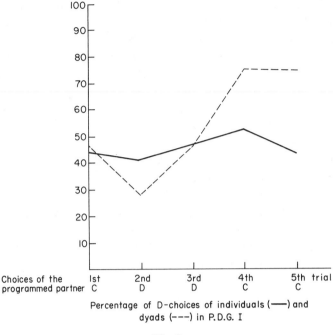

Choices of the          1st        2nd        3rd        4th        5th  trial
programmed partner  C          D          D          C          C

Percentage of D-choices of individuals (——) and
dyads (–––) in P.D.G. I

Fig. 2

more defensive than individuals at the very first trial of the game, thus before they had seen the reactions of the other party. In their response to the first motive questionnaire, dyads as a group ($m = 5.88$) felt more strongly motivated "to lose as little as possible" than individuals ($m = 4.12$, $P < 0.01$). This result could imply that dyads or groups were predisposed at the very beginning of the game to behave more defensively, regardless of the actions of the other player. As we have seen, this greater defensiveness of the dyad did not show up in their actual choice behaviour. Only after the other party played two Ds after a first cooperative C-choice, the dyads may have felt trapped and exploited. If this is the case, the initial defensive orientation was strengthened and motivated them to the overt choice behaviour of choosing more often a "D" than a "C" in the fourth and fifth trial in order to minimize a maximum possible loss.

After a first choice dyads seem also to have had more of a long term perspective than individuals. They ($m = 4.44$) were more likely than individuals ($m = 3.21$) to "take the following choices into account" ($P < 0.04$). It is also quite clear that our motive questionnaire was much more sensitive in picking up subtle differences in motivation than could be inferred from the dichotomous choices afforded by the PDG. This difference in defensive orientation between dyads and individuals became even more apparent in their answers to the motive scale at the end of the game when dyads actually made more competitive/defensive choices. Dyads, as compared with individuals, would "like to lose as little as possible" ($m = 5.48$ and 4.06, $P < 0.01$), "at least not more than the other party" ($m = 4.34$ and 2.71, $P < 0.01$) and were motivated to be more "cautious" than individuals ($m = 4.38$ and 3.56, $P < 0.10$). There was a slight tendency on the part of dyads to have a stronger "individualistic" orientation than individuals: "they wanted to earn as much for themselves as possible" ($m = 5.14$ and 4.21, $P < 0.10$) and were "less interested in maintaining a good relationship with the other party" than individuals ($m = 4.73$ and 5.71, $P < 0.07$). There were no significant differences between individuals and dyads with regard to the competitive and cooperative orientations measured by the motive scale.

## Discussion

The results of the present study seem in accord with the goal-expectation theory of Pruitt and Kimmel. From the beginning dyads have a longer time perspective than individuals, which according to their theory should facilitate the development of the long-range goal of mutual cooperation. However, when the other party seemingly does not want to cooperate or even threatens to exploit their own party, dyads become more non-cooperative or defensive in their behaviour and orientation than individuals.

There is also some support for the second hypothesis. The questionnaire data suggest that dyads have a stronger "individualistic" orientation and are less interested in developing a good relationship with the other party than individuals.

Since we have no information about the prevailing normative orientations of our subjects before and after the group discussion we have no hard evidence for or against the polarization hypothesis.

In the experiments reviewed earlier, individuals were either compared with dyads (Pylyshin et al., 1965) or triads (Lindskold et al., 1969, 1977). After this experiment the next logical step seems to be to try to replicate these findings and to find out whether the greater defensiveness in behaviour and orientation of the group is due to the unique properties of the dyad or whether it is characteristic of larger groups in general. It has been argued that larger groups usually have more resources at their disposal than smaller groups (Steiner, 1972). Provided they are able to solve their greater problems of motivation and coordination, which may result in "process loss", larger groups should be better able to analyse the structure of the game and act accordingly than smaller groups. Therefore, triads are more likely than dyads to strive for the goal of mutual cooperation in order to maximize their own outcomes.

### Experiment 2: group size and defensiveness of males and females in a PDG

In the second experiment a three-member group or triad was added. To enlarge our subject pool, we employed male as well as female subjects. Wilson (1971) has reviewed a number of studies, including his own, which shows that the initial double cross by the opponent followed by later unconditional cooperation set the stage for a higher level of later cooperation of groups and individuals. Apparently, an increase in positive rewarding behaviour after an earlier antagonistic reaction has more impact on liking — and presumably on mutual cooperation — than constant rewarding behaviour (Aronson and Linder, 1965). Lindskold (1978) has pointed out that the initial antagonism conveys the impression of having the capacity and willingness to be damaging; the switch, as a contrast, may more clearly create the impression that the other party is truly conciliatory. By extending the game with a few cooperative moves of the pro-grammed opponent it is possible to find out whether males and females, groups and individuals, differ in their tendency toward greater cooperation toward the end of the game.

If groups tend to strengthen and enhance the prevailing normative orientations of the individual members (Myers, 1978; Moscovici and Zavalloni, 1969; Rabbie and Visser, 1972; Rabbie and de Brey, 1972; Visser, 1975), one would expect that groups would be more extreme in exhibiting the differential motivational orientations of males and females than isolated individuals.

## Method

In total 96 students of the University of Utrecht, 48 male and 48 female subjects, participated in the experiment. There were eight boys and eight girls in the individual condition, 16 boys and 16 girls in the dyad condition and 24 boys and 24 girls in the triad condition. Apart from these changes, the second experiment was very similar to the first one. The game was extended from a five to a seven trial game, in which the programmed partner played C, D, D, C, C, C, C. This extension would give us the opportunity to find out how long the defensive behaviour would persist after the critical fourth trial at which point the subjects would have received two consecutive D-choices from their opponent. A modified and enlarged version of the motive scale was introduced at the 1st, 4th and 7th trial of the game. In order to check on the possible effects of responding to this questionnaire on the subsequent choice behaviour the motive scale was administered either before or after they made their fourth choice. For the present discussion the results of this experimental variation will not be reported here.

## Results

All (100%) of the male and female dyads chose a D on the fourth and critical trial, while 44% of the individuals and 56% of the triads chose this course of action ($P < 0.002$). As expected dyads chose more Ds than individuals, but surprisingly these data also indicate that they chose more Ds than triads. For the other choices no significant differences were obtained between individuals, dyads and triads.

Women are more defensive or competitive in playing Ds than men at the second ($P < 0.01$), fifth ($P < 0.05$) and sixth ($P < 0.01$) trial of the game. Probably for this reason they were able to earn more money playing against a non-contingent strategy in which the other party made consistently a cooperative choice after the fourth trial. The average amount of money earned by women and men was respectively Dfl. 1.76 and Dfl. 1.53 ($P < 0.02$). This result runs counter to the assumption that men are more outcome oriented than women and are inclined to act accordingly playing against a non-contingent strategy (Rubin and Brown, 1975).

The significant differences in choices between individuals, dyads and triads at the fourth critical trial indicates that dyads were not only more defensive or non-cooperative in their orientation than individuals, as was suggested by the previous experiment, but they seemed also more defensive or non-cooperative than the three member group at this trial!

This impression was supported by the answers to the motive scale which was administered at the first, fourth and seventh trial of the game. Generally dyads described themselves as more "cautious" ($m = 4.94$) than either individuals ($m = 3.25$) or triads ($m = 4.27$, $P < 0.05$). Just as in the first experiment the greater cautiousness of the dyad appeared already at the first trial ($P < 0.11$), thus before they could have seen the reactions of the other party. At this first trial too, dyads ($m = 5.19$) did not want to "lose more than the other party" in comparison with individuals ($m = 2.75$) and triads ($m = 4.56$, $P < 0.05$). Apparently intra-group interaction, especially among dyads, creates a greater awareness of the risky aspects of the PD situation even at the very beginning of the game.

It was hypothesized that women, because of their greater interpersonal responsiveness, would react more defensively and vindictively after the initial double cross of the fourth choice than males who were more interested in maximizing their own gains (Rubin and Brown, 1975). However, the choice behaviour data indicate that women behaved more defensively and non-cooperatively than males on the second, fifth and sixth trial of the game. Thus before the double cross, in response to the initial cooperative choice of the opponent, women react more defensively and competitively than men. It might be that at the beginning of the game women are more suspicious than men about the possible actions and intentions of the other party, which induces them to react more defensively despite the cooperative first choice of the other.

The "long term goal of mutual cooperation" (Pruitt and Kimmel, 1977) becomes more important over time. Except for the understandable dip at the fourth critical trial ($m = 4.52$), people are more motivated "to earn together as much as possible" at the end of the game ($m = 5.56$), than at the beginning ($m = 4.94$, $P < 0.05$). There is also a greater interest in "developing an understanding with the other party" at the end of the game ($m = 5.27$) than at the fourth ($m = 4.88$) or at the beginning of the game ($m = 3.83$, $P < 0.001$).

In accord with these questionnaire data, a trend analysis indicated a significant linear increase in cooperative choice behaviour over time

$(P < 0.05)$. Apparently, despite initial antagonistic behaviour of the opponent, people become more cooperative in their behaviour and orientation over time, provided that the other party, after his earlier "lapse", behaves consistently in a cooperative way (Wilson, 1971; Harford and Solomon, 1967).

It was hypothesized that groups are likely to strengthen the normative orientations of the individual member. This hypothesis would imply that groups of men and women would become either more outcome- or relationship-oriented than individual men or women. At the behavioural level, this hypothesis receives no support. The interactions between sex and group size in the choice data were not significant. Other questionnaire results indicate that the different normative orientations of men and women are best represented in the dyad. Since the members in the dyad have to achieve consensus in order to make a decision at all, they can only persuade each other by an appeal to a common norm. In the triad, on the other hand, people can make decisions by majority vote and are less dependent upon the persuasiveness of the arguments (Burnstein, 1978).

## Experiment 3: group size and avoidance of internal conflict

In the two previous experiments we have found that especially male dyads tend to be more defensive in their behaviour and orientation than individuals and triads, particularly when they are faced with a "tricky competitive opponent" who threatens to exploit them. One possible explanation could be that dyads compared with larger groups are more strongly motivated to resolve conflicts among themselves. If they do not succeed they will cease to exist (Simmel, 1955). It is probably for this reason that dyads show less open hostility, but more tension in their verbal behaviour than larger groups (Bales and Borgatta, 1955; O'Dell, 1968). Slater (1958) has found that dyads may become so preoccupied with developing and maintaining good relationships among themselves that this kind of "pussy-footing" will hamper their effective functioning. In case of disagreement it is easier to reach a decision in a triad than in a dyad, since triads can decide by majority vote. This "super-individual" feature of the triad lessens feelings of personal responsibility for the groups' decision, including the adverse effects such a decision may have for the inter-personal relationships within the group (Steiner, 1972).

Thus, it can be expected that members of the dyad will feel more attracted to their group than members of a triad (Thomas and Fink, 1963). They will find it more difficult to reach agreement in the dyad than in the triad and they will feel more responsible for what happened in the group in the dyad than in the triad. Consequently there are strong pressures in the dyad to reach agreement and avoid open antagonism in the group. When dyads are threatened by the other party, a D-choice is probably more effective in minimizing internal conflict than a C-choice, since it leads to relative gain when the other party chooses a C or to a minimal loss when the adversary chooses a D. Mutual recriminations and reproaches are hereby minimized. Therefore it is expected that dyads will be more defensive in their behaviour and orientation than either individuals or triads, especially when they have reasons to believe that the other party is trying to exploit them. It is likely that the tendency to avoid internal conflict would be the strongest among those dyads or other groups who are motivated to maintain and enhance their own identity. It is probable that a longer time perspective would strengthen these feelings of identity within the group (Rabbie and Wilkens, 1971). The stronger the tendency to maintain and enhance group identity, the more likely is it that groups as compared with individuals are motivated to avoid internal conflicts by playing a D rather than a C against an exploitive opponent. This tendency will be strengthened when they are told by the experimenter to avoid internal conflicts among themselves.

## Method

In this study 120 male students at the University of Utrecht had to play a PDG against a programmed partner, who played a non-contingent C, D, D, C strategy during the first four moves and a tit-for-tat strategy until the 7th trial of the game.

The tit-for-tat strategy was added to find out whether in the long run groups are more likely than individuals to strive for the goal of mutual cooperation in order to maximize their own earnings when they are faced with a contingent strategy of the other player (Pruitt and Kimmel, 1977; Wilson, 1971). In the conflict avoidance condition half of the subjects, divided into individuals, dyads and triads, were told that we were interested in the decision making process leading up to each choice, particularly how groups or individuals would be able to avoid internal conflicts and to achieve consensus about the choices they had to make. In order to vary the time perspective of the subjects they were also told that they would work together as a "unit" on another task after the first seven trials. An effort was made to phrase these instructions in such a way that they would be equally applicable to individuals as to groups. In the no conflict avoidance condition these instructions were omitted. After the 7th trial subjects in both conflict conditions were told to continue to the 12th and last trial. During this period a tit-for-tat strategy was followed. The motive scale was administered after the 3rd, 6th and 12th trial. In order to obtain information about the tenability of the polarization hypothesis subjects were asked to fill out the motive questionnaire prior to the group's discussion in the dyad and triad condition at the fourth critical trial. A comparison between these individual and collective judgements would reflect the degree and direction of the group polarization. We also obtained other observational and questionnaire material, but these results will be reported elsewhere (Van Oostrum, 1977).

## Results

In view of space limitations we will limit the presentation of the results to the effects of the size of the group. It should be noted that the conflict avoidance condition produced no main and only a few interaction effects with the group size variable. Generally these significant interactions were in the predicted direction. Dyads tend to play more Ds in the first ($P < 0.08$) and the second trial ($P < 0.05$) of the game than individuals and especially as compared with triads.

Consistent with the hypothesis, these differences between individuals, dyads and triads are particularly pronounced in the condition when they are told to avoid internal conflict among themselves. There is no indication that groups were more likely than individuals to maximize their gains by using the optimal cooperative strategy during the tit-for-tat strategy of their opponents (Wilson, 1971). No significant differences in cooperative choices between individuals, dyads and triads were obtained during the tit-for-tat strategy. In both the conflict avoidance and no conflict avoidance condition dyads expected more often than individuals and triads that the other party would play a D at the first ($P < 0.06$) and the second trial ($P < 0.07$).

There is some question as to what extent the discussion in the group is a necessary condition for the non-cooperative choice behaviour of the dyad on the first two trials. When subjects are asked at the very first trial to indicate individually which choices they would prefer, before they have had the opportunity to discuss these proposals with the other members of the group, it was found that the individual members of the dyad were more likely to propose a D than either individuals, or individual members in the triad, especially in the conflict avoidance condition ($P < 0.05$). This finding raises the question as to whether the group polarization hypothesis, which requires intra-group comparisons and argumentation, is a viable explanation for the differences in behaviour and orientation between individuals and groups in these experiments.

It was expected that dyads would react more defensively than individuals and triads after the exploitive C, D, D moves of the programmed opponent. However, after the third choice of the opponent, no significant main effects or interactions were obtained between group size and the conflict avoidance conditions. Thus the main hypothesis in the study received no support.

To find out whether any group polarization did occur the motive questionnaire was administered after the third trial, first individually and again after a group discussion. If we first look at the individual judgements prior to the discussion, dyads do not differ significantly from individuals and triads on defensive motives. However, individual members of the dyad ($m = 5.12$) are more strongly motivated "to earn as much as possible" than either individuals ($m = 3.50$) and members of the triads ($m = 4.38$, $P < 0.05$). Individual members of the dyad are also more competitively oriented: "they try more to win from the other party" ($m = 3.75$) than either individuals ($m = 2.25$) and members of the triad ($m = 2.70$, $P < 0.025$). These data indicate that during the first two trials dyads may have played more Ds than individuals and triads not because of defensive but for offensive reasons. At this stage they do not seem to realize that inter-group cooperation is a better strategy for achieving this goal than non-cooperation. After the discussion in the group these significant differences between individuals, dyads and triads tend to disappear. Groups score lower than their individual members on individualistic and competitive moves on items such as "to earn as much as possible" ($m_{ind} = 4.75$, $m_{gr} = 3.97$, $P < 0.01$) and "to win from the other party" ($m_{ind} = 3.23$, $m_{gr} = 2.50$, $P < 0.01$). Apparently some group polarization did in fact occur, but it tends to minimize rather than sharpen the differences in orientation between individuals and groups. This might be another reason why the polarization hypothesis is probably incorrect in explaining the differences in orientation between individuals, dyads and triads in these games.

There is some support for the notion that individuals are more "relationship oriented" than groups: after both the sixth ($P < 0.05$) and twelfth trials ($P < 0.01$) individuals reported a stronger desire "to develop a positive relationship with the other party" than either triads and especially dyads. Apparently, dyads are more preoccupied with their internal relationships than with the relationship to the other party. Just as in the previous experiment, at the initial stages in the game, male dyads choose more Ds than either individuals or triads. However, in this study this happened at the very first few trials of the game, thus before they could have felt exploited by the other party. Moreover, in contrast to the previous experiments the dyads in this study tend to give more competitive than defensive reasons for their choice. This confronts us with the problem that the motivational meanings of the choices in the PDG are very ambiguous (McClintock, 1972). A task is needed which provides the subjects with more response alternatives, which makes it easier to make more unequivocal inferences about the cooperative, competitive, or individualistic motives of the subject. Tajfel et al. (1971) have developed a task which seems to meet these criteria. In the following experiment we will describe this task.

## Experiment 4: group size and inter-group cooperation in an allocation task

In our modified version of the Tajfel et al. (1971) task subjects have to make a choice in a series of trials between two rows of numbers forming a matrix. The top row in each matrix stands for rewards or penalties awarded to their own party. The other row represents rewards and penalties rewarded to the other party. Two examples of the matrices used in this experiment are presented in Table 1.

By composing different types of matrices, it is possible to make

TABLE 1

*Examples of matrices employed in Experiment 4*

| Matrix R− | MIP MD | | | | | MF | | | | | | MJP |
|---|---|---|---|---|---|---|---|---|---|---|---|---|
| Own party | 14 | 13 | 12 | 11 | 10 | 9 | 8 | 7 | 6 | 5 | 4 | 3 | 2 |
| Other party | −5 | −3 | −1 | 1 | 3 | 5 | 7 | 9 | 11 | 13 | 15 | 17 | 19 |

| Matrix R+ | MD | | | | | | MF | | | | | | MIP MJP |
|---|---|---|---|---|---|---|---|---|---|---|---|---|
| Own party | 2 | 3 | 4 | 5 | 6 | 7 | 8 | 9 | 10 | 11 | 12 | 13 | 14 |
| Other party | −5 | −3 | −1 | 1 | 3 | 5 | 7 | 9 | 11 | 13 | 15 | 17 | 19 |

inferences about the motives or goals which may guide the subjects while making their choices. Following Tajfel *et al.* (1971, p. 163) we may distinguish between different types of motivational variables.

(1) MJP (maximum joint payoff) can be defined as that choice in a matrix which results in the highest possible payoffs to both parties. This choice is represented in the 13th column of the matrices R− and R+ in Table 1.

(2) MIP (maximum individualistic payoff) is defined as that choice of the matrix which corresponds to the highest number of points which can be awarded to one's own group. This choice is represented in the 1st column of matrix R− and in the 13th column of matrix R+. Thus MIP and MJP are negatively correlated in matrix R−, but positively correlated in matrix R+.

(3) MD (maximum difference in favour of own party). This choice represents the greatest possible difference between points awarded to own and other party in favour of own party. As can be seen in Table 1, MD and MIP are positively correlated in matrix R−, but negatively correlated in matrix R+.

(4) MF (maximizing fairness) is defined as that choice which represents the minimal difference in payoff between the two parties.

If it is assumed that groups are more rational and "outcome" oriented, and less "relationship" oriented than individuals it is to be expected that:

(1) Groups are more likely to maximize their individual profit (MIP) than individuals.

(2) Individuals will be more fair (MF) to the other party than groups, i.e. they tend to minimize the differences between themselves and the other party.

(3) Groups are likely to maximize their joint profit (MJP), provided

MJP and MIP are positively correlated. When these scores are negatively correlated, i.e. when the maximum possible profit can only be achieved by rewarding the least for the own and the most for the other party, groups are less likely to maximize their joint profit than individuals.

(4) Generally, when groups are better able than individuals to solve the problem to gain as much for themselves as possible it is to be expected that, given the particular reward structure of the game, groups will earn more money with this task than individuals.

In these hypotheses no distinction is made between the choice behaviour of dyads and triads. It was suggested earlier that triads are likely to make more effective decisions than dyads in maximizing their outcomes, since they have more resources or members at their disposal, decisions can be made by majority vote and as a consequence members will feel less personally responsible for the group's decision (Steiner, 1972). There is also less concern and mutual responsibility for the inter-personal relationships in the triad than in the dyad. It was hypothesized that the deviant behaviour of the dyad in the previous PDG experiments, was due to the concern about the inter-personal relationships in the group. The parties in the PDG are more interdependent in terms of their outcomes than in the Tajfel task (McClintock, 1977). Therefore the choices made in the Tajfel task will involve less risk for the inter-personal relationships in the dyad than the decisions made in the PDG. Assuming that the process loss for dyads and triads will be about the same, the number of resources will determine the actual outcomes (Steiner, 1972). Therefore, it is predicted, in view of the hypotheses formulated earlier that dyads will occupy an intermediate position in performance between individuals and triads.

## Method

In a 3 x 2 experimental design male students of the University of Utrecht subdivided into individuals, dyads and triads played 40 trials in the modified Tajfel et al. (1971) task in which they were able to award money to themselves or to the other party or to penalize themselves or the other party.

In the first 20 trials half of the subjects received information about the actual choices of the other party, in the other half the feedback about the choices of the other party was omitted. In view of space limitations the results of this experimental variation are discussed elsewhere (Visser *et al.*, 1976). The types of matrices differed from one another to the degree that the MJP and MIP scores correlated negatively or positively with each other and in the total amount of money which could be awarded to own and other party. Each matrix involves 13 choices of allocation to own and other party. The response alternatives constitute a 13 point scale. For each motive measured (MJP, MIP, MD, MF) the directions of the scales were made comparable, permitting the summation of responses across matrices. During the second phase, both parties in the feedback and no-feedback condition received information about the choices of the other party. After the first and second phase of the experiment questionnaires were administered about evaluation of own and other party, attribution of motives to own and other party etc. These findings will be discussed elsewhere.


## Results

As expected groups are more likely to maximize their individual profits (MIP) than individuals. The mean MIP choices for individuals, dyads and triads over the 40 choices were respectively 7.68, 8.29 and 9.16 ($P < 0.001$). Consistent with our second hypothesis, individuals score higher on "maximizing fairness" (MF) than groups. The mean MF scores for individuals, dyads and triads were respectively 3.75, 4.38 and 4.94 ($P < 0.02$).

Groups are more likely than individuals to maximize their joint profit (MJP), provided that in this way they are also able to maximize their individual profit (MIP). In the matrices in which MJP and MIP are positively correlated the mean MJP scores for individuals, dyads and triads are respectively 9.03, 10.72 and 11.83. In the matrices when the MJP and MIP indices are negatively correlated, no difference between individuals ($m = 7.67$), dyads ($m = 8.15$) and triads ($m = 7.51$) could be found. This interaction between group size and the R− and R+ matrices is highly significant ($P < 0.01$). When we sum over the R− and R+ matrices no significant differences between individuals ($m = 8.35$), dyads ($m = 9.44$) and triads ($m = 9.67$) could be obtained ($P < 0.17$). We were also interested in whether groups are more likely to maximize the differences between themselves and others than individuals. On the basis of the "positive social identity hypothesis" of Tajfel *et al.* (1971) and Turner (1974), one would expect that groups would be more strongly motivated to differentiate themselves from the other party than individuals. In the matrices we used, the MD scores were perfectly negatively correlated with the MJP scores. Since no significant differences were obtained for the MJP scores between individuals, dyads and triads, this hypothesis receives no support.

As a consequence of the higher MJP and MIP scores of groups than individuals, groups earn more money than individuals. The average amount of money earned by individuals, dyads and triads was respectively Dfl. 8.65, 10.74 and 11.14 ($P < 0.001$).

The answers to the motive questionnaire confirm the impression based on the choice behaviour of our subjects. Consistent with the higher MIP scores of groups than individuals, triads ($m = 4.48$) report more often than dyads ($m = 2.79$) and individuals ($m = 2.24$) that they would like to "earn as much for themselves as possible", regardless of the outcomes of the other party ($P < 0.002$). The greater individualistic orientation of groups as compared with individuals is also reflected in their endorsement of the statement: "Whatever the other party does, it is a matter of principle to make a choice whereby the other party gains as much as possible". Individuals (mean rank order position 7.90) were more likely to stress the importance of this statement than dyads ($m = 9.05$) and triads ($m = 10.85$, $P < 0.005$). Triads ($m = 5.21$) and dyads ($m = 5.23$) wanted "to lose as little as possible" as compared with individuals ($m = 4.01$, $P < 0.04$). In view of the higher MF scores of individuals than groups, it is not surprising that triads ($m = 7.85$) are more likely than dyads ($m = 8.10$) and individuals ($m = 9.45$) to stress the importance of the statement: "In a task like this one should *not* give the other party as much as oneself, since that would make one more vulnerable to him, if he refuses to reciprocate" ($P < 0.10$).

In the previous PDG studies dyads seem to differ from individuals and triads in their choice behaviour and orientation. As predicted in this study there is not a curvilinear but a linear relationship between group size and the main dependent variables. The larger the group, the more people tend to maximize their individualistic profits, the less they strive for maximum fairness and the more they try to achieve as much as possible for both parties, provided their individualistic gains are thereby maximized. In this particular task, people are less outcome-dependent on the other party than in a PDG. For this reason the behaviour of the other party has fewer repercussions for the internal affairs of the dyad than in the PDG. Under these circumstances they seem better able to devote themselves to the impersonal and rational task of earning as much for themselves as possible.

## Conclusion

The experiments reported in this paper strongly suggest that groups may have different ways of handling inter-party conflicts than individuals. However, our knowledge about the processes by which these differences come about are still very incomplete and rudimentary.

Myers (1978) reviews considerable research evidence which indicates that intra-group discussions enhance inter-group polarization. This does not seem to happen in our experiments. In the third study, which was specifically designed to obtain information on this issue, it was found that prior to the discussion, individual members of the dyad and triad were more extreme in their proposed choice behaviour and motivations than after the discussion. The intra-group discussion tends to diminish rather than strengthen the inter-group polarization. Obviously, further research should focus on the nature of these intra-group interactions.

There is some support for the goal expectation theory of Pruitt and Kimmel (1977). They have asserted that in the strategic environment of these experimental games, people try to be as rational as possible in pursuing their goal of maximizing their own gain. If mutual cooperation seems the most rational way of achieving this goal, people will cooperate, if not, they will compete. According to the questionnaire data it appears that in the present studies groups act more in this impersonal strategic frame of mind than individuals. However, it should be noted that in only one of the four studies groups were able to earn more money than individuals. A greater insight and a stronger outcome orientation does not guarantee higher earnings in the conditions of the present games.

Pruitt and Kimmel (1977) assume that the greater rationality of groups than of individuals is simply a matter of insight in the reward structure of the game. In their view in the setting of the PDG "conventional social norms, attitudes and sentiments, and most social motives, have relatively little impact on behaviour, because they seem irrelevant to the task at hand" (p. 370). However, it was argued earlier that the social isolation and deprivation of individuals in the minimal social situation of the two-person PDG, would make them more socially dependent upon the relationship with the other party (Gewirtz and Baer, 1958). Therefore, individuals would be more "relationship" than "outcome" oriented as compared with groups. In support of this hypothesis it was found in the present and other studies (van Oostrum, 1977) that individuals expressed a greater need to establish a good relationship with the other party and at the same time made more cooperative choices than groups. These findings suggest, contrary to the opinion of Pruitt and Kimmel, that social motives may have some impact on behaviour in the PDG.

A recent content analysis of the discussions of high school and university students in a PDG suggested that the definition of the situation may have a strong impact on how the game is played, especially at the earlier stages. When the game is played as a test of strength, as was the case with our high school students, people will compete much more with the other party, then when the situation is defined as a way of earning money. These results may imply that both normative and rational considerations play a role in the choice behaviour in these strategic games. When both types of considerations are congruent with one another, they lead to a similar choice behaviour, e.g. mutual cooperation. When they are in conflict, as in the case of our high school students, the normative orientations may become so dominant that people will compete rather than cooperate. In order to assess the relative strength of these utilitarian and social considerations experiments are needed in which individuals and groups have equal insight in the reward structure of the game, but differ in the degree of social isolation they experience and/or the subculture they belong to.

We are still quite puzzled about the differences in behaviour and orientation between dyads and triads. It has been pointed out that larger groups have more resources at their disposal than smaller groups. When they are equally successful in solving problems of coordination and motivation larger groups should have a higher actual productivity than smaller groups (Steiner, 1972). If it is assumed that higher outcomes reflect a greater actual productivity, there is some support for this hypothesis in the fourth study. The outcome interdependence of the two parties in the Tajfel *et al.* (1971) task is much less than in the PDG. Therefore intergroup conflict has much less impact on the intra-group relations and created much less "process loss" in the Tajfel than in the PDG-situation. As a consequence more money was earned as the group increased in size. In the PDG studies no significant differences in earnings between individuals, dyads and triads were obtained. There is also another difference between the two bargaining tasks. The dilemma in a PDG had no unique solution. The game will be played dependent upon such motivational and cognitive factors as the motivational orientation of the players, e.g. whether they want to compete, cooperate or to maximize their own individualistic gains (Rubin and Brown, 1975); what kind of attributions they make about the competitive or cooperative orientations of their partners (e.g. Kelley and Stahelski, 1970); their "cognitive representations of the game" (Abric, 1970), e.g. whether they see it just as a game, a test of strength, an opportunity to earn money (van Oostrum, 1978) a task which may involve ethical issues (Rabbie *et al.*, 1975), or as a strategic environment in which people try to maximize their individualistic gains (Pruitt and Kimmel, 1977). When there are differences of opinion within the group about these issues, an implicit or explicit agreement should be reached, before the dilemma can be "solved" effectively. From this point of view, the PD situation can be considered as an "intellective" as well as a "judgemental" task (Laughlin and Adamopulous, 1978).

We have argued earlier that there will be stronger pressures to reach agreement and to avoid open antagonisms in a dyad than in a triad in which decisions can be made by majority vote. If the exploitive behaviour of the other party evokes defensive reactions, it is likely that dyads as compared with individuals and triads will tend to choose an alternative which minimizes conflict among them. Presumably the desire for cohesion and mutual acceptance is greater for members in the dyad than in triads (Steiner, 1978). In the experiment which was specifically designed to test the conflict-avoidance hypothesis, dyads did indeed play more Ds than individuals and triads, especially in the conflict-avoidance condition, but only at the first two trials of the game. Thus before they had reason to believe that the other party intended to exploit them. Moreover, dyads gave mainly competitive rather than defensive reasons for their choice. The avoidance of conflict hypothesis receives thus only scant support.

At this point we are uncertain whether the deviant behaviour and orientation of the dyad, especially in the second experiment after the exploitive moves of the programmed partner, is due to the peculiar composition of these groups, to short term defensive considerations, which take precedence over long range cooperative aims (Pruitt and Kimmel, 1977) or to the unique properties of the dyad as compared with the triad (Simmel, 1950; Steiner, 1972). The only way to find out is to examine the actual decision making process in these dyads and triads. With this aim in mind we have developed category systems to analyse the verbal (Muller *et al.*, 1978) and non-verbal interactions during the game (Kalma and van Rooy, 1977). A computer program to analyse the voice qualities of the participants is in preparation (Kalma and Tempelaars, 1978).

Finally, these experiments were conducted as a reaction to the dominant trend in experimental social psychology in this area to use individuals rather than groups as the main unit of analysis. This preference is understandable. The study of individuals in minimal social situations is more convenient, less costly and provides much more experimental control over the relevant experimental variables, than studying freely interacting individuals as members of groups, which may have interdependent relationships with other groups. The employment of individuals rather than groups in our experiments has led to a tendency to explain large scale social conflicts in terms of intra-individual (Steiner, 1974) or inter-personal processes (Tajfel, 1972). When we use groups rather than individuals in our research we are forced to develop theories which take account of both intra- and inter-group processes and the complex ways in which these processes at different levels may interact with each other. These future theories may be more complex, less elegant and rigorous than conceptualizations which stay at one particular level of explanation (Doise, 1978). However, this loss of elegance and rigour might be counterbalanced by a greater external and ecological validity (Schlenker and Bonoma, 1978). Therefore, if we want to increase our understanding of the decision making process in international relations by studying game behaviour in the laboratory (Deutsch, 1969) we should examine the game behaviour of interacting groups rather than of isolated individuals, preferably in a setting which simulates some of the features of the organizational context in which such decisions are usually made (van der Linden and Rabbie, 1976; Rabbie and van Oostrum, 1977; Rabbie and Bekkers, 1978, Weick, 1965).

# References

Abric, J. C. Image de la tache, image du partenaire et coopération en situation de jeu. *C. Psychology*, 1970, 13.2, 71–82.

Aronson, E. and Lindner, D. Gain and loss of esteem as determinants of interpersonal attractiveness. *Journal of Experimental and Social Psychology*, 1965, 1, 156–171.

Bales, R. F. and Borgatta, E. F. Size of group as a factor in the interaction profile. In A. P. Hare, E. F. Borgatta and R. F. Bales (Eds). *Small groups: Studies in Social Interaction.* New York: Knopf, pp. 496–513, 1955.

Barnlund, D. C. A comparative study of individual, majority and group judgment. *Journal of Abnormal Social Psychology*, 1959, 58, 55–60.

Blake, R. R. and Mouton, J. S. Reactions to intergroup competition under winlose conditions. *Management Science*, 1961, 420–435.

Brickman, P. *Social Conflict, Readings in Rule Structures and Conflict Relationships.* Lexington Mass.: Heath and Co., 1974.

Burnstein, E. *Persuasion as argument processing.* Paper presented to the International Symposium on Group Decision Making, August 6–11, 1978. Schlosz Reisensburg, West-Germany.

Davis, J. H. *Social Interaction as a combinatorial process in group decision.* Paper presented at the International Symposium on Group Decision Making 6–11 August, 1978, Schlosz Reisensburg, West-Germany.

Deutsch, M. Socially relevant science: Reflections on social studies of conflict. *American Psychologist*, 1969, 24, 1076–1092.

Deutsch, M. The social psychological study of conflict: rejoinder to a critique. *European Journal of Social Psychology*, 1974, 4, 441–456.

Deutsch, M. and Gerard, H.B. A study of normative and informational social influence upon individual judgment. *Journal of Abnormal and Social Psychology*, 1955, 51, 629–636.

Doise, W. Images, réprésentations, idéologies et expérimentations psychosociologue. *Social Science Information*, 1978, 17, 41–69.

Festinger, L. A theory of comparison processes. *Human Relations*, 1954, 7, 117–140.

Gewirtz, J. and Baer, D. M. Deprivation and satiation of social reinforcers as drive conditions. *Journal of Abnormal and Social Psychology*, 1958, 57, 165–172.

Harford, R. and Solomon, L. "Reformed sinner" and "lapsed saint" strategies in the Prisoners' Dilemma Game. *Journal of Conflict Resolution*, 1967, 11, 104–109.

Horwitz, M. and Rabbie, J. M. Individuality and membership in the intergroup system. In: H. Tajfel (Ed.) *Social Identity and Intergroup Relations.* Canbridge: Cambridge University Press and Paris: Editions de la Maison de l'Homme.

Janis, L. L. *Victims of Groupthink: A Psychological Study of Foreign Policy, Decisions and Fiascos.* New York: Houghton Mifflin, 1972.

Kalma, A. and Tempelaars, C. *Programma voor het analyseren van een aantal fysische parameters van de stem in sociale interactiesituaties.* In preparation ISP, Utrecht, 1978.

Kalma, A. and van Rooy, J. *Een categoriesysteem van de analyse van non-verbaal interactiegedrag in een experimentele "setting".* Internal Rapport, ISP, Utrecht, 1978.

Kelley, H. H. and Stahelski, A. J. The social interaction basis of cooperators' and competitors' beliefs about others. *Journal of Personal and Social Psychology*, 16, 66—91, 1970.

Laughlin, P. R. and Adamopoulos, J. *Social decision schemes on intellective tasks*. Paper presented to the International Symposium on Group Decision Making, August 6—11, 1978. Schlosz Reisensburg, West-Germany.

Linden, W. J. van der and Rabbie, J. M. Doel, Differentiatie en integratie in gesimuleerde organisaties. *Nederlands Tijdschrift voor de Psychologie*, 1976, 31, 305—320.

Lindskold, S. Trust Development, the G.R.I.T. proposal, and the effects of conciliatory acts on conflict and cooperation, *Psychological Bulletin*, 1978, 85, 772—793.

Lindskold, S., Cahagan, J. and Tedeschi, J. T. The ethical shift in the Prisoners Dilemma Game. *Psychonomic Science*, 1969, 15, 303—304.

Lindskold, S., McElwain, D. C. and Wayner, M. Cooperation and the use of coercion by groups and individuals. *Journal of Conflict Resolution*, 1977, 21, 531—550.

McClintock, Ch. G. Game behavior and social motivation in interpersonal settings. McClintock (Ed.) In *Experimental Social Psychology*. New York: Rinehart and Winston, 271—297, 1972.

McClintock, Ch. G. Social motivation in settings of outcome interdependence. In Druckman, D. (Ed.). *Negotiations, social psychological perspectives*, Beverley Hills, 1977, pp. 49—77.

Meyers, D. G. *Polarizing effects of social interaction*. Paper presented to the International Symposium on Group Decision Making, August 6—11, 1978, Schlosz Reisenburg, West Germany.

Meyers, D. G. and Lamm, H. The group polarization phenomenon, *Psychol. Bulletin*, 1976, 83, 602—627.

Moscovici, S. and Zavalloni, M. The group as a polarizer of attitudes. *Journal of Personal and Social Psychology*, 1969, 12, 125—135.

Muller, J., Danse, J. and Lodewijkxs, H. Scoring manual of verbal interaction behavior in the Prisoners' Dilemma Game. In preparation ISP, Utrecht, 1978.

Nemeth, Ch. A critical analysis of research utilizing the PDG paradigm for the study of bargaining. In Berkowitz, L. *Advances in Experimental Social Psychology*, 1972. New York and London: Academic Press.

Nemeth, Ch. Whose ideology? A rejoinder to M. Plon. *European Journal of Social Psychology*, 1974, 4, 437—439.

O'Dell, J. W. Group size and emotional interaction. *Journal of Personality and Social Psychology*, 8, 75—78, 1968.

Oostrum, J. van. *Group size and future perspective in an intergroup game*. Unpublished report. ISP, Utrecht, 1977.

Oostrum, J. van. *Effects of group size and counterstrategy on the normative orientations of young adolescents and adults*. Intern Rapport, ISP, Utrecht, 1978.

Pilisuk, M., Potter, P., Rapoport, A. and Winter, J. A. War hawks and peace doves. Alternative resolutions of experimental conflicts. *Journal of Conflict Resolution*, 9, 491—508, 1965.

Pines, A. The shift to competition in the prisoner's dilemma game. *Social Behaviour and Personality*, 4(2), 177—186, 1976.

Plon, M. On the meaning of the notion of conflict and its study in social psychology. *European Journal of Social Psychology*, 1974a, 4, 389—436.

Plon, M. On a question of orthodoxy. *European Journal of Social Psychology*, 1974b, **4**, 457—467.

Pruitt, D. G. and Kimmel, M. J. Twenty years of experimental gaming: Critique, synthesis, and suggestions for the future. *Annual Review of Psychology*, **28**, 363—392, 1977.

Pylyshin, Z., Agnew, N. and Illingworth, J. Comparison of individuals and pairs as participants in a mixed motive game. *Journal of Conflict Resolution*, 1966, 211—220.

Rabbie, J. M. Effects of expected intergroup competition and -cooperation. Paper presented at the *Annual Convention of the American Psychological Association*, USA, August 31, 1974.

Rabbie, J. M. Mini crowds, an experimental study of audience behavior. Paper presented to the *General Meeting of the European Association of Experimental Social Psychology*, Weimar, March, 1978.

Rabbie, J. M. *Experimental studies on intergroup cooperation and competition.* Unpublished manuscript. Institute of Social Psychology, University of Utrecht, 1979.

Rabbie, J. H. The effects of intergroup competition and cooperation on intra- and intergroup relationships. In: V. I. Derlega and J. L. Grzelak (Eds) Cooperation and Helping Behaviour: Theories and Research. New York and London: Academic Press (in press).

Rabbie, J. M. and Bekkers, F. Threatened leadership and intergroup competition. *European Journal of Social Psychology*, **8**, 9—20, 1978.

Rabbie, J. M. and de Brey, J. H. C. The anticipation of intergroup cooperation and competition under private and public conditions. *International Journal of Group Tensions*, **1**, 230—251, 1971.

Rabbie, J. M. and van Oostrum, J. *Motivational orientation and strategy of other groups in a Prisoner's Dilemma Game.* Intern Rapport ISP, 1975.

Rabbie, J. M. and Visser, L. Bargaining strength and group polarization in intergroup negotiations. *European Journal of Social Psychology*, **4**, 401—416, 1972.

Rabbie, J. M. and Visser, L. *Motives in individual- and intergroup conflict.* Unpublished report of the Institute of Social Psychology, Utrecht, 1975.

Rabbie, J. M. and Wilkens, G. Intergroup competition and its effect on intra- and intergroup relations, 1971. *European Journal of Social Psychology*, **1**, 215—234.

Rabbie, J. M., van Oostrum, J. and Visser, L. *The effects of influence structures upon the intra- and intergroup relations in simulated organizations.* Paper presented to the International Conference on Socialization and Social Influence, Grzegorzewice, Poland, September 1977.

Rapoport, A. *Strategy and conscience.* New York: Harper and Row, 1964.

Rubin, J. S. and Brown, B. R. *The Social Psychology of Bargaining and Negotiation.* New York and London: Academic Press, 1975.

Schlenker, B. R. and Bonoma, Th. V. Fun and games, the validity of games for the study of conflict. *Journal of Conflict Resolution*, **22**, 7—38, 1978.

Sherif, M. *In Common Predicament.* Boston: Houghton Mifflin, 1966.

Simmel, G. The significance of numbers for social life. In A. P. Hare, E. F. Borgatta and R. B. Bales (Eds). *Small Groups* (rev.ed) New York: Knopf, pp. 9—15, 1955.

Slater, P. Contrasting correlates of group size. *Sociometry*, 1958, 21, 129—139.

Steiner, I. D. *Group Process and Productivity*, New York and London: Academic Press, 1972.

Steiner, I. D. Whatever happened to the group in social psychology. *Journal of Experimental Social Psychology*, 1974, 10, 94–108.

Steiner, I. D. *Heuristic models of groupthink.* Paper presented to the International Symposium on Group Decision Making, August 6–11, 1978, Schlosz Reisensburg, West-Germany.

Tajfel, H. Experiments in a vacuum. In Israel and Tajfel (Eds). *The Context of Social Psychology: a critical assessment.* London and New York: Academic Press, 1972.

Tajfel, H., Billig, M. G., Bundy, H. P. and Flament, Cl. Social categorization and intergroup behavior. *European Journal of Social Psychology*, 1971, 1, 149–178.

Thomas, E. J. and Fink, C. F. Effects of group size. *Psychological Bulletin*, 1963, 60, 371–384.

Turner, J. C. Social comparison and social identity: Some prospects to intergroup behavior. *European Journal of Social Psychology*, 1974, 5, 5–34.

Turner, R. M. and Killian, L. W. *Collective Behavior.* 2nd ed. Englewood Cliffs, N.J., Prentice Hall, 1972.

Visser, L. De invloed van de achterban op cooperatieve en competitieve intergroeps onderhandelingen. Intern Rapport, ISP, Utrecht, 1975.

Visser, L. *Ingroup-outgroup differentiation of groups engaged in conflict.* Internal Report ISP, 1978.

Visser, L., Räkers, A., Hezewijk, R. and Sopacua, M. Groupsize and decisions under uncertainty. Internal Report, ISP, Utrecht, 1976.

Weick, K. E. Laboratory experimentation with organizations. In J. G. March *Handbook of Organizations,* Chicago: Rand McNally, pp. 194–260.

Wilson, W. Reciprocation and other techniques for inducing cooperation in the Prisoners' Dilemma Game. *The Journal of Conflict Resolution*, 1971, 15, 167–195.

# 16
# The Effect of Experience on Information Exchange and Cheating in an Asymmetrical Bargaining Situation

Helmut W. Crott, Roland W. Scholz and Beate Michels

## The role of experience in bargaining

In more than 20 years of research in bargaining only a few studies have been concerned with the effect of experience, i.e. its impact on the process of conceding, the dynamics of motivational orientations, the use of threats and promises and the differential payoff. Since most studies suggest that their results and the consequent con- clusions are more or less directly related to real life social interaction, it is important to study the effects of experience for at least two reasons:

(1) The inexperienced subject will possibly be ambiguous regarding his primary bargaining goals (e.g. to be fair, to maximize his outcome, to maximize the difference between his and his partners' outcome). If time is provided to reflect on one's own intentions possibly certain goals will become more salient and others will diminish in importance. Hence, the analysis of experience effects can give us some ideas about the accentuation of motives during the course of interaction if the subjects' reactions are relatively systematic.

(2) Increasing experience usually puts the subject in a position to study the (average) partner's concession behaviour, his reactions to soft and hard bargaining, and, depending on the character- istics of the experimental situation, his attitudes and intentions.

This study was conducted at the Sonderforschungsbereich 24, Sozial — und wirtschafts- psychologische Entscheidungsforschung, Universität Mannheim (West Germany), and financed by the Deutsche Forschungsgemeinschaft and the Land Baden-Württemberg.

Thus, experience essentially establishes a kind of competence power.

## Unilateral v. bilateral experience

Studies which include experience as an independent variable are almost exclusively concerned with the effects of balanced experience (both partners are equally experienced). In this manner the effects of the perceived intentions of the partner (McClintock and McNeel, 1967), reflection time (Rapoport and Chammah, 1965), individual and group strategy planning (Bass, 1966; Druckman 1967, 1968, Kahn and Kohls, 1972) and repeating the same game several times (Crott and Möntmann, 1973) have been investigated. The results turned out to depend very much on the structure of the experimental situation (e.g. Prisoners Dilemma Game or Maximizing Difference Game v. Bargaining game). Under some conditions "cooperation", in other instances tough behaviour seems to be fostered by experience. The cooperative tendency usually shows in PDG studies, possibly, as Conrath (1970) pointed out, not as a consequence of an increase in cooperative motivation but because of the ambiguous nature of the "cooperative" choice in the PDG. Choosing cooperatively allows for long term profit maximization in PDG as well. Thus, experienced subjects might realize in face of the symmetry of the PDG situation that on the average it is in their own interest to choose cooperatively, instead of defectively. The study by Crott and Möntmann (1973) compared the performance of two inexperienced subjects with that of the two experienced subjects in a bargaining game. Subjects had successively to play the same bargaining game with the same partner three times. As expected in this case of balanced experience no effect on the payoffs could be found. The only difference noticed was that the experienced subjects needed a greater number of offers to reach agreement (see Möntmann 1971), i.e. bargaining became tougher with increasing experience.

A couple of studies have been carried out by Crott and co-workers in order to evaluate the effect of asymmetrical experience conditions on the bargaining process and its outcome. The situation was usually a bargaining situation in which only pareto-optimal solutions were negotiated. The case in which one seller and one buyer are negotiating for the price of a single object may be quoted as an illustration of such a situation. The seller wants the highest price possible, the buyer strives for a low price. Their profits depend on the agreed price and are inversely related. Experience was operationalized in these experiments by playing the same game several times within a given period (e.g. 10 days). Thus the subject had to play three or four times against an inexperienced partner who took part in the experiment for the first time. Crott and Müller (1976) found that in such a bargaining task with complete information (both partners knew each other's payoff matrices) the experienced subject was able to bargain to better result.

Crott et al. (1980) found comparable results for the condition of incomplete information (subjects did not know the partner's profit table). Moreover some insight into the tactics of the experienced subjects could be gained by looking at the concession process. Under incomplete information the experienced subject tends to increase his first demand but does not change the speed of concession, whereas under complete information he holds the first demands fairly constant, but with increasing experience his concession frequency becomes lower. Extreme demands might appear insolent to an informed partner, evoking his resistance, and therefore it may be more promising to wear him down in the course of interaction by making concessions slightly less frequently or slightly smaller. On the other hand, with incomplete information the partner knows nothing about the profit table of his counterpart, and hence it may be more efficient to announce high initial demands but show readiness for well-balanced concession behaviour.

The authors conclude from these findings that under conditions of conflict increasing bargaining skill enables the more experienced subjects effectively to evade the partners' attempts to establish a fair solution. In this case — because no differences in investments were perceivable — this would be the equal split. Actually two inexperienced or two equally experienced subjects usually agree on a solution that gives equal profits to both partners. Among other things it was also hypothesized that the motivational orientation of experienced subjects should divert them away from fairness and cooperation to outcome maximization.

## Power conditions and their effect on motivational ratings

Subsequent studies by Crott and co-workers showed that this is true under conditions of low power. When both parties have no opportunities to employ sanctions the individualistic orientation increases with growing experience, whereas social orientation decreases from the first to the third state of experience. In these experiments subjects had to rate their own behaviour on a five point scale in 15 20 items considering different bargaining goals. The factor analytic structure of the questions constantly showed three factors: (1) fairness and cooperation; (2) egoism and outcome maximization; and (3) competition and rivalry. In the following we will refer to those three tendencies as (1) social, (2) individualistic and (3) competitive motivational orientation. Accordingly the sum of the scores of the respective items showed a tendency for individualistic ratings to increase and for social ratings to decrease. The competitive ratings remained mostly unchanged. However, when subjects were allowed to employ punishments (condition of mutual high power) the individualistic ratings decreased whereas the social tendency increased. In fact, equally experienced players usually imposed punishments in the first session (when both were inexperienced) and thereby got into an "exchange of blows" which turned out to be disadvantageous for both parties (cf. Müller and Crott, 1978). Consequently they avoided the use of sanction in the second and third sessions. For mixed groups, in which one partner is experienced, the other not, the same trend on ratings of the own behaviour was observed across the three stages of experience. However, subjects were not able to avoid the detrimental spiral of punishments. The inexperienced subject usually started by punishing and this was followed by similar action from the experienced player. Apparently the experienced player was not able to prevent the naive subject from using sanctions and so he felt impelled to do likewise.

Bearing in mind the limited situational variation in these experiments, one could tentatively conclude from these results that experience tends to foster task-related egoistic behaviour and to reduce concern with aspects of fairness and cooperation. This holds for the case in which experience provides an excess in competence power. When the advantage of experience is reduced because the partner can exert punishment power (as in the experiments mentioned in the last paragraphs) the ratings of the subjects indicate that both participants would like to get on with each other. As indicated by the subjects ratings under these conditions, individualistic objectives decrease whereas social tendencies increase. Nevertheless, in mixed experienced groups they are not able to stop punishing each other to their mutual loss.

Though many questions remain open (e.g. what causes the change in the motivational orientation of experienced subjects?), this series of experiments shows that experience affects the process of concession making and the point of agreement, as well as the subjective correlates of the bargaining process in interaction with situational characteristics.

## The interpretation of bargaining behaviour by equity and dissonance theory

Except for the experiment by Crott and Möntmann (1973), in the studies which have been mentioned in the preceding sections subjects had to bargain under symmetrical payoff conditions, i.e. both partners had identical payoff tables. From the viewpoint of equity theory asymmetrical bargaining situations are of special interest because an asymmetry which is not related to investments provides an unjustified advantage for one of the partners.

According to equity theory, equal division is the just solution in such cases, because the advantage of the one player is not based on investments. As has already been pointed out, if the information is complete under such circumstances, equal divisions are in fact negotiated (Crott and Möntmann, 1973). Furthermore it could be shown whenever the favoured player (e.g. as the instructed helper of the experimenter) refuses to accept an equal division, the opponent at a disadvantage tends to employ penalties against his partner (Crott *et al.*, 1976). Besides the tendency to agree on equitable divisions, the tendency to maximization of one's own payoffs is postulated within equity theory. As goals are incompatible, non-equitable solutions are also realized in social exchange.

Adams (1963, 1965) has connected equity theory with dissonance theory. He postulates that both persons with undue advantage and persons at a disadvantage notice a contradiction between the accepted equity norm and the deviating results, which causes cognitive dissonance for both. Uneasiness over a non-equitable solution (distress) is an accompaniment of dissonance, and thus is experienced by both participants. They will therefore try to reduce this dissonance either by altering the actual division or by psychological restoring of equity. The reduction of dissonance, for example, can be expressed in the search for justifications for an inequitable division. If the interpretation of dissonance holds true, then another way of acting should also be noticeable that, as far as we know, has not been discussed up to now in connection with equity theory. According to Festinger (1957), striving for cognitive equilibrium leads not only to corrective, but also to preventive measures. Not only is the existing dissonance reduced, but potential dissonance is also avoided. This should result in information, which was suitable to produce dissonance, not being taken up from the start. Less directly it is explicable by the dissonance interpretation of equity theory that the favoured player withholds information on his payoff situation. With the impression of being in a more advantageous position, the player also realizes that by passing on information he makes the situation more transparent for the opponent. The partner's resistance would actually restrain the player from gain maximization and it would also increase his dissonance because it points to his unjustified advantage, to which he does not like to admit.

This assumption was examined in a preceding experiment (Crott et al., 1980) with an experimental design similar to the following study. The task was a modified form of the Siegel and Fouraker bargaining situation, in which non-pareto-optimal solutios were also possible. The players were incompletely informed, i.e. each player knew only his own payoff alternatives and not those of his opponent. However, the rules allowed the possibility of exchanging information on payoff alternatives during the course of the bargaining session. Even false information could be exchanged. Furthermore the situation was asymmetrical, so that one bargainer had higher payoffs than the other. The defined roles of the favoured and the handicapped player were assigned to the subjects at random, i.e. the differences in the payoff possibilities were not justified by special investments or other activities. Thus, an agreement that divides the payoffs in proportion to the maximum payoffs was accordingly more advantageous to the player in the better position than a solution that divides up the payoffs equally (Fig. 1 shows the bargaining situation). In addition, some information and communication conditions were varied which cannot be more specifically described here. There were no differences in the frequency of receiving and giving information between the favoured and the handicapped player. However, the favoured player gave incorrect information (bluffed) more often. Under these circumstances he was also able to achieve significantly better results. This finding indicates that the mechanisms with which the attempt was made to preserve one's own

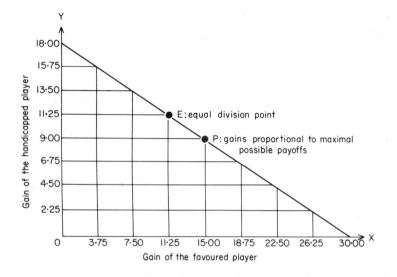

Fig. 1. Graphical presentation of the bargaining game.

payoff advantage are larger than could be assumed by reflection on dissonance theory. The frequency of information does not change. Instead, the subjects try more often to cheat each other. The subjects presumably take into consideration that a lack of interest in available information and, even more, the refusal to give information about one's own situation might sooner cause distrust than cheating, which they hope will remain undiscovered. Whether this interpretation holds true or not, defence and withholding information does not generally seem to occur in interactive situations of this kind, according to the study by Crott *et al.* (1980).

However, it is conceivable that in this earlier study the subjects did not have enough experience to employ more differentiated methods like withholding information. This study should present a better basis for the analysis of the information policy of the subjects. This is, above all, to be attained by having one participant (experienced player) play against a partner who is taking part in the experiment for the first time (inexperienced player), at intervals of several days. Besides, for reasons that will be explained in the description of the experimental design and the hypotheses, the receiving and giving of information was either obligatory or voluntary.

## The experiment: situation characteristics and theoretical expectations

METHOD

*Subjects*
The subjects were 164 male German university students who voluntarily participated in the experiment; they received a gratuity of 10 DM plus the payoffs they achieved in the negotiation.

*Procedure*
Each of the subjects was led into a cubicle without having seen the other beforehand. In the cubicle the subjects found the experimental instructions and the payoff tables.

They were instructed that they had to bargain with their partners in the other cubicle and that there were different alternatives which were of different value for themselves and for their partner. Each subject got a table with the 45 alternatives shown in Fig. 1 and the corresponding payoff for himself. The assignment to the role of player A (favoured player) and player B (disadvantaged player) was made at random (see also independent variables and experience conditions below). It was not explicitly mentioned that the roles were different. Subjects were told that they had to reach an agreement within a maximum time of 90 min on one of the 45 alternatives. The game is graphically shown in Fig. 1. Each point within this graph, and thus also each point on the diagonal line, represents a possible agreement; the corresponding benefit (payoff) for player A and B can be read off the $x$ and $y$ axes in the diagram. Note that with this system a number of alternatives gives the same amount to the player but different amounts to his opponent, since each crossing point including the intersections with the axes and the diagonal constitutes an alternative. Figure 1 further shows that, on principle, the subjects can agree on solutions that are not pareto-optimal. All solutions that do not lie on the dark line are not pareto-optimal. In the pareto-optimal range the solution indicated by point P represents the distribution proportionally to both players' maximal payoff (15 DM: 9 DM) and that indicated by E and equal split (11.25 DM: 11.25 DM).

Figure 1 was not, however, shown to the negotiators. Instead, each party was given a payoff table in which the alternatives and the corresponding payoffs were numbered from 1—45 in a random sequence. The opponent's payoffs were not indicated in this table. As mentioned, the sequence of alternatives was random to prevent the participants from being able to infer the payoff structure (cf. Kelley and Schenitzki, 1972).

Bargaining took place by a simultaneous exchange of offers. The offers simply consisted of the number of the alternative the subject proposed as the solution of bargaining. In each cubicle there was a switchboard on which subjects could indicate their offers. After each player had indicated his offer on the switch panel, the two respective numbers flashed up next to each other for 10 s on the recording device (luminous panel), visible to both subjects through a window in the cubicle. However, subjects could not see each other during the negotiation. The operation of the recording device and (in the perspective experimental condition) the procedure for information exchange were demonstrated to the subjects. After half a minute, which depending on the experimental condition could be (voluntary condition) or had to be (obligatory condition) used for information exchange or communication, the next bid could be placed. Subjects were informed that they themselves as well as their opponent might give false information (bluff). Negotiation offers and information on the opponent's payoff table were to be recorded by the subjects. Then a trial run was held with numerical examples that were not listed in the payoff table. In addition, with the help of some questions, the participants' comprehension of the payoff tables was checked. Terms such as "opponent" or "partner" as well as comparisons with economic or political negotiations (cf. Eiser and Bhavnani, 1974) on the part of the experimenter were avoided; no advice on negotiation behaviour was given.

As soon as an agreement was reached (choice of the same alternative and thus appearance of the same number at the screen), the participants answered a questionnaire designed to measure their perceptions of their own negotiation behaviour and that of their opponent as well as of the entire situation.

The subjects then left the experimental rooms separately. Before leaving each participant was told that they had to play a lottery with a random machine in the lobby. The conditions for participation in the lottery were written on a conspicuous table which also could be seen before the experiment. According to the instructions, subjects had a 50% chance of taking part in a session of the experiment within one week, and a 50% chance of having to withdraw and get paid. The subjects were told that there was a maximum of four repetitions. The random mechanism was manipulated in such a manner that all favoured players participated exactly three times and the handicapped only once. It should be mentioned that both the experienced and the inexperienced partner got the same role each time. Neither the experienced nor the inexperienced players were told that they were to play against a more or less sophisticated partner.

*Independent variables*

Information conditions: $i_1$ : In the voluntary condition a total of 24 dyads negotiated with the possibility of exchanging information on the payoff tables through written questions and answers. The question was the number of the alternative, the answer, the corresponding payoff (or some other number if the partner decided to bluff). Thus, a negotiator could (at a maximum of once per bid) inquire after his opponent's payoff if the alternative interested him and (also voluntarily) answer his opponent's inquiry. $i_2$: In the obligatory condition (24 dyads altogether), one question and one answer per negotiation bid was required for each player.

*Experience conditions*

$e_1$ first level of experience, i.e. first session of player A and B

$e_2$ second level of experience, i.e. second session of player A, first session of player B

$e_3$ third level of experience, i.e. third session of player A, first session of player B.

The experience factor is considered as a repeated measurement factor, for the interaction on the bargaining result in each consequent session is influenced by the behaviour of both players in former sessions. It should be mentioned that no information was given about the stage of experience of the partner. By the nature of the recruitment system subjects could only conclude that some of them were experienced, others not.

By the nature of the task the role of players A and B constitutes a third factor. This factor is relevant only for some independent measures, namely those measures which are not unique for the dyad but the for single subjects. Because player A and B bargained at the same time, and because some of the dependent variables are influenced by interaction, the role factor is also regarded as repeated measurement factor. The whole experiment was replicated twice with four dyads per cell. Thus a two level replication factor was introduced.

### Dependent variables

The following variables entered into the statistical analysis: (a) the number of pieces of information obtained; (b) the number of pieces of information given under voluntary information condition; (c) the number and size of bluffs, i.e. of false pieces of information given and the difference between real and cheated payoff value; (d) the length of the bargaining session; (e) the payoffs of player A and B; and (f) the post-experimental questions on the negotiation session and on the evaluation of the opposing player.

### Hypotheses

(1) In accordance with the argumentation of the dissonance theory it is expected that the favoured player at the first experience stage under the condition of voluntary information (1a) asks for less information and (1b) gives less information. As already pointed out, this hypothesis is not likely to hold true according to the results of the study by Crott *et al.* (1980).

(2) At the beginning we discussed whether only experienced players are able to withhold information as a deliberate technique. As a result we could expect players with increasing experience to give information (i.e. answer the opponent's questions) less often under the condition of voluntary information.

From the "avoidance of dissonant information" hypothesis one could expect that the experienced player asked for information less often. However, if this were the case, it might also be explained by the assumption that the experienced players knew the situation better, i.e. this would not necessarily indicate avoidance of dissonance. Therefore we will not formulate a hypothesis regarding increasing information avoidance by the experienced player. Crott *et al.* (1978a) postulate two further points.

(3) The frequency of bluffs increases with growing experience, for the subjects try to obtain agreement on alternatives advantageous to themselves by using bluffs.

(4) With growing experience the favoured player achieves better results. This could be expected according to hypotheses 1–3, if one assumes that the information policy or the bluffing of the

experienced player's results under the condition of voluntary information. For only on this basis can the player avoid giving information
on his payoff table to the opponent. On the other hand, bluffing, in
line with hypothesis 3, should work out more evenly under both
information conditions.

RESULTS

*Results relating to the hypotheses*
According to the first hypothesis the favoured player should ask for
less information and give less information than the handicapped
player at the first state of experience (both players, favoured and
handicapped, are inexperienced). There is no evidence in favour of
this assumption. Both players ask for and give information almost
equally often as the study by Crott *et al.* (1980) has already shown,
i.e. hypothesis 1 does not hold true.

Hypothesis 2 was based on the consideration that only experienced
bargainers are able to use means of retaining information. However, the data present no basis for this, either. Requested information
was refused in only 4% of the cases and there was no tendency to
give less information with increasing experience. Withholding information is evidently hardly employed as a means of bargaining.
Accordingly, the two hypotheses that are derived by reflections on
the dissonance theory could not be confirmed.

The second group of hypotheses (3 and 4) have a more empirical
basis. They proceed from the observation made in previous studies
that tendencies aimed at payoff in maximization increase with
growing experience and that this is shown by a more frequent use
of bluffs. First, it is noticeable that bluffing is made use of relatively
often. On only 24 of the 96 occasions did the subjects not employ
the means of bluffing and in only 3 of the 48 dyadic bargaining
sessions did neither participant give false information. The share of
false information in proportion to the total amount of given information comes to 31%. In accordance with hypothesis 3, the number
of bluffs increases with growing experience.

Under $e_1$ false information from the advantaged player was given
on an average of 4.0, under $e_2$ 4.9 and under $e_3$ 6.6. This trend is
significant ($\bar{\tau} = 0.23$; $P < 0.5$ one-tailed). Even if the number of
bluffs is related to the total amount of information given (relative
bluff frequency) on account of the different lengths of bargaining
time and thus to be able to compare the dyads better under the

conditions $e_1$, $e_2$ and $e_3$, this trend remains significant ($\bar{\tau} = 0.23$; $P < 0.05$ one-tailed). Hypothesis 3 can thus be confirmed. Hypothesis 4 also proves true: with growing experience player A's payoffs increase ($P \leqslant 0.05$ repeated measurement analysis of variance). The trend does not depend on the conditions of information exchange. Table 1 shows the payoffs of the experienced player A and of the inexperienced player B at the three levels of experience.

TABLE 1

*Mean gains of player A and player B dependent on level of experience*

|  | Mean $E_1$ | Mean $E_2$ | Mean $E_3$ |
|---|---|---|---|
| Player A ($r_1$) advantaged | 12.65 | 15.93 | 15.23 |
| Player B ($r_2$) disadvantaged | 9.35 | 8.01 | 8.35 |

It can be inferred from the comparison of Fig. 1 and the mean values of Table 1 that the subjects are generally able to negotiate pareto-optimal solutions (85%), especially under conditions $e_2$ and $e_3$.

### Post hoc *Analysis*

The following will report on some results that were not explicitly predicted in the hypotheses. The subjects used the means of bluffing in different ways. A distinction can be made between understatement and overstatement-bluff. While in the understatement bluff the player's own payoff possibilities were represented as being low, in the overstatement bluff a higher payoff is alleged. Both kinds of bluffs are employed. The favoured player A uses understatement bluffs more often than player B. However, the difference is not significant.

The employment of overstatement bluffs had not been expected by the authors. Overstatement bluffs have not yet been described in the literature on the subject, possibly because experiments studying bluff behaviour almost exclusively deal with symmetrical bargaining situations. On the given background the authors also implicitly presumed in the formulation of hypothesis 2 that all cheating reflects the attempts of the subjects to play down their own payoff possibilities. However, a considerable part of the cheating by the disadvantaged subjects were overstatement-bluffs. The disadvantaged and inexperienced player used the means of overstatement bluffs in all dyads, in which this type of bluff was employed more frequently than the favoured player ($P \leqslant 0.001$; in 13 of the 16 independent observational units the overstatement bluff was used). An interpretation of the function of understatement and overstatement bluffs will be attempted in the discussion section.

The question as to how often final agreement occurs on an alternative, on which false information was given at any time during the bargaining session, is interesting. After all, this is the case in 19 (of 48) dyads. It is always a matter of the alternative 15 DM for A, 9 DM for B. For this the favoured player declares lower values than 15 DM (e.g. 9 DM) in order to feign a more equitable distribution. It is therefore presumable that the willingness to agree on the part of the disadvantaged player is based on an equity cheat. It should also be recorded that the handicapped participant makes an initial bluff significantly more often than the favoured player (in all 14 − of 16 − independent observational units in which a player bluffed in one of the three repetitions, the disadvantaged player made initial bluffs more often; $P \leqslant 0.001$).

In the post-experimental questionnaire the subjects had a large number of questions to answer that referred to their own behaviour, their opponent's behaviour and to the bargaining process. Among other things they were to rate their own bargaining behaviour on a 7-point scale between "not at all" and "very much" on the basis of 17 statements. The items had as themes the three aspects that, in previous studies, turned out to be factors of answering behaviour: these are (1) fairness and cooperation; (2) rivalry and competition; and (3) payoff maximization and egoism. This factor structure also resulted in the analysis of the data presented here; because of the low number of subjects the factor analysis is only of little value so that we will omit it. The variance analyses of the answers to the questions indicated main effects of the experience and role factors. It is therefore presumable, as already observed in earlier studies, that the bargaining parties influence each other in their behaviour or in their evaluations. The results support the assumption formulated at the beginning that with increasing experience behaviour is seen as more egoistical and selfish. By combining the items according to the factors the data from Table 2 result.

TABLE 2

*Mean score of questionnaire of subjects' own motivation in bargaining dependent on condition of information*

|  | $e_1$ | $e_2$ | $e_3$ |
|---|---|---|---|
| Justice and cooperation | 5.10 | 4.53 | 4.51 |
| Maximization of gains and egoism | 4.54 | 4.78 | 5.14 |
| Rivalry and competition | 3.23 | 3.43 | 3.89 |

An analysis of variance brings up a significant effect on the averaged item scores of fairness and cooperation ($F = 3.82$; d.f. $= 2$; $P \leqslant 0.04$). An inspection of Table 2 shows that there is a decrease in fairness and cooperation items whereas the reverse can be observed for the egoism items. However, the results were only marginally significant ($F = 2.64$; d.f. $= 2$; $P \leqslant 0.09$). The tendencies aimed at rivalry and competition also increased, however, due to the higher error variance this increase was not significant, as expected ($F = 1.95$; d.f. $= 2$; $P < 0.16$). Besides this the favoured player rated his behaviour as more egoistic ($F = 7.60$; d.f. $= 1$, $P < 0.02$) than the handicapped player.

Some more information was gained from the post-experimental questionnaire. The subjects were asked how high they evaluate the payoff possibilities that the game presented them. The favoured player rated them significantly higher than the handicapped players ($F = 6.84$; d.f. $= 1$, $P < 0.02$). The difference in the payoff possibilities was accordingly reflected in the subjective evaluation of the subjects. The subjects were further asked how much they had tried to mislead their opponents with false information. The intention to mislead increased significantly from the first level of experience to the third ($F = 5.68$. d.f. $= 2$, $P < 0.006$). A further result showed that the favoured player finds information from his partner by comparison less helpful ($F = 7.79$, d.f. $= 1$, $P < 0.01$). Finally, by a candid question, we wanted to find out whether the subjects had noticed the experimenter cheating. For example, we wanted to find out whether the subjects had noticed that one payoff matrix was asymmetrical and that the favoured player could play against the the inexperienced player several times. With this question we also wanted to give the subjects the opportunity to express suspicion of the programmed "generator of chance" and possibly doubt about the genuineness of the opponent. Unfortunately, the results on this question were unprofitable. In only 17 out of 96 observations did the subjects even give an answer. The answers mainly came from the handicapped players (13 out of 17) and referred almost entirely to aspects of lack of transparency in the situation and the difficulty of being able to assess the partner's honesty.

*Summary and discussion of the results*

Hypotheses 1 and 2 on information behaviour that were derived by considerations on equity and dissonance could not be confirmed. This is not surprising against the background of the previous results (Crott *et al.*, 1980). Our study replicated previous known results and showed beyond them that better knowledge of the situation is not sufficient to trigger information behaviour that corresponds to the hypotheses.

One might object that refusing or rejecting information should occur only after a state of dissonance has been reached, i.e. after some information has been exchanged, so that the favoured player could form the impression of being at an advantage. However, there is not even a trend in information refusal and rejection over the course of a negotiation session.

Another argument supported by the dissonance theory would state that only small and medium degrees of dissonance could cause information rejection and refusal. Whatever a small or medium dissonance might be, in the given situation we deal with emergent dissonance, which should develop step by step synchronized with the reception of information. In this case the favoured player should be able to select the degree of dissonance suitable for the production of defensive protection and denial of information.

As Maryla Zaleska pointed out in her contribution to the discussion of this paper, subjects might not have realized their advantage or disadvantage, especially in face of the fact that false information could be exchanged. Thus there would be no reason for dissonance avoidance on the side of the favoured person and therefore no reason for withholding information. In fact, we got no valid information about the subjects' perception of their role from our open-ended question. On the other hand, the dissonance hypothesis requires that subjects do not fully realize their position. As soon as they get the faintest idea of their advantage they should employ information avoidance and information hiding strategies. There are two indications that suggest that subjects realize their different roles. First, the differential use of the under- and overstatement bluff on the part of the favoured and the handicapped player indirectly points to a difference in role perceptions. However, this does not indicate whether both players were aware of the discrepancies in the payoff tables. Possibly only the handicapped player felt that his position was less favourable and therefore used overstatement bluffs (see also discussion of bluff behaviour below). Second, we can compare the present study with the experiment mentioned earlier by Crott et al. (1980). In this study, in which two inexperienced subjects bargained with each other, two conditions were identical with the conditions in the present experiment (namely $i_1 e_1$ and $i_2 e_1$), others differed in control for bluffing (no bluffing allowed) and communication conditions (verbal communication possible). One post-experimental question asked subjects directly to estimate the other's gain possibilities. Under all experimental conditions subjects realized the differences in gain possibilities, i.e. favoured subjects perceived the partners maximal gain possibilities as significantly lower and handicapped subjects perceived them as significantly higher than their own maximal gain possibilities. However, the estimated differences were considerably lower than the real difference.

In connection with the results of the post-experimental questionnaire we can presume that for experienced subjects aspects of fairness and tendencies to cooperation diminish in the given situation, whereas payoff maximization and egoistical behaviour increase. In order to realize these goals, cheating seems more suitable than warding off and refusing to give information. The latter might arouse the bargaining partner's suspicion.

The negotiated results show that the favoured player succeeds in using his advantage. He achieves significantly higher payoffs than his opponent, especially on the second and third levels of experience. In accordance with previous studies (Crott and Müller, 1976, Crott et al., 1978) the experience effect is already fully realized on the second level; the third level brings no improvement. In case the advantage of experience was based on an information policy that corresponds with hypothesis 2, the experience should effect the result mainly under the condition of voluntary information exchange. However, this is not the case: the result of the experienced player improves, whether the exchange of information is obligatory or voluntary. Considering the finding that the players hardly made use of the possibility of withholding information, this result is not surprising. As the number of bluffs increase under both conditions of information exchange with experience (in contrast to the small and constant rate of information refusal), it is reasonable to assume that the experience advantage is realized by bluffs.

On making our hypotheses we proceeded on the assumption that with growing experience cheating of the understatement type increases. As the inequality of the roles is not justified by achievement (or other investments), the experienced player should try to screen his advantageous situation and thus try to dispose his partner to be more willing to make concessions. This is in fact the case, but beyond that the inexperienced disadvantaged player also bluffs to a high degree. Altogether he bluffs more frequently, whereby a surprisingly large amount of the cheating is overstatement bluffing.

On the basis of these data we cannot present a conclusive interpretation of bluff behaviour. However, we find the assumption plausible that the handicapped player uses the means of overstatement bluff in order to indicate to his partner, that he, too, has alternatives with high payoff possibilities. If he then suggests an alternative, whose payoff lies far beneath the feigned payoff, he thereby seems very willing to make a compromise. He thus calls upon the partner to make similar compromises.

Accordingly, overstatements were interpreted as attempts to produce equity. The handicapped player hinders the favoured player in realizing his advantage. By exaggerations he tries to give the impression that he must relinguish as much as his partner by agreeing, e.g. on an alternative that divides the payoffs equally (11,25:11,25).

The use of overstatement bluff against an experienced partner does not seem to be very successful, because the experienced partner achieves better results in spite of his opponent's efforts. The reason for this could be that the inexperienced player uses the overstatement with very little conviction. On account of incomplete information it is impossible for the inexperienced player to distinguish the alternative which gives him 0 DM and his partner 24 DM (0,24) from the alternative that gives him 0 DM and his partner 0 DM as well, without examining the alternative and receiving dependable answers (for example, at (0,24)). If then he also declares that his payoff is 24 DM, then this alternative is very attractive for his partner and the partners might aim at this alternative. But if the inexperienced player suddenly resists this alternative he then becomes untrustworthy and his behaviour is probably considered as bluffing. Controlled use of overstatement bluff is thus hardly possible if the opponent's payoffs are not known.

Bluff behaviour by the favoured player, on the other hand, can be clearly interpreted. This player tries to disguise his advantage by using understatement. He is successful in this, as can be inferred from the fact that he had made false statements in many cases in the course of bargaining on negotiated alternatives that feign a more equitable distribution of the payoffs of this alternative.

The study should make a contribution to the role of considerations on fairness in inter-personal conflicts and to the analysis of efforts to produce equity and of the resistance to such attempts. We were especially interested in the effect of experience as a prerequisite for acquiring competence. Although some questions, for instance, about the function and differentiated use of understatement and over-statement bluff, could only be answered tentatively, the results still show that it is necessary for the development of an elaborate equity theory to examine differences in roles, status and power as well as their significance for motivational structure and its dynamics.

## References

Adams, J. S. Toward an understanding of unequity. *Journal of Abnormal and Social Psychology*, 1963, 67, 5, 422–436.

Adams, J. S. Inequity in social exchange. In: Berkowitz, L. (Ed.), Advances of Experimental Social Psychology, Vol. II, 276–299. New York and London, Academic Press, 1965.

Bass, B. M. Effects of the subsequent performance of negotiators of studying issues of planning strategies alone or in groups. *Psychological Monographs*, 1966, No. 614.

Conrath, D. W. Experience as a factor in experimental gaming. *Journal of Conflict Resolution*, 1970, 14, 192–202.

Crott, H. W. and Möntmann, V. Der Effekt der Information über die Verhandlungsmöglichkeiten des Gegners auf das Verhandlungsergebnis. *Zeitschrift für Sozialpsychologie*, 1973, 4, 209–219.

Crott, H. W. and Müller, G. F. Der Einfluß des Anspruchsniveaus und der Erfahrung auf das Ergebnis und den Verlauf dyadischer Verhandlungen bei vollständiger Information über die Gewinnmöglichkeiten. *Zeitschrift für Experimentelle und Angewandte Psychologie*, 1976, 4, 548–568.

Crott, H. W., Lump, R. R. and Wildermuth, R. Der Einsatz von Bestrafungen und Belohnugen in einer Verhandlungssituation. In Brandstätter, H. and

Schuler, H. (Eds), Zeitschrift für Sozialpsychologie, Beiheft 2, Entscheidungsprozesse in Gruppen, 147–165, 1976.

Crott, H. W., Kayser, E. and Lamm, H. The effect of information exchange and communication in an asymmetrical negotiation situation. *European Journal of Social Psychology*, 1980, 10, 149–163.

Crott, H. W., Muller, G. F. and Hamel, P. L. The influence of the aspiration level of the level of information and bargaining experience on the process and outcome in a bargaining situation. In: H. Sauerman, (Ed.) *Contributions to Experimental Economics*, 1978b, 7, 211–230.

Druckman, D. Dogmatism, prenegotiation exprience and simulated group representation as determinants of dyadic behaviour in a bargaining situation. *Journal of Personality and Social Psychology*, 1967, 6, 279–290.

Druckman, D. Prenegotiation experience and dyadic conflict resolution in a bargaining situation. *Journal of Experimental Social Psychology*, 1968, 4, 367–383.

Eiser, J. R. and Bhavnani, K. K. The effect of situational meaning on the behaviour of subjects in the Prisoner's Dilemma Game. *European Journal of Social Psychology*, 1974, 4, 93–97.

Festinger, L. A Theory of Cognitive dissonance. Stanford, Stanford University Press, 1957.

Kahn, A. S. and Kohls, J. W. Determinants of toughness in dyadic bargaining. *Sociometry*, 1972, 35, 305–315.

Kelley, H. H. and Schenitzky, D. P. Bargaining. In McClintock, C. G. (Ed.): Experimental Social Psychology. New York: Holt, Rinehart and Winston, 298–337, 1972.

McClintock, C. G. and McNeel, S. P. Prior experience and monetary reward as determinants of cooperative and competitive game behaviour. *Journal of Personality and Social Psychology*, 1967, 5, 282–284.

Möntmann, V. Experimentelle Untersuchungen von Verhandlungssequenzen unter unterschiedlichen motivationalen Bedingungen. Diplomarbeit am Sozialwissenschaftlichen Institut der Universität Mannheim, 1971.

Müller, G. F. and Crott, H. W. Behaviour orientation in bargaining: The dynamics of dyads. In H. Brandstätter, J. H. Davis and H. Schuler (Eds) Dynamics of Group Decisions. Beverly Hills: Safe, 1978 (in press.)

Rapoport, A. and Chammah, A. Prisoners' Dilemma: a study of conflict and cooperation. Ann Arbor: University of Michigan Press, 1965.

# 17
# A Simulation Study of Third Parties in Industrial Decision-making

Geoffrey M. Stephenson and Janette Webb

## Introduction

The development of increasingly complex employment legislation and the interest in industrial relations as a specialist area of study point to the increasing interest of government and public bodies in the regulation and control of employment in Britain. Where industrial disputes arise, employment legislation has encouraged the use of various forms of third-party intervention (conciliation/arbitration), with the aim of overcoming impasse, strikes and lockouts, which are seen as harmful to the community.

Systematic research on the practical use and techniques of third-party intervention is however minimal. There is no prevailing theory of the functions of third-party intervention (in industrial relations or other spheres) and there is little debate about when different forms of intervention might be usefully employed or how strategies fitting to particular types of disputes might be chosen. Published material has been largely anecdotal, unsystematic in nature and not concerned with the detailed practices of third-party intervention. Instead it describes the third-party's task as an "art", not susceptible to systematic analysis by the methods of social science (e.g. Cole, 1961; Meyer, 1960).

Whilst earlier work (see Morley and Stephenson, 1977, for a summary) has studied, for example, pre-intervention effects of mediation — the mediator as "face-saver" or impartial chairman — the "base-line" effect of the mere presence of a third-party has been largely ignored. Yet there is general agreement in American relations literature that the mere presence of a third-party changes the bargaining climate (Meyer, 1960; Peters, 1958; Rehmus, 1965). However, even at this most "basic" level of analysis, contrasting arguments lead to opposite predictions about the effect of a third-party's presence. The first argument is derived from articles written by mediators and officials of US mediation agencies where the mediator is described as the "voice of the community" (Cole, 1961, p. 51). He represents the "pressure of public interest" and is invested with "moral authority" (Warren and Bernstein, 1949, p. 444). The role of mediator as a representative of the wider community can also be inferred from McGrath's (1966) "tripolar" model of negotiation, which suggests that the acceptability of a bargaining settlement to the community is an influential force on party representatives. This argument leads to a prediction of increased willingness to concede, and more compromise solutions, resulting from emphasis on "reasonable" courses of action, with less recourse to aggressive tactics in the form of strike or lockout.

The opposite prediction can, however, be derived if it is argued that the third-party, in bringing "temperate speech" (Meyer, 1960, p. 61) and increased "politeness", decreases the probability of personal clashes between participants (Peters, 1958). Since the third-party is invested with status, which is external to the parties, the formality of negotiation is increased and parties become more aware that their case is open to evaluation by an independent party. It has been demonstrated in experiments by Morley and Stephenson (1977) that the more formal the communication system, the lower the occurrence of interpersonal exchange, resulting in increased attention to the negotiation task and presentation of case. Any differences in strength of case, which are inherent in the situation, are, consequently, more likely to become apparent. To the extent that the third-party has control over the situation, party representatives must convince him or her of the validity of their bargaining position, resulting in increased orientation to presentation of case and decreased emphasis on interpersonal relations. The prediction derived is, therefore, one of fewer compromise solutions and more straight victories for one side. It is, of course, possible to envisage the fulfilment of both predictions in experimental test, depending on the design of the situation and the role of the third-party as presented to the negotiators.

One experiment which has tried to measure the effects of a silent observer on process and outcomes (Belliweau and Stolte, 1977) seems to offer some evidence for the latter argument. The presence of a third-party increased the number of offers made by negotiation dyads, but had no effect on number of agreements reached. Increased attention to the task may well have resulted in an increased number of offers, without any necessary effect on the number of agreements made. They do not analyse the form of agreements, so no conclusions can be drawn about whether the presence of an observer affected the type of agreements made, to the benefit of one or both sides or, in any way, improved the quality of agreements. The results of the experiment point to the limitations of using number of agreements as the sole indicator of the success of "mediation". Any particular resolution may benefit one party more than the other, or potentially satisfy both parties. A more objective and meaningful measure of success of outcome, such as that provided by the inclusion of differential strengths of case as a factor in experimental design (e.g. Morley and Stephenson, 1977) provides a better means of explaining the effects of the third-party's presence on both content and outcome of negotiation.

The experiment by Belliweau and Stolte also demonstrates the importance of a system of content analysis which describes more of the debate than "number of offers": "The correlation between number of offers . . . and the number of agreements was quite weak ($r = 0.21$)" (p. 248). As long as participants have sufficient background material to allow a full discussion of the issues, a category system for content analysis should encompass all forms of communication, in order to offer a convincing explanation of the effect of a third-party's presence.

THE AIM OF THE PRESENT EXPERIMENT

The present experiment aimed to evaluate the effect on outcomes of the mere presence of a third-party. Two variables were manipulated: the *status* of the third-party (expert or naive), and *strength of case* (management strong or union strong). We had one principal expectation that the party with the stronger case would be more likely to win when a third-party, particularly the expert, constituted a third member of the negotiation group. This and other expectations are discussed in the following section.

## Method

This experiment focused on the effect of the presence of absence of a third party. However, the identity of the third-party is clearly an important factor determining the effectiveness of his presence, so the "status" of the third-party was systematically varied between conditions. In the "Naive" condition, the third-party was described as a third year undergraduate attending as part of his course work. In the "Expert" condition, on the other hand, the third-party was described as a postgraduate student highly experienced in the social psychology of bargaining. In each case the observer was instructed to maintain an interested but neutral attitude, avoiding eye-contact as far as possible. Our first expectation, following the argument in the Introduction, was that the third-parties, and especially the expert, would elicit a more pronounced inter-party orientation than would occur in the Alone condition (Hypothesis 1).

An inter-party orientation would be manifested in the process of debate and decision-making. This was to be detected using Conference Process Analysis (see Morley and Stephenson, 1977), which is a category system especially designed for describing behaviour in negotiation groups, and is particularly sensitive to comparisons which bear directly on the question of the participants' concern with his task as representative of his party (see also Stephenson *et al.*, 1977, for an example of the detailed use of this system in the description of an industrial wage negotiation).

In addition, however, we would expect the actual agreements reached, or outcomes, to differ between the experimental conditions. The presence of the third-party and, in particular, the expert, should encourage the participants to achieve a solution which can be publicly justified as being in some sense "fair". To test this hypothesis we systematically varied strength of case between the two parties in dispute, giving first one and then the other side the stronger case. Settlements should reflect relative strengths of case more in the "third-party" than in the "alone" condition, this being reflected in a significant interaction between third-party presence and strength of case (Hypothesis 2).

THIRD-PARTY PRESENCE AND ROLE RELATIONSHIPS

In this experiment subjects enacted the role of management or trade union representative. Each participant would, no doubt, have his own conception of what behaviour typically attaches to such roles. It is interesting to consider what effect the presence of the third-party would be expected to have on the enactment of these roles.

It might be thought that the presence of a third-party would make participants more self-conscious about their representative roles, such that the differences in their respective positions would be more salient than when no third-party was present. In this case, it would be expected that behaviour would become more conventionalised, and reflect commonly held stereotypes about management-union relationships. Stephenson *et al.* (1976) showed that when the role relationship was more apparent (as in "face-to-face" rather than "audio-only" interactions), students defending attitudes favourable to management were more likely to take the initiative. In that experiment, as in this one, such students were selected for roles according to their attitude scores on standardized tests of attitudes towards industrial relations. The authors suggested that social class differences between the two groups of management-oriented and union-oriented subjects may have contributed to the interaction between role and medium of communication. Similarly, in the present instance, it may be expected that social class differences would be more salient in the third-party conditions, and contribute to any interaction between role and presence of a third-party. In particular, we anticipated that management subjects would be more likely to seek to validate their position as managers by taking the initiative in the "third-party" than in the "alone" condition. This would have the effect of making victories for management less likely to occur in the "alone" than in the other two conditions (Hypothesis 3).

## Procedure

Undergraduate students were given a test of attitudes towards industrial relations (see Stephenson and Dewey, 1976) the results of which were used to select a group of 18 students distinctly favourable towards trades unions and a further 18 who were favourable towards management. These were randomly paired to form 18 dyads, each dyad consisting of one subject favourable towards managements and another favourable towards trades unions. The task of each dyad was to come to an agreed decision on a dispute affecting the "Townsford Company". Instructions were as follows:

*Instructions*
This is an experiment about industrial relations. You have been assigned the role of union (management) representative in a mock industrial dispute.

Please read these thoroughly — you have 30 minutes study time. You will then be asked to take your assigned role in the negotiation, with another person, who has the opposing role. You will have 30 minutes in which to reach agreement with the opposing side. You may make notes, during the study time, if you wish. You will be able to keep both notes and information sheets throughout.

*Assignment as Company (Union) Negotiator*
You have been selected by the Townsford Company (the Union) to represent it in its negotiations with the Union. Negotiations for a new 2-year contract broke down last week. You are to do the best you possibly can to get a good settlement of the contract for the company (union). It is essential to the company (union) that the contract be settled in this bargaining period. We realise that this involves compromises on both sides, and you are appointed to carry out binding negotiations for us.

Five major issues were to be negotiated — sick pay, hourly wage rate, cost of living increases, night shift differential, and holiday pay — and handouts were given to subjects describing the rates paid by other firms, including an average for other industries in the country (the "going rate"):

*Data from an Independent Community Survey (last year)*
The following table gives information on Townsford, four other textile plants and averages for non-textile industries in the country. The Moss plant and the Rose plant employ highly skilled workers.

| | Townsford | Moss | Rose | Baxter | Kraft | Average for other industries in the country |
|---|---|---|---|---|---|---|
| No. of workers | 100 | 300 | 90 | 150 | 300 | 60 |
| Sick pay scheme | 1/4 | 3/4 | 3/4 | 4/4 | 0 | 1/2 |
| Hourly wage rate | 80p | 83p | 83p | 75p | 77p | 85p |
| Cost of living increases | No comp. | Yes full comp. | Yes full comp. | No comp. | Yes full comp. | Half compensation |
| Night shift differential | 2 | 4 | 5 | 4 | 1 | 4 |
| Paid vacation | 3 wks for 1 year | 3 wks for 1 year | 3 wks for 1 year | 3 wks for 1 year | 3 wks for 1 year 4 wks for 20 years | 3 wks for 1 year 4 wks for 15 years |

*Issues for Bargaining*

1. *Sick Pay Scheme*
    Past contract: Company pay 1/4 of normal wages minus state benefit.
    Union demanded that company make up wages in full.
    Company refused to pay more than 1/4 of difference.

| Company | Proportion of company payment | | | | Union |
|---|---|---|---|---|---|
| | 1/4 | 2/4 | 3/4 | 4/4 | |
| Total money value per 2 years | 0 | 12 000 | 24 000 | 36 000 | |

2. *Wages*
    Past contract: 80p per hour.
    Union demanded an increase of 8p per hour.
    Company refused outright.

| Company | Increase per hour | | | | | | | | | Union |
|---|---|---|---|---|---|---|---|---|---|---|
| | 00 | 01 | 02 | 03 | 04 | 05 | 06 | 07 | 08 | |
| Total money value per 2 years | 0 | 2000 | 4000 | 6000 | 8000 | 10 000 | 12 000 | 14 000 | 16 000 | |

3. *Sliding Pay Scale to conform to Cost of Living*
    Past Contract: pay scale is fixed through the term of the contract.
    Union demanded pay increase in proportion to increase in the cost of living.
    Company rejected outright.

| | No compensation | Quarter compensation | Half compensation | Three-quarters compensation | Full compensation | |
|---|---|---|---|---|---|---|
| Company | | | | | | Union |
| Total money value per 2 years | 0 | 5000 | 10 000 | 15 000 | 20 000 | |

4. *Night Shift Differential*
    Past Contract: an extra 2p per hour is paid for night work.
    Union demanded a 2p increase to 4p per hour.
    Company rejected.

| Company | 0 | ½ | 1 | 1½ | Increase per hour 2 | 2½ | 3 | 3½ | 4 | Union |
|---------|---|---|---|-----|-----|------|------|------|------|-------|
| Total money value per 2 years | 0 | 250 | 500 | 750 | 1000 | 1250 | 1500 | 1750 | 2000 | |

5. *Vacation Pay*
   Past Contract: 3 weeks paid vacation for all workers with one year's service.
   Union want 4 weeks paid vacation for workers with 10 years of service.
   Company rejected.

| Company | 3 wks for 1 yrs service | 3 wks for 20 yrs service | 4 wks for 15 yrs service | 4 wks for 10 yrs service | Union |
|---------|-------------------------|--------------------------|--------------------------|--------------------------|-------|
| Total money value per 2 years | 0 | 500 | 2000 | 5000 | |

In addition, Background Information was provided which provided the manipulation of "strength of case" as follows:

*Union Strong Case*
   *Townsford Textile Company — Background Information*
   The Townsford Company is a small textile company located in a large northern town. Townsford is highly respected for its quality work in the dyeing and finishing of raw woven fabrics. It employs approximately 100 men. Townsford's men are among the most skilled to be found in the area.
   The general business conditions of the town are good and the financial conditions of Townsford are stable. Townsford is operating at full capacity and has a six month backlog of orders. Profits are not as high as at previous times, however, since the company has not raised the prices in several years in order to maintain a good competitive position with other sections of the industry. The Company has been able to maintain a 6% share-holders' dividend and has made recent purchases of more modern equipment. Consequently, with the co-operation of the union, restrictive and protective practices, e.g. over-manning, inter-departmental transfer and task flexibility, were decreased.
   The personnel policies at Townsford are not the most modern but are average for the plant size. The past president of the company, who retired three months ago, valued the reputation of Townsford as a "good place to work". His successor is viewed with some suspicion by the workers, due mainly to his statements about changing more of the work procedures to achieve greater efficiency.

For the last 25 years, a majority of the employees have been members of the union. Relations of the union with the company, for the most part, have been quite good with grievances promptly discussed and settled. The first strike occurred, however, three years ago and lasted 15 days. The workers lost the fight for a sliding scale wage based on increases in the cost of living index but did get the sick pay scheme, a 2 pence per hour wage differential for night shift workers and several other minor fringe benefits.

Townford's wage scale of 80p per hour compares unfavourably with most other textile firms; it is considerably lower than those textile firms which employ workers of equivalent high skill and produce a similar high quality product. Wages in the industry have not increased in proportion to increases in the cost of living or increases in other industries.

Despite occasional small wage increases, over a period of years Townsford's workers have slipped from a relatively high pay scale to a position roughly equivalent to that of lowly skilled workers in other industries. This has caused some unrest among the workers, and there is some danger of the workers shifting into these other higher paying industries. Unemployment is below normal in the area, and it has been difficult to obtain replacements who meet the skill requirements at Townsford.

Townsford gives seven paid holidays and three weeks of paid vacation to all workers with at least one year of service. The company also pays some sick pay contributions and grants other fringe benefits. More detailed information on Townsford and other firms may be found in the table that accompanies this background information.

The three year contract has now expired. Negotiations for a further two year contract broke down in the final week with both sides adamant in their positions. The only agreement reached was that each side would select a new bargaining agent to represent it, scheduled to meet today (the day before the strike) in an attempt to reach a quick solution and avoid a long strike.

*Management Strong Case*

*Townsford Textile Company — Background Information*

The Townsford Company is a small textile company located in a large northern town. Townsford is repsected for the consistent quality of its work in the dyeing and finishing of raw woven fabrics. It employs approximately 100 men, at the middle range of skill for the area.

General business conditions of the town are good, but the financial conditions of Townsford are increasingly unstable. The backlog of orders has fallen, while profits have decreased with the rising costs of raw materials and transport.

The company has raised its prices to cover a recent wage increase, but is unable to pass full costs on to customers, if it is to maintain a competitive position with other sections of the industry. If the Union would co-operate with the Company in the purchase and manning of more modern equipment, improvements in efficiency would in the long-term aid the company's financial position. The Union have, however, refused any discussion of re-organization and consequent reduction of restrictive practices.

The personnel policies at Townsford are not the most modern but are better than those of most plants of the same size. The past president of the company, who retired three months ago, valued the reputation of Townsford as a "good place to work". His successor intends to continue with the same objectives.

For the last 25 years a majority of employees have been members of the union. Relations of the union with the company have been quite good, with grievances promptly discussed and settled. The first strike occurred, however, three years ago and lasted 15 days. The workers did not get a sliding-scale wage based on increases in the cost of living index, but obtained an hourly wage rate increase, a sick-pay scheme, a 2p per hour wage differential for night shift workers and several other fringe benefits.

Townsford's wage scale compares very favourably with most other textile firms. It is 4% below textile firms which employ workers of a higher level of skill, producing a higher quality product, but ranks higher than firms employing workers of a similar level of skill. Wages in the industry have increased in proportion to increases in other industries, and to some extent, with increases in the cost of living.

With fairly regular wage increases over a period of years, Townsford's workers have remained on a high pay scale, relative to that of lowly skilled workers in other industries.

Unemployment is at an average level in the area: it should not be very difficult to obtain replacements of similar skill. Management are, however, reluctant to dismiss employees of some years standing.

Townsford gives seven paid holidays and three weeks of paid vacation to all workers with at least one year of service. The company also pays some sick pay contributions and grants other fringe benefits. More detailed information on Townsford and other firms may be found in the Table that accompanies this background information.

The three year contract has now expired. Negotiations for a further two year contract broke down in the final week with both sides adamant in their positions. The only agreement reached was that each side would select a new bargaining agent to represent it, scheduled to meet today (the day before the strike) in an attempt to reach a quick solution and avoid a long strike.

The effectiveness of the manipulation of strength of case was determined in advance by successively re-writing the material until independent groups of subjects rated the respective information as more or less equally favourable to the Union or management respectively.

The 18 dyads were randomly allocated to one of three third-party conditions as follows:

*Expert Observer* — In this condition the observer was described as an experienced postgraduate student who had considerable knowledge of bargaining and negotiation, and would like to sit in on their discussions.

*Naive Observer* — In this condition the observer was described as an undergraduate student who would like to sit in on their discussions.

*Alone* — In this condition the subjects came to their decisions with no other person present.

The six dyads in each condition were randomly allocated to three Strong Union Case and three Strong Company Case conditions. All sessions were audio taperecorded, and recordings later transcribed in full.

## Results

The outcomes are presented in Table 1 in terms of deviations from "going-rate" (i.e. the company average figure) summed across all five issues.

TABLE 1

*Settlement-points summed over the 5 issues, and expressed as deviations from the "going-rate" in 18 dyadic negotiation groups*

| Strength of case | Third-party status | | |
| --- | --- | --- | --- |
| | Naive observer | Expert observer | Alone |
| Management strong | −13 000 | −19 500 | 1 000 |
| | −1 500 | 9 500 | 6 000 |
| | 250 | −9 000 | 1 500 |
| Union strong | 6 500 | 4 000 | 15 500 |
| | 23 250 | −11 000 | 10 500 |
| | 0 | −4 000 | 8 500 |

| | $\bar{x}$ |
| --- | --- |
| Management strong | −£2 750 |
| Union strong | £5 917 |
| Naive observer | 2 583 |
| Expert observer | −5 000 |
| Alone | 7 167 |

EFFECTIVENESS OF EXPERIMENTAL MANIPULATION

We may first observe that the manipulations of strength of case appear to have been effective, the unions averaging £5917 above the going-rate when their case is strong, but conceding an average of £2750 below the going-rate when the management case is strong. Employing Mann-Whitney U test, this difference reaches statistical significance in the Alone condition at the 5% level, and over all conditions at the 10% level.

*Does third-party presence assist party with stronger case (Hypothesis 2)*
Next we may note a distinct lack of evidence for the expected inter-action between third-party status and strength of case. We had expected that the Observer conditions would exaggerate the effect of strength of case. Unfortunately for the hypothesis, the Alone con-dition finds most impressively for the unions in both Union Strong and Management Strong conditions, and the Expert condition shows least difference between Management and Union Strong conditions. Although the strength of case manipulation was effective, there is no evidence for its differential effectiveness in the presence of a third-party.

*Does the presence of a third-party influence which side will be victorious?*
*(Hypothesis 3)*
From our earlier discussion of the findings of Stephenson *et al.* (1976), we suggested that the third-party presence should induce the management representatives to assume a more authoritative role, and, hence to influence the outcome in favour of his side. Indeed, it seems that this occurred. In the Alone condition, the unions con-sistently scored above the "going-rate" — to the tune of more than £7000 on average — whereas in the two Observer conditions, and especially in the Expert Observer condition, management were considerably more successful, the average in the Expert groups being £5000 below the "going-rate" (see Table 1). Again employing Mann-Whitney U, the six groups in the Alone condition score sig-nificantly higher ($P < 0.05$) than those in the two third-party groups combined, and significantly higher than those in the Expert con-dition ($P < 0.021$). The Alone and Naive Observer conditions differed at only the 10% level of significance. In this experiment, the external observer strengthened the hand of management, regardless of strength of case, thus supporting Hypothesis 3.

*Do the third-parties increase task orientation? (Hypothesis 1)*
Rarely have the outcomes of experimental negotiation groups been effectively related to the process of decision-making. Here we can

examine the results of applying Conference Process Analysis (CPA) categories to the transcripts of all the groups in the study. The results will be considered in the light of the principal findings with respect to outcomes.

CPA provides two sets of rules, first for dividing transcripts into Acts, each "act" making a single "point", and a second set for classifying each act according to its Mode, Resource and Referent (see Morley and Stephenson, 1977, Chapter 10). The version employed in this investigation is portrayed in Table 2.

TABLE 2

*Conference Process Analysis (CPA) categories employed in the classification of each "act" (after Morley and Stephenson, 1977)*

| Mode | Resource | Referent |
|---|---|---|
| 1 Offer | *Structuring activity* | 0 No referent |
| 2 Accept | 1 Procedure | 1 Self |
| 3 Reject | *Outcome activity* | 2 Other |
| 4 Seek | 2 Settlement-point | 3 Party |
| | 3 Limits | 4 Opponent |
| | 4 Positive consequences of outcomes | 5 Both persons |
| | 5 Negative consequences of outcomes | |
| | 6 Other statements about outcomes | |
| | *Acknowledgement activity* | |
| | 7 Acknowledgement Plus | |
| | 8 Acknowledgement Minus | |
| | *Information activity* | |
| | 9 Information | |

To illustrate the use of CPA categories, let us examine how the following hypothetical exchange could be coded:

A. Perhaps it would be best if we agreed to treat this negotiation as a package deal.

B. I think that's a reasonable suggestion.

A. On second thoughts, no. Wouldn't it be best to examine each issue one by one?

B. Trust you to suggest that. It's to your advantage.

A. OK. Let's just split down the middle on every issue.

|                                                                     | Mode    | Resource                 | Referent     |
| ------------------------------------------------------------------- | ------- | ------------------------ | ------------ |
| A. Perhaps it would be best if we agreed to treat this negotiation as a package deal. | Offer   | Procedure                | Both persons |
| B. I think that's a reasonable suggestion.                          | Accepts | Procedure                | Self         |
| A. On second thoughts, no.                                          | Rejects | Procedure                | No referent  |
| A. Wouldn't it be best to examine each issue one by one?            | Seeks   | Procedure                | No referent  |
| B. Trust you to say that.                                           | Offers  | Acknowledgement minus    | Other        |
| B. It's to your advantage.                                          | Offers  | Acknowledgement minus    | Opponent     |
| A. OK.                                                              | Accepts | Acknowledgement minus    | No referent  |
| A. Let's just split down the middle on every issue.                 | Offers  | Settlement point         | Both persons |

## INCIDENCE OF CPA ACTS*: A FURTHER TEST OF THE EFFECTIVENESS OF EXPERIMENTAL MANIPULATION

As a further indication of the effectiveness of the strength of case, we examined the total incidence of CPA acts, however classified. Strength of case had a marked effect. When the union case was strong, the shop stewards contributed 56.0% of all acts, management only 44.0%. With a strong management case, this figure rose to 53.9% and that of the union fell to 46.1%, the differences being statistically significant beyond the 5% level.

### OVERALL EFFECTS OF THIRD-PARTY PRESENCE

In the Introduction we contrasted two approaches which would lead one to have contrasting expectations of the third-party presence. One argument, deriving largely from those in the practical business of mediation, suggested that participants should be more "reasonable" in some sense. The other, deriving from laboratory studies by Morley and Stephenson (1977) suggested that the presence of the third-party would reduce the salience of inter-personal exchange and, hence, increase the inter-party orientation of the negotiation group. By inter-party orientation we mean the concern of the participants with being effective representatives, at the expense of maintaining an

*Two sessions were recorded so poorly that no transcript was available for analysis. Results are, therefore, based on 16 negotiations only.

TABLE 3

*Predicted and obtained association of CPA categories with presence of third-party*

|  | Predicted Positive Association | Result | Predicted Negative Association | Result |
|---|---|---|---|---|
| *Modes* | Offer | * | Accept | ** |
|  | Reject | * |  |  |
|  | Seek | * |  |  |
| *Resources* | Limits | * | Procedure | ** |
|  | Negative consequences of outcomes | ** | Settlement-point | ** |
|  | Acknowledgement minus | ** | Acknowledgement minus | — |
|  | Information | ** |  |  |
| *Referents* | Party | ** | No referent | ** |
|  | Opponent | ** | Self | * |
|  |  |  | Other | ** |
|  |  |  | Both persons | ** |

*Code:*
** Both Third-party (Expert and Naive) conditions differ from Alone condition in predicted direction.
* One Third-party condition differs from Alone condition in predicted direction.
— Neither Observer condition differs from Alone condition in predicted direction.

harmonious relationship. Morley and Stephenson (1977) and Stephenson *et al.* (1976, 1977) have discussed the differences that exist between interaction in situations which favour inter-personal and those which favour inter-party exchange. We suggest that the third-party will increase the representatives' awareness of their role obligations, and that inter-party exchange will be strengthened at the expense of the inter-personal relationship.

On the basis of results obtained in the studies cited above, deductions were made about the correlation of each CPA category with task orientation, and predictions then made concerning the association between each CPA category and third-party presence. Table 3 lists these predictions. In general it will be seen that we expect third-party presence to increase emphasis on the representative role (e.g. use of Party and Opponent as referents), to increase belligerence (e.g. use of Limits, Negative consequences of outcomes, and Acknowledgement minus as Resources, and Reject as a Mode) and to increase presentation of case, and probing of opponent's case (e.g. use of Modes — Offer, Seek; and Resource — Information). Conversely, third-party presence should decrease inter-personal considerations (e.g. use of Referents — Self, Other and Both persons;

and use of Resource — Acknowledgement plus) and decrease movement towards a conclusion (e.g. use of Resources — Procedure and Settlement points; and use of Mode — Accept). The tendency not to refer specifically to Parties and Persons (uses of No Referent) has frequently been shown to be associated with an interpersonal orientation to an encounter.

In 13 out of 19 instances, both the Naive and Expert observers had the effect we had predicted, i.e. those negotiation groups with third-parties present had a higher or lower incidence of the CPA strategy than the Alone groups, as predicted in Table 2. The only exceptions were Modes — Offer, Reject and Seek; Resources — Limits and Acknowledgement plus; and Referent — Self. Of these, only one (Acknowledgement plus) indicated the reverse trend to that predicted in both observer conditions. The overall pattern, however, was clearly in the expected direction, with nearly twice as many categories (13) fulfilling expectations as would be expected by chance (6.33). This yields a $\chi$-square of 11.86 (2 d.f.; $P < 0.01$). For example, the Referent dimension in particular points to the increased interparty orientation in the third-party conditions. In the Alone condition there is less reference overall to persons and parties, and what reference there is tends to persons. In the third-party conditions, on the other hand, references tend towards the Parties. Differences in the Modes show greater positive response in the Alone condition, and on the Resource dimension the third-party groups are more likely to criticize and carp (Acknowledgement minus, Negative consequences of proposed outcomes), whereas the Alone groups are more constructive (Positive consequences of proposed outcomes).

"Procedure" has frequently been shown to be associated with a joint problem-solving approach to the business in hand (see especially Stephenson, 1978; and Stephenson et al., 1977), and the increased incidence of Settlement Points and Other Statements about Outcomes may well indicate a greater readiness actually to come to agreement than in the third-party condition. There, on the other hand, participants seem to "talk around" the issues more (use of Information). The (unexpected) increased Acknowledgement plus probably indicates an increased formal politeness in the third-party condition. The overall pattern suggests that by increasing the emphasis on representation of parties the presence of third-parties increases interparty conflict, and makes an inter-personal, problem-solving approach to the issues less likely to occur.

## FURTHER CPA ANALYSIS OF INTERACTIONS OF THIRD-PARTY AND ROLE

Although the overall pattern of results indicated that the presence of third-parties would, if anything, enhance interparty conflict and exchange, ANOVA showed no statistically significant differences between conditions on individual CPA categories. There were, however, a number of statistically significant interactions, which, although largely unexpected, are sufficiently interesting to merit some tentative discussion. We have seen that one of the principal effects of condition on outcomes concerned the apparent effect of the observer, especially the Expert, on the balance between the parties. Observers increased the success of management, a finding which we thought was due partly to a heightening of management's conventional "leadership" role when under public scrutiny. Is there any evidence for this in the CPA results? There was some evidence (but not at a statistically significant level) for increased role differentiation whereby management become more critical and less conciliatory in the third-party conditions, with the union representative moving the opposite way, in a number of instances. For example the union representatives show more Acknowledgement plus (i.e. "praise" and "respect") towards management in the third-party conditions, management representatives less. With respect to Negative Consequences of Proposed Outcomes — statements concerning the drawbacks of proposals — the union side tend to decrease this form of belligerence when a third-party is present, whereas the management representatives rather increase such behaviour, and, Positive Consequences of Proposed Outcomes shows the reverse pattern.

Further evidence for role differentiation when exposed to third-parties comes from two highly significant 3-way interactions, in which it would appear that Strength of Case may affect tactical adaptation to the mediator's presence. The use of Mode Reject is of interest here. Let us again consider how management changes from the Alone to the third-party conditions. The patterns of change are quite different according to whose is the strong case, and the direction of change depends on the status of the third-party. When the union has a strong case, management rejects their proposals consistently if the observer is Naive ($\bar{x} = 4.46$) but adopts the reverse strategy when the observer is said to be an Expert ($\bar{x} = 0.78$). "Naivety" and "Expertise", however, elicit quite the opposite trends when management itself has the strong case.

TABLE 4

*Percentage of CPA acts classified by Mode: Reject calculated separately for Management and Union contributions in different third-party conditions according to strength of case*

| Third-party status | Union Strong Case | | Management Strong Case | |
|---|---|---|---|---|
| | Mgmt. | Union | Mgmt. | Union |
| Naive | 4.46 | 2.98 | 0.20 | 1.38 |
| Expert | 0.78 | 3.32 | 1.35 | 0.76 |
| Alone | 1.92 | 1.42 | 0.80 | 2.66 |

Analysis of Variance: Mode — Reject

| Source | SOS | d.f. | VE | F | d.f.2 | P |
|---|---|---|---|---|---|---|
| A | 12.771 | 1 | 12.771 | 2.32 | 10 | 0.158 |
| B | 2.856 | 2 | 1.428 | 0.26 | 10 | 0.776 |
| C | 1.989 | 1 | 1.989 | 2.28 | 10 | 0.162 |
| AB | 11.808 | 2 | 5.904 | 1.07 | 10 | 0.377 |
| AC | 0.752 | 1 | 0.752 | 0.86 | 10 | 0.375 |
| BC | 1.745 | 2 | 0.872 | 1.00 | 10 | 0.401 |
| ABC | 13.645 | 2 | 6.822 | 7.82 | 10 | 0.009 |

A — Strength of Case
B — Observer Presence/Absence
C — Management/Union Role

This indicates that participants in the two roles are affected differently by the presence of a third-party, and that these differences vary according to the status of the third-party. The picture is filled in by two further 3-way interactions. Table 5 shows the incidence of Resource Limits, that is statements which "set limits" to an agreement without making a specific proposal of a settlement point. Limits are frequently employed as an excuse for intransigence: e.g. statements to the effect that "it is the Board" or "the workforce" who insist on a particular figure: the negotiator's hands are tied. It is interesting to note first the difference between the two management conditions in the Alone groups. When management have the upper hand they are more likely to set limits ($\bar{x} = 5.50$) than when the union is strong ($\bar{x} = 1.60$). This picture changes with the advent of a "mediator"; then, given a strong case, the management representatives show the reverse pattern. The presence of the third-party makes them less likely to shelve responsibility by setting limits, i.e. they exploit their advantage less in the presence of a third-party. On the other hand, when the union has the stronger case, the third-party presence seems to encourage management representatives to

TABLE 5

*Percentage of CPA acts classified as Resource: Limits calculated separately for Management and Union contributions, in different third-party conditions according to strength of case*

| Third-party status | Union Strong Case | | Management Strong Case | |
|---|---|---|---|---|
| | Mgmt. | Union | Mgmt. | Union |
| Naive | 6.53 | 1.89 | 3.08 | 6.25 |
| Expert | 3.45 | 4.24 | 1.39 | 2.23 |
| Alone | 1.60 | 3.14 | 5.50 | 3.03 |

Analysis of Variance. Resource: Limits

| Source | SOS | d.f. | VE | F | d.f.2 | P |
|---|---|---|---|---|---|---|
| A | 0.082 | 1 | 0.082 | 0.01 | 10 | 0.943 |
| B | 14.010 | 2 | 7.005 | 0.45 | 10 | 0.648 |
| C | 0.124 | 1 | 0.124 | 0.03 | 10 | 0.874 |
| AB | 20.431 | 2 | 10.215 | 0.66 | 10 | 0.537 |
| AC | 3.187 | 1 | 3.187 | 0.67 | 10 | 0.433 |
| BC | 3.522 | 2 | 1.761 | 0.37 | 10 | 0.700 |
| ABC | 46.278 | 2 | 23.139 | 4.84 | 10 | 0.033 |

A — Strength of Case
B — Observer Presence/Absence
C — Management/Union Role

adopt this particular form of intransigence, and the incidence of Limits increases.

Table 6 portrays the results for the use of *Referent* Self. The Referent dimension is used only when a person or party involved in the negotiation is explicitly referred to in the act, and "Self" is coded only if the act contains no other referent. Use of the Referent dimension has proved a particularly useful indicator of task involvement and conflict, with references to Party (one's own side) and Opponent (the other side) being particularly good indicators of the involvement of the negotiators as *party representatives.* Inspection of Table 6 shows that this time it is variation in the union representative's behaviour which largely accounts for the statistically significant interaction. The unions, when they have strength, are more "self-opinionated" when Alone, whereas when faced by strong management, they become more self-opinionated when in the presence of third-parties, especially the Expert.

In summary, it is clear that for both management and union representatives their response to one another, and to differences in their relative power positions, is determined, at least in part, by the

TABLE 6

*Percentage of CPA acts classified as Referent: Self, calculated separately for Management and Union contributions, in different third-party conditions according to strength of case*

| Third-party status | Union Strong Case | | Management Strong Case | |
|---|---|---|---|---|
| | Mgmt. | Union | Mgmt. | Union |
| Naive | 5.47 | 8.64 | 5.27 | 9.16 |
| Expert | 8.43 | 7.82 | 8.74 | 12.65 |
| Alone | 5.11 | 17.12 | 6.81 | 5.89 |

Analysis of Variance. Referent — Self

| Source | SOS | d.f. | VE | F | d.f.2 | P |
|---|---|---|---|---|---|---|
| A | 3.538 | 1 | 3.538 | 0.15 | 10 | 0.706 |
| B | 28.054 | 2 | 14.027 | 0.60 | 10 | 0.569 |
| C | 98.532 | 1 | 98.532 | 10.18 | 10 | 0.009 |
| AB | 71.878 | 2 | 35.939 | 1.53 | 10 | 0.263 |
| AC | 12.650 | 1 | 12.650 | 1.31 | 10 | 0.279 |
| BC | 19.438 | 2 | 9.719 | 1.00 | 10 | 0.400 |
| ABC | 108.270 | 2 | 54.135 | 5.59 | 10 | 0.023 |

presence of a third-party, and his status as Expert or Naive observer. In general, management differentiates more — acts more strategically — between conditions. But the general, and most important, finding is that the significance of their role relationship is changed by the presence of a third-party.


## Conclusions

(1) The mere presence of a third-party, especially an Expert, is sufficient to change the agreements reached by negotiation groups.

(2) Third-party presence does not necessarily favour the party with the stronger case, there being no evidence for the expected interaction between third-party status and strength of case in the present experiment.

(3) The main effect of a third-party is to increase the salience of the role relationship between the participants, so as to strengthen the position of the higher status role. This is reflected in the present instance in a tendency for management representatives to improve their performance markedly in the third-party conditions.

(4) There was evidence to suggest that the importance of the

inter-personal relationship was reduced in the third-party conditions, which, compared with the Alone condition, gave evidence of greater concern with inter-party disagreement than with cooperative problem-solving.

(5) CPA analysis suggested that the effect of the third-party presence on role relationships varies in complex ways according to strength of case.


## Acknowledgements

Our thanks are due to Dr Ian Morley of the University of Warwick who discussed with us the design of the experiment, and to the Social Science Research Council for financial support.


## References

Belliveau, L. M. and Stolte, J. F. The structure of third-party intervention, *Journal of Social Psychology*, 1977, **103**, 243—250.

Cole, D. L. Government in the Bargaining Process: the role of mediation, *Annals of the American Academy of Political and Social Science*, 1961, V. 333, 43—58.

McGrath, J. E. A social psychological approach to the study of negotiation. In Bowers, R. V. (Ed.) *Studies on Behaviour in Organisations: a research Symposium*. University of Georgia Press, Athens, 1966.

Meyer, A. S. Function of the mediator in collective bargaining, *Industrial and Labor Relations Review*, 1960, V. **13**, 159—165.

Morley, I. E. and Stephenson, G. M. *The Social Psychology of Bargaining*. London, Allen and Unwin, 1977.

Peters, E. The Mediator: a neutral, a catalyst, or a leader?, *Labor Law Journal*, 1958, V. 9, 764—769.

Rehmus, C. M. The mediation of industrial conflict: a note on the literature, *Journal of Conflict Resolution*, 1965, V. IX, 118—126.

Stephenson, G. M., Ayling, K. and Rutter, D. R. The role of visual communication in social exchange, *British Journal of Social and Clinical Psychology*, 1976, **15**, 113—120.

Stephenson, G. M., Kniveton, B. M. and Morley, I. Interaction analysis of an industrial wage negotiation, *Journal of Occupational Psychology*, 1977, **50**, 231—241.

Stephenson, G. M. and Dewey, M. E. Final report to the Social Science Research Council for Grant Ref. HR3106/2 Some factors affecting attitudes to industrial relations at the plant level: an exploratory study, 1976.

Stephenson, G. M. The characteristics of negotiation groups. In Brandstätter, H., Davis, J. H. & Schuler, H. (Eds) *Social Decision Processes*. Sage, 1978.

Warren, E. L. and Bernstein, I. The Mediation Process, *Southern Economic Journal*, 1949, V. XV, 441—457.

# 18
# Preparation for Negotiation: Conflict, Commitment and Choice

Ian E. Morley

If a theorist is seriously interested in the processes used by a subject in arriving at a decision, it is essential to devise a technique for exploring the predecisional behaviour (Pitz, 1977).

One approach to the study of inter-group relations has been to investigate negotiations between representatives of organizational groups, at industrial (e.g. Balke *et al.,* 1973; Morley, 1979a; Morley and Stephenson, 1977; Stephenson, 1971a, 1978a, b, 1979), national (e.g. Zartman, 1971, Druckman, 1973; Steinbruner, 1974; Winham 1977), and community levels (e.g. Chalmers and Cormick, 1971, Brehmer and Hammond, 1977). Yet the way in which negotiators prepare for negotiation is surprisingly little understood, for four main reasons.

Firstly, social psychologists have paid relatively little attention to the processes which occur in formal negotiation groups (Morley, 1979b; Morley and Stephenson, 1977). Secondly, studies of negotiation and studies of decision-making have proceeded more or less independently, to the detriment of both. Psychologists interested in decision-making have tended to study forms of social decision-making which pose strategic dilemmas, but which do not involve negotiation or the expectation of negotiation (Morley, 1979b). Psychologists interested in negotiation have too often reduced the study of strategic decision-making to the study of bid and counterbid (Morley and Stephenson, 1977; Winham, 1977). Thirdly, research on negotiation has led to relatively little development of theoretical ideas (Patchen, 1970; Morley, 1979b) and what theory there is tends to ignore organizational mechanisms of decision of the sort outlined by Friend and Jessop (1971). Finally, social psychologists have paid little attention to the importance of continuity in certain kinds of bargaining relationships, particularly those which occur between union and management negotiators (Brown and Terry, 1975).

Whatever the reasons, social psychologists have not studied pre-negotiation planning in any detail. The purpose of this chapter is to review literature relevant to the study of preparation for negotiation and to indicate some of the directions future research might take. Essentially, I want to follow Marsh (1974) and argue that the process of negotiation "is one of progressive commitment" in which "planning and action are... successive stages of single process" (p. 3). Negotiation is also a form of joint decision making and to understand what is going on it is important to explore the ways in which negotiators formulate and define the cognitive and social problems they are likely to face (Allison, 1971; Pitz, 1977; Zartman, 1977; Snyder and Diesing, 1977).

The first part of this chapter uses the work of Howard Elcock (1972) to illustrate some of the difficulties encountered by negotiators as they prepared for the Paris Peace Conference of 1919. The object of the exercise is to characterize some of the ways in which negotiation may change when negotiators act as representatives rather than individuals; participate in bargaining relationships extended over time; and operate in settings which challenge their ability to comprehend what is going on. Hopefully, this will help to identify some of the directions future research might take.

The special problems faced by representatives are discussed with reference to Joseph McGrath's tri-polar model of negotiation groups. It is argued (against McGrath) that formal negotiation should not be regarded as a process in which conflicting group interests observe or distort inter-personal processes (such as discussion or problem solving) which would otherwise occur. The treatment of continuity and complexity introduces aspects of negotiation not included in McGrath's model. In particular, it is argued that if we are to understand bargaining as a process of joint decision making it may be important to consider bargaining modules which are "rational" or "irrational" in the sense outlined by Snyder and Diesing in their *Conflict Among Nations*.

The second part of this chapter outlines the results of experimental manipulations of pre-negotiation experience, paying particular attention to an unpublished study conducted by Maryon Tysoe, Geoffrey Stephenson and myself. The role of *commitment,* outlined by McGrath, is considered in some detail. Finally, in the third section, I discuss some of the ways in which social psychologists might go on to study the pre-decision behaviour of members of negotiation groups drawing heavily on the work of Steinbruner (1974), Snyder and Diesing (1977), and Payne *et al.* (1978).

## The Paris Peace Conference of 1919

Elcock's (1972) *Portrait of a Decision* describes the events which preceded the Paris Peace Conference of 1919 and the course of the negotiations which led to the Treaty of Versailles (which included a Covenant for the League of Nations and dealt with issues of German war guilt, reparation, disarmament, and the like). The treatment is that of an historian who is trying "to reveal something of the motives, personalities and actions" (p. xii) of negotiators who "believed that no possible successors could do better" (p. xii) but were roundly condemned as knaves and fools by writers such as J. M. Keynes (in *The Economic Consequences of the Peace*). Of course it is easy to be wise after the event, and to demonstrate some of the complexities of the task Elcock points out that:

> The negotiators at Paris had to reach decisions relating to the whole future of the world, by a process of discussion, investigation and inevitably compromise, against a background of war, starvation, pestilence and unrest which made them all feel that their time was limited. If peace and prosperity were not restored quickly, Europe would succumb to Bolshevism and anarchy. Their task was not made any easier by the fact that, in addition to their own strong opinions, they were the servants of democratic Parliaments and electorates who were making extreme demands which, inevitably, the statesmen could not entirely satisfy... These were perhaps, the most important background factors. (Elcock, 1972, pp. xi–xii)

I would add that the Conference seems to me to provide a striking example of the "social negotiations" Walton and McKersie (1965) define as involving subprocesses of distributive bargaining, integrative bargaining, attitudinal structuring and intra-organizational bargaining. Consequently, the negotiators had to deal with uncertainties arising from the nature of their representative role obligations (compare Oppenheim and Bayley, 1970; Chalmers and Cormick, 1971) as well as uncertainties arising from the complex nature of their task (compare Friend and Jessop, 1971; Winham, 1977). They were also subjected to many of the stresses of consequential decision-making which have been elaborated by McGrath (1966), Janis (1959), and Janis and Mann (1977). Some examples may help to show the kinds of problem I have in mind.

NEGOTIATORS AS REPRESENTATIVES OF GROUPS

By and large social psychologists have shown much more interest in inter-personal bargaining than formal negotiation, as both Geoffrey Stephenson and I have argued elsewhere (Morley and Stephenson, 1977; Morley, 1979b; Stephenson, 1978b). However, in the early sixties Joseph McGrath and his associates developed a "tri-polar" or "tri-forces" model which attempted to predict the outcomes of formal negotiations by measuring the major psychological "forces" acting on each of the participants. The model is called a "tri-polar" or "tri-forces" model because McGrath assumes that three sets of forces are involved. The net effect is that:

> Each participant. . . is subjected to. . . (1) a force, R toward the position held by his reference group; (2) an opposed force, A, toward agreement with other negotiating parties; and (3) a third force, C, toward attaining a high quality, creative or constructive solution to the problem as judged from the point of view of the broader social system (McGrath, 1966, pp. 110–111).

Broadly speaking McGrath's position may be summarized as asserting (1) that the concept of commitment is central to a distinctively psychological formulation of the processes of joint decision-making involved in negotiation[2]; and (2) that the greater the commitment of negotiators to Party positions the smaller the probability that effective decisions will be made.

More precisely, McGrath's model contains four component parts (Morley et al., 1978). Firstly, there is a list of some of the factors which increase or decrease the net R-, A-, and C-forces acting on the negotiators. Secondly, there is a proposition asserting that the net R-force "pressure" is a more important determinant of outcomes than the net A- or C-force "pressure". Thirdly, it is assumed that the greater the R-force pressure acting on negotiators the smaller the overall effectiveness of the negotiation. In contrast, A- and C-force pressures are assumed to be directly related to task success. Finally, task success is defined by a "multipartisan" criterion in which "overall effectiveness" is measured by the product of ratings of the agreements, obtained from officials of each of the parties concerned (including judges representing the position of "the broader community" within which the negotiation takes place).

The force, R, is generated when the cognitive, attitudinal, and social commitments[3] of negotiators are made explicit and salient by their role obligations to represent the vested interests of organizational groups (Vidmar and McGrath, 1967, p. 7)[4]. What is being asserted is that:

> ... It is not only the divisive nature of the task or differing members attitudes *per se* that results in conflict, but also the demand on the group members to represent the interests and viewpoints of their respective reference groups. Such a role structure promotes among the group members a perception of their relationship in the problem-solving session as being at least partially contrient. They must represent their respective reference groups as well as work together to set forth an acceptable and constructive solution" (Vidmar and McGrath, 1967, p. 45).

Apparently, strong R forces produce conflicts which prevent negotiators working out the problems posed by the negotiation task.

I would like, however, to discuss a number of difficulties with this point of view. Basically, what McGrath has done is to base his model of negotiation upon organizational groups (assigned a "standard decision task") that *turn in to* negotiation groups. In such cases:

> ... the group members (may) perceive themselves primarily as members of, and representatives for, their own departments. As departmental representatives they attempt to insure that their department gets its "fair share" of the resources to be allocated. The decision group's *formal* goal is obstructed by conflicting group interests and can only be realized *along with* a satisfaction of those interests. Often results are not to the organization's best advantage (Vidmar and McGrath, 1967, p. 3).

Notice that the group members are not supposed to be acting as representatives of groups, nor engaged in a negotiation task. The clear implication is that, in negotiation groups also, role obligations act to distort[5] the inter-personal process of discussion or problem-solving which otherwise would occur. But negotiation groups are not the same as discussion groups or problem-solving groups (Stephenson, 1971b; Morley and Stephenson, 1977; Morley, 1979a, c). Nor is formal negotiation that in which interpersonal processes are held in check by organizational constraints (Stephenson, 1978b).

To be fair, Vidmar and McGrath (1967) wrote only that "the conflict inherent in some decision-making groups is similar to the conflict in formal negotiation groups" (p. 3): but the only differences they have identified are differences in the force C. In standard decision making groups the force C is simply a pull towards the organizational goal formally given to the members of the group. In formal negotiation groups participants are seen as "*ex officio* agents" of a wider community to which both Party and Opponent belong: that is, the force is "analogous to the 'pull' toward the position of a generic or universalistic reference group" (McGrath, 1966, p. 112).

There are two rather different ways in which the "wider community" or "generic reference group" might be conceptualized. In labour negotiations, both union and management may be under pressure from the public at large so that "the welfare of the general public' is an "external criterion" by which outcome may be judged (McGrath, 1966, p. 110). But in international negotiations the only community to which all parties belong is that sharing some sort of values, principles, hopes, fears, or whatever.[6] Harold Nicolson's *Peacemaking, 1919* gives an example of the kind of idealism which may be involved:

> We were journeying to Paris, not merely to liquidate the war, but to found a new order in Europe. We were preparing not peace only, but Eternal peace. There was about us the halo of some divine mission. . . . (Nicolson, 1964, pp. 31–32).

It is to McGrath's credit that he has recognized the importance of feelings of this kind. For example, Clemenceau justified a decision to stand firm during the debate on war reparations by saying:

> France is the country which has suffered most of all from the war and today her people are convinced that we are not demanding enough from Germany. *I am convinced that we have done what is reasonable* {despite R pressure to do otherwise} but if I retreat one step further I know that I will arouse a general revolt against myself (Elcock, 1972, p. 318, my emphasis).

There seems little reason to doubt that Clemenceau meant what he said. His behaviour may be described (following Midgaard, 1976) as:

> the result of an attempt to strike a balance between the requirements of co-operative negotiations and the requirements of securing certain minimal interests of one's own in pure bargaining (p. 122).

Thus, it seems that Vidmar and McGrath may have succeeded in identifying a variety of distributive bargaining (Walton and McKersie, 1965) which combines elements of "pure bargaining" with elements of "co-operative negotiation" in the way that Midgaard suggests. This is important and worthy of further consideration, but Midgaard's "co-operative negotiations" represent an "ideal type", not the general case (compare Morley, 1979a). The original model of the "standard" decision-making group is, perhaps, most relevant to cases of intra-organizational conflict or inter-departmental conflict rather than cases in which the group exists primarily to manage a formal negotiation task.[7, 8]

THE IMPORTANCE OF CONTINUITY

Preparation for negotiation occurs in the context of relationships extended over time. That is to say, the separation between preparation and negotiation is heuristic and should not blind us to the importance of historical relationships between the participants and/or the parties. Here I would like to note a number of points which do not fit very well into the framework provided by McGrath:

(a) Negotiators were subject to constraints produced by a number of previous wartime commitments (see e.g. Elcock, 1972, p. 52).

(b) Many of President Wilson's reactions against Germany were engendered by the terms of the Treaty of Brest-Litovsk, concluded between Germany and Bolshevik Russia. Temperley (1920) reports Wilson as saying that:

> ...the men who act for many... are enjoying in Russia a cheap triumph in which no brave or gallant nation can take pride. A great people, helpless by their own act, lies for the time at their mercy. Their fair professions are forgotten. They nowhere set up justice, but everywhere impose their power and exploit everything for their own use and aggrandisement... (p. 41; quoted in Elcock, 1972, p. 19).

(c) Negotiators must not only decide what to do; they must decide what to say. Public comments made at the time$_1$ may be used to structure negotiations at time$_2$. Elcock reports that the day after the Armistice was signed (12 November 1918) the Germans responded to President Wilson's "Fourteen Points" speech (8 January 1918) by pointing out:

> The Germany Government has accepted the terms laid down by President Wilson in his address of January 8th and in his subsequent addresses on the foundation of a permanent peace of justice. Consequently, its object in entering into discussions would only be to agree upon practical details of the application of these terms (Elcock, 1972, p. 37).

For a more extensive treatment of the importance of continuity in negotiating relationships the reader is referred to Harbison and Coleman (1951), Walton and McKersie (1965), Anthony and Crichton (1969), Brown and Terry (1975), Morley and Stephenson (1977), Batstone *et al.* (1978) and Morley (1979c).

COMPLEX SETTINGS AND PROCESSES

The general impression given by Elcock (1972), Nicolson (1964), and Keynes (1961) is that the negotiators at Paris found it extremely difficult to monitor what was going on.[9] The negotiations were complex because of the "size" or "variety" of the data base and the "uncertainty", "ambiguity", or "discretionary content"[10] associated with each of its elements. According to Winham (1977) each challenges the negotiator's comprehension, but for different reasons: size or variety creates problems of information overload; uncertainty, ambiguity, and discretionary content make it difficult to structure decisions so that clear statements of preference can be made. The effects of each kind of complexity will be considered in turn.

(1) As the size or variety of the data base is increased negotiators *may not have time to study important documents and work out what is going on.* Nicolson (1964, pp. 153—4) has vividly portrayed the problems of information overload which characterized the proceedings at the Paris Peace Conference. And, in another context, Irving Janis has noted that:

> Washington bureaucrats quipped that the reason McNamara looked so good, in comparison to the others who participated in the White House Meetings, was that the long drive gave him eight extra minutes to do his homework in the back of his limousine (Janis, 1971, p. 114).

Negotiators may be subjected to the same kinds of time pressure or to other forms of organizational stress. This may be why Daniel (1976) found that only one fifth of the establishments included in his survey systematically attempted to cost how long they could afford any interruption to work.

(2) As the size or variety of the data base is increased parties are *less likely to agree that concessions have been exchanged.* For example, Midgaard and Underdal (1977) have argued that as the number of formal parties to a negotiation is increased: "the negotiation situation tends to become less lucid, more complex, and therefore in some respects more demanding" (p. 331).

Furthermore, multilateral negotiations imply that there will be "more values, interests, and perceptions to be accommodated" (Midgaard and Underdal, 1977, p. 332). Individual concessions may be embedded in a mass of detail and "screened out much of the time" (Winham, 1977, p. 359). Data from Winham's simulation of the "Kennedy Round" trade negotiations showed that:

> more than half the time the participants either failed to agree on the nature of concessions or failed to agree when concessions were made to them (p. 358).

Bilateral negotiations led to more congruent perceptions than multilateral negotiations in three of the four analyses reported (Winham, 1977, Table 12.2, p. 359). Thus, the more complex the negotiations the harder it will be to establish that a genuine "breakthrough" has been made.

(3) Increasing the size or variety of the data base will increase the uncertainties involved *so that it will be harder for each party to judge the other's "resolve" and to assess its relative bargaining power.* As Midgaard and Underdal have pointed out:

> since there are more interests to consider, there will probably also be more uncertainty as to the interests and motives of some of the others and as to their perception of one's own utilities (pp. 331–2).

Uncertainty provides the link between bargaining power and bargaining process (Snyder and Diesing, 1977; Morley and Stephenson, 1977; Morley, 1979a). For example, Snyder and Diesing have argued that when governments begin crisis bargaining:

the parties are either uncertain or mistaken about relative bargaining power, primarily because they cannot know the value of each other's interests at stake and hence how firm the other ultimately will be. Coercive, persuasive, and perhaps accommodative tactics attempt to communicate one's own resolve... weaken the adversary's resolve... and gain information about the adversary's interests and resolve. Toward the end of the confrontation stage, the parties develop fairly clear, if not correct, pictures of mutual resolve and hence relative bargaining power, and then a process of resolution occurs — either compromise or one-sided capitulation depending on the revealed power relations. Process is therefore practically inseparable from power since it is through process that the true power relations become manifest in the parties' values and perceptions (p. 281–1).

Similarly, Morley and Stephenson (1977) have suggested that the first stage of industrial negotiations functions to establish strength of position, setting the standard against which future settlements will be judged. In their view negotiators:

... are assessing the form of the parties with respect to the particular course on which the present contest will take place" (Morley and Stephenson, 1977, p. 288).

"Form" or "strength of position" is determined by consideration of the merits of the arguments (strength of case) and by consideration of the costs each protagonist is ready to incur in pursuit of a given demand (bargaining power). In general, participants will agree what sized concessions from Party should be exchanged for what sized concessions from Opponent only after an exploratory[11] process of negotiation (Chamberlain, 1951; Morley, 1979a). However, we may surmise that the difficulty of establishing an exchange rate for concessions is directly proportional to the complexity of the negotiation task, or, possibly that in multilateral negotiations there is no criterion of bargaining power "that is precise and feasible as well as compelling" (Midgaard and Underdal, 1977, p. 334). At the very least we can agree with Midgaard and Underdal (1977) that:

... as the number of parties increases, there will be ample room for the art of creating suggestive clues... and a more prominent role for chance as a determinant of bargaining outcomes (p. 334).

Elcock's *Portrait of a Decision* provides several examples of this art, including one case in which Lloyd-George was able to reverse the

British position without other members of the "Council of Four" perceiving his change of front (Elcock, 1972, pp. 315–6).

(4) Negotiators may have to exercise their discretion by trading off values one against the other (Steinbruner, 1974) without adequate knowledge of policy decisions made outside the negotiation (Elcock, 1972, pp. 28, 52, 58). *Complexity of this kind may make negotiators feel uncertain about value judgements of their own.* In some cases this may lead to differences within teams of the kind reported by Balke *et al.* (1973) in their "reenactment" of negotiations at the Dow Chemical Company, in the United States. Judgements of sample contracts showed that:

> ... the contract evaluation policies of the union did not vary from nego-
> tiator to negotiator. Union negotiators, however, had three management
> policies rather than one, with which to cope (Balke *et al.*, 1973, p. 322).

Negotiators did not estimate accurately the importance they attached to each of the issues, and changed policies "from the evaluation of one contract to the next" (Balke *et al.*, 1973, p. 323).

(5) To the extent that policy changes result in ambiguous or misleading signals being sent to the other side we may hypothesize that, *as negotiations become more complex, it will be harder for negotiators to estimate what would be acceptable to their opponents at the bargaining table* (Balke *et al.*, 1973; Brehmer, 1975; Brehmer and Hammond, 1977). The negotiators studied by Balke *et al.* (1973) were dealing only with four key issues; they:

> were confident that they understood their counterpart's policies, a belief
> based on years of association and negotiation. Yet they were wrong (Balke
> *et al.*, 1973, p. 320).

(6) As negotiators face increasingly difficult problems of balancing benefits against costs *they are more likely to use decision procedures which are "cognitive" or "cybernetic" rather than "analytic" in origin.* (Steinbruner, 1974; Winham 1977). Analytic procedures are derived from the assumption that people strive to maximize their values under the constraints they face: i.e. they strive toward the ideal of rational choice (Steinbruner, 1974, p. 8). According to Steinbruner:

> The quintessential analytic decision maker is one who strains toward as
> complete an understanding as possible of the causal forces which determine

outcomes. He seeks to predict the flow of events and, where he has leverage, to manipulate them to his advantage. The processing of information while making decisions is all done for the purpose of constructing and improving the blueprint from which the optimal choice emerges. (Steinbruner, 1974, pp. 35–6).

As far as possible the optimal choice is one which maximizes subjectively expected utility; or rather,

> the maximization equations represent the ideal limit that a good decision approaches as it becomes more careful and exact (Snyder and Diesing, 1977, p. 345).

Walton and McKersie (1965) and Marsh (1974) have described industrial negotiations from this point of view. In contrast, the picture which emerges from Elcock's *Portrait of a Decision* suggests that negotiators were preoccupied with problems of uncertainty control, central to what Steinbruner has called the "cybernetic paradigm".

Like many other multilateral negotiations the Paris Peace Conference did not develop primarily to resolve specific items in dispute (see Winham, 1977, p. 352). And, as in other cases, negotiation consisted of:

> adapting to the complex environment created by the demands and offers of other nations (Winham, 1977, p. 353).

In such cases negotiation may begin without much idea of what would constitute an acceptable agreement (Iklé and Leites, 1962; Iklé, 1964; Winham, 1977; Snyder and Diesing, 1977; also see McKersie and Hunter, 1973; Warr, 1973). Snyder and Diesing (1977) have reported that the negotiators they studied did not establish minimum goals until late in the process of negotiation, and, in many cases, did not set minimum goals at all. Fisher (1969) makes a similar point by outlining a hypothetical case in which Fidel Castro calls up the President of the United States with the message:

> . . . economic sanctions have gone on long enough. You win: send down your terms. I will sign anything you can realistically expect me to sign. You must be practical — I have domestic problems. I am not going to commit political suicide. But anything within the realm of reason, I will sign. (Fisher, 1969. p. 25)

How long, Fisher asks, would it take the White House to prepare such a draft?

At Versailles, President Wilson was "obsessed" with the League of Nations although he had not considered in detail the problems such an organization would face (Elcock, 1972, p. 51). In general, the American delegation found it difficult to consult with President Wilson and was, therefore, unable to work out a coherent point of view. General Bliss advised his Secretary of State that:

> The Allies. . . know exactly what they are going to ask in the ways of territorial concessions. Their demands will be immediately accompanied by their reasons and arguments. Are we agreed that the Alsace—Lorraine of 1871 shall be ceded? Or the Alsace—Lorraine of 1814?. . . Are we agreed on a principle with which we will meet a demand for the cession of the entire left bank (of the Rhine)? How are we going to get the President's views or instructions on such questions? (Elcock, 1972, p. 58).

In fact Wilson failed to give appropriate direction to his aides and, himself, remained "shockingly ignorant of the European situation" (Elcock, 1972, p. 55). Consequently, negotiations proceeded from positions which were, in general, defined by a British or French draft. The President:

> . . . had to take up, therefore, a persistent attitude of obstruction, criticism and negation if the draft was to become at all in line with his own ideas and purpose (Keynes, 1961, p. 24).

Of course part of the problem is that what is acceptable can only be determined when negotiation has shown what is available (Winham, 1977). In Winham's opinion the result is:

> that negotiators proceed with more understanding of and attention to the process of negotiation than where this process will lead. The process is a programmed set of operations that has evolved out of considerable experience. It consists of tabling a position, decomposing and aggregating the relevant information wherever possible, and then setting about, point by point, to reconcile the differences between the parties (Winham, 1977, p. 353).

The negotiation is thus a kind of "grooved thinking" (Steinbruner, 1974) in which negotiators follow simple decision rules which guide their behaviour irrespective of what the others will do meantime (Kelley and Thibaut, 1969, pp. 48—9; Kelley, 1964; Kelley and

Schenitzki, 1972; Kelley *et al.*, 1967; Morley and Stephenson, 1977). The procedures generate outcomes, but psychologically the negotiator:

> is not engaged in the pursuit of an explicitly designed result. The psychological effects of uncertainty are therefore held to a minimum. . . . The responses are "action sequences", of the character of a recipe, established by prior experience. They are programs which accept and adjust to very specific and very limited kinds of information (Steinbruner, 1974, pp. 66–7).

A settlement emerges as a result of running the programs, but the settlement need not be conceptualized in advance. Settlements may thus be "accumulated from the bottom up" by fragmenting decisions into smaller units, by following established procedures and precedents, and by paying particular attention to a few key variables such as domestic support for a policy (Winham, 1977, p. 353; Steinbruner, 1974). The risk is, of course, that negotiators will fail to appreciate trade off between different aspects of an agreement and become dissatisfied with the bargain they have obtained.

The "cognitive paradigm" is concerned with the way in which negotiators form strong, categorical (i.e. non-probabilistic) beliefs in the face of extreme uncertainty in their environment. It derives from principles of cognitive and social psychology which have been outlined very elegantly by Steinbruner himself, and by Abelson (1976) and Jervis (1976). What is suggested is that

> the mind constantly struggles to impose clear, coherent meaning on events, uses categorical rather than probabilistic judgements in doing so, and thus expects to anticipate outcomes exactly rather than having to assign probabilities to a range of outcomes (Steinbruner, 1974, p. 112).

In other words the mind "imposes an image" on the environment and "works" to preserve it (Steinbruner, 1974, p. 123).

Decision makers unfamiliar with an organization and its business may adopt the image provided by a sponsor. When sponsors disagree, and uncertainty is high, this may produce a "syndrome of uncommitted thinking" in which the decision maker defines the same decision problem in different ways at different times, (Steinbruner, 1974, p. 129). Here, Steinbruner's analysis provides an interesting supplement to Janis' account of vacillation in "emergency" decision making (Janis and Mann, 1977; Janis, 1978).

In other cases the image of the environment may derive from commitments to "abstract and extensive belief patterns" (Steinbruner, 1974, p. 131) which are stable over time and maintained by a variety of inconsistency management techniques (Holsti, 1967, Steinbruner, 1974, pp. 132–3; Snyder and Diesing, 1977, pp. 331–2; Elcock, 1972, pp. 51, 193–4, 197, 307). The result is a "syndrome of theoretical thinking" (Steinbruner, 1974) which has much in common with the "irrational bargaining module" outlined by Snyder and Diesing (1977).

If Snyder and Diesing are correct, analytic cybernetic, and cognitive perspectives each have something to contribute to a model of negotiation. However, they emphasize some of the similarities between cybernetic and cognitive process and argue that, broadly speaking, negotiators may be divided into two groups: those who are "rational" in an information processing sense and those who are not (Snyder and Diesing, 1977, pp. 282–339).

"Rational" bargainers begin with tentative diagnoses of what is going to use information obtained from negotiation to adjust estimates:

> of the opponent's specific aims, interests, degree of resolve, and capabilities in the particular conflict (Snyder and Diesing, 1977, p. 337).

In contrast "irrational" bargainers have rigid belief systems which render expectations and strategy immune to change. Incoming information which does not fulfil expectations is denied, ignored, or distorted in a variety of ways (Jervis, 1976).

Distinctions of this kind, which help to identify different kinds of negotiation (compare Snyder and Diesing, 1977, pp. 284, 335), seem to me to deserve much more attention from psychologists than they have received to date.

## Experimental research: a brief review

Let me repeat that social psychologists have not studied preparation for negotiation in any great detail. Nevertheless, I would like to make the most of the literature that is available. Hopefully, a brief outline of research on role reversal, strategy versus study preparation, conflicts of interest and value dissensus, group polarization, and issue emphasis, will serve to introduce the comments to follow in Part III of my paper. For more comprehensive treatments the reader is referred to Morley and Stephenson (1977) Morley (1979a), Druckman (1977) and Tysoe (1979).

PREPARATION IN REVERSED ROLE GROUPS

Courses designed to teach the skills of formal negotiation often use "gaming simulations" (Morley and Stephenson, 1977) to introduce students to some of the complexities of the real life tasks they will have to face. However, some participants may be required to negotiate in reversed roles, whilst others may not. More precisely, two-party negotiations allow:

(a) Standard groups,[12] in which party A is represented by members of party A and party B is represented by members of party B. Thus, all participants operate in their standard role.

(b) Cross-assigned groups, in which party A (say) is represented by members of party A and party B is represented by other members of party A. Some participants operate in their standard role; others operate in reversed roles. Other variations are possible — witness Campbell (1960) — but do not require elucidation at this stage.

(c) Reversed role groups, in which party A is represented by members of party B and party B is represented by members of party B and party B is represented by members of party A. Here, there is a mutual exchange of roles. All participants operate in reversed roles.

Most training for negotiation occurs in cross-assigned groups (Pocock, 1970; Tysoe, 1979) but techniques of role-reversal are used (occasionally) in policy or planning meetings. For example, after three months of negotiation and debate Lloyd George:

> ... decided that it was desirable that the British Delegation should make clear in writing the limits to which they were prepared to go (Hankey, 1963, p. 100).

Essentially, the object of the exercise was to prepare "a complete synopsis of the future Treaty" (Hankey, 1963, p. 100). On Saturday March 22nd 1919, Lloyd George, General Smuts, General Sir Henry Wilson, Sir Maurice Hankey, and Philip Kerr, met in a hotel near the Palace of Fontainebleau. Hankey (1963) reports that Lloyd George:

proposed to begin with a rather general inquiry on a plan in vogue at that time. . . namely to assign a particular role, e.g. ally, enemy or neutral, to selected individuals who would be invited in turn to address the meeting from the point of view allotted to them. . . . We were given half an hour to prepare our thoughts and to meet again for a cup of tea and discussion (p. 100).

General Wilson spoke as a German officer and a Frenchwoman. Hankey himself spoke for the average Englishman. Presumably, the main effect was to produce a heightened awareness of R-forces previously known (compare Wilson, 1970, p. 73). In any case the synopsis was completed two days later, on Monday March 24th, and sent immediately to Clemenceau and President Wilson.

However, social psychologists interested in experimental research have not started from a consideration of cases of this kind. No one (to my knowledge) has studied the effects of "staff conferences" of the sort used by Lloyd George (i.e. preparation in cross-assigned groups) upon negotiations in which all participants take their standard roles (i.e. negotiation in standard groups). Instead, it has been assumed that commitment to Party positions generates perceptual distortions which, quite literally, prevent negotiators seeing issues in the same way (see Bass, 1966, p. 2): leading to two main lines of research. Firstly psychologists have compared the performance of representatives and non-representatives on the same negotiation task (e.g. Druckman, 1967; Druckman et al., 1972; Benton and Druckman, 1974; Lamm, 1975).[12] Secondly, they have attempted to show that, in some sense, negotiations are more efficient in reversed role groups than in cross-assigned groups than in standard groups:[13] either because negotiation takes less time, or leads to a greater number of agreements, or because the agreements obtained are judged as "better" in terms of an "overall" (multipartisan) criterion such as that used by McGrath. It is this second line of research that I wish to discuss.

Two studies have compared the "efficiency" of standard and cross-assigned groups. Vidmar and McGrath (1965) (SD3)[14] studied two-person negotiations in which group members represented organizations with different philosophies about housing on the campus of the University of Illinois. Quality of agreement was measured in terms of a combined merit score equal to the product of ratings made by a trained judge assuming, in turn, the viewpoint of Party A, Party B and the general Community. (Ratings obtained from officials of the organizations concerned produced inter-rater reliabilities which were "extremely low", confirming the finding of Balke *et al.* that organizational officials cannot always substitute for each other without marked change in contract evaluation policies.) Differences between the experimental treatments were in the predicted direction but did not reach acceptable levels of statistical significance. Settlements from cross-assigned groups were, however, judged to be of higher quality when rated from a neutral point of view ($P < 0.10$).

Campbell (1960) studied four-person groups role-playing an industrial negotiation. Each side, union and management, was represented by a two-man team. In standard groups team members identified strongly with the party they were to represent. In cross-assigned groups terms were made up of one subject who identified strongly with Party and one who identified strongly with Opponent. Negotiation efficiency was measured in terms of speed (times to agreement) and quality ("approximation of the decisions reached in the negotiations to the *community* standard for similar companies"; "the going rate"), (Campbell, 1960, p. 37, my emphasis). There were no statistical differences between the treatments with respect to measures of time to agreement and absolute deviation from the going rate. Cross-assigned groups, however, did negotiate contracts with smaller algebraic deviations from the going rate than standard groups.

Only one published study, by Stephenson *et al.* (1976)(SD3) has compared the performance of reversed role and standard negotiation[15] groups. The probability of reaching agreement was higher in reversed role groups and more varied settlements were obtained (i.e. settlements with greater absolute deviations from compromise). Measures of "overall effectiveness", such as McGrath's product score, were not obtained.

Here I would like briefly to describe a study by Morley *et al.* which compared the performance of reversed role and standard negotiation groups with respect to each of the dependent variables identified above (also see Morley *et al.* 1979; Morley, 1979c; Tysoe, 1979). Two consecutive RPD3[14] negotiations were included in a course on "communications training" run by a large manufacturing company. The first, Exercise Venture,[16] required teams of negotiators to reach agreement on hours of work and shift premiums for five grades of worker. The second, Exercise Negotiations, was derived from Bass's (1966) research and required pairs of subjects to negotiate five financial issues: as in Bass's Experiment One pressure to reach agreement was increased by setting a deadline and increasing the time costs assoociated with each ten minutes of negotiation time. Half of the subjects completed Exercise Venture in reversed role groups and half in standard groups. Half of the teams prepared for Exercise Negotiations in unilateral strategy groups and half in unilateral study groups (see Bass, 1966). Strategy instructions required team members to formulate a package of agreements, prepare for concessions, and decide issues on which to stand firm. In contrast, study instructions asked subjects to strive for greater understanding of the other point of view in comparison to their own, rather than to formulate detailed plans.

Two predictions were derived from McGrath's tri-forces model: (1) that product ratings of agreements at time$_1$ (Exercise Venture) would be higher in reversed role and standard groups; and (2) that product ratings of agreements at time$_2$ (Exercise Negotiations) would be higher when negotiators reversed roles at time$_1$ than when they did not. Hypothesis 1 received some support since the mean product was higher in reversed role groups than standard groups and the trend approached significance at the 0.05 level. With respect to hypothesis 2, product scores were higher where participants had previous experience in reversed role rather than standard groups, but differences between treatments were small and not statistically reliable ($F < 1$). To be fair to McGrath it should be noted that, in this case, product scores were derived from ratings provided by the negotiators themselves rather than from ratings of judges trained to adopt the relevant points of view.

Two predictions were derived from Campbell's (1960) research: (3) that settlements at time$_1$ would have smaller algebraic deviations from the local going rate in reversed role groups than standard groups; and (4) that settlements at time$_2$ would have smaller algebraic deviations from the going rate when negotiators reversed roles at time$_1$ than when they did not. Hypothesis 3 received no support; Hypothesis 4 was supported only for subjects who prepared for negotiations in *study* groups.

The finding that role reversal produced more varied settlements than negotiation in standard groups (Stephenson *et al.*, 1976) was not supported in the present case, either at time$_1$ or at time$_2$. Presumably, effects of this kind vary with the details of the negotiation task used.

PREPARATION IN STRATEGY AND STUDY GROUPS

Bass (1966)(RPD3), Druckman (1967, 1968)(RPD3), Kahn and Kohls (1972) (GEE1)[14], and Klimoski (1972) (RPD3) have compared the effects on subsequent negotiations of instructions to study the issues rather than formulate specific plans. Their work is too well known to merit detailed treatment here, and has been reviewed elsewhere (Morley and Stephenson, 1977; Tysoe, 1979). What is of interest, however, is the suggestion that the effect of studying issues is to reduce negotiators' commitments to Party positions. Presumably, the argument could be spelled out as follows: R forces would be decreased to the extent that study preparation fostered a "problem solving" rather than a "win-lose" orientation (Druckman, 1968) and to the extent that Party's demands were formulated with less clarity than would otherwise be the case (McGrath, 1966).

Simultaneously, A forces would be increased to the extent that study preparation induced a "bilateral focus" (Walcott et al., 1977) which helped "delineate the region of validity in the other's stand or position" (Druckman, 1968, p. 368). Therefore, negotiations should be more "efficient" when subjects prepare by studying the issues rather than by preparing detailed strategic or tactical plans.

The data obtained by Bass (1966) and Druckman (1967, 1968) are, of course, consistent with this view. When experiments set a deadline and associate "financial" costs with negotiation time, studying issues rather than formulating specific plans (apparently) increases the probability that agreements will be obtained, leaves negotiators closer together when agreements cannot be reached, and leads to faster speeds of negotiation. Results of this kind were, however, simply not obtained in the study by Morley et al. which has been described above. Furthermore, the contracts did not have the characteristics which would be expected from consideration of McGrath's research. The hypothesis that product ratings of agreements would be higher when negotiators came from unilateral study rather than unilateral strategy groups was confirmed only for subjects given previous experience in reversed role groups. In addition, differences between strategy and study treatments seemed not to follow from differences in commitment to Party positions.

The effects of strategy and study preparation require a different kind of explanation. For example, Morley et al. (1978) have summarized their findings as follows:

... strategic planning produced conflicts which were "resolved" by finding compromise or near compromise solutions. The effects of the study treatment seem rather more complex, however. . . When negotiators operated in standard roles at time$_1$ and went on to study issues at time$_2$ settlements were more likely to diverge from compromise and favour the union side. Presumably, study may lead either to increased sympathy with the position advocated by the other side or increased awareness of the weaknesses in the other's case. One interpretation of our data is to say that the former is more likely than the latter when participants have just engaged in an exercise in reversed role groups (p. 10).

Ultimately, to understand what is going on we shall have to explore the nature of the study and the plans which are formulated in much more detail (Bass, 1966; Morley *et al.*, 1978).

CONFLICTS OF INTEREST AND VALUE DISSENSUS

Druckman and Zechmeister have conducted a series of studies (Druckman and Zechmeister, 1970; Druckman, 1971; Zechmeister and Druckman, 1973; Druckman *et al.*, 1977) designed to explore the consequences of linking conflicts of interest to general principles of the kind outlined by Schelling (1960, e.g. pp. 30, 34). Subjects were asked to take the role of political decision makers empowered to decide policies for dealing with urban racial problems, and to allocate government funds accordingly. Not surprisingly, linking conflicts of interest to dissensus about more basic values (system-maintenance v. social change) made agreements harder to obtain and decreased the number of pairs who negotiated MJP (maximum joint profit) outcomes by apportioning the entire funds available. However, what is important about this work is that it draws our attention to the facts: (1) that conflicts with an "ideological link" may be perceived as zero-sum (under certain circumstances) and therefore end in deadlock or unilateral domination;[17] and (2) that variables such as "own" v. "assigned" solutions will affect the way negotiators view their decision-making task (also see Daniel, 1976, p. 70).

GROUP POLARIZATION

In certain industrial contexts bargaining proposals may also be "linked" to unwritten rules of custom and practice (C & P) that arise when junior managers and foremen

... bend rules and create increasingly liberal precedents in their efforts to maintain good working relationships with their men (Brown, 1973, p. 107).

Brown's book on *Piecework Bargaining* contains two key arguments: first, that C & P rules "drift on a broad front" (p. 115); and second, that "the further C & P drifts, the stronger it makes the pieceworker at the ratefixer's expense" (p. 118). Indeed, Brown has argued that C & P leniency is the *major* determinant whether bargains will be favourable to management or the worker. But what is of interest here is the finding that *individuals* and *gangs* negotiated changes in rates in fundamentally different ways.

The earnings of individuals showed a "stable ranking pattern" within a given machining group, implying that each person gained fairly small increases whenever he bargained. In contrast some gangs, located in factories with very lenient C & P rules showed a "vintage ranking pattern", implying that wage increases leapfrogged gangs to the top of the earnings distribution in a very competitive way. There are, without doubt, some straightforward reasons for differences of this kind (e.g. the gangs bargained less frequently) but, as Brown himself has noted it is also possible that "Group activity tends to reinforce and polarize attitudes and more extreme bargaining behaviour can be expected to result" (p. 63). Brown's discussion of gangs of fitters in Factory A (p. 80) suggests the operation of a "runaway norm" (Raven and Rubin, 1976) and the more "competitive" behaviour of the gangs is consistent with research on extremity shifts in laboratory negotiation groups (Rabbie and Visser, 1972, RPD3; Lamm and Sauer, 1974, DG2).

Rabbie and Visser's study is particularly interesting since it includes a manipulation of bargaining strength (labour shortage v. over-employment). Subjects prepared for negotiation in three-man groups: but did not, in fact, go on to negotiate the three issues presented to them. Group activity tended to raise the aspirations of the strong, but lower the aspirations of the weak: suggesting that the vintage ranking pattern of earnings would be less marked for gangs in factories where C & P rules favoured management rather than workers.

Gopi Bannerjee and I are attempting to reproduce Rabbie and Visser's work at the University of Warwick, manipulating bargaining strength by varying *strength of case* (Morley and Stephenson, 1977) and observing the effects of polarization (if any) on subsequent negotiations.

ISSUE EMPHASIS

Bonham (1971) and Jervis (1976, pp. 211–216) have suggested that differences in issue emphasis may lead to a kind of tunnel vision in which:

> Actors. . . overestimate the degree to which each understands what the other is going to say. . . they rarely take into full account the degree to which the other may be concerned with different tasks and problems (Jervis, 1976, p. 216).

Bonham used a laboratory task to simulate certain aspects of the disarmament negotiations which took place between 1946 and 1961. Issue emphasis was manipulated by instructing some negotiators to give priority to reducing arms and others to give priority to problems of inspection. Differences in issue emphasis led to extremes of interaction. In some cases negotiators exchanged fewer messages and tried "to avoid the problem" (p. 306). In other cases negotiators exchanged more messages but made more attacks on the motives of others and were less likely to reciprocate concessions. That is to say:

> . . . differences between nations in the relative saliency of the issues may lead to misunderstanding, hostile interaction, few concessions, and a lower probability of eventual agreement (Bonham, 1971, p. 313).

It is important to establish whether such conclusions generalize to other contexts (and, if so, why). From this point of view Rabbie and Visser's (1972) finding that group polarization was more likely to occur on important than unimportant issues is, perhaps, of some relevance.

## Conclusions

The research which I have outlined demonstrates some of the "antecedent conditions" which may be expected to affect the process and outcomes of negotiation groups. However, what is provided is *empirical evidence of input-output correlations rather than a detailed examination of the cognitive and social processes involved.*[19] Only two of the studies cited (Zechmeister and Druckman, 1973; Bonham, 1971) present data describing the process of negotiation. None show how negotiators structure their negotiation task.

Elsewhere, I have argued that studies of negotiation should pay more attention to the processes which lead to the outcomes reported in experimental research (Morley, 1973, 1979b; Morley and Stephenson, 1977) (see also McGrath and Julian, 1963). Here, I want to add that to understand the process of negotiation we need to explore the ways in which negotiators formulate and define the problems they are likely to face. In other words, I want to argue that preparation and process are linked by virtue of the fact that they are *the intra-group and inter-group phases of a complex decision making task.*

There is much that is worthwhile in social psychological studies of negotiation (Druckman, 1977; Morley and Stephenson, 1977), including those I have discussed above, but what is missing is a perspective which *emphasizes the decisions negotiators have to face and locates them within the framework of a general theoretical account of decision making under risk and uncertainty.*

I am not, however, advocating a return to models such as the SEU framework used by Walton and McKersie (1965). Quite properly models of this kind have been viewed with a great deal of suspicion (Abelson, 1976; Milburn and Billings, 1976; Fischhoff, 1976; Slovic *et al.,* 1976; Morley, 1979a). However, a general theory of negotiation requires some account of the ways in which people search for information and choose between alternatives on the basis of the information they obtain. Personally, I think that psychologists could learn a great deal from the accounts of historians (also see Slovic *et al.,* 1976, pp. 177—8): but wherever it comes from, and however it is formulated, *a theory of individual decision making is required.* In addition, some thought must be given to the problem of extending the theory to cover decisions made by groups (see e.g. Steinbruner, 1974, pp. 36—8, 71—8, 124—5; Waddington, 1975).

Of course, individual decision making has been studied much more extensively in cognitive than social psychology and the recent emphasis upon "bounded rationality" (e.g. Slovic, 1972; Simon, 1976a), and heuristic judgement (e.g. Tversky and Kahneman, 1974; Fischhoff, 1976; Pennington *et al.,* 1980) is of considerable interest in the present context (Steinbruner, 1974; Jervis, 1976). Nevertheless, descriptive theory ". . . has not been developed to the point where a systematic model will lead to testable predictions" (Pitz, 1977, p. 420). Janis and Mann's (1977) work shows the value of further effort for cognitive and social psychologists alike (Morley, in press).

However, if we are to develop a theory of decision making likely to illuminate the study of negotiation groups, at least three kinds of move will have to be made. Firstly, it seems important to explore similarities and differences between rational/analytic theories and theories of bounded rationality outlined by Steinbruner (1974), Snyder and Diesing (1977), and Janis and Mann (1977). It is also important to remember that the theories identify "modes of thinking" (Steinbruner) or "decision procedures" (Snyder and Diesing which are likely to vary with the nature of the task (Steinbruner, 1974, p. 136; Snyder and Diesing, 1977, p. 344; Winham, 1977), incorporate elements of bureaucratic politics (Snyder and Diesing, 1977, pp. 348–351), and cannot be assumed automatically to refer to personality types (Steinbruner, 1974, p. 136).

Secondly, social psychologists should pay more attention to the processes which precede (or interrupt) inter-group phases of the decision making task. At the very least this would involve asking questions of the kind outlined by Porat (1969, 1970)[19] and Rabbie and Visser (1972) in previous studies of the goals set by members of negotiation groups. More ambitiously, attempts could be made to collect and analyse verbal protocols (Carroll and Payne, 1976, 1977; Payne et al., 1978); monitor the acquisition of information (Stabell, 1978; Payne et al., 1978); or build computer simulations such as those discussed by Coddington (1968) and Simon (1976b). (Essentially, I am recommending that social psychologists adapt and use techniques more commonly employed in the cognitive domain.)

Finally, I would recommend that experimental studies attempt to build some of the complexities identified by Winham and Steinbruner into laboratory simulations of negotiation groups. Some attempts in this direction have already been made (Stephenson, 1979; Bartos, 1970; Evan and MacDougall, 1967) but much remains to be done. To study negotiation at all we must simplify what is going on (Bartos, 1970; Morley, 1979b), but it is important to recognize that some processes (e.g. concession making) cannot be characterized independently of the contexts in which they occur.

## Notes

1. This paper is a revised version of a draft, "Role playing, role reversal and training in negotiation", presented at a Conference on Group Decision Making organized by the European Association of Experimental Social Psychology (August, 1978: Castle Reisensburg, Nr. Gunzburg, Federal Republic of Germany.

An early version of the present paper was presented to the Social Psychology Research Unit, The University of Kent, under the heading "How negotiators prepare for negotiation: a review of some experimental research" (November 1978: Canterbury). I would like to thank Ivan Steiner, Geoffrey Stephenson, and Nigel Kemp for the Criticism and the encouragement they gave me. Hermann Brandstätter provided valuable editorial comment which helped clarify a number of points.

2. Janis and Mann (1977) have argued that the concept of commitment is central to psychological formulation of any "consequential" decisions.

3. An extended discussion of the part played by cognitive, attitudinal and social commitments is given by Tysoe (1979).

4. Notice that this would lead to the surprising prediction that the smaller the decision latitude of negotiators the greater the effects of person variables, such as the attitudes of negotiators towards their reference groups. Contrast Druckman (1977, p. 30).

5. I am indebted to Stephenson (1978b) from whom I have borrowed this form of words.

6. Pressures from public opinion of the sort faced by Lloyd George and Clemenceau must be regarded as contributing to the force R rather than the force C, e.g. Lloyd George was returned to office in December, 1918, "allegedly on a platform of 'Hang the Kaiser' and 'Make Germany Pay'" (Elcock, 1972, p. 6).

7. Note that even when negotiations are "co-operative" participants have a role obligation to reach agreement in a given time, based on Party's "investment in resolution of the problem" (McGrath, 1966, p. 112). Consequently, if the force R exists only when negotiators are given role obligations, so do some components of the force A.

8. McGrath's model does have the advantage, however, of emphasizing that institutional goals are not always independent of personal "needs" and the relationships which come to the fore "at the bargaining table". (Morley and Stephenson, 1970, 1977).

9. Those who would like to explore the complexities in more detail will find Temperley (1920—1924), Mantoux (1964) and Burnett (1965) particularly useful.

10. See Friend and Jessop (1971, p. 87).

11. The term "exploratory" should not be taken to mean that negotiation is tentative or off the record. Negotiators gain information about the others' interests and resolve from "vehement demands and counter-demands, arguments and counter arguments" (Douglas, 1962, p. 13). For further detail see Morley and Stephenson (1977), Morley (1979c), and Stephenson (1979).

12. A related line of research has attempted to explore the effects of different relationships between representatives and reference groups. Recent reviews of the literature have been given in Klimoski (1978), Breaugh and Klimoski (1977), Klimoski and Breaugh (1977) and Haccoun and Klimoski (1975).

13. Researchers have also considered some of the cognitive and perceptual consequences of participation in cross-assigned groups. See Stern *et al.* (1973, 1975).

14. Morley and Stephenson (1977) and Morley (1979b) have produced a 4 × 3 classification in which laboratory negotiation tasks are described in terms of experimental paradigm they employ and the structure of the issues they include. There are four experimental paradigms — distribution game (DG), game of economic exchange (GEE), role-playing debate (RPD), and substitute debate (SD), and three types of issue — Type 1, Type 2 and Type 3. Combining the two

dimensions — e.g. (SD3) — thus allows the description of experimental tasks in a convenient shorthand form.

15. Muney and Deutsch (1969) have investigated the effects of role reversal during the discussion of opposing points of view. Their data "strikingly failed to confirm the superiority of role-reversal over self presentation as a method of developing favourable interpersonal attitudes, mutual understanding, and agreement in circumstances where there is a pronounced initial conflict of attitudes" (p. 354).

16. During course 1 Exercise Barchester, which required participants to negotiate an overmanning dispute, was used instead of Exercise Venture. Exercise Venture was used on all other courses.

17. Other explanations of Druckman and Zechmeister's data may be possible since the measure of deviation from crompromise was not independent of the amount of money allocated (Druckman and Zechmeister, 1970, p. 436; Zechmeister and Druckman, 1973, p. 75). Suppose, therefore, that A made concessions early in negotiation, inadvertently raising B's level of aspiration, so that concessions were not returned in kind (Siegel and Forraker, 1960; Bartos, 1970). If A became intransigent A and B would be unlikely to agree on other issues and B would have obtained the lion's share of the funds divided between the two.

18. Similar conclusions have been presented in recent reviews of decision-making and cognition (e.g. Pitz, 1977; Payne *et al.*, 1978) so that this tendency is by no means confined to research on negotiation.

19. My own experience suggests that subjects are very unhappy with forced choice procedures of the kind used by Porat, and will give very different replies if asked verbally to report what they were trying to do.

## References

Abelson, R. P. Social psychology's rational man. In Benn, S. I. and Mortimore, G. W. (Eds), *Rationality and the Social Sciences*. London: Routledge & Kegan Paul. pp. 58–89, 1976.

Allison, G. *The Essence of Decision*. Boston: Little, Brown, 1971.

Anthony, P. and Crichton, A. *Industrial Relations and the Personnel Specialists*. London: Batsford, 1969.

Balke, W. M., Hammond, K. R. and Meyer, G. D. An alternate approach to labor-management relations. *Administrative Science Quarterly*, 1973, **18**, 311–327.

Bartos, O. J. Determinants and consequences of toughness. In Swingle, P. (Ed.), *The Structure of Conflict*. New York and London: Academic Press. pp. 45–68, 1970.

Bass, B. M. Effects on the subsequent performance of negotiators of studying issues or planning strategies alone or in groups. *Psychological Monographs: General and Applied*, 1966, **80**.

Batstone, E., Boraston, I. and Frenkel, S. *Shop Stewards in Action: The Organization of Workplace Conflict and Accomodation*. Oxford: Blackwell, 1978.

Benton, A. A. and Druckman, D. Constituents' bargaining orientation and intergroup negotiations, *Journal of Applied Social Psychology*, 1974, **4**, 141–50.

Bonham, M. G. Simulating international disarmament negotiations, *Journal of Conflict Resolution*, 1971, **15**, 299–315.

Brehmer, B. Social judgment theory and the analysis of interpersonal conflict. *Umea Psychological Reports No. 87*. Umea, Sweden: University of Umea, 1975.

Brehmer, B. and Hammond, K. R. Cognitive factors in interpersonal conflict. In Druckman, D. (Ed.), *Negotiations: Social Psychological Perspectives*. Beverley Hills: Sage. pp. 79–103, 1977.

Breaugh, J. A. and Klimoski, R. J. The choice of a group spokesman in bargaining: member or outsider. *Organizational Behaviour and Human Performance*, 1977, 19, 325–336.

Brown, W. *Piecework Bargaining*. London: Heinemann Educational, 1973.

Brown, W. and Terry, M. The importance of continuity to an understanding of bargaining, paper presented at a symposium on Psychology & Industrial Relations, Nottingham: Annual Conference of the British Psychological Society, April, 1975.

Burnett, P. M. *Reparation at the Paris Peace Conference: From the Standpoint of the American Delegation, Vols. I and II*. New York: Octagon Books, 1965.

Campbell, R. J. *Originality in Group Productivity, III: Partisan Commitment and Productive Independence in a Collective Bargaining Situation*, Office of Naval Research Contract Nonr-495(15)(NR 170-396). Columbus, Ohio: Ohio State University Research Foundation, 1960.

Carroll, J. S. and Payne, J. W. The psychology of the parole decision process: a joint application of attribution theory and information processing psychology. In Carroll, J. S. and Payne, J. W. (Eds) *Cognition and Social Behavior*. London: Wiley. pp. 13–32, 1976.

Carroll, J. S. and Payne, J. W. Judgments about crime and the criminal: a model and a method for investigating parole decisions. In Sales, B. E. (Ed). *Perspectives in Law and Psychology, Vol. I, The Criminal Justrice System*. London: Plenum Press. pp. 191–239, 1977.

Chalmers, W. E. and Cormick, G. W. (Eds) *Racial Conflict and Negotiations: Perspectives and First Case Studies*. Ann Arbor, Mich.: Institute of Labor and Industrial Relations, University of Michigan — Wayne State University and the National Center for Dispute Settlement of The American Arbitration Association, 1971.

Chamberlain, N. W. *Collective Bargaining (1st edition)*. New York: McGraw-Hill, 1951.

Coddington, A. *Theories of the Bargaining Process*. London: George Allen and Unwin, 1968.

Daniel, W. W. *Wage Determination in Industry*. London: P. E. P., 1976.

Douglas, A. *Industrial Peacemaking*. New York: Columbia University Press, 1962.

Druckman, D. Dogmatism, pre-negotiation experience and simulated group representation as determinants of dyadic behaviour in a bargaining situation. *Journal of Personality and Social Psychology*, 1967, 6, 279–90.

Druckman, D. Prenegotiation experience and dyadic conflict resolution in a bargaining situation. *Journal of Experimental Social Psychology*, 1968, 4, 367–83.

Druckman, D. The influence of the situation in interparty conflict. *Journal of Conflict Resolution*, 1971, 15, 522–554.

Druckman, D. Human factors in international negotiations: social psychological aspects of international conflict. *Sage Professional Paper in International Studies 02-020*. Beverley Hills: Sage, 1973.

Druckman, D. (Ed.) *Negotiations: Social Psychological Perspectives.* Beverley Hills: Sage, 1977.

Druckman, D. and Zechmeister, K. Conflict of interest and value dissensus. *Human Relations,* 1970, 23, 431–8.

Druckman, D., Solomon, D. and Zechmeister, K. Effects of representational role obligations on the process of children's distribution of resources. *Sociometry,* 1972, 35, 387–410.

Druckman, D., Rozelle, R. and Zechmeister, K. Conflict of interest and value dissensus: two perspectives. In Druckman, D. (Ed.), *Negotiations: Social Psychological Perspectives.* Beverley Hills: Safe, pp. 105–131, 1977.

Elcock, H. *Portrait of a Decision: The Council of Four and the Treaty of Versailles.* London: Eyre Methuen, 1972.

Evan, W. M. and MacDougall, J. A. Interorganizational conflict: a labor-management bargaining experiment. *Journal of Conflict Resolution,* 1967, 11, 398–413.

Fischhoff, B. Attribution theory and judgement under uncertainty. In Harvey, J. H., Ickes, W. J. & Kidd, R. F. (Eds), *New Directions in Attribution Research.* Hillsdale, N. J.: Lawrence Erlbaum Associates, 1976.

Fisher, R. *Basic Negotiating Strategy: International Conflict for Beginners.* London: Allen Lane, 1969.

Friend, J. K and Jessop, W. N. *Local Government and Strategic Choice.* Oxford: Pergamon Press, 1971.

Haccoun, R. R. and Klimoski, R. J. Negotiator status and accountability source: a study of negotiator behaviour. *Organizational Behaviour and Human Performance,* 1975, 14, 342–359.

Hankey, (Lord) *The Supreme Control at the Paris Peace Conference 1919.* London: George Allen and Unwin, 1963.

Harbison, F. H. and Coleman, J. R. *Goals and Strategy in Collective Bargaining.* New York: Harper, 1951.

Holsti, O. Cognitive dynamics and images of the enemy. In Farrell, J. C. and Smith, A. P. (Eds) *Image and Reality in World Politics* New York and London: Columbia University Press, p. 16–39, 1967.

Ikle, F. C. *How Nations Negotiate.* New York: Harper and Row, 1964.

Ikle, F. C. and Leites, N. Political negotiation as a process of modifying utilities. *Journal of Conflict Resolution,* 1962, 6, 19–28.

Janis, I. L. Decisional conflicts: a theoretical analysis. *Journal of Conflict Resolution,* 1959, 3, 6–27.

Janis, I. L. *Victims of Groupthink: A Psychological Study of Foreign-policy Decisions and Fiascos.* Boston, Mass.: Houghton-Mifflin, 1972.

Janis, I. L. Counteracting the adverse effects of concurrence — seeking in policy-planning groups: theory and research perspectives. Paper presented at Conference on Group Decision Making organized by the European Association of Experimental Social Psychology; Castle Reisensburg, Near Grunzburg, Federal Republic of Germany, August 6–11, 1978.

Janis, I. L. and Mann, L. *Decision Making: A Psychological Analysis of Conflict, Choice and Commitment.* New York: The Free Press. London: Collier MacMillan, 1977.

Jervis, R. *Perception and Misperception in International Politics.* Princeton, N. J.: Princeton University Press, 1976.

Kahn, A. S. and Kohls, J. W. Determinants of toughness in dyadic bargaining. *Sociometry,* 1972, 35, 305–15.

Kelley, H. H. Interaction process and the attainment of maximum joint profit.

In Messick, S. & Brayfield, A. H. (Eds) *Decision and Choice.* New York: McGraw-Hill, pp. 240—50, 1964.

Kelley, H. H. and Schenitzki, D. P. Bargaining. In McClintock, C. G. (Ed.), *Experimental Social Psychology.* New York: Holt, Rinehart and Winston, pp. 298—337, 1972.

Kelley, H. H. and Thibaut, J. W. Group problem-solving. In Lindzey, G. and Aronson, E. (Eds), *Handbook of Social Psychology, Vol. 4.* Reading, Mass.: Addison-Wesley, pp. 1—101, 1969.

Kelley, H. H., Beckman, L. L. and Fischer, C. S. Negotiating the division of a reward under incomplete information. *Journal of Experimental Social Psychology,* 1967, 3, 361—98.

Keynes, J. M. *Essays in Biography.* London: Mercury paper edition, 1961.

Klimoski, R. J. The effects of intragroup forces on intergroup forces on intergroup conflict resolution. *Organizational Behaviour and Human Performance,* 1972, 8, 363—83.

Klimoski, R. J. Simulation methodologies in experimental research on negotiations by representatives. *Journal of Conflict Resolution,* 1978, 22, 61—77.

Klimoski, R. J. and Breaugh, J. A. When performance doesn't count: a constituency looks at its spokesman. *Organizational Behaviour and Human Performance,* 1977, 20, 301—311.

Lamm, H. Some recent research on negotiation behaviour. Paper presented at the European Association of Experimental Social Psychology Conference, Bielefeld, West Germany, April, 1975.

Lamm, H and Sauer, C. Discussion induced shift toward higher demands in negotiation. *European Journal of Social Psychology,* 1974, 4, 85—88.

McGrath, J. E. A social psychological approach to the study of negotiation. In Bowers, R. (Ed.) *Studies on Behaviour in Organizations: A Research Symposium.* Athens, Georgia: University of Georgia Press, pp. 101—34, 1966.

McGrath, J. E. and Julian, J. W. Interaction process and task outcomes in experimentally created negotiation groups. *Journal of Psychological Studies,* 1963, 14, 117—38.

McKersie, R. B. and Hunter, L. C. *Pay, Productivity and Collective Bargaining.* London: MacMillan, 1973.

Mantoux, P. *Paris Peace Conference 1919: Proceedings of the Council of Four (March 24—April 18).* Geneva: Librairie Droz, 1964.

Marsh, P. D. V. Contract Negotiation Handbook. Gower Press, 1974.

Midgaard, K. Cooperative negotiations and bargaining: some notes on power and powerlessness. In Barry, B. M. (Ed.), *Power and Political Theory: Some European Perspectives.* London: Wiley, pp. 117—137, 1976.

Midgaard, K. and Underdal, A. Multiparty conferences. In Druckman, D. (Ed.), *Negotiations: Social Psychological Perspectives.* Beverley Hills: Sage. pp. 329—345, 1977.

Milburn, T. W. and Billings, R. S. Decision-making perspectives from psychology: dealing with risk and uncertainty. *American Behavioural Scientist,* 1976, 20, 111—126.

Morley, I. E. Behavioural studies of industrial bargaining. In Stephenson, G. M. and Brotherton, C. J. (Eds). *Industrial Relations: A Social Psychological Approach.* London: Wiley. pp. 211—236, 1979a.

Morley, I. E. The character of experimental studies of bargaining and negotiation.

In Brandstätter, H., Davis, J. H. and Schuler, H. (Eds). *Dynamics of Group Decisions*. Beverley Hills: Sage. pp. 175–206, 1979b.

Morley, I. E. Leadership and negotiation: a comparison of some British and American research. Paper presented to a Workshop on European Perspectives in the Application of Social Psychology, Cartmel, Cumbria; European Association of Experimental Social Psychology; 2–6 January, 1979c.

Morley, I. E. Review of Janis, I. L. and Mann, L. (1977), Decision making: a psychological analysis of conflict, choice and commitment. *British Journal of Psychology*, 1979, 70, 170–171.

Morley, I. E. and Stephenson, G. M. Strength of case, communication systems, and the outcomes of simulated negotiations: some social psychological aspects of bargaining. *Industrial Relations Journal*, 1970, 1, 19–20.

Morley, I. E. and Stephenson, G. M. *The Social Psychology of Bargaining*. London: George Allen and Unwin, 1977.

Morley, I. E., Tysoe, M. and Stephenson, G. M. Role reversal and preparation for negotiation in management training groups. Paper presented at London Conference of the British Psychological Society, December 1977, 1978.

Muney, B. F. and Deutsch, M. The effects of role reversal during the discussion of opposing viewpoints. *Journal of Conflict Resolution*, 1968, 12, 345–360.

Nicholson, H. *Peacemaking, 1919*. London: Methuen, 1964.

Oppenheim, A. N. and Bayley, J. C. R. Productivity and conflict. *Proceedings of the International Peace Research Association, 3rd General Conference*. Essen: Netherlands: Van Gorcum, 1970.

Patchen, M. Models of cooperation and conflict: a critical review. *Journal of Conflict Resolution*, 1970, 14, 389–407.

Payne, J. W., Braunstein, M. L. and Carroll, J. S. Exploring predecisional behaviour: an alternative approach to decision research. *Organizational Behaviour of Human Performance*, 1978, 22, 17–44.

Pennington, D. C. Rutter, D. R., McKenna, K. and Morley, I. E. Estimating the outcome of a pregnancy test: women's judgements in foresight and hindsight. *British Journal of Social and Clinical Psychology*, 1980, 19, 317–324.

Pitz, G. F. Decision making and cognition. In Jungermann, H. and G. de (Eds) *Decision Making and Change in Human Affairs*. Dordrecht-Holland: D. Reidel. pp. 403–424, 1977.

Porat, A. M. *Planning and Role Assignment in the Study of Conflict Resolution: A Study of Two Countries*. Technical Report No. 28. Rochester, NY: Management Research Center of the College of Business Administration, University of Rochester, 1969.

Porat, A. M. Cross-cultural differences in resolving union-management conflict through negotiations. *Journal of Applied Psychology*, 1970, 54, 441–51.

Rabbie, J. M. and Visser, L. Bargaining strength and group polarization in intergroup negotiations. *European Journal of Social Psychology*, 1972, 2, 401–416.

Raven, B. and Rubin, J. *Social Psychology: People in Groups*. London: Wiley, 1976.

Schelling, T. C. *The Strategy of Conflict*. New York: Harvard University Press. Reissued as Oxford University Press paperback (1968). References are to OUP edn. 1960.

Siegel, S. and Fouraker, L. E. *Bargaining and Group Decision Making.* New York: McGraw-Hill, 1960.

Simon, H. A. *Administrative Behaviour: A Study of Decision-Making Processes in Administrative Organization.* (3rd edn.). New York: Free Press, 1976a.

Simon, H. A. Discussion: cognition and social behaviour. In Carroll, J. S. and Payne, J. W. (Eds) *Cognition and Social Behaviour.* London: Wiley. pp. 253—267, 1976b.

Slovic, P. From Shakespeare to Simon: speculations and some evidence about man's ability to process information. *Oregon Research Institute Research Bulletin,* 1972, **12**, (2).

Slovic, P., Fischhoff, B. and Lichtenstein, S. Cognitive processes and societal risk taking. In Carroll, J. S. and Payne, J. W. (Eds), *Cognition and Social Behaviour.* Hillsdale, N. J.: Lawrence Erlbaum Associates. pp. 165—184, 1976.

Snyder, G. H. and Diesing, P. *Conflict Among Nations: Bargaining, Decision Making, and System Structure in International Crises.* Princeton, N. J.: Princeton University Press, 1977.

Stabell, C. B. Integrative complexity of information environment perception and information use: an empirical investigation. *Organizational Behaviour and Human Performance,* 1978, **22**, 116—142.

Steinbruner, J. D. *The Cybernetic Theory of Decision.* Princeton, New Hersey: Princeton University Press, 1974.

Stephenson, G. M. Inter-group relations and negotiating behaviour. In Warr, P. B. (Ed), *Psychology at Work.* Harmondsworth: Penguin. pp. 347—73, 1971a.

Stephenson, G. M. Negotiation and collective bargaining. In Warr, P. B. (Ed), *Psychology at Work* (2nd edn.) Harmondsworth: Penguin. pp. 187—207, 1978a.

Stephenson, G. M. Intergroup negotiations and bargaining. Paper presented at the British Psychological Society Social Psychology Section One Day Conference on 'The Social Psychology of Intergroup Behaviour'. University of Bristol, November 18th, 1978b.

Stephenson, G. M. Interparty and interpersonal exchange in negotiation groups. In Brandstätter, H., Davis, J. H. and Schuler, H. (Eds), *Dynamics of Group Decisions.* Beverley Hills: Safe pp. 207—228, 1979.

Stephenson, G. M. Skinner, M. and Brotherton, C. J. Group participation and intergroup relations: an experimental study of negotiation groups. *European Journal of Social Psychology,* 1976, **6**, (1), 51—70.

Stern, L. W., Sternthal, B. and Craig, C. S. (1973) Managing Conflict in distribution channels: a laboratory study. *Journal of Marketing Research,* 1973, **10**, 169—179.

Stern, L. W., Sternthal, B. and Craig, C. S. (1975) Strategies for managing interorganizational conflict: a laboratory paradigm. *Journal of Applied Psychology,* 1975, **60**, 472—482.

Temperley, H. *A History of the Peace Conference of Paris, Vol. I.* London: Oxford University Press (Reprinted 1969), 1920.

Temperley, H. W. V. *A History of the Peace Conference of Paris, Vol. VI.* London: Oxford University Press. (Reprinted 1969), 1924.

Tversky, A. and Kahneman, D. Judgment under uncertainty: heuristics and biases. *Science,* 1974, **185**, 1124—1131.

Tysoe, M. *An Experimental Study of the Efficacy of Some Procedural Role*

*Requirements in Simulated Negotiations.* Ph.D. Thesis: University of Nottingham, 1979.

Vidmar, N. and McGrath, J. E. *Role Assignment and Attitudinal Commitment as Factors in Negotiation.* Technical Report No. 3. AFOSR Contract AF49 (638)-1291. Urbana, Ill: Department of Psychology, University of Illinois, 1965.

Vidmar, N. and McGrath, J. E. *Role Structure, Leadership and Negotiation Effectiveness.* Technical Report No. 6, AFOSR Contract AF49 (638)-1291. Urbana, Ill.: Department of Psychology, University of Illinois, 1967.

Waddington, J. Social decision schemes and two person-bargaining. *Behavioural Science,* 1975, 20, 157–165.

Walcott, C., Hopmann, P. T. and King, T. D. The role of debate in negotiation. In Druckman, D. (Ed.), *Negotiations: Social Psychological Perspectives.* Beverley Hills: Sage pp. 193–211, 1977.

Walton, R. E. and McKersie. R. B. A Behavioural Theory of Labor Negotiations: An Analysis of a Social Interaction System. New York: McGraw-Hill, 1965.

Warr, P. B. *Psychology and Collective Bargaining.* London: Hutchinson, 1973.

Wilson, A. *War Gaming.* Harmondsworth: Penguin Books, 1970.

Winham, G. R. Complexity in international negotiation. In Druckman, D. (Ed), *Negotiations: Social Psychological Perspectives.* Beverley Hills: Sage pp. 347–366, 1977.

Zartman, I. W. Negotiation as a joint decision-making process. In Zartman, I. W. (Ed.) *The Negotiation Process: Theories and Applications.* Beverley Hills: Sage p. 67–86, 1977.

Zechmeister, K. and Druckman, D. Determinants of resolving a conflict of interest: a simulation of political decision-making. *Journal of Conflict Resolution,* 1973, 17, 63–88.

# V
# Social Influences on Individual Judgement

# Introduction

Gisela Stocker-Kreichgauer

The papers presented in this section, while departing from very different theoretical orientations, concentrate on individual behaviour within or caused by social interaction and not on the social interaction itself.

In continental phenomenological psychology, as in philosophy, it has been pointed out that man has a double nature as an individual and as an *animal sociale,* i.e. as a member of groups of different sizes and different characteristics, such as the family, the class at school, the working group, and various other political, ideological, and cultural assemblages. Contrary to Leibniz's theory of monads, man is not considered to be a "windowless monade" developing his innate abilities exclusively by determination of inner laws. He is regarded instead as endowed by a genetic potential dependent on external stimulation and practice, which include feedback loops enabling the individual to control his behavioural progress in different areas such as cognitive, social, and motor skills.

The individual's social adjustment has two aspects. In the first place individual behaviour can be affected by social influence such as pressure toward conformity. A person feeling under social pressure in a group, whether real or imaginary, not only has to solve the problems in question but also has to take into account his own actual social position within the group and his possible future status when submitting or resisting to the pressure of the group members. Conformity and non-conformity of the individual may have very different roots in individual motivation, as Asch pointed out. Hatcher, in his chapter in this volume discusses conformity behaviour under the view of individual arousal reduction. Other explanations such as curiosity about others' reactions, sympathy, and the desire to be accepted by others may also be valid and work in combination with the arousal variable.

Secondly, individual behaviour can be addressed to its social content, indicated here as social or person perception, as social emotions and social motivation. It is obvious that the two areas of social adjustment are intimately linked to each other, and they are therefore often studied in combination.

The two main prerequisites of social influence on an individual's behaviour are the perception, and the cognitive and social-emotional elaboration of social stimuli by the individual. Both depend on genetic factors and on maturation as well as on the actual condition of the individual and his learning history. The work of Gabriel Mugny and Willem Doise pertains to cognitive development by social influence, accentuating the maturation of cognitive functions as a prerequisite of such stimulating effects of social influence.

Social influence which is effective on the individual can be seen as giving the individual, in his cognitive and emotional as well as motivational potential, his first structure. This works usually in a cumulative way, rarely by one-trial-learning, and enables the individual to react in future situations in a similar way to that learned in the past. Changes in the social expectations and/or the confrontation with changed behaviour of others may force the individual to change his learned structures and to find a new adjustment by developing new structures, or by finding a way to integrate the past and the present demands of the social environment into modified structures. These changes often take place when the individual enters a new phase of cognitive maturation or when he leaves one social assemblage to join another one.

The cognitive preconditions of effective social adjustment are various and very complex in their interaction. First there should be mentioned the ability to discriminate various stimulus situations and to accentuate those stimuli relevant for differential reactions in a given situation. Secondly, the individual must be able to choose the best reaction for the situation with regard to his own objectives; he has to anticipate various feedbacks from his partners and his own organism (external and internal feedback caused by the reaction) and to discern the actual feedback from other stimuli existing in the situation. He also has to control his behaviour guided by continuous feedback evaluation, drawing comparisons between the expected and the actual feedback, and modifying his objectives on the basis of these data if necessary.

The goals of the individual in a given social context may be related to different dimensions. On the cognitive dimension the individual may aim at some knowledge about social interrelations between others or between others and himself as well as, with a more diagnostic intention, about personality traits underlying other persons' behaviour. With regard to the individual's emotional aims he may be interested in reducing fear and arousal as well as increasing his pleasure and satisfaction. Concerning the motivational dimension, the individual may seek satisfaction of his various social motives, such as the desire of affiliation or dominance, while on the action dimension the individual may strive towards dealing with other people in a manner dictated by the other three dimensions mentioned above. The individual acquires manifold impressions corresponding to the different goal dimensions from his social environment; these are often worked out as attitudes toward special aspects of social situations, persons, and behaviours in social contexts.

The active and constructive role the individual takes in social interaction must be stressed. The individual, when changing roles from source to receiver of information in a social interaction, not only selects from the social environment the stimuli relevant for himself and accentuates them in his interactional behaviour, but also determines to some degree by his communication strategy the frame within which his partner can react, thus influencing in an indirect manner his own social environment (interactionism). Furthermore, the individual not only influences his own social environment by his choices in the actual situation but also by choosing special social environments conducive to the attainment of his short-term and long-term objectives. This is less true for experimental laboratory situations where the experimenter sets the conditions under which the individual has to work, though even this leaves to the individual possibilities of inner emigration and sabotage often not apparent to the experimenter, since the individual's usual behaviour is not generally known.

Mugny and Doise who, like Piaget, stress the essential role of social interaction in cognitive development, report in their paper some recent experimental results relating to the development of cognitive structures of children facing socio-cognitive conflict. Children not able to solve a special task when working alone are confronted with solutions of peers or of the experimenter himself, differing from their own incorrect answers to the task. In early developmental stages of the cognitive abilities necessary to solve the task children do not gain by the conflicting answers, presumably because they place their own and the partner's solution additively side by side. In later cognitive development they gain the ability to change the different points of view and to choose the one which seems themselves most appropriate to the task. The cognitive progress, tested in a single-group—single-procedure, often survives the social situation by internalization of the new solution strategy, which is made apparent by progress between the two single tests, which use differing tasks to exclude mere memory effects. The cognitive processes related to such progress are located in the memory of the child as well as in the actual functioning in problem solving. Cognitive structures learned in the past are modified or abandoned in favour of other cognitive processes of higher complexity including the perception of the relativity of different points of view. The new cognitive structures are prepared by cognitive maturation and actualized by socio-cognitive conflict. Mugny and Doise accentuate in their paper that similar results are found when the children are confronted with different types of tasks, such as spatial transformations, length conservation when the position of the objects is varied, and a cooperative game using a "moveable pencil" within a tracing task. Concerning the underlying theory of cognitive development, the authors refer to the studies of Piaget. Future experiments about the role of social interaction in cognitive development include systematic observations of the interaction stages in order to find the relations between specific interactional variables and cognitive progress.

Hatcher, in contrast to Mugny and Doise, uses an evolutionary approach to social behaviour. He chooses the arousal or activation level of the individual as the critical variable in behaviour prognosis, proposing that the individual will try to hold a subjectively optimal level of arousal.

Hatcher's hypothesis is

"that if the arousal level of the organism in question differs from the optimum, there will be a tendency, increasing with the magnitude of the difference, to emit that response whose PEA-value (PEA means potential effects on arousal) most closely represents a return to that optimal level.

Concerning the PEA-value of responses, Hatcher states that it varies inter- and intra-individually depending on genetic and learned factors.

When isolating the arousal level as the critical variable in behaviour prognosis, it must be realized that every behaviour can be evaluated by the individual on different dimensions. For example, it can be regarded relative to its external, material, and social, consequences as well as to its internal consequences related to cognitive, emotional, and motivational dimensions including effects on self-evaluation responses. The individual may accentuate one special expected consequence as Hatcher points out in his arousal hypothesis, or may balance many different supposed consequences when choosing his reaction. The rules governing the accentuation and balance processes are not clear at present.

The range of tolerance of arousal differences from the optimum level needs to be studied, the question of whether the optimum level should be regarded as a point or as an area on the subjective arousal scale. It is plausible that the optimum level is subject to intra-individual changes depending on internal variables and on situational variables including the freedom in choice of behaviour. Perhaps there are even periodical changes associated with the feeling of pleasant tension and relaxation within the individual. Additionally, the individual may choose one behaviour or a series of behaviours with calculated additive affects on arousal: this presumably would depend on the subjective attribution of the arousal by the individual and his expectation of being able to change it within different time intervals (immediately, in the long run, or at all).

The advantage of simplicity in behaviour explanation and prognosis implied by the optimal arousal hypothesis leads to a high level of abstraction in that area. Hatcher attempts to submit his hypothesis to an experimental test in an Asch-type situation in which two responses are possible: conformity and independence. Arousal of subjects was manipulated by exposing them to differentially exciting films. Hatcher gives evidence that conformity behaviour seems to be less arousing than independent behaviour and tests the hypothesis that subjects in the more aroused group will show more conformity than subjects in the less aroused group. He also gives an impression of the difficulties of arousal manipulation and arousal measurement arising in that context. Hatcher uses two kinds of arousal measurement, the physiological measurement of the subjects' heart rate in the experimental situation itself and subjects' ex-post ratings of arousal taken at the end of the experiment. The problems of such ex-post measures are discussed, as are possible cognitive interpretations of the results.

# 19
# Social Interactions in Cognitive Development

Gabriel Mugny and Willem Doise

One explanation of collective polarization phenomena refers to the cognitive structures developed by groups in specific situations. At the Ottobeuren Conference, Doise (1978) argued that, although isolated individuals can deal with a problem from quite heterogeneous viewpoints and thereby give quite different responses, this is often no longer the case in a group situation, where a more unidimensional approach to a given problem takes the place of the multidimensional individual ones. Through the reanalysis of a previous experiment as well as by some new experiments, the authors were able to show how different indices (such as response variability, hierarchical structure of different criteria, transitivity of choices) indicate that the groups having to reach a consensus (and it may be generalized to situations where consensus is not requested but where group members confront their viewpoints):

> organize the task material to a greater degree than individuals who make decisions, on the same material, alone. It is a process which takes place when there is collective polarization, which probably accounts for some of this organization. Indeed, once a dimension is made salient or, if the criteria of decisions are well hierarchicalized, judgments and decisions can become very clearcut, as demonstrated in group polarization studies. (Doise, 1978, p. 79.)

Of interest here is the fact that the same cognitive processes underlie decisions made by groups of children of 10—12 years of age

The experiments presented here have been realized within the scope of the contract No. 1.343.0.76 with the F.N.R.S.

(Doise, 1973) who had to express their preferences for eight different pictures (constructed following three dichotomous criteria). The groups presented more hierarchical choices than did individuals alone. In the same vein, groups having to express their preferences for professions (by a paired comparisons technique) showed fewer intransitive choices than individuals working alone.

In the preceding experiments with children, no individual post-measures were taken, so that no subsequent effect of social interaction could be assessed. Indeed, the pretest/post-test paradigm in studying the effects of such interactions may take a quite different meaning with children than with adults, since it is necessary to consider children as developing cognitive structures, whereas most of the experiments on group polarization seem to deal with the actualization of potential, preconstructed attitudes. Therefore, the effects of social interaction in cognitive development will be the focal point of this chapter.

## Hypothesis and general design of the experiments

HYPOTHESIS

Our main hypothesis was that social interactions intervene in cognitive development (taken in the Piagetian sense); this means that cognitive development would be intimately linked to the social interactions in which children participate. In essence, we attempted to produce situations in the laboratory which would allow us to look at how social interaction is related to cognitive development in "natural settings." Thus, what cognitive development realizes in "naturalistic settings." we, as social scientists, tried to actualize through our experimental paradigms. The aim of this chapter, then, is to report some experiments performed in Geneva, showing how group situations do or do not lead children to construct more structurized cognitive solutions during the interaction than those same children could do working individually, as well as how they lead individuals to internalize such cognitive structures, i.e. to show individually some cognitive progress during the post-test.

We also hypothesized that one important mechanism of social interaction is that of socio-cognitive conflict. In a study dealing with the social origin of decentrations, Smedslund (1966) developed the idea that children can progress when confronted with the centrations of others, even when the latter are in error. Centrations are here to be understood (in the Piagetian sense) as more elementary cognitive schemes which have to be coordinated in more complex cognitive structures in order to give rise to operational thinking. As the rationale of our thesis, we are placing the role of the socio-cognitive conflict in its very core. If a child, all by himself, approaches reality with successive and different centrations, these differences become explicit when two individuals are engaged at the same time on the same problem with opposing centrations. Such simultaneity unveils the more urgent necessity of coordinating those insufficient centrations.

SUBJECTS

Since our interest was the social development of concrete operational thought, the subjects we have used in most of our experiments are pupils in public schools for children (approximately 5–6 years of age) and in elementary schools (about 6–8 years old) in the Geneva region. When this is not the case, the experimental place will be indicated. In general, one half of the pupils are girls, and the other half boys. (If perhaps this could not be exactly arranged in a given case, we have endeavoured to have a similar proportion of girls and boys across different experimental conditions.)

GENERAL PARADIGM

The general paradigm of the experiments presented here follows the individual-group-individual procedure. During the first phase, subjects are individually pretested on one task (and sometimes on related ones) in order to establish indvidual scores and/or their cognitive level on the task. In the second phase, subjects interact in groups of two or three, or with an adult experimenter, in different experimental conditions. During the third phase (these phases are separated from each other by approximately one week) the subjects are individually post-tested in order to establish their new score and/or their new cognitive level in the task (and sometimes in related ones). The prepost difference in scores and/or in cognitive level constitutes the main interest of these experiments, even though emphasis is also given to the group process during the experimental phase.

The experimental plans were designed allowing for comparisons of the different conditions of interaction among themselves. Sometimes individual control conditions have also been employed.

In principle, the experimenter avoided interfering, beyond the standardized norms, with the procedure of interactions. The interaction times varied from one group to another. However, certain precise limits were imposed, for example, ten minutes per item in the Task I. Where individual controls were employed care was taken to insure that the average time of their task performance would not differ from other experimental conditions (for instance, by increasing the number of items).

Finally, it should be mentioned that the original data are presented in the tables in a summary way, i.e. without detailed statistical (ordinarily non-parametric) measures. The interested reader may consult the original papers for the appropriate statistics. Also, the analysis will centre only around the significant results.

TASKS

We will now summarize three different tasks which were used in the various experiments presented here. For the first task involving spatial transformations, a detailed description is given by Mugny and Doise (1978) and for the second one, a task of length conservation, by Doise *et al.* (1976). The materials and instructions for the third paradigm are reported by Doise and Mugny (1975). In the rest of the paper, we will refer to each paradigm as Task I, Task II, and Task III, respectively. Only those procedural differences that are important for a specific experiment will be added to the experiment's description.

*Task I (spatial transformation)*
As represented in Fig. 1, subjects have to make a copy (on Table 1) of a "village" made by the experimenter on Table 2, with three or four toy houses. For a simple item, the orientation of the support of the village, indicated by a mark (a lake or a mountain for the children) is the "same" (in the frontoparallel plane) for the model village and for the copy. Difficulty is introduced in the critical trials by modifying the perceptual relations between the marks and the child in the copy and in the model village (see Fig. 1), and by forbidding the subject to move away from their assigned position. Usually, in the individual tests, a simple item (introducing the task for the subjects) is followed by two complex items. The children's best performance on those two items is used as the criterion for the classification at one of three different levels. (1) At an initial level

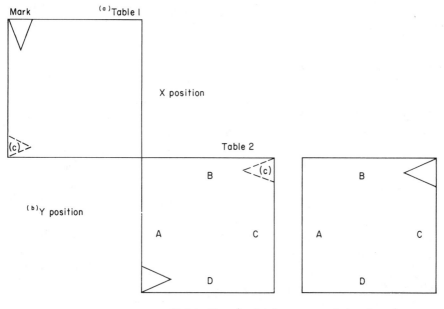

Model village (each letter corresponds to a house)

(b) Complex item          (b) Simple item

Fig. 1. Schema of Task 1.
(a) Subjects have to make on Table 1 the same village as the one made by the experimenter on Table 2.
(b) During the individual test subjects are standing in the Y position. The example of simple and complex items is given for subjects in the Y position. For each single experiment the position the subjects occupy during the interactive phase will be precisely given.
(c) Position of the marks for the experiment discussed in the sections "The conflict of opposed centrations" and "Sociocultural handicap and Task 1".

(NC: no compensation), subjects do not make the transformations or compensations necessary for a correct copy; they only apply a 90° rotation to the village without taking the changes in orientation of the marks into account. (2) At an intermediary level (PC: partial compensation) subjects are capable of partial compensations: they take into account the change of orientation, but they realize the necessary inversions for only one spatial relation (for instance, left/right, or front/behind). (3) At a final level, (TC: total compensation) they are able to transform correctly both relations together.

In this task, the progress is established when an initially NC subject becomes PC or TC during the post-test, or when an initially PC subject becomes TC.

### Task II (length conservation)

Two equal rulers are placed parallel to each other, and all children participating (from five years at least) accept that they are of equal length. But, if one displaces one ruler so that the ends do not coincide any more, the subjects state at a first stage (NC: non conservers) that one ruler is longer than the other. If one again places the rulers so that their ends coincide, these subjects once more accept their equality in length. If one moves the other ruler, they will again think that one ruler is longer, because they are centred on one difference, not taking the complementary one into account. At an intermediary level (I) subjects sometimes accept the conservation, often without argument, and sometimes they do not. At a superior stage (C: conservers), they always recognize the conservation of the length, notwithstanding the perceptual arrangements, and they are able to present arguments about it.

This was the case of the equal length conservation test. Let us look now at the unequal length conservation test. When two unequal chains are put in parallel ( ═════ ), children easily notice the unequal length of both chains. When the longer chain is modified so that the two ends of the chain correspond ( ⌒‿⌒ ), NC (non conservers) subjects think that now the two chains are of equal length; the intermediate subjects continue to judge the longest chain as correct. When the modifications of the longest chain is accentuated in such a way that it perceptually seems shorter ( ∿∿ ), intermediate as well as NC subjects judge the shorter chain as being the longest. C (conservers) subjects are correct in all items and can argue for the length conservation.

In this task progress is established when an initially NC subject becomes I or C during the post-test, or when an initially I subject becomes C.

### Task III (cooperative game)

The "cooperative game" (see Fig. 2) may be played by one child (turning around the game), or two or three children. Three pulleys are tied to a "moveable pencil" (which makes a drawing line), which had to be moved so that it follows as exactly as possible the "road" delineated on a protocol sheet. Subjects complete this task as

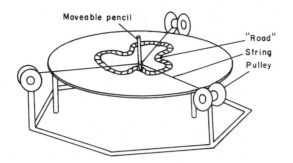

Fig. 2. Schema of the cooperative game.

individuals during a pre- and post-test, and as individuals or in groups during an experimental phase. The individual performance is evaluated on only one-third (in length) of the "road." Subjects have to manipulate the three pulleys, turning around the bale if necessary. When not manipulated, a pulley is blocked so that the subject cannot move it even by pulling very strongly on another one.

The performance score is evaluated as follows. The "road" to be followed is divided into three parts (in width). If the drawing remains in the central part of the "road," it means that there is no problem for the subjects (scored: $+1$); if the drawings touch one of the external thirds of the "road," it means that subjects have some difficulty (scored: $0$); if the drawing line goes out of the "road", it means that subjects have a serious problem of coordination (scored: $-1$). This scoring is applied to the 60 divisions of half a centimetre in the length of the "road." If the child realizes the task all the way without any difficulty, the score would by $+60$; if the drawing line always goes out of the "road," the score would be $-60$. Thus, in this paradigm, distinctions are not made in terms of stages (as would be possible), but in terms of performance scores. Let us say only that the scores are globally very similar to what we would have obtained from a stage analysis.

## INTRA-SITUATIONAL AND EXTRA-SITUATIONAL FACTORS IN SOCIOCOGNITIVE INTERACTIONS

The experiments presented here are of three types. The first type manipulated intra-situational factors in groups where the subjects were seen as "inter-changeable." In the second type, subjects were no longer considered "inter-changeable," since extra-situational variables (such as norms, status, or whether or not the subject was a foreigner) were manipulated. The last set of experiments attempted to provide a link between the first two types by manipulating both intra-situational and extra-situational variables within a single experimental setting.

### Intra-situational variables

Initial experiments (Doise *et al.*, 1975) have shown that group solutions were cognitively more advanced than individual solutions and that internalization took place for an important number of subjects who had participated in the group situations. A clinical observation of the first experiment reported by the authors, involving Task I, indicated that the best solutions took place in groups where a confrontation of divergent strategies between the two children was taking place.

The first four experiments discussed here manipulated different intra-situational variables, introducing sociocognitive conflicts. These experiments considered intra-situational factors linked to the children's cognitive abilities in the task, and to the opposed centrations of different partners interacting in different positions. Subjects were considered as inter-changeable, meaning that their own status or social position was not related to the task, as will be the case in the next section. The conflict here was induced simply by intra-situational arrangements.

### Extra-situational variables

Two other experiments are presented which manipulated the nature of the inter-individual conflict by introducing variables, such as the targets of a sharing task or the nationality of subjects in a task related to the concept of a foreigner, while keeping the intra-situational arrangements constant. Such variables, even in relation to a direct inter-individual situation, have their origin in a system of social relations external to the situation. They are linked to norms, status, etc., and as such are extra-situational variables.

### Sociological factors

Finally two experiments will be discussed where cognitive differences between children of contrasted socioeconomical levels were studied before and after the children participated in inter-individual interactions. The main hypothesis was that sociocultural differences in cognitive development are often found in experiments using paradigms which extract children from their sociopsychological conditions of development. If social interactions are at the source of such development, it is possible to expect that participating in such interactions would diminish, if not eliminate, such differences in cognitive development between subjects of different socioeconomic levels.

## Experiments

### EXPERIMENTS REFERING TO THE INTRA-SITUATIONAL MANIPULATION OF THE SOCIOCOGNITIVE CONFLICTS

*Cognitive abilities in the group composition: design and hypotheses*
One way of changing intra-situational dynamics is to put individuals with different cognitive abilities together. In a situation using Task I (Mugny and Doise, 1978b) subjects were divided into three categories corresponding to three cognitive levels: NC, inferior level; PC, intermediary level; and TC, superior level, depending on their ability to find the correct solution. This classification was made relative to the pretest performances. One week later, subjects participated in a collective situation, where experimental conditions were produced by putting together children of the same or different cognitive levels. The interaction conditions were as follows: an NC with another NC (no conflict condition), an NC with a PC, and an NC with a TC (conflict conditions). A last condition put two PC subjects together (low conflict condition). Our main hypothesis was that subjects interacting with other subjects of a different cognitive level would progress more than subjects interacting with other subjects of the same cognitive level, even if they interact with a partner of a level lower than their own.

*Results.* A frequency count of the number of groups whose best performance was correct or better than the initial performance of the more advanced member is presented in Table 1.

These results may be summarized in the following way: considering only the groups where an NC subject was involved, it appears that the group performances increased in accuracy as the partner's cognitive level increased. This means that the groups NC x NC produced the least correct solutions (most of them belonging to the NC level),

TABLE 1

*Frequencies of groups whose best performance during the interaction is correct or better than the initial level of the more advanced member*

| Experimental conditions | |
|---|---|
| NC + NC ($n =$ 9) | 2 |
| NC + PC ($n =$ 11) | 6 |
| NC + TC ($n =$ 11) | 9 |
| PC + PC ($n =$ 6) | 5 |

the NC x TC condition the most correct solutions, with the performances of NC x PC condition falling in between the other two conditions. The NC x PC condition is of special interest in that, although none of the subjects in these groups were able to give a correct solution during the pretest, more than one half of the groups produced at least one correct solution, thus exemplifying the originality of group cognitive products. The PC x PC conditions appeared to be more "creative" than hypothesized, since most groups produced at least one correct solution during the interaction. This result, however, might have been due to the cognitive fluctuation of the intermediate subjects.

The results obtained from the individuals' post-test repsonses are presented in Table 2. Interestingly enough, individual changes at the post-test do not follow the same pattern as the group results. In the NC x NC condition, no conflict existed, and only two of the 15 subjects of this condition progressed. In the NC x TC condition, where the group performances were the best, only one of the 11 NCs

TABLE 2

*Frequencies of progress at the post-test*

| Experimental conditions | |
|---|---|
| NC$^a$ + NC$^a$ ($n = 15$) | 2 |
| NC$^a$ + PC ($n = 11$) | 7 |
| NC$^a$ + TC ($n = 11$) | 1 |
| PC$^a$ + NC ($n = 9$) | 8 |
| PC$^a$ + PC$^a$ ($n = 12$) | 6 |

[a]Subjects taken into account for the progress index

progressed. However, in the NC x PC condition, seven of the 11 NCs progressed, as did eight of the nine PCs, while in the PC x PC condition, half of the subjects progressed.

*Discussion.* Thus, the cognitive levels of each of the partners had a great effect on the group performance, an effect which cannot be explained only by the partners' initial levels. For instance, in the NC x PC interactions, group elaborated new solutions which none of the children were capable of formulating at the pretest. Furthermore, individual improvements were not linked to group performances in a simple linear way. NC subjects progressed only when paired with intermediate subjects, and not when confronted with correct subjects. We observed that there was a covariation between cognitive level and attitudes during the interactions in that the TC subjects imposed their solution on the group, thus hindering the NC subjects' participation, without making explicit the reasons behind their strategies, as if they were unable to decentrate from the obvious correct solution. On the other hand, the PC subjects, who had not yet elaborated the correct solution and had more doubts and difficulties, made much more explicit the dimensions problematical for them, and allowed the NC subject to intervene more often, thus facilitating his participation in the original group performance.

In conclusion, it may be noted that conflict of different levels of centration can be useful for improving group performances as well as individual performances at the post-test. However, improvements in individual performances are dependent on the level of conflict, since when TC and NC subjects were paired together the NC subjects did not improve. Finally, the higher cognitive strategies developed by the NC x PC and PC x PC groups, as well as the individual improvements shown by the members of these groups during the post-test, tend to indicate that the process underlying cognitive development is not reducible to simple observational learning.

### The conflict of opposed centrations: design and hypothesis

This experiment (Doise *et al.*, 1976) was run in order to show that the conflict of centrations hypothesis was not reducible to a "modelling effect" (see, for instance, Rosenthal and Zimmerman, 1972). Using Task II, two experimental conditions were studied. In the incorrect model condition, the usual equal length conservation test was used with the child giving his responses first, and an adult experimenter responding second. The children were all NC (non-conservers) at the pretest and judged that one ruler was longer when displaced. The experimenter, sitting in front of the child, gave in turn his response, which consisted of incorrectly judging whichever line the subject did not choose as longer. The subjects were thus confronted with a response which was similarly incorrect but exactly opposite of their own. The experimenter gave the same but inverse argument for his response as the child: "because this ruler is longer here," ignoring the other complementary difference.

In the correct model condition, the child was confronted with the correct response given by the adult experimenter using the argument of compensation (the double difference).

In the control condition, the task was the same but subjects were run individually. Starting with the rulers in line, four different configurations were obtained by alternatively displacing each ruler in the two opposite directions. After each of these displacements, subjects were asked whether the rulers were of the same length or not. This was the condition of intra-individual conflict. (Note that the number of items was double the number of experimental conditions in order to insure a similar amount of time working with the material for each subject.)

Our main hypothesis was that both experimental conditions, the correct model condition as well as the incorrect model condition, would lead to improvement since they both would induce conflict of centrations imbedded in a social situation. In the control condition, these conflicts of centration would be less social and more individual, thus, subjects should not progress.

*Results.* The results of the experiment are presented in Table 3. These results showed that not only did the children improve when faced with a correct model, but they also improved when faced with an incorrect model with a similar but opposite centration.

TABLE 3

*Frequencies of progress at the post-test*

| Experimental conditions | Conservation test | |
|---|---|---|
| | Equal lengths | Inequal lengths |
| Control ($n = 13$) | 0 | 1 |
| Incorrect model ($n = 20$) | 9 | 13 |
| Correct model ($n = 19$) | 18 | 9 |

Furthermore, this improvement generalized, to a large extent, to unequal length conservation. (Note that we do not here insist on this generalization: A detailed discussion concerning problems with the "authenticity" of the operative changes will be found in Perret-Clermont, 1980.) However, in the control condition conflict was difficult to obtain, and as such, improvement was minimal. These results were replicated in a study by Mugny *et al.* (in press) which, in addition, showed that conflicts of the same sort between children produced the same effect.

This experiment shows how manipulating the opposition of centrations, which are produced by the same pre-operational scheme, induces socio-cognitive conflicts leading to cognitive restructuring. It indicates, as the preceding experiment suggested, that observing a correct model is not necessary to obtain a socially initiated progress. Furthermore, observational learning can be integrated into our explanation, since a sociocognitive conflict may also be aroused when subjects are confronted with a correct model. However, in the correct model case, facilitating cues for resolving such a conflict may be given by the model itself.

*The conflict induced by opposed spatial positions: design and hypothesis*
In the first experiment described in this section it appeared that inter-actions between two NC subjects led to no improvement, whereas the second experiment indicated that even a similar centration may lead to progress, if it is opposed to the subject's own centration. This effect was replicated in this experiment using Task I, where two NC subjects were placed in two different positions: one in the X position and one in the Y position, the items being complex in both positions. (See "marks" (c) and note c in Fig. 1.) This opposition of same level subjects in different positions should lead to a socio-cognitive conflict, since the same incorrect strategy displayed from two opposed points of view implies that the children will put the houses in different places. The design of the experiment was elaborated during the Fourth European Summer School in Social Psychology at Oxford (1976) and is described by Doise and Mugny (1979).

Thus, in the experimental condition, two subjects had to perform the task together from different positions. In the control condition, subjects (working individually) changed their point of view (from X to Y or from Y to X) after having produced a copy of the village from the first point of view. This first copy was not removed, making it possible for the children to see a difference between the first copy and the one they would need to make in their new position.

*Results.* The results of this experiment (see Table 4) indicated that even NC subjects can improve when interacting together, if they have to produce copies from two opposed spatial positions. On the

TABLE 4

*Frequencies of progress at the post-test*

| Experimental conditions | |
| --- | --- |
| Individual ($n = 19$) | 6 |
| Collective ($n = 21$) | 13 |

other hand, subjects working alone showed less improvement even if the procedure was such that it was possible for the child to see a difference between his first copy made from one point of view and the copy he would need to make from the second point of view.

*How children progress even if the problem is not difficult: design and hypothesis* Task I presents the possibility of providing different degrees of difficulty in different positions. For instance, in Fig. 1 subjects in Position Y have to resolve the difficulty induced by the different orientations of the model and of the cardboard copy. On the other hand, subjects viewing the same stimulus set up from the X position have no problem at all, since from this perspective the solution only requires a 90° rotation, of which all subjects at the ages studied (5–8 years old) are capable. The question of how to induce progress in children in such a position who have already produced a correct solution and have no reason to develop new cognitive orientations, was addressed by the following study run in Bologna (Carugati *et al.,* 1978).

The principle of the experiment was quite simple. NC level subjects were placed in the X position where the solution was evident to them, without any doubt. In front of them were placed one or two subjects of the intermediate level (this was not a choice, but resulted from the levels obtained at the pretest). From this interaction, a sociocognitive conflict would have to arise, since intermediate subjects did not place all the houses correctly at the pretest, whereas

subjects in the X position did. Progress was expected for the intermediate subjects, since they were confronted with other subjects
defending a correct position. The major focus then was on the NC
subjects in the easy position, in an attempt to see which conditions
would enhance cognitive development.

The main hypothesis was that, when confronted with only one
partner in the difficult position, it would be easier for the child in
the X position to impose his view without having to "decentrate"
than when confronted with two partners in that difficult position,
since they could support each other in their wrong solution and
force the subject who has the evident response to make a stronger
cognitive effort toward understanding, and even convincing the
others of the correctness of his position.

*Results.* The results given in Table 5 are only for subjects in the easy
position (other reasons led us to hypothesize the same progress for
subjects in the difficult position in both experimental conditions).

TABLE 5

*Frequencies of progress at the
post-test*

| Experimental conditions | |
| --- | --- |
| One partner ($n = 12$) | 2 |
| Two partners ($n = 7$) | 5 |

These subjects improved significantly more when confronted with
two children in the opposed position than when opposed by only
one child. This progress can only be explained in terms of the social
dynamics involved in the situation, since from a strictly cognitive
point of view there was no problem at all for these subjects. These
results once again rule out interpretations based solely on ideas of
reinforcement or imitation, and exemplify the importance of the
social dimension in sociocognitive conflict for inducing cognitive
development.

EXPERIMENTS REFERRING TO EXTRA-SITUATIONAL FACTORS OF
SOCIOCOGNITIVE CONFLICT

In the preceding section we discussed how it was possible to induce
sociocognitive conflicts and subsequent individual advancements in
cognitive development by manipulating variables inscribed in the

definition of the experimental situation itself. In the present section, we will examine how variables external to the experimental situation can enhance such socio-cognitive conflicts.

*Attribution of bracelets to himself and to an adult: design and hypothesis*
In an experiment involving Task II (Doise *et al.*, 1978a) NC subjects, non-conservers at the equal and at the unequal length conservation tests, were used in the experimental phase during which an unequal length situation was used, following a procedure similar to the pretest and post-test designs described previously. After having compared the two lengths, subjects had to attribute the longest bracelet (20 cm) to a big cylinder or to the experimenter's wrist, and the little bracelet (15 cm) either to a little cylinder or to their own wrist. Subjects were then confronted with a contradictory situation in which they first incorrectly judged the shorter bracelet as long (on critical trials where the longer bracelet was folded) and then later had to correct this judgement. This contradiction was enhanced by the experimenter who systematically made counter-suggestions. The two experimental conditions were logically the same, the only difference being that the attribution of bracelets was made to either impersonal cylinders or to the adult and to the subject himself. We hypothesized that more progress would appear in the "wrist" condition, since the sociocognitive conflict is directly socially relevant in this condition and since there are pre-existing norms the child recognizes, for instance, that adults are bigger and need "more," and so on.

*Results.* The results, given in Table 6, confirmed the above hypothesis. In order for a sociocognitive conflict to be most useful for enhancing cognitive development, it must be relevant to the regulation of social relations. This is the case when subjects' responses establish a direct relationship with the experimenter. This is not so much the case when subjects' responses apply to an impersonal environment.

*Acquiring reversibility in the notion of being a foreigner: design and hypothesis*
Piaget and Weil (1951) have shown that initially children have a quite absolute definition of the notion of a foreigner. It is only later that children recognize that they themselves are foreigners when visiting a foreign country. Intermediate levels may also be

TABLE 6

*Frequencies of progress at the post-test*

| Experimental conditions | Conservation test | |
|---|---|---|
| | Equal lengths | Inequal lengths |
| Bracelets ($n = 18$) | 10 | 11 |
| Cylinders ($n = 17$) | 2 | 2 |

distinguished, for instance when children always consider themselves as native, but recognize that a foreigner may be a native while in his own country.

V. Jacq (doctoral research, in progress) has studied the development of the notion of being a foreigner. She has found that foreigners acquire the reciprocity of the notion sooner than Swiss children do. This is a clear demonstration of how one's own position intervenes in cognitive development. The study described here looks at different social interactions which can induce progress in conceptualizing the notion of a foreigner. We will consider only two of the conditions used in this study. In one condition, two Swiss subjects of the same cognitive level had to imagine that they were travelling through different countries. In the other condition, one Swiss and one foreign child had to imagine the same situation except that they were to imagine that the country they were travelling through was the foreign child's homeland. The hypothesis was that in the latter condition both Swiss and foreign children would progress more in their ability to conceptualize the notion of being a foreigner than children in the other condition.

*Results.* The results showed that little progress was found in the Swiss–Swiss condition, whereas in the Swiss–Foreign condition the Swiss children progressed significantly more than the Swiss children in the first condition. This is another illustration of how variables external to the experimental situation may influence the mastering of some cognitive notions. The same experiment showed that progress obtained in these interaction situations concerning the notion of being a foreigner generalized to mastering the notions of being a brother or a sister. Other research, in progress, has also shown the reverse generalization in that interacting children who were led to better understand the notion of being a brother of a sister also showed progress toward understanding the notion of being a foreigner.

EXPERIMENTS REFERRING TO SOCIOPSYCHOLOGICAL AND
SOCIOLOGICAL FACTORS IN COGNITIVE DEVELOPMENT

The results of the experiment by Jacq show that subjects defined as
"native" or "foreign" in the experimental situation differ in their
ability to acquire an understanding of the reciprocal operation
concerning the notion of a foreigner. This shows that the social
characteristics of children intervene in their cognitive development.
Another social characteristic which plays a role of great importance
in cognitive development is social class. It is unnecessary to cite the
impressive number of studies related to this problem, most of them
showing an important "handicap" in cognitive development for the
lower classes relative to the higher classes. Many explanations have
been given, relative to motivation differences, to linguistic differentiation, etc. and even to hereditary factors. Our theoretical framework has led us to conceive of a somewhat different approach to
this problem which integrates the "sociocognitive" factors of cognitive development.

The usual methodological paradigm used in estimating differences
between children of different social classes relates only to the individual level, and views cognitive abilities as if they were invariant
rather than treating them as constantly developing. However, our
experiments have confirmed that even quite limited social interactions can play a dynamic role in cognitive development, relative to
specific notions, and can often imply important generalizations, as
Perret-Clermont (1980) points out. (It could also be hypothesized
that more systematic and continuous social interactions would lead
to still more general cognitive changes.)

An extension of these ideas to the social class problem is that the
usual paradigm isolates the individuals whose cognitive abilities are
being evaluated from conditions supportive of development (i.e.
social interaction). To clarify this point, we could make the hypothesis that higher class children have already had the occasion to
actualize their cognitive potential when evaluated, since they have
interacted more often with peers and adults in relation to the type
of notions involved in the tasks used. Alternatively, children from
the lowest classes would not have yet been able to elaborate these
cognitive instruments.

If lower and upper class subjects were tested individually, for
instance, with Task I or Task III, a difference between the two
classes of subjects in the usual direction would be predicted. This is

the point at which most studies concerning social class differences stop. However, if these same subjects were allowed to interact with other subjects in a way similar to the various studies described previously, and a second, post-test measure was taken, our reasoning would lead us to expect that the differences found at the pretest would be less, if not absent, at the post-test. The following two experiments were designed to test these ideas.

*Sociocultural handicap and Task I: design and hypothesis*

The different conditions of the relevant experiment (Mugny and Doise, 1978a) have already been described in the first section. During the experimental phase subjects performed as individuals or as collective work groups (dyads) with Task I in situations made up to facilitate intra-individual conflicts or inter-individual conflicts of centrations.

During the first phase, subjects, coming from either a very poor suburban school near Barcelona or from a school frequented by upper middle or upper class students, were tested individually. The results showed that the distribution of lower class subjects split somewhat equally into the inferior, intermediate, and superior levels, while more than half the upper class subjects fell into the superior category. The differences between these two samples was highly significant.

After the pretest, the children were placed in collective situations designed to produce intra-individual and inter-individual conflicts: a post-test comparison of the two samples was made. Our prediction was that the differences between the two samples on the post-test would be less than those found on the pretest, especially for subjects in the inter-individual conflict condition.

*Results.* In order to simplify the presentation, only the instances of progress will be given in Table 7. Let us consider the instances of progress that appeared in the collective as well as the individual conditions. For the higher classes, the collective condition was slightly better than the individual condition (both conditions showing progress), but the difference did not reach significance. For the lower class subjects, the collective condition was significantly better than the individual one. One consequence of these results is that, in reality, the differences between social classes did not disappear, but rather were increased for subjects in the individual condition. In the

TABLE 7

*Frequencies of progress at the post-test*

| Experimental conditions | |
|---|---|
| Individual, high social class ($n = 17$) | 9 |
| Individual, low social class  ($n = 22$) | 9 |
| Collective, high social class ($n = 14$) | 10 |
| Collective, low social class  ($n = 19$) | 13 |

collective condition differences were slightly diminished, though still significant. However, these results may be attributable to a simple ceiling effect, since the correct subjects (more than a half in the high class) could not show improvement at the post-test due to the nature of the task. The discussion of the following experiment will make this point clear.

*Sociocultural handicap and Task III: design and hypothesis*

The same ideas led us to a second experiment using similar populations (Mugny and Doise, 1979), but involving Task III. Furthermore, subjects were systematically divided into three school degrees: ages 5–6, 6–7, and 7–8. The task was used in such a way so that even the more advanced children could still progress considerably at the post-test.

At the pretest the performance scores obtained by the higher class were significantly better than those obtained by the lower class. A finer analysis shows that this difference exists for each age, but that it reaches significance only for the age 6–7. Let us add that the quality of the performances increased with age.

During the experimental phase, subjects again had to respond to the same cooperative game, either working alone, or in groups of two or three. The two collective conditions will be considered together, since no differences appeared between them. One week after this phase, subjects were post-tested with the hypothesis that differences between social classes would become less obvious, especially for subjects having interacted in the experimental phase.

*Results.* The pattern of progress is summarized in Table 8. Results showed that for the lower class there was no progress at ages 5–6, either in the collective or in the individual conditions. For ages 6–7, progress appeared only in the collective condition, while for ages 7–8 progress in both the individual and collective conditions was

TABLE 8

*Progress pattern* (0 = *no significant progress;* + = *significant progress*)

| Social class and age | Experimental conditions | |
|---|---|---|
| | Individual | Collective |
| High social class, age 5—6 | 0 | + |
| age 6—7 | 0 | + |
| age 7—8 | + | + |
| Low social class, age 5—6 | 0 | 0 |
| age 6—7 | 0 | + |
| age 7—8 | + | + |

significant. The higher class pattern is similar, but one year in advance. Thus, for ages 5—6 only the collective condition yielded progress, while for ages 6—7 (even if progress in the individual condition did not reach significance) the difference between collective and individual conditions was no longer significant. At ages 7—8 both collective and individual conditions led to significant progress. Thus, the pattern of progress was the same in both classes. In the first phase, collective work leads to progress, whereas individual work does not. At the subsequent stage, both individual and collective work was equally productive. We probably observed a progressive individual internalization of the cognitive processes involved in a specific cognitive performance. Paradoxically, this internalization first takes place in the context of a social interdependence (Doise *et al.*, 1978b).

An important finding of this study was that, at the post-test, the difference between the two samples (for all ages together) was no longer significant. However, considering the ages separately, the results were more complicated. Although there were no differences found between the two samples for the older children (ages 6—7 and 7—8), a difference did appear for children in the 5—6 year age group. This suggests that the difference between the two classes was only present in the early stages of acquisition rather than the later stages, which would seem to indicate that there were no differences between classes in potential cognitive abilities.

The results of this study would seem to lend some support to our hypothesis that social class differences in cognitive tasks could be the consequence of a methodological artifact. Furthermore, our results suggest that development processes are basically similar for both classes (at least in the tasks used), even if the elaboration of some abilities appears sooner in the upper classes. However, this would not be a hereditary difference but rather a psycho-sociological one.

## Conclusions

It was not within the scope of this paper to discuss other approaches to the study of social factors in cognitive development, as for instance those following from different social learning theories. Such an analysis is presented elsewhere (Mugny *et al.*, 1978).

In the first section of this paper we have limited our discussion to the presentation of experiments where a sociocognitive conflict was induced by intra-situational variables. We have seen how much conflicts lead subjects to elaborate more advanced cognitive operations. In a second section, factors were introduced which gained meaning from putting the experimental situation in a more general framework. Each time, the child was led to elaborate new cognitive instruments in order to establish or to conserve a relationship governed by pre-existing norms. For instance, he had to establish through his responses a specific sharing relationship with the experimenter. In the same vein, foreign subjects acquired the notion of reciprocity in relation to the concept of a foreigner sooner than did native children. Finally, we have seen how social class differences related to cognitive processes can be interpreted differently when the children are allowed to work together, which we consider to be the "natural" condition of cognitive development.

On the one hand, then, extra-situational factors such as the social categories to which children belong intervene in cognitive development. On the other hand, sociocognitive conflict, depending on specific intra-situational factors, appears to be a fundamental process through which cognitive development takes place. Considering all these experiments together, it appears that differences due to social factors (external to the experimental condition) were modified by the sociocognitive conflicts produced experimentally. Is this not an example of an articulation between psychological and sociological models (Doise, 1978), which has to be the real scientific object of socio-psychological research?

# References

Carugati, F. and Mugny, G. Psicologia sociale dello sviluppo cognitivo: imitazione di modelli o conflitto socio-cognitivo? *Giornale di Psicologia*, 1978, 2, 323–352.

Doise, W. Le structuration cognitive des décisions individuelles et collectives d'adultes et d'enfants. *Revue de Psychologie et des Sciences de l'Education*, 1973, 8, 133–146.

Doise, W. Groups and individuals. *Explanations in Social Psychology*. Cambridge, Cambridge University Press, 1978.

Doise, W. Actions and judgements: collective and individual structuring. In H. Brandstätter, J. Davis, H. Schuler (Eds). Dynamics of Group Decisions. Beverley Hills, Safe, 1978.

Doise, W. and Mugny, G. Recherches socio-génétiques sur la coordination d'actions motrices interdépendantes. *Revue Suisse de Psychologie*, 1975, 34, 160–174.

Doise, W. and Mugny, G. Individual and collective conflicts of centrations in cognitive development. *European Journal of Social Psychology*, 1979, 1, 105–108.

Doise, W., Mugny, G. and Perret-Clermont, A.-N. Social interaction and the development of cognitive operations. *European Journal of Social Psychology*, 1975, 5, 367–383.

Doise, W., Mugny, G. and Perret-Clermont, A.-N. Social interaction and cognitive development: further evidence. *European Journal of Social Psychology*, 1976, 6, 245–247.

Doise, W., Dionnet, S. and Mugny, G. Conflit socio-cognitif, marquage social et dévelopment cognitif. *Cahiers de Psychologie*, 1978, 21, 4, 231–243.

Doise, W., Deschamps, J.-C. and Mugny, G. *Psychologie Sociale Experimentale*. Paris, Armand Colin, 1978b.

Mugny, G. and Doise, W. Factores sociologicos y psicosociologicos en el desarollo cognitivo. *Anuario de Psicologia*, 1978a, 18, 1, 21–40.

Mugny, G. and Doise, W. Socio-cognitive conflict and structure of individual and collective performances. *European Journal of Social Psychology*, 1978b, 8, 181–192.

Mugny, G. and Doise, W. Factores sociologicos y psicosociologicos en el desarrollo cognitivo: una nueva ilustracion experimental. *Anuario de Psicologia*, 1979, 21, 3–25.

Mugny, G., Giroud, J.-C. and Doise, W. Conflit de centrations et progrès cognitif, II: nouvelles illustrations experimentales, *Bulletin de Psychologie* (in press).

Mugny, G., Lévy, M. and Doise, W. Conflit socio-cognitif et développement cognitif: l'effet de la présentation par un adulte de modèles "progressifs" et de modèles "régressifs" dans une épreuve de représentation spatiale. *Revue Suisse de Psychologie*, 1978, 37, 22–43.

Perret-Clermont, A.-N. *Social Interaction and Cognitive Development in Children*. London and New York, Academic Press, 1980.

Piaget, J. and Weil, A. M. Le développement, chez l'enfant, de l'idée de patrie et des relations avec l'étranger. *Bulletin International des Sciences Sociales*, 1951, 3, 605–621.

Rosenthal, T. L. and Zimmerman, B. J. Modeling by exemplification and instruction in training conservation. *Developmental Psychology*, 1972, 6, 392–401.

Smedslund, J. *Les origines sociales de la décentration*. In: Psychologie et Epistémologie. Themès Piagétiens. Paris: Dunod, pp. 159–167.

# 20
# Arousal and Conformity

J. Hatcher

In the last 50 years, and especially in the last 25, the concept of arousal or activation has played an increasingly important role in the thinking and theorizing of psychologists. While the applications of this concept historically have dealt mainly with the effects of arousal on learning on performance, there have been recent indications that the concept may be equally relevant for social behaviour. Evidence of this type has come primarily from the fields of aggression (Zillman *et al.*, 1972), attitude change (Nuttin, 1975; Zanna and Cooper, 1976), and helping behaviour (Piliavin, 1969).

We shall attempt here to relate the concept of arousal to conformity behaviour. We would define arousal as a state of excitement ranging from a comatose state to one of excitement, and would propose that this state be measured by one or a combination of physiological measures such as heart rate, skin conductance, blood pressure etc. Our point of departure shall be that of optimal-arousal theory, which is the idea that behaviour is organized around the maintenance of an optimal level of arousal; when events in the inner or outer environment of the organism precipitate a deviation from the optimum, the organism will tend to act in such a way as to minimize or neutralize the disturbance. We assume that this tendency will increase with the size of deviation from the optimal level. We would further assume that in any situation, an organism faces a choice between several response alternatives which have been associated with certain changes in arousal level in similar situations in the past, and that these arousal effects have been conditioned to the responses themselves. These effects will be called the potential effect on arousal of the response, or its PEA value. A response which in the past has consistently led to increases in the arousal level will thus carry a positive PEA value. The same response is conceived as

possibly carrying different PEA values for different individual
organisms, depending on the particular learning history and/or
genetic make-up involved. Similarly, the PEA value of a certain
response is considered to be quite flexible, capable of changing as
quickly as the situation.

It is proposed here that, if the arousal level of the organism in
question differs from the optimum, there will be a tendency, increasing with the magnitude of the difference, to emit that response
whose PEA value most closely represents a return to the optimal
level. If the present level coincides with the optimum, the organism
should tend to perform that response which will maintain the
optimal level.

It is predicted here (concerning the following experiments) that in
a case in which two groups of subjects at different levels of arousal
face two mutually exclusive responses, one of which leads to a higher
level of arousal than the other, that the group with the higher level of
arousal will emit more of the lower PEA value response than the
group with the lower level of arousal. Figure 1 represents the possible
combinations of two groups of subjects when it is known that
Group I is, on the average, more aroused than Group II.

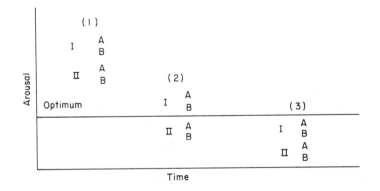

Fig. 1.

In the first example both groups are supra-optimally aroused, in
the second Group I is supra-optimally aroused while Group II is
sub-optimally aroused, and in the third example both groups are
sub-optimally aroused. It is assumed for illustrative purposes that
response A leads to a slight increase of arousal, while response B
leads to a slight decrease. In the first example in which both groups

are supra-optimally aroused, we would expect each group to emit predominantly response B, since both groups should prefer a decrease to an increase of arousal; we would expect Group I, being more aroused than Group II, to be relatively more prone to emit the arousal-reducing response B than would Group II, which lies close to the optimum.

In these predictions one must exercise care in choosing an adequate arousal manipulation, for it is essential that the arousal manipulation has no effect on the PEA values of the responses in question. The best way to obtain the relative PEA values in a given situation is to measure the changes in the arousal levels of the organisms as they emit those responses in that situation. Although physiological measures of arousal are not perfect, it should be remembered that only relative values are needed. If one cannot measure the effects on arousal of certain responses as they naturally occur, one may request subjects to emit a certain response in a certain situation, and then measure the arousal effects of this response, as did Lanzetta *et al.* (1976).

Two experiments shall now be described which provide a test of the above predictions.

## Experiment

OBTAINING THE RELATIVE PEA VALUES OF CONFORMITY AND INDEPENDENCE

Our first concern in attempting to apply the results of a conformity experiment to our thinking is to determine the relative PEA values of conforming or not conforming in such a situation. Relevant data can be produced from several experiments.

Concerning agreement versus disagreement in general, Smith (1936), in an early study, obtained data indicating that the GSR to disagreeing with a neutral statement was higher than for agreeing. Also, more relevant for our needs, the GSR to disagreeing with the bogus majority response was consistently higher than for agreement.

The context of the above study was somewhat far removed from the typical conformity situation, however; we shall therefore turn to experiments which have measured the arousal effects of conformity or non-conformity in situations more similar to an Asch-type (1956) conformity situation.

Studies conducted by Kurt Back and his associates included

physiological measurements to the effects of certain experimental treatments, and of the effects of different modes of responding in typical conformity situations. The arousal measure used in this case was the level of free fatty acid (FFA) in the blood. This procedure involves taking blood samples at various times during the experiment, and thus does not provide a continuous measure, but is nevertheless a sensitive measure of the effects of events or actions during an experiment.

Back *et al.* (1973) used this technique to study the effects of cohesion and perceived ability relative to others on subsequent conformity and on the physiological arousal levels of the subjects involved. A blood sample was also taken at the end of the conformity trials to determine the effects of different modes of responding. The differences in instruction led to differences in FFA levels during the instruction period; more importantly from our point of view, decrease in FFA level and conformity during the trials sequence were positively related. Although this was not the case when subjects were told that they were greater in ability than their fellow subjects, this may have been due to the ability manipulation itself, it would not necessarily be less arousing to agree with those less competent than oneself than to disagree. From this study, Back *et al.* draw the conclusion that conformity is an arousal-reducing behaviour.

Another experiment, by Back *et al.* (1970) found that a "high strain" group (high anxious, strangers, with drug) when compared to a "low strain" group (low anxious, friends, without drug) exhibited significantly more conformity and also declined in FFA level during the trials sequence. Again the conclusion was reached that conformity is, in part, a manner of reducing excessively high autonomic arousal.

Finally, a study by Costell and Liederman (1968), using continuous measure of skin potential during a conformity task, found that subjects who conformed showed an initial sharp increase on the first few trials when almost all subjects were independent; thereafter their arousal levels underwent steady decreases throughout the trials. Independent subjects, on the other hand, experienced a decrease in arousal to the initial conflict, but increased in arousal during the trials, never reaching, however, the initial level of the conforming subjects.

Taking these data as a whole, it seems safe to say that in general, conformity in an Asch-type situation seems to carry a lower PEA value than independent responding.

## CHOOSING AN AROUSAL MANIPULATION

As cautioned above, care must be taken in choosing a manipulation of arousal, as the manipulation itself must have no effects on the relative PEA values of the responses to be measured. Direct manipulation of arousal by pharmaceutical means was rejected as impractical because of the parental consent needed with subjects of university age, and because, due to the minute chance of an adverse reaction, the presence of a doctor would be required at all times. The second method described above was thus employed, that of using a manipulation which may have cognitive effects and thus may alter the PEA values of some responses in the situation, but whose cognitive effects would seem to be totally extraneous to the responses being measured.

A violent—peaceful film contrast was decided upon, as this is known to create different levels of arousal from research concerning aggression, yet has no obvious relationship to conformity or independence in an Asch-type conformity situation. Also, the use of films could be reconciled readily with an adequate cover story which would further distance the films themselves from the behaviour being studied.

## PREDICTION

Following our examples given earlier, given two groups of subjects at different levels of arousal, and two responses of which it can be said that one carries a higher PEA value than the other, then the prediction can be made that the more aroused group will emit proportionately more of the lower PEA value response. Thus, assuming the films to have the desired effects on arousal, we should predict more conformity following the violent film than the peaceful film.

## SUBJECTS AND DESIGN

Subjects were 66 volunteers from the dentistry class of the Katholieke Universiteit te Leuven, who responded to a request by the experimenter for volunteers. No pay was offered, as this is not customary at the KUL. Both males and females were included, and were assigned to conditions by chance, the only stipulation being that approximately equal proportions of each sex would be represented in each condition.

Aside from the violent and peaceful film conditions, a conformity control, or no-film condition was included so the effects of the film conditions, if any, would be more clear. A baseline condition was also included to check the ambiguity of the stimuli.

## STIMULI AND APPARATUS

The stimuli were lines identical in ratio to those of Asch (1956), projected on a white screen 7 m from the cubicles of the subjects. The slide containing the standard line, i.e. the left-hand slide, was raised about 20% of its height relative to the slide containing the comparison lines, to prevent the use of a seam on the projection screen for comparison purposes. Each slide was projected for the entire duration of the trial, which was approximately 30 s. The sequence of majority answers followed Asch (1956).

Subjects sat in individual cubicles from which they could neither see nor easily hear one another, and responded on a Crutchfield-type (1955) apparatus through which the majority answers were also induced. Subjects always answered fourth out of five "subjects". Their cue to respond was the flashing of the others' responses, and the illuminating of the response panel. The former was designed to insure attention to the responses of the others.

## PROCEDURE

As each subject arrived at the laboratory, he or she was escorted to one of the cubicles by the experimenter. From three to five subjects participated in each session, though they arrived separately and consequently had no idea how many subjects had already arrived or arrived subsequently. After all subjects had arrived, the experimenter entered the large room of the laboratory upon which all of the cubicles faced, sat down at the control panel, and welcomed the students, apologizing in the process for his poor Dutch. He then turned on the tape-recorded instructions.

Subjects in the two film conditions heard the experiment described as concerning the effects of colour stimulation on black-and-white perception, which was said to be a relatively new field within perception. The subjects were told that in order to test for these effects, they would first be shown a short colour film to ensure that they had all been exposed to colour stimulation of the same quantity and quality. It was emphasized that due to the nature of the study, it was necessary that the black-and-white perceptual task follow immediately after the film segment. Instructions for responding were then given, and a practice trial administered. The experimenter then left the central room and entered one of the cubicles where the film projectors were housed. He then started either the violent film, a segment from an American film *The Strawberry Statement* of nine minutes duration, and depicting police breaking up a student protest; or the peaceful film, entitled *People and Animals on Sunday* (Dutch title *Mensen en Dieren op Zondag*), a segment also of nine minutes showing scenes at an outdoor zoo on Sunday. The soundtrack of the violent film consisted of screams, the drone of machinery, etc. while that of the peaceful film contained soft music; there was no commentary to either film. Immediately upon completion of the film segment, the experimenter unplugged the film projector, activated the slide projectors, and projected the first slide; the delay between the end of the film segment and the projection of the first slide never exceeded five seconds.

In the conformity control, or no-film condition, the procedure was somewhat different. First of all, since this condition was intended to check the base level of conformity in this student population, and since there was no film to justify the cover story of the two film conditions, subjects in this condition were simply told that the experiment concerned judging the lengths of lines, with there being no mention of colour stimulation. Finally, a problem existed as to the time difference involved. It was felt that to provide some task or other treatment equal to the length of the films would be likely to produce arousal confoundings, as it proved impossible to conceive of a task that could be guaranteed to have no arousal effects. It was thus decided to use no time delay equal to the length of the films, as this would give an idea of the rate of conformity before the projection of the films, thus enabling their effects to be determined more clearly (for similar reasoning, see Zillman and Johnson (1973)). In this condition, therefore, the experimenter, after the practice trial, entered the control cubicle and immediately started the slide sequence.

Subjects in the baseline condition received the same description of the experiment as those in the no-film condition, but answered, of course, without seeing the responses of the other subjects.

When the 18 trials were completed, subjects filled out questionnaires containing, among other items, self-report ratings concerning their nervousness during the instructions, film (if applicable) and trial phases of the experiment. The usefulness of this type of retroactive rating is admittedly less than might be hoped, but it was felt that to obtain such ratings during the experiment itself would not only be distracting, but could lead as well to the subjects becoming sensitive to this factor, this possibly affecting their behaviour. The questionnaire also contained ratings of the films on violent–peaceful and interesting–uninteresting continuums, and a final question designed to tap any suspicion the subject may have had concerning any aspect of the experiment. After the questionnaire was completed, the subjects were fully debriefed, and pledged to silence concerning the experiment.

RESULTS

Turning first to the retroactive self-report measures of nervousness, we can see in Table 1 that subjects in the violent film condition rated themselves as significantly more nervous during the film than did subjects in the peaceful film condition ($t = 3.92$, $P < 0.001$). There were no differences between the ratings of these two conditions during the instruction or trial phases of the experiment, while there was a tendency ($t = 1.75$, $P < 0.10$) for the no-film subjects to rate their nervousness during the instructions as higher than the two film conditions combined. It should be noted that the interest scores for the two films did not differ, while the violent film was rated as significantly more violent than the peaceful film.

TABLE 1

| Condition | | Phase of experiment (1 = very nervous, 7 = very relaxed) | | | Film rating | |
|---|---|---|---|---|---|---|
| | $n$ | Instructions | Film | Trials | Int–Unint | Peace–violent |
| Violent | 18 | 4.39[a] | 3.72[b] | 4.44 | 2.89 | 6.50[b] |
| Peaceful | 20 | 4.18 | 5.38[b] | 4.53 | 3.40 | 2.35[b] |
| No-film | 19 | 3.74[a] | — | 4.53 | — | — |
| Baseline | 9 | 4.44 | — | 4.78 | — | — |

[a]$P < 0.10$    [b]$P < 0.001$

Concerning the conformity scores, as can be seen in Table 2 the film conditions differed in the predicted direction, conformity in the violent film condition being 27.2% compared to 18.3% for the peaceful film condition. This difference, however, is not significant by a $t$ test ($t = 1.08$), as both conditions exhibited a large degree of variability. The data are also quite severely skewed, with a disproportionately large number of subjects with zero conformity

TABLE 2

| Condition | $n$ | Total responses (critical trials) | Conf. resp. | % Conf. |
|---|---|---|---|---|
| Violent film | 18 | 213[a] | 58 | 27.2 |
| Peaceful film | 20 | 240 | 44 | 18.3 |
| No film | 19 | 228 | 73 | 32.0 |
| Baseline | 9 | 108 | 1 error (0.9%) | |

[a]Three critical trials lost due to procedural malfunction.

responses. Resorting to less-powerful non-parametric tests, subjects in the violent film condition conform a greater percentage than those from the peaceful film condition on ten of the twelve trials (sign test, $P = 0.038$, two-tailed), while the overall distributions of conformity v. non-conformity responses in the two conditions differed on a $\chi^2$ test ($\chi^2 = 4.62$, $P < 0.05$, one-tailed). This most surprising result, however, came from the no-film condition. This condition was expected to fall somewhere between the two film conditions, assuming that the films resulted in increases or decreases in arousal; however, the conformity in this condition was highest of all, reaching a figure of 32%. This still did not differ from the peaceful film on a $t$ test ($t = 1.55$), but differed on the above non-parametric tests even more strongly than did the violent film. On no test did the violent and no-film conditions differ significantly.

The baseline group committed one error, for a rate of 0.09%.

Suspicion on the part of the subjects was difficult to assess. Very few subjects showed any hints of suspicion when simply asked on the questionnaire if any aspect of the situation seemed strange of bothersome, though a common complaint was that seeing the responses of the others made them nervous. Responses to a more leading question implying that there was another purpose to the experiment other than the one mentioned by the experimenter provoked more response. To this question, five subjects from the peaceful film condition, six from the violent film condition, and eleven from the no-film condition gave responses that could be classified as suspicious. It is impossible to determine when these suspicions arose, of course, since several of the above subjects manifested high rates of conformity. No subjects were dropped from the analysis.

Finally, it should be noted that females conformed slightly more than males in all conditions, though this difference was far from significant.

DISCUSSION

Considering the violent—peaceful film contrast, the results can be seen as supporting the prediction of the theory of increased emission of the lower PEA value response, conformity, in the condition of the higher arousal, in this case assumed to be the violent film condition. This support cannot be called overwhelming, however, since the difference between the two conditions, while not small as conformity differences go, is too weak to allow full confidence in the effect. One other shortcoming in this case is the lack of a physiological measure of arousal. The self-ratings of arousal would indicate, to the extent to which they can be trusted as rough measures of arousal, that subjects in the two conditions entered the trials phase of the experiment at different levels of arousal; it would be preferable to have more precise information to that effect.

The results of the no-film condition are also rather puzzling. This condition produced a higher-than-expected level of conformity, at least assuming the arousal of this group to fall somewhere between those of the two film conditions. Of course, this assumption may have been incorrect; it is possible that arousal upon entering the experimental situation is rather high, and that this arousal decays over the span of the experiment. The difference in time between the film and no-film conditions may have thus led to the arousal levels in the no-film group being elevated at the time of the control group relative to the film conditions. This would imply that the violent film, instead of producing increased arousal, may only serve to arrest the decrease in arousal associated with increased exposure to the experimental situation. Evidence of this type is presented by Zillman and Johnson (1973), who found that arousal levels which were elevated due to provocation decreased somewhat to a violent film, but much more to a neutral film.

It is also possible that, due to the differences in the cover story and general description of the experiment, subjects in the no-film condition may have experienced different arousal effects during this phase of the experiment. For example, the description of the task as involving the judging of the lengths of lines may have led to a higher level of arousal than describing the experiment as concerning the effects of colour stimulation on black-and-white perception; the former description may have produced more of a "test" atmosphere. This difference could have also produced differences in the PEA values of conforming or not conforming in the two experimental situations. Subjects in the film conditions may have been less disturbed by the prospect of disagreeing with the responses of their fellow subjects, since they had been led to believe that the colour stimulation may have some effect on black-and-white perception. In fact, several subjects in the no-film condition offered the comment that they were very surprised by the apparent disagreement of the others over what seemed to be a very simple discrimination. This comment did not occur during the debriefing of the film conditions.

The only piece of evidence that can be offered in support of the no-film condition being more aroused than the film conditions is the tendency for subjects in that condition to rate their nervousness during the instructions to have been higher than the two film conditions ($P < 0.10$). This is suggestive, but not conclusive, of course.

Due to the encouraging but indecisive results of the first experiment, it was felt that a replication was in order, both to check on the consistency of the results, as well as to clarify them.

## Replication

PROCEDURE, STIMULI, AND SUBJECTS

The same stimuli and apparatus were used as in the initial experiment. A heart-rate measure was incorporated as well, primarily to check the effects of the films, but also to provide information as to possible effects in the no-film condition. This measure required having the subjects sit for five minutes before the experiment began, taking the measure during the last two minutes of this period as the base rate in terms of which later measurements could be expressed. Heart rate was measured by a small light and a photo-sensitive cell attached to the ear of the subject by a small clip and a piece of tape.

The procedure remained unchanged for the two film conditions. For the no-film condition, however, the cover story and description of the experiment were altered to make them more equivalent to those of the film conditions. Instead of being told that the task concerned the judging of the lengths of lines, subjects in the no-film condition this time heard the experiment described as concerning the effects of colour stimulation on black-and-white perception. They were then told that, since everyone was constantly exposed to colour stimulation, they, who would see no film, would be compared to subjects who first saw a black-and-white film. After this, the procedure proceeded as before, with again no time delay equal to the length of the films.

The same films were used as before, though the length of the films was shortened to eight minutes due to an accident with the violent film. The same questionnaires were employed and the subjects were again fully debriefed.

Serving as subjects this time were 57 male and female students of the physical therapy class of the KUL, a student population comparable to that of the first study. Subjects were assigned to conditions as before.

RESULTS OF THE REPLICATION

Again turning first to the self-report data, one can see basically the same effects as before as far as the two film conditions are concerned. Subjects in the violent film condition again rate themselves as relatively more nervous during the film than do their peaceful film counterparts. The film ratings are also as before, differing as to rated violence but not rated interest. Subjects in the no-film condition, however, again give surprising data, this time rating their nervousness as having been lower than in the film conditions, both during the instructions ($t = 2.77$, $P < 0.01$ for both film conditions) and the trials ($t = 2.48$, $P < 0.02$, and $t = 3.34$, $P < 0.01$ for the violent and peaceful film conditions, respectively), as can be seen in Table 3.

TABLE 3

| Condition | $n$ | Phase of experiment (1 = very nervous, 7 = very relaxed) | | | Film rating | |
|-----------|-----|--------------|-------|--------|-----------|---------------|
|           |     | Instructions | Film  | Trials | Int–Unint | Peace–violent |
| Violent   | 16  | 4.0[a]       | 3.81[a] | 3.56[a] | 3.31    | 4.38[a]       |
| Peaceful  | 16  | 4.0[a]       | 4.81[b] | 3.25[a] | 3.27    | 2.00[b]       |
| No film   | 16  | 4.8[b]       | —     | 4.40[b] | —       | —             |
| Control   | 9   | 4.0[ab]      | —     | 4.78[b] | —       | —             |

Differing subscripts differ at at least $P < 0.05$ (vertically).

The conformity scores of the two film conditions strongly resembled those of the first experiment, the violent film displaying 29.2% conformity compared to 19.8% for the peaceful film condition. Again, this difference was not significant by a $t$ test ($t = 0.81$), though the distribution of conformity and non-conformity responses

TABLE 4

| Condition | $n$ | Total responses (critical trials) | Conf. resp. | % Conf. |
|---|---|---|---|---|
| Violent film | 16 | 192 | 56 | 29.2 |
| Peaceful film | 16 | 192 | 38 | 19.8 |
| No film | 15 | 180 | 23 | 12.8 |
| Baseline | 9 | 108 | No errors | |

TABLE 5

| Condition | $n$ | Phase of experiment | | |
|---|---|---|---|---|
| | | Instructions | Film | Trials |
| Violent film | 14 | $1.026^{ab1}$ | $0.986^{a2}$ | $1.007^{a12}$ |
| Peaceful film | 12 | $1.022^{ab1}$ | $0.951^{a2}$ | $1.012^{a1}$ |
| No film | 13 | $1.008^{a1}$ | — | $1.000^{a1}$ |
| Baseline | 9 | $1.043^{b1}$ | — | $0.970^{a2}$ |

HR expressed as % of baseline.
Differing letters (vertically) = $P$ of at least $< 0.05$ ($t$ test).
Differing numbers (horizontally) = $P$ of at least $< 0.05$ (paired $t$).

in the two groups differed at the 0.10 level ($\chi^2 = 3.13$). As can be seen in Table 4, the no-film group again produced surprising data, this time conforming only 12.8%. This almost differs from the violent film condition at the 0.10 level ($t = 1.68$, $t_{0.10} = 1.697$, two-tailed), and differs significantly on the non-parametric tests used in the first experiment. Females again conformed more than males in all conditions, this time significantly so ($F = 5.46$, 1/41, $P < 0.025$). Although the sex X condition interaction was not significant ($F = 1.33$, 2/41, $P < 0.28$), this was especially true in the peaceful film condition, where males averaged 0.37 conformity responses on the twelve critical trials compared to 4.5 for females. Violent film rates were 2.6 and 4.7.

The heart rate data were averaged for each 20 s of the experimental period, including instructions, and expressed as a percentage of the base rate. Table 5 gives the mean heart rates for the different phases of the experiment, and Fig. 4 shows the heart rates of the two film conditions during the films. Concerning the means, there was a tendency for violent film subjects to exhibit higher heart rates during the film than their peaceful film counterparts, but this did not reach significance. Interestingly, as in the Zillman and Johnson (1973) study, each film actually resulted in a decrease in arousal compared to the instructions.

The reduced *n* in Table 5 are due to malfunctions of the heart rate apparatus resulting in illegible records for some subjects, spread fairly evenly over conditions.

A look at the continuous record of the heart rates of the film conditions during the viewing of the films is more informative. An analysis of variance revealed a weak repeated measures effect ($F = 1.37$, 24/528, $P < 0.11$) and a slightly stronger repeated measures X conditions effect ($F = 1.45$, 24/528, $P < 0.08$). This would indicate that, while the overall heart rates of the two conditions did not differ significantly, there was a tendency for them to differ over time.

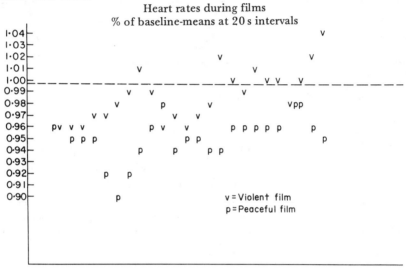

Fig. 2.

Suspicion was not a factor in this experiment, only four subjects giving responses that could be classified as suspicious. No subject was dropped from the analysis.

DISCUSSION OF THE REPLICATION

The results of the replication further support the different effects of violent and peaceful films on subsequent conformity. The data from these conditions mirror almost exactly those of the first experiment, though in neither experiment alone can the effect be called a strong one. Self-rating data are also in line with those of the first experiment concerning these two conditions.

TABLE 6

*Heart rate and conformity correlations*

| Conditions | | I | II | III | IV |
|---|---|---|---|---|---|
| | | | Intervals | | |
| Violent film | Males | $-0.71^b$ | $-0.62^b$ | $-0.70^b$ | $-0.62^b$ |
| | Females | $-0.55$ | $-0.81^b$ | $-0.21$ | $-0.69^a$ |
| | All | $-0.57^b$ | $-0.58^b$ | $-0.41^a$ | $-0.55^b$ |
| Peaceful film | Males | * | * | $0.03$ | $-0.80^b$ |
| | Females | $0.66^a$ | $0.35$ | $0.08$ | $0.19$ |
| | All | $0.39^a$ | $0.18$ | $-0.20$ | $-0.14$ |
| No film | Males | $-0.23$ | $0.51$ | $-0.28$ | $0.61$ |
| | Females | $-0.14$ | $0.24$ | $0.58^a$ | $0.43$ |
| | All | $-0.14$ | $0.22$ | $0.39^a$ | $0.30$ |
| All subjects | | $-0.18$ | $-0.19$ | $-0.28^b$ | $-0.29^b$ |

$^a P$ 0.10
$^b P$ 0.05
*Too few cases for correlation to be computed.

The no-film condition again produced perplexing results. Barring some random variation within the subject pool, which would be argued against by the similarities of the violent and peaceful conditions with those of the previous experiment, it would seem that the change in cover story accounted for this change in conformity rates. From our point of view, this could not have occurred due to differing PEA values of conformity and non-conformity between this and the film conditions, as the description of the situation was almost identical. In order to interpret these results within the framework of the theory's predictions, the position would have to be taken that the no-film group was actually, in this experiments, less aroused than the film conditions. This would seem a dubious possibility, if the self-ratings of nervousness and, to a lesser degree the heart rates, did not indicate that this may well have been the case.

If the no-film condition really was less aroused than the film conditions, then the degree of conformity in the replication can be argued to be a function of the degree of arousal present at the time. This is dampened a bit, however, by the fact that the self-ratings do not discern a difference between the two film conditions during the trials, while the heart rate shows no difference among the three conditions. It is possible of course, that the arousal caused either by the film or by whatever factor is operating in the no-film condition may be clouded by the arousal effects of the modes of responding within the various conditions. Fortunately, the heart rate during the trials allows a check of such an hypothesis. The trials period was divided into four intervals, each containing three critical trials, and mean conformity and mean heart rate were computed for each subject for each interval, thus allowing correlations to be computed. Table 6 gives these correlations.

It can thus be seen that, in general, there exists a negative correlation between conformity and heart rate, this being especially true in the violent film condition. This would seem to indicate that subjects in this condition upon conforming, experienced reductions in arousal, and that if such conformity had not occurred, the arousal levels of this condition during the trials would have been higher.

## Discussion of the two experiments combined

STATISTICAL TREATMENT

Rosenthal (1978) discusses several methods for combining the results of independent experiments in order to arrive at a probability value for the findings as a whole. Using the method of adding probabilities, a one-tailed $P$ of 0.065 is obtained for the $t$ tests of conformity between the two film conditions. Combining the results of the non-parametric tests yields a $P$ of less than 0.01 for the distributions of conformity and non-conformity responses in the two film conditions. When applied to the number of trials on which a greater percentage of violent film subjects conform than peaceful film subjects, a $P$ of less than 0.005 is reached.

An analysis of variance was also performed on the combined data, with replication as a factor. This yielded only a significant sex effect ($F = 4.37$, 1/92, $P < 0.05$). No other main effect or interaction approached significance.

GENERAL DISCUSSION

The two experiments described above make a fairly strong case for the degree of conformity in an Asch-type situation being a function of the level of arousal of the various conditions, all else being equal. The two film conditions show this effect; so do the no-film conditions as far as measures of arousal such as self-reports can be trusted. Interestingly, the opposite effects of the no-film conditions in the two experiments still follows this general relationship, although it is not clear exactly which feature of the changes in cover story are responsible for the reversal of the effect.

While the above experiments were designed to lessen or eliminate the effects of cognitive factors, one may nevertheless attempt to interpret the above results in cognitive terms. It could be suggested, for example, that subjects in the violent film condition may come to identify with the students in the film, somehow transfer this identification to their fellow subjects, and feel subsequently less inclined to disagree with them. This interpretation, and others of this nature, suffer from one important weakness. Despite the thorough nature of the debriefing and the inclusion of a leading question to tap any ideas the subject may have entertained during or after the experiment, not one subject mentioned any such connection. Perhaps it should be explained that subjects from other faculties rarely serve as subjects for psychological experiments here at the KUL. They are consequently very unsuspicious concerning procedures or decisions which may provoke more suspicion in more experienced subject pools. In a word, the subjects seem to have simply accepted the cover story at face value.

While I cannot anticipate each interpretation that may apply to the above data, it should be pointed out that in these particular experiments there did not exist a great deal of time for complex thought or reflection, as the time between the films and the trials was miniscule, and the intervals between trials not long. One further observation along these lines will be offered. Anyone suggesting an attribution-type interpretation explanation of the above results would seem to have difficulty explaining why the subjects in the violent film condition did not attribute their arousal to the film, and consequently display low degrees of conformity.

In summary, there is no particular evidence indicating that the differences in conformity between conditions to be due to cognitive factors or operations. On the other hand, the self-ratings, and to a lesser degree the heart rate measures, indicate that differences in arousal did exist. This, coupled with the significant negative correlation between conformity and heart rate in the condition assumed to be highest in arousal, the violent film condition, would seem to indicate that our interpretation of the differences in conformity as being due to the different levels in arousal in the various conditions is the most plausible one in this case.

## References

Asch, S. E. Studies of independence and conformity. *Psychological Monographs,* 1956, 70, 9 (Whole no. 416).

Back, K., Bogdonoff, M., Shaw, D. and Klein, R. An interpretation of experimental conformity through physiological measures. *Behavioral Science,* 1963, 8, 34—40.

Back, K., Oelfke, S., Brehm, M., Bogdonoff, M. and Nowlin, J. Physiological and situational factors in psychopharmacological experiments. *Psychophysiology,* 1970, 6, 749—760.

Costell, R. and Liederman, P. Psychophysiological concomitants of social stress: the effects of conformity behavior. *Psychosomatic Medicine,* 1968, 30, 298—310.

Crutchfield, R. Conformity and character. *American Psychologist,* 1955, 10, 191—198.

Lanzetta, J. T., Cartwright-Smith, J. and Kleck, R. E. Effects of nonverbal dissimulation on emotional experience and automatic arousal. *Journal of Personality and Social Psychology,* 1976, 33, 3, 354—370.

Nuttin, J. *The Illusion of Attitude Change.* London and New York: Academic Press, 1975.

Piliavin, I., Rodin, J. and Piliavin, J. Good Samaritanism: an underground phenomenon? *Journal of Personality and Social Psychology,* 1969, 13, 289—299.

Rosenthal, R. Combining results of independent studies. *Psychological Bulletin,* 1978, 85, 1, 185—193.

Smith, C. E. A study of the autonomic excitation resulting from the interaction of the individual opinion and the group response. *Journal of Abnormal and Social Psychology,* 1936, 31, 138—164.

Zanna, M. P. and Cooper, J. Dissonance and the attribution process. In J. H. Harvey, W. J. Ickes and R. F. Kidd (Eds) *New Directions in Attribution Research,* Hillsdale, N.J.: Lawrence Erlbaum, 1976.

Zillman, D. and Johnson, R. Motivated aggressiveness perpetuated by exposure to aggressive films and reduced by exposure to nonaggressive films. *Journal of Research in Personality,* 1973, 7, 261—276.

Zillman, D., Katcher, A. and Milavsky, B. Excitation transfer from physical exercise to subsequent aggressive behavior. *Journal of Experimental Social Psychology,* 1972, 8, 247—259.

# VI

# Groupthink

# Introduction

Gisela Stocker-Kreichgauer

On the basis of the analysis of case studies of American policy planning groups whose decisions and recommendations lead to "historic fiascoes", Janis (1972) developed the concept of "groupthink". Groupthink is described by Janis as a concurrence-seeking tendency of highly or moderately cohesive groups which leads to the following dysfunctional cognitive and behaviour phenomena in group decision-making:

> (1) incomplete survey of alternatives, (2) incomplete survey of objectives, (3) failure to examine risks of preferred choice, (4) failure to reappraise initially rejected alternatives, (5) poor information search, (6) selective bias in processing information at hand and (7) failure to work out contingency plans. (Janis and Mann, 1977, p. 132)

Janis found these phenomena when analysing accounts of historic decisions including memoirs of the policy makers themselves.

Choosing the method of analysis of real decisions of great public importance, Janis avoided the well-known shortcomings of laboratory experiments, which decrease the external validity of the findings. On the other hand the advantages of experimental studies (laboratory research) have to be relinquished in case study analyses of historic decisions — the control and manipulation of relevant variables necessary to determine cause-effect-relations, the possibility of directly observing the subjects' interactions during group discussion, the measurement of theoretically relevant dependent variables during the group decision or at its end, and so on.

Analysis of historical records is restricted to the limited data that are available, much of which may be of dubious relevance or reliability. The investigator has to use the historical material as best he can when reconstructing the actual decision process. He needs to know about the formal working arrangements accepted by the group members, their linguistic style and emotional expressiveness, in-group code words, allusions to present or past events, speaking order, informal status of group members, and power structures of the group. The investigator should also be acquainted with the different degrees of knowledge of group members about the problem to be solved, since it is plausible that facts and arguments known by all group members — regardless of their relevance — will be treated somehow differently by speakers and listeners than those that are not common knowledge. The same argument analysed from tape-recordings may have a totally different meaning when given by different speakers or within different groups.

The researcher should also be acquainted with the details of the historic events. He should be able to notice when an account has omissions, exaggerates or reduces the importance of the real events. Otherwise his reconstruction of facts and therefore his conclusions drawn from the material are defective and open to criticism.

In connection with the analysis of historical records (and also with the observation of real decision groups in organizational settings) there is still another problem to be mentioned: groups working together for a long time and being engaged on important problems displace a good deal of interaction from their formal group sessions to informal meetings before the final decision is made. They speak to each other about their views of the problem to be decided and their preferences, partly to obtain more confidence in their own beliefs and preferences (social validation), partly to influence others' preferences and to gain supporters for their own point of view (informal coalition formation). The observed (or recorded) session of the group can become a mere "theatre session" about a problem already decided, often with pseudo-arguments given in the discussion, while the real arguments and causes of action remain in the dark.

If the investigator does not have access to tape-recordings of the decision session itself but must build up his analysis on summaries or minutes that report only the most important events, he has still another difficulty to overcome: the author of the summary may have felt free to put in his own ideas instead of giving an unbiased statement of the facts. The research data may be distorted not only by the author's views and intentions but also by general conventions about how to write minutes.

Last but not least there is a decisive advantage of document analysis of real and important decisions with serious consequences, like the ones Janis has studied. The group members have to make complex decisions for which they have to state the reasons to the general public and therefore will feel much more responsible than subjects in laboratory experiments who have to decide about problems which do not affect them personally (low ego-involvement). Laboratory subjects also have to undergo artificial interference and sometimes unintelligible restrictions of their behaviour repertoire. Furthermore, they must interact with an experimenter who is in control of the situation and who can influence the kind of inter-actions that take place within decision-making groups. They are likely to think about the experimental hypotheses that are being studied, which can affect their behaviour, especially when they have doubts about the cover story presented to them by the experimenter. The study of real decisions is almost free from these side effects of laboratory studies and can therefore obtain results having greater external validity. As Janis points out, there should be a systematic, coordinated attempt of research on group decision making to use a variety of different methods, including content analysis of real decisions, laboratory studies, field experiments and case studies to combine the advantages and avoid the shortcomings of the different research methods.

Janis worked out a careful plan for the combination of the different research methods and has emphasized the need for doing field experiments using well-qualified decision makers representing appropriate expertise and varying viewpoints for a policy-planning group. The experimenter can induce high ego involvement by promising that the group's recommendations will be circulated to people who have the power to change the current unsatisfactory policy. These field experiments are proposed by Janis as a means for testing the conclusions drawn from his case study analyses of groupthink. Such field studies might bring about a better understanding of group decision processes in the future. In the paper presented here Irving Janis presents a description of symptoms of groupthink and their antecedent conditions, such as high cohesiveness and insulation of the group, directive leadership, and lack of methodical procedures for search and appraisal of information and of alternatives. He gives examples of symptoms of defective decision making, like incomplete survey of alternatives, poor information search, and selective bias in processing information at hand. Janis also presents ten prescriptive hypotheses derived partly from comparative case studies, from the stress literature, and from social psychology. These hypotheses specify how to avoid groupthink in order to bring about more effective group decisions. Janis indicates how these hypotheses can be tested by using a multiple methodological approach.

Ivan Steiner presents in his paper a survey of three lines of experimental research in social psychology showing obvious similarities with Janis's work on groupthink. He re-analyses laboratory experiments based on three different paradigms — the horse-trading model, the risky shift model, and a normative model. Steiner proposes alternative hypotheses about how the group decisions reached by different experimental arrangements (kind of leadership, differences in status, differences in initial preferences concerning the issue) can be explained. His explanations are in line with Janis's conception of causes, symptoms, and behavioural consequences of groupthink, thus creating a connection between traditional experimental social psychology of group performance and the concept of groupthink derived from analysis of real policy decisions. Differing from Janis's proposition that cohesion of groups is an antecedent condition of groupthink, Steiner from his experimental review (mostly including *ad hoc* or transitory groups composed of strangers who had no reason to expect their associations to continue) suggests that the members' desire for cohesion or for approval are the factors that promote groupthink. Group cohesion therefore may be the effect rather than the cause of groupthink.

# 21
# Counteracting the Adverse Effects of Concurrence-seeking in Policy-planning Groups: Theory and Research Perspectives

Irving L. Janis

This paper discusses the concurrence-seeking or "groupthink" phenomena described by Janis in *Victims of Groupthink* (1972) and the more recent explanatory hypotheses developed by Janis and Mann (1977) that have direct implications for improving the quality of decision making by policy planning groups. First I shall present a set of analytic and prescriptive hypotheses that specify how changes in the antecedent conditions that foster groupthink increase the probability of effective group work in carrying out the tasks of search and appraisal when the members are engaged in making policy recommendations or decisions. Then I shall describe the type of research needed to test the hypotheses (some of which is now underway). This will include: (1) laboratory experiments to develop new interventions and to test them in a preliminary way; (2) field experiments with *ad hoc* policy planning groups (e.g. with American graduate students in economics and policy sciences who volunteer to prepare a position paper on proposed means for dealing with the dangers of replying upon atomic fission as a source of energy, to be circulated within the US Department of Energy and other relevant governmental agencies); and (3) field experiments in organizational settings (starting with aides who are relatively low in the organizational hierarchy and then, if the evidence shows that certain interventions are effective, replicating the study by moving up the hierarchy to higher-level policy planners).

## Background

One of the first requirements for carrying out research on the effectiveness of interventions designed to improve the quality of policy-planning is to specify criteria that can be used as dependent variables. In my earlier research (Janis, 1972; Janis and Mann, 1977), I have reviewed the extensive literature on decision-making and have extracted seven major criteria to use in judging whether a decision made by a person or group is of high quality. Such judgements pertain to the decision-making procedures that lead up to the act of commitment to a final choice (cf. Etzioni, 1968; Hoffman, 1965; Maier, 1967; Simon, 1957; Taylor, 1965; Young, 1966; Wilensky, 1967). As applied to policy-planning groups, the seven procedural criteria are as follows: the group (1) thoroughly canvasses a wide range of policy alternatives; (2) takes account of the full range of objectives to be fulfilled and the values implicated by the choice; (3) carefully weighs whatever is found out about the costs or drawbacks and the uncertain risks of negative consequences, as well as the positive consequences, that could flow from each alternative; (4) intensively searches for new information relevant for further evaluation of the policy alternatives; (5) conscientiously takes account of any new information or expert judgement to which the members are exposed, even when the information or judgement does not support the course of action they initially prefer; (6) re-examines the positive and negative consequences of all known alternatives, including those originally regarded as unacceptable, before making a final choice; and (7) makes detailed recommendations or provisions for implementing and executing the chosen policy, with special attention to contingency plans that might be required if various known risks were to materialize.

Janis and Mann (1977) point out that although systematic data are not yet available on this point, it seems plausible to assume that failure to meet any of the seven criteria is a defect in the decision-making process. The more such defects are present before the policy-planners commit themselves, the greater the chances that they will undergo unanticipated setbacks and post-decisional regret, which make for reversal of the decision. If this working assumption is valid, we would expect that any improvement with regard to meeting the seven criteria will increase the chances that the policy-makers will fulfill the main objectives they themselves (and the other leaders of their organization) wanted to achieve when they initiated the process of working out a new policy.

One major source of defective decision-making has been described in my analysis of fiascos resulting from foreign policy decisions made by presidential advisory groups (Janis, 1972). I call attention to a *concurrence-seeking tendency* that occurs among moderately or highly cohesive groups. When this tendency is dominant, the members use their collective cognitive resources to develop rationalizations in line with shared illusions about the invulnerability of their organization or nation and display other symptoms of "groupthink".

A number of historic fiascos appear to have been products of defective policy-planning on the part of a misguided government leader who obtained social support from his group of advisors. My analysis of case studies of historic fiascos suggests that the following groups of policy advisors were dominated by concurrence-seeking (referred to as "groupthink"): (1) Neville Chamberlain's inner circle, whose members supported the policy of appeasement of Hitler during 1937 and 1938, despite repeated warnings and events indicating that it would have adverse consequences; (2) Admiral Kimmel's group of Naval Commanders whose members failed to respond to warnings in the fall of 1941 that Pearl Harbor was in danger of being attacked by Japanese planes; (3) President Truman's advisory group, whose members supported the decision to escalate the war in North Korea despite firm warnings by the Chinese Communist government that United States entry into North Korea would be met with armed resistance from the Chinese; (4) President John F. Kennedy's advisory group, whose members supported the decision to launch the Bay of Pigs invasion of Cuba despite the availability of information indicating that it would be an unsuccessful venture and would damage United States' relations with other countries; (5) President Lyndon B. Johnson's "Tuesday luncheon group", whose members supported the decision to escalate the war in Vietnam, despite intelligence reports and other information indicating that this course of action would not defeat the Vietcong or the North Vietnamese and would entail unfavourable political consequences within the United States. In all these "groupthink"-dominated groups, there were strong pressures toward uniformity, which inclined the members to avoid raising controversial issues, questioning weak arguments, or calling a halt to soft-headed thinking. Other social psychologists (Green and Conolley, 1974;

Raven, 1974; Wong-McCarthy, 1978) have noted similar symptoms of groupthink in the way Nixon and his inner circle handled the Watergate coverup.

Eight main symptoms of groupthink run through the case studies of historic decision-making fiascos (Janis, 1972). Each symptom can be identified by a variety of indicators, derived from historical records, observers' accounts of conversations, and participants' memoirs. The eight symptoms of groupthink are:

(1) An illusion of invulnerability, shared by most or all of the members, which creates excessive optimism and encourages taking extreme risks.

(2) Collective efforts to rationalize in order to discount warnings which might lead the members to reconsider their assumptions before they recommit themselves to their past policy decisions.

(3) An unquestioned belief in the group's inherent morality, inclining the members to ignore the ethical or moral consequences of their decisions.

(4) Stereotyped views of rivals and enemies as too evil to warrant genuine attempts to negotiate, or as too weak and stupid to counter whatever risky attempts are made to defeat their purposes.

(5) Direct pressure on any member who expresses strong arguments against any of the group's stereotypes, illusions, or commitments, making clear that this type of dissent is contrary to what is expected of all loyal members.

(6) Self-censorship of deviations from the apparent group consensus, reflecting each member's inclination to minimize to himself the importance of his doubts and counter-arguments.

(7) A shared illusion of unanimity concerning judgements conforming to the majority view (partly resulting from self-censorship of deviations, augmented by the false assumption that silence means consent).

(8) The emergence of self-appointed mind-guards — members who protect the group from adverse information that might shatter their shared complacency about the effectiveness and morality of their decisions.

In our recent book, Leon Mann and I have elaborated on the theory of concurrence-seeking, or "groupthink", as a defective pattern of decision making that is fostered by certain social conditions affecting most, if not all, members of a group. Our assumption is that the symptoms of groupthink are behavioural consequences of

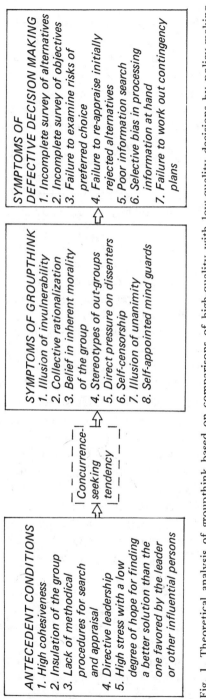

Fig. 1. Theoretical analysis of groupthink based on comparisons of high-quality with low-quality decisions by policy-making groups. From I. L. Janis and L. Mann, *Decision-making: A psychological analysis of conflict, choice and commitment.* New York: Free Press (1977).

a coping pattern of defensive avoidance, which is mutually supported by the group members.

The schematic analysis in Fig. 1 (from Janis and Mann, 1977) shows the major antecedent conditions of concurrence-seeking, which lead to the symptoms of groupthink. The main variables shown in this figure form the basis for the independent and dependent variables that need to be investigated in comparative case studies, field experiments, and other systematic investigations. This analysis leads us to attempt to develop interventions that change the antecedent conditions in such a way that group processes are less likely to produce the symptoms of groupthink, with the result that symptoms of defective decision-making will also be less likely to occur.

One of the factors listed as an antecedent condition in Fig. 1 is the lack of methodical procedures for search and appraisal. Among the procedures that may help to prevent groupthink are various interventions derived from our recent work on preventing defective coping patterns in individual decision making (Janis and Mann, 1977). The key concepts on which the new interventions are based come from an analysis of the research literature on psychological stress bearing especially on the cognitions that determine how people react to warnings and fear-arousing messages that urge protective action to avert health hazards or other serious threats. From this research literature, we extracted five basic patterns of coping behavior that affect the quality of decision-making. One of the patterns — vigilance — results in careful information search, unbiased information processing, and other characteristics of high-quality decisions. The other four patterns are occasionally adaptive in saving time, effort, and emotional wear-and-tear; but much more often they result in defective decision-making if the decision maker is confronted with a vital choice that has serious consequences for himself, for his family, or for the organization on whose behalf he is making the decision. The four non-optimal patterns of decision-making behavior that are contrasted with the fifth pattern, vigilance, are (1) unconflicted adherence to old policy — "business as usual"; (2) unconflicted change to a new course of action; (3) defensive avoidance; and (4) hypervigilance. In line with our approach to decision-making in terms of stress dynamics, we have proposed a general model of the same five coping patterns to apply to the analysis of all consequential decisions that generate decisional conflict.

TABLE 1

*Manifestations of conflict and related symptoms of stress for each of the five basic patterns of decision-making*

| Pattern of Coping with Challenge | Subjective Beliefs (Indicators of Mediating Psychological Conditions) | Level of Stress | Degree of Vacillation of Preference for Alternative Courses of Action |
|---|---|---|---|
| 1. Unconflicted adherence | ● No serious risk from current course of action | Low: persistently calm | No vacillation |
| 2. Unconflicted change | ● Serious risk from current course of action<br>● No serious risk from new course of action | Low: persistently calm | No vacillation |
| 3. Defensive avoidance | ● Serious risk from current course of action<br>● Serious risk from new course of action<br>● No better solution can be found than the least objectionable alternative | Variable: from low to high (predominantly pseudo-calm with breakthrough of high emotional arousal when signs of threat become salient) | Little or no vacillation (except when signs of threat are salient) |
| 4. Hypervigilance | ● Serious risk from current course of action<br>● Serious risk from new course of action<br>● A better solution can be found<br>● Insufficient time to search for and evaluate a better solution | High: persistently strong anxiety | Very high rate of vacillation or practically none (perseveration) |
| 5. Vigilance | ● Serious risk from current course of action<br>● Serious risk from new course of action<br>● A better solution can be found<br>● Sufficient time to search for and evaluate a better solution | Moderate: variations within inter-mediate range, with level depending upon exposure to threat cues or reassuring communications | Moderate to high rate of vacillation (depending on content of new information) |

From Janis and Mann (1977).

TABLE 2

*Criteria for high-quality decision-making*

| Pattern of Coping with Challenge | 1. Thorough Canvassing of Alternatives | 2. Thorough Canvassing of Objectives | 3. Careful Weighing of Consequences | 4. Thorough Search for Information | 5. Unbiased Assimilation of New Information | 6. Careful Re-appraisal of Consequences | 7. Thorough Planning for Implementation and for Contingencies |
|---|---|---|---|---|---|---|---|
| A. Unconflicted adherence | − | − | − | − | + | − | − |
| B. Unconflicted change | − | − | − | − | + | − | − |
| C. Defensive avoidance | − | − | − | − | ± | − | − |
| D. Hypervigilance | − | − | ± | + | ± | ± | ± |
| E. Vigilance | + | + | + | + | + | + | + |

Note: + = The decision-maker meets the criterion to the best of his ability.

− = The decision-maker fails to meet the criterion.

± = The decision-maker's performance fluctuates, sometimes meeting the criterion to the best of his ability and sometimes not.

All evaluative terms such as "thorough" and "unbiased" are to be understood as intrapersonal comparative assessments, relative to the person's performance under the most favorable conditions that enable him to display his cognitive capabilities to the fullest possible degree. From Janis and Mann (1977).

The mediating psychological conditions that are assumed to give rise to each of the five coping patterns are shown in the second column of Table 1. Many research studies we reviewed (Janis and Mann, 1977, Chapters 8–14) indicate that the beliefs listed here can often be modified, whether the decision maker is a private consumer or a member of a top-level government policy-planning group. When those beliefs are changed, there are observable changes in the level of stress and in the degree of vacillation, as described in the third and fourth columns of Table 1. Some of the interventions we are planning to develop are based on the assumption that among members of policy-planning groups, the individual beliefs that give rise to the various defective coping patterns can be changed in the direction of the four basic beliefs specified for the coping pattern of vigilance.

Table 2 shows the behavioral consequences pertaining directly to the seven criteria for high-quality decision-making. These consequences for group decisions have not yet been investigated systematically. Later on in this paper I shall indicate how this might be done in the context of policy-making groups.

Interventions designed to counteract the defective decision-making patterns, which may prove to be effective in preventing groupthink, include the balance-sheet procedure and stress inoculation for post-decisional setbacks. (These procedures and the series of research studies that indicate their value for individual decision makers are described in Janis and Mann, 1977, Chapter 14.) The same basic procedures, which could easily be modified for use in group meetings, might prove to be effective in preventing defensive avoidance and promoting vigilance among members of decision-making groups.

Not all cohesive groups suffer from groupthink, though all may display some of its symptoms from time to time (Janis, 1972). A group whose members are highly competent and who have properly defined roles, with traditions and standard operating procedures that facilitate critical inquiry, is probably capable of making better decisions than any individual in the group who works on the problem alone (see Davis, 1969; Steiner, 1966). And yet the advantages of having policy decisions made by groups are often lost because of psychological pressures that arise when the members work closely together, share the same values, and above all, face a crisis situation in which everyone realizes at the outset that whatever action the group decides to take will be fraught with serious risks and that there is little hope for obtaining new information that will point to a satisfactory solution. In these circumstances, the leader and the members of his in-group are subjected to stresses that generate a strong need for affiliation.

As conformity pressures begin to dominate, the striving for unanimity fosters the pattern of defensive avoidance, with characteristic lack of vigilance, unwarranted optimism, "sloganistic" thinking, and reliance on shared rationalizations that bolster the least objectionable alternative. That alternative is often the one favored by the leader or other influential persons in the policy-making group on the basis of initial biases that remain uncorrected despite the availability of impressive evidence showing it to be inferior to other feasible courses of action.

### Prescriptive hypotheses to be tested

In my analysis of the conditions that foster groupthink (Janis, 1972), I suggest ten prescriptive hypotheses.

One general hypothesis, which pertains to the effects of training, is presented in my discussion of the question, "Is a little knowledge of groupthink a dangerous thing?" (pp. 222–224). The training hypothesis is as follows:

> *Hypothesis 1.* Information about the causes and consequences of groupthink will have a beneficial deferring effect.

Impressive information from case studies can augment the members' resolve to curtail group encroachments on their critical thinking and can increase their willingness to try out antidote prescriptions, "provided . . . that they are aware of the costs in time and effort and realize that there are other disadvantages they must also watch out for before they decide to adopt any of them as a standard operating procedure" (p. 223).

Six more prescriptive hypotheses pertain to decision-making procedures that can be carried out within the policy-making group itself and can usually be put into operation if the chairman of the group decides to try them out:

> *Hypothesis 2.* The leader, when assigning a policy-planning mission to a group, should be impartial instead of stating preferences and expectations at the outset.

This practice requires each leader to limit his briefings to unbiased statements about the scope of the problem and the limitations of available resources, without advocating specific proposals he would like to see adopted. This allows the conferees the opportunity to develop an atmosphere of open inquiry and to explore impartially a wide range of policy alternatives.

*Hypothesis 3.* The leader of a policy-forming group at the outset should assign the role of critical evaluator to each member, encouraging the group to give high priority to airing objections and doubts.

This practice needs to be reinforced by the leader's acceptance of criticism of his own judgements in order to discourage the members from soft-pedaling their disagreements.

*Hypothesis 4.* At every meeting devoted to evaluating policy alternatives, one or more members should be assigned the role of devil's advocate.

In order to avoid domesticating and neutralizing the devil's advocates, the group leader will have to give each of them an unambiguous assignment to present his arguments as cleverly and convincingly as he can, as a good lawyer would, challenging the testimony of those advocating the majority position.

*Hypothesis 5.* Throughout the period when the feasibility and effectiveness of policy alternatives are being surveyed, the policy-planning group should from time to time divide into two or more subgroups to meet separately, under different chairmen, and then come together to hammer out their differences.

*Hypothesis 6.* Whenever the policy issue involves relations with a rival organization or out-group, a sizable block of time (perhaps an entire session) should be spent surveying all warning signals from the rivals and constructing alternative scenarios of the rivals' intentions.

*Hypothesis 7.* After reaching a preliminary concensus about what seems to be the best policy alternative, the policy-planning group should hold a "second chance" meeting at which every member is expected to express as vividly as he can all his residual doubts and to rethink the entire issue before making a definitive choice.

Three additional hypotheses specify procedures that require the participation of other units and persons in the organization outside of the policy planning group:

*Hypothesis 8.* One or more outside experts or qualified colleagues within the organization who are not core members of the policy-planning group should be present at each meeting on a staggered basis and should be encouraged to challenge the views of the core members.

*Hypothesis 9.* Each member of the policy-planning group should discuss periodically the group's deliberations with trusted associates in his own unit of the organization and report back their reactions.

*Hypothesis 10.* The organization should routinely follow the administrative practice of setting up several independent policy-planning and evaluation groups to work on the same policy question, each carrying out its deliberations under a different chairman.

The last three of the above ten prescriptive hypotheses, in contrast to all the others, cannot be applied unless cooperation is obtained from the key persons throughout an organization, with appropriate directives issued by the chief executive or the board of directors.

## What type of research can be done?

In the preceding sections, I have presented a number of analytic and prescriptive hypotheses concerning the conditions under which the quality of group decisions can be improved by preventing groupthink. Five analytic hypotheses are represented in Fig. 1, which lists the key situational factors that are expected to increase the concurrence-seeking tendencies of the members of a group and thereby decrease vigilant search and appraisal. The ten prescriptive hypotheses are intended to reduce or moderate the influence of one or more of these five factors. All of these hypotheses must be validated before they can be applied with any confidence. Each of the proposed remedies may prove to have undesirable side effects and other drawbacks, but these hypotheses appear sufficiently promising to warrant the trouble and expense of being tested as potentially useful means for counteracting groupthink whenever a small number of policy-planners or executives in any organization meet with their chairman or chief executive to work out new policies. Some of the anti-groupthink procedures might also help to counteract initial biases of the members, prevent pluralistic ignorance, and eliminate other sources of error that can occur independently of groupthink.

The next question that arises is: How can the analytic and

prescriptive hypotheses be tested? My answer is that the full range of behavioral research methods could be used, including comparative case studies, experiments in social psychological laboratories, and field experiments in natural settings.

In limited ways, comparative case studies can provide evidence pertinent to analytic hypotheses about the causes and consequences of groupthink. One study that illuminates some of the politically relevant consequences of groupthink was completed by Phillip Tetlock when he was a graduate student at Yale working with me. Tetlock systematically re-investigated the Bay of Pigs fiasco and the two other historic fiascos in US foreign policy that were analyzed in the main case studies presented in my book on *Victims of Groupthink* (1972). Tetlock carried out systematic content analyses of the relevant public speeches made by the President of the United States and by the Secretary of State during the period when each of the three policy decisions was being made, which presumably would reflect the quality of their thinking at that time. He compared the content analysis results from the three groupthink decisions with those obtained from comparable public speeches made during the time when two non-groupthink decisions were being made (the Marshall Plan and the Cuban Missile Crisis), both of which I had also analyzed for comparative purposes in *Victims of Groupthink*. Using a measure of cognitive complexity developed by Peter Suedfeld, Tetlock found that when the groupthink decisions were being made, the public speeches obtained significantly lower scores than when the non-groupthink decisions were being made. Tetlock also found that when the groupthink decisions were under discussion there were certain signs of stereotyped thinking in the public speeches. In our future research, we plan to apply the comparative method used in Tetlock's study to other verbal products produced in connection with group meetings, including memoranda, memoirs, minutes, and verbatim transcripts of the sessions.

A somewhat different type of comparative study has been initiated by William Wong-McCarthy, when he was a Yale graduate student working with me. Wong-McCarthy systematically compared two samples of Watergate tapes from two different periods. One sample was from a period when Nixon and his main advisors (Haldeman, Erlichman and Dean) were keenly aware of the threat of public exposure, felt little hope for finding a better solution than to continue the cover-up policy, and displayed coordinated group action. The other sample was from a period when the in-group disintegrated as more and more devastating revelations implicated one member after another. He found that the transcripts of the meetings held during the period of coordinated action contained significantly more supportive statements, which are symptomatic of groupthink, than those meetings held during the period when the participants were no longer a cohesive group. This comparative method in which each policy-making group is used as its own control could be extended to obtain objective data on the relationship between various external conditions and blind ratings of the symptoms of groupthink — provided, of course, that the investigators can obtain recordings or detailed minutes of group meetings.

Concurrently with the fully controlled experimental research I shall describe shortly, my co-workers and I are planning to continue conducting quasi-experimental studies based on existing records of historic policy decisions. We hope to obtain the cooperation of other social scientists in developing a cross-organization file that will contain indexed case studies of policy-planning. One purpose is to provide comparative case study material for the *discovery phase* of the research, to suggest plausible hypotheses about the conditions under which high-quality policy-making is facilitated. We expect to pursue the most promising hypotheses in designing the field experiments on the effects of interventions intended to improve the quality of group decisions. A second purpose is to build up a data bank on a large sample of high-quality versus low-quality policy decisions for the *verification phase* of the research. The data bank will provide correlational evidence for testing the hypotheses (derived from a few comparative case studies) with large samples of policy decisions. For example, the conditions shown in the causes-of-groupthink model in Fig. 1 above, which were inferred from a small number of comparative case studies, might be tested systematically by comparing 25 high-quality decisions with 25 low-quality decisions made by governmental committees. The comparison would focus on degree of group cohesiveness, degree of insulation of the group, extent to which methical procedures were used, and other variables specified by the model.

The first step in constructing the file will be to insert duplicate copies of case studies of policy decisions that have been published as books or journal articles. (Copyright permission would have to be obtained before photocopying any articles for insertion in the data file). Typical examples are Paige's (1968) book on the Truman administration's decision to enter the war in Korea and Allison's (1971) book on policy decisions made during the Cuban Missile Crisis. The second step will be to index and code the material in ways that can be useful for comparative analysis. One set of coding categories pertains to the quality of the decision-making procedures. For this purpose the seven major criteria for judging the adequacy of decision-making procedures, as stated  earlier, will be used. We plan to operationalize the seven categories in terms of indicators that can be used to rate the degree to which each criterion is met. These operational definitions will be used to rate each decision in the file. The ratings or scores, in turn, will be used to sub-divide the case studies into three main categories – policy decisions arrived at by (1) high-quality procedures (high or moderate scores on all seven criteria), (2) medium-quality procedures (mixed scores), and (3) low-quality procedures (low scores on the seven criteria). A selective search of the case study literature will be made early in the development of the file in order to build up a series of cases in all three categories. These could form the basis for a series of comparative studies looking into leadership practices, standard operating procedures, and other conditions that might be related to high-quality decision-making.

The final step will be to carry out systematic correlational investigations using the case study material in the file. These studies should enable us to determine the degree to which specific conditions (and interacting sets of conditions) are related to the quality of policy-making procedures. The file might also be useful for cross-cultural and cross-national studies, to see to what extent the causes and consequences of groupthink tend to be the same or different under varying social conditions.

The comparative methods I have been discussing so far are quasi-experimental and suffer from a number of obvious disadvantages with regard to achieving experimental control over the independent variables under investigation, but have the great advantage of high external validity by dealing with real-life desicions by policy makers. The reverse advantages and disadvantages are to be expected, of course, for laboratory experiments, where relatively high control over the variables can be achieved but at the expense of obtaining findings that may prove to have little validity outside the laboratory. Controlled field experiments in actual organizational settings might prove to be feasible, in which case we can hope to observe cause-and-effect relationships that will have a high degree of external validity. If field experiments as well as laboratory experiments and comparative case studies of historic decisions all point to the same general conclusion when we are testing a hypothesis about the conditions that foster groupthink, we can feel reasonably confident about the generality of the findings.

When I speak of controlled field experiments I have in mind studies in which the investigator firstly, introduces an experimental intervention under natural conditions with policy planners facing real decisions and, secondly, determines the effects of the intervention by comparing groups assigned on a random basis to the experimental and control conditions. No such studies bearing on groupthink have been carried out as yet.

Prior to attempting to carry out field experiments in order to test the interventions specified by the prescriptive hypothesis, I think it is sensible to develop and test them first in laboratory experiments. A few laboratory studies that have already been carried out are indirectly relevant to the causes and consequences of groupthink. Some of the symptoms noted in my studies, for example, are similar to those observed in experiments on group polarization effects (see Davis, 1969). An article by Myers and Lamm (1975) discusses the dozens of laboratory experiments carried out during the 1960s that purported to demonstrate that the average individual was more prone to take risks after participating in a group discussion than when making a decision on his own (e.g. Brown, 1965, 1974; Kogan and Wallach, 1967; Stoner, 1961; Wallach *et al.*, 1962). They also take account of more recent findings and analyses that call into question the generality of the so-called "risky-shift" tendency (e.g. Cartwright, 1971; Pruitt, 1971). Their analysis of the accumulated evidence, in agreement with Davis (1969) and others, points to a group polarization tendency such that the group decision enhances whichever point of view, risky or conservative, that is initially dominant within the group (see, for example, Lamm and Sauer, 1974; Moscovici and Zavalloni, 1969; Rabbie and Visser, 1972).

> Some of the literature cited presents experimental demonstrations of groupthink processes which Irving Janis (1972) has proposed to help explain decision fiascoes . . . For example, his suggestion that group members "show interest in facts and opinions that support their initially preferred policy and take up time in their meetings to discuss them, but

they tend to ignore facts and opinions that do not support their initially preferred policy" (p. 10) is confirmed by a recent finding that discussion arguments more decisively favor the dominant alternative than do written arguments (Myers and Lamm, 1977.)

More direct evidence bearing on the conditions that foster group-think comes from a few other laboratory experiments. In a simulation experiment of the historical decision by Mexican authorities which led to the Alamo episode, Crow and Noel (1975) found symptoms analogous to those of groupthink. When consensus was induced as an experimental condition, many groups chose a much more aggressive course of action than many individual members initially preferred.

Flowers (1977), in "a laboratory test of some implications of Janis's groupthink hypothesis", divided 40 teams of students into different treatment groups and asked all of them to work on the same hypothetical decision (imagining that they were a group of school administrators deciding what to do about a formerly good teacher who as a result of illness had become incompetent). Group leaders were trained to conduct meetings according to two different leadership styles. One was an *open* style — in line with prescriptive hypotheses about preventing groupthink, the leader avoided stating his own position on the issue until after the others in the group had discussed their own solutions, continually encouraged free discussion of alternatives, and explicitly conveyed the norm of airing all possible viewpoints. The second leadership style was *closed* — the leader stated his own position at the outset, did not encourage free discussion of alternatives, and explicitly conveyed the norm that the most important thing was for the team to agree on its decision. Flowers found that, as predicted, the teams exposed to the open leadership style offered significantly more solutions to the problem and during their discussion cited significantly more facts from the information made available to them before arriving at a consensus than the teams exposed to the closed leadership style.

Another variable investigated in Flower's laboratory experiment was cohesiveness of the groups, which she manipulated by comparing groups of acquaintances with groups of strangers. Contrary to one of the analytic hypotheses about factors that promote groupthink, the teams made up of acquaintances, who were assumed to be more cohesive, did not differ significantly from the teams made up of strangers on either measure of decision-making activity. Flowers suggests that the failure to find the predicted differences may imply that cohesiveness is not a necessary condition for groupthink, but she also points out that the student groups she studied might differ on many dimensions from the groups described in *Victims of Groupthink* — such as degree of consequentiality of the decision, salience of real rivals or enemies, length of time the group works together, and quality of interaction among the members. Any of these different factors could prove to be an interacting variable that moderates the effects of differences in cohesiveness. Another possibility is that differences in decision-making activities at relatively low levels of cohesiveness (strangers versus mere acquaintances) may be too slight to be detected, whereas differences between low and high degrees of cohesiveness (e.g. strangers versus close friends who are somewhat dependent upon each other for self-esteem enhancement) might emerge quite clearly.

The laboratory experiments I have just described illustrate the type of research that can provide some pertinent evidence and that can help investigators to pose more sharply the issues to be pursued in much more costly experiments dealing with real-life decisions by policy-making groups in natural settings. Additional studies are discussed by Ivan Steiner in his chapter in this volume.

Among the additional variables specified in Fig. 1 that could be assessed in laboratory studies are the following:

(1) *Insulation of the group.* The laboratory environment permits control over communication from outside the group. The flow of information and contact with neutral non-group members can be restricted to produce a high degree of insulation.

(2) *Lack of methodical procedures of search and appraisal.* The tendency of problem-solving groups to avoid planning and discussion of procedural methods has been pointed out by Hackman and Morris (1974). They discuss the assumptions apparently made by many decision-makers in public and private institutions that everyone already knows how to go about the task and that discussion about how to tackle the problem is a waste of time. It is therefore unlikely that methodical procedures will be used unless a group is specifically instructed to employ the balance sheet procedure, which I mentioned earlier, or other methodical procedures.

(3) *High stress with low hope.* A number of stressful policy-planning tasks could be compared in order to determine the ones

most likely to produce concurrence-seeking. Stress and hope could be varied by modifying the difficulty of the decision and the resources available to work on it.

By testing the prescriptive hypotheses in controlled experiments we can expect to gain some further information about the effects of the antecedent conditions. Insulation of the group, for example, is counteracted by Prescriptive Hypotheses 8 and 9, which involve having outside experts at each meeting, and consultation with "home-base" colleagues. The antecedent condition of lack of methodical procedures for search and appraisal is counteracted by Prescriptive Hypotheses 3, 4, 5, 6, and 7. Also, low hope of finding a better solution than the one stated by the leader (Antecedent Condition 5) is counteracted by Prescriptive Hypothesis 2, which requires that the leader be impartial in stating the problem without expressing a preference for a particular solution. Consequently, the effects of these antecedent conditions can be evaluated as part of the study of the relative effects of the different prescriptive hypotheses.

## Perspectives for controlled experiments on groups making real decisions

Increasing criticism of laboratory studies (cf. Argyris, 1968; McGuire, 1973; Meehl, 1966; Rosenthal and Rosnow, 1969) has spurred efforts to develop approaches which avoid some of their short-comings. As I mentioned earlier, laboratory experiments have the advantage of control over the manipulation of independent variables and therefore more certain identification of cause-effect relations than is the case with survey or field studies. However, the many background variables that are held constant by the nature of the experimental setting potentially could affect the extent and direction of the relationships observed between the independent and dependent variables. Often these "interactions" contribute to the failure of observed relationships to hold up in new, untested situations.

A research strategy that may help to solve this problem without going to the enormous expense in time and effort of doing field experiments in large organizations is to carry out small laboratory-like experiments using *ad hoc* groups of qualified policy-planners who agree to cooperate with our research team in exchange for having the opportunity to participate in policy-planning on an issue about which they are deeply concerned. Working with advanced graduate students in administrative sciences and related fields at Yale University, I have developed the prototype for this type of field research: (1) announcements are made to recruit well-qualified candidates for a policy-planning group with the promise that their policy recommendations will be circulated to people who have the power to change the current unsatisfactory policy. (2) Volunteers are selected with an eye to representing appropriate expertise and varying viewpoints, comparable to what is done when a government agency sets up a group to recommend policy changes. (3) The working sessions of the planning group are recorded and are unobtrusively observed by one or more members of the research team. (4) When the group submits its final report on policy recommendations, the head of the research team carries out his promise by circulating it, via informal university social networks, to key persons in the local, state or federal government who could initiate a change in policy.

As an example, about 12 years ago, in collaboration with David Adams, who was a psychology graduate student at that time, I recruited a policy-planning group of administrative scientists, economists and political scientists from among the graduate students at Yale University to prepare a "white paper" for the US Government on proposals for overcoming economic deterrents to ending the war in Vietnam. The members of the group were highly motivated to do a good job and reinforced each other's hopes that the product of their deliberations could have a positive effect on the policy-planning in Washington. When the group submitted its "white paper", I had it duplicated and, with the aid of various federal government advisors on the faculty in the Law School and in the Department of Political Science, circulated it to a number of key government officials. The group's efforts were rewarded by encouraging responses from several officials, including a detailed critique of the group's "white paper" indicating that even though it was not going to bring about an immediate end to the Vietnam war, at least it was being read carefully and taken seriously. The data obtained from the tape recordings of those sessions of the *ad hoc* planning group were used to investigate phases in group development, which turned out to be parallel to those I had reported on the basis of research on self-study groups in management training workshops and mutual aid groups in anti-smoking clinics and weight-reduction clinics (Janis, 1966).

I am planning to use this prototype in the following way: announcements will be sent to community organizations — such as the local chapters of the American Civil Liberties Union and the League of Women Voters — calling for qualified volunteers to participate in making policy recommendations on a controversial policy that many people would like to change, e.g. involving restrictive abortion laws, failures to implement rules about equal opportunity employment, lack of control over industries that are polluting the local atmosphere, etc. The attempt will be made to select issues for which qualified persons in the community are likely to volunteer. For each issue, at least 14 volunteers are needed, which is sufficient to set up two equivalent groups, one of which will be given the procedures of the anti-groupthink program developed earlier in laboratory experiments, while the other will serve as a control group Using several different issues as replications in an analysis of variance design, the effectiveness of the intervention procedures can be determined. Because of the educational value of the anti-groupthink research program, cooperation of management training workshops can be expected. In exchange for the training provided to the participants, workshop administrators would be asked to permit the training to be given in a sequence so that the performance of trained groups could be compared with those that are untrained until the end of the workshop period.

An alternative would be to obtain a large pool of volunteers to work on a popular problem so that ten or more groups of seven or eight each can be set up to work on the same policy issue. All of those groups would have the same policy-planning assignment, with half of the groups first being given the anti-groupthink program while the other half is not. In all such studies, the seven criteria for high-quality decision-making could be used as dependent measures. Other measures could also be obtained to ascertain the effectiveness of the anti-groupthink program. These might include, in addition to manifestations of the eight symptoms of groupthink, blind ratings by well-qualified judges of the quality of the policy recommendations and the arguments for them in the "white papers" produced by each of the policy-planning groups.

This approach used in introducing anti-groupthink interventions would be similar to "process counselling", which is oriented toward improving interaction processes within policy-making groups by changing group norms concerning problem-solving strategies "to help group members discover and implement new, more task-effective ways of working together" (Hackman and Morris, 1975). Some suggestive evidence is cited by Hackman and Morris in support to the assumption that task effectiveness and creativity of solutions might be increased by inducing participants to engage in a preliminary discussion of the strategy of solving the problem before they start to work on it. They point out, however, that while a few pertinent studies show promising results, other studies indicate that interventions designed to improve problem-solving procedures give rise to only temporary improvements with little or no carryover to subsequent problem-solving tasks (Hackman *et al.*, 1974; Maier, 1963; Shure *et al.*, 1962; Varela, 1971). The interventions we propose to develop and test differ from these earlier efforts in that we try to counteract certain of the conditions that motivate the participants to rely on group consensus, which interferes with open-minded, vigilant problem-solving.

After evidence from *ad hoc* planning groups is available concerning the effectiveness of an anti-groupthink program, the heads of local and national organizations could be approached. Professional services might be offered free of charge to introduce the program to executive groups in their organization in exchange for the opportunity to obtain additional data on its effectiveness. It would be desirable to try out the program first with executive groups that are relatively low in the organizational hierarchy and then, if evidence shows it to be effective, to move up in the hierarchy to top level groups of policy makers. I have started to discuss this idea with a few high-level executives and they seem to be highly receptive to the proposed research. It seems to me, therefore, that controlled field experiments on preventing groupthink in actual organizational settings will prove to be feasible.

If sufficient progress is made from field experiments with *ad hoc* groups, I see no reason why the necessary arrangements could not be made to test the most promising interventions in a few organizations interested in improving the quality of policy-making procedures. And if I permit myself to be a little grandiose about imagining what might be done in the future, I can envisage the same type of research on prescriptive hypotheses being carried out in many different organizations in different countries, so as to accumulate evidence on the generality of the conclusions in different organizational and national contexts.

## References

Allison, G. T. *Essence of Decision: Explaining the Cuban Missile Crisis.* Boston: Little, Brown, 1971.

Argyris, C. Some unintended consequences of rigorous research. *Psychological Bulletin,* 1968, 70, 185—197.

Brown, R. *Social Psychology.* New York: Free Press, 1965.

Brown, R. Further comments on the risky shift. *American Psychologist,* 1974, 29, 468—470.

Cartwright, D. Risk taking by individuals and groups: An assessment of research employing choice dilemmas. *Journal of Personality and Social Psychology,* 1971, 20, 361—378.

Crow, W. J. and Noel, R. C. An experiment in simulated historical decision-making. In M. G. Hermann and T. W. Milburn (Eds), *A Psychological Examination of Political Leaders.* New York: Free Press, 1975.

Davis, J. H. *Group Performance.* Menlo Park, Calif.: Addison-Wesley, 1969.

Etzioni, A. *Active Society.* New York: Free Press, 1968.

Flowers, M. L. A laboratory test of some implications of Janis's groupthink hypothesis. *Journal of Personality and Social Psychology,* 1977, 35, 888—896.

Green, D. and Conolley, E. "Groupthink" and Watergate. Paper presented at the annual meetings of the American Psychological Association, 1974.

Hackman, J. R. and Morris, C. G. Group tasks, group interaction process, and group performance effectiveness: A review and proposed integration. Technical Report No. 7, August, 1974. Contract No. N00014-67A-0097-0026, NR170-744, Organizational Effectiveness Research Program, Psychological Sciences Division, Office of Naval Research. (Republished in L. Berkowitz (Ed.), *Advances in Experimental Social Psychology,* Vol. 8. New York and London: Academic Press, 1975.)

Hackman, J. R., Weiss, J. A. and Brousseau, K. *Effects of task performance strategies on group performance effectiveness.* Technical Report No. 5, Department of Administrative Sciences, Yale University, 1974.

Hoffman, L. R. Group problem solving. In L. Berkowitz (Ed.), *Advances in Experimental Social Psychology,* Vol. 2. New York and London: Academic Press, 1965.

Janis, I. L. Field and experimental studies of phases in the development of cohesive face-to-face groups. *XVIII International Congress of Psychology abstracts of communication: Problems of mental development and social psychology.* Moscow, USSR: International Union of Scientific Psychology, 1966, p. 397.

Janis, I. L. *Victims of Groupthink: A Psychological Study of Foreign-policy Decisions and Fiascoes.* Boston: Houghton Mifflin, 1972.

Janis, I. L. and Mann, L. *Decision-making: A psychological analysis of conflict, choice and commitment.* New York: Free Press, 1977.

Kogan, N. and Wallach, M. Risk taking as a function of the situation, the person and the group. In G. Mandler *et al., New Directions in Psychology,* Vol. 3. New York: Holt, Rinehart and Winston, 1967.

Lamm, H. and Sauer, C. Discussion-induced shift toward higher demands in negotiation. *European Journal of Social Psychology,* 1974, 4, 85–88.

Maier, N. R. F. *Problem Solving Discussions and Conferences: Leadership Methods and Skills.* New York: McGraw-Hill, 1963.

Maier, N. R. F. Group problem solving. *Psychological Review,* 1967, 74, 239–249.

McGuire, W. J. The yin and yang of progress in social psychology: Seven koan. *Journal of Personality and Social Psychology,* 1973, 26, 446–456.

Meehl, P. Theory testing in psychology and physics. *Philosophy of Sciences,* 1967, 34, 103–115.

Moscovici, S. and Zavalloni, M. The group as a polarizer of attitudes. *Journal of Personality and Social Psychology,* 1969, 12, 125–135.

Myers, D. G. and Lamm, H. The polarizing effect of group discussion. In I. Janis (Ed.), *Current Trends in Psychology: Readings from American Scientist.* Los Altos, Calif.: Kaufmann, 1977.

Paige, G. D. *The Korean Decision.* New York: Free Press, 1968.

Pruitt, D. Conclusions: Toward an understanding of choice shifts in group discussion. *Journal of Personality and Social Psychology,* 1971, 20, 495–510.

Rabbie, J. M. and Visser, L. Bargaining strength and group polarization in intergroup negotiations. *European Journal of Social Psychology,* 1972, 2, 401–416.

Raven, B. H. The Nixon group. *Journal of Social Issues,* 1974, 30, 297–320.

Raven, B. H. and Rubin, J. Z. *Social Psychology: People in Groups.* New York: Wiley, 1977.

Rosenthal, R. and Rosnow, R. *Artifact in Behavioral Research.* New York and London: Academic Press, 1969.

Shure, G. H., Rogers, M. S., Larsen, I. M. and Tassone, J. Group planning and task effectiveness. *Sociometry,* 1962, 25, 263–282.

Simon, H. *Administrative behavior* (2nd ed.). New York: Macmillan, 1957.

Steiner, I. D. Models for inferring relationships between group size and potential group productivity. *Behavioral Science,* 1966, 11, 273–283.

Stoner, J. A. F. A comparison of individual and group decisions involving risk. M.S. thesis, Mass. Institute of Technology, 1961.

Taylor, D. W. Decision making and problem solving. In: J. March (Ed.) *Handbook of Organizations.* Chicago: Rand McNally 1965.

Tetlock, P. E. Identifying victims of groupthink from public statements of decision makers. *Journal of Personality and Social Psychology,* 1979, 37, 1314–1324.

Varela, J. A. *Psychological solutions to social problems.* New York and London: Academic Press 1971.

Wallach, M. A., Kogan, N. and Bem, D. J. Group influence on individual risk taking. *Journal of Abnormal and Social Psychology,* 1962, 65, 75–86.

Wilensky, H. L. *Organizational intelligence.* New York: Basic Books 1967.

Wong-McCarthy, W. Symptoms of groupthink in the Watergate tapes: Results of a content analysis. Unpublished paper, 1978.

Young, S. *Management: a system analysis.* Glenview, Illinois: Scott, Foresman 1966.

# 22
# Heuristic Models of Groupthink

Ivan D. Steiner

In a fascinating book Irving Janis (1972) has examined the deliberations leading to the Bay of Pigs invasion and other US military fiascos. Participants in the decision-making process are described as having been *Victims of Groupthink,* a mode of thought in which strivings for unanimity override the motivation to realistically appraise alternative courses of action. Groupthink is said to be most likely to occur in highly cohesive groups that are insulated from the judgements of outsiders — especially if the leader actively promotes his own preferred solution to problems. These conditions encourage an "in-group v. out-group" mentality that denigrates any opposition and creates the illusion of in-group invulnerability and moral rectitude. In such a climate members of a decision-making body censor their own and one another's comments, exert direct pressure on any "disloyal" participant who challenges the prevailing stereotypes or assumptions, and nurture the impression of unanimity within the group.

On reading Janis' account of group process in the American White House, I was struck by the parallel between the events he described and other happenings that have been studied by social scientists. My thoughts ranged from lynching crowds and social movements to laboratory research on the "risky shift" and group decision-making. To be sure, such diverse phenomena differ from one another and from the proceedings described by Janis, but there are also obvious similarities. In all of them people communicate selectively and are influenced by what their associates do, or fail to do. Censorship by self and others is often apparent, and can sometimes be inferred even when it is not. Most importantly, social interaction generates an outcome or decision that is a "biased" composite of the initial preferences of the participants, but one that is accepted, defended, or at least tolerated, by all. Sometimes this biased composite is a notoriously bad solution to the problem confronting the group.

Some of the differences among these assemblages are rather striking. Cohesion is not always high, and sometimes seems to be a consequence, instead of a cause, of behavioral harmony. Formal institutionalized leadership of the kind described by Janis is sometimes lacking, and emergent leadership, if it occurs at all, may play a facilitating rather than a determining role. But in spite of such differences, something approximating groupthink occurs in all of them. Information and insights favoring one side of an issue receive disproportionate attention, and social pressure guide the interaction process toward a conclusion that may deviate rather markedly from the initial consensus among members.

Much of social psychology is relevant to an understanding of such processes. In this paper I will concentrate on three lines of research that seem especially pertinent. None of them deals with all the symptoms of groupthink, but each provides a heuristic model for interpreting certain aspects of the phenomenon.

## The horse-trading model

> A man bought a horse for $60 and sold it for $70. Then he bought it back for $80 and again sold it for $90. How much money did he make in the horse business?

Although almost all American college students "solve" this problem immediately, only about 40 percent reach the correct answer. Furthermore, when invited to reconsider, only about 10% of those who have erred discover the correct solution.

The horse-trading problem is far less consequential than those confronted by the groups Janis examined. It does not call for specialized knowledge or entail complex planning or military strategy. But experimenters have found it a convenient issue for group deliberation. Small groups of subjects with contrary opinions can readily be induced to discuss the problem and arrive at a single solution. Participants' interactions can be observed and the accuracy of their joint decision can be appraised. Because such decisions are sometimes outrageously inaccurate even when certain members of groups have the ability to decide correctly, we may surmise that something akin to groupthink is occurring.

Maier and Solem (1952) assembled college students into five or six-person groups, each of which was asked to select a "representative." Approximately half of the groups were told their representative would refrain from expressing any opinion concerning the problem they were about to discuss. The remainder of the groups were advised their representative would serve as a discussion leader who would "encourage the participation of all members and ask questions so as to cause the group to think together rather than as individuals." Discussion leaders were prohibited from expressing their own opinions, but were instructed to try to obtain group agreement on an answer. After each member had worked alone on the problem for one minute, groups were instructed to begin their discussion. After the one-minute initial exposure to the problem, and again after eight minutes of discussion, subjects recorded their own personal decisions on cards. On the second of these occasions they were told they were free to change their decision if they wished.

Sixty-three of Maier and Solem's 67 groups contained at least one person who had solved the problem correctly while working alone. If discussion had been maximally productive, all of the members of those groups should have recorded the correct answer at the conclusion of the session, but less than 80% of them did so. Final accuracy was significantly higher in groups with a discussion leader charged with responsibility for encouraging all members to participate than in groups with inactive leaders. However, this finding held only for groups in which a minority of members had solved the problem correctly when working alone; if three or more individuals had been correct, the sheer weight of majority opinion seemed to assure acceptance of the true answer.

Because Maier and Solem did not attempt to observe and record the actions of their groups, we can only speculate concerning what happened. It is plausible to believe that a single individual with the ability to solve the problem might have been reluctant to suggest his solution was superior to that of his colleagues, or may not have pressed his case very strongly. Without a leader who encouraged him to present and explain his solution he may have remained silent or have been "howled down" by the majority who were committed to a different answer. The same kind of censorship may have occurred when a minority of two correct members confronted a majority who believed the man had netted $10 in the horse-trading business.

If this interpretation is correct, some of Maier and Solem's groups were victims of groupthink — or, at least, one aspect of it. Important contributions that might have permitted everyone to make the correct decision were suppressed. But this apparently happened less often when, as Janis recommends, the leader encourged and legitimized the presentation of all points of view. (It should be noted that none of Maier and Solem's leaders was permitted to express or advocate his own solution to the problem. Thus none of them biased the outcome in a way that Janis believes President Kennedy influenced the decision to invade at the Bay of Pigs.)

In real-life decision-making conferences outcomes may be affected by the prestige or power of those who favor particular options. Torrance (1954) had members of B-26 bomber crews generate their own individual solutions to the horse-trading problem before engaging in discussion and reaching a joint decision. Crews consisted of a pilot (highest prestige and power), navigator, and gunner (lowest prestige and power). Although gunners produced almost as many correct solutions as pilots when working individually, they were markedly less successful in getting their decisions accepted by crewmates who had reached other conclusions. Navigators, who displayed greater competence than either pilots or gunners when working alone, nevertheless failed to match pilots' success rate during the discussion period. When *ad hoc* groups were formed by assembling a pilot from one crew, a navigator from another, and a gunner from a third, the effects of status were greatly reduced.

Because data concerning "who did what" during the discussions are not available, we cannot be sure how the effects of status differences were generated. Perhaps low status discussants sometimes failed to voice their correct solution, or advocated it in a meek and unconvincing fashion. Or, they may at least have delayed their comments until others had committed themselves to other solutions. On the other hand, it is possible that the arguments of low-status members, though vigorously pressed, were less persuasive and acceptable because they represented the thoughts of a low-status person. Another possibility is that high-status members found the views of their low-status associates to be persuasive but were unwilling to acknowledge that their subordinates had been more perceptive or "intelligent" than themselves. Each of these alternative hypotheses would account for the impact of status on group outcomes, and several of them appear to be more plausible when persons of unequal status know they will continue to function with one another in the future (intact crews) then when they realize their present behaviour has no implications for future relationships (*ad hoc* crews).

Although Janis did not stress the effect of status differentials on the deliberations that led to the Bay of Pigs disaster, he noted the probable impact of ribbon-bedecked Chiefs of Staff, and cited President Kennedy's subsequent lament over having assumed "that the military and intelligence people have some secret skill not available to ordinary mortals." The biasing effect of the source on the acceptance of messages has been widely documented by research on attitude change (cf. McGuire, 1969) and appears to be an integral component of groupthink.

High status persons are probably inclined to be more confident of their judgements than are low-status persons — at least when the issue concerns matters that are relevant to their status. Consequently, it is possible that differences in confidence, rather than differences in status *per se*, may have been partly responsible for the effects noted by Torrance. Johnson and Torcivia (1967) asked college students to work alone on the horse-trading problem and then to rate their confidence in the decision they reached. Two-person groups were formed by pairing a subject who had solved the problem correctly with one who had not. Groups were allowed 15 minutes to reach a single solution. Seventy-two percent of the pairs agreed upon the correct answer whereas 100% should have done so if groups had made the best possible use of members' resources. In half of the 36 pairs the member with the correct answer had indicated greater confidence than his partner, and in all but one of these groups the correct answer was accepted. Members of the remaining pairs had indicated equal confidence or the "incorrect member" had reported greater confidence than his colleague; only half of these groups settled upon the correct solution.

We cannot be sure whether more confident members of groups pressed their judgements more strongly than their less confident associates, or whether high confidence conferred a greater measure of immunity to contrary arguments. In any event, confidence was a strong determinant of the groups' decisions, and would probably have produced a large number of "bad" solutions had it not been positively associated with individual competence to solve the problem. In the kinds of situations examined by Janis there can be no assurance that confidence will always be linked with "correctness." Indeed, it seems probable that the representatives of the Central Intelligence Agency and the Joint Chiefs of Staff, having participated in the planning of the Bay of Pigs invasion, were much more confident of its military and political potential than were other members of the conference group.

All of the above studies document a point that is perhaps obvious: groups often fail to reach "good" decisions even when one or more members possess the knowledge or insight that permit a good decision to be made. Success requires that the necessary knowledge and insights be presented to others in the group and that they react favorably to it. Thomas and Fink (1961) studied the fate of individuals' solutions to the horse-trading problem as groups considered the issue. College students who had worked alone on the problem were assembled into groups and asked to arrive at a decision. However, they were told their final report might be either unanimous or divided, and no pressures were exerted to obtain unanimity. As the discussion proceeded, the experimenter marked a tally sheet each time a participant (a) stated the correct answer; (b) rejected an incorrect answer; (c) expressed a rationale for the correct answer; (d) stated an incorrect answer; or (e) gave a rationale for an incorrect answer.

Groups manifested a strong tendency to converge on a single (not necessarily correct) solution. Six of the 44 groups were "unanimous" even before discussion began; after deliberating, 28 groups were unanimous. Exchange of opinion led to a marked increase in agreement but did not greatly influence the correctness of members' judgements. Although 29 of the groups contained at least one member who had solved the problem correctly, only 15 groups succeeded in producing a unanimously correct report. Thomas and Fink's observational data indicated that the correct solution had a greater chance of being proposed by someone if it were known by several (rather than only one) members, and a greater chance of being proposed many times. The more frequently it was proposed by someone, the greater was its chance of being supported by others, and the larger, in general, was the proportion of the members who endorsed it at the conclusion of the discussion. In 18 groups only one member had solved the problem correctly when working alone; six of these groups produced unanimously correct solutions at the conclusion of the discussion. In all six of them the person who solved the problem correctly talked more often than anyone else, while in only one of the other 12 groups was that the case. Although the number of persons originally favoring the correct solution was important, a single individual who persistently offered a supporting rationale for his correct solution was sometimes able to persuade his associates.

Hoffman and Maier (1964) conducted a study which, though it did not employ the horse-trading problem, highlights the relevance of such research to an understanding of groupthink. Groups of three or four persons were asked to recommend a solution to the "Parasol Assembly" problem (Maier, 1952) for which a number of proposals of varying quality are possible. As deliberations proceeded two observers tallied instances of support for, and opposition to, every solution that was mentioned. Hoffman and Maier subsequently derived a score for each such solution by subtracting the number of opposing comments from the number of supporting arguments offered by the group. As might be anticipated, the solution accepted by the group was almost invariably the one that had received the largest score. Of greater pertinence to our present concern, however, was the finding that once support for a specific solution had exceeded opposition by a certain margin (15 more instances of support than of opposition in their study), it was almost assured of acceptance. This critical margin was sometimes achieved early in the discussion, and subsequent deliberations rarely altered the eventual outcome. In some cases a recommended solution attained the necessary margin even though only one or two members of the group argued in its favor, but in 80% of the groups whatever proposal first achieved the critical margin was adopted as the group's recommendation.

Hoffman and Maier's conclusions were remarkably similar to some of Janis' findings concerning groupthink in real decision-making conferences. They observed that the majority of the solutions recommended by their groups were of poor quality, and suggested that mediocre performance was in large part due to a tendency to adopt a solution without truly considering other alternatives. Objectively sound proposals offered after an inferior solution had received the crucial margin of support had little chance of being accepted. Like Janis, Hoffman and Maier emphasized the value of attempting to "bring forth all solution possibilities before any are evaluated.'

It should be noted that none of the studies reviewed in this section attempted to create a high level of cohesion or endeavored to establish strong in-group v. out-group relationships. The fact that procedural flaws similar to those characterizing groupthink occured even when groups could be presumed to have low-cohesion suggests that group solidarity may be less critical than Janis believed.

## The risky-shift model

Discussion of the horse-trading problem ordinarily led participants to converge upon a single solution, but not always the one that had been most widely favored before discussion began. Discussion of the problems employed in "risky shift" research has been found to have similar effects: the major consequence is convergence on a position that approximates, but does not quite match, the mean of the judgements expressed by participants before discussion began. During the 1960s a great deal of effort was expended to explain why group decisions were systematically, even if only slightly, more extreme than the average of the individuals' initial preferences. Most of this research was predicated on the assumption that there was something special about risk-taking that accounted for the effects of discussion, but recent years have brought evidence that the "risky shift" is only a special case of a more general phenomenon.

A popular early theory maintained that risk is a value for almost everyone (at least in American society). When discussion makes it evident to some portion of the members of a group that they have not been as loyal to that value as their colleagues, they shift to more risky positions. On the other hand, those who have already taken a risky stance have less reason to alter their views. Consequently, convergence occurs at a point that is displaced in the more risky direction. This formulation was challenged by the discovery that, when discussing certain issues, groups regularly shift toward greater caution, a fact that was rationalized by the assumption that caution, too, is sometimes a value. A new perspective became appropriate when it was noted that risky shifts tended to occur if the mean of the individual judgements had been somewhat risky even before discussion began, and cautious shifts were manifested (though to a lesser degree) if the mean of the individual judgements had been somewhat cautious.[1] The effect of discussion was, therefore, to accentuate an already existing tendency. That this polarizing effect of discussion was not uniquely related to risk and caution became evident when investigators obtained similar results with other kinds of issues. Myers and Bishop (1970) found that groups shifted toward more extreme positions following a discussion of racial attitudes, and Moscovici and Zavallone (1969) obtained parallel findings when high school students discussed President De Gaulle. Other investigators (e.g. Gouge and Fraser, 1972; McCaulay, 1973) also reported evidence of the generality of such shifts.

Myers and Bishop (1971) examined the communicative acts of groups that shifted toward more extreme positions on issues that did not concern risk or caution. Analysis of tape-recorded records of discussion sessions revealed that: (a) the more extreme the mean of the participants' initial opinions was, the greater was the proportion of oral statements favoring the "dominant" view; and (b) the greater the proportion of statements favoring the dominant view, the greater was the margin by which the group's decision shifted in the direction of that opinion. However, the group's initial mean did not predict the magnitude of its shift, a finding that may reflect regression and ceiling effects. Although initial means did not directly determine polarization, they predicted the flavor of discussion rhetoric which was a significant predictor of shifts. Myer and Bishop's conclusions are quite parallel to those of Thomas and Fink (1961) who, as we have already noted, found that decisions concerning the horse-trading problem were not necessarily dictated by the initial distribution of subjects' judgements, but were strongly affected by the ratio of supportive to opposing arguments expressed concerning each possible solution.

Vinokur (1971) proposed an explanation of risky and cautious shifts that is consistent with the findings of Myers and Bishop and of Thomas and Fink. After reviewing evidence concerning each of many theories advanced to account for risky and cautious shifts, Vinokur concluded that most could be rejected and none seemed completely adequate. His own formulation pictures the discussion process as one in which partially shared information is exchanged. Any individual can probably think of at least one or two reasons to be risky, and a reason or so to be cautious, in almost any situation. Some people will think of more reasons than others, and different persons are likely to think of different reasons. But in many situations, it will be easier to adduce arguments favoring risk, or favoring caution. Consequently, the initial judgements of subjects will tend to cluster in either the risky or cautious sectors of the continuum, though some will be more extreme than others, and an occasional individual will produce a highly deviant judgement. During discussion people exchange, or pool, their arguments, and most participants can be expected to learn more new reasons for favoring the view that is already dominant in the group than for accepting the contrary conclusion. However, information exchange will not be a completely equalitarian process. Persons who are initially aware of many more arguments (and/or stronger arguments) favoring one alternative than the other will not only be extreme but confident because extremity of initial position implies greater confidence (Burnstein, 1969; Clausen, unpublished data; Osgood et al., 1957), and because confidence encourages vigorous presentation of one's views (Gurnee, 1937; Johnson and Torcivia, 1967; Thorndike, 1938), participants whose initial opinions are extreme can be expected to communicate their arguments more strenuously than those whose judgements are moderate. Consequently, a "majority wins" principle will not always prevail, but shifts toward greater extremity should be commonplace.

Vinokur's explanation of risky and cautious shifts emphasizes the rationality of group discussion. To be sure, the arguments that are exchanged may not always be as valid as they seem, critical information or insights may be unavailable or remain unexpressed, and the most confident people may not always be correct. But people are assumed to evaluate the evidence that is presented during discussion and to reach final conclusions that reflect the comparative weights of the arguments they have heard. They are not alleged to alter their judgements simply for the sake of agreement, or to avoid the criticism or rejection deviant status might bring. In the language of Deutsch and Gerard (1955), their judgemental changes reflect "informational" rather than "normative" conformity. In one way or another something approximating Vinokur's "rational" view of risky and cautious shifts has tended to displace many of the earlier, more normative, explanations.

The "rational" view seems, at first glance, to have little relevance to groupthink. There is an absence of "mindguards" and overt censorship. Leaders do not prejudice the ultimate verdict or manipulate the deliberative process in ways that inhibit the expression of minority views. There is little emphasis on in-group v. out-group relationships, and participants can hardly be regarded as a cohesive group. But discussants are persuaded by what they hear, which tends to be arguments on one side of the issue (Nordhoy, unpublished data), and more confident members of the group exert a disproportionate influence on the ultimate decision. Most importantly, the "rational" model describes a process by which groups move toward acceptance of extreme positions that many of their members would not ordinarily have supported.

Although the rational model may be more successful than any other single formulation in accounting for the many findings of risky-shift research, it is not entirely consistent with certain critical data. Shifts toward greater extremity have sometimes (e.g. Teger and Pruitt, 1967) been obtained when group members merely reveal their individual judgements on cards. Although such effects have not always been obtained, and are not as strong as those that follow presentation of pro- and con-arguments, they suggest that something in addition to the rational evaluation of shared arguments may be happening. Perhaps people do sometimes become more risky or cautious for purely normative reasons — because it is uncomfortable to be an extreme deviant. Or, on learning that most of his associates disagree with his position, the deviate may conclude that he is wrong and they are right; they probably have information or insights that are not available to him. In this connection it should be recalled that even the staunch non-conformers in Asch's (1951) classic studies reported doubts concerning the accuracy of their own sense data. The distinction between normative and informational influence is sometimes rather tenuous, and learning that many other people do not share one's view may prompt a reassessment of the evidence on which one's own opinion is based.

Another finding that is not easily subsumed by the "rational" model concerns subjects' initial assessments of various responses to risky and cautious-shift items. When considering risky-shift items Levinger and Schneider's (1969) subjects reported they most strongly admired choices more risky than those they had personally endorsed, and admired positions less risky than their own on items that had been found to yield cautious shifts. Madras and Bem (1968) obtained supportive evidence for the former, but not the latter, kind of items. If subjects were rational evaluators of pro- and con-arguments, they should presumably have endorsed the decision they most admired (i.e. the one most favored by arguments with which they were familiar), and we are left to speculate why they did not always do so. A possible explanation is provided by early research conducted by Allport (1924). Subjects who believed their judgements of the pleasantness-unpleasantness of odors would be compared with those of other persons gave less extreme ratings than did subjects who believed no such comparison would occur. The former apparently minimized the possibility of being an extreme deviant by expressing slightly less extreme views than they really held. In the absence of knowledge about how others would respond, they presumably made the reasonable assumption that associates, if they disagreed at all, would render verdicts less extreme than those they personally felt appropriate. (That experimental subjects actually assume others will be less extreme than themselves has been documented for risky-shift items by Levinger and Schneider, 1969, and Wallach and Wing, 1968, and for a public issue by Steiner, 1954.) Confronted by the likelihood of deviant status if they express their true opinions, subjects apparently "hedge their bets" by endorsing positions a little more moderate than they prefer; they succumb to normative pressures even before discussion begins. When such compromises are a widespread phenomenon, discussion should serve to dispel pluralistic ignorance and result in a shift toward greater extremity even if no new substantive arguments are presented. The pertinence of such normative influences to an understanding of groupthink will be examined in the next section of this paper.

## A normative model

Previous to the Second World War the great mass of middle- and upper-income families in America consumed very little visceral meat. When the war brought a severe shortage of their preferred cuts, they did not, as might have been expected, shift to heart, kidney, or sweetbread. In an effort to promote such a change the government sponsored numerous radio and newspaper announcements concerning the availability of these nutritious substitutes. The importance of protein in the diet was stressed, and semi-technical information about the dietary advantages of serving visceral meats was presented. Recipes by which such foods might be made especially tasty were published, and their consumption was sometimes depicted as a patriotic contribution to the war effort. But the mass-media campaign had little effect on buying practices.

Opinion surveys revealed that people had indeed "learned" information contained in these public announcements. Furthermore, they believed it; many housewives acknowledged the wisdom of shifting to visceral meats when other kinds were unavailable, and some reported personal willingness to do so. Why, then, had they not purchased and served such foods? Their responses to this question were often evasive, but sometimes communicated a belief that visceral meats were for the uncultured or poverty-stricken. To comply with the government's appeal would therefore require them to violate what they believed to be a widely accepted standard; they might even incur the disrespect of friends and neighbors. The position of housewives who held this combination of views was not unlike that of subjects in risky-shift studies, or in Allport's research on odor-judging. Like experimental subjects, they apparently moderated their public actions in order to avoid possible censure.

It was at this point that Lewin (1947) demonstrated the effectiveness of group discussion. Groups of female Red Cross volunteers either listened to a lecture on the merits of serving visceral meats or were asked to discuss the matter among themselves. At the conclusion of the discussion, but not after hearing the lecture, participants were asked to indicate, by a show of hands, their willingness to prepare and serve one of the recommended dishes. Follow-up interviews suggested that the discussion procedure had been markedly more successful than the lecture in securing compliance.

The superior effectiveness of discussion could hardly be attributed to more thorough communication of substantive information. Women in both kinds of groups had already been exposed to a widespread publicity campaign that covered the basic facts. The lecturer reviewed the information transmitted by the mass media, discussed cooking techniques, and emphasized the favorable responses of other families to these less expensive meats. But the lecture did not enable individual housewives to discover that many of their associates were, like themselves, "privately" willing to make the change. It did not dispel pluralistic ignorance about the judgements of others; each listener could continue to believe that she alone was convinced of the wisdom of serving the "socially inappropriate" foods. During discussion, however, participants could scarcely have avoided transmitting cues about their own personal feelings as they exchanged information about nutrition, recipes, or the cost and availability of foods. According to Lewin, sooner or later someone in such a group "breaks the ice." Perhaps an especially uninhibited person says, "I'm willing to try it if you are, Mary." Because nobody remonstrates or is openly critical of the ice-breaker, others who share her view are embolden to say so, and some who were originally hesitant or even opposed decide that visceral meat are, after all, acceptable during wartime. The overt vote at the conclusion of the discussion provides dramatic evidence that the old standard is no longer operative, and proclaims the existence of a new one.

According to this interpretation, discussion succeeded because it altered people's conceptions of a norm that had formerly restricted their actions. It created an atmosphere in which widely shared doubts about the appropriateness of that norm could be expressed by at least a few persons whose overt behaviors initiated a "spiralling process" and led to the establishment of a new standard of conduct. Probably such a sequence of events can be expected to occur only when many persons are already privately convinced that actions contrary to the existing norm are justified. Discussions of the kind conducted by Lewin would surely fail to convince housewives they should serve arsenic for breakfast or ground-up glass for dessert. Discussion should lead to a rapid change in norms only when substantive information already available to participants strongly favors a change.

Some of the "group decision" research conducted by Lewinians (e.g. Coch and French, 1948) entailed prolonged deliberation of the benefits to be gained by establishing a new standard, and thus may be regarded as having involved a great deal of "informational influence." Other studies (e.g. Radke and Klisurich, cited in Lewin, 1947) appear to have examined instances in which "informational influence" led to the creation of a norm where none had previously existed. Lewin conceived group change to be the result of a three-step process: unfreezing, moving, and freezing at a new level. When no standard existed at the beginning of a group's discussion, there was nothing to be unfrozen.

Because the decision to serve visceral meat seems to have been a highly reasonable one, the relevance of Lewin's normative model to the subject of groupthink is not immediately apparent. It becomes so when one realizes that the substantive information favoring replacement of an existing norm may be extremely faulty. If disenchantment with an old norm reflects rumor, misinformation, or prejudice, the "unfreezing–movement–freezing" process may lead to decisions that are as ill-founded as those taken by the groups Janis studied. Such conditions have sometimes been responsible for the actions of lynching crowds.

Because lynchings were once rather common in the United States, they have received considerable attention from scholars. By the 1930s social scientists had accumulated extensive anecdotal evidence concerning many of them (cf. Cantril, 1941; Raper, 1933). Participants and observers were interviewed, official records and newspaper reports were examined, and local gossip was recorded and evaluated. Although data of this kind are often unreliable, the consistency with which certain patterns were discerned by different investigators suggests that major conclusions were probably correct.

It is apparent that some lynchings are carefully planned in advance by a small band of conspirators who calmly and methodically conduct the affair at the appointed time. Because little is known about the steps by which conspirators reach their decisions, this type of lynching will not concern us further. Instead, we will focus on instances in which the decision to lynch was reached by an already assembled collection of persons who proceeded to "take the law into their own hands."

One of the most common conclusions concerning such events is that many of the persons who become involved are already privately convinced the victim should be lynched. They have heard rumors of rapes, killings, impending uprisings, or other crimes that threaten the welfare and security of good people. Back-yard gossip has encouraged them to attribute many of their own misfortunes and frustrations to the misconduct of persons like the victim. Numerous conversations with neighbors have convinced them that existing legal machinery cannot, or will not, punish wrongdoers or prevent offences against innocent citizens. "Informational influence" has already prepared them to favor vigilante action when the lynching victim is reported to have committed a crime against the good people. Although individuals with this mental set are privately willing or even eager to destroy the victim, they are nevertheless aware of a broad societal code that forbids such action, and they know that prominent members of the local community and church have condemned lynching. Few of these privately-convinced individuals would be willing publicly to proclaim that the victim should summarily be killed, and even fewer would attempt, single-handedly, to accomplish the deed. Their actions are moderated by uncertainty concerning the support they might receive from others and by fear of reprisals.

Nobody knows how many of the persons who became involved in lynchings fitted this pattern. Research during the first third of the century suggested that many did not, and that a few were strongly opposed to the activities in which they were induced to participate.

The initial step in the sequence that led to lynching was often an unplanned conversation about an offense the victim was alleged to have committed (e.g. rape, theft, or failure to abide by "caste rules"). Only a handful of people were likely to be involved in the initial discussion which typically occurred on a street corner or in a gas station or saloon. However, the small group tended to become an assemblage of considerable size as others, interested in the topic or prompted by curiosity, joined in. As numbers grew, conversation generally gave way to short impromptu speeches about the heinous character of the "crime" or its perpetrator. After "information" of this kind had been exchanged, someone "broke the ice" by declaring that the offender should be lynched. It seems not to have mattered very much who the ice-breaker was; in some instances he was the town drunk or an irresponsible youth whose advice would ordinarily have been ignored. What did matter was that this proposal was not immediately contradicted by anyone else. Instead, it was publicly supported by one or more others. The uncontested overatures of a vociferous minority appear to have initiated a "spiralling process." Vigorous presentation of only one side of the issue legitimized its espousal by others who would not have dared to take the lead, and defined social reality for many who were originally undecided. Consequently, the initial action of a few soon became the openly avowed policy of the majority. Unfreezing, movement, and freezing occurred in rapid succession.

Why did those who deplored lynching fail to voice their judgements? There is widespread agreement among scholars that such persons sometimes attempted to remonstrate. But they delayed until the spiralling process had begun, and were then forcefully suppressed by the emerging majority. Or they were at least intimidated by threats. Although there may have been many potential deviates in the crowd, each was confronted by what seemed to be a unanimous majority. Like subjects in Asch's (1951) classic studies of conformity, they were inclined to avoid social pressures by "going along." Or they employed strategies not available to Asch's subjects: they remained silent or left the group. The effect of "mindguards" and self-consorship was to accentuate the apparent unanimity of the majority, and thus to promote the "freezing" of a new norm that supported lynching.

Once the spiralling process had generated an "impression of universality" (Allport, 1924), lynch crowds tended to manifest a high degree of cohesion. Total strangers sometimes treated one another as life-long acquaintances, and friendly exchanges were common. A festive atmosphere often characterized the proceedings, and lynch crowds were known to sing hymns or "Happy Days Are Here Again" as they marched off to assault their victim.

Perhaps, as Janis suggests, cohesion encourages groupthink. But the intense cohesion of lynching crowds can most accurately be described as a consequence of processes that resemble groupthink. My own reading of Janis' book leads me to suggest it was the desire for cohesion, rather than cohesion itself, that promoted groupthink in the conferences he studied. From this point of view, the essence of groupthink is an extreme emphasis on cohesion-building or cohesion-maintaining behaviors that interferes with rational decision-making. The desire for cohesion may be especially strong when people have no other basis for establishing the validity of their beliefs (Festinger, 1950), when their beliefs are contrary to the views (norms) of the larger society (Festinger et al., 1956; Hardyck and Braden, 1962), or when they and their associates are subject to attack by external sources (Burnstein and McRae, 1962; Cartwright and Zander, 1968; Lott and Lott, 1965). Some or all of these circumstances seem to have prevailed in the instances discussed by Janis and in the case of lynching crowds.

Janis observed that groupthink is sometimes accompanied by an illusion of invulnerability. Participants feel they are "invulnerable to the main dangers that might arise from the risky action in which the group is strongly tempted to engage." Cantril (1941) noted that members of lynching crowds feel they are immune from prosecution or censure; what they are doing is right, and, even if it were not, nobody would hold them personally responsible. The impression of universality establishes a new norm that conveys a feeling of moral rectitude and exemption from criticism. The constraints that formerly prevented the individual from engaging in barbarous action are replaced by social prescriptions that endorse those behaviors.

In the case of the Bay of Pigs deliberations, President Kennedy's leadership may have been largely responsible for the rapid acceptance of a new norm. Janis suggests that Kennedy's talent, charisma, and record of past successes created a mood of euphoric compliance. Perhaps his apparent support of the invasion plan hastened the "movement" stage of Lewin's three-step process, and stimulated the illusion of universality and invulnerability in discussants who might otherwise have avoided these pitfalls. But evidence from lynching crowds indicates that similar effects may be obtained in the absence of strong facilitative leadership. When there is widespread private disapproval of a norm, a vociferous minority that suppresses potential opposition can sometimes accomplish the same results.

In Lewin's visceral meat studies, as in lynching crowds, the critical communication concerns how people feel about an issue, rather than information about the issue itself. Participants knew that others (at least those who are heard) favor an action or conclusion they are already prepared to accept. Substantive information favoring that position is also communicated, but serves primarily to reveal a readiness to establish a new norm, or to justify its endorsement after it has already been accepted by many discussants. Perhaps the Bay of Pigs conferees ignored readily available facts and engaged in one-sided discussion of the issue because their "secret agenda" called for a rapid normative change.

## Conclusions

In certain respects the groups examined in this paper were quite different from those studied by Janis. In most instances they were *ad hoc* or transitory groups composed of strangers who had no reason to expect their associations to continue. The initial level of cohesion was conparatively low, and formal leadership was generally lacking. The issues under discussion were often rather inconsequential and, except in the case of lynching crowds, members probably had little reason to believe their actions might have important effects on their own status or welfare. But in spite of these differences, some of the symptoms of groupthink appeared in each of them.

All three lines of research reveal that groups make selective use of information (or misinformation) at their disposal, that there is suppression or self-censorship of certain opinions, that some persons are more influential than others, and that a group's decision may not be a very accurate reflection of the mean of its members' initial views. Some of the research suggests that what was expressed first during discussion tends to have greater impact than what is said later, and may even determine subsequent developments. Although the risky-shift literature is not concerned with the "goodness" of group decisions, both the horse-trading studies and research on lynching crowds supports Janis' conclusion that groups sometimes reach notoriously bad decisions. Truth does not necessarily emerge victorious over untruth even when it is known by someone in the group.

When very different kinds of research yield similar outcomes there is reason to suspect that rather pervasive forces are at work. Janis identifies cohesion as the underlying cause of the more evident symptoms of groupthink. As I have already suggested, I believe *desire for cohesion* more accurately describes the factor that is primarily responsible, and that cohesion is more likely to be a consequence than a cause of failure to examine all sides of an issue in a dispassionate manner. However, I am now convinced that this suggestion should be ammended slightly. What is desired by subjects in the experimental studies or horse-trading and risky shift is apparently the acceptance and approval of one's associates rather than membership in a tightly-bonded, cohesive group. To be sure, in the conferences studied by Janis, and in lynching crowds, cohesion may be desired as a means of diffusing responsibility and minimizing doubts about the correctness of the group's decision. But responsibility-diffusion and doubt-reduction are unlikely to have been critical considerations in the experimental groups examined above, or in many committee situations where I have observed something akin to groupthink. Instead, members appear to have avoided controversy because normative pressures (i.e. the desire to be accepted as a good colleague) outweighed the need to reach the best possible decision. Consequenty, I suggest that groupthink is promoted by the desire for cohesion or personal acceptance and approval.

Two other factors may either favor or inhibit groupthink. Prior public commitments are known to limit conformity (Deutsch and Gerard, 1955), and thus may be expected to restrict an individual's willingness to remain silent about arguments favoring his own initial view. If most members of a group have made the same public commitment, or a minority has made the same commitment and others have made none at all, we may anticipate the occurrence of groupthink that supports that commitment. But if different members are committed to different views, groupthink should be suppressed.

Self-interest should operate as does prior commitment to encourage or inhibit groupthink. It is interesting to recall that the military members of the group that endorsed the Bay of Pigs invasion were already committed in a semi-public fashion to that action, and that their self-interest also favored it. Several other participants had been unaware of the plan and thus may be presumed to have had no compelling personal reason for either supporting or opposing the invasion.

Whatever the causes of groupthink may prove to be, Janis' book should have a salutary effect on social psychology. It dramatically illustrates the relevance of the field to important real-life events. We may hope that it will stimulate a revival of research into group decision-making.

## Note

1. It has regularly been found that subjects are initially more risky on issues that yield a risky shift than on those that yield a cautious shift. However, the mean of the individual responses to Belief—Dilemma items that produce a risky shift is often approximately 0.5 instead of a more risky 0.3 or 0.2. It should be noted that a mean of 0.5 does not indicate neutrality with respect to risk-taking: it represents a willingness to accept an option that has a 0.5 chance of failure, and therefore can be interpreted as a rather high level of risk-taking. Initial reactions of Belief—Dilemma items that yield a cautious shift have ordinarily been unmistakaly cautious (see Vinokur, 1971).

## References

Allport, F. H. *Social Psychology*, New York: Houghton Mifflin, 1924.

Asch, S. Effects of group pressures upon the modification and distortion of judgement. In H. Guetzkow (Ed.), *Groups, Leadership, and Men.* Pittsburgh: Carnegie Press, 1951.

Burnstein, E. An analysis of group decisions involving risk. *Human Relations* 1969, 22, 381–395.

Burnstein, E., and McRae, A. V. Some effects of shared threat and prejudice in racially mixed groups. *Journal of Abnormal and Social Psychology*, 1962, 64, 257–263.

Cantril, H. *The Psychology of Social Movements.* New York: Wiley, 1941.

Cartwright, D., and Zander, A. *Group Dynamics: Research and Theory.* New York: Harper and Row, 1968.

Clausen, G. S. Risk taking in small groups. Unpublished doctoral dissertation, Ann Arbor, Michigan, University of Michigan, 1965.

Coch, L., and French, J. R. P., Jr. Overcoming resistance to change. *Human Relations,* 1948, 1, 512–532.

Deutsch, M., and Gerard, H.B. A study of informational social influences upon individual judgement. *Journal of Abnormal and Social Psychology,* 1955, 51, 629–636.

Festinger, L. Informal social communication. *Psychological Review,* 1950, 57, 271–282.

Festinger, L., Riecken, H., and Schachter, S. *When Prophesy Fails.* Minneapolis: University of Minnesota Press, 1956.

Gouge, C., and Fraser, C. A further demonstration of group polarization. *European Journal of Social Psychology,* 1972, 2, 95–97.

Gurnee, H. Maze learning in the collective situation. *Journal of Psychology,* 1937, 3, 437–444.

Hardyck, J. A., and Braden, M. Prophesy fails again. *Journal of Abnormal and Social Psychology,* 1962, 65, 136–141.

Hoffman, L. R., and Maier, N. R. F. Valence in the adoption of solutions by problem-solving groups: Concept, method, and results. *Journal of Abnormal and Social Psychology,* 1964, 69, 264–271.

Janis, I. L. *Victims of Groupthink.* Boston: Houghton Mifflin, 1972.

Johnson, H. H., and Torcivia, J. M. Group and individual performance on a single-stage task as a function of distribution of individual performance. *Journal of Experimental Social Psychology,* 1967, 3, 266–273.

Levinger, G., and Schneider, D. J. A test of the risk is a value hypothesis. *Journal of Personality and Social Psychology,* 1969, 11, 165–169.

Lewin, K. Group decision and social change. In T. M. Newcomb and E. L. Hartley (Eds), *Readings in Social Psychology.* New York: Holt, Rinehart and Winston, 1947.

Lott, A. J., and Lott, B. E. Group cohesiveness as interpersonal attraction: A review of relationships with antecedent and consequent variables. *Psychological Bulletin,* 1965, 64, 259–309.

Madras, G. R., and Bem, D. J. Risk and conservatism in group decision making. *Journal of Experimental Social Psychology,* 1968, 4, 350–365.

Maier, N. R. F. *Principles of Human Relations.* New York: Wiley, 1952.

Maier, N. R. F., and Solem, A. R. The contribution of a discussion leader to the quality of group thinking: The effective use of minority opinions. *Human Relations,* 1952, 5, 277–288.

McCauley, C. R. Extremity shifts, risk shifts and attitude shifts after group discussion. *European Journal of Social Psychology,* 1972, 2, 417–434.

McGuire, W. The nature of attitude and attitude change. In G. Lindzey and E. Aronson (Eds), *The Handbook of Social Psychology.* (2nd ed.) Reading, Mass.: Addison-Wesley, 1969.

Moscovici, S., and Zavalloni, M. The group as a polarizer of attitudes. *Journal of Personality and Social Psychology,* 1969, 12, 125–135.

Myers, D. G. and Bishop, G. D. Discussion effects on racial attitudes. *Science,* 1970, 169, 778–779.

Myers, D. G. and Bishop, G. D. Enhancement of dominant attitudes in group discussion. *Journal of Personality and Social Psychology,* 1971, 20, 386–391.

Nordhoy, F. Group interaction in decision making under risk. Unpublished master's thesis, Boston, Massachusetts Institute for Technology, 1962.

Osgood, C. E., Suci, G. J., and Tannenbaum, P. H. *The Measurement of Meaning.* Urbana: University of Illinois Press, 1957.

Raper, A. *The Tragedy of Lynching.* Chapel Hill: University of North Carolina Press, 1933.

Steiner, I. D. Primary group influences on public opinion. *American Sociological Review,* 1954, 19, 260—267.

Teger, A. I., and Pruitt, D. G. Components of grouprisk taking. *Journal of Experimental Social Psychology,* 1967, 3, 189—205.

Thomas, E. J., and Fink, C. F. Models of group problem solving. *Journal of Abnormal and Social Psychology,* 1961, 63, 53—63.

Thorndike, R. L. The effect of discussion upon the correctness of group decisions, when the factor of majority is allowed for. *Journal of Social Psychology,* 1938, 9, 343—362.

Torrance, E. P. Some consequences of power differences on decision-making in permanent and temporary three-man groups. *Research studies, State College of Washington,* 1954, 22, 130—140.

Vinokur, A. Review and theoretical analysis of the effects on group processes upon individual and group decisions involving risk. *Psychological Bulletin,* 1971, 76, 231—250.

Wallach, M. A., and Wing, C. W., Jr. Is risk a value? *Journal of Personality and Social Psychology,* 1968, 9, 101—106.

VII

# 23
# Recent Research on
# Group Decision Making

Hermann Brandstätter

Group decision making has been praised as a panacea to overcome increasing task complexity, to solve social conflicts, and to secure cooperation. Others have warned against the loss of time and effort on problems that are better handled by individuals, or against the deleterious effects of "group think" on decision quality. Research on group decision making has often been stimulated by practical problems and some of its findings may be useful in improving group problem solving within organizations. But more than for its social relevance, this research deserves attention for its potential for developing a social psychological theory of inter-personal behaviour.

Conceiving of "Group Decision Making" as a fuzzy concept, the typical situation to which it is related may be described as exchanging ideas about the structure of and the possible solutions to a problem of some importance, and collectively choosing an action from a number of alternatives, with risks involved.

Most experiments deal with single components or single stages of the complex process only. Usually they exclude defining the problem, or generating possible solutions to it. The risk of choosing a non-optimal alternative may be perceived as virtually zero, if the selected alternative is evident to all members of the group as the correct or the best one. The importance (values at stake) may be minimized, and there may be no more than a rudimentary implication of action, if the group decides on what "should be done" instead of on what "will be done", or even less if only opinion (attitude) change is studied. Collectivity of choice may be reduced by imposing all the responsibility on the group leader, if he has to decide alone after having discussed the problem with the group.

If one strives for a theoretical integration of very heterogeneous experimental results, if one wants to assess their relevance to the understanding of group behaviour in highly complex "natural" settings, a comprehensive classification system of group decision situations is needed, describing basic aspects of the relation between group members and task, of the inter-personal relations within the group, and of the relations of group members to their reference groups or constituency. It should be applicable to experimental settings as well as to natural ones.

Any classification system of group decision situations is useful in as far as it lends itself to a theoretical integration of a great variety of experimental results, of historical documents on important decision processes, and of observations in natural settings.

Recently Witte (1979) dealt with this problem, trying to select those dimensions that are both easy to handle in describing a situation, and relevant in theoretical terms. Witte distinguishes two kinds of variables. The one class of variables comprises different aspects of the information used by the group members in choosing a specific alternative. The other class of variables refer to antecedent conditions that determine the weights of the informational variables, which in his model are additively combined. There is supposed to be a hierarchical order within both classes of variables. If in the first class of variables, the antecedent conditions, a higher ranked variable is rated as extreme (high or low), the lower ranked variables are not considered further in determining the weights of the informational variables. From the hierarchical order within the class of informational variables follows that lower ranked variables are less general.

There are six antecedent varibales, most of them roughly differentiated by three ordinal categories only (low, medium, high) in the following hierarchical order

(1) Awareness of a theory on group behaviour (AT).

(2) Group atmosphere (GA), i.e. average rating of mutual liking; (1) negative, (2) neutral, (3) positive.

(3) Distribution of individual choices (DIC); (1) no variance (2) medium variance (3) extreme variance.

(4) Verifiability of choice (VC) which is low, if there is neither a clear objective nor a clear social standard for orientation; (1) low (2) medium (3) high.

(5) Commitment to a constituency (CC) which is especially

relevant in negotiations; (1) low (2) medium (3) high.

(6) Uniformity pressure (UP), defined as pressure for conforming with social values, objective standards, or small group standards.

There are four informational variables:

(1) Social value (SV) or objective standard (OS). SV is defined as the solution to the problem which is seen as most congruent with the values of a reference group. OS is defined as the solution to the problem that can be verified as the correct one.

(2) Group standard (GS), defined as the weighted mean of the individual choices within the group. Different weights may be given to the members according to their status.

(3) Weighted scale value of arguments exchanged during the discussion (AR). The weight of the argument represents how convincing it is.

(4) Individual value (IV), a term introduced in order to take into account those components of the information processing which are specific to the individual members. It is a kind of residual category.

Combining the two types of variables we arrive at a hierarchical order of predictions of a group members choice. The prediction follows a rule: "if the antecedent conditions are in a specific state, then combine the informational variables in a specific way in predicting the group members final choice Y". Table 1 presents Witte's model of individual choice behaviour (Y) in a group decision situation (1979, p. 161). The model cannot be explained in detail. We may look at just one example: it predicts that the individual choice will be the average of social value, group standard, and argumentation, $\hat{Y} = (SV + GS + AR)/3$, if there is no awareness of a theory (AT = 0), if group atmosphere, distribution of individual choices, and verifiability of choice all are medium (GA = 2; DIC = 2; VC = 2).

Reanalysing the data of various kinds of group experiments and performing his own experiments, Witte tested the applicability of his model. Much depends on how one categorizes a specific group situation with respect to the first set of variables that determines how to combine the informational variables. Although some of the *post hoc* categorizations can be doubted, on the whole Witte's approach seems to be more than a first step towards a better theoretical integration of otherwise very heterogeneous and poorly related experimental results. Witte's model, focusing on only one stage of the entire decision making process, i.e. on converting individual

TABLE 1

*Witte's model of individual choice behaviour in group situations (Witte 1979, p. 161)*

|            | If | Then |
|------------|------|------|
| Awareness | $AT = 0$ | Go to GA |
| of theory | $AT = 1$ | $\hat{Y} = AR$ |
| Group | $GA = 1$ | No social interaction |
| atmosphere | $GA = 2$ | Go to DIC |
|  | $GA = 3$ | $\hat{Y} = GS$ |
| Distribution | $DIC = 1$ | $\hat{Y} = GS$ |
| of individual | $DIC = 2$ | Go to VC |
| choices | $DIC = 3$ | Group falls apart |
| Verifiability | $VC = 1$ | $\hat{Y} = SV$ |
| of choices | $VC = 2$ | Go to CC |
|  | $VC = 3$ | $\hat{Y} = (GS + AR)/2$ |
| Commit- | $CC = 1$ | $\hat{Y} = (SV + GS + AR)/3$ |
| ment to a | $CC = 2$ | $\hat{Y} = (SV_1 + GS_1 + AR_1 + SV_2 + GS_2 + AR_2)/6$ |
| constituency | $CC = 3$ | No agreement possible |
| Uniformity | UP varies | The higher UP, the less amount of variance has to |
| pressure | continuously | be explained by the residual category IV |
|  |  | (individual value) |

preferences into a group choice, does not lend itself to a comprehensive analysis of the whole process, especially if the decision task is poorly structured, as is the case in most real-life group decisions.

In a recent conference paper Burnstein (1980) tries to overcome this restriction by designing a process model comprising all stages from identification of the problem, over development of possible solutions to selection of one of the alternatives considered, the latter being the only stage, that has been extensively studied in experiments. This model provides for various feedback loops and thus becomes more appropriate in describing complex decision processes in natural settings, where quite often a new idea coming up in the group, or a new event in an ever changing environment, leads to a redefinition of the problem, to a new access to, search for or design of alternative solutions, and to a new selection of an alternative which seems to be more adequate. The feedback (cybernetic) model of group decision making seems to be particularly useful in analysing the documents of crucial political decisions in the past.

Having discussed two recent contributions to the field of group decision research that I consider most stimulating, I will try to give a brief and selective review of the relevant publications during the past two years, when we saw remarkable productivity in the field of small group research in general, and of group decision making in particular. It is not so much the number of reports on single experiments, which amounts to about 40 each year, but the coincidence of several reviews and general discussions of lasting problems, that strikes us most.

A whole issue of the *Journal of Applied Behavioral Science* (Volume 15, 1979, Number 3) tries to give an answer to the question of "What's happened to small group research?" Among others Zander (1979a) adds to his annual review article on recent research (Zander, 1979b) a historic viewpoint by looking back over four decades of research, Hoffman (1979) reconsiders the significance that experimental research on group problem solving has for organizations, and Mills (1979) presents his thoughts about "changing paradigms for studying human groups". In a volume of the *American Behavioral Scientist* Newcomb (1978) gives his historic perspective on themes and theoretical concepts of small group research. In the same volume McGrath (1978) presents a selective overview of problems that have been studied up to now. He expresses his hope for a better balance of empirical and theoretical research, and for higher social significance of small group research in the years to come.

Volume 11 of *Advances in Experimental Social Psychology* contains an extensive review article on polarization of attitudes and behaviour by Lamm and Myers (1978). They give a systematic account of the well established empirical evidence of polarization following group discussion: if on average individuals prefer one side of an issue, this tendency usually becomes more prominent by group discussion. Studies simulating real life situations like jury decisions, and naturalistic observations, show that the group polarization phenomenon has some significance outside the laboratory. In the second part of the paper they evaluate the explanatory power of theoretical concepts like social decision rules, responsibility diffusion, informational influence, social comparison, finding the last two concepts the most useful.

After all one would expect that group polarization is by now an exhausted field of research. But Burnstein and Vinokur's radicalism in stressing persuasive argumentation as the only source of group polarization (Vinokur and Burnstein 1978a, b) may stimulate some

more experiments, that will eventually show that persuasive argumentation is not the whole story of group polarization. In a review
of relevant research Singleton (1979) states that the concepts of
social comparison and conformity tendency are needed in addition
to the concept of persuasive argumentation in order to explain group
induced shifts in choice. Goethals and Zanna (1979) show that social
comparison is most effective in choice shift if the subjects not only
know the others' choice but perceive them also as comparable to
themselves on relevant ability. Greenberg (1979) finds a polarization
effect in reward allocation by groups, and takes several possible
explanations into account. Madsen (1978) favours the concept of
persuasive argumentation showing that the influence of issue importance on choice shift is mediated by the perceived persuasiveness
of the arguments presented in the discussion. Schaefer (1978) gives
an example of how decision theory is able to explain some aspects of
the risky shift phenomenon. Another reference to normative models
of decision making is made by Dickson (1978), showing that group
decisions come closer to maximization of expected value than
individual decisions.

As yet the problem of commitment to group decisions has been
widely neglected. Castore and Murnighan (1978) were interested in
just this by looking at the determinants of support for group
decisions, comparing majority rule with formal voting, discussion to
unanimity, discussion to majority agreement, and choice by an
experimenter appointed executor, considering the level of prediscussion agreement among group members as well as the congruence between the individual's preference and his group's decision.

Models of jury decision making are discussed in a critical review
by Penrod and Hastie (1979). The influence of authoritarianism on
group polarization in mock juries has been studied by Bray and
Noble (1978).

Minority influence has been studied with the colour judgement
test by Moscovici and Lage (1978), relating it to the context of a
social norm that gives a high value to originality of thinking. As
expected salience of originality norm facilitates minority influence.
Paicheler (1979) discusses the function of social norm in the
influence of an extremist male or female confederate on all female
or all male group members, respectively. Wolf (1979) shows, with
female subjects, that a deviate is most influential if group cohesion
is high, if the deviate member behaves consistently, and if there is

no opportunity to reject the deviate. But the deviate was also quite influential in the high cohesion/low consistency/possibility of rejection situation, a result which was unexpected, and which points to the importance of context in which a minority member behaves consistently or inconsistently.

Bargaining is a topic which was as frequently studied during the past two years as choice shift. Goodge (1978) gives a critical account of research on inter-group conflict. Müller (1979) studied the motivational orientations of bargainers. He found in a questionnaire study that subjects would try to maximize their own gain only if the situation was characterized as promising high gains and providing no information on the partner's outcome. If the subjects knew the partner's outcome, they tried to reach a fair agreement. Low gain possibilities induced competitive (maximizing differences) behaviour. Komorita and Kravitz (1979) looked for variations in bargaining behaviour depending on a variation of alternatives left in the case that agreement would not be reached. Slusher (1978) was interested in the effect of counterpart strategy, prior relations between the parties, and consistent pressure in simulated management-union negotiations. Wall (1979) studied the effects of mediating strategies (mediator rewarding concessions — mediator suggesting concessions) on bargaining outcomes. Brenenstuhl and Blalack (1978) focused on the question of whether subjects who prefer the role of management or union but have to play the opposite role in a negotiation game, behave differently and get different results from those whose role is congruent with their attitudes. They also made an effort to enhance ego involvement by giving grades according to their bargaining efficiency. Stephenson and Kniveton (1978) and Foddy (1978) focused on non-verbal aspects of bargaining. In the experiment of Stephenson and Kniveton with two role playing management and union representatives each, the seating position (opposite or mixed) made a difference in the inter-personal orientation and in the bargaining outcome. Foddy instructed his subjects to compete or to cooperate in a bargaining game (dividing 9 points) and observed the length and frequency of gaze and eye contact. Cooperation was positively related to the length of eye contact. Hoggatt and Selten (1978) used a bargaining game with incomplete information on the other's outcome. He compared the subjects behaviour with a normative model, and designed a computer program simulating the subjects' bargaining behaviour. A step into applied field research was done by Cialdini *et al.* (1979) by having subjects bargain in the new car showroom. His results — tough prior consumer bargaining on a car gives an advantage in subsequent bargaining — were meant as a help in strengthening the position of the consumer.

There were few studies on group problem solving with objectively verifiable solutions. Bray *et al.* (1978) studied the effect of group size, problem difficulty, and sex on the proportion of solution and the time needed for solution. Kanekar *et al.* (1978) had different types of groups, varying in degrees of inter-dependence of group members, and in scholastic level, solve anagrams. Kabanoff and O'Brien (1979) looked after the combined effect of task type and type of cooperation on group performance. Zaleska (1978) used the horse-trading problem with university students and trade school students to which the verifiability of the correct solution was supposed to be high or low. Group performance was superior to individual performance with university students (high verifiability) only. This study included also an analysis of the communication behaviour, whereas most other studies consider only the outcome of the decision process. Mugny and Doise (1978) and Doise and Mugny (1979) reported their research on socio-cognitive conflict and cognitive development as defined by Piaget. Shiflett (1979) contributes to the construction of a general model of small group productivity. He conceives of the existing models as specifications of his general model.

The research group I belonged to at the University of Augsburg systematically studied the influence of social emotions on the attitude change of participants and observers of group discussion in laboratory and field settings (Brandstätter, 1978; Schuler and Peltzer, 1978; von Rosenstiel and Stocker-Kreichgauer, 1978; Rüttinger, 1978; Brandstätter and Klein-Moddenborg, 1979). Cognitive consistency, attribution, social reinforcement, and emotional conditioning were the basic theoretical concepts in our research. Some reports on it have been published in a book edited by Brandstätter *et al.* (1978). It also contains contributions by Davis, Lambert, Zaleska and Doise in a chapter on cognitive aspects of cooperative interaction, and contributions by Morley, Stephenson, Mikula, and Crott on mixed-motive interaction, mainly bargaining.

Some articles deal with methods of group process analysis. Bezdek *et al.* (1978, 1979) discuss the potential of fuzzy set theory for modelling group preference structures. Gottman (1979) discusses special analytic methods as a device in detecting cyclicity in social interaction. Kraemer and Jacklin (1979) suggest a technique that allows for the statistical analysis of individual behaviour measures in dyadic interaction by taking mutual dependency into account.

I have not included in my review work on coalition behaviour and on matrix games. Although it may also be subsumed under the heading of research on group decision making in a broader sense, the experimental situations used in this kind of research differ remarkably from the typical group decision situation as it was defined at the beginning of this review. Nevertheless I want to mention two review articles, one of Murnighan (1978) on models of coalition behaviour in game theoretical, social psychological, and political perspectives, and one of Schlenker and Bonoma (1978) on the "validity of games for the study of conflict".

During the last few years social psychologists began to raise some doubts on whether social psychology is directed towards the really important problems and on whether experimentation should still be the principal method in analysing social interaction. They are concerned about its neglect of cultural context in its past development and in its present differentiation. They point to its oversimplification and artificiality and they complain about its irrelevance to the solution of real problems (Gergen, 1978; Jahoda, 1979). Are there any signs in the recent literature on group decision-making that mirror these doubts and the search for a new approach? Generally, the experiment is still the dominant method in the field of group decision research; there still seems to be little concern with its limitations, and rather little broadening of the view in theoretical and methodological terms. But there are exceptions, two of them I have mentioned briefly, that point into the direction future research on group decision-making could take.

It will be necessary to find a better way of combining comprehensive but rather subjective intuitive understanding and restricted but precise experimental analysis. In my research group we started to collect information on the assumptions people have about how subjects would respond to a specific experimental situation. We used to ask social psychologists, as well as people belonging to the same population from which the participants in the main experiment come, to state their subjective probabilities of specified hypotheses and to give their reasons for them. This usually gave us a better idea of what might happen within an experimental situation than we had

before, and sometimes this led us to to a modification of the experimental design.

Another way to use the insight people have in their own experience
and behaviour is to have them describe and interpret the process of
decision making in which they recently have participated. This
should be especially valuable in a situation where observation is not
feasible. We have to accept that experiments can only provide us
with markers on the map representing our knowledge of the field.
Whether we can trust them, and how we fill the space between them,
has to be decided by considering all other available sources of information, including personal experience and intuition.

## References

Bezdek, J., Spillman, B. and Spillman, R. A fuzzy relation space for group
    decision theory. *Fuzzy Sets and Systems*, 1978, 1, 255–268.
Bezdek, J. C., Spillman, B. and Spillman, R. Fuzzy relation spaces for group
    decision theory: an application. *Fuzzy Sets and Systems*, 1979, 2, 5–14.
Brandstätter, H. Social emotions in discussion groups. In Brandstätter, H.,
    Davis, J. H. and Schuler, H. (Eds). *Dynamics of Group Decisions*,
    Beverly Hills: Sage, 1978, 93–111.
Brandstätter, H. and Klein-Moddenborg, V. A modified proportional change
    model of attitude change by group discussion. *European Journal of Social
    Psychology*, 1979, 9, 363–380.
Brandstätter, H. and Schuler, H. Social decision situations: integration and appli-
    cation. In Brandstätter, H., Davis, J. H. and Schuler, H. (Eds). *Dynamics of
    Group Decisions*, Beverly Hills: Sage, 1978, 263–270.
Bray, R. M. and Noble, A. M. Authoritarianism and decisions of mock juries:
    Evidence of jury bias and group polarization. *Journal of Personality and
    Social Psychology*, 1978, 36, 1424–1430.
Bray, R. M., Kerr, N. L. and Atkin, R. S. Effects of group size, problem diffi-
    culty, and sex on group performance and member reactions. *Journal of
    Personality and Social Psychology*, 1978, 36, 1224–1240.
Brennenstuhl, D. C. and Blalack, R. O. Role preference and vested interest in a
    bargaining environment. *Simulation and Games*, 1978, 9, 53–65.
Burnstein, E. *Stages in group decision making: The decomposition of historic
    narratives*. Paper presented at the Social Psychology and Social Policy
    Workshop, Canterbury 1980.
Castore, C. H. and Murnighan, J. K. Determinants of support for group decisions.
    *Organizational Behavior and Human Performance*, 1978, 22, 75–92.
Cialdini, R. B., Bickman, L. and Cacioppo, J. T. An example of consumeristic
    social psychology: Bargaining tough in the new car showroom. *Journal of
    Applied Social Psychology*, 1979, 9, 115–126.
Davis, J. H. Spitzer, C. E., Nagao, D. H. and Strasser, G. Bias in social decisions
    by individuals and groups: an example from mock juries. In Brandstätter, H.,
    Davis, J. H. and Schuler, H. (Eds). *Dynamics of Group Decisions*, Beverly
    Hills: Sage, 1978, 33–52.

Dickson, J. W. The effect of normative models on individual and group choice. *European Journal of Social Psychology*, 1978, 8, 91—107.

Doise, W. Actions and judgments: Collective and individual structuring. In Brandstätter, H., Davis, J. H. and Schuler, H. (Eds). *Dynamics of Group Decisions*, Beverly Hills: Sage, 1978, 75—91.

Doise, W. and Mugny, G. Individual and collective conflicts of centrations in cognitive development. *European Journal of Social Psychology*, 1979, 9, 105—108.

Foddy, M. Patterns of gaze in cooperative and competitive negotiation. *Human Relations*, 1978, 31, 925—938.

Gergen, K. J. Experimentation in social psychology: a reappraisal. *European Journal of Social Psychology*, 1978, 8, 507—527.

Goethals, G. R. and Zanna, M. P. The role of social comparison in choice shifts. *Journal of Personality and Social Psychology*, 1979, 37, 1469—1476.

Goodge, P. Intergroup conflict: a rethink. *Human Relations*, 1978, 31, 475—487.

Gottman, J. M. Detecting cyclicity in social interaction. *Psychological Bulletin*, 1979, 86, 338—348.

Greenberg, J. Group vs. individual equity judgments: Is there a polarization effect? *Journal of Experimental Social Psychology*, 1979, 15, 504—512.

Hoffman, L. R. Applying experimental research on group problem solving to organizations. *The Journal of Applied Behavioral Science*, 1979, 15, 375—391.

Hoggatt, A. C. and Selten, R. Bargaining experiments with incomplete information. In Sauermann, H. (Ed). *Bargaining Behavior*. Tübingen: Mohr 1978, 127—178.

Jahoda, G. A cross-cultural perspective on experimental social psychology. *Journal of Personality and Social Psychology Bulletin*, 1979, 5, 142—148.

Kabanoff, B. and O'Brien, G. E. The effect of task type and cooperation upon group products and performance. *Organizational Behavior and Human Performance*, 1979, 23, 163—181.

Kanekar, S., Libby, C. Engels, J. and Jahn, G. Group performance as a function of group type, task condition and scholastic level. *European Journal of Social Psychology*, 1978, 8, 439—451.

Komorita, S. S. and Kravitz, D. A. The effects of alternatives in bargaining. *Journal of Experimental Social Psychology*, 1979, 15, 147—157.

Kraemer, H. C. and Jacklin, C. N. Statistical analysis of dyadic social behavior. *Psychological Bulletin*, 1979, 86, 217—224.

Lambert, R. Situations of uncertainty: Social influence and decision processes. In Brandstätter, H., Davis, J. H. and Schuler, H. (Eds). *Dynamics of Group Decisions*, Beverly Hills: Sage, 1978, 53—66.

Lamm, H. and Myers, D. G. Group-induced polarization of attitudes and behavior. In Berkowitz, L. (Ed). *Advances in Experimental Social Psychology*, New York and Lonson: Academic Press, 1978, 11, 145—195.

Madsen, D. B. Issue importance and group choice shifts: A persuasive arguments approach. *Journal of Personality and Social Psychology*, 1978, 10, 1118—1127.

McGrath, J. E. Small group research. *American Behavioral Scientist*, 1978, 21, 651—674.

Mikula, G. and Schwinger, T. Intermember relations and reward allocation: theoretical considerations of affects. In Brandstätter, H., Davis, J. H. and Schuler, H. (Eds). *Dynamics of Group Decisions*, Beverly Hills: Sage, 1978, 229—250.

Mills, T. M. Changing paradigms for studying human groups. *Journal of Applied Behavioral Science*, 1979, 15, 407–423.
Morley, I. E. Bargaining and negotiation: the character of experimental studies. In Brandstätter, H., Davis, J. H. and Schuler, H. (Eds). *Dynamics of Group Decisions*, Beverly Hills: Sage, 1978, 175–206.
Moscovici, S. and Lage, E. Studies in social influence IV: Minority influence in a context of original judgment. *European Journal of Social Psychology*, 1978, 8, 349–365.
Müller, F. Orientierungsdominanz in Verhandlungssituationen. *Psychologie und Praxis*, 1979, 23, 51–58.
Müller, G. and Crott, H. Behavior orientation in bargaining: the dynamics of dyads. In Brandstätter, H., Davis, J. H. and Schuler, H. (Eds). *Dynamics of Group Decisions*, Beverly Hills: Sage, 251–262.
Mugny G. and Doise, W. Socio-cognitive conflict and structure of individual and collective performances. *European Journal of Social Psychology*, 1978, 8, 181–192.
Newcomb, T. M. Small group research. *American Behavioral Scientist*, 1978, 21, 631–650.
Murnighan, J. K. Models of coalition behavior: Game theoretic, social psychological, and political perspectives. *Psychological Bulletin*, 1978, 85, 1130–1153.
Paicheler, G. Polarization of attitudes in homogeneous and heterogeneous groups. *European Journal of Social Psychology*, 1979, 9, 85–96.
Penrod, S. and Hastie, R. Models of jury decision making: A critical review. *Psychological Bulletin*, 1979, 86, 462–492.
Rosenstiel von, L. and Stocker-Kreichgauer, G. Vicarious social reinforcement. In Brandstätter, H., Davis, J. H. and Schuler, H. (Eds). *Dynamics of Group Decisions*, Beverly Hills: Sage, 1978, 133–148.
Rüttinger, B. Friendliness and group consensus: field study. In Brandstätter, H., Davis, J. H. and Schuler, H. (Eds). *Dynamics of Group Decisions*, Beverly Hills: Sage, 1978, 149–153.
Schaefer, R. Eine entscheidungstheoretische Analyse des Risky Shift Phänomens. *Zeitschrift für Sozial Psychologie* 1978, 9, 186–204.
Schlenker, B. R. and Bonoma, T. V. Fun and games: the validity of games for the study of conflict. *Journal of Conflict Resolution*, 1978, 22, 7–38.
Schuler, H. and Peltzer, U. Friendly versus unfriendly nonverbal behavior: the effects on partner's decision making preferences. In Brandstätter, H., Davis, J. H. and Schuler, H. (Eds). *Dynamics of Group Decisions*, Beverly Hills: Sage, 1978, 113–132.
Shiflett, S. Toward a general model of small group productivity. *Psychological Bulletin*, 1979, 86, 67–79.
Singleton, R. Jr. Another look at the conformity explanation of group induced shifts in choice. *Human Relations*, 1979, 32, 37–56.
Slusher, E. A. Counterpart strategy, prior relations, and constituent pressure in a bargaining simulation. *Behavioral Science*, 1978, 23, 470–477.
Stephenson, G. M. and Kniveton, B. K. Interpersonal and interparty exchange: An experimental study of the effect of seating position on the outcome of negotiations between teams representing parties in dispute. *Human Relations*, 1978, 31, 555–566.
Stephenson, G. M. Interparty and interpersonal exchange in negotiation groups. In Brandstätter, H. Davis, J. H. and Schuler, H. (Eds). *Dynamics of Group Decisions*, Beverly Hills: Sage, 1978, 207–228.

Verhagen, J. Expertness, participation, coorientation and social influence. In Brandstätter, H., Davis, J. H. and Schuler, H. (Eds). *Dynamics of Group Decisions*, Beverly Hills: Sage, 1978, 155–174.

Vinokur, A. and Burnstein, E. Novel argumentation and attitude change: The case of polarization following group discussion. *European Journal of Social Psychology*, 1978a, 8, 335–348.

Vinokur, A. and Burnstein, E. Depolarization of attitudes in groups. *Journal of Personality and Social Psychology*, 1978b, 36, 872–885.

Wall, J. A. Jr. The effects of mediator rewards and suggestions upon negotiations. *Journal of Personality and Social Psychology*, 1979, 37, 1554–1560.

Witte, E. H. *Das Verhalten in Gruppensituationen. Ein theoretisches Konzept.* Göttingen: Hogrefe, 1979.

Wolf, S. Behavioural style and group cohesiveness as sources of minority influence. *European Journal of Social Psychology*, 1979, 9, 381–395.

Zaleska, M. Individual and group choices among solutions of a problem when solution verifiability is moderate or low. *European Journal of Social Psychology*, 1978, 8, 37–53.

Zaleska, M. Some experimental results: majority influence on group decisions. In Brandstätter, H., Davis, J. H. and Schuler, H. (Eds). *Dynamics of Group Decisions*, Beverly Hills: Sage, 1978, 67–74.

Zander, A. The study of group behaviour during four decades. *The Journal of Applied Behavioural Science*, 1979a, 15, 272–282.

Zander, A. Psychology of group processes. *Annual review of Psychology*, 1979b, 30, 417–451.

# Author Index

# Subject Index